THE IMPACT OF
CHINESE SECRET SOCIETIES IN MALAYA

The Royal Institute of International Affairs is an unofficial body which promotes the scientific study of international questions and does not express opinions of its own. The opinions expressed in this publication are the responsibility of the author.

The Institute gratefully acknowledges the comments and suggestions of the following who read the manuscript on behalf of the Research Committee: Professor Maurice Freedman and John Gittings.

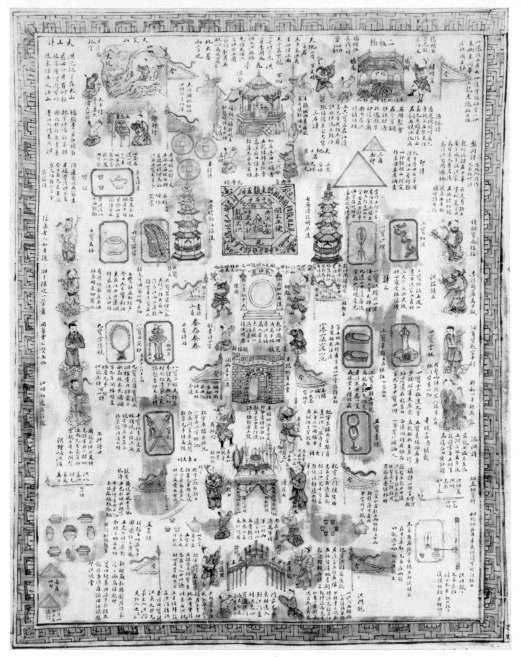

1 *Conventionalized Portrayal of Ghee Hin (Triad) Ceremony. From Cowan's Wall-Sheet, 1897*

The eight Immortals are pictured, four down each side.
The Ten Treasures are shown, five at each side in vertical frames.
Up the middle, starting from the bottom are: The Hung Gate, The Hall of Loyalty and Righteousness, The City of Willows, The Heaven and Earth Circle, A Diploma, (above which is the phrase 'In the centre is a nine-storied pagoda'), The Hung Flower Pavilion.
Top right is the Two-Planked Bridge. Top left is the Flaming Mountain, below which is the Fruit-seller.
The Diploma is flanked by two seven-storied pagodas, above which are (left) the Three Cash, and (right) the Triangular Seal.
Also shown are tobacco pipes, an opium lamp (bottom right), arrangements of tea-cups and pots, and of rice-bowls and chopsticks.
Bottom left are the seals of the First and Second Lodges, to the right of which is the statement that the Penang Ho Seng was a First Lodge Society, and the Singapore Ghee Hin a Second Lodge Society.

THE IMPACT OF
CHINESE SECRET SOCIETIES
IN MALAYA

A HISTORICAL STUDY

WILFRED BLYTHE, C.M.G.

Issued under the auspices of the
Royal Institute of International Affairs

OXFORD UNIVERSITY PRESS

LONDON   KUALA LUMPUR   HONG KONG

1969

Oxford University Press, Ely House, London W.1

GLASGOW NEW YORK TORONTO MELBOURNE WELLINGTON
CAPE TOWN SALISBURY IBADAN NAIROBI LUSAKA ADDIS ABABA
BOMBAY CALCUTTA MADRAS KARACHI LAHORE DACCA
KUALA LUMPUR SINGAPORE HONG KONG TOKYO

Printed in Great Britain by Richard Clay (The Chaucer Press), Ltd,
Bungay, Suffolk

To the memory of all those who served in the Chinese Protectorate Department in the Straits Settlements and the Malay States, and of the late Percy Maude Roxby, one time Professor of Geography in the University of Liverpool, who first set my feet upon the way.

CONTENTS

Part 1

ORIGINS AND HISTORY

Part 2

ATTEMPTS AT SUPPRESSION

Part 3

TWENTIETH-CENTURY MALAYA

Part 4

POSTWAR MALAYA

PLATES

Abbreviations used in text

(For Abbreviations of Official Sources see p. 546)

BEFEO:	*Bulletin de l'École Française d'Extrême Orient*
CCP:	Chinese Communist Party
CDL:	China Democratic League
CJSA:	*China Journal of Science and Arts*
FMS:	Federated Malay States
IGP:	Inspector-General of Police
IOL:	India Office Library
JAS:	*Journal of Asian Studies*
JAOS:	*Journal of American Oriental Society*
JIA:	*Journal of the Indian Archipelago and East Asia*
JMBRAS:	*Journal of the Malayan Branch of the Royal Asiatic Society*
JSBRAS	*Journal of the Straits Branch of the Royal Asiatic Society*
JSEAH:	*Journal of South East Asian History*
JP:	Justice of the Peace
Keesing:	Keesing's Contemporary Archives
KMT:	Kuomintang
MCA:	Malayan Chinese Association
MCP:	Malayan Communist Party
MPAJA:	Malayan People's Anti-Japanese Army
MPAJU:	Malayan People's Anti-Japanese Union
NDYL:	New Democratic Youth League
OCAJA:	Overseas Chinese Anti-Japanese Army
PAP:	People's Action Party
PRO:	Public Record Office, London
RAS Trans.:	*Royal Asiatic Society Transactions*
SFP:	*Singapore Free Press*
SMCYYC:	San Min Chu Yi Youth Corps
SPA:	Singapore People's Alliance
ST:	*Straits Times*
UMNO:	United Malay Nationalist Organization
SATU:	Singapore Association of Trade Unions

FOREWORD

THIS book fills a serious gap which until now has been left largely vacant in the written histories of Malaya and Singapore. Its contents are composed by the most knowledgeable among non-Chinese (and for that matter probably also Chinese) authorities on the intriguing subject of Chinese secret societies in those lands. From my close working association with Wilfred Blythe through a decade in South East Asia after the war I am familiar with his deep knowledge, understanding, and wisdom on that and related subjects. His volume will occupy an essential place on the bookshelves in any library claiming to cover the affairs of the Far East in general and those of South East Asia in particular.

For the last several generations the 'Overseas Chinese' have played a very significant part in the story of Malaya, and a dominant part in that of Singapore. Much has been written on the subject by scholars, historians, and other literary types; yet almost none of them has probed adequately into the crucial influence exerted on the local Chinese communities by the traditional system of secret societies which the original emigrants from China brought with them to Malacca, Penang, and Singapore many generations ago, which spread later into the Sultanic Malay States, and which has flourished more or less continuously in those adopted homes ever since. The societies have given some odd twists to various important developments right up to the present day. In their unique and generally clandestine social, political, and sometimes criminal ways they have contributed powerfully to events. Although their rivalry to the established government was something new in South East Asia when it first appeared there, it was as old as history in China itself. Mr Blythe gives a brief sketch of its origins in ancient Cathay, and then describes in great, revealing detail its reincarnation on the Malay Peninsula. His extraordinary story sometimes reads like a detective novel conceived on a grand scale. For example, he writes on page 345 'The [Ang Bin Hoey] society . . . exerted such a terrorizing influence over the general public that information which might lead to the arrest of its criminals was unobtainable except from detectives and informers, and of these . . . six had been shot dead, two were missing, one had been drowned, and one shot and wounded.'

However, it is much more than a tale of crime. It touches unceasingly, and sometimes commandingly, the everyday lives, economic activities and official governance of the Chinese population, incidentally throwing sharp lights and shades on the character, social organization, and politics of the Chinese, who can boast a longer continuous civilization than any other race on earth. This book is therefore a vivid piece of research, not into a scrap of dead history concerning a comparatively unimportant (however interesting) section of the human family, but into an age-long established and still persisting facet in the make-up of one of the most important peoples still alive and very much kicking, both in their own homeland and overseas. As is well known, they are not only a characterful, able, and cultured people, but often also an enigmatic one to others than themselves. Mr Blythe describes how the somewhat baffled Western-type colonial governments could not fully comprehend the Oriental complexities of the secret societies' organizations, activities, and purposes, and how they strove to cope with the problems these presented according to Occidental political notions and legislative methods which never wholly succeeded in dealing effectively with them. As a background to all this he sketches briefly the history of the mixed Chinese, Malay, and other racial populations in the varied lands on the Malay Peninsula, including their latest vicissitudes during the Second World War, the Japanese Occupation, the formation and later modification of the Malayan Union, the Communist rebellion in the jungle, and the establishment and then partial break-up of Malaysia. He sets down his complicated combinations of facts coherently and clearly, and comments enlighteningly on successive situations. Moreover his book will have enduring value because it cannot now be complemented or replaced at any time by an equally authoritative work. Most of the police records and other documents concerning fairly recent events which he analyses have been destroyed since he studied them, and can never be consulted again.

I am happy to introduce this excellent book to the reading public.

MALCOLM MACDONALD

PREFACE

KNOWLEDGE of the impact of Chinese secret societies in Malaya gained during almost thirty years' experience in the Chinese Affairs Department (the Chinese Protectorate) of the Malayan Governments was augmented through a three years' research project in Malaya sponsored jointly by the University of London and the University of Malaya (then situated in Singapore). For arranging this sponsorship I am indebted to the late Sir Alexander Carr-Saunders, former Director of the London School of Economics and Political Science. My thanks are also due to Dr Charles B. Fahs of the Humanities Division of the Rockefeller Foundation for his interest in the project, and to the Trustees of the Foundation for financial assistance in carrying it out.

I am grateful to the Governments of the Federation of Malaya and of Singapore for placing at my disposal all the material available in their records touching the subject under research, and to the police officers of all ranks who co-operated in the project with such enthusiasm. To my many colleagues (Chinese and European) in the Chinese Affairs Departments who, throughout the country, conducted enquiries, collected information, and translated documents, I am particularly indebted. The warmth of comradeship was very evident.

It was my good fortune to be the Secretary for Chinese Affairs in the Malayan Union (later Federation of Malaya) during the immediate postwar period when a remarkable upsurge of secret-society activity occurred. All documents and paraphernalia seized by the police in raids on initiation ceremonies and on secret premises (including manuscript notebooks of ritual verses) together with copies of statements made to the police, passed through my hands. Later, during the period of the research project, a great deal of information about postwar developments and ritual practices came from the interrogation of secret-society members (including ritual practitioners), some of whom were in police hands, and others who were reached through my own long familiarity with underworld channels. Comments on these sources will be found in Appendix 2. I had hoped to include an account of ritual variations and deviations, but in order to keep the book within bounds the decision had to be taken to concentrate on the impact of the societies and include only the minimum of esoteric material.

I wish to refer to my late friend Mervyn Llewelyn Wynne of the Malayan Police whose researches were published as a restricted document in 1941 under the title *Triad and Tabut*. The Malayan Governments in 1957 approved the distribution of existing copies to suitable university and institutional libraries. Though I differ from his conclusions at a number of points, his work has been both an inspiration and a source of information not otherwise available. To his son, Mr O. R. W. Wynne, I record my thanks for permitting access to his father's manuscripts and notes intended for further chapters. One other book calls for mention: the original book of prints from wood-blocks belonging to the Triad societies in Singapore and Penang at the time of their dissolution in 1890 which was given to the then Governor, Sir Cecil Clementi Smith. The gift to me of this book by Lady Clementi is acknowledged with gratitude.

Most regrettably my former colleague, Victor Purcell of Cambridge, died before publication of this book. His prompt response to many enquiries needing reference to library sources to which, at times, I had no means of access was of the greatest help. So, too, was the similar response by my former colleague, Hugh Bryson, of the British Association of Malaya. I have also to thank Professor Raymond Firth and Professor Maurice Freedman of the London School of Economics for their advice and continuing interest during a very protracted period of preparation, and Professor D. C. Twitchett of the School of Oriental and African Studies, University of London, for comments on Chapter 2.

For proposals to reduce the original very long and detailed study to proportions suitable for publication as a single volume I must thank Mr John Gittings, formerly of Chatham House and at present Assistant Editor of the *Far Eastern Economic Review*, Hong Kong, and for co-operation in achieving this I most warmly thank Miss Hermia Oliver and Miss Katharine Duff, whose careful and zealous editing of a complicated script not only reduced my labours but re-kindled my enthusiasm. To Miss Duff, too, must go a special word of commendation for undertaking the daunting task of preparing the index.

It is impossible adequately to express what I owe to my wife who has been completely involved in the project from the start: finding and copying material (how many thousand pages), drafting, editing, and arguing. This work is a tribute to her steadfast dedication over many years, without which it would never have been accomplished.

The romanization of Chinese words raises difficulties when dealing with people whose normal speech may be any one of five major and several subsidiary Chinese dialects. The apparently simple solution of putting everything into Mandarin (Kuo Yu) does not suit. I have kept to local usage—mainly Hokkien, Cantonese, or Hakka—but even so, the romanization of these sounds may vary. Though disclaiming any precise system, I hope that I have avoided ambiguity.

Grouville, Jersey   W. B.
February 1968

1

INTRODUCTION

THIS study attempts to give some account of the traditional role of secret societies in China, their introduction to the Straits Settlements and the Malay States, their influence on the Chinese population, and the various attempts made by the Governments of this region to deal with the problems thus produced.

We shall see that in China ritualistic societies existed for centuries born of social needs, based on a combination of self-protection and spiritual satisfaction. Once established, such societies frequently deteriorated through the easy profits of power into tyrannical groups of bullies and extortioners battening upon the weaknesses of the public, providing a shelter under which entrepreneurs and traders at every level who were prepared to pay and obey could operate in comparative safety, and yet retaining an aura of chivalry as the poor man's protector and champion. In particular, the Triad Brotherhood, composed of societies of this type with a common ritual, had, since the seventeenth century, been a potent influence in south China throughout the whole of the region from which immigrants to Malaya came.[1]

To the first flood of immigrants arriving in the late eighteenth and early nineteenth centuries, conditions of life in the new country were such that the Triad societies or similar organizations became an even greater social necessity than in the homeland, replacing to some degree the various groupings of family, village, and clan which were operative in China, and frequently offering to the immigrant the one power group to which he could cleave.

In this way the various societies, most of which used the Triad ritual, became the governing bodies of their members. In some places, such as Singapore, separate dialect groups formed their own societies, while in others, of which Penang was an example, societies included in their membership men of various dialects, and even men not of Chinese ethnic stock. At times, too, place of residence or type of employment was the criterion of eligibility, or there might be a combination of several of these factors. But whatever its composition, the society with a secret ritual and binding blood-oath of loyalty provided the individual with a social background, a body politic in miniature, in and through which he found authority, protection, assistance, a sense of kinship, and, through the ritual bond, possibly some measure of spiritual content, in a foreign land where the ruling power was completely alien in race, language, religion, manners, and customs. In these circumstances, reliance by the immigrant on the society was inevitable, to which must be added that the pressure exerted upon him to join was virtually irresistible, for engagement to labour invariably carried with it the

[1] See below, ch. 2.

inescapable implication of belonging to the secret society in control at the place of employment.

This system of domination of the rapidly increasing immigrant community by the society organizations meant that many of the powers which, in British practice at least, were normally in the hands of the Government were wielded by the societies which had their own disciplinary codes including the death penalty, and were disinclined to recognize any authority superior to their own. The existence of this intermediate layer of extra-legal jurisdiction by non-government bodies caused, at times, the best-intentioned policies and legislation to be nullified and the authority of the Government to be set at nought. The societies, indeed, operated a system of control more readily accepted by the Chinese community than that of the Government, and the story of these societies in Malaya concerns, to a large degree, the efforts of British-controlled Governments to use the machinery of English law to deal with this disturbing manifestation of an alien culture.

For while each society was able to govern its own members (subject, however, to jealousies and rifts within the society, and even, at times, subdivisions and separations) there was no provision in this system for any central control acknowledged by all to have supreme power. And as individual societies were constantly in conflict one with another through economic rivalry, competing claims to rights of protection or control, or simply through frictions and affrays between members of different societies, the division of the community into these fraternity groups fostered antagonisms between them on such a scale as to cause murders of revenge, public riots, and other serious disturbances of the peace.

A partial exception to this lack of central control did exist at Singapore where a central organization composed of officers from all the tribal branches of the dominant Ghee Hin Triad fraternity assumed the function of arbiter of disputes between constituent societies or their members.[2] In this way the danger of inter-society antagonisms (within the Ghee Hin organization) developing into threats to the public peace was minimized though never entirely removed. But Triad societies outside the Ghee Hin group, and other non-Triad ritualistic societies owed no allegiance to this central body, so that there were still enough divisions to give scope for public disputes.

In the early years the criminal offences which came to light: assaults, murders, extortion, and public affrays, were regarded as being purely a police problem, a matter of having an adequate and properly-trained police force to ensure that the criminals were brought to book, and efforts were made by successive Governors to improve the size and quality of the force for this purpose. But it was soon apparent that the problem was not as straightforward as this. The normal pattern of complainant and witnesses making statements to the police and then being taken to court to give evidence against an accused person was not valid in this community, for the person committing the crime, if found, was shielded by his secret society which, indeed, might have instigated the crime and would certainly take steps to ensure that no one dared to testify against him. Furthermore, there was no senior police or other government officer who spoke even one of the half-dozen dialects of the immigrants, and no Chinese members of the police force to carry out investigations. Reliance was perforce placed upon

[2] See App. 1, p. 526.

interpreters who themselves were members of secret societies and therefore subject to pressure. And the same would have been true of any Chinese constables who might have been recruited.

There was, therefore, in this network of fraternities embracing the entire Chinese population a social system working against the police and thwarting their efforts to maintain public order. Not that the societies had any particular animus against the Government but merely that each society was traditionally a sufficient government for its members and resented outside interference. Because of this the authorities found themselves forced to consider whether this all-embracing power assumed by the societies should not, in the interests of peace and good government, be curtailed, and if so by what means.

Thoughts naturally turned to legislative controls, first of all to the prohibition of known secret societies by name, but here at once difficulties were encountered. Such a prohibition could readily be evaded by change of name or, if the society was dissolved, by re-forming a new society with a different name. There was also some difficulty in distinguishing between fraternities which were regarded as being inimical to the welfare of the State, and others such as Clan associations which had large memberships and exercised considerable control over their members but were, apparently, welfare societies. The trouble was that the 'inimical' societies also could and did claim to be welfare societies, and with the limited means of investigation available it was some time before the different categories of associations could be sorted out, and the 'secret societies' distinguished.

Societies may be 'secret' in two different ways: they may be clandestine organizations working underground with the identities of their leaders and members carefully concealed, or they may be 'open' societies whose officials are known or knowable, but which have a secret ritual (usually of initiation) and an oath of secrecy binding the members not to reveal the affairs of the society to non-members or, above all, to the authorities. It is, of course, possible for a society to be 'secret' in both these ways.

The Chinese secret societies of early Malaya were secret in the sense that they had a secret ritual and oath. There was no secret about their existence, or in general, about their office-bearers, though when trouble occurred there might be attempts to evade responsibility. And the rituals of all these societies included an oath of secrecy the breaking of which was punishable with death.

Once it was realized that the ultimate sanction for the power exerted by the secret societies lay in this oath, it seemed reasonable to suggest that the law should provide for the prohibition of any association whose members were required to take any oath not authorized by law. In this way it was thought that the stranglehold might be broken. But, as was pointed out by J. R. Logan, the Penang lawyer, it was improbable that any conviction would ever be obtained under such a law for it would never be possible to prove that an oath was, in fact, administered. The suggestion was abandoned.

Meanwhile, police and administrative officers responsible for keeping order found it necessary to establish a *modus vivendi* with the leaders of the secret societies so that in times of disturbance they might be induced to control their members and to reach agreement by arbitration or conciliation. Indeed, a system was adopted (illegally in the early years) whereby the leaders of contending societies were sworn in as special constables and made to accompany the police

B

through the streets in times of riots so that the danger to which they were exposed would sharpen their appreciation of the need for pacification.

While this uneasy relationship between the authorities and the societies continued, ways were sought through the framing of legislation to strengthen the hands of the police in times of disturbance. Suggestions which were put forward from time to time came, naturally, from European officials or leading members of the European unofficial community, and among them were: registration of all inhabitants and the appointment of headmen as District Peace Officials, the registration of all secret societies and their office-bearers and members, and the granting of powers of banishment to the Governor. None of these proposals was acceptable to the Government of India whose sanction was necessary before any such measures could be introduced for the Straits Settlements were still administered as an offshoot of India. The fact was that the climate of liberalism which pervaded governmental circles whether in India or in England was antipathetic to restrictive legislation of this nature. Indeed, even the Governors of the Straits Settlements who were faced with this problem continued in the belief that it was primarily a police problem and that special legislation was unnecessary. It was not until 1866 that the retiring Governor, Cavenagh, reached the conclusion that some further measures of control should be introduced.

In the Malay States at that time there was no British control. In the tin-mining areas of Perak, Selangor, and the territory now known as Negri Sembilan, the Malay rulers and chiefs, having made their own arrangements with the secret society leaders as to the amount of taxation to be paid by the miners and the holders of the revenue 'farms', then left the Chinese communities to their own resources, and when inter-society fighting even amounting to civil war took place they were powerless to intervene.

The transfer of the Straits Settlements to the control of the Colonial Office in 1867 coincided with a vicious secret society riot in Penang, the immediate result of which was the introduction of an Act for the Better Preservation of the Peace which empowered the Governor in Council to issue a proclamation whenever a state of disturbance was feared, whereupon the carrying of arms or offensive weapons became an offence. Powers were also given to the Governor in Council to remove from the Colony any person, not being a British subject, and there were other powers for dispersing mobs and requiring normal trading to continue. This Act, though intended as a temporary measure in force for only one year, was found to be so useful that it was renewed from time to time until in 1872 it was incorporated into the body of permanent law. There was no attempt, however, in this Act to deal with societies as such.

But once the Penang Riots were over, a Commission which sat to investigate its causes made recommendations which resulted in the introduction of a Bill aimed at controlling the secret societies. Though the Bill was stated to be 'for the suppression of Dangerous Societies', by the time its provisions had been whittled down in Council it contained no powers of suppression but provided for the registration of all societies of ten or more persons (with the exception of the Freemasons), whether dangerous or not. Once registered, a society which had illegal objects or was likely to be a threat to the public peace could be called upon to furnish detailed information as to members, ceremonies, rules, and accounts, and the office-bearers might be required to find sureties not to infringe the law. Societies participating in riots could be fined and required to pay compensation for injury to persons or property. This law, passed in December 1869, like the previous Act, began as a temporary measure for one year, but in 1872 became permanent.

As a result of the introduction of this new law it was possible to remove some of the more stringent provisions of the Peace Preservation Act, one of the most important amendments being the restriction of the scope of banishment to office-bearers of Dangerous Societies participating in riots during the existence of a proclamation. It was hoped that these two laws would act as a deterrent to the society leaders and that the powers provided would rarely be used.

But despite the increased powers thus vested in the Government, disturbances within the Chinese communities still continued. Not all of these were attributable to secret society action, some were natural responses to the imposition of unpopular restrictive municipal legislation, but the impression remained that the Chinese population contained unruly elements which were insufficiently restrained and which, in conjunction with the widespread secret society organization, were a danger to public order. Discussions and debates canvassed the possible benefits of restriction of Chinese immigration and the extension of the 'Capitan'[3] system so that a leader of each 'tribe' would be responsible for the behaviour of all its members. To a measure designed to control immigration the Government would readily have agreed, but the vested interests of the merchants and entrepreneurs in the business of importing cheap labour created such a strong opposition to any restrictive measure that no development along these lines was pursued. As for the extension of the Capitan system on the lines adopted in the Dutch East Indies, this was a form of regimentation unlikely to be approved by any British Government except as a last extremity.

Once again, too, the possibility of introducing Chinese constables into the police force was debated, but the danger of corruption through secret society influence was held to be too great. The one additional positive step taken was the appointment of a European government officer with a knowledge of Chinese as an interpreter, though it was also laid down that he would assist the Government in any matters concerning the Chinese community.

This officer (W. A. Pickering) arrived in Singapore early in 1872, and in the following year was appointed to be a 'Protector'. From the outset his advice was sought by the Government on all Chinese affairs, and the responsibility for carrying out the registration of societies was transferred to his hands from those of the police, resulting in a more thorough and accurate record. Before long he had established a position of influence among the leaders of the secret societies in Singapore, and this greatly increased the importance of this channel of communication between the Government and the Chinese population. He soon realized the danger of allowing the societies to exist at all, and would have favoured a system of regimentation on the Dutch pattern, but as this was not acceptable, and as he considered that the societies were too strong to be suppressed without the introduction of some such system to take their place, he continued the existing practice of exerting influence upon the society leaders through consultation and instruction backed, as they knew, by the sanctions which the Government now possessed. In this way pressure was brought to bear on these leaders to control mob activities and riotous outbursts, and this method

[3] Capitan or Kapitan: a term used throughout Malaya (probably from the Portuguese) to denote the 'captain' or headman of a community.

of liaison between the Protector and the societies continued to be an accepted feature of administrative practice in the Straits Settlements.

It was never able to achieve more than partial effectiveness, and that only in times of crisis, for the societies suffered from no inhibitions in the continuance of their 'protection' activities, the promotion of illicit gaming, the exploitation of brothels, the adjudication of their 'courts', and the inter-society quarrels, jealousies, and vendettas. Loss of face arising from any of these sources might at any moment erupt into violence and a riot be precipitated. Nevertheless, the establishment of the Chinese Protectorate, as Pickering's department was called, undoubtedly did ensure more effective control than had previously existed.

It was in the Malay States, and particularly in the Larut area of Perak, that the full viciousness of government by the secret societies was seen, areas where the primitive Malay Government was completely overwhelmed by aggregations of thousands of Chinese miners recognizing no authority but that of their leaders who were also headmen of their secret societies. The chaos resulting from two bloody civil wars between competing Chinese factions among the miners led to the intervention of the British in the Malay States in 1874. Thereafter it was made plain in each of the States which came under British influence that secret societies were prohibited, and though the natural result of this policy was that the societies continued to exist clandestinely, it did clear the way for the authorities to take action against such societies and their members whenever they came to light and demonstrated to the Chinese community that membership carried with it the risk of prosecution and imprisonment if discovered, and that active organizers or officials of such societies might expect to be banished to China.

In the Straits Settlements the old policy of toleration continued, despite the accumulation of evidence of the obnoxious grip exerted by the societies on the Chinese community and the knowledge of their complicity in riotous outbreaks, which evoked bitter comment and criticism of the Government's policy from unofficial members of the Legislative Council. Pickering's view of the danger of suppressing the societies unless they were replaced by other controls prevailed in official circles until 1888 when a new Governor (Sir Cecil Clementi Smith), with experience of governing Chinese in Hong Kong where secret societies were prohibited, and (as Colonial Secretary) in the Straits Settlements where they were tolerated, vigorously insisted on the need for suppression, overruled Pickering, and, in 1889, obtained the agreement of the Legislative Council to a Societies Ordinance which required all societies of ten or more persons to register, and empowered the Governor in Council to refuse to register any society which had among its objects purposes incompatible with the peace or good order of the Colony. It also provided for an order of dissolution to be made against any society if it appeared necessary for the public safety or welfare to take such action. The punishment for assisting in the management of an unlawful society might extend to three years' imprisonment, and for membership to a fine of $500 and/or imprisonment for six months.

The law came into force on 1 January 1890 and, with some amendments specifically outlawing societies which used a Triad ritual and making it an offence to be in possession of Triad documents or other paraphernalia, remained the basic law through which the control of secret societies was exercised until the Japanese conquest of Malaya. All prosecutions under this law required the sanction of the Protector of Chinese (in his capacity of Registrar of Societies) and this same official had the power to order photographs and fingerprints of individuals to be taken if, after interrogation, he was satisfied that they had not told the truth concerning their connexion with unlawful societies. Side by side with this law of control and suppression went the Banishment Ordinance under which, eventually, any person other than a British subject could be banished at any time if his removal was considered by the Governor in Council to be necessary for the peace or welfare of the country.

Legislation on similar lines was adopted throughout the Malay States (although Johore did not fall into line until 1916) and the use of the powers provided in these two laws was sufficient to hold in check the more serious outbursts of mass secret society violence such as had for so long menaced the public peace. In addition to these restrictive and repressive measures, the extension of branches of the Chinese Protectorate throughout Malaya provided a poor man's tribunal to which all Chinese had access without payment of court or lawyers' fees and where an official trained in their language and customs could hear accusations, adjudicate on claims, arbitrate in disputes, and reconcile quarrels, thus removing some at least of the grounds which normally led to inter-society warfare.

But although this position of equilibrium was achieved, and on the whole maintained until the Japanese invasion, the secret society virus still continued to infect the Chinese community, developing robustly wherever official pressure was relaxed or could only with difficulty be effectively exercised. The concept of the secret society as part of the social fabric still remained even though tempered with the knowledge that such organizations were unlawful, and the public were constantly faced with the dilemma of deciding which was the greater danger: to report the activities of these societies or to yield to their demands. As has been suggested above, the pressure upon the public varied considerably, tending to be stronger in areas remote from control or where officials were lax, or where detectives or other officers were open to bribery. Under such circumstances the ritualistic Triad societies frequently continued to exist. But the pressure was never completely absent even in the urban areas where, very often, the secret societies had degenerated into or been replaced by hooligan gangs which, as a consequence of police action, had discarded the ritualistic trappings of the old societies but retained the techniques of extortion, pressure, and reprisal, working upon the ingrained traditional fears of the community.

The scene was diversified during the last thirty years before the Japanese war by the emergence of Chinese political societies reflecting the political movements taking place in China. Some of these societies, such as the Chung Woh T'ong and the Chi Kung T'ong, were direct offshoots of the Triad Brotherhood, using its ritual, while others, such as the Kuomintang (KMT), though not so closely bound to Triad fashioned their rules on the Triad pattern with oaths of secrecy and punishments for disobedience; and one and all were prepared to use the traditional pressure techniques to gain their ends. This new development must be taken into account when painting the picture of comparative calm during this period, for the political societies provided other channels through which the urge for fraternal contact could be satisfied, and, though there were cases of public disturbance directly attributable to political societies, they were not, on the whole, engaged in criminal activities on the same level as the old societies. The later establishment of a Communist Party in Malaya, almost entirely of Chinese organization and membership, though quite different from the Triad pattern, provided yet another nucleus for an organization, but one which had the avowed object of disturbing the peace, and frequently did so.

Nevertheless, the vigilance of the various sections of the police; the Special Branch in the political field, the CID in the criminal, and the Chinese Protectorate over the whole of the activities of the Chinese community, enabled the governments in Malaya to maintain a reasonable balance of order, upset from time to time by the viciousness of Singapore gangs or the mob-appeal of China-based political organizations. The governments were, however, increasingly conscious that the effectiveness of the banishment laws which provided the main sanction on which they relied for keeping the peace in the society world was steadily being eroded by the increasing number of members who were locally-born and who, for this reason, could not be removed. It was necessary, too, to take into consideration the effect on the relations between Great Britain and China of action taken against the China-based political groups. But despite these limiting factors the incidence of crime and of public disturbance was kept within reasonable bounds; indeed, when the multi-racial nature of the population and the multi-tribal composition of the large Chinese section of the population are taken into account, the relative freedom from serious trouble originating with the secret societies may even be regarded as remarkable.

Shortly before the Japanese war there were officers of the Chinese Protectorate who drew attention to the great amount of useless work entailed in the keeping of records of all registered and exempted societies, of which only very few could be regarded as dangerous, and suggested that the Societies Ordinance might well be replaced by one on the Hong Kong model where a simple law empowered the Governor in Council to declare a society to be unlawful if its activities were prejudicial to public peace or welfare. Oddly enough, at the same time there were officials in Hong Kong who were suggesting that the Hong Kong law was inadequate and advocated the introduction of a law on the Singapore model. The Japanese occupation of both colonies effectively closed the discussion.

The Postwar Scene

The occupation of Malaya by the Japanese army introduced a régime in which the niceties of judicial procedure in operation during the period of British control were no longer observed. Hundreds of secret society members were executed out of hand; others fled to the jungle to join the resistance groups, most of which were organized by the Malayan Communist Party (MCP), while others found employment as informers to the Japanese on the criminal activities of their brethren and on any anti-Japanese moves they could discover.

But while the Japanese administration was ruthless in exterminating undesirable elements, it did not succeed in eradicating the secret society virus. Indeed, it is known that on the Perak coast the Japanese officer in charge was in league with a local secret society in the promotion of smuggling, and as the Japanese in many parts of the country were engaged in smuggling and black-market activities it is reasonable to assume that the secret societies were also involved as active agents. But very little information is available, and it would appear that such secret societies as were not thus protected moved with great caution, though initiation ceremonies did take place.

With the surrender of the Japanese army and the entry of British troops there came a complete change of climate. The policy of freedom of association laid down by the British Government coupled with the feeling of elation induced by the liberation led to a proliferation of societies of all kinds throughout Malaya. The Government of Singapore were disinclined to abandon the old Societies Ordinance, and in the rest of Malaya, now organized under one central government as the Malayan Union (later to become the Federation of Malaya), it was soon evident that the abandonment of the controls formerly operating under the Societies Ordinance and the Banishment Ordinance encouraged Triad societies to come out into the open again and to assume overall powers in the Chinese community similar to those which existed in the early days of Penang.

Although there had been an announcement of the non-implementation of the old Societies Ordinance, no public mention had been made of the intention to introduce a law on the Hong Kong model which also banned Triad societies, and it was therefore generally assumed that Triad societies were no longer unlawful. It was five months before this omission was remedied, and in the meantime the Triad societies had developed to such an extent that, in Penang in particular, they presented a serious challenge to the Government. Thousands of members were recruited and initiated with the full ceremony and the blood-oath, and every section of the community of Penang from millionaire to beggar was subjected to taxation and extortion levied by branches of this society. In the rest of Malaya the domination of Triad, though not as complete as this, was very widespread.

Once the enforcement of the anti-Triad sections of the old Societies law was announced, it was possible, through prosecutions and the reluctant use once again of the powers of banishment against those society members proved to have been involved in criminal acts, to put a damper on the overt activities of the Triad societies. This gradually took effect, though the under-manned, ill-equipped, and overworked police force could not give to the problem the attention it deserved, and the abolition, for political reasons, of the Chinese Protectorate added to the difficulties.

But apart from the Triad societies, all other associations were lawful, and the public found themselves fleeced and pressured by a legion of newly-formed associations, often under the guise of Benevolent Societies, together with Communist organizations and KMT branches in addition to a vastly increased criminal fraternity with arms readily available. The subsequent introduction (1947) of a law providing for voluntary registration of societies proved, after two years of trial, to be a failure, and once again legislation on the lines of the prewar law was passed requiring all societies to apply for registration. The Singapore Government had already obtained the consent of the Secretary of State to the re-enforcement of the prewar Societies Ordinance, so that the Federation and Singapore were now, once again, on the same basis, and in both territories the efficiency of the police force was increased by reorganization which created specialist sections of the CID to deal solely with secret societies.

Meanwhile a new threat to peace had made its appearance in the shape of the revolt organized by the MCP which by sabotage and terrorism created even more violent and dangerous disturbances than had previously occurred, and led to the assumption by the Government of special emergency powers under which any person likely to be a threat to the public peace could be arrested and detained without trial. These powers were widely used, not only against those believed to be connected with the Communist movement but also against known and sus-pected secret society organizers and members, with the result that some weaken-ing of the secret society fabric took place. From time to time there were revivals of Triad activity, but so long as these emergency powers continued and were used in this fashion it was always possible to contain the threat which, despite the operation of the new Societies Ordinance and the now freer use of the powers of banishment, would otherwise probably have been a serious embarrassment to the Government. Significantly, in Singapore, where similar Emergency Regulations were brought into force, a later decision not to use these powers against persons unconnected with the Communist movement, and the release of those secret society members who had been arrested under the Regulations before this deci-sion was taken, led at once to an increase of crime and lawlessness due directly to the societies and their gangsters.

In the Federation no such relaxation of the use of the powers of detention took place, and the police made full use of them to ensure that the advent of inde-pendence in 1957 did not lead to increased society activity on the pretext that once the British had left the societies would provide protection for the Chinese community against a Malay-majority Government. The withdrawal of British control and the introduction of a popular franchise added a further dimension to the sphere of secret society influence in the local political field, and the same was true later in Singapore under similar circumstances.

The formation of local political parties and the consequent campaigning and canvassing for elections proved an irresistible opportunity for the employment of secret society personnel with their usual techniques of intimidation and pressure. In addition, repeated attempts were made to induce the Singapore Government to consent to the formation of an 'umbrella' organization with membership open to all Triad Brethren, a combination which, had it been permitted to exist, would have had very powerful political implications.

When, in the Federation, the Communist revolt was eventually defeated and the Emergency Regulations were withdrawn, the powers of arrest and detention continued to operate for they had, in the meantime, been embodied in the permanent law, together with other provisions relating to known secret society members and other criminal types whose identity cards could be stamped with a special symbol and who were liable to double penalties should they commit an offence.

Singapore obtained a new transitional Constitution with an elected Chief Minister and Council of Ministers in February 1955, and the first legislative step taken by the newly-elected Government (April 1955) was the cancellation of the Emergency Regulations. But it was soon discovered that the main powers of arrest and detention were still needed, and they were reluctantly embodied in a new Ordinance which was to be in force for one year. In practice the same dis-tinction as previously obtained continued to be observed, and the law was not applied to criminals who had no Communist connexion, so that it was of no use to the police in their war against the secret societies whose criminal activities were rapidly increasing.

There were signs of a deterioration in internal security encouraged, no doubt, by the assumption that an elected people's government would not be disposed to risk its popularity by harsh measures. Clandestine Communist organizations promoted and exacerbated industrial disputes, strikes, and riots, creating a climate of disorder in which the secret society gangsters flourished. Much thought was given to forms of legislation which might check the rising power of the societies, and several additional powers were given to the police and to the courts, but eventually it had reluctantly to be admitted that nothing short of the powers of arrest and detention without open trials, as used against the Communists, would suffice to relieve the public of the daily menace of the gangs which by extortion, murder, and affrays made life intolerable; and legislation was passed vesting the Government with these powers. The sincerity of the Singapore Government in wishing to avoid this step is unquestionable, but having examined every possible alternative and tried those that were feasible, they were forced into the same position as that which the Government of the Federation had adopted, and, once again, both territories possessed similar laws for use in the control of secret societies and their members.

The position had now been reached where it was accepted that normal judicial procedures as embodied in English law were clearly inadequate to deal with this Chinese social problem in Malaya (in which term Singapore is, of course, included).

It may be argued that the assumption of exceptional powers of this nature has proved to be advisable in many if not most of the newly-emergent States once the colonial power has been withdrawn, but usually this has been because of fears of political subversion, akin to the use of Emergency Regulations in Malaya to counter Communist subversion. In Malaya, on the other hand, these powers were equally required for dealing with secret societies not as political organizations seeking the overthrow of the Government but as disturbers of the public peace by their criminal acts.

The question which now arises is whether any judicial system other than the English would be any more successful in solving this problem. Certainly neither the Government of the Ch'ing dynasty in China nor that of the Japanese army (during its comparatively short period) whether in China or Malaya was able to keep secret societies suppressed to the point of extinction. Both these administrations were ruthless in the imposition of the death penalty, though it must also be remarked that the severity of the law was sometimes tempered in practice by the corruptibility of the lower ranks of both administrations. Has the present People's Government of China had any greater success? Little has been heard in recent years of secret societies in China, though there was clear evidence that they still existed and were a nuisance to the Government in 1961 and were ruthlessly suppressed. But if history is any guide this will not eradicate the virus.

The prevalence of gangs of youthful hooligans is now a commonplace in most countries, and there can be no doubt that the postwar universal climate of turmoil and indiscipline has aggravated the problem in Malaya as elsewhere. But (apart, perhaps, from the Sicilian Mafia) gangs in western countries seldom have the historical, traditional, ritualistic background of a brotherhood such as the Triad, and it may well be that much more radical treatment than the passing of repressive legislation and the incarceration (or, as in China, the execution) of secret society members is necessary if this cancer is to be removed; the abandonment, perhaps, of those items of Chinese history, mythology, and tradition which stimulate successive generations to emulate the achievements of the Heroes of Liang Shan.[4]

[4] See below, p. 19.

It would seem that the Communist Party in China has some such aim in view: the utilization of the tremendous acclaim accorded to these heroes of Chinese traditional history by transforming them into the progenitors or prototypes of Communist comrades, thus assimilating them into the Communist ethos with the intent that the ineradicable popular admiration and enthusiasm for these heroes shall be deflected to the party, its leaders, and its achievements.

Mao Tse-tung in 1927 referred to this transference of old urges in these terms:

the members of the secret societies [in Hunan] have all joined the peasant associations in which they can openly and legally play the hero and vent their grievances, so that there is no further need for the secret 'mountain', 'lodge', 'shrine', and 'river' forms of organisation. In killing the pigs and sheep of the local bullies and bad gentry and imposing heavy levies and fines, they have adequate outlets for their feelings against those who oppressed them.[5]

And it may well be that in the course of a generation or two of indoctrination in the new 'history' a new tradition will emerge sufficiently strong to supplant the old and to turn the energies of those who would formerly have become Triad devotees into channels through which they will become equally fervid supporters of the party and the Government. But this will not be known in our time.

There is, perhaps, something to be learnt from the history of the Chinese in Malaya before the 1930s when the gap between the Straits Chinese and their China-looking brethren was wider than it is today. Members of the latter group (comprising the majority), though among them were many who were locally-born, were educated at Chinese schools on the Chinese pattern. Often their parents were born in China, so that at school and at home they were imbued with the traditional Chinese ethos, of which secret societies were a natural component. The Straits Chinese, on the other hand, came from families which had been born locally, often for generations, and educated in English at western-type schools offering western history, ethics, and behaviour patterns, so that the original Chinese ethos was progressively diluted, and the loyalties and enthusiasms of Chinese tradition had largely lost their appeal. As a result, the proportion of Straits Chinese interested in secret societies was relatively small, and it is reasonable to assume that had English school education been available to the whole of the Chinese child population during the nineteenth century, the impact of secret societies in the present century would have been significantly reduced.

To suggest that this could ever be, however, is to assume the impossible, for although considerably more extensive English education could well have been provided, the massive flow of people from and to China, as well as financial considerations, precluded any such all-inclusive educational policy. Today the position is very different. No longer do hundreds of thousands of labourers stream in from China annually to revivify the Triad tradition and, in due course, bringing wives and families with them. For years now the door has been closed to immigration, and there is every reason, economic, social, and political, why it should never again be opened. The number of China-born children in Malaya is rapidly decreasing, and already the provision of an educational system based on local needs is taking shape.

What is hinted at here, then, is a basic cultural change, though the pattern of

---

[5] *Selected Works* (Peking, 1964), i. 53, quoted by Stuart Schram in 'Mao Tse-tung and Secret Societies', *China Quarterly*, July–Sept. 1966, p. 5.

the future would need to be not so much a western-type system as a Malayan-type, providing local symbols to replace those of Chinese tradition to hold the interest, enthusiasm, and loyalty with which students are so generously endowed. There is no doubt, however, that any such change will be strenuously resisted by the China-looking group, just as all previous moves to reduce the China political influence in their schools have been resisted, but if the large Chinese community is to be assimilated as citizens of an independent country, sooner or later this cultural adjustment must be brought about.

The wide powers now possessed by the governments in Malaya would seem to be essential in present circumstances if the peace is to be preserved, but the detention of hundreds of secret society members, while it takes the thugs off the streets and gives a welcome respite to the public and to the police, can scarcely be regarded as a final solution. If the detainees through education or indoctrination and the learning of trades can be transformed into useful citizens and be provided with work on release, that is all to the good. That was the aim of the Pulau Senang scheme which, praiseworthy though it was, ended in catastrophe through too great a belief in the efficacy of reformation and too little provision of security precautions.[6] But any such schemes deal only with those who are already in the grip of the societies, and there must be many among them who are not responsive to such treatment. Nor must it be thought that this is primarily an economic problem—of finding jobs for the youthful population as it emerges—though unemployment certainly aggravates the condition. It is essentially an ethical problem.

It is hoped that this study through a review of the history of secret societies in Malaya will reveal their deep-seated nature and their widespread impact, actual and potential, on the daily life of the Chinese even at the present time, and that it will help to place the problem in its sociological setting. It is for the administrators on the spot who are in touch with the public and who, in these days of elected governments, draw their authority and power from the people, to devise experiments and policies which may be applicable and feasible, for that which is possible may well vary from one election to another. In this they will deserve the greatest measure of sympathy and understanding, for the problem is not the least intractable of those faced by the Governments both in Kuala Lumpur and in Singapore.

[6] See below, pp. 520–3.

2

THE CHINA BACKGROUND

BECAUSE of the deep-seated nature of the secret society organism in the Chinese social system it is advisable, before considering the activities of these societies in Malaya, to mention briefly a few of the concepts, religious, ethical, and social, which lay behind the secret society tradition in China, and to give some indication of their influence in that country up to recent times.

A propensity to form groups for mutual support and the attainment of common objectives has long been a characteristic of the Chinese social pattern. The family and the clan were natural associations of blood relations with well-understood obligations between members, but a similar sense of commitment extended to other types of associations: to those formed of men of a particular district or province living away from their home areas, to associations of traders or workers, separately or jointly as guilds which maintained discipline within particular groups and protected the external interests of their members. To those individuals who had left their ancestral villages to seek work elsewhere in China or abroad, surrounded by strangers of different language groups, such associations were of paramount importance in relieving their feeling of isolation and ignorance. Through them they could meet men of their own speech and of similar territorial origins, organized as a 'friendly society' with a governing body of elders of recognized prestige able to help the newcomer in the solution of his problems and the settlement of disputes.

Many such associations, in addition to having meeting places for business and social purposes and providing a traditional tribunal readily accessible, also had benevolent schemes for the provision of benefits in sickness, unemployment, or death, either through regular monthly subscriptions or by levies on members. Even if no such scheme existed there would be, at least, provision of a coffin and a set of funeral regalia, including lanterns bearing in large characters the name of the society. All members, no matter how humble or indigent, were thus assured of the prestige of a ceremonial burial. This may seem of small importance to the western mind, but a Chinese attached great significance to the funeral rites which enabled the spirits of the dead to proceed on their way with decorum. To the labourer working away from home and family it was a great comfort to know that provision had been made for his funeral and that his body would not be abandoned in a hole or thrown into the river like that of a dog, and his spirits left to howl bewildered in space. According to Chinese folk-lore the most important thing in life is to be buried with proper respect.

In the organization of these groups there was invariably a religious element: the worship of ancestors in the family and clan, and the adoption of a tutelary deity by other groups to be honoured at fixed times by fêtes, sacrifices, and theatrical performances. In each group there developed a sense of solidarity and collective interest and of reliance upon their own organization rather than upon the state. Each had its own exclusiveness, jealously guarding the interests of its members and latently hostile towards outsiders.

Among secret sects, brotherhoods, and societies there has frequently been a still greater emphasis on religious ritual, reflecting the traditional philosophical and ethical beliefs of the people. Elements from the worship of natural features abound: of Heaven and Earth, the planets, the sun and moon, and the recognition of the existence of a system of natural law—the Tao—governing the relationship between all the constituents of the universe, in particular Heaven, Earth, and Man, producing a divine harmony of universal tranquillity and justice: 'T'ai P'ing.'

Confucianism makes its contribution through its emphasis on the relationship between individuals—the principle of 'Yi' (justice or right conduct between men) and 'Chung' (loyalty to the group), in addition to the concept of the family nature of the political structure with the emperor as father of the people, responsible for their welfare. Ancestor worship is reflected in the provision of 'ancestors', real or imaginary, by such groups as part of their ritual.

The influence of popular Taoism is to be found in sects and cults practising various hygiene techniques: breathing exercises, the avoidance of alcohol or of meat or grain foods, the drinking of pure water, the search for an elixir, the interaction of Yin and Yang in the perfection of harmony. Alchemy and occultism were frequently employed, as well as the mystical significance of numbers, in particular the multiples of the number three: 18, 21, 36, 72, and 108, and the use of the perfect number, five. Throughout popular Taoism, too, ran a streak of anarchy, of opposition to control, which added to its suitability for incorporation in the rituals of rebellious sects and movements.

Buddhism, too, in its Chinese development, provided many features readily absorbed into ritualistic practice. Kuan Yin, the Goddess of Mercy, with her ship of salvation, appears in the ritual of the secret Triad Brotherhood, as does Bodhidharma under the name of 'Ta Mo' (a sinification of 'dharma'). The monastery at which he lived in the sixth century—that of Shao Lin in Honan— was renowned as the home of the 'warrior monks' who taught the art of Chinese boxing,[1] and the Triad Brotherhood has made use of this historical item in the composition of a mythical account of its own origin.[2]

The famous seditious White Lotus sect prominent from the twelfth century onwards with a high Taoist content in its ritual, 'borrowed' its title from a Buddhist devotional school founded in the fifth century.[3]

In ways such as these, strands from the complicated fabric of the Chinese ethos have been woven into the rituals of secret associations, creating a popular emotional appeal with a sense of continuity and authority.

These fraternities took various forms. Some started as religious sects, variants of Taoism or Buddhism, or perhaps adopting a ritual combining elements from both; others were frankly seditious from the start, and others, again, were media through which rogues and charlatans fleeced the public. Couling rightly calls attention to the difficulty of tracing the history of any particular sect: 'Societies

[1] J. J. M. De Groot, 'Militant Spirit of the Buddhist Clergy', *T'oung Pao*, 1891
[2] B. Favre, *Les Sociétés Secrètes en Chine* (1933), 116–32, 200–2.
[3] P. Pelliot, 'La Secte du Lotus Blanc et la Secte du Nuage Blanc', *BEFEO*, iii (1903); S. Couling, *Encyclopaedia Sinica* (1917), p. 467.

originally political became also religious with the addition of new blood or in new conditions, and vice versa; some died out or were persecuted into silence, to be revived, perhaps under a new name and in another place with or without modification in doctrine and organization . . .'[4]

One special form of relationship within the Chinese social pattern should be mentioned, that of sworn brotherhood which, though of great antiquity, was popularly exemplified by the legend of the Peach Garden Trio of the second century A.D. It concerned three strangers, Liu Pei, Kuan Yu, and Chang Fei who, at a time when the throne was threatened by revolt, bound themselves by an oath of brotherhood to be loyal to each other until death, to save the state and serve the people. It is from this legend that the figure of Kuan Yu has emerged, deified as Kuan Ti, the God of War, the symbol of courage, devotion, and loyalty. His picture is widely encountered not only in temples but in houses and association premises in a position of honour as the tutelary deity. Sworn brother relations are still a common feature of Chinese life, even in the commercial world, and whenever the oath is taken it supersedes all other ties and is binding until death. This same link of sworn brotherhood is a usual ingredient of secret societies.

SECRET SECTS AND SOCIETIES

Although the formation of associations known as secret sects or secret societies with seditious aims was rooted in antiquity, the exact period at which such combinations emerged is open to conjecture.

Needham[5] suggests a relationship between secret societies of the first bronze founders of 1600 B.C. or earlier and the 'legendary rebels' who received favourable mention in Taoist texts. Favre,[6] however, has pointed out that the Spring and Autumn Annals which purport to tell the story of the middle Chou period made no mention of any secret societies, though the various afflictions affecting the state which are therein recorded—politics, massacre, and distress resulting from the disintegration of the central feudal authority—might be expected to include such groups. Eberhard[7] suggests that the seeds of the secret society as a medium of expression by an excessively-oppressed peasant class are to be found in the sects of shamanistic origin which existed in the third century B.C.; and the circumstances surrounding the revolt which led to the foundation of the Han dynasty in 202 B.C. and placed a commoner, Liu Chi, on the throne tend to support the presumption that the rebels were then organized on a secret society pattern.

In the period of turmoil and brigandage before the founding of the Eastern Han dynasty in A.D. 25 many such bodies were in existence. The 'Red Eyebrows' were responsible for the defeat of the old and the setting up of the new dynasty, and among other rebellious bands of the period were the 'Copper Horses', the 'Iron Shins', the 'Green Groves', and the 'Big Spears'.[8]

By this time it is also known that a class of wanderers had come into existence, uprooted peasantry, the victims of flood, famine, war, or oppressive taxation, wandering gipsies, stopping wherever sustenance could be found. These vagabonds were everywhere unwelcome, for like locusts they were all-devouring.

[4] Couling, p. 501.   [5] *Science and Civilization in China* (1954–6), ii. 119.
[6] Favre, p. 43.   [7] W. Eberhard, *A History of China* (1950), p. 60.
[8] W. Stanton, 'The Triad Society or Heaven and Earth Association', *China Review*, xxi & xxii (1899), reprinted Hong Kong, 1900, p. 1.

They rejected the authority of the state which had failed to ensure their livelihood and were treated as outlaws and bandits. This was the raw material readily available for the formation of secret sects and societies whose members were banded together by a ritual of initiation and an oath of loyalty and secrecy, and who acknowledged no authority but that of their leaders.[9]

This class of vagabond outlaws later came to be known as 'Han Liu'—(in the tradition of Han)—thus linking them in popular fancy with the founder of the Han dynasty, the first commoner to reach the throne by popular revolt. In their own jargon they were 'good fellows of the rivers and lakes', and to them were attracted rebellious spirits, unemployed, dispossessed, criminals, and fugitives from the law, men who were 'on the waters', living in the hills or marshes, but with points of contact throughout the community.[10]

Once such a society was established in an area, the whole locality rapidly became enmeshed. Landlords, shopkeepers, and all who had a source of income found it worth while, indeed, essential to existence, to pay for the society's protection.

In addition to the tradition of robbing the rich to pay the poor, such societies were invariably opposed to established authority. In this they were frequently representative of the attitude of the people at large who regarded government officials as venal oppressors, and such bands of 'heroes' able to keep such officials in check by fear of death could, with some justification, claim to be upholders of 'Yi', justice for the common man.

This mistrust and dislike of government officials was so ingrained that recourse to the court of a magistrate was avoided like the plague, and every effort was made to settle disputes by means outside the framework of official legal processes. In this system of conciliation and arbitration the various voluntary associations played their important parts, but here, too, the secret society found a field for the enjoyment of power and profit. Local secret societies became the reservoirs of power, the source of the unofficial sanctions necessary in the final stages of the working of the extra-legal machinery. The power which they possessed rested upon readiness to kill should their demands be refused or their commands disobeyed, and over all was fear. Among members there was not only the fear of death at the hands of their comrades should the oaths of loyalty and secrecy be broken, but also the fear of the gods instilled through a religious ritual of initiation, the revelation of which, or of other business of the society, would be known to the gods and punished by inescapable death.

Over the centuries, at times of aggravated social discontent caused by flood, famine, conscription, or excessive taxation, a leader would emerge from the rabble and be credited with extraordinary powers. Rumours of unusual natural phenomena would circulate, and the news that a leader was at hand would spread over the countryside. He might be a Taoist or a Buddhist priest, or lay claim to being the Maitreya, the Buddha reincarnate, drawing to his banner the superstitious, credulous, bemused masses with promises of better things to come. Or he might claim to be the scion of a previous dynastic family come to regain the ancestral throne, thus appealing to the sense of historical continuity. Or again, he might be one who had failed in the official examinations with a grievance against authority on that account, or, perhaps, just a man with blood on his

---

[9] M. Loewe, *Imperial China* (1966), pp. 132, 180–1.
[10] Mao Tse-tung, *Selected Works* (1955), i. 20.

hands, a fugitive from justice, a lusty hero 'on the waters' with nothing to lose, calling upon the people to help him to overthrow injustice.

Ch'i Yi (Hei Yi) was the term for an uprising of the people (Rising in the name of Justice). The local magistrate was frequently the first victim, both as the representative of the object of hatred, the Government, and to ensure that the authority of his seal could not be employed against the rebels. Thereafter the movement snowballed in frightening fashion, and the terror of mob rule caused all to submit. The military power was rarely adequate to quell the rising, so the troops joined the rebels to escape annihilation. A rebellion had been born, and was likely to sweep through the country like a prairie fire, uprooting the population, devastating the crops, and eventually leading to the overthrow of the ruler and his line. The genesis of such a movement, the core of the original rebel band, was a local secret society, and, as the movement spread, other similar groups joined in, for it was the tradition of them all to oppose constituted authority.

The secret sects and societies were, in fact, as much a part of the constitutional machinery of China as are the political party and the ballot box in the West. They were the ultimate instruments for the relief of oppression, and opened a way for changing a Government with which the people were dissatisfied. In addition, these fraternities gave to their members a feeling of security and of strength in numbers, as well as providing through ritualistic practices a means of satisfying to some degree the inborn desire of man to relate himself to the universe and to enjoy a private refuge shared only by the elect. That the people were exchanging one tyranny for another was inevitable, but there was always hope that the new régime would be better than the old, particularly for those who had helped it to power.

The second century A.D. saw the emergence of a number of Taoist sects which, though apparently religious in origin, rapidly became seditious as their leaders took advantage of the opportunities for mass organization offered by the political and agrarian discontent which marked the closing years of the Han dynasty. Of these, the Five Pecks of Rice sect, so named from the nature of its 'entrance fee', was of particular importance in that it was able to set up a small independent state in Shensi, and continued to be a political force until A.D. 339 when it failed in an attempt to overthrow the Eastern Chin dynasty.[11] It was also of importance because it became the principal sect of popular Taoism whose founder, Chang Tao-ling, was officially granted the posthumous title of 'Celestial Master' which remained with the Chang family until 1927, when their palace-temple on the Dragon and Tiger mountain in Kiangsi was destroyed.

A similar sect of the same period was known as the sect of Universal Peace (*T'ai P'ing*) which also began as a health sect, but was soon involved in palace intrigue and started the Yellow Turban rebellion.[12] At one time the rebels controlled two-thirds of the kingdom, for the peasantry, wearied of famine conditions and sick at heart, eagerly accepted the message of hope offered by the movement.[13] The Yellow Turban rebellion was crushed in the year A.D. 184 when

[11] H. F. MacNair, ed., *China* (1946), ch. XVII, p. 285; Favre, pp. 64–69; H. Welch, *The Parting of the Way* (1957), pp. 115–16.

[12] Favre, p. 61; Welch, pp. 117–18; V. Y. C. Shih, 'Some Rebel Chinese Ideologies', *T'oung Pao*, xliv (1956), pp. 163–70; L. Wieger, *Textes historiques* (1929), i. 773.

[13] Calamities due to natural causes occurred in the following years: floods, 175; droughts, 176, 177, 182, 183; epidemics, 173, 179, 182 (H. S. Levy, 'Yellow Turban Religion and Rebellion at the end of the Han', *JAOS*, lxxvi (1956), pp. 214–22).

the Peach Garden Trio (to which reference has already been made) swore their oath of brotherhood and volunteered to save the country.

During the Sui dynasty (A.D. 581–618) the conscription of large numbers of men for public works led to widespread revolts, one of which has continued to live in the legends of secret societies to this day. It is known as the revolt of Wa Kang, in which a number of men determined to resist the insatiable demands of the Government banded themselves together and took to the hills. There they lived as outlaws, typifying the 'righteous revolt' and defying the state and its officials. In popular presentations of traditional heroes on the stage or in books, this band, formed in the early seventh century, is portrayed as a shining example of the rightness of the people in resisting official oppression.

To the twelfth century tradition ascribes the formation of an even more famous band of outlaws whose organization and behaviour still form the pattern of secret societies. The band's exploits are related in the Chinese novel, *Shui Hu Chuan* (The Story of the River Bank), which had behind it some centuries of folk-lore before achieving widespread popularity throughout China about the year 1660.[14] The story tells of a group of men, 108 in number, of whom 36 were chiefs and 72 of lower rank, thus following the orthodox numeration of the 36 celestial and 72 terrestrial stars. Each of these men had been outlawed, and all gathered together in the mountain lair of Liang Shan which was set in a lake in Shantung, and was inaccessible to all who did not know the secret passages. There, in the Hall of Loyalty and Righteousness (*Chung Yi T'ong*), they swore oaths of mutual fidelity, secrecy, and obedience, taking Heaven as Father, Earth as Mother, the stars as Brothers, and the Moon as Sister, and drinking a mixture of blood and wine. Within the organization all class distinctions were eradicated, and all relationships through birth or marriage disregarded. All members were recognized as brothers of one family, and whether they were 'clever, uncouth, rustic, or romantic, skilled in the use of pen or tongue, of sword or lance, adept at running, thieving, or cheating, each man followed his own bent, and used his talent in the field to which it was best suited'. They took as their motto 'Loyalty and Righteousness' (*Chung Yi*), and used their strength to oppose oppressors and extortionate government officials. It was part of their legend that if a royal pardon were offered they would be willing to take service with the emperor and go to the frontiers, thus demonstrating their loyalty and patriotism.

It is not surprising that this story frequently earned the disapproval of the country's rulers. During the Ch'ing dynasty, first in 1799 and again in 1851, both years of unrest, the printing and circulation of this book were banned because of its seditious nature. But in modern times the *Story of the River Bank* has re-appeared, published in the early 1930s under the auspices of the Chinese Communist Party, and described in a preface as the earliest Communist literature of China, 'as suitable to this day as the day it was written'.[15] That this story was one of the powerful influences shaping the pattern of his early thought has been acknowledged by Mao Tse-tung,[16] and the book, re-edited by the party, is now widely used for government propaganda purposes.[17]

The twelfth century, too, saw the founding of the most notorious of China's

[14] There are two translations in English: *All Men are Brothers*, by Pearl Buck (1933), and *Water Margin*, by J. H. Jackson (1937).   [15] *All Men are Brothers*, pp. vi–ix.

[16] Edgar Snow, *Red Star Over China* (1937), pp. 129–32, 138; Ping-chia Kuo, *China: New Age and New Outlook* (1956), pp. 32, 38, 65–66, 88.

[17] Sing. Leg. Ass., Sess. Paper Cmd. 14 of 1959, p. 3 (Communist Literature in Singapore).

c

rebellious sects, the White Lotus, which from its foundation about 1129 adopted the title of the Buddhist religious fraternity founded in the fifth century. This led to considerable confusion, but the sect had nothing in common with the high ideals and pure practices of the school. It was from first to last an insurrectionary society bound together by a ritual of semi-religious origin with elements from hygiene cults, sexual practices, Manichæism, Taoism, and Buddhism.[18] In 1281, and again in 1308, the sect was proscribed by imperial edict.[19] Nevertheless, during the next sixty years there were several uprisings claiming connexion with the White Lotus. This was a period of widespread famine during which one-sixth of the population was said to be starving.[20] The final rebellion which in 1368 overthrew the Mongol dynasty of Yuan and established the Chinese dynasty of Ming was led by the Red Turbans, but to the end the White Lotus was associated with the movement.

Once again a man of the people reached the throne through popular revolt. He was of the surname Chu, and took the dynastic title of *T'ai Tsu* (First Ancestor) and the reign title of *Hung Wu* (Extensive and Martial). He is commonly known as the 'Beggar Emperor' and his success in freeing China from alien rule has stimulated secret society leaders ever since. In particular, the Triad Society of later years regarded him as its First Ancestor, and adopted the character '*Hung*' as the 'family name' of its members.

Throughout the centuries there were repeated outbreaks of revolt sponsored by sects claiming the name and ritual of the White Lotus. During the Manchu dynasty of Ch'ing (1644–1911) numerous edicts and announcements from the throne proscribing heterodox sects mentioned the White Lotus by name,[21] but the society survived to reappear among the groups which coalesced to form the Boxer movement leading to the uprising of 1900.

This brief outline of the White Lotus is given to indicate the persistence and all-pervasiveness of this type of seditious sect. Though repeatedly outlawed and its members exterminated, it contrived to continue to exist in the minds of the people and in due course reappeared. Someone would claim direct lineage from a previous leader and, using known elements of the previous ritual, with variations and additions, would reassert the magnetism which the sect held for the impoverished and distressed peasantry. During the Mongol and Manchu dynasties there was an added ethnic patriotic appeal in the call to overthrow the rule of the foreigner, but it would be a mistake to regard this as a primary reason for the formation of these associations. The Ming dynasty, of Chinese ethnic stock, also had its fair share of uprisings, and, in the end, suffered the usual fate of extinction through rebellion.

Throughout north and central China, the area in which the White Lotus was predominant, there were many other similar sects.[22] In more recent times its

[18] Chan Wing-tsit, *Religious Trends in Modern China* (1953), p. 158; De Groot, *Sectarianism and Religious Persecution in China* (1903–4), pp. 164–5; J. Kesson, *The Cross and the Dragon* (1854), pp. 250–1; V. Purcell, *The Boxer Uprising* (1963), p. 147.

[19] E. H. Parker, *China, Her History, Diplomacy, and Commerce* (1917), p. 303.

[20] Eberhard, p. 251.

[21] Though not, as stated by J. S. M. Ward and W. G. Stirling, *The Hung Society, or The Society of Heaven and Earth* (1925) (i. 3), in 1662. The Sacred Edict of Kang Hsi was issued in 1670 and denounced unorthodox sects. The proscription of sects by name, including the White Lotus, was issued in 1673 (see De Groot, *Sectarianism*, p. 153).

[22] Couling, p. 501, refers to a paper by Rev. F. H. James (1890) dealing with 52 secret sects out of over 100 in Shantung alone.

place as the most extensive secret association in that region has been taken by the Ko Lao Hui (Elder Brother Society), with its Shanghai affiliates, the Ch'ing Pang (Green Group) and the Hung Pang (Red Group), the former of which also held sway in the Yangtze valley.[23]

The foundation of the Ko Lao Hui was connected with the special Hunan militia organized by Tseng Kuo-fan to undertake the task of dislodging the Taiping rebels from Nanking. This force has been described as being 'very little different from a religious army'.[24] and it would seem that this form of organization was continued when the militia was disbanded after the fall of Nanking in 1864, and a wave of dissatisfaction swept through its members because their pensions were stopped.[25] The influence of this association spread rapidly and fostered conspiracies.[26] After the revolution of 1911, in the period of warlordism, the Ko Lao Hui became the real government over large tracts of country, with the warlords as its local leaders.

Many of the powerful figures in the Communist Government of China today graduated in the school of the 'Elder Brother' and there learned the technique of harnessing the traditional rebellious urge of the masses to the chariot of political ambition.[27]

During the twentieth century the Ch'ing Pang has been the ruling power in its own zone. Its hand, or that of the smaller Hung Pang, has been found in innumerable forms of vice and crime—in smuggling (particularly opium), gambling, extortion, prostitution, and protection. From 1927 T'u Yueh-sheng, the head of the Ch'ing Pang, was the overlord of Shanghai in politics, business, and the underworld.[28]

Between the Mandarin-speaking provinces of north and central China and the southern provinces of Fukien, Kwangtung, and Kwangsi, with their numerous local languages, there are cultural barriers which may have prevented the southern spread of the White Lotus, and in the south, the principal secret association has been the Heaven and Earth Society, also known as the Three Dots Society and as the Three United Society, from the last of which designations the anglicized form, Triad Society, derives.

The date of the Triad Society's foundation, according to its own claim, was 1674, twenty-six years after the establishment of the Manchu dynasty of Ch'ing. The society's main slogans were 'Obey Heaven and follow the Way', and 'Overthrow Ch'ing, Restore Ming'. Its ritual and precepts contained elements from ancestor worship, astral worship, popular Taoism, Buddhism, and Confucianism, with the typical oath of secrecy and brotherhood sealed by the drinking of a mixture of blood and wine.[29]

[23] Originally called the An Ch'ing Pang after its town of origin in Anhwei province on the Yangtze. Popular usage has substituted the homophone meaning 'green' for the original 'ch'ing'.

[24] Li Chien-nung, *The Political History of China 1840–1928* (1956), pp. 66 and 68, quoting Inaba Iwakichi.

[25] W. J. Hail, *Tseng Kuo-fan and the Taiping Rebellion* (1927); F. Boyle, 'Chinese Secret Societies', *Harper's Mag.*, Sept. 1891; C. W. Mason, *The Chinese Confessions of C. W. Mason* (1924), p. 245.

[26] J. D. Ball, *Things Chinese* (1925), pp. 614–15; Chan Wing-tsit, p. 161; J. Hutson, 'Chinese life in the Tibetan foothills', *New China R.*, Feb. 1920.

[27] Agnes Smedley, *Battle Hymn of China* (1943), p. 113; Snow, pp. 65–68, 129–38, 212–14, 352.

[28] Y. C. Wang, 'Tu Yueh-sheng, 1888–1951', *JAS*, May 1967.　　　　　[29] See App. 1, p. 529.

As with the Heroes of Liang Shan, candidates on joining were deemed to have been born into a new family. They took the family name of 'Hung', adopted from the reign title of the founder of the Ming dynasty whom they chose to regard as their 'First Ancestor'. This was the basis of the Hung Brotherhood to which, later, the Ko Lao Hui and its affiliates of the north adhered, adopting the same mythical traditional history as the Triad fraternity but retaining their individual organizational patterns and rituals. And wherever societies of the Hung Brotherhood existed, whether in China or overseas, they claimed to be the guardians of the true Chinese ethos.

From the outset, as its second slogan implied, the Triad Society was a seditious brotherhood, and its tentacles spread throughout the southern provinces where innumerable local societies sprang up. For although all used the same ritual there was no central organization. Its disturbing influence was reflected in the promulgation of special laws proscribing such brotherhoods, and, in 1792, mentioning the Heaven and Earth Society by name.[30] This was six years after a serious revolt organized by a local Triad society of long standing had taken place in Formosa in which the magistrate was killed. Thereafter, the activities of the Brotherhood came increasingly to official notice,[31] and from 1817 onwards risings fostered by Triad societies became endemic throughout the three southern provinces despite the public beheading of thousands of their members.

Two Triad rebellions which had residual consequences in the Straits Settlements took place in 1853, one at Amoy in Fukien province, and one at Shanghai. In the first of these the 'Small Sword Society', of which many members had previously lived in the Straits Settlements, raised the banner of revolt and captured Amoy in May. After a desultory campaign against imperial troops sent to retake the city, an arrangement was reached whereby in November the rebels left the city and sailed away in junks for Singapore and elsewhere in the Southseas. At Shanghai, in September, a rebellion was organized and conducted by Triad men hailing from Fukien and Kwangtung, of whom there were said to be 150,000 in the city. The arrest and torture of some members of the Brotherhood alleged to have been engaged in unlawful activities had angered their fellows who rose in revolt. The city was captured and remained in rebel hands for nearly eighteen months when, once again, an agreement was made which permitted the Triad forces to decamp. They left during the night of 17 September 1855, and some of these, too, sailed for the Straits Settlements.[32]

Both these risings took place during the early years of the Taiping rebellion which ravaged the country from 1850 to 1864, and almost overthrew the Manchu dynasty. The Taiping rebellion was not a Triad revolt, although in popular Chinese accounts of the Brotherhood it is frequently so regarded. This is, in part, because the leader, a Hakka from Kwangtung province, was of the surname Hung, but it is also likely that he was supported in the early stages by a Triad leader with the Ming dynastic surname of Chu, who (but for his capture in 1852) hoped to use the Taiping movement to carry him to the throne. Thereafter,

[30] Sir G. T. Staunton, trans., *Ta Tsing Leu Lee* (1810), App. xxiii, pp. 456 ff.
[31] According to Favre, it was 'officially noticed' in connexion with seditious movements in 1749, 1789, 1814, 1817, and 1832. See also Stanton, pp. 10–11 & 20–24.
[32] Stanton, pp. 15–20; A. Wylie, 'Chinese Researches', *Shanghae Almanac*, 1854.

the other Triad headmen left the movement, having found that the discipline imposed by its stringent rules was not to their liking.[33]

The leader of the Taiping rebellion, who had frequently failed his literary examination and had subsequently become mentally deranged, had received some instruction in Christianity and believed that he had been chosen as the deliverer of his country. Into the religious ritual with which he bound his followers he introduced pseudo-Christian elements, and called his fraternity the 'Society of God-worshippers', initiation into which was by baptism. At its height the rebellion overran most of China, and is believed to have cost 20 million lives. On his death in 1864 Nanking, which had been held by the rebels for eleven years, surrendered to the imperial forces, and the last remnants were defeated near Amoy a year later.[34]

Meanwhile, authentic Triad groups were in constant revolt in the south, and by 1854 every district in Kwangtung and most of Kwangsi was in open rebellion, while Kiangsi and Fukien were also affected. Most of the important towns of the Canton delta were in Triad hands, and Canton itself was invested for a time. When, eventually, imperial troops regained control it was estimated that during the subsequent suppression 1 million people were executed in Kwangtung province alone.[35]

A further cause of unrest in Kwangtung during the period 1855-68 was the antagonism existing between the indigenous Cantonese and the Hakkas who, as their name meaning 'visitors' or 'guests' implies, were regarded as foreigners, though they had been settled in the southern provinces since their ancestors were driven southwards from Shantung perhaps as early as the second century B.C. Local antipathies led eventually to vicious internecine warfare in which the Hakkas were driven from their lands and roamed the countryside in armed bands. It was not until the end of the Taiping rebellion that imperial troops were available to deal with the problem by disarming the Hakkas and transferring them to lands elsewhere, but in the struggle it was estimated that over 150,000 people perished.[36] Many refugees, both from these disturbances and from the Triad revolts, escaped to join the Taiping movement in Kwangsi, while many more fled to the safety of Hong Kong, America, and the South Seas. Despite the severity of the suppression, pockets of the Triad Brotherhood continued to exist, and disturbances caused by them were reported in 1877, 1886, 1892, and 1898.

While it is true that the overthrow of the Ch'ing dynasty was a declared aim of the Triad Brotherhood, economic factors during this dynasty were particularly conducive to revolt. There have been few periods in the history of China when there has not been agrarian discontent, but during the Ch'ing dynasty this was aggravated by a population explosion without any comparable increase in the area of cultivable land. From the beginning of the Han dynasty to the beginning of the Ming, a period of some 1,600 years, the population of China had remained reasonably static between 50 and 60 millions. During the Ming dynasty (1368-1644), a period of 276 years, this had increased to 100 millions, and by

[33] Hail, ch. 3; Lindley, *Ti-Ping Tien Kwoh, the History of the Ti-Ping Rebellion* (1913), i. 52.
[34] Cdr. Brine, *The Taeping Rebellion in China* (1862); S. W. Williams, *The Middle Kingdom* (1900-1), ii. 631; Li Chien-nung, pp. 53-81; MacNair, *Modern Chinese History* (1927), pp. 335 ff.
[35] Stanton, p. 21; Williams, ii. 582 ff.; Hsiao Kung-chuan, *Rural China* (1960), pp. 710-11 n.
[36] Eitel, 'History of the Hakka People', *China R.*, ii (1873-5); Ball, pp. 281-2.

1850, when the Taiping rebellion began, the population was of the order of 400 millions.[37] This greatly magnified the problem of a starving peasantry, and the peasants formed about 80 per cent of the population.

During the last quarter of the nineteenth century another factor in the social and political pattern began to emerge as students educated abroad absorbed ideas which were not merely seditious but revolutionary, and on their return to China, instead of calling for the reinstatement of a previous dynasty, planned to associate the people permanently with the Government through representative institutions as found in the West.

Sun Yat-sen, while a student at a missionary hospital in Canton, joined the Triad Brotherhood about 1886,[38] and after completing his medical studies in Hong Kong, and having decided to devote himself to the revolutionary cause, made contact with branches of the Brotherhood in China, in Honolulu, and at other places abroad. He soon discovered, however, that his enthusiasm for the proclamation of a republic was received with great reserve. Triad tradition postulated an emperor of Chinese ethnic stock, not a foreign-style president of a republic.[39]

In 1894, therefore, Sun founded his own society, the Hsing Chung Hui (Revive China Society), which in its organization followed the traditional secret society pattern with the swearing of a blood-oath of brotherhood and the use of secret signs and language.[40] An early attempt to sponsor a revolt at Canton in 1895 was unsuccessful, and Sun went abroad. Later, in 1899, he tried to obtain the support of the secret societies throughout China by arranging a conference at Hong Kong at which leaders of the Hsing Chung Hui, the Triad Brotherhood, and the Ko Lao Hui of the Yangtze valley met and agreed to co-operate,[41] but little further developed because there was no centralized control of either the Ko Lao Hui or the Triad Brotherhood, and local leaders were preoccupied with day-to-day happenings in their own areas.

In 1900 Sun attempted, by intriguing with the Japanese Governor-General of Formosa, to start a rebellion in South China through a local Triad society, but at the last moment the Japanese withdrew their support. In the north, the failure of the Boxer rising, originally an anti-Manchu secret society revolt which, by Court intrigue, was diverted into an anti-European channel, was also a setback for the revolutionaries.

In 1905 the Hsing Chung Hui, preponderantly a southern party, amalgamated with its counterpart in the north, the Hsing Hua Hui, which had considerable support from the Ko Lao Hui, to form the T'ung Meng Hui, a sworn brotherhood on the secret society pattern with the death penalty for betrayal of trust.[42]

[37] Eberhard, p. 290; Ping-chia Kuo, pp. 12–13; L. C. Goodrich, *A Short History of the Chinese People* (1957), p. 202.

[38] J. Ch'en and R. Payne, *Sun Yat-sen, a Portrait* (1946). Li Chien-nung, p. 145, refers to Sun's close friendship at this time with Cheng Shih-liang, a Triad member. T'ang Leang-li, *The Inner History of the Chinese Revolution* (1930), p. 20, says that Sun at this time joined the Ko Lao Hui. Sun, in his Memoirs, does not disclose whether he was a member of any Hung society, but he could hardly fail to be.

[39] Sun Yat-sen, *Memoirs of a Chinese Revolutionary* (1918), pp. 190–8; T'ang Leang-li, pp. 24–27; C. Glick and Hong Sheng-hwa, *Swords of Silence* (1947), pp. 108–9.

[40] B. Martin, *Strange Vigour; Biography of Sun Yat-sen* (1944), p. 101; T'ang Leang-li, p. 29.

[41] J. Hutson, 'Chinese Secret Societies', *CJSA*, (1929); Glick and Hong, p. 153.

[42] T'ang Leang-li, pp. 49–50; Martin, p. 104; Li Chien-nung, p. 201.

This society was responsible for a series of minor rebellions in 1907–8, mainly on the Kwangsi–Yunnan–Indochina border, and its influence increased considerably.[43] By 1911 it was said to have 100,000 members in seventeen provinces, and in April of that year attempted a rebellion at Canton which was quickly suppressed. In October, however, a rising took place at Wuchang, the capital of Hupeh, and, unexpectedly, spread rapidly, leading to the declaration of the Republic on 1 January 1912, and to the subsequent collapse of the Manchu dynasty.

Throughout this revolutionary struggle the main role of the traditional secret societies was that of fifth columnists, though when the battle came their way they followed their natural urge to join in the revolt. The Triad Brotherhood also rendered assistance to the revolutionary cause by the provision of funds, and for this support the Brethren in America and Malaya were chiefly responsible, though there were many among them who preferred monarchical reform, and only fell into line with the revolutionaries when it became clear that the monarchy was finished.

With the establishment of the Republic secret societies were no longer unlawful and came out into the open as power groups, still with the secret rituals of sworn brotherhood, but claiming freedom from legal restraint. Before long, every official and military leader who hoped to advance in his career found it essential to belong to the local society,[44] and the way was clear for the usurpation by the societies of the powers and sanctions of the Government with the consequent fragmentation of authority throughout the country. When, eventually, warlordism became the pattern of regional government, it was from these societies and from their own positions in the hierarchy of the Brotherhoods that the warlords drew their support.

Political developments, including the establishment of a parliament, led to a change in the constitution and aims of the T'ung Meng Hui, which from being a revolutionary society became a political party. With the absorption of certain other small parties which had sprung up, its name was changed to Kuomintang (National Party) (August 1912), and thereafter, with some further changes in constitution and title, the Kuomintang (KMT) provided the nominal government of China until superseded by the Communist Party in 1949.

Sun Yat-sen was fully aware of the dangers inherent in relying on the secret societies to obtain the support of the masses. He realized that members were obedient only to their own immediate leaders, and were traditionally opposed to governmental authority. Nevertheless, such was their influence, that during a reconstitution of the KMT in 1919 he urged the Hung Brethren to abolish their ritual, change the name of the Brotherhood, and become fully identified with his party.[45] His appeal failed. Although some Triad members joined the KMT, and, on the whole, the Brotherhood supported Sun, Triad leaders refused to allow the Brotherhood to be completely absorbed. It was always possible, they argued, that the cause of the revolution might be betrayed, and the Brotherhood would then need to be in a position to fight for the liberty of the people.

[43] Li Chien-nung, p. 221.

[44] K. S. Latourette, *The Chinese; Their History and Culture* (1951), p. 681; A. D. Barnett, *China on the Eve of the Communist Takeover* (1963), pp. 127–9.

[45] From July 1914 to October 1919 the party was called the Ke Ming Tang (Revolutionary Party).

Therefore, they must continue as a separate organism, responsible to no political party, and governed only by their own statutes and their own loyalties.[46]

Seeking help elsewhere, in 1921 Sun made contact with the Third International at Moscow, and was persuaded to permit individual members of the recently-formed Chinese Communist Party (CCP) to join the KMT. In 1922, in difficulties because of the ambitions of one of his warlords, General Ch'en Chiung-ming (a Hakka from the Waichow (Fui Chiu) area of Kwangtung, who aspired to become the semi-independent ruler of Kwangtung and Kwangsi, thus jeopardizing Sun's plans for a united China), and impressed by the manner in which the Russian revolution had resulted in a strong republican government, Sun approached the Russian special envoy to China, Adolf Joffe. In January 1923 a joint manifesto was issued by Sun and Joffe in which Russia pledged herself to assist the KMT in its fight against Imperialism and in the accomplishment of the national revolution, while undertaking not to make any propaganda in China for the Communist order of society which was acknowledged to be impracticable for China.[47] A young Russian revolutionary organizer, Michael Borodin, was sent to Sun as his adviser, and at a Congress of the KMT held in January 1924 a new party constitution, based on the Moscow model, was adopted, and the Congress agreed to the admission to the KMT *en masse* of members of the CCP. At the same time, members of the KMT who were members of secret societies or of open organizations were urged to expand their membership within such societies or associations.

The reorganized KMT made a great appeal not only to the Communist members now enrolled under the Nationalist banner but also to the new generation of students anxious to find a focus for their own revolutionary ideals. To Sun Yat-sen the revivification of the party offered the possibility of regaining lost ground and of providing a fresh impetus to the work of completing the revolution. But not all of his colleagues were of the same mind. Quite apart from their distrust of the Communists, some feared that they themselves might be displaced by the energetic fresh elements now swarming into the party. A split occurred, Sun and most of the prominent leaders, including Wang Ching-wei and Chiang Kai-shek, forming a Political Council of the KMT under Sun's chairmanship, and excluding therefrom the reactionary 'Old Comrades'.

Meantime, in 1923 a voice had been heard emanating from overseas Chinese in America, who, disturbed by the spectacle of political confusion in China, resolved to bring their influence to bear.

The original Chinese emigrants had fled to the west coast of America (California and British Columbia) in the 1850s, when the Imperial troops were 'cleaning up' after the Triad rebellions. They were refugees from Shanghai, Amoy, and Kwangtung, all were southerners, most were Cantonese, and the majority were Triad members who continued to group themselves into local societies. They adopted the generic name of Chi Kung T'ong (Achieve Justice Society), and were known as the Hung Men,[48] or, in English, as the Chinese Freemasons. Throughout the Pacific and American zone wherever Chinese settled Chi Kung T'ong (i.e. Triad) societies appeared, in Mexico, Panama, the Philippines, Peru, Australia, New Zealand, and as far east as Cuba. On the Double Tenth 1923 a Triad conference was convened at San Francisco to attempt to

[46] Glick and Hong, p. 232.   [47] MacNair, *China*, p. 140.
[48] Hung Men (Mandarin), Hung Mun (Cantonese) = Hung Family.

organize the political opinion of the Brotherhood concerning developments in China where, instead of the realization of the Three Principles of the People as enunciated by Sun Yat-sen, there was warlordism, oppression, and corruption. Some delegates were of the opinion that Sun and his KMT had outlived their usefulness, and the Sun–Joffe agreement of January 1923 had done nothing to allay their fears.

An item which received general approval was a proposal to establish a focus for the national spirit of the Hung Men by building at Shanghai a Memorial Hall including an ancestral temple. This was to be a public acknowledgement of the legality of the Brotherhood and a visible memento of its patriotic spirit. (The hall was opened on 12 September 1925, and an old Triad leader, Chiu Yuk, well known in America and Australia, was appointed to be the director of this headquarters.) But a motion to form from among the members a political party to be known as the China Min Chi Tang[49] (Democratic Party of China), with the object of participating in the political development of China and pressing for the formation of a democratic government in the place of the dictatorship of the KMT, caused considerable dissension. The proposal implied a criticism of Sun Yat-sen, and as some members had been his close associates or staunch supporters it aroused opposition. Furthermore, as Sun himself had found in China, many members disliked the idea of using the old-established mystic Brotherhood as a modern political party, preferring to retain the traditional forms under which the local societies had complete liberty of action and were not under the instructions of a central political body. Eventually, though the proposal to form a Min Chi Tang received the assent of most of the delegates, such was the strength of the opposition that the decision was not implemented.

There were, however, certain developments in Hong Kong where a band of supporters of General Ch'en Chiung-ming formed in March 1923 by Hakkas from Waichow seized the opportunity of the expression of anti-KMT feeling at San Francisco in October to declare itself to be the World Chi Kung Party (Ng Chau Chi Kung Tong), and from the safety of Hong Kong circulated propaganda to all Chinese communities overseas, soliciting funds and support for General Ch'en Chiung-ming in opposition to Sun and his party. This propaganda had some influence on the large Waichow Hakka population in Malaya where the General, ten years earlier, had, with Sun, taken refuge from the wrath of Yuan Shih-k'ai. This party was later called the China Chi Kung Tong.

In 1926 yet another minor political association with Triad connexions re-appeared in Hong Kong. This was the Chung Woh T'ong (Society of Central Harmony), founded in 1898 by four of Sun Yat-sen's collaborators from among Triad members with revolutionary sympathies. It was revived by its leader, Yau Lit, who disapproved of the growing Communist influence within the KMT.[50]

The death of Sun Yat-sen in March 1925 had not immediately weakened the KMT's close contacts with Russia and the Communists. Leadership of the so-called National Government at Canton had fallen to Wang Ching-wei, one of Sun's most faithful colleagues from the days of the Tung Meng Hui; Borodin

[49] In Cantonese: Man Chi Tong.
[50] Originally Yau Lit had formed Chung Woh T'ong centres in Kowloon and Tokyo and from 1901–9 in Malaya. He returned to China from Siam in 1912, and attached himself to Yuan Shih-k'ai. After the latter's death he retired to Hong Kong, where he studied Confucianism and smoked opium, but played no part in politics until roused by the Communist threat.

had become a virtual dictator in the political councils of the KMT; among the Chinese masses the organization of labour and peasant groups on Communist lines had greatly expanded; and workers and students had drawn together in a common cause of anti-imperialism.

But early in 1926 Wang Ching-wei's position was challenged. At the Second National Congress of the KMT held in January, Chiang Kai-shek was elected to the Central Executive Committee of the party, and open rivalry between him and Wang became increasingly evident. Seeing the mass movements slipping into Communist hands, Chiang secretly planned to remove the vital control-centres of the Communist machine. On the night of 20 March the principal Communist officials attached to the army, the navy, and the Military Academy were arrested, the Russian advisers in Canton were placed under house arrest, and a detachment was sent to raid the headquarters of the Canton–Hong Kong strike organization with instructions to remove all arms. Wang Ching-wei temporarily withdrew to Europe, and at a plenary session of the Central Executive Committee held on 15 April restrictions on Communists within the KMT or in government employ were approved, Chiang Kai-shek was appointed head of the KMT party and Commander-in-Chief of the Northern Military Expedition which aimed at defeating the northern warlords and bringing the whole of China under the control of the National Government.

Hankow was captured in October (1926), and became the seat of government in place of Canton, but on reaching the Lower Yangtze and Shanghai, Chiang found the Labour unions and the Communists in control. He was able to avoid a head-on clash with the masses by intriguing with the leaders of the Ch'ing Pang and the Hung Pang. This was made the easier as, according to popular belief, he had been admitted to membership of the Ch'ing Pang in 1911 when stationed in Shanghai.[51]

The task of bringing the victory-flushed mass organizations to heel by the gangs began at Nanchang on 17 March 1927, when on Chiang's orders the local KMT branch was dissolved and its left-wing leaders arrested, labour unions and students' organizations were closed down, and a newspaper suppressed. The same process was followed at Kiukiang, Anking, and Wuhu, Nanking was by-passed, and Chiang went on to Shanghai. At this stage (1 April) Wang Ching-wei returned from Europe and took charge of the Hankow Government. Both he and Chiang stressed their devotion to the common cause and repudiated any suggestion of a split or difference between them, and in a circular telegram Chiang pledged his loyalty to Hankow, and stated that thereafter all matters relating to the welfare of the country and the KMT would be handled by 'Chairman Wang' or carried on under his guidance (thus effectively placing the responsibility for what he himself was planning to do upon the shoulders of Wang and the Hankow Government).

These plans were implemented when at 4 a.m. on the morning of 12 April armed parties of the Ch'ing Pang, wearing white armbands, and purporting to be members of a 'white' labour union, made simultaneous attacks on premises in Shanghai occupied by Communist and leftist labour groups. Those who were seized were led out to execution or shot down if they resisted. The next day remnants of the General Labour Union attempted to organize a general strike,

   [51] H. R. Isaacs, *The Tragedy of the Chinese Revolution* (1951), p. 81; Wang, *JAS*, May 1967, p. 437.

and after holding a mass meeting, marched on the military headquarters. They were met with a barrage of machine-gun bullets, and over 300 men were killed. Thereafter the gangs were in charge, and conducted a house-to-house search for members of Communist unions, or their sympathizers.[52] With Shanghai thus 'pacified', a similar technique was adopted at other centres under the control of the Nationalist Army, at Ningpo, Foochow, and further south at Amoy, Swatow, and Canton.

The Hung Brotherhood portrays this purge of Shanghai and other cities as meritorious, in that the country was saved from the scourge of Communism. A more objective appraisal tends to show that the gangs acted in the interests of the side from which the most lucrative rewards could be expected. Certainly, their influence over the population was maintained without interference either by Communists or by Nationalist troops, and they were left in control of the gambling, opium, brothel, and extortion rackets which they might otherwise have lost. They were also in a stronger position than ever to exert pressure on those with wealth, for they now acted as agents for the financial needs of Chiang Kai-shek's local administration.[53]

Moscow, stunned by these drastic purges, urged its agents to introduce a full revolutionary programme into China, and to win over the left wing of the KMT into an alliance with the Communist Party against Chiang Kai-shek. But Wang Ching-wei had decided to discard the Communists, and to work for the control of the labour unions through the KMT. In this he and Chiang Kai-shek were agreed. In December (1927) he left again for Europe, the Northern Expedition continued, and in June 1928 was brought to a successful conclusion by the defeat of Chang Tso-lin and the capture of Tientsin and Peking. In the same month Nanking was declared to be the new capital of China.

Despite this evident success, it cannot be said that Chiang Kai-shek had the whole-hearted support of the country. Not only was he opposed by the Communists who had been expelled from the KMT, but also this latter party was by no means homogeneous, and as the years went by the number of cliques into which it was divided increased. Wang Ching-wei returned from Europe in February 1929 and headed a faction in opposition to the Nanking Government. A month later the Canton–Kwangsi clique of generals in the south was in revolt, and in September declared war on Chiang. Throughout the country there were innumerable 'bands'—secret society groups—ravaging the countryside and defying the Government in the tradition of the 'Heroes of Liang Shan'. The incidence of these rebellions was widespread in central and south China, reaching a notable virulence in Hopei, Honan, and Shantung. The local secret societies had filled the vacuum caused by the lack of powerful centralized control, and had become a law unto themselves. At the National People's Convention in May 1931 Chiang Kai-shek declared that the spread of Communism was due to the inability of the National Government to divert the troops engaged in the suppression of rebellions.

In addition to these problems of internal security, the shadow of Japan loomed in the north, leading in September 1931 to the Mukden Incident which marked

[52] Isaacs, *Chinese Revolution*, chs 9–11

[53] For an account of the all-embracing power wielded by T'u Yueh-sheng and the gangs in Shanghai in 1931, see Isaacs, *Five Years of KMT Reaction* (1932), chapter headed 'Gang Rule in Shanghai'. Also Y. C. Wang's biography of T'u.

the beginning of the Japanese invasion of Manchuria, to an attack on Shanghai in 1932, and to a full-scale invasion of China in 1937. Chiang Kai-shek's policy of 'trading space for time' was widely criticized in China, and when, in December 1936, he was kidnapped at Sian he was forced to agree to a united front with the Communists against the Japanese. There was already a Red Army in being in Shensi, under the leadership of Mao Tse-tung, Chu Teh, and Chou En-lai. This army had originally been composed of 'rovers of rivers and lakes', attracted to the Communist movement by the latter's seditious nature and egalitarian doctrine. According to Mao, the majority of this early army were 'yu min' (vagrants), including secret society elements whose leaders he welcomed into the fold.[54]   In this way, many of the disturbing and destructive elements from rural areas were brought under Communist control by the provision of continuous employment and discipline on active military service or on schemes of develop-ment, while at the same time through indoctrination the traditional spirit of patriotic heroes, responsible for the salvation of their country, was maintained. An outstanding example of the shift from brigandage to Red Army was pro-vided by General Ho Lung, a regional leader of the Elder Brother Society who, with his followers, went over *en bloc* to the Communist cause.[55]

Japan openly showed her hand on 7 July 1937, a date which under the title of Double Seventh is entered in the long list of China's Days of Remembrance. Both Peking and Shanghai were attacked, and thenceforth the watchword for China was 'National Salvation', under which the entire resources and capacity of the whole Chinese nation (including all Chinese overseas) were pooled, irre-spective of party, in united resistance to the invaders.

Japanese troops advanced rapidly. Shanghai, much ruined, was abandoned in November. Among those who had participated in its defence were T'u Yueh-sheng and his Ch'ing Pang fraternity. Nanking fell in December, and the Chinese Government moved to Hankow. Less than a month later that city was also abandoned, and the Government moved on to Chungking in the far west where it remained until the end of the war.

Nevertheless, the conquest and subjugation of the whole of China proved an impossible task. Chinese guerrilla bands constantly harassed lines of communi-cation and isolated posts, and this very effective limiting warfare which kept Japanese garrisons confined to centres of population owed much to the wide-spread influence of the tradition of the Hung Brotherhood. The Elder Brother societies in the north and the Triad societies in the south were ubiquitous, and the presence of Japanese on China's soil provided opportunities, by the simple means of ambushing military detachments or killing Japanese-sponsored officials, of fulfilling the patriotic duty of eliminating the country's enemies, and of satis-fying the equally traditional urge of defying the Government in power.

The Chinese Communist Red Army, operating originally from its Shensi base, also conducted substantial guerrilla operations, seizing and holding the rural hinterland over wide areas, but avoiding frontal operations in which it might have been destroyed.[56]

[54] Schram, 'Mao Tse-tung and Secret Societies', *China Quarterly*, July–Sept. 1966, p. 6.
[55] Isaacs, *Chinese Revolution*, pp. 400–1; Ping Chia-kuo, pp. 64–66; Smedley, pp. 113, 336; R. C. North, *Chinese Communism* (1966), p. 109.
[56] By 1945 it was 900,000 strong and controlled 300,000 square miles, containing 95 million inhabitants (W. W. Rostow, *The Prospects for Communist China* (1954), p. 28).

As their initial military invasion slowed down and eventually came to a stand-still, the Japanese introduced a Chinese puppet government with the title of 'Reformed Government', in the hope of rallying part, at least, of the Chinese people to the support of the new régime. To this end, Wang Ching-wei, who had left Chungking on a mission to Hanoi, was prevailed upon to head this Chinese Government under Japanese control, set up in November 1938 at Nanking.

The Japanese were well aware of the importance of secret societies in the political field, not only from their own experience and intrigues in Manchuria and north China but more particularly because of the impact of such societies in Japan.[57] In the penetration of Manchuria they had used their own societies, and in occupied areas pressure was exerted on known Chinese secret society leaders to form friendship societies to be used for propaganda, for indoctrination of students, and as intelligence agencies.

With the appointment of Wang Ching-wei as head of a Reformed Government the way was clear for an extension of this technique. At Shanghai the Ch'ing Pang leaders were drawn into the net. T'u Yueh-sheng, who had with-drawn to Hong Kong and later moved to Chungking, had maintained his allegi-ance to Chiang Kai-shek, but other prominent leaders who had remained in Shanghai found it profitable or advisable to support the Reformed Government.

One of these leaders (Chang Hsiao-lin), at the instance of the Japanese, organ-ized the Citizens' Union and was later murdered by a Chungking agent for his pains, as was his successor in office (Chi Yun-ching) and, later still, a third leader (Kao Chin-pao). Three other societies organized by Ch'ing Pang leaders on Japanese instructions were eventually amalgamated at Nanking in May 1940 to form the 'Maintenance of Friendship between China and Japan Society'. Branches were formed in forty occupied towns and the organization published its own newspaper: *Today's Nanking Newspaper of the People*.

Also under government auspices was a strong-arm organization known as the 'Mobile Unit' in which many of the ruffians of the Ch'ing Pang were enrolled.[58]

Japanese policy implemented by the Reformed Government was to infiltrate all organizations which had supported the KMT Government. Usually this caused an internal split among the leaders, leaving the people puzzled as to which section was authentic. The party supporting the Reformed Government then assumed the role of the legitimate association and issued manifestoes and instructions to the branches and members. Where this was not successful or expedient, an exactly similar society was organized with the same name, operat-ing under reliable supporters of the Reformed Government, and once again the bemused public was bombarded with propaganda announcing the legitimacy of this cuckoo in the nest.

It was in pursuance of this policy that in November 1940 Wang Ching-wei set up an organization at Canton designed to appeal to the Triad fraternity in south China and overseas. This organization was given the grandiose name of the 'Five Continents [i.e. world-wide] Overseas Chinese Union of the Hung Family', and on 29 November 1940 it issued a Manifesto to all Brethren extolling the glories of the Brotherhood at the time of the foundation of the Republic,

---

[57] Between 1931 and 1936 Japanese secret societies were responsible for the murders of 2 premiers (Hamaguchi and Inukai), 2 Finance Ministers (Inouye and Takahashi), 1 General (Watanabe), and 1 Admiral (Saito). See R. Storry, *The Double Patriots* (1957).

[58] *Sin Chew Jit Po* (Singapore), 26 May 1941.

emphasizing that the purpose of the Brotherhood was to serve patriotically the best interests of the country, and pointing out that this could best be done by supporting the Peace Campaign recently inaugurated by Wang Ching-wei and the Japanese Premier. At the same time a circular telegram was sent to 'the Brethren of the Hung Family Organizations and of the Chi Kung T'ong in the various towns of countries of the Five Continents'. Following the same propaganda line, the circular invited members of the Brotherhood to return to China to help 'Mr Wang' in national reconstruction through peace.

In Hong Kong territory an attempt was made to spread propaganda in support of the Peace Campaign through Chung Woh T'ong members at Kowloon. Yau Weng-cheung, the adopted son of the late founder of the society, Yau Lit, was persuaded to establish at the Yau Lit School in Kowloon a society styled the 'Chung Woh T'ong Sino-Japanese Goodwill Society', whose object was to build up a Fifth Column for the support of the Japanese. During 1941 a large-scale organization operating under the name Chung Woh Company was uncovered in Hong Kong, and documents found at its premises laid stress on the great importance of winning over the Hung Brotherhood for the purpose of spreading the Peace Movement of the Wang Ching-wei Government.

In these ways the sympathy and support of the Hung Brethren in China and overseas, whether under Japanese domination or not, was canvassed for the new régime. These methods were the forerunners of a pattern of infiltration, fragmentation, and parallelism which was to develop much further in the post-war years when the KMT and the Communists were vigorously competing for the allegiance of the Hung Brotherhood.

Meanwhile, at Chungking as the war dragged on, the KMT Government and the Communist Party, though both engaged in the common cause of resisting the Japanese, were unable to reach any agreement on political collaboration. In March 1945 Chiang Kai-shek announced that he proposed to convene a National Assembly in November to inaugurate a constitutional government, whereupon all political parties would have legal status and enjoy equality.[59] After the collapse of Japan in August 1945 he broadcast similar proposals (3 September),[60] but fear of a Communist takeover led to postponement of the proposed Assembly. One effect of the declaration, however, was the revival of a number of minor political groups, including the Chung Woh T'ong and the China Chi Kung Tong, who saw possibilities of prestige in a future parliament, while the KMT set out to woo the masses through the Hung Brotherhood by instructing that their societies should be formed into National Reconstruction Associations to participate in the rehabilitation of China.

The possibility of political developments and concern over the lack of an effective government in China due to the KMT–Communist split also caused members of Triad societies overseas, and particularly the Chi Kung T'ong of America, to take an interest in the affairs of the mother country. Already in March 1945 a conference had been held in New York at which it was decided, with some dissidents, to reorganize the Brotherhood as a political party to work for the introduction of a constitutional democratic government in China.[61] In July 1946 a 'World Conference' was held at Shanghai under the leadership of Szeto Mei-tang, a veteran Triad leader of America who had been at Chungking

[59] Keesing, v. 724–7, 9–16 June 1945.   [60] Ibid., vi. 7705–10, 2–9 Feb. 1946.
[61] See Manifesto of 1 Jan. 1946 at App. of Glick and Hong.

during the war. There was considerable objection to the proposal to absorb the Brotherhood into a political party, and, instead, a political party sponsored by the Brotherhood was formed with the title of Chung Kuo Hung Men Min Chi Tang, or China Hung Family Democratic Party, with the shortened form of Min Chi Tang.[62]

From the outset this party was penetrated by KMT agents determined that if this new Triad political organization was to come into being it should be firmly aligned with the KMT. Once the party acquired the taint of supporting dictatorship, the democratically-inclined groups of Chinese in America withheld their support, and rifts within the party widened. When the National Assembly at last met in November 1946 the claims of the Min Chi Tang to recognition were ignored, and no seats were offered to its representatives. This attempt by the Triad Brotherhood overseas to enter politics in China had its repercussions in Triad circles in Malaya.

The National Assembly was boycotted by the Communists, and thereafter that party's military offensive against the KMT Government was intensified. At the same time a campaign of Communist infiltration of democratically-inclined political groups began, and through suggesting the formation of a democratic front sought to isolate the KMT. In October 1947 the China Democratic League (CDL), an alliance of several intellectual democratic groups which, for years, had been trying to provide a middle way between the Communists and the KMT, was outlawed for alleged complicity with the Communists and for denouncing through its branches in Hong Kong and Singapore the issue of a total mobilization order by the Government. Many of its leaders were arrested: others fled to Hong Kong and America.[63]

In May 1948 the Communist Party announced the shrewd proposal to call together a political consultative council to prepare a coalition government of all parties except the KMT, and thereafter leaders of the democratic groups in Hong Kong and south China quietly made their way to the north to prepare for the meeting. The China Chi Kung Tong, opposed as always to the KMT, was represented by General Li Chi-shen who had become its titular head, and even the veteran Triad leader from America, Szeto Mei-tang, who with the failure of the Min Chi Tang had forsworn politics, arrived in Peking in August 1949. In September, after three months of preparatory talks, the full meeting of the People's Political Consultative Conference was held at which members of the new Central Government were elected, and on 1 October the inauguration of the Central Government of the People's Republic of China was proclaimed.

Leaders of the groups represented at the Conference were given posts in the new Government, and specific duties were allocated. In this way the appearance of common participation in the business of government was preserved. As with the KMT Government, an Overseas Affairs Commission was appointed to maintain contact with and seek support from Chinese overseas. To this Commission Szeto Mei-tang was appointed, and on its Standing Committee were six members of the China Chi Kung Tong, including one each from Hong Kong and Malaya. It soon became apparent that the sole role of the China Chi Kung Tong was to act as a propaganda link with Chinese overseas, for in April 1950 it was announced that although the promotion of overseas branches should continue,

[62] In Cantonese, Chung Kwok Hung Mun Man Chi Tong
[63] Keesing, vi. 9017–18, 14–21 Feb. 1948.

party activities in China should cease. The political representation of this group of Triad Brethren thus ceased to be significant.

The fate of the rank and file of the Hung Brotherhood in China is largely a matter for conjecture. Some, particularly of the Ko Lao Hui in the north, have been absorbed into the Red Army, but there were many areas in the north and west where local allegiances were stronger than the influence of Communism, and where secret societies such as the 'Red Spears' and the 'Long Hairs' resisted attempts to impose a Communist system of control. In the south, with its ever-present undercurrent of revolutionary enthusiasm and its many loyalties to local generals of Kwangsi and Kwangtung, it is certain that the persuasive force of the Communists met with considerable resistance, particularly in the rural areas.

By mid-1950 a surprising number of Third Forces, all avowedly both anti-Communist and anti-KMT, had set up organizations in Hong Kong in the hope of receiving financial aid from America for alleged guerrilla projects. Most of the promoters were charlatans, but there was a Kwangsi group which made a genuine attempt to keep anti-Communism alive under direction from General Li Tsung-jen (then in New York), and a similar group in Kwangtung under the orders of General Chang Fa-kuei, a former Commander-in-Chief of the Chinese army. With both these groups the Chung Woh Tong, which, like the China Chi Kung Tong, had re-emerged in 1946 and had transformed itself into a party, claimed to be connected.

That secret societies were still a thorn in the flesh to the new Government is clear from a decree issued on 2 January 1951 declaring that all secret societies (T'ongs) were dissolved as being 'contrary to the best interests of the people'. This was followed on 23 February by the issue of regulations authorizing the death penalty or imprisonment for life for, among others, members of secret societies. Article 8 of the Regulations mentioned in particular 'those who utilize feudalistic secret societies to engage in counter-revolutionary activities'.[64] Here we have a modern version of the old Imperial Edicts clearly directed against the same class of turbulent subjects. It was officially announced that these Regulations were necessary because anti-Communist elements were becoming increasingly active in various parts of the country, that many peasants were not supporting the Government's land reform, and that armed defiance was spreading. In Kwangsi province alone 3,000 officials sent to enforce the Communist administrative measures had been killed.[65]

The immediate result of the promulgation of these penalties was a series of mass executions throughout the country, and it is reasonable to assume that the majority of the victims were secret society members. That the virus was by no means exterminated is clear from a report by the Minister of Public Security in June 1956 wherein it was stated that during the previous year twenty-seven 'pretenders to the throne' had been arrested, some of them having hoped to set up 'new imperial dynasties, and claiming to be emperors', a pattern which recalls many secret society leaders of revolts in past centuries and indicates that tradition still had its appeal.[66]

Meanwhile, in Formosa, where Chiang Kai-shek and the rump of the KMT Government had settled under American protection, an attempt was made to rally members of the Hung Brotherhood overseas to the support of 'Free China'.

[64] *Ta Kung Pao* (Hong Kong), 23 Feb. 1951.
[65] Keesing, viii. 11419A, 21–28 Apr. 1951.   [66] Ibid. x. 14943, 23–30 June 1956.

In October 1956 a 'Reunion of the Overseas Brethren of the Hung Family of China' was held there, with the aim of electing a Central Executive Committee of the Brotherhood overseas, to be incorporated within the KMT party framework. The Convention was well-attended, and every effort made to convince the delegates that the duty of the Brotherhood as the watch-dog of the people's interests was to do everything in its power to resist Communist aggression, but little of practical value seems to have resulted.[67]

The Hung Brotherhood overseas which, as it consists almost entirely of southern Chinese, is the Triad fraternity abroad thus finds itself the recipient of advances and propaganda from both the Communist People's Government and the KMT Government in Formosa, each of which covets the support which such a wide-based mass movement might be expected to provide. The evidence of recent years seems to indicate that while local societies may be used for the support of local influences, attempts to organize the Brotherhood, with its multiplicity of language divisions and local loyalties, as a homogeneous political entity are unlikely to succeed.

Whether the elements of the old Chinese ethos which have been incorporated into the secret society tradition will survive the inundation of Communism remains to be seen, but the indications are that despite outbursts of iconoclasm the development will be along the lines of synthesis between old and new rather than complete rejection of the old and the substitution of a new political and cultural system of foreign origin. It is reasonable to assume that much of the traditional attitude will persist even though overlaid by modern political forms, and that a tradition so deep-rooted and widespread as that which underlies the formation of secret societies will not easily be eradicated.

[67] Report printed in Chinese (154 pages plus photographs).

Part 1
ORIGINS AND HISTORY

1. The Malay Peninsula

3

THE PIONEERS

1. THE EARLY SETTLEMENTS AND THE COMING OF THE CHINESE

THE importance of the Chinese in the economic, social, and political life of Malaya at the present time is so obvious that it requires no emphasis, but this development is, historically speaking, of recent growth. Although there had been small numbers of Chinese at Malacca since the foundation of the Malay kingdom there in the fifteenth century, it was not until British influence penetrated Malaya through the founding of Settlements, first at Penang, and then at Singapore, that the Chinese arrived in large numbers and became a significant factor in the life of the country.

In 1786 Francis Light, captain of a 'Country Ship' sailing from India, landed on the point of what is now known as Penang Island and hoisted the flag, 'taking possession of the Island in the name of His Britannic Majesty and for the use of the Honourable East India Company'. This was no buccaneering enterprise, but the result of an agreement reached with the Sultan of Kedah, and it laid the foundation for the development of Malaya. The next step was the founding of Singapore by Stamford Raffles in 1819, and when Malacca was acquired by treaty from the Dutch in 1824, it became the third British Settlement on Malayan soil.

As, throughout this book, there will be repeated references to the administrative framework of these three Settlements, a brief account of the arrangements made by the British for their governance is expedient.

Penang was originally placed under the administrative control of the Presidency of Bengal with a Superintendent (Francis Light) in charge. In 1800 his title was changed to Lieutenant-Governor, and in 1805 the status of Penang was raised to that of a Presidency, on the same footing as Madras, Bombay, and Bengal. Singapore under a Resident was subordinate to Raffles in Bencoolen (Sumatra) from 1819 to 1823, when it was placed under the Bengal Government. In 1826 Singapore and Malacca were united with Penang in a single administrative unit known initially as the 'Incorporated Settlement of Prince of Wales's Island, Singapore and Malacca', and until 1830 constituted the Fourth Presidency of India. The seat of government was in Penang, and each 'Station' had its own Resident Councillor under the Governor/President of the whole 'Settlement'.

In 1830 the Fourth Presidency was abolished and reduced to a Residency under the jurisdiction of Bengal. The seat of government remained in Penang where the Resident was in control, and each of the three Stations was in charge of a Deputy Resident.

Almost at once (for reasons connected with the Charter of H.M. Court) it was found necessary to restore the titles of Governor and Resident Councillor, but the Governor was given no separate power and was still required to refer every administrative detail to Bengal. In 1832 the seat of government was moved to Singapore, which had far outstripped both Penang and Malacca in importance. In 1851 the 'Straits Settlements', as they were then termed, were removed from the jurisdiction of Bengal and placed directly under the Supreme Government of India. In 1867 the control of the Settlements was transferred from the Government of India to the Colonial Office, and the Settlements became a Crown Colony.

The Malay States of the mainland gradually came under British protection, and each accepted a British 'Resident' or 'Adviser'. In 1896 the four States of Perak, Selangor, Negri Sembilan, and Pahang agreed to form a federation known as the Federated Malay States, with a federal legislature and a British 'Resident General', later known as 'Chief Secretary'. The Governor of the Straits Settlements was also the High Commissioner for the Malay States, whether federated or unfederated. After the Japanese war, all nine Malay States, together with the Settlements of Penang and Malacca, were combined in a confederation known as the 'Malayan Union', a title which was later changed to 'Federation of Malaya'. This political entity was granted self-government on 31 August 1957. Singapore was excluded from this confederation, and remained as a separate territory which in June 1958 was given full internal self-government as a separate State.

The next development was the combination of the Federation of Malaya with Singapore and the Bornean territories of Sarawak and Sabah (formerly known as British North Borneo) to form the Federation of Malaysia, which was inaugurated on 16 September 1963 with the headquarters of the Central Government at Kuala Lumpur. Later, differences between the political leaders of the Federation of Malaya and those of Singapore led to a partial disruption in which Singapore was excluded from the Federation of Malaysia on 9 August 1965 and became an independent republic within the Commonwealth.

The agreement of 1786 granted Penang Island to the East India Company as a trading station and refitting base for ships of war, in return for military aid to Kedah in the event of any external attack, and the payment to the Sultan of an annual subsidy of $6,000. In order that a settlement and a refitting station could be established, Light's first care was the encouragement of a flow of labour, for at the time of its cession the island was practically uninhabited. His efforts met with an immediate and almost spectacular response. A Capitan China from Kedah, eager for an extension of his power into the new Settlement, arrived with a present of fishing nets, and Indians from the Coromandel Coast, Malays from Kedah and Sumatra, and Chinese from Malacca, Siam, the Dutch Indies, Sarawak, and China were all drawn to Penang by the prospect of trade.

There was, however, one hitch in the arrangements, for the Company refused to ratify the provisions of the original agreement concerning the defence of Kedah. This brought the local administration into disrepute with many of the early European residents, as well as causing the Sultan to attempt, unsuccessfully, to recover the island by force. There were said to be further plans for this purpose involving a rising of the Chinese in Penang in 1799, but in 1800 the Sultan was obliged not only to confirm the original agreement (without the aid clause) by treaty, but to cede a strip of territory on the mainland, now known as Province Wellesley. In return, his subsidy was increased to $10,000 annually.

Despite the extension of cultivation of sugar-cane, pepper, rice, and nutmegs made possible by the additional territory, Penang, for a variety of reasons, did not fulfil the high hopes of its founders. It was fever-ridden, the death-rate was high, and there was little hard wood for ship repairs. Furthermore its distance from the spice islands prevented any significant interference with Dutch trade, while the Straits of Malacca were such a notorious hunting-ground for pirates that the Company's ships from the Celebes feared to make the passage through the Straits to Penang.

Stamford Raffles, an official of the East India Company who had lived in Penang for some years and was aware of its limitations, saw and seized the opportunity in 1819 of establishing a trading station in a more central and dominating position at the southern end of the Straits. There he obtained permission from the Malay ruling house to set up a trading establishment at Singapore, where, again, the population was very sparse, totalling only some 150 Malays at the riverside, said to have settled there only in 1811, with a few Chinese, probably Tiechius, some of whom had established gambier plantations on the slopes not far from the river. According to Raffles, 'There were not, perhaps, fifty-three Chinese on the island.' So that, once again, there began a mass immigration of Chinese labourers and traders composed of elements similar to those at Penang.[1]

Malacca was in a different category. Chinese had settled there at least as early as the fifteenth century, and the territory had been under European control (Portuguese and Dutch) since 1511. It was not until 1824 that Malacca finally became British territory by virtue of a treaty with the Dutch whereby the British exchanged their settlement at Bencoolen in Sumatra for the Dutch settlement of Malacca. The transfer did not, however, take place until April 1825. Already there were many Chinese families, mostly Hokkiens, settled at Malacca, some of which had been there for hundreds of years.

Agriculture, fishing, and trading provided a livelihood for the main body of the earliest Chinese settlers. On Singapore Island it was not long before small groups were settled on the streams around the coast. These groups followed the pattern of villages in China by being composed mainly of relatives of one surname with a patriarchal headman. Traces of this survive in the names Lim Chu Kang, Chua Chu Kang, and Yio Chu Kang, denoting rivers controlled by people of surname Lim, Chua, and Yio respectively. In the early days there were other 'Chu Kangs' which have now disappeared, bearing the surnames Chan, Tan, Lao, and Chu.

When, in the 1830s, owing to the failure of their spice plantations on Singapore Island, Chinese settlers went further afield into south Johore to plant pepper and gambier, they took this same system with them, and many such settlements were made on the Johore rivers, where they were known as 'Kangkas', each with a headman known as the 'Kangchu', Lord of the River.

The system of indirect rule through the headman of the various communities was the common pattern in the East, particularly in areas where multi-racial

[1] *SFP*, 2 Oct. 1856; W. Bartley, 'Population of Singapore in 1819', *JRASMB*, xi/2 (1933); *Memoir of the Life and Public Service of Sir T. S. Raffles*, by his widow (London, 1830), app., p. 10.

populations came under the control of western powers. It was adopted in the sixteenth century by the Portuguese in Malacca, and was followed in their eastern colonies by the Dutch, the French, and the British, all of whom appointed 'captains' of communities who were, in some degree, responsible to the supreme authority for the acts of all members of their communities, and who therefore exercised great power within their own groups.

In early Penang, 'captains' of the Chinese, Malay, and 'Chulia'[2] communities were appointed by the Government to assist in maintaining order, and were authorized to try petty cases between their own countrymen. Similar systems were introduced in Singapore and retained in Malacca. This also became the accepted pattern for dealing with Chinese communities as they grew up in the Malay States, where the practice of officially appointing 'Capitans China' was not discontinued until late in the nineteenth century.

In territories controlled by the Dutch and the French, even greater responsibility was placed upon the Captains. In Indo-China, for example, the French divided the various Chinese-language groups into 'Congregations', each with its own headman, to whom every immigrant of his group was assigned on arrival and for whom the headman was responsible, being obliged to produce each individual if called upon to do so by the authorities. Although in Malaya the system never went as far as this, each group in the Chinese community had its own headman with the prestige of a leader, and even smaller territorial or sub-dialect groups had their own locally-acknowledged 'captains'.

The spread of the Chinese population to the mainland, and particularly to the states of Perak, Selangor, and Negri Sembilan, was intimately connected with the development of tin-mining. Tin had been mined in Malaya for centuries and was exported from Malacca, but both production and export seem to have been in the hands of Malays, with perhaps a sprinkling of Chinese labourers. Close at hand, however, in Siam, at Junk Ceylon (Ujong Salang, i.e. Tongkah), there were Chinese employed in the tin industry in 1787, for Francis Light in a despatch of that year refers to them.

The earliest reliable figures for the Malay States relate to 1824, when some 400 Chinese were working in Perak as mining labourers and traders, and 200 were employed in tin mines at Lukut, which was then in Selangor but in February 1878 was incorporated in Negri Sembilan. In 1828 there was a settlement of nearly 1,000 Chinese miners further inland at Sungei Ujong, with headquarters at Rasah.[3] These figures are small when it is remembered that there had been Chinese in near-by Malacca for centuries, and that, not much further afield, Siam, Java, and Borneo each had about 100,000 immigrant Chinese by this time.[4]

The 1850s, however, witnessed the enterprise of some Malay chiefs who brought increasing numbers of Chinese into the Malay States for the development of mines, and from then onwards floods of male Chinese immigrants poured into the country. By 1901 Chinese formed 65 per cent of the population of Selangor, and 46 per cent of that of Perak, being about equal in numbers with the Malays in that State. The peak was reached in 1913 when 250,000 Chinese were employed in tin mining in the Federated Malay States.

[2] Mohammedan Indians, from the Coromandel coast.
[3] R. J. Wilkinson, 'Sungei Ujong and Notes on Negri Sembilan', *JSSBRAS*, 1921.
[4] Raffles, Despatch on the 'Singapore Institution', 1823 (SSR(M2), Lett. fr. Beng.); *Memoir*, p. 255.

Although the rapid expansion of mining accounted in the main for the great influx of labour from China during the nineteenth century, the introduction of rubber planting on a commercial scale from 1895 led, from 1905, to further large demands for labour. Much of this was recruited from India, but many thousands of Chinese also came to Malaya for work on estates.

The direct employers of this immigrant Chinese labour were invariably Chinese owners, lessees, or contractors who arranged through brokers to obtain the labour required from the importing agents for work on indenture, a system known as the 'selling of piglets', in which there were many abuses, and in 1822, when Raffles visited Singapore from Bencoolen, he decided that some regulation was essential. On 1 April 1823, four years after the founding of Singapore and only two months before he finally left the Settlement, he published an Ordinance providing for the protection of immigrants from China, part of which ran:

As it frequently happens that free labourers and others are brought from China and elsewhere as passengers who have not the means of paying their passage, and under the expectation that individuals resident in Singapore will advance the amount of it on receiving the services of the parties for a limited period in compensation thereof, such arrangements are not deemed objectionable provided the parties are landed as free persons, but in all cases the amount of passage money or otherwise is limited to twenty dollars, and the period of service by an adult in compensation thereof shall in no case exceed two years, and every agreement shall be entered into with the free consent of the parties in presence of a Magistrate, and duly registered.

The intention was good, but as there was no machinery other than the police and the magistracy to see that the law was enforced, it was many years before the abuses were seriously tackled. Such cases as were brought before the magistrate were dealt with according to law, and occasionally the *sin-khehs* (new arrivals) were set at liberty after signing a bond promising to pay the passage money. But action on complaints was not enough. A whole system of supervision was needed, and, as will later be seen, was eventually provided. Meantime, despite the hardships involved, the importation system, by bringing him to this new land, offered the landless Chinese peasant chances of livelihood, of self-advancement, even of wealth such as were beyond any possibility of procurement in his native land. Writing as early as 1794 about the Chinese settlers at Penang, Francis Light commented:

They are indefatigable in the pursuit of money. . . . They do not wait until they have acquired a large fortune to return to their native country, but send annually a part of their profit to their families. This is so general that a poor labourer will work with double labour to acquire two or three dollars to remit to China.

But he added: 'They are excessively fond of gaming, there is no restraining them from it; this leads them into many distresses and frequently ends in their ruin.'[5]

The Chinese immigrants without exception had their origin in the three southern provinces of China—Kwangtung, Kwangsi, and Fukien—and with rare exceptions that has been true of all Chinese immigrants ever since. They fell into five main groups—Cantonese (including Kwangsais) from the provinces of Kwangtung and Kwangsi, Hakkas from all three provinces, Tiechius from Swatow and its vicinity in northern Kwangtung and southern Fukien, Hailams (or Hainanese as they are now generally called) from the island of Hainan off the

[5] Quoted in 'Notices of Penang', *JIA*, v (1851), p. 9.

coast of Kwangtung, and Hokkiens, mainly from Chuan Chiu and Amoy in the province of Fukien, with whom were also grouped the Hokchius, the Hokch'ias, and the Hinghwas, from Foochow and the north of the province.

It is not always easy in the early records to distinguish clearly between them all. Cantonese (from both Kwangtung and Kwangsi), Hakkas, Hainanese, and sometimes Tiechius were liable all to be classified as 'Macaos' because their port of assembly for emigration was Macao. (After its foundation in 1842, Hong Kong was to become the main outlet for emigrants from Kwangtung and Kwangsi.) The words 'Hakka' (or its Hokkien equivalent 'Kheh') and 'Tiechiu' do not appear in early documents, though men of these groups were certainly among the early immigrants. Tiechius were sometimes referred to as 'Ahyas', though the origin of the term is unknown. The Hokkiens were called 'Chinchews' because many of them came from the port of Chuan Chiu, north of Amoy.

Most of the early arrivals were 'Macaos'. They formed the bulk of the Chinese labouring and artisan population, the swarm of indentured labourers. The Tiechiu section of this group usually engaged in agriculture, and at Penang, Province Wellesley, and Krian they established sugar-cane plantations. In Singapore they were engaged in growing gambier and pepper. Many of the Cantonese and Hakkas also took to agriculture, but once the mines were operating, it was there that they were to be found in large numbers, preferring the gambler's chance of quick profits (they worked on a share system) should they strike a rich patch.

The Hokkiens were not to be compared in numbers with the 'Macaos', but were important commercially. Some of the Hokkien families who had been established at Malacca or Rangoon or in the Dutch Indies islands for many years were attracted to Penang, where they set up as traders rather than as manual labourers. But their northern compatriots, the Hokchius, the Hokch'ias, and the Hinghwas were, as a rule, engaged in labour.

The language barriers between the various groups were formidable. Natives of Kwangtung and Kwangsi had one basic speech which we call Cantonese, and which was not understood by the natives of Fukien. Within the Cantonese language are district variants, some of which are sufficiently close to the standard speech of Canton to be intelligible to most Cantonese, others which are not. The Tiechius had a different language again, more akin to Hokkien than to Cantonese. The Hakkas spoke a language, with several variants, closer to Mandarin than the other southern vernaculars, while men from the island of Hainan had their own dialect showing kinship with both Hokkien and Cantonese, but not understood by either group.

Within the Hokkien group differences were even more pronounced. There are over 100 local dialects in common use in the province of Fukien, and though only a few of these were represented among the immigrants, some, such as Foochow (Hokchiu), Hokch'ia, and Hinghwa were quite unintelligible to speakers of other Hokkien dialects, as they were to all the 'Macaos'.

Not only did the languages differ but there were quite wide differences between the customs of many of the groups. Even more important was the fact that each group, and each territorial subdivision of each group, brought with it to Malaya the jealousies and antipathies, the clannishness and suspicion which were part of the normal pattern of life in China.

But from whatever province or prefecture or district in China these men came, and whatever the differences of language and custom, they had one thing in common. In China, in their villages, matters concerning the daily life and welfare of the people were dealt with by organizations of the people and not by the Government. Whenever the Government moved, it boded ill for the people, for it meant the collection of taxes, the conscription of men for fighting or for labour, or the restriction in some other way of individual liberties. With such experience, the immigrants were unlikely to look upon the foreign Government of the Straits Settlements any more favourably than they regarded their own. Although the Manchus were aliens, the British were even more alien, and therefore still more remote from their cognizance. The various territorial language groups, Cantonese, Hokkiens, Hakkas, Tiechius, Hainanese, formed their separate clusters which were still further subdivided into provincial, prefectural, and district associations, and even into clan organizations.

This was an entirely male population in its early stages, for until 1863 there was no regular immigration of women, and the men of each group looked to its own leader for security and jurisdiction. The pattern was admirably suited to the formation of secret societies, and as all the immigrants were already familiar with, and many were members of, the Triad societies of south China, it was not long before societies of this same Brotherhood took root in Malaya, and became the principal control centres of the Chinese population.

Most of the available information concerning the Chinese in Malaya comes from contemporary documents written by Europeans, including official reports and despatches, press comments, and some articles in journals. It would be idle to deny that these sources often reveal the superior attitude of the early mercantile colonists and missionary enthusiasts, who reflected the belief of Victorian England in the progress of western civilization, elevating its representatives above the level of the rest of mankind. The age of objective anthropological assessment had not yet dawned, and the writings of the period, both official and unofficial, were plentifully sprinkled with evidence of a disdain which was augmented by the unruly nature of many of the Chinese immigrants and by the lack of persons of any educational standing among them.

Nevertheless, writers such as Logan and Vaughan maintained a reasonably objective approach, and many of the permanent officials and Governors viewed the problems of their Asian citizens with such a degree of humanity and understanding that critics among the mercantile community frequently deplored what they considered to be the Government's lack of resolution when dealing with 'native' problems.

There are no records of what the Chinese immigrants thought of this impact of West and East, but there can be little doubt, if the evidence of Chinese annals dealing with westerners in China is any guide, that they were even more contemptuous of the westerners than the latter were of them.

2. SECRET SOCIETIES IN EARLY MALAYA[6]

Although there is no information about the existence of specific secret societies among the Chinese community of Penang in its earliest years, it is clear that

[6] For an account of the traditional history and ritual of the Triad Brotherhood, see App. 1, p. 528.

Francis Light was well aware of the propensity for secret combination of his Chinese settlers. In January 1794, less than eight years after Penang's foundation, he wrote: 'speaking a language which no other people can understand, they are able to form parties and combinations in the most secret manner against any regulation of government which they disapprove'.[7] In 1799 this tendency to oppose government regulation was alleged to have developed into a seditious conspiracy, in which it was said some 500 persons had taken oaths of secrecy and fidelity to their leader (a Chinese servant of one of the European planters), with the intention of setting up a jurisdiction 'independent of the Company's authority, under a Captain and Magistrates of their own choosing'.[8] When this leader and four others were arrested by the Acting Superintendent, Mr Caunter, further rumours spread through the town, that a plot existed 'for surprising the fort, that the Malays secretly instigated by the Rajah of Queda were in league with the Chinamen, and that scaling ladders were actually provided by the latter for that purpose'.[9]

There are grounds for doubting whether this 'conspiracy' ever existed. At the time there was strong disagreement between the European community and the administration, and ill feeling had gone to such lengths that the officials were even prepared to accuse several members of the European community of having urged the Chinese to plot against the Government. It seems unlikely that any outbreak actually occurred, or this would have been mentioned in the accounts of these early years, and it is probable that the European employer of the alleged 'leader' of the 'conspirators', Mr Roebuck, put his finger on the truth when he gave it as his opinion that the story of the plot had been put about by the Capitan China on account of a personal quarrel with this 'leader' on whom he wished to take revenge.

Looking back, it seems natural to expect that the Capitan China was the head of a Triad society, and it may be that Mr Roebuck's employee was starting a rival society in which he had already enrolled some 500 members, to the discomfiture of the Capitan China.[10] The taking of oaths of secrecy and fidelity and the setting up of a jurisdiction under a leader of their own choosing with disciplinary control, as was alleged to be the object of the 'conspiracy', fits in very well with the supposition that what was afoot was the organization of a Triad society.

The first specific reference to a Triad society in Malaya occurs in an article describing the Sam Hop Wui, written by Dr Milne, a missionary who was on the staff of the Anglo-Chinese College in Malacca.[11] He mentions a Chinese tailor in Malacca 'who committed murder at the close of 1818, shortly after the transfer

[7] *JIA*, v. 9, quoting Light.
[8] Ibid., p. 117, quoting Caunter.
[9] Ibid., pp. 117 ff., quoting Caunter.
[10] When we come to consider the details of the societies formed in early Penang, it will be noticed that only one of them is given a date of foundation as early as 1799, and even this society was not one of the more notorious Triad societies. This, however, would not preclude the existence in Penang of a group of members of a Triad society from Siamese territory, in particular Junk Ceylon, where Chinese had already settled and were in close contact with Penang. It is possible that the 'conspiracy' was really the beginning of a struggle for power between two Triad groups attempting to establish themselves on Penang Island.
[11] Sam Hop Wui: Three United Society, one of the titles of the Triad Brotherhood. The article was written in 1821, and was sent to China for further investigation in July of that year. Milne died in June 1822, leaving the article unfinished (*RAS Trans.*, i/2 (1827), pp. 240–50).

of the Colony,[12] and made his escape from the hands of justice taking refuge in the tin mines beyond Malacca territory.' This man was a chief of the society, and his escape was attributed to the assistance of his fellow members. According to Milne:

In foreign colonies, the objects of this Association are plunder and mutual defense. The idle, gambling, opium-smoking Chinese (particularly of the lower class) frequently belong to this fraternity. What they obtain by theft or plunder is divided in shares, according to the rank which the members hold in the society. They engage to defend each other against attacks from Police officers; to hide each other's crimes; to assist detected members to escape from the hands of Justice.

He adds that 'in such places as Java, Singapore, Malacca, and Penang, when a Chinese stranger arrives to reside for any length of time he is generally glad to give a trifle of money to this brotherhood to be freed from their annoyance'.

Milne's account of Malacca is paralleled by Major Low's account of Province Wellesley, when he put it on record that the Chinese at Batu Kawan sugar plantations nearly all belonged to one kongsi,[13] 'and were very turbulent before 1829, having turned out on several occasions to the sound of a buffalo horn against the civil power'. Of these 'occasions' there is no record, but Low goes on to recount that:

When a Chinese is apprehended for, or accused of a crime, however atrocious it may be, his whole Kongsi are unanimous in their endeavour to get him off. Subscriptions for counsel, high bribes to adverse witnesses to keep them away, and to forthcoming ones to perjure themselves; dreadful threats to conscientious witnesses and connivance at the escape or secreting of the accused are the means resorted to as a matter of course. When one Kongsi is opposed to another by the criminal accusation of an individual of one of them, no bounds can be assigned to the use which is made of these illegal means.[14]

By 1824, only five years after the foundation of the Settlement, a Triad society was already well in evidence in Singapore, and there is a description of a visit paid to its headquarters at 'Tangling Tuah' by Munshi Abdullah bin Abdul Kadir, a protégé of Raffles and teacher of Malay to Dr Milne of Malacca. Abdullah devoted an entire section of his journal, the *Hikayat Abdullah*,[15] to an account of the T'in Tei Wui in Singapore, describing the society as consisting of many thousands of men, living deep in the jungle, some owning plantations but the majority living by robbery, piracy, and murder. There was a master, four captains, section leaders, and 'scores of satellites who looked after the rank and file and caught people, forcing them to join . . . by ordeals, by oath-taking and by the drinking of blood'. Those unwilling to join were tortured or even killed.

Through the good offices of a Chinese friend from Malacca who was a member of the society, Abdullah was able to pay a visit to the headquarters, accompanied

[12] Transfer of the Colony refers to the retrocession to the Dutch in 1818. Malacca was in British hands during the Napoleonic wars.

[13] Cantonese Kung Sz. The original meaning was a business partnership, but this was extended to mean any partnership or group of persons with common interests. In Malaya the term is also applied to the premises occupied or used by the group.

[14] Quoted by T. J. Newbold and F. W. Wilson, 'The Chinese Secret Triad Society of the Tien-ti-huih', *JRAS*, vi (1840–1), p. 133.

[15] The trans. of Dr A. H. Hill in *JMBRAS*, xxvii/3 (1955) has been followed, except that 'T'in Tei Wui' has been substituted for 'Thian Tai Huey'. The writing of the *Hikayat* was not begun until 1840.

by his friend and four other Chinese. There was no beaten track, they went 'over and under trunks of trees and zigzagging through swamps, and standing water'. Starting at 5 a.m. it was four o'clock in the afternoon before they reached their destination, 'three large huts, each at least 180 feet in length, inside which men swarmed like maggots'. The huts were surrounded by a deep and wide ditch crossed by a narrow bridge easily removed to prevent a surprise incursion. Abdullah was eventually lodged in a small room off the main hall, from which he could see what was going on through a chink in the wall. At the sound of a bamboo gong, 500 or 600 men from all three huts assembled, practically all of whom smoked opium at hundreds of opium lamps in the hut. Abdullah gave a vivid account of the initiation ceremony which he then saw. After uproarious eating and drinking, gongs were sounded and drums beaten, and all sat down in rows facing 'the idols of their ancestors', the master sitting on a high chair in the middle. Two men, followed by eight men holding drawn swords, stood on either side of him; others lit pieces of paper in front of the shrine.

A candidate for initiation, his hair dishevelled, and wearing no shirt, was dragged forward. As he knelt before the master with head bowed low, sword-bearers shouted and brandished their weapons about his neck. An exchange of questions and answers took place during which the man declared that his parents were dead and asked for admission to the society.[16] He agreed to swear allegiance and secrecy, and an attendant then made a small cut in his finger and caught the blood in a bowl which already contained the blood of the others present mixed with spirit.[17] The initiate and the master and the others present then drank from the bowl before the 'idols' of their ancestors.

After the initiation ceremony there followed a dramatic scene during which a man who refused to join the society was questioned. This man, brought before the master with hands bound, was ordered to make obeisance but refused, whereupon he was beaten with a bamboo. When asked if he wished to become a member or not he at first gave no answer, but eventually said that he did not. The sword-bearers then brandished their weapons in threatening fashion, and when he still refused to join he was thrown to the ground and belaboured with bamboos until he shrieked in agony. As he still persisted in his refusal the master ordered him to be killed the following morning when, said the account, 'he was put to death for refusing to join the Society'. 'In this way,' said Abdullah, 'they had assassinated scores of men, all of them forcibly abducted from Singapore, for this was how the Society's men set about enlarging its membership.' Moreover, if members broke their oaths of allegiance and revealed any of its secrets to outsiders, they were put to death without mercy.

Abdullah was thoroughly alarmed at what he had seen, and begged his friend to take him away from the 'accursed place' as soon as it was light. He made no mention of having seen the death sentence carried out on the recalcitrant prisoner, and it is likely that his statement that 'he was put to death' was based on presumption rather than on observed fact. It is possible, too, that his account of the number of men involved was exaggerated, but there is no reason to quarrel

[16] Meaning that the initiate renounced his worldly parents and was reborn as a child of the Hung Family (see App. 1).

[17] The present custom is that only the new members have their fingers pricked and only they drink the 'blood-wine'. In this account there is no mention of 'cutting a cock'. See App. 1 for details of initiation ceremony.

with the general picture which he presented. He also referred to robberies and a piracy committed by members of the society and carped at the inactivity of the Government in the face of the misdeeds of the society men who were 'quite unrestrained, free to do exactly as they liked without shame or consideration for others', and came to the conclusion that the reason was that it was difficult to drive a road into the interior because 'in those days, not many of the Company's convicts had yet come to Singapore'.

Abdullah also recorded a rumour that it was the intention of the T'in Tei Wui to attack the town of Singapore, but his Chinese friend said that the plan had not yet been concerted with their comrades in Penang and Malacca. If true, this information might add significance to the allegations of conspiracy at Penang in 1799.

It is possible that lack of experience on the part of British officials of the activities of Chinese secret societies had given the latter added confidence. In this the British differed from their Dutch confrères, who from their earliest contacts with China in 1622 had been aware of the power exercised by secret societies among the Chinese in Formosa, and in 1662 had been driven out of their base in that island by Koxinga (Cheng Ch'eng-kung), the pirate chief and leader of the secret society of the area. In 1677 they had warned their ships of the danger of 'Koxinga' pirates in the Straits of Malacca.[18] Throughout the East Indies they had had experience of insurrections caused by secret societies, and both there and in Malacca had ruthlessly suppressed them. British officials, ignorant of the strength of the potential threat, ruled with a less repressive hand, and as a result secret societies increased in strength and in audacity. By 1825 in all three Settlements—Singapore, Malacca, and Penang—they were causing anxiety, and the necessity of obtaining information concerning their personnel and activities was becoming increasingly apparent. In addition to the threat to internal security there seemed also to be a danger that they might be used to further the designs of the Siamese in expanding their influence throughout the peninsula. During their tenure of Malacca the Dutch had contracted treaty alliances with both Perak and Selangor under which they engaged to defend these states, which were in constant danger of being overrun by the Siamese. When, in 1824, the treaty between England and Holland was signed providing for the transfer of Malacca to the British, the Dutch treaties with these Malay States lapsed, and the way was open to the Siamese to plan a southward expansion.

Kedah was the first victim of Siam's aggression. It was overrun in 1821 by the Raja of Ligor, and though the king escaped and was granted asylum in Penang, many members of his family were taken prisoner, and half the population were slaughtered. In June 1823 the Raja of Ligor informed the Governor of Penang that the King of Siam had granted him jurisdiction over Kedah, and demanded that the ex-king of Kedah be surrendered and that attempts to recover Kedah territory engineered from Penang should cease. The Governor refused to interfere,[19] and in April 1825 news was received in Penang that the Raja of Ligor was fitting out an armada of 300 armed prahus at Trang in Kedah for the alleged purpose of attacking Perak and Selangor.

The Governor of Penang, Robert Fullerton, however, was disposed to believe that the real purpose of this fleet was to attack Penang, a belief founded on

---

[18] Victor Purcell, *The Chinese in Southeast Asia* (1965), p. 241.
[19] SSR(A18), Pg Cons., Council Mtg, 10 July 1823, pp. 2–7.

information received from several sources, some of which spoke of the intention to hire 200 men in Penang to set the town on fire preparatory to attack. The Raja of Ligor was the son of a Chinese father, and his prime minister was Chinese. Furthermore, it was known that they had contacts with the Chinese community in Penang, and a prisoner in the House of Correction gave information which appeared to link the machinations of the Raja with those of a Chinese secret society in the Settlement.[20]

The prisoner was a Hokkien, who stated that eight months previously his employer, a 'Macao' Chinese goldsmith, had invited him to join a 'Kungsee or Club' to which he himself belonged. This was the 'Ghee Chin' and was 'very numerous'.[21] All persons on joining were compelled to take an oath that they would 'when required or on any public commotion join the members thereof'. He understood that they had stores of spears and other weapons which were deposited in different places, some at the house or premises of the arrack farmer. Not having the means of paying the entrance fee, which he said was M$5.00, and not wishing to take the oath prescribed, he had not joined the society.

He also gave information about two other similar clubs of the Macao Chinese, the 'Hoosing Club' and the 'Hysan Club', and said that a certain Lowe Achong was a member of both these clubs, and when recently visiting Ligor 'was desired to communicate to the Siamese that there were but few people now at Penang, and that it was a good opportunity for attacking it if the Siamese were inclined to do so'. (This Lowe Achong had been employed by Captain Burney as a go-between with the Raja of Ligor.'[22]

This information was given on 6 May 1825 and was at once forwarded by the Superintendent of Police, R. Caunter, through the Sitting Magistrate, R. Ibbetson, to the Governor, together with his own comments on these Chinese 'clubs'. He wrote:

There are seven or eight Chinese Clubs or Hooeys[23] in this Island, some of which have been established several years. The avowed object of these institutions is the relief of indigent brethren and particularly to defray in a decent manner the funeral expenses of a member dying without that means. Owing to the known propensity of the Chinese to conspiracies these Hooeys are, I understand, strictly forbidden in China. Here they are found chiefly, if not solely, among what are termed Canton or Macao Chinese, of whom there may be about 3,000 on this island. The Chinchew Chinese may, if they please, become members of these associations, and some of the Chinchews are said to belong to them, but they are chiefly composed of the Canton Chinese, between whom and the Chinchews great jealousy and often hostility prevails.

When the Raja of Ligor was at Kedah 2½ to 3 years ago, he carried on a good deal of secret correspondence with the Canton or Macao Chinese of this place, got numbers of them to go in some junks he equipped and sent them to cruise to the northward of and about Junk Ceylon, where they were suspected, and I believe with some truth, to have committed some atrocious acts of piracy.[24]

[20] SSR(A20), Pg Cons., Council Mtgs 3 & 19 May 1825. Also H. Burney, *The Burney Papers* (1910), ii. 121 ff.
[21] By Ghee Chin was meant the Ghee Hin, also found as 'Gehin' and as 'Nghee-hung Kwun'.
[22] SSR(D8), Penang's Letts to India, pp. 80–83, No. 523, 14 May 1825.
[23] The word Hoey (Hokkien), Wui (Cantonese), which appears in various romanizations (Hooey, Huay, Hway, Hui, etc.), means an association. But it was used by contemporary European writers as a synonym for a secret society and as such is used throughout the book.
[24] SSR(H14), Pg, Letts & Ords in Council, 1825, Council Mtg, 12 May.

In response to this report, Caunter was informed that 'security against the evil-disposed being the principal object, the stricter judicial forms applicable on ordinary occasions in the apprehension of suspected persons must be dispensed with'. He was required to employ every means in his power to prevent the assembly of such 'kongsees' or clubs in future, and was reminded that many persons similar to those described had already been in the service of the Raja of Ligor

and moreover that several atrocious robberies have been committed by parties of armed Chinese on this Island. However such associations may profess to be for charitable or useful purposes, they must at all times be regarded with jealousy and are certainly dangerous to the peace of Society, and it will hereafter be a matter for consideration to frame a Regulation either for their total suppression or at least placing so under the direct cognizance of the Police as to prevent the perversion of the objects of their institution, to the disturbance of the peace and danger to Government.

Finally, he was directed to retain in custody Lowe Achong, believed to be the headman of one of the societies, 'for examination before the Council'.[25]

Caunter's investigations did nothing to substantiate the fears of the Governor, and he reported that no information had been obtained to prove that meetings of the clubs had ever been held for bad or improper purposes, nor had arms of any description been found. It was his opinion that the object of the clubs was partly to raise alms for charitable purposes, such as for the relief of sick or distressed brethren or providing funerals for the indigent, and partly convivial, to raise subscriptions for a good dinner at their meetings two or three times a year. There were several of these societies among the Cantonese and Macao Chinese (but not the 'Chinchoos') in the island, some of which had been in existence for twenty or thirty years. Only one of them admitted members under an oath. He believed that such societies must be beneficial to the Chinese in a foreign country where they would have no relations or friends to help them when in need, but 'considering the peculiar character of the Chinese and other circumstances, it would perhaps be good policy to place all such associations under control and regulation, and prohibit any oaths or tests of that nature being administered to them'.

Caunter forwarded a translation of a Malay version of the oath said to be administered to new members of the Nghee-hung Khoon club at the time of beheading a cock, and which appeared to be harmless, though it included an undertaking to be secret. He added that the word translated as 'secret' (*diam*) could equally mean 'quiet, orderly'.[26]

This attempted exculpation of Lowe Achong and the almost laudatory account of the activities of the clubs were so at variance with what the Governor himself believed that he arranged to examine the four leading Chinese traders of Penang on the subject. The examination was conducted by the Governor together with the Chief Judge on 9 June. Not only did the merchants unanimously confirm that Lowe Achong was the head of the 'Hysan' (Hai San) kongsi, but they had a good deal to say about the kongsi itself. From the nature of their remarks it may be assumed that these merchants were not themselves 'Macaos'; they were probably Hokkiens. According to them, the Hai San kongsi had been established

[25] SR(H12), Pg, Lett. & Ords in Council (1824–5), lett. 516, 9 May 1825, pp. 473–6.
[26] S.R(H14), Pg, Lett. & Ords in Council, 1825, pp. 892–5· fr. Supt of Police, R. Caunter, to John Anderson, Sec. to Govt, 21 May 1825. Produced at Council Proc. of 24 May 1825.

about two years and consisted of about 1,000 members 'of the lowest class of Macao Chinese—day-labourers, carpenters, gardeners, etc. They are all poor, not a merchant or respectable trader among them; they are looked upon as bad characters; good people do not join such clubs.' So said the merchants, but evidently this was not the whole truth, for on further questioning, while they agreed that it would be most advisable to put a stop to such clubs, they thought that it would not be easy to discover the names of the *better* people who were members. According to these informants, the Macao Chinese who were employed in the service of the Raja of Ligor a few years previously belonged to the Hai San and Ghee Hin clubs. They understood that Achong went to Ligor to endeavour to get the appointment of Captain China at Perak, and that he was proposing to take some 200 Chinese from Penang Island to Perak to make certain of this. As for the Ghee Hin club, it was 'equally numerous and the persons composing it equally bad as the Hysan Club'. Many of the members, they said, were seafaring people and they were connected with the Chinese residing in Pegue, Siam, and the adjoining countries.[27]

This information tended to confirm not only the undesirable nature of the Hai San kongsi but also its earlier connexion with the Raja of Ligor in 1823, and Lowe Achong's position as its headman. But the Governor had also received additional news of the immediate evil intention of the Raja of Ligor from a letter dated 6 June, sent by a native chief in the Raja's service to his brother, a respectable inhabitant of Province Wellesley, in which the writer said that the Siamese 'beyond all doubt will attack Pulo Penang. They are now preparing and only waiting until the white men are off their guard so that they may attack them by stealth.'[28]

Thus, confirmed in all his suspicions, Governor Fullerton immediately addressed a strong letter to the Raja of Ligor refusing to allow him to send armed prahus through the channel between Penang Island and the mainland on their way to attack Selangor, and warning him that if any of them came to the island, he would consider that they came with hostile intent and would treat them accordingly.[29] The Governor produced this information at a meeting of Council the next day (10 June), when he severely reprimanded the Police Department and its Superintendent, for failure 'to watch and discover the machinations of the evil-disposed'. This reprimand was embodied in a letter sent to the Superintendent of Police in which Caunter was informed that 'in consequence of information obtained by the Hon'ble the Governor from a variety of channels', there seemed 'not a vestige of doubt' that Lowe Achong was at the head of the Hai San kongsi, and that 'if any persons were engaged to aid the views of the Raja of Ligor' it was next to certain that they would be members of the Hai San kongsi and it would be very desirable to obtain, by a seizure of papers or otherwise, the names of those belonging to it. 'Had an immediate search taken place at the house where they are known to assemble instead of trusting to the asseveration of the reported heads, the names of all the parties and the precise objects of these

[27] SSR(A18), Pg Cons., 1823–5, 10 June 1825, pp. 253–5.
[28] Ibid. pp. 209–10: lett. fr. Chori Teang to his brother, Syed Jaffar, 6 June 1825. Forwarded by Mr Maingy to the Actg Sec. to Govt, John Anderson, and read at the Council Proc. at Ft Cornwallis, Pg, 10 June 1825.
[29] Ibid. pp. 243–53, App. 6 to President's Min. Lett. fr. Gov., Robert Fullerton, to Raja of Ligor, 9 June 1825. Read at Council Proc., 10 June 1825, at Ft Cornwallis, Pg.

meetings would have been ascertained.' It was still hoped that a clue might be obtained leading to the discovery of the Chinese employed by the Raja of Ligor. In the meantime a due regard to the preservation of order required that Achong should be kept in custody, and not allowed to communicate with anyone. The letter expressed the Governor's regret that on this occasion the police had shown itself to be 'so deficient as to the Clubs alluded to' and surprise that they had even been allowed to exist, composed as they were

of the very lowest and most worthless of the Population, a class of People without tie or connection on the Island, ready for any mischief, holding such meetings with closed Doors, administering Oaths of Secrecy, etc. It is difficult to conceive an instrument better fitted for the subversion of any regular Government.

The Governor in Council was only restrained from submitting a proclamation for the immediate suppression of these clubs by the hope that the discovery of members might still be possible, and the letter ended by requesting a thorough investigation into the nature and objects of the 'Kongsees', with the utmost vigilance 'in discovering any evil-disposed persons who may be conniving with the Emissaries of the Raja of Ligor'.[30]

Council proceedings on 16, 23, and 30 June 1825 were acrimonious, since both Mr Ibbetson and Mr Clubley, magistrates in Penang, took the Governor to task for being unduly apprehensive in regard to the Raja of Ligor and unnecessarily censorious of the police. They were also concerned that the Governor had instructed the police to dispense with the 'stricter judicial forms applicable on ordinary occasions in the apprehension of suspected persons'. As to this last, the Governor, at the end of a long Minute, declared:

None can admire more than I do the open and public enquiry and all the safeguards which British Jurisprudence has placed between the subject and unfair or undue accusation when trial and punishment are the object. But in a case like this, a Police Officer has other duties to perform. If conspiracy and sedition are at work, the secret machinations of the disaffected should be secretly traced and counteracted. To that case the best of Governments are sometimes reduced, and the public and ostentatious enquiry at the Police Office is just the cause best calculated to defeat the object and enable the really guilty to escape discovery, and it is just because the enquiry has been so conducted that it has failed.[31]

Already, apparently, some uneasiness was felt as to whether the judicial procedure designed for England was entirely suited to the very different social conditions of Penang.

When forwarding to the Government the information which he had collected about the societies, together with books and documents seized from their premises, Caunter reiterated that he still believed that the 'clubs' existed for charitable purposes. He had no reasons for supposing otherwise. Nevertheless, in deference, one feels, to the strong line taken by the Governor, he agreed that the 'clubs' were possibly 'impolitic, particularly among the Chinese, who are . . . a most intriguing people', so that 'their suppression was, in his opinion, very desirable'.

[30] SSR(I29), Misc. lett., 1825, pp. 44–47, No. 603: J. Anderson, Act. Sec. to Govt, to R. Caunter, Supt of Police, Ft Cornwallis, 10 June 1825; ibid. p. 75, No. 650: fr. J. Anderson to R. Caunter, Ft Cornwallis, 16 June 1825.
[31] SSR(A18), Pg Cons. (1823–5), 23 June 1825, pp 394–491. See also ibid. Mtgs of 16 June 1825, pp. 312–24, & 30 June 1825, pp. 514 & 518.

It is evident that Caunter had no clear idea of the real nature of the 'clubs' or of the differences between them, for he wrote:

In China, associations of this kind, namely, Hooey Khoons,[32] are permitted, I understand, but then they are under certain regulations, and their number of members limited. Hoeys of this description must not be confounded with another kind of Hoey, namely, Tin Tee Hoeys which are secret associations and confederacies formed for seditious and other illegal purposes.

That three of the Penang associations were of this type was not revealed to him by his informants.

When so little was known of the objects, organization, and activities of the Chinese societies it was very easy to go astray. No European had any experience of direct dealing with the Chinese. All were entirely dependent on their interpreters for communication, and the interpretation was of poor standard and not necessarily disinterested.

Caunter listed seven 'clubs' in Penang, all being composed of 'Macaos', i.e. Cantonese or Hakkas.[33] The three principal ones with the approximate dates of foundation were (in the romanization of Cantonese given by Caunter): the Ngee Hung (1801), the Woh Sung (1810), and the Hoy San (1823). In later years they were usually referred to in official documents by their Hokkien romanizations, i.e. Ghee Hin, Ho Seng, and Hai San.[34] The remaining clubs appear to have been district associations.

In 1826 a Hokkien society, the Chun Sim, popularly known as the Chin Chin, was formed because the 'Macao' societies developed such an overbearing attitude towards the Hokkien community that the latter started a society to 'lower the tone' of the Macao men.[35] The name of this society appears in a list supplied by Caunter's successor, John Patullo, in 1829.[36] By this time all four societies had branches in the country districts as well as headquarters in Georgetown.

The three original 'Macao' Hoeys in Penang, the Ho Seng, the Ghee Hin, and the Hai San, were three distinct foundations of the Triad Brotherhood. This was not generally realized at the time but appears from later information. Vaughan, writing in 1854, suggested that the first two were 'nearer to the famous Triad Society of China' than was the Hai San which, according to him, was formed in Penang.[37] This implies that the Ghee Hin and the Ho Seng were imported from elsewhere, and it seems probable that they came from either Siam or Burma. These two societies are known to have continued to exist side by side in Rangoon at least until 1954.[38]

There is no room for doubt that all three societies were Triad foundations, and this is corroborated by their diplomas as published on Cowan's wall-sheet of

[32] Hooey Khoon = Hoey Kwan (Hokkien), Wui Kwun (Cantonese): an association of men from a particular province, prefecture, or district in China.

[33] SSR(A18), Pg Cons., 23 June 1825, pp. 415–28.

[34] The normal Cantonese romanizations are: Yi Hing, Woh Shing, and Hoi San. M. L. Wynne, *Triad and Tabut* (1941), pp. 76 ff., erroneously treated the Woh Sung and the Ho Seng as two different societies.

[35] 'Report on Chinese Associations in Prince of Wales Island', by W. T. Lewis (1843). Encl. 16 to Despatch 23 of 1843, Samuel Garling, Actg Gov. to Sec. to Govt. Calcutta (IOL).

[36] SSR(A66), 1829, pp. 64–72.

[37] 'Notes on the Chinese of Pinang', *JIA*, viii (1854). The article was anonymous but was known to have been written by J. D. Vaughan, then Supt of Police, Penang.

[38] *Kwong Wah Jit Poh* (Penang), 11 Nov. 1954.

1897.[39] Not only so, but it can now be said that they claimed to represent three different Lodges of the original Brotherhood.[40] The Ho Seng purported to be a First Lodge society, the Ghee Hin a Second Lodge society, and the Hai San a Third Lodge society. Thus although all members were Brethren of the Triad fraternity, this division into three groups was liable to result in rivalry or antagonism whenever the interests of the groups failed to coincide. In the absence of any 'vatican' of the Brotherhood competent to decide disputes between lodges, the society leaders were left to the normal methods of conciliation, arbitration, and eventually physical force to arrive at settlements in such cases.

Patullo, in his report of 1829 on the composition and activities of the Chinese societies at Penang, made it clear that he did not share his predecessor's complacency about their harmless nature. He gave warning that they had often been made use of for 'very bad ends', including giving protection to murderers and robbers. He referred to the difficulty of getting at the truth of society activities in the face of their 'spirit of combination', and drew attention to the unnecessary and complicated forms which had to be gone through for the punishment of the most trivial offences. 'The application of English Law', he wrote, 'can never be adapted to meet the petty offences which are daily, nay hourly, committed. The forms to be gone through and the loss of time prevent, I have no doubt, many persons bringing offenders forward. . . .'

Patullo stressed particularly the 'rival spirit of competition which exists between the Macao and Chinchew classes of Chinese in almost every speculation, and especially in the excise farms'. This suggestion of a connexion between the excise farms and the Hoeys was well justified. A revenue system based on the farming out of monopolies had been in force in Penang from the earliest days of its existence as a dependency of Bengal, and at one time covered the sale of opium, spirits, toddy and bhang (from 1808), sireh leaf, pork, ataps, tobacco, oil, ghee and hogs' lard, nibong, firewood, timber, and salt. There was also a gambling farm until 1811, when it was discontinued as a result of a Presentment by the Grand Jury, at the instance of the 'Recorder', as the Judge was then called. By 1825 only five of these farms remained: those of opium, spirits, toddy and bhang, sireh leaf, and pork, the last of these having been introduced at the request of the leading Chinese to provide funds for the establishment and maintenance of a hospital and poor house for needy Chinese. At a later date, pawnbroking was added to the list.

Singapore and Malacca followed the same revenue system. Revenue from gaming was not abolished until 1826 in Malacca and 1829 in Singapore.[41] Invariably the farms for opium, spirits, pork, and pawnbroking were held by Chinese, and the system was a perfect setting for the machinations and intrigues of secret societies in support of their leaders. It was a subtle business, for while every influence that could possibly be brought to bear came into play, it was necessary to see to it that by agreement between possible tenderers the field of competition should be reduced to avoid paying to the Government any more than was unavoidable. To obtain the rights to a farm meant an immediate increase in wealth, prestige, and power, and in this struggle, secret societies throughout Malaya have played a prominent part.

[39] See App. 2, p. 535 and Plate 4   [40] For Lodges, see App. 1, p. 532.
[41] GD 181, to S. of S., 27 Aug. 1869.

It may be noted that of the four 'leading merchants' examined by the Governor in May and June 1825 on the subject of the Hoeys in Penang, three at least appear to have been holders of farm licences.[42] Caunter, at the same period, gave it as his opinion that the Raja of Ligor's principal agents were 'our Chinese traders', and suggested that 'some of our Chinchoo merchants' were holding farms under him in Kedah.[43] The Hokkien merchants on their part stated that Lowe Achong, 'notorious' as the head of the Hai San kongsi, was hoping to be made Capitan China in Perak, as a reward for his assistance to the Raja of Ligor. And there is evidence that in July 1823, some 'Amoy Chinese' from Penang had attempted to take by force the gambling, opium, and arrack farms in Perak from a Cantonese.[44] Finally, in June 1829, Patullo referred to the illicit smuggling of spirits and opium into Penang 'from the other side' (Province Wellesley), caused by the rival spirit of competition between the Macao and Chinchew classes of Chinese.

Writing in 1835 on the subject of the connexion (in Singapore) between the farmers and the Hoeys, the Recorder of Penang, Sir Benjamin Malkin, had this to say:

> The revenue derived at Singapore from the opium farm has increased very remarkably of late and the solution I have generally heard of it has been that some Chinese connected with the Hooeys or Fraternities in the Island have become the Farmers, and have been able to afford a much larger rent than their predecessors, from the additional power which this connection gives them of detecting any smuggling. In short, they gain the advantage of having besides their establishment of peons an irregular body of spies and intelligencers scattered in great numbers over the Island.[45]

It is certain that the giants of the Chinese community down to the time when the revenue-farm system was abolished were invariably the holders of licences for these farms, and equally certainly, and indeed, inevitably, they were the headmen or patrons of secret societies.

In May 1830 we find some support for Patullo's view of the undesirable nature of Hoey activities when the Superintendent of Police, Penang, H. Nairne, brought to the notice of the Governor in Council a case in which the headman of a society was prosecuted and discharged 'on account of the victim of his assault being too terrified to testify against him'. He added:

> The Hon. the Governor will see how dangerous it is for the due preservation of the public peace to allow the Chinamen on any pretext whatsoever to keep any house professedly for the purpose of a Congsee, as they are so constructed that it is impossible when the doors are shut for any person outside to hear any cries that may be uttered by a person undergoing punishment.

Nairne was convinced that sinister proceedings took place at all the 'Congsees', and suggested that the Chinese should be prohibited from continuing to be members of these societies, on penalty, if convicted, of six dozen lashes and a

[42] SSR(I20), Pg, Misc. Lett. (1806–30), No. 412, p. 199, 4 June 1817; SSR(I27), Pg, Misc. Lett. (Out), 1824–5, No. 460, p. 659, 26 Apr. 1825.

[43] SSR(A18), Pg Cons., pp. 428–36, 23 June 1825: Caunter to Anderson, 22 June 1825.

[44] SSR(F5), Lett. fr. Native Rulers, 1826–32, pp. 128–9: Raja of Perak to Gov., R. Fullerton, 2nd Moharram 1244 (= 31 July 1828).

[45] Encl. 8 to Gov., Letts to Beng., No. 23, 1 Apr. 1843 (IOL).

year's working on the roads. Though ostensibly charitable they were 'made use of as a powerful combination of carrying on their own malpractices which are strictly prohibited by their own laws in China'.[46]

The Council, finding itself in some difficulty as to the nature of these societies, resolved 'that the Superintendent of Police forward to Government a distinct definition and description of a Congsee in order that the same be brought to the notice of Legal Authority for an opinion as to such coming within the intent and meaning of "unlawful assemblies"'. But the Superintendent had to confess that he had nothing to add to what had already been said by Caunter and Patullo, and suggested that the best way of breaking up the 'Congsees' would be 'not to allow them to have any processions on their great day'. The only objection he could see to this was that former Governors had indirectly sanctioned the Hai San by giving a grant of land to the 'Congsee' and their heirs for ever.[47]

In the end the Council decided in June 1830 to send copies of the Patullo report of 1829 to the Resident Councillors at Singapore and Malacca asking for reports as to the existence of such associations at their Settlements and their effects and objects, 'and any further information on the subject which can be gathered as to their general constitution and management'. In the meantime, Nairne did the best he could to control the societies by appointing Malay Penghulus (village headmen) in the country districts in order that 'a strict registry of the people of all tribes may be kept . . . as the strongest check to persons of bad character resorting to the Island'.[48]

Singapore already had its secret society problems. At a Council meeting held on 2 March 1830 the Resident Councillor, Kenneth Murchison, tabled a Minute to the effect that the most important subject of a local nature which he had to submit was the unsettled state of the population in the interior of Singapore Island, where 'large and formidable gangs of Chinese of the most daring and atrocious character are assembled, who make irruptions into the town at night, and in fact subsist by plunder, and set the police at defiance'. Bearing in mind the information obtained in 1824 by Abdullah on his visit to the secret society hideout, it is reasonably certain that the marauders referred to were members of the T'in Tei Wui.

The Minute continued:

This evil is rapidly increasing from the annual influx of additional numbers in the junks, whilst the means of subsistence do not advance in the same proportion. If the Island were well intersected by roads, and under efficient police control, this state of things would be of less consequence . . . but in the present state of the Island, it is alarming and demands immediate interposition.

He proposed that a strong party of police and troops should at once be employed under the personal orders of the magistracy to make a tour of surveillance in order to ascertain the haunts and the strength of the robbers and to seize and disperse them wherever possible. He also suggested that strong and well-armed police parties, if necessary supported by troops, should be posted permanently at out-stations; that the country should be well intersected by roads and pathways;

[46] SSR(A70), Pg Cons., 1830, pp. 101–7: lett. fr. H. Nairne, Supt of Police, to Sec. to Govt, J. Patullo, 21 May 1830. Laid before Council on 31 May 1830.
[47] Ibid. 1829, pp. 195–6.
[48] SSR(I39), 1830, Pg, Misc. Lett., pp. 78–81, 23 July 1830: H. Nairne to R. Ibbetson.

and finally that measures should be adopted for restraining or regulating the future influx of Chinese.[49]

A quick survey was carried out which revealed that a good deal of rice cultivation was in progress, and the Governor believed that the occupation and cultivation of land on the island had been carried to a much greater extent than the Government was aware. A further survey, estimated to take three years, was undertaken, but in the meantime only 'occasional inspection' was possible.[50]

When the letter from Penang was received, asking for a report on the Hoeys existing at Singapore, Murchison framed a questionaire on the subject of their organization, objects, and membership, and asked his Assistant Resident, S. G. Bonham, to furnish the replies. This document gives us our first detailed picture of the secret societies in Singapore.[51]

According to Bonham's account, dated 17 September 1830, there were at that time three Hoeys in Singapore, the Thean-ti Hoey (T'in Tei Wui), the Quan-ti Hoey (Kwan-ti Hoey), and the Shoo So-kong Hoey. These societies were 'not connected but were constantly at variance'. The Shoo So-kong Hoey had only been formed during the previous four months, and was believed to be 'more a religious institution than for any other purpose'. The second, the Quan-ti Hoey, was believed to be nearly extinct, for Bonham had been told that its members had joined the T'in Tei Wui. If this was so, there must have been a later revival, for the Quan-ti Hoey was very much alive sixteen years later. Bonham regarded the T'in Tei Wui as the strongest and the most dangerous.

He considered that the Hoeys comprised no particular class.

Natives of Hokien, Macao, and Malacca being within my personal knowledge combined in the first-mentioned association [the T'in Tei Wui] and even the principal office-bearers of it. The poorer classes comprise naturally the majority, but were the rich and poor of this Settlement on a par as to numbers, I have no doubt the latter would greatly preponderate, the former having little to gain from it, the latter everything in as far as rapine and robbery are concerned, and being screened from justice.

Bonham admitted, however, that 'it is generally believed . . . by the Chinese whom I have conversed with that the expenses of Marriages and Funerals of the Members are sometimes defrayed by the different Hways to which such members may belong'.

It should be noticed that the 'natives of Malacca' were considered to be a separate category of Chinese. They were the Chinese born in Malacca, whose forebears had lived there for generations. They were the 'Baba' Chinese, and were readily distinguishable from the more recent immigrants. According to Bonham, it was generally believed that nearly all of the 'real Chinese' were connected with the T'in Tei Wui, and that a great portion of the 'Malacca Chinese' were connected either with the T'in Tei Wui or the Shoo So-kong Hoey, but none of the *respectable* Malacca Chinese belonged to the T'in Tei Wui.

He believed that all Chinese in the country districts of Singapore belonged to the T'in Tei Wui, with a total membership of not less than 2,500–3,000.

[49] SSR(A68), Sing. Cons., 2 Mar. 1830, pp. 9–11.
[50] Ibid. 12 Mar. 1830, SSR(B10), Lett. to London, p. 133, 30 Apr. 1830.
[51] SSR(R9), Gov., Lett. to Beng., 1843, pp. 1–57. Encl. 4: No. 23, 1 Apr. 1843, fr. S. Garling to G. A. Bushby, Sec. to Gov. Ft William. (The encls were obtained from the IOL Records.)

In the country [he wrote] the planters are made to enter the Hways; if they do not, they are robbed and plundered and eventually driven out of their plantations. I fear, however, that little persuasion is necessary, as if the greater portion was averse to the Institution it would not be possible to compel them to enter.

As to the real object of the Hoeys he believed that it was

general rapine and robbery among the lower classes and the assumption of an improper degree of power and importance among the higher. The object of both I believe to be to screen offenders from justice when apprehended, by perjury and subornation of perjury, and before apprehension to assist in effecting such offenders' escape as far as lies in their power.

His account confirms Abdullah's statement that there were heads of sections within the society. The principal headman of the T'in Tei Wui was Tan Yu Guan, and under him, each different tribe had its own headman, who was first consulted before 'any members of the tribe can go forth to do good or evil'.[52] On certain occasions grand assemblies were held before the principal members of the Hoey to try and to punish members who were alleged to have infringed its regulations. The usual punishment was whipping, but it was asserted that even executions had taken place, and it was clear, he said, that the people were dreadfully afraid of this assembly, and were much indisposed to talk on this subject at all, much less to become informers.

He briefly described the society's initiation ceremony, which included the decapitation of a white cock, whose blood was collected in a cup containing arrack. The initiates as well as other members present cut their forefingers and mingled the blood with that of the cock, each member taking a sip. At the same time the Twa Hia (elder Brother, Hokkien dialect) or Chief administered oaths whereby they swore 'to abide with each other through good and through evil, not to reveal the secrets of the club to others or to any member of their own club, but to obey the regulations of their own Hway'. The Quan-ti Hoey ceremony was the same, except that the cut was made on the tongue instead of the forefinger; that of the Shoo So-kong Hoey comprised the burning of a piece of yellow paper 'containing probably some written deprecation if they do not follow what is dictated to them'.

It was Bonham's opinion that most of the robberies that occurred in the town of Singapore and certainly all the gang robberies which took place in the country were perpetrated by people belonging to the T'in Tei Wui, and with the concurrence of their chiefs, some of whom he believed shared in the proceeds. Asked whether he was aware of any benefit arising from Hoeys, and whether they maintained their own sick or destitute members, he replied:

I have no hesitation in saying that no benefit can possibly arise from such a combination, and if I may judge from the multitude of diseased and destitute subjects that constantly present themselves to our view in the public streets, I may infer that the care and relief of these unfortunate objects is not a matter of primary consideration to them, if one at all.

Bonham believed that the Hoeys in the three 'Stations' of the Straits Settlements assisted one another, and had information that a society in Penang had

[52] By 'tribe' is meant language group, e.g. Hokkien, Cantonese, Hakka, Tiechiu, Hainanese, etc.

contributed 200 Spanish dollars towards the building of the club-house of the T'in Tei Wui in Singapore.

Not all the material in Bonham's letter is based on known fact: surmise clearly enters from time to time, but he had clearly been to some pains to obtain whatever information was available.

Nowhere is any mention made as yet in Singapore of the name Ghee Hin, which we have seen was already used in Penang for the local formation of the T'in Tei Wui and was later to be adopted in Singapore. It is to be noted, too, that the Singapore T'in Tei Wui embraced Chinese of all tribes, each under its own headman, whereas the Triad societies in Penang were basically 'Macao', though other tribes were not excluded.

What the Quan-ti Hoey was we can only conjecture. We do know that about this time there was a society of this name at Rhio, the archipelago of the Dutch Indies immediately to the south of Singapore, and that the Dutch authorities took stringent repressive measures against it, including deportation of members to Singapore. It was the rival of the T'in Tei Wui and, as we have seen, was a 'secret society' of the Triad type, including a blood oath in its initiation ceremony.

As for the Shoo So-kong Hoey, it may have existed, as Bonham believed, mainly for religious purposes, and perhaps was not a 'secret society'. It did not, apparently, require a blood-oath for initiation, though the burning of a written paper is frequently a characteristic of secret sects. This society is referred to again in 1846, romanized as 'Choo Soo Kong'.[53]

Bonham had decided ideas as to how best to deal with these obnoxious Hoeys. He believed that it would be impossible to abolish them as long as the present judicial system existed. If only the law permitted, he would propose that whenever the police were convinced that a robbery had been committed by members of a Hoey, they should seize some of its leaders and fine them double the amount of the property stolen. They, in turn, would have to impose a levy on members, and 'finding it a losing trade would soon abandon it'. 'Were some few acts of injustice at first committed by the authorities,' he remarked, 'it would be more than balanced by the blessings it would eventually confer on Society in general.'

Bonham was not alone in believing that the laws of the Straits Settlements were inadequate to deal with the menace of the societies. An article in the *Chinese Repository* in 1833[54] referred to the growth of Triad societies in the Straits Settlements and the enmity existing between the Hai San and the Ghee Hin. No redress was possible for their victims, for no witnesses would dare to give evidence, so no conviction was ever obtainable. The editor hoped

that the authorities . . . will be on the alert . . . with something like martial law for those lawless persons who make it dangerous to give evidence in the usual way. . . . These brotherhoods do not seem to aim at taking the external name of a government, but to avail themselves of the substance. They wish to be the 'gentlemen regulators' for all poor Chinese, and to leave the gentlemen European governors and residents in quiet possession of their titles and salaries.

This theme of the inadequacy of the judicial code as conceived in England to deal with these societies is one which was constantly to recur throughout official correspondence. Always the problem has been how to vest in the police or the

[53] *SFP*, 12 Mar. 1846.   [54] Vol. ii. Sept. 1833, pp. 230-3.

judicial officers or the executive adequate powers for the control of these societies without violating the basic principles of British justice.

Malacca

Although the Penang authorities had written to Malacca in 1830 concerning secret societies there, no reply similar to Bonham's report on Singapore has been traced. We know, however, from Milne's account of 1821 that the Triad Brotherhood already existed in Malacca in 1818, though called by the general name of Sam Hop Wui and not by any specific title.[55] When Dutch control was resumed during the period 1818 to 1824, it is likely that secret society activity was severely suppressed, but we also know from Newbold and Wilson's account that the Brotherhood had, in 1826, 'again reared its head under the more lenient and perhaps too liberal policy of the English', and that an affray took place in the town when a party of 'men from the plantations' belonging to the society met to celebrate and became noisy and quarrelsome. Four Chinese were charged in court, and three of them were sentenced to terms of imprisonment varying from three months to two years. Two 'leaders' were made responsible for keeping the peace.[56] The same source affirms that all members of this society at Malacca were 'either Canton or Macao men, no Fokien man being allowed to enter their body'. There were also said to be five headmen in Malacca, though whether this refers to different societies or to office bearers within one society is not stated.

We do, however, know from another account concerning Malacca in 1834 that both the Hai San and the Ghee Hin societies were 'numerously represented among the immigrant Chinese, but scarcely a member of the native-born or wealthy classes belonged to them', and it seems likely that these two societies had been in existence in Malacca territory for some time.[57] Indeed the murder committed by the Malacca tailor in 1818, reported by Milne, may well have been the result of rivalry between the headmen of these two societies even at that early date, and the inexorable hunting down of a fugitive in 1826 by members of the murderer's society who accused him of having sympathized with the victim of the murder, as recorded by Newbold and Wilson, again arouses the suspicion that a feud existed between two rival societies.

Newbold visited the premises of a Triad society in Malacca in 1835, and gave the figure of 4,000 as its membership 'from the different plantations and tin mines in the interior, added to those at Malacca itself'. He gave no indication of any awareness of the existence of two societies within the Brotherhood, and whether his figure of membership relates to one society or to the Brotherhood as a whole is therefore a matter for conjecture. In his total he probably included not only men from Malacca territory but also others from Rasah in Sungei Ujong, from Linggi on the borders of Malacca territory, and from Lukut in Selangor, at all of which places Chinese miners had been established for some time. Malacca was the port of entry for all these areas, and was the control centre of the Triad organizations within them.

In these mining areas there is evidence not only of conflict within the Chinese communities themselves but of antagonism between the Chinese miners and the Malays of the riverine villages. Rivers were the only highways permitting penetration of the dense jungle up to the foothills where the tin was found.

[55] See above, p. 46.   [56] *JRAS*, vi (1840-1), pp. 120-58.
[57] Lett. fr. Mgte, PW, to RC Penang; 9 May 1860. Encl. in GD 108 of 5 June 1860 (IOL).

Established on a river mouth or a confluence, a Malay chief could levy toll on all tin being shipped downstream and on all supplies travelling upriver. This was his normal source of revenue, and the high rates charged were frequently the cause of disputes. One such clash is reported at Rasah in 1828, when there were nearly 1,000 Chinese miners in the area. According to one account, Malays raided the treasure chest of the Triad society. Another account of the incident relates that the Chinese, presuming upon their numbers, attacked the Malays but were defeated and had to abandon the mines. Most of the refugees went south to Lukut where the mines could absorb them. The mines at Rasah were reopened in 1830 by 400 Chinese miners brought from Malacca, but they were driven out again three years later.[58]

Lukut was the scene of a similar outbreak in 1834, when 300 or 400 Chinese miners attacked their Malay employers in an attempt to seize the mines. They burned down the houses and massacred the inmates, but were later driven out by Malays avenging the outrage.[59] As time went on, the Chinese miners in the Malay States, organized in their secret societies, were to become a major problem not only to the Malay chiefs but also to the British Government of the Straits Settlements, particularly in Penang and Malacca, where traders and financiers of the tin-producing industry lived.

[58] T. J. Newbold, *Political and Statistical Account of the British Settlements in the Straits of Malacca* (1839), ii. 33–34; Wilkinson, *JSBRAS*, 1921.
    [59] Newbold.

4

THE GROWING PROBLEM

1. 1843–52

THE rapid increase of the immigrant Chinese population naturally led to an expansion of membership of the Triad societies and to an extension of their activities. Newbold, writing in 1839, remarked that the ends of justice were frequently defeated at Penang, Malacca, and Singapore, by bribery, false swearing, and sometimes by open violence owing to combinations of the fraternities formed for the purpose of screening guilty members from detection and punishment.[1] At Singapore in particular gang-robbery was rapidly increasing, so much so that by 1843 there was considerable public alarm. A public meeting was called on 10 February, with Thomas Oxley, Sheriff, in the chair.

According to a leader in the local newspaper of the time, the *Singapore Free Press* (16 February 1843), the meeting was attended by all sections of the inhabitants. Respectable Chinese merchants who were present admitted that it was common practice among Chinese traders and shopkeepers to pay protection money to the societies. The meeting considered that the societies should be broken up and urged the Government to enact a law to effect this. It was also recommended that those discovered paying or receiving protection money should be liable to punishment. A suggestion that some Chinese should be appointed as police peons was strongly opposed by influential Chinese present, who believed such action would make matters worse. 'This,' said the article, 'shows either that they must not entertain very high notions of the integrity of their countrymen; or that they know that the influence of the secret societies is so universal that it could not fail to cause Chinese Peons to swerve from their duty to the public.'

The actual terms of the resolution were

that it is highly expedient a law should be passed having for its object the suppression of these Brotherhoods so long as the same may be effected or influenced by legal enactments, and in particular it should be made penal for any person or persons to pay or receive any sum of money as protection money . . .

The 'influential Chinese present' no doubt sat with their tongues in their cheeks as the last part of this resolution was passed, for it is highly improbable that any of them had not at some time paid protection money, and they must have known well that they would have to do so again when called upon. It is of great interest to find that at this early period the leading Chinese themselves strongly objected to the recruitment of Chinese into the police force, no doubt because, as suggested in the press, they realized that such action would only

---

[1] Newbold, i. 13–14.

introduce one more level of extortion and one more complication in settling matters between themselves and the societies.

There were letters to the press too, one of which gave some details of the initiation of members to the T'in Tei Wui, and added: 'All Chinese, to whatever tribe they belong or whatever dialect they speak are admitted as members.' According to the writer, this society had been in existence in Singapore 'for the last twenty years', which would put the date of its formation at Singapore at about 1823. He estimated its membership at between 20,000 and 30,000, and he commented:

> The man who performs the duties of Chief Secretary in the Brotherhood is . . . well known for his abandoned habits, vindictive disposition and reckless conduct, and being moreover a man of great force of character and natural shrewdness and cunning, he exercises much influence over the other members.

The writer regarded as useless the proposal that payment of protection money should be made illegal. He supported more drastic methods: 'Seize the heads and chiefs of these assemblies whilst they are sitting in secret conclave; lay hands upon their books, papers, chops, etc.; put the rulers in prison, and if it can be done transport them to Bombay out of the place . . .'[2]

At a session of Oyer and Terminer held in Singapore in March 1843, the Recorder, Sir William Norris, opening the proceedings, referred to the activities of gang robbers belonging to the Triad society which 'of late assumed such a character of boldness and audacity as naturally enough to excite very general and considerable alarm'. He appealed to well-disposed Chinese, the leading and more respectable members of the Chinese community, to come forward and boldly denounce and disavow all future participation in such 'illegal societies'.

The recommendations of the public meeting were submitted through the Singapore Chamber of Commerce to the Acting Governor of the Settlements, Samuel Garling, who thereupon collected all the information he was able to obtain on the subject which he incorporated in a monumentally prolix despatch, with no fewer than seventeen enclosures, to the Government of Bengal.[3]

These enclosures may be put into three groups—those connected with the resolutions of the public meeting of February 1843; the measures the Governor proposed to take to improve the situation; and a collection of earlier reports concerning secret societies, including Dr Milne's article (written in 1821), Caunter's report of 1825, Bonham's report of 1830, and a new report by W. T. Lewis, then Assistant Resident and Superintendent of Police, Prince of Wales Island, written in 1843 at Garling's special request. Apart from differences in orthography, the only divergence in this last report is that according to Lewis the Hai San Society existed at Penang before the Ghee Hin. The contrary is affirmed by Caunter and by Patullo. Garling seems to have overlooked Patullo's list and description of the Penang Hoeys in 1829, for it is nowhere mentioned.

An important enclosure was a letter from the Resident Councillor of Singapore (Mr Church) dated 14 February 1843, in which he suggested that English law and rules of procedure were unsuited 'to our mixed and vicious population' and that the Superintendent of Police 'in his capacity of sitting Magistrate'

---

[2] *SFP*, 23 Feb. 1843.

[3] SSR(R9), Gov., Lett. to Beng., No. 23, 1 Apr. 1843, pp. 1 ff. For the encls, which are not included in the above filing, see Ft William, 24 May 1843, Judicial Dept, Proc. of the Deputy Gov. of Beng. (IOL).

should have powers of summary punishment by fine, imprisonment with hard labour, or public whipping, as at Hong Kong. As it was, he had to hand over to another tribunal to adjudicate a simple and petty assault. There was no doubt whatever that the evil of the societies was

> materially promoted by the notorious fact that nine-tenths of the Chinese population are supposed to be members of the Hoeys and on the occasion of robberies . . . instead of the Chinese householders rendering aid to the police, they are entirely passive, and not infrequently afford shelter and protection to the depredators.

He believed that the problem was seriously aggravated by unrestricted immigration from China. During the past six weeks 5,494 Chinese had been reported at the office as having landed, and the actual number was no doubt greater. The vast majority were 'in a state of utter destitution', but because of the low price of gambier and other circumstances, the difficulty of finding employment for such an influx was obvious. Unless there were to be a demand for more labour, there would have to be some restriction 'to the importation of vagabonds from China'.

Church therefore proposed that the nakhodas and owners of junks be informed that they would not be allowed to land Chinese emigrants unless resident householders engaged to provide for them for six months and to become responsible for their good behaviour. This, however, did not go forward as one of the recommendations in the despatch, for Garling was 'disposed to believe that the mercantile community of Singapore who are markedly jealous of the freedom of their port do not altogether concur in this view of Mr Church'.

The principal purpose of the despatch was twofold; first, to obtain sanction for an expansion of the police at Singapore, and second, to suggest the passing of a law for the suppression of Hoeys. There were also other less important items, such as the provision of a secret service fund, the facilitation of the collection of the assessment, and the sanctioning of the punishment of whipping in certain cases. A draft Bill entitled 'Act for the Suppression of Clubs and Associations of a secret and dangerous character in the Straits Settlements' was enclosed, and it listed the following names of associations: San Ho Huay, Thean Te Huay, Kung Kea, Guan Te Huay, Gheen Hin, Hoye San, Ho Sing. These correspond with the following equivalent titles already mentioned, i.e. Sam Hop Wui, T'in Tei Wui, Kung Kea (probably meaning 'Hung Ka', or Hung Family), Quan-ti or Quan-tec or Kwan Tec, Ghee Hin, Hai San, Ho Seng. It may be assumed that at the time of this despatch, this list covered all the secret societies known to exist in the Settlements.

The Bill declared that all clubs and associations known as Hoey or Chinese Brotherhood and bearing any of these titles, and all other clubs and associations holding or professing similar objects and principles were 'utterly suppressed and prohibited as unlawful combinations and confederacies'. Also, any club or association whose members were required or admitted to take any oath not required or authorized by law were declared to be unlawful combinations and confederacies—the Lodge of Freemasons being specifically excluded.

The punishment proposed for membership was transportation for seven years, or imprisonment with hard labour not exceeding three years. Office-bearers were liable to transportation for life.

Attached to this draft Act was a long commentary by James Richardson

Logan, Law Agent of the Court of Judicature of Prince of Wales Island, Singapore, and Malacca, in which he not only gave his own views on the policy of suppression but redrafted the whole Act.[4] Logan considered that the taking of an oath was an insufficient criterion on which to base an Act for the suppression of societies. Among other things, he pointed out that it would never be possible to prove that an oath had been taken, nor indeed was it known whether in fact all members of the various groups involved in the commission of crimes had taken oaths. He thought that under an Act which adopted this single criterion no conviction would take place. He also discussed the possibility of introducing a division of the Chinese into classes, or a division of the Settlements into districts in the nature of 'Hundreds' and 'heavily amercing each class for crimes committed by any of their members', but concluded, reluctantly one feels, that such a system 'would be utterly inconsistent with the liberal and just principles of government which have hitherto rendered the British Eastern Settlements so attractive to emigrants, and could never be contemplated save as a last resource'.

He spoke of the difficulties arising from lack of precise knowledge of the Hoeys. Although 'a vast amount of crime' had been committed in Penang through the agency of these societies and the magistrates had all along been aware of their existence, no legal evidence had ever been obtained tracing a crime to them, nor had direct evidence ever been presented of anyone being a member, nor had initiation ceremonies, oaths, or the exact constitution of any Hoey ever been described 'by persons who could speak confidently from actual knowledge'. It did not seem that the Chinese Government's knowledge of the laws, ceremonies, and working of the San-tien or Theen-te Society was 'more certain or complete than our own', or that they had ever induced any member to become an informer or reveal the society's secrets.[5]

On the subject of recruiting Chinese police, Logan was undecided. It was obvious that no authentic information would ever be procured by the present police, who neither spoke the language nor associated with the Chinese, and so a first step would be to employ a certain number of Chinese peons and Jamadars.[6] But the Hoeys were so powerful, and 'the lower Chinese so grossly corrupt', and the dangers of bribery and intimidation so obvious that it was doubtful whether the fidelity of the best-selected Chinese could be depended upon, while it was certain that if they were not faithful they would do much evil.

The Bengal Government's reply to Garling's proposals is, in its brevity, in striking contrast to his despatch. The proposals for strengthening the police and facilitating the collection of assessment were approved, but Logan's comments seem to have had their effect, for the legislative proposals received the curt reply that the Deputy Governor of Bengal did not consider it necessary to employ particular legislation for the suppression of the societies. 'The strengthening of the Police now sanctioned will, if properly employed in the Settlements, effectually secure the protection of life and property in the Settlements without the aid

---

[4] Logan is better known as the editor of the *Journal of the Indian Archipelago*. The title 'Law Agent' does not mean that he held an official position, but merely that he was entitled to practise in the court.

[5] This is the first mention by a Malayan commentator of the 'San-tien Society', namely the 'Three Dots Society', that has been traced. The name was known in Canton in 1831 (see *Chinese Repository*, vol. ii, Jan. 1836, p. 424). It is clearly used as an alternative name for the 'T'in Tei Wui' (Heaven and Earth Society).

[6] Indian police officers.

of special enactments which, indeed, would probably in these cases entirely fail of their object.'[7] In the meantime Garling had forwarded yet a third draft Act[8] prepared by Mr Napier, Law Agent, Singapore, but it met with no better fate. Thus none of the three draft Bills ever reached the public eye, and the policy of complete freedom of association continued.

But despite the assurance of the Bengal Government, it was not long before Singapore was the scene of a riot due directly to secret society activity. The occasion was the funeral of Ho Yam Ko, 'Elder Brother Ho Yam', described as being the founder and president of the T'in Tei Wui (which is also at this time called the Ghee Hin).[9] For some time past Ho Yam had been unable to take any part in the management of the T'in Tei Wui owing to ill-health, but he still continued to be the nominal head and was given full funeral honours. The funeral took place on 3 March 1846, and the usual police permit for a procession was issued, on condition that there should be no disturbance and that no greater number of persons than usually attended a funeral should be present.

Clearly the police were apprehensive, and when the time came a crowd of several thousand persons assembled at Rochore, determined to form a procession through the town as far as Telok Ayer Street before going to the cemetery. According to the Ghee Hin members, the purpose of this was to perform ceremonies in front of the house of an influential member of the Hoey. But the headman of the rival society, the Kwan Tec Hoey,[10] believed that the Ghee Hins intended to sack the houses of several people belonging to the Kwan Tec, and the police therefore diverted the procession before it reached Kampong Glam, along a road leading straight to the burial ground. This was a great public loss of face, and the thwarted Ghee Hins attacked the police. To make matters worse, the police used as an interpreter to pass their orders to the Ghee Hins none other than Ho Cheo Tek, the headman of the Kwan Tec. He and one police peon were severely injured; the military were called out, and accompanied the funeral almost to the grave. Those who led the attack were described as 'apparently coolies from the jungle, armed with pieces of iron and wood'. A leading Chinese merchant in Singapore known as 'Whampoa', who had a place of business in Telok Ayer Street, Whampoa & Co, was quick to deny in the press that he was in any way connected with the Hoeys.[11]

A funeral procession among the Chinese is an occasion of great importance at which the wealth, power, and prestige of the deceased are reflected by the magnificence of the coffin and accoutrements, by the size of the procession, and by the number of associations sending representatives, each with their own

[7] SSR(S10), Gov. Lett. fr. Beng., 1843, pp. 52–53; Under-Sec. to Govt of Beng. to the Act. Gov. of Prince of Wales Is., Sing. & Mal., no. 489, Ft William, 24 May 1843.

[8] Ibid. p. 65, no. 587, 19 June 1843.

[9] *SFP*, 10, 11, & 18 Mar. 1846. See also Bonham's report of 17 Sept. 1830, p. 58 above.

[10] The Kwan Tec Hoey is the Quan-ti Hoey of Bonham's report (see above, p. 58). In the manuscript documents of this period, there is considerable confusion in the spelling of this title, partly due to mistaking capital 'T' for capital 'Y', as, for example, in Quan Yah, Quan Yat, Quan Quay. Even in this printed article it is spelt Kwan Tec, Kwan Taec, and Kwan Toec.

[11] 'Whampoa' was the Admiralty contractor for stores, and his name was Ho Ah Kay. He was a Cantonese born at Whampoa, Canton, China. Later (1853) he became a naturalized British subject, and later still, odd though it may appear, became the first Chinese Consul at Singapore (5 Oct. 1853). He was also appointed Consul for Russia and for Japan. In 1867 he was awarded the CMG. He died in 1880, and his bones were later taken to China for burial. His portrait hangs in the Victoria Memorial Hall, Singapore.

F

distinguishing banners, lanterns, hats, and fans, bearing the characters of the title of the society. The occurrence of secret society fights at the funerals of their leaders was to be a not unusual feature in Malaya. A procession provided a setting for the display of power and arrogance by the society, and opportunity was frequently sought, when members were thus massed together bearing the emblems and insignia of their brotherhood, to insult members or officials of rival societies, as a result of which a quarrel would flare up.

One indication of the increasing interest taken in the activities of the Hoeys is to be found in the repeated 'Presentments' made on the subject by the Grand Juries at the various Settlements.

There was no Legislative Council in those days, but the leading citizens had an opportunity of putting forward their views at meetings of the Grand Jury, of which they were members. At the sessions of Oyer and Terminer and at the Quarter Sessions, the Grand Juries were wont to discuss recent events in their particular Settlements, and record their views in 'Presentments' which therefore formed a channel for the expression of opinion of at least this section of the public, with the added advantage that it could not escape official attention. It is likely too that some of the Recorders of the time (as the Judges were then known) were happy to have this opportunity to plague the executive by conveying to the Government these opinions put forward by the juries, which were frequently couched in robust language far from complimentary to the Government. Not surprisingly, the Residents, Governors, and even at times the Government of India were inclined to regard the fulminations which the Presentments frequently contained as ill-informed, ill-considered, or out of place. But nevertheless they fulfilled a need, and on one occasion Governor Butterworth, in reproving the Resident Councillor, Penang, for his criticism of a Presentment very properly remarked:

I beg that all strictures on the Presentments of the Grand Juries may be avoided. These Presentments are made under a solemn oath and however erroneous many of the views of the Grand Juries may be on the matter presented, there can, I hope, be no doubt that these views are conscientiously entertained, whilst putting them to paper gratifies the parties, and ensures even imaginary grievances being fully considered.[12]

At the meeting of the Criminal Sessions which took place after the clash between the Ghee Hin and the Kwan Tec societies, the Grand Jury submitted an acid Presentment on the subject of the police and the control of the Hoeys, which moved the Governor to comment on forwarding it to Bengal: 'The length of this Presentment may be attributed, as stated by one of the jurors, to want of occupation by the Mercantile Community between the arrival and departure of the overland mail, and the tone and spirit with which it is penned, to the nature of the parties composing the Grand Jury.'[13] In his account of the clash between the two Hoeys which had prompted the Presentment, the Governor referred to the bitter enmity existing between them, and commented that there had been 'considerable excitement amongst the different Hoeys or Secret Societies in all places where the Chinese are located, more especially at Rhio, from whence numbers emigrated to Singapore, and endeavoured to foment disturbances, but happily without any permanent effect'. He recalled Garling's proposed Bill for

[12] SSR(U17), Gov., Lett. to RCs, 1849, pp. 118–21: No. 152, 11 Apr. 1849.
[13] SSR(R13), Gov., Lett. to Beng., 1845–6, pp. 445–57: No. 66, Pg, 7 May 1846.

putting down the societies but feared that any attempt to carry this into effect would prove futile, 'as these Societies appear to exist among all Classes of the Chinese wheresoever located'. His own suggestions, however, were very unspecific. He thought that seeking out the leading men of the Hoeys with a view to binding them over to keep the peace might be effective, but that such a public recognition of these societies might not be becoming, and it might be thought that if it was possible to discover these headmen they should be arrested and punished, not merely bound over. As to the police force, it was impracticable to obtain a perfect organization, 'for we can only look to the refuse of the Natives from the Coromandel Coast, who annually seek employment in the Settlements. The Chinese being wholly untrustworthy, and the Malays too indolent to be placed on watch by themselves.'

Once again the reply from the Government of Bengal was to the effect that 'His Honor adheres to the opinion expressed by the late Deputy Governor that it is not necessary to employ particular legislation for their suppression, and that such enactments would in these cases '"entirely fail in their object" '.[14]

But the Quarter Sessions renewed the attack with a further Presentment in July 1846, in which an attempt was made to remove the control of the police from the hands of the Governor, placing it instead in the hands of the court. They insisted that the power to appoint the Superintendent of Police lay with them, and *not* with the executive government, and it was necessary in consequence for the Government of India to introduce an Act to make clear that all constables and subordinate peace officers should be appointed by the Governor, and that the Superintendent of Police should continue to be appointed by the Governor of Bengal.[15]

Nevertheless, a Presentment of May 1848 dared to criticize the appointment of a Mr Jackson to the post of Superintendent of Police and Assistant Resident, and strictures were passed on the local authorities as on the Bengal Government. This called forth a reproof, and Bengal instructed the Governor to inform the Grand Jury 'that in introducing into their Presentment matters such as this, they were travelling altogether beyond the proper province of a Grand Jury, to which it will be expedient for them in future to confine themselves'. In forwarding the Presentment in the first instance the Governor had remarked that: 'The Secret Societies existing among the Chinese have been brought to the notice of Government from time to time, and remedies suggested. I will not therefore dilate on this subject. I am of opinion that the Chinese are the best and most peacable Colonists in the world.' He received the usual reply from Bengal: 'On the subject of Secret Societies among the Chinese, a reference on this subject was formerly made to the Supreme Government who declined to legislate regarding these Societies.'[16]

In September 1849 the Singapore Grand Jury again called the attention of the Government to the threat of the Hoeys, and cited a case in which an assault had been made on Chinese Roman Catholic converts who had plantations in the interior of the island. In forwarding this to Bengal, the Governor reiterated his objection to the introduction of legislation, but proposed to use every endeavour

[14] SSR(S13), Gov., Lett. fr. Beng., p. 120, No. 1605, 29 July 1846.
[15] Ibid. p. 132 (encl. in No. 1715 of 15 Aug. 1846), 1 Aug. 1846. Also S13, pp. 153, and encl., forwarding No. 1964, Ft William, 23 Sept. 1846.
[16] SSR(R17), Gov., Lett. to Beng., 1848, pp. 65–66: No. 74, 21 June 1848; SSR(S16), Gov., Lett. fr. Beng., 1849, p. 2: No. 36, 5 Jan. 1849.

'to exercise a vigilant supervision over the interior of the Island', adding that with the dense jungle in which these people located themselves, it was extremely difficult with limited means to do all that could be desired. As to the assault on the Chinese Christians, he was clearly of the opinion that they were as much to blame as were the members of the Hoeys.[17]

One incident illustrating the control exercised by the Ghee Hin Society in Singapore over the Chinese population received publicity in the press in June 1850. A boat belonging to five Chinese was stolen, and after a search of fourteen days the owners discovered it in the Serangoon river with a number of weapons in it. At the same time they seized three men in charge of the boat and set off with them for the police station. On the way they met one Tan Ah Tow, a head-man of the Ghee Hin Society, who ordered them to release the captives and to appear at the kongsi house at Rochore on 9 June when he would hear the case and adjudicate. Afraid to disobey, the five men did as they were ordered. When the case was heard at the kongsi house only one of the three thieves was present, but there were about thirty other Chinese with the headman in the chair. He directed the five men to return all the articles found in the boat, but allowed them to keep the boat itself, and decreed that they should be punished. This the five refused to accept, whereupon the headman ordered them to be beaten, and they were set upon with fists, stones, and bamboo umbrella handles. The headman, Tan Ah Tow, was later charged in court with misprision of felony and aggravated assault, and sentenced to imprisonment for six months and a fine of $200. The *Singapore Free Press* commented that during the trial the court house was packed with a number of leading men of the society who manifested great satisfaction at the penalty. Some were even overheard saying that if it were levied by a collection, this would come to 1 cent a head, as there were 20,000 members in the island. Each member paid an entrance fee of 2 dollars on joining and was bound to pay any sum when called upon by the kongsi, though there was no monthly contribution. It was a common occurrence to see a Hoey raising sums of $500, $1,000, and $2,000 in a few days and it was known to the police that $20,000 was raised in eight days during the funeral riot of 1846 already described, as well as the burial expenses which came to nearly $5,000.

By 1850 there were signs that the Hoeys, and in particular the T'in Tei Wui (Ghee Hin), were extending their campaign of intimidation against the Chinese converts to the Roman Catholic Church who were scattered over the island as planters and whose numbers were steadily increasing. According to Buckley, on the slightest pretence the plantations belonging to Christian Chinese[18] were sacked and pillaged, individuals being carried off and held to ransom for large sums. The conversion of Chinese in the interior not only withdrew members from the societies but also placed throughout the island men who would be opposed to their interests, so that the societies 'were thus deprived of that complete immunity from surveillance which constituted one of the sources of their power'.[19]

The climax was reached early in 1851. In February there was trouble among

[17] SSR(R19), Gov., Lett. to Beng., 1849–50, p. 187: No. 134, Sing., 8 Oct. 1849. This Presentment was published in the *SFP* of 5 Oct. 1849.
[18] The term used by English writers of the period for Christian converts is the Hokkien expression 'Hong Ka' (Those who have received the Faith).
[19] C. B. Buckley, *Anecdotal History of Old Times in Singapore* (1902), ii. 542.

the Chinese in the jungle at Kranji and Bukit Timah which developed into a general attack on the Christian Chinese. The disturbances lasted for more than a week, and it was said that over 500 Chinese were killed, among them many of the well-to-do converts who had become planters.[20] Indian convicts were sent out in gangs to pursue the rioters into the jungle and disperse them, and in the end it was necessary to call out the troops.[21]

The Grand Jury once more made its usual representations asking for legislative action against the Hoeys, but the Governor remained firm in his opinion that 'no legislative enactment except one of the most arbitrary nature leading to the abandonment of the gambier plantations in the jungles would eventually suppress them'.

At the criminal sessions a number of exemplary sentences, for periods varying from seven to fourteen years, were passed on some of those arrested, and the Governor hoped that these would tend to check such lawless proceedings in the future. He concluded by saying that he was happy to add that: 'the heathen proprietors of gambier plantations who are respectable people and located in the town have come forward on the present occasion and subscribed a sum of money to remunerate the Christian Chinese for the losses they have sustained'.[22] Perhaps the reason for this gesture was the fear that otherwise measures would be taken which might result in the closing down of their plantations in the interior.

After this there was a period of peace in Singapore, but as no action had been taken against the Hoeys they continued to flourish and expand. In October 1852 Constable Berthier with a Jamadar and two peons raided an initiation ceremony of the Ghee Hin off the Tanah Merah road, and found some 250 people present. He seized a number of books and papers, flags with inscriptions, diplomas on printed cloth, a 'red execution truncheon', stamps, and pins to draw blood. In referring to this, the *Pinang Gazette* of 23 October wondered whether the English Acts against secret confederations were to be considered to be in force in the Settlements; otherwise Berthier's action might have been illegal.

Is it not a little strange [said the *Gazette*] that after all the trouble the Chinese Secret Societies have given to the executive, and resolutions of public meetings, presentments of Grand Juries, and memorials to the Legislature that have been directed against them, these Acts have never been practically made part of the law of this Settlement. If they in fact are not, it is quite impossible for the Police to deal with these Societies.

The editorial further remarked:

the first step in dealing with these societies is to put an end to the singular system of coquetting with them, in which both the executive and the police have so much indulged, and into which they have no doubt felt themselves drawn by their uncertainty as to the state of the law. The Government should either openly recognize their existence as fully as it does that of the Chamber of Commerce or any other unchartered association, or it should have no dealings with them whatever. The Chinese are a shrewd people, well able to draw the right conclusions from the inconsistent and humiliating policy of the ruling power, now denouncing Hoes through its Judges on the benches of the Court of Judicature, now leaguing with their leaders through its Superintendent of

---

[20] J. F. A. McNair and W. D. Bayliss, *Prisoners their own Warders* (1899).
[21] Song Ong Siang, *One Hundred Years History of the Chinese in Singapore* (1923).
[22] SSR(R21), pp. 299–302, Gov., Lett. to Beng., No. 37 of 18 Mar. 1851.

Police, and now recognizing them through its Governors and Resident Councillors as more powerful in the Settlement than itself, and virtually confessing its inability to protect life and property without their aid.

It was suggested that the first step necessary was to introduce a system of registration of office-bearers and members, which might be accompanied by some concrete advantages such as being able to obtain secure titles to their houses and land. It might then happen that the societies themselves would one after another apply to be registered. The *Gazette*, however, counselled caution:

> The Ghee Hin is believed to have about thirteen thousand members at Singapore. They have been allowed to develop their society unchecked, to build halls, to acquire property, and to follow the coffins of their chiefs to the grave in crowds to which the burial of an African king affords the only parallel. It would be equally unjust and foolish to attempt suddenly to enforce the law against fifteen thousand men, even if we had ample proof of their having taken unlawful oaths.

This was a fair statement of the dilemma with which the Government was confronted. The existence of the Hoeys was not in the interests of the public in general. By protecting their members from the operation of the law, the societies encouraged criminal acts. While those who were members of a particular Hoey were exempt from the attentions of the criminal elements within it, the rest of the public was fair game, and the decent members of the Hoeys were prevented by blood-oath from betraying the criminal members to the authorities. But despite this vicious character, the Hoeys had been permitted to exist from the earliest days of the Settlements, they embraced a very large section of the Chinese population, including a high admixture of criminals, and to interfere with them might bring a hornets' nest about the ears of the Government, for the forces at its command might very easily be overcome. Moreover, the Hoeys served a useful purpose as friendly societies for their members, and, above all, were the most valuable channels of communication between the Government and the masses. There was no electorate. There was not even a body of leading citizens comprising representatives of the various associations as a sort of electoral college. Apart from the English-language press, the only channel of public opinion was the Grand Jury, and both the press and the jury reflected in the main the views of the European traders, not of the Chinese masses.

That was why there had been the 'singular system of coquetting with them'. There was also the added difficulty of trying to find any equitable principle on which to base a law which would prohibit societies such as the Hoeys which engaged in nefarious activities, and yet would permit other societies such as district or clan associations and the Freemasons (to which many of the leading European citizens belonged) to function without restraint.

In December 1852, perturbed by the spread of secret societies, Samuel Garling, then Sitting Magistrate at Singapore, submitted a memorandum to the Government. The Governor (Butterworth) was away on leave, but the Officiating Governor, E. A. Blundell, took the same view as his chief, that the control of secret societies was a matter for the police and the magistracy and not for special legislation, and he considered that 'a highly discriminating, patient and zealous Sitting Magistrate such as Mr Garling, aided by the active and intelligent body of police now serving under Mr Dunman, ought to suffice to counteract the evil of Secret Societies without the necessity of any recourse to legislative enactments'. Surprisingly, he based this opinion on what he called 'the vast change for the better which had been yearly observable as regards safety of life and property in Singapore', and continued:

If we compare the state of the island during the past year with that which existed in 1842, 1832, and 1822, we shall find that the evils of secret societies have at each period been diminished, and that within the last few years they have been reduced to a comparative minimum, and yet this has been effected by an improved system of Police without any legislative assistance.

He was unwilling to refer the matter again to the Government of India, but suggested to the Resident of Singapore that a considerable sum of money be put at the disposal of the police and secret service funds for the purpose of obtaining information relative to the secret societies.[23]

Were the *Pinang Gazette* and Samuel Garling over-apprehensive, or was Blundell over-complacent? The divergence of view probably rests on different bases of appraisal. There had been no recent attack to justify Blundell in reopening the matter with India. He looked at the number of serious crimes which could be attributed to the Hoeys and found that through the years there had been an improvement. Garling, on the other hand, knew from his experience as Sitting Magistrate that the influence of the Hoeys was such that it was almost impossible to pin any crime on to one of their members. Certain it was that the overall influence of the Hoeys showed no sign of diminution.

Malacca

Presentments of the Grand Jury were not confined to Singapore, for Malacca faced a similar problem at the tin mines which had been opened 'upwards of twenty miles or more from the Town . . . in an uninhabited and uncleared part of the country, verging on an imaginary line of frontier separating us [Malacca territory] from the petty Malay States of Johole, Segamat and others'.[24] As early as 1833 several mines had been started at Naning by J. B. Westerhout, and in 1840 he helped a Chinese to open one at Durian Tunggul which proved to be profitable. Other Chinese followed suit, and from about 1846 the mines were worked 'on an extensive and increasing scale', the labour force expanding from 2,000 in 1848 to 4,000 in 1850.[25]

According to Blundell, the miners, brought direct from China to the mines, were utterly ignorant of any laws, habits, or customs other than those of their own country. They were an entirely male community, encouraged in drinking, smoking opium, and gambling by their employers as means of gain, and were left entirely to themselves with no interference by the police except on extraordinary occasions of crimes brought to public notice. Furthermore they were 'unprotected against the lawless, half-savage though scanty population of the frontier Malayan countries'. They developed, in consequence, an independence of the Malacca authorities in all matters of external administration, though, said Blundell, they were fully conscious of general dependence on British power.

[23] SSR(U), vol. 24, 1852–3, Gov., Lett. to RCs, pp. 126–30: No. 422, 29 Dec. 1852, fr. Gov- (Blundell) to RC Sing. Also S22, Gov., Lett. fr. Beng., 1855: encl. 221, 26 Sept. 1855 (Com‐ ment No. 52).
[24] GD 51, 8 May 1852.
[25] Blundell: as no. 23; J. H. Croockewit, 'The Tin Mines of Malaya', *JIA*, viii (1854), p. 113; J. B. Westerhout, 'Notes on Malacca', ibid. ii (1848), p. 172.

The mines were fiercely attacked by Malays in 1848, and as a means of defence for the future the Chinese miners secured supplies of arms and built stockades, measures which caused some apprehension in Malacca. At the same time there was again trouble between the Hai San and the Ghee Hin societies, and the head of the former, described as 'a wealthy and intelligent Tin-miner', was charged with having murdered a member of the rival society. He was eventually acquitted, and the lawyer who defended him later recorded (1860) that

the Hai San had then [1848] attained a position which has never been reached by any other Chinese Secret Society in the Straits, either before or since, chiefly owing to the Tin mines at Kessang having been discovered and worked exclusively by members of the society, which, at that time, included not only many individuals of the native-born Chinese community, but Malays, Boyanese, and Klings, and it was currently reported that some members of the upper class of Indo-Europeans had also been admitted.[26]

In August 1849, as a result of this turbulence, the Malacca Grand Jury followed the lead of Singapore in formulating a Presentment on the subject of the Chinese Hoeys, suggesting 'the expedience of placing some check upon them', but it too made no impression, the Deputy Governor of Bengal agreeing with the Resident Councillor, Malacca, and Governor Butterworth, that the evils complained of could not be remedied 'by the enforcement of any special or penal enactments; a course to which, moreover, the Government of India had already objected'.[27] Steps were taken, however, to introduce some control by posting police at the mines and by the provision of funds for the improvement of river and road communications throughout Malacca territory, and these measures had some effect. But in 1851 an attempt to enforce the excise laws in the mining areas led to armed resistance. By this time the miners numbered between 5,000 and 6,000, and before order was restored troops had to be called in.

Once again the Grand Jury of Malacca submitted a Presentment. Blundell, the officiating Governor, was a former Resident Councillor of Malacca and was well aware of the problem. He also, in March 1852, sat with the Recorder at the criminal sessions at Malacca and heard the depositions of witnesses which, according to the Recorder, presented 'a frightful description of the state of the Mining District'.[28]

There was an obvious need to establish closer contact with and control over the mining community, and Blundell ordered a rapid survey of the area to show the positions of the mines, roads, and paths, and sanctioned the upkeep by convict labour of roads for the use of carts and carriages to and through the mining areas. The building of a police post at the mines was begun, comprising a barrack inside a stockade sited in a large clearing where people were encouraged to build houses and shops to form a village. In addition there were to be four smaller police posts at specified places in the area. Blundell sanctioned for one year the use of one-tenth of the tin revenue for the maintenance of this country police force 'for the protection of the mines from external aggressions and internal disturbance'. He also drew attention to the importance of frequent visits to the tin districts by the Resident Councillor, the Magistrates, and the Super-

---

[26] Lett. fr. Mgte, PW, to RC Pg, 9 May 1860: encl. to GD 108, 5 June 1860 (IOL).
[27] SSR(S16), Gov., Lett. fr. Beng., 1849, p. 128: No. 1108, Ft William, 17 Aug. 1849.
[28] Lett. fr. Recorder to RC, Mal., 23 Mar. 1852. Encl. to Blundell's despatch No. 51, 8 May 1852 (IOL).

intendent of Police, and instructed that all disputes should be settled summarily on the spot if possible.[29]

As a result of these measures, he was able to report in April 1852 that order had been re-established, the miners felt themselves protected, and there was every prospect of their numbers being considerably increased. Good houses and shops were rising around the police station, and several new mines had been opened. The increase in the revenue from tin and from opium was an indication of the rise in prosperity. In acknowledging his report, the Government of India did not allow Blundell to forget that he should have obtained their sanction before authorizing the allocation of one-tenth of the tin revenue for the upkeep of the special police.[30]

Penang

The only record of disturbance in the northern Settlement at this time relates to trouble at Bukit Mertajam in Province Wellesley caused by Chinese cultivators in January 1850, when the police found it necessary to call the Malay community to their aid before the riot was quelled and the participants disarmed.[31] But already the seeds of future trouble were being sown by the formation in Penang of a new secret society known as the 'Kien Tek' but frequently referred to as the 'Toh Peh Kong' (more correctly 'Toa Pek Kong'), which was the name of its tutelary deity in the Hokkien dialect.

This society, founded in 1844 under a leader Khoo Teng Pang, was a Hokkien association originating in a break-away of Ghee Hin members, mostly Straits-born Hokkiens. Its rules provided for hereditary membership, son succeeding father, and it was laid down that any member who joined the Ghee Hin, the Ho Seng, or the Hai San would be immediately expelled, and his children and grandchildren would not be permitted to succeed him. Though apparently antipathetic to all the established Triad hoeys (at least at the time of its foundation), it was particularly antagonistic to the Ghee Hin, and always remained so.[32]

2. THE SINGAPORE RIOTS, 1854

The middle of the nineteenth century was a significant period in the history of Chinese migration. In China the Taiping rebellion began in 1851 and brought in its train untold suffering and misery. At the same time the Triad revolts and the Hakka–Cantonese struggle swept across the southern provinces. During this same period the construction of railroads in America, the discovery of gold in Australia, and the mining of tin deposits in Malaya provided outlets for large numbers of Chinese manual labourers and rebels who would otherwise have faced starvation or violent death in the chaotic conditions then existing in the southern provinces of their homeland.

The 'Small Sword' rebellion at Amoy ended in November 1853, and it is known that after the evacuation of the city, the rebels took ship to Singapore. This is not surprising, for the leaders of the revolt were Singapore-born. There

[29] Lett. fr. Gov. to RC, Mal. No. 145, 4 May 1852. Encl. in GD 51, 8 May 1852.

[30] SSR(R24), Gov., Lett. to Beng., No. 51, 8 May 1852; SSR (R25), ditto, No. 44, 17 Apr. 1853; SSR (S22), Gov., Lett. fr. Beng., 99, 26 Sept. 1855 (Comments 7 & 15).

[31] SSR(U19), Gov. to RCs, 1849–50: No. 57, Sing., 5 Feb. 1850.

[32] Draft Report of the Penang Riot Commission, 1868, p. ix, para. 14: Report of the Commission on Chinese Labour in the Colony, 1876.

was thus an immediate influx of Triad fighters. Four Hokkien junks which arrived at Singapore in December 1853, and a fifth which arrived in January 1854 were said to have belonged formerly to the Emperor of China, and to have been captured from him at Amoy during the rebellion. They were flying a three-cornered flag which, according to reports, was intended to signify that they belonged to the T'in Tei Wui. On examination, the junks were found to contain between them 28 cannon, 26 matchlocks, 10 iron Lillas (small swivel guns), a number of spears, and a quantity of gunpowder. Eleven other cannon and 13 barrels of gunpowder had been removed before the junks were examined.[33] It was estimated that during that junk season 20,000 Chinese immigrants arrived in Singapore as compared with the more usual 8,000 or 10,000. They were completely destitute and ready for any mischief, and it was not long before trouble started.

On 5 May 1854 a period of rioting began in Singapore which lasted for ten or twelve days and ranged throughout the island wherever there were Hokkien and Tiechiu inhabitants. The day-to-day details of the fight have been recorded; over 400 people were killed and more than 300 houses were destroyed.[34]

The evidence as to the participation of societies in the riots is by no means conclusive. According to Buckley,

a quarrel arose between the Hokkiens and the Tiechius because the former refused to join in a subscription to assist the rebels who had been driven from Amoy by the Chinese Imperial troops. The Tiechius belonged to the Macao group, and were joined in the struggle by the other Macao elements, the Cantonese and Hakkas.

There was, in China, a long-standing feud between Tiechius and Hokkiens, of which this quarrel was undoubtedly a further manifestation, but whether it also corresponded to an alignment of secret societies in Singapore cannot be affirmed. Almost certainly District and Clan Associations would be involved.

The immediate cause of the outbreak was an extremely trivial incident. Two Chinese, a Hokkien and a Tiechiu, quarrelled about the weight of a catty of rice which one bought from the other. High words ensued, and the bystanders joined in.

Blows followed, and the report being rapidly circulated through the neighbouring streets, the adherents of each faction came pouring in by hundreds to take part in the broil, which then assumed a very alarming character. The fighting spread into the adjoining streets, in all of which the shops were at once closed, and sticks, stones and knives were used freely on the streets, and bricks thrown from the upper windows whenever an opportunity offered of assailing their enemies on the street.

Shops were smashed and looted, and before nightfall troops were called out to restore order. The following morning, Saturday, 6 May, fighting and plundering again broke out all over the town, wherever Tiechius or Hokkiens lived. These outbreaks were dealt with by the police, the marines, and sepoys, together with the greater part of the European residents and a few of the commanders of merchant ships lying in the harbour who were sworn in as special constables. The vigilance of the authorities in the town area was highly commendable, but the trouble spread to the country districts, and from Monday onwards the countryside was ravaged by the mobs in the Tanglin, Bukit Timah, and Paya

---

[33] SSR(AA31), Lett. to Gov., 4 Jan. 1854.
[34] *SFP*, 5 May 1854 ff.; also Buckley's *Anecdotal History*, ii. 585.

Lebar areas. In the Paya Lebar and Siglap districts the Hokkiens suffered severely, huts being everywhere burned by their enemies, who murdered men, women, and children, in many instances mutilating the corpses.

Some of the rioters had come over from Johore, and the Temenggong was asked for 200 Malays whom he readily supplied. These, together with sepoys and special constables, were landed from ships round the coast at various points and converged on the town down the principal tracks, rounding up rioters whenever found. At Bedok a stockade built to hold a great number of men was destroyed. Eventually the riots subsided, after days of murder, fire-raising, robbery, and wanton destruction of houses, plantations, gardens, and fruit trees.

In reporting the riots to the Government of India, the Governor made it clear that at no time were they directed against the local government. It had been entirely a party feud, as was evident from the fact that although there were over 500 prisoners in jail, not a single policeman had been killed or wounded in apprehending them and in suppressing the disturbances. He, himself, sometimes alone, and on other occasions with the Resident Councillor and the Magistrates, walked all over the town without molestation. Unfortunately, in the town the 'two Clans living opposite to each other in almost every street' turned out to fight the moment the police absented themselves. The Governor grieved to add that in the country some fearful crimes had been committed owing to the protection afforded by the density of the jungle, where the gambier and pepper plantations were located, to which access could only be gained 'by traversing deep swamps over planks merely supported by heavy timber loosely thrown under them'.

The authorities received no assistance from the leaders of the Chinese community who, though sent for, could not be induced to leave their homes. The Governor believed that this feud had been smouldering for some time

the embers of which, as far as I can gather, were brought from Amoy to this place, where they would very possibly have expired but for the lawless set, the very refuse of the belligerents in China that have crowded into this Island during the past year, to the number of fifteen to twenty thousand, who have rekindled them in connection with the Hoeys to serve their own ends by plundering both parties. . . .[35]

It would appear that some of the unwelcome immigrants may have returned to China immediately after the riots had subsided, for the *Straits Times* of 16 May 1854 reported the departure of more than twenty junks at this time.

The immediate result of the riots was a request to India for an increase in the military forces stationed in the Straits Settlements. The great influx of 'the very refuse of the belligerents in China', the widespread nature of the riots, and the brutal atrocities which accompanied them, had shown that at any moment, on the flimsiest pretext, the whole of the Chinese population could become embroiled in a hideous massacre. A number of other immediate measures were introduced for enlarging and increasing the efficiency of the police force, for opening up the interior of the island by bridle paths, and for controlling the traffic on the river to prevent vagabonds landing from junks. But at long last, the Governor had also come to the conclusion that 'some stringent enactment for

[35] SSR(R26), Gov., Lett. to Beng., 1854, pp. 78–86, Nos 42, 13 May 1854, & 43, 17 May 1854, pp. 87–119.

the management of the Chinese is very necessary', and six months later the draft of such an enactment was forwarded to the Government of India.

On 28 June 1854 the Governor reported to India that 515 men were arrested during the riots, but only 245 could be identified. They were brought to trial on 6 June at a Special Criminal Session. Two men were sentenced to death, 15 to transportation to Bombay, 63 were committed to the House of Correction, 90 were released on recognizances to appear and receive judgement when called upon, and 75 were acquitted.[36]

With 500 men being questioned and half of them tried in court, one would expect that if these riots had been fostered or fomented by rival Hoeys some inkling of this would have reached the outer world and resulted in vigorous denunciations in the press. But there is no real evidence of the riots being directed by any particular Hoeys. There does, however, appear to have been some organized combination of Tiechiu, Cantonese, and Hakka societies, for the Governor closed his despatch of 28 June 1854 by reporting that

perfect peace and order have prevailed since my last communication on this subject (the riots), and that the combination of the Macao, Canton and other minor sects which had been formed with the leading class opposed to the Hokien people has been broken up so completely that one party refused to participate in the Law expenses of the other which were very heavy, two Legal Practitioners having been engaged during the whole of the trial on the part of the Defence.[37]

The local press had much to say. An article in the *Straits Times* of 30 May 1854 implied that the system of organization of the Chinese community which included the Hoeys was dangerous, and accused the Government of 'blind confidence and mistaken leniency' in the face of constant warnings by the press, which had year after year dwelt on the state of affairs in the Settlement resulting from the character and habits of the increasing Chinese population, and the encouragement of their tendencies to combined outbreaks by the system adopted by the local Government of temporarily suppressing them by using the influence of heads of Hoeys and other leading Chinese to effect compromises between feuding parties. In order to re-establish governmental control stringent laws should be passed for the suppression of meetings of more than a limited number of Chinese and for the registration of the regulations and names of members and office-bearers of all societies. The Government should enforce the existing law against unlawful assemblages and any other laws the legislature might pass. In the meanwhile, it should be announced that the existing law—which had hitherto been a dead letter—would be enforced.

The *Singapore Free Press* of 19 May was more forthright, but had no evidence of the participation of specific Hoeys, merely a presumption that they must have been at the bottom of the trouble.

The first and monster grievance, and indeed the root from which all the others spring exists in the Hoes or secret societies of the Chinese; for there seems now to be no manner of doubt that the late tumultuous riots in the town and country which have produced the loss of hundreds of human lives and the destruction of much property arose from an ill-feeling originating in the proceedings of these illegal bodies and that the dispute about the chupa of rice was merely the pretext.

[36] SSR(R26), Gov., Lett. to Beng., 1854, pp. 158–61, No. 59, 28 June 1854.
[37] Ibid.

And after reporting the opening of the trial of those arrested, it said: 'If these people can, in a dispute in which their strength is divided against themselves, carry on a riot for ten days . . . what may they not be able to accomplish should they become bold enough to act for an object common to all the members of their Hoes . . . The Hoes *must* be suppressed.'

Buckley, too, nowhere suggests that secret societies had anything to do with these riots, and Vaughan, writing in 1878, used these and other inter-tribal fights to illustrate his contention that the Hoeys were not the only disrupting factor in the social life of the Chinese in the Straits Settlements. He regarded it as a popular error that most of the riots that had occurred from time to time originated with the secret societies. In the greatest of the Singapore riots, that of 1854, Hokkiens were ranged against the Macaos, Khehs, Tiechius, and Hailams. 'The solemn obligations of the secret societies were cast to the winds, and members of the same Hoey fought to the death against their brethren.' In 1870–1, 1872, and again in 1876 the riots were between Hokkiens and Tiechius. Clan riots also occurred frequently. 'In all these disturbances the vows of the secret societies were sacrificed to the claims of family and district feuds.' The societies were additional elements of discord, but so were any new elements introduced among such an inflammable population. 'In Hongkong', he wrote, 'riots are unknown chiefly because the mass of the inhabitants are Cantonese. Limit the immigration of Chinese to the Straits from one province in China and peace would be the result.'[38]

In the light of subsequent knowledge it is certain that in trying to justify his thesis that secret societies were only one, and not the most important one, of the disruptive factors in the Chinese community in the Straits, Vaughan tended to overstate his case, for there is ample proof that Chinese from the same province in China were quite capable of indulging in violent strife and bloody warfare both in China and in Malaya. Indeed, Vaughan's own statements about fights between groups of different surnames is in itself evidence of this. But the greatest danger of all lay in the possibility of one of these sectional interests, whether tribe, clan, province, or district, coinciding with the interests of a particular secret society.

Vaughan's remarks about the 1854 riot are of particular interest because although all the tribes mentioned did, as he said, belong to one Hoey, the T'in Tei Wui or Ghee Hin Society, each tribe had its own separate branch, a Hoey within a Hoey. On the evidence available, it is not possible to say whether the Hokkien section of the Ghee Hin, which was the strongest of all the sections, organized itself on this occasion to fight against the other branches of the same society, all of which came from Kwangtung province. Judging from later quarrels between different sections of the society there would be nothing improbable in this.

What is quite certain is that the trouble was caused by the influx of Triad fighters from China after their withdrawal from Amoy in 1853. They comprised 'Macaos', Hokkiens, and Tiechius, but which of these groups predominated is not known. If Buckley is correct in saying that the Hokkiens refused to join in a subscription to assist these rebels, it may be that they were mainly Tiechius. But whatever they were, they had created great devastation at Amoy both by their own depredations and indirectly through the vengeance wreaked upon the unfortunate inhabitants by the imperial troops. Their arrival at Singapore

[38] J. D. Vaughan, *The Manners and Customs of the Chinese of the Straits Settlements* (1879.

introduced to local Triad circles a new and violent element, already organized through experience at Amoy, and whose members had their own loyalties within their own group. They did not arrive as indentured labourers, but as adventurers with no ties or obligations outside their own group, and with the taste for blood and violence already awakened. To this extent at least, the riots of 1854 may properly be attributed to the interplay of Triad groups.

It also seems quite probable that these intruders from Amoy formed the Ghee Hok Society in Singapore at this time. The first official reference to this society that has been traced occurs in a 'List of the different Secret Societies in the Island of Singapore' prepared by the Acting Commissioner of Police, C. B. Plunket, and dated 1 May 1860.[39] In this list the number of members is given as 800, and they are said to be Tiechius. We find too that at a later date (1885), the branch of the Ghee Hok at Penang, opened about 1875, was described as being 'chiefly Tiechiu'.[40] There is therefore some ground for believing that it was the Tiechiu element among the Triad fighters from Amoy which was responsible for the riots of 1854 and for the formation of this new addition to the Triad complex of Singapore.

Once the excitement caused by the riots and the trials of those involved had died down, the Governor considered the introduction of legislation to strengthen the hands of the Government in dealing with such outbreaks. A copy of an Ordinance in force in Hong Kong (No. 7 of 1846) was obtained and sent to the magistrates for consideration, and a Draft Act for the suppression of outrages in the district of Malabar was also studied.

The Governor was encouraged in his search for additional powers by a despatch from the Government of India in which he was informed that the Governor-General in Council was happy to be able to express his entire concurrence in the opinion recorded by the local magistrates that the measures he had adopted for the suppression of the recent riots were the best and safest that the means at his disposal permitted. After expressing satisfaction with the conduct of the various individuals and services concerned in the suppression of the riots, the despatch continued:

I am directed to convey to you the assurance that the Government of India will be ready to take into immediate consideration any measures you may propose as calculated to prevent the recurrence of outrages so disgraceful and so disastrous. While it would be premature for the Government of India to express any definite opinion on the several enactments to which you have referred, the Governor-General in Council considers that the most stringent measures would be greatly preferable to the possibility of the recurrence of such outrageous tumults as you have lately suppressed.[41]

After consultation with the Resident Councillors of the three Settlements, and with the Bench of magistrates in Singapore, a draft act 'for the Better Preservation of the Public Peace' was framed by the Clerk of the Court of Judicature, Singapore, and was sent to the Government of India in November 1854, for consideration. It was accompanied by the comments of the three Residents, and of the Singapore Bench, and was intended, in the first instance, to apply to Singapore only. The Act was drafted under four main heads:

[39] Encl. to GD 108, 5 June 1860 (PRO). See App. 3, p. 538.
[40] Pg *AR*, 1885.
[41] SSR(S21), 1854, Gov., Lett. fr. Beng., p. 98: GD 665, 16 June 1854.

1. Registration of the inhabitants.
2. The Governor to have power of banishment.
3. Registration of secret societies.
4. Appointment of Chinese Headmen as District Peace Officials.

In a long covering despatch the Governor offered his comments. He disliked the idea of registration of the inhabitants, but allowed the clause to stand. As to the powers of banishment, he thought that he would have difficulty 'in adequately conveying to His Lordship his sense of the expediency of investing a single individual with power so great, and so liable to be abused'; opposed too, as it was, to 'the principles and spirit of modern laws which, however, were unsuited in some respects to the state of society in the Settlements'. The Governor then set out his view of the special circumstances.

The clannish nature of the Chinese people, their spirit of combination, their inclination to intrigue, their impatience of control under a foreign government, their tendency to take the law into their own hands, their habits and ideas so opposed to the spirit of our laws, and their proneness to settle all their differences, grave and trivial by their own self-constituted tribunals instead of seeking justice at our Courts, all require peculiar legislation to be dealt with effectively. These evils are perpetuated by certain chiefs or Headmen at whose bidding those over whom they exercise any influence are ready to engage in the most serious outrages against persons of an opposite Clan, regardless of all consequences.

These headmen were not permanent settlers or resident merchants, but merely temporary sojourners on the Island, 'frequently for a single season, intending to return to their own land the moment they can gather sufficient funds'. Therefore their deportation was not as great a hardship as it might seem.

This was an exaggeration, for undoubtedly there were leaders of the T'in Tei Wui who were residents of long standing. The Governor supported his plea by adding that the power to deport was deemed essential 'by the most experienced officer in the Straits, Mr Church, the Resident Councillor at Singapore, as well as by all the Magistrates, including Tan Kim Seng, a Chinese of high respectability'.

On the subject of registration of societies, the Governor reiterated his opposition to the introduction of legislation for total suppression, stating that, though such legislation might have been expedient if introduced at the time of the first formation of the Settlement, it 'would prove a complete failure at this period'. The Draft Act proposed to require these societies to register at the police office their nature and object, their rules and regulations, the names and places of residence of all the office-bearers and members, their places of meeting, and appointed days of assembling. All societies and associations not so registered would be held to be illegal combinations and confederacies, and their members subject to transportation or local imprisonment. There were also provisions for the meetings to be held with open doors and before eight o'clock at night, and for the Superintendent of Police and his delegates to have a right of entry. 'All this', wrote the Governor, 'will at all events check that propensity to band together which is the dangerous characteristic of the Chinese, who are in all other respects in my opinion the best Colonists within the tropics or possibly in any part of the world.'

The proposal to appoint 'Peace officials' or 'District Constables' applied not only to the Chinese but to 'all classes of native inhabitants'. It was hoped that it would be possible

> to select men of character and standing sufficiently independent to point out the turbulent and evil-disposed persons of their Districts, and to give information of their plots, combinations, conspiracies or intended outbreaks, and who would encourage their countrymen to bring their complaints before the constituted authorities instead of, as at present with the Chinese, before the chief of the Hoeys.

The last section of the Draft Act enabled the Governor to extend its provisions to Penang, Province Wellesley, and Malacca and the despatch concluded:

> I would observe that the riots above referred to [May 1854] have clearly demonstrated the refractory character of the Chinese, which, with their preponderating numbers over the other classes of the community and the evil influence of the Secret Societies that the existing laws have hitherto been found powerless to meet, render imperatively necessary some such stringent provisions as those embodied in the Draft Act now submitted, in the earnest hope that it may receive the early sanction of the most Noble the Governor-General of India in Council.[42]

The despatch containing the Draft Act for the Better Preservation of the Public Peace was acknowledged from Fort William on 31 January 1855, and the Governor was informed that it had been transferred to the Legislative Council for consideration.[43] On 3 October 1855 the Honourable the Court of Directors, London, commenting to the Governor-General in India upon the Singapore Narrative of 1854, which included the story of the May riots, said:

> It was sufficiently clear that not only were the Police numerically insufficient, but that the powers conferred by Law were entirely inadequate to control the Chinese. Application was therefore properly made for more stringent enactments, which will be further noticed when they come under your consideration and are reported to us.[44]

But apparently the proposed new law never came into being. No further mention of it has been traced in later documents, and it can only be presumed that the Legislative Council in India decided against its enactment.

This was the swansong of Governor Butterworth, who retired on grounds of ill-health in 1855 and died the following year in England. He had been Governor from 1843, and for years, despite public criticism formulated mainly by the European community, with the leading merchants of the Chinese, Arab, and Indian communities in the background, had adhered to the policy of freedom of association, and had regarded the control of the evil doings of the Hoeys as a function of the police force. This force he endeavoured to strengthen in order that it might be able to deal effectively with this social canker. At the same time he supported the policy of providing adequate funds to enable the police and the magistracy to obtain information about the proposed unlawful activities of the Hoeys.

But in the end, while still maintaining that suppression was impossible, he reached the conclusion that the existing laws were inadequate. He was succeeded by a no less doughty opponent of suppression, E. A. Blundell, who, as Resident

---

[42] SSR(R27), Gov., Lett. to Beng., 1854–5, pp. 18–38: GD 110, 27 Nov. 1854.

[43] SSR(S22), Gov., Lett. fr. Beng., 1855, p. 41: Despatch 148, Ft William, 31 Jan. 1855. Sec. to GOI (C. Beddon) to Gov., Prince of Wales Is., Sing., & Mal.

[44] Ibid. pp. 222 & encl. London comment, 3 Oct. 1855, forwarded to Singapore from India.

Councillor first of Malacca and then of Penang, was well acquainted with the machinations of secret societies.

3. THE NUISANCE OF PUBLIC PROCESSIONS

Disturbances of the public peace were not confined to those caused by Chinese secret societies, nor was the Chinese community the only one to cause anxiety from time to time.

The celebration of their festival days by the various communities was frequently accompanied by hooliganism and lawlessness, while the streets were often blocked by processions or 'wayangs' (theatrical performances) played on stages set up at the side of a road or in a public square. The principal Hindu festivals were the Hoolie[45] and the Dusserah,[46] the Indian Muslims celebrated Moharram,[47] and the Chinese celebrated the lunar New Year. On all these occasions there were liable to be faction fights in the streets between rival groups participating in the processions, for these festivals were regarded as opportunities for paying off old scores, and the injuries of one year were nursed for the next.

As early as May 1842, on account of previous unpleasant experience, the Government had refused to permit one such Indian procession in Singapore, and had forbidden the 'Tabut' to be carried round the town.[48] In 1849 the Singapore Grand Jury called attention to the desirabliity of limiting the celebration of festivals by the Asian population, in particular those which took place at the principal festivals mentioned above.[49]

The Governor was in favour of introducing some measure of control, but in asking his Resident Councillors to what extent such limitation was practicable, he pointed out that these processions had been tolerated from the earliest period of the Settlement, and even the convicts had been allowed to participate in some of them, so that they had now become part of their religion. He consequently considered that every indulgence should be granted 'consistent with the safety and convenience of Her Majesty's subjects'.[50]

In 1852 the police at Penang endeavoured to introduce measures of control over Chinese processions and wayangs, with the result that a deputation of Chinese waited upon the officiating Governor asking for the withdrawal of the restrictions. Mr Blundell gave it as his opinion that so long as the religious practices of the Chinese did not cause any obstructions on the public thoroughfares, or endanger in any manner the person of the passers-by, they should not be subject to interference by the police. This once again begged the question, for the complaint of the police was that these processions and wayangs did obstruct the thoroughfare and endanger the safety of passers-by. On this occasion, Mr Blundell granted permission to the deputation to 'erect posts on the edge of the road or street opposite their dwellings, for hoisting paper lanterns, and to burn paper in iron pans on the edge of the road opposite their doorways', but thought that wayangs should cease at 10 p.m. except on special occasions, though this should be at the discretion of the magistrates.[51] Again, in 1852, there was a collision between convicts and police in Singapore at the Moharram festival, and

---

[45] Hindu carnival of Krishna at the vernal equinox.   [46] Hindu autumnal festival.
[47] Islamic new year festival.   [48] Buckley, p. 375.
[49] SSR(U17), Gov. to RCs, 1849, No. 165, 19 Apr. 1849: Grand Jury Presentment, para. 13.
[50] SSR(U18), Gov., Lett. to RCs, 1849, pp. 246–9, No. 418, 12 Oct. 1849.
[51] SSR(U24); Gov., Lett. to RCs, 1852–3, pp. 2–3, No. 311, 7 Oct. 1852.

G

by late 1855 the police had once more reached the conclusion that these processions should be prohibited.[52] In October 1855 the Resident Councillor, Singapore, addressed the Governor suggesting that all future proposals to hold public processions on the occasion of the Moharram and Dusserah festivals should be disallowed.[53]

The Indian population of the Straits Settlements included not only merchants, traders, and labourers but also the regiments of Sepoys which from time to time were posted from India. These were usually the Madras Native Infantry, though there were occasionally regiments from Bombay and Bengal. Both Muslim and Hindu elements were included. It was customary for these troops to participate in these public processions. The convicts transported from India formed another Indian group described as 'thugs and dacoits from different parts of the Bengal presidency'.[54] From 1787 onwards there was a penal settlement for criminals from India at Bencoolen, the British Factory on the west coast of Sumatra, and at the time of the handing over of Bencoolen to the Dutch in 1825 in return for Malacca, these convicts, to the number of some 800 or 900, were removed from Bencoolen to Penang, and from there were distributed to the prisons at the three Settlements. From that date they were Penal Settlements for India until 1860, and for Ceylon until 1867, when the Straits Settlements were separated from British India. After 1844, when transportation of criminals to Tasmania ceased because of the determined opposition of the inhabitants, the Straits Settlements, despite protests, also became Penal Settlements for Hong Kong. This ceased in 1856, when it was considered that such practice was

dangerous to the community, in as much as the convicts are objects of interest to the Secret Societies existing among their countrymen, all of whom possess great influence and considerable pecuniary means to assist and protect their members against constituted authority.[55]

On the expiry of their sentences many of the Indian convicts elected to stay in the Straits and were absorbed into the Indian population. Even those who were still serving sentences were, at these times of festival, 'accustomed to enjoy a degree of licence strangely inconsistent with their condition . . . their procession the noisiest to be seen on the public streets'.[56]

The Indian processions were not, however, totally prohibited in 1855. After consulting the Resident Councillors of Penang and Malacca, the Governor decided that this was inadvisable. He pointed out that if the Mohammedan and Hindu processions were disallowed, Chinese processions must be similarly controlled. He thought that sufficient powers would be conferred upon the police by a new Act about to be introduced to restrict and modify the processions, so that in the course of a few years the desire to form them might diminish.

In the meantime a considerable amount of control could be exercised under the existing law, and in particular, during the Moharram and the Dusserah festivals, all processions of convicts should be prohibited.

Accordingly, at the Moharram festival in September 1856 the convicts in Singapore were refused permission to carry their Tabut in procession through

[52] Narrative of 4th quarter of 1852, 27 Apr. 1853, paras 64–67. Comment on this at SSR(S22), Gov., Lett. fr. Beng., No. 99, 26 Sept. 1855.
[53] SSR(U30), Gov., Lett. to RCs, 1855–6, encl. of 31 Oct. 1855 in No. 531, 5 Nov. 1855.
[54] McMair, *Prisoners Their Own Warders.*
[55] *SFP,* 20 Nov. 1856.   [56] Ibid. 18 Sept. 1856.

the public streets, and were told that their demonstrations must take place within their own lines. As a result, some hundreds of the convicts forced their way out of their lines, and carrying their Tabut and lighted by torches, marched in procession to the house of the Resident Councillor, where they conducted themselves in 'a most tumultuous and insubordinate manner', later demonstrating similarly outside the Government Offices.[57]

In Penang the police were able to limit the period of the festival to five days instead of ten or more, and this was achieved without incident. The *Pinang Gazette* (13 September 1856) urged the Government to take advantage of the new Police Act to frame some general rules to 'check nuisances of this kind' in order to 'enforce the right of the public to the use of the streets' and prevent the blocking of thoroughfares by processions. It suggested that some open ground should be made into a park and the Superintendent given power to authorize its use for 'native Tamashas'. It commented that every race, clan, sect, and association laboured under the delusion that 'its feasts are of such paramount importance that the public are bound to respect and give way to them'. Half the pleasure of the revellers consisted in their sense of power in compelling the authorities and the public 'to submit to the nuisance and allow a temporary triumph and supremacy to their native creeds'. This was a sentiment which should not be indulged.

The 'new Act' to which both the Governor and the press referred was the Police Act, which together with a 'Conservancy Act' was introduced in June 1856, to have effect from 1 November of that year. In the event, the introduction of these Acts was to have effects far different from those which were so confidently envisaged.[58]

In the first place the Police Act, which made it clear that control of the police vested in the Government, was vigorously opposed by most of the JPs who had long maintained that the appointment and control of the police should be in the hands of the Superintendent, subject only to the control and direction of the Court of Quarter Sessions; and on publication of the new Act a number of them resigned. A public meeting was held in Singapore on 29 July 1856, at which resolutions were passed objecting to this 'arbitrary and unconstitutional measure'. It was contended that as the police were paid for out of the Assessment Fund, the ratepayers who furnished the fund should have a share in their control.[59]

Among other things, the two Acts between them provided for rules to be made governing the conduct of assemblies and processions, prevention of obstructions in streets, roads, and places of public resort, the licensing of music in the streets, and the regulation of markets. They were very comprehensive, the Police Act having 118 sections and the Conservancy Act 142 sections. An abstract was prepared and translated into Chinese for the information of the public, but the appearance of a document (in so far as it was understood at all) containing all those powers, provisions, restrictions, and requirements was too much to be

[57] Ibid.
[58] The Acts were:

(a) India Act, XIII of 1856: An Act for regulating the Police of the towns of Calcutta, Madras and Bombay, and of the stations of the settlement of Prince of Wales' Island, Singapore and Malacca.

(b) India Act, XIV of 1856: An Act for the Conservancy and improvement of the towns of Calcutta, Madras and Bombay, and the several stations of the settlement of Prince of Wales' Island, Singapore and Malacca.   [59] *SFP*, 31 July 1856.

borne. The Government was, of course, faced with a difficulty common to all non-representative governments, and particularly to governments alien in language and culture to the mass of the people. The Acts made provision for increased police control, which no doubt the enormous influx of immigrants had rendered advisable or even essential. Essential, that is to say, from the point of view of the administrator brought up in the tidy tradition of England of even 100 years ago, but of doubtful importance when viewed by the local populace of Singapore, who were more accustomed to the press of crowds in the streets and market-place, and did not regard sanitation or noise with western eyes or ears. In other words, it was not a body of law which the people themselves found necessary and had brought into being through their own customary channels. It was something imposed upon them from outside.

There is no doubt that throughout the centuries of Britain's colonial history, nothing has been more generally advantageous to the peoples under her rule than the introduction of her legal system, and, in particular, the impartiality of its application. In Malaya, at least, it is highly improbable that the legal system of any of the various components of the population would have been found to be so generally acceptable as was the British, which brought all men together on equal terms. Nevertheless, as it was not a natural growth from the peoples to whom it was applied, it was not at all times regarded as the well-intentioned instrument which the paternal Government believed it to be. The writer well remembers a stalwart old Malay charged in court with a breach of the law retorting: 'What is this "Loh"? It is not Adat [Customary Law], it is not Shara' [Religious Law]. What then is it? It may be your Adat or your Shara', but it is not mine and I will have none of it.'

To the Chinese during the early years in Malaya, the introduction of laws controlling their conduct in everyday affairs was even more repellent. In China there were no such laws. The law was the instrument of an oppressive government, and every artifice of bribery, deceit, and evasion was employed to avoid coming into contact with it. The ordinary intercourse of the people was controlled not by law but by the customary procedure of the people themselves and their representative organizations. Therefore, the appearance of an official law to regulate their daily affairs, accompanied by legal processes and punishments for infringement, was most unwelcome. Besides, such laws, in one way or another, invariably meant some interference with the livelihood of at least part of the public. The removal of hawkers from certain areas, the insistence of adequate width of passage-way in the streets and markets, the licensing and limitation of hours for open-air theatrical performances, all these meant less opportunity for earning by the people concerned. Added to this was the almost insurmountable difficulty of conveying the meaning of the new regulations to the public.

By the end of 1856 the Chinese community in Singapore was becoming uncomfortable about these new powers which were about to be enforced. Their uneasiness was considered to arise

partly from the stringent nature of many of the provisions, partly from the injudicious and overbearing manner of the police in putting these new Acts into force, and partly from the abstract in the native languages conveying a very imperfect, and in some cases erroneous idea of their contents.[60]

[60] *SFP*, 8 Jan. 1857.

There was also rising discontent in Penang. Even before the powers vested in them by the new Act, the police at Penang had refused permission for the holding of 'certain noisy processions through the streets of the town' as being subversive of order. In September 1856 the Chinese community presented a petition to the Governor stating that from the commencement of their residence in the Settlement, they had been permitted to carry on their religious ceremonies and marriage and funeral processions without the interference of the police. They requested that this might continue. They received a curt reply from the Governor:

This being a British Settlement, under English Law, it cannot be allowed in justice to other inhabitants of different creeds and habits that the streets of the town should be rendered dangerous to passengers in carriages or on horseback by the firing of crackers and by processions accompanied by the beating of gongs, or that the peace, quiet and good order of the town should be nightly disturbed by wayangs in various parts of it.

The Chinese coming to a British Settlement must learn to modify their habits and religious ceremonies in deference to fellow settlers of other creeds. There were already two places at which wayangs might be held. The question whether the firing of crackers was indispensable at wedding ceremonies 'should be finally settled'. The carrying of idols in procession, which was decidedly dangerous to passers by, must be strictly limited and controlled. At the Chinese New Year a certain number of days might be permitted for Chinese festivals 'within enclosures, being private property', and here they could at all times hold wayangs and other amusements. Funeral processions must be allowed, 'but the course through the streets should be prescribed'.

This letter, signed by Blundell, and dated Penang, 8 September 1856, was published in the *Straits Times* of 11 November, 1856, and with the coming of the New Year the uneasiness felt by the Chinese communities in Singapore and Penang was transformed into open defiance.

5

REACTIONS TO MEASURES OF CONTROL

1. SINGAPORE, 1857

ON 2 January 1857 there was a general strike, and the commercial life of Singapore came to a standstill. Shops were closed, public markets deserted, and supplies to European households intercepted with the use of threats and intimidation.

The business community were extremely perturbed, and a public meeting was convened by the Sheriff and was attended by the leading Europeans as well as three Chinese merchants, Whampoa, Tan Kim Seng, and Tan Kim Cheng, the last-named being the head of the Hokkien Hoey Kwan (Provincial Association). A deputation was formed to wait on the Governor to inform him of the position, and to beg him to issue a proclamation calling upon people to return to their business, stating that he would be at all times ready to listen to proper complaints, and that the translation of the Police and Conservancy Acts should be revised.

The Governor had already anticipated the wishes of the meeting by issuing a proclamation along these lines, stating that the new Acts had been misrepresented and misapprehended, and announcing that a revised translation would be made within one month. At the same time, big guns were moved into position on Government Hill (now Fort Canning) and Pearl's Hill, covering the town. Some handwritten placards of an inflammatory nature were found pasted over some of the government proclamations announcing that no faith should be put in the Governor's promise, that he only wished to gain time and make preparations, and that the Chinese community was ready with arms to sweep every barbarian off the island. There is no doubt that in addition to the local grievances there was an undercurrent of ill-will because of the outbreak of hostilities between Britain and China.[1] British ships were blockading the port and river of Canton, and bad feeling against foreigners had also spread to Amoy and Foochow, so that the home area of the majority of Chinese immigrants in Malaya was affected. During the next few days further posters appeared, announcing that as the English had suffered reverses at Canton, now was the time to exterminate them in Singapore. As most of the towkays (employers) had sided with the barbarians, they too should be eliminated.

Fortunately the trouble did not develop. Leading members of the Chinese community were prevailed upon to intervene, and after the first day's strike, business went on as usual. Indeed, some of the shops had opened in the evening of the first day. But the leading citizens had been badly shaken, and at the resumed public meeting on 3 January a long and animated discussion took place on the misgovernment of the Settlements by the East India Company, and the

---
[1] The 'Lorcha Arrow' war.

probable advantage that would result were Singapore, Penang, and Malacca placed under the direct rule of the Crown. Eventually the following resolution was passed:

That the evident reliance of the people during the present disturbances on the orders of certain headmen, is another prominent proof of the dangerous combination of the Chinese Secret Societies, whose growing power has long been subversive of public order and security; and this meeting is of opinion that the Hon'ble East India Company, whether in Council or by means of the Legislative Council is deeply to blame for having treated with marked negligence and disdain the urgent petitions and remonstrances of the inhabitants of this Settlement; who have ever sought by legal means to restrain the authority which these secret combinations have obtained, and which threaten, at no distant period, to produce the most serious results.[2]

The Governor, in reporting the strike to the Governor-General in India, said that the Chinese population of Singapore took their 'national mode of evincing their dissatisfaction by closing their shops and intimidating or inducing the natives of India to follow their example'. He admitted that the translation of the abstract of the Acts which had been posted up in the town was defective and he commented at some length on the general question of the organization of the strike, which he believed demonstrated a 'power and spirit of organization among the Chinese which has excited a considerable degree of alarm and apprehension'. He considered that it was undeniable that the secret societies constituted the framework of the organization, and their leaders 'may have objects in view far beyond the mere redress of Police grievances', but their power and influence among their own people could not be combated with existing means. The European community were much dissatisfied that no law had been passed to prohibit the associations, but he did not believe that any such legislation could be effective. Experience in Europe and in Ireland supported this view, and indeed laws of repression might well increase the element of secrecy. Associations of all kinds were a natural feature of Chinese life, and the problem was how best to control those which had become dangerous.

Instead of legislative enactments the Governor proposed two measures. The first was the creation of a well-organized and efficient police. He pointed out that Singapore was fast becoming one of the great cities of the east. Its trade and shipping were second only to Calcutta, and though the size of its population could not yet compare with those of the Presidencies, it contained a more turbulent and ill-affected mob than was to be found in the Indian cities, above all, a mob distinct and separate in language, habits, and character from the classes from which the police could be recruited. He also considered that the Commissioner of Police in Singapore should not hold other administrative posts but should be able to devote all his time to his duties, and that to ensure an efficient police, it was absolutely necessary to select the best man as Commissioner and to pay him well.

The Governor had some hesitation in proposing the second measure which he then put forward. He proposed that

the Governor of the Straits Settlements should be vested with the power of deportation on his sole responsibility and wholly irrespective of the law. . . . The Governor should have the power of apprehending and of sending out of the Colony any individual who,

2 *SFP*, 8 Jan. 1857.

from the evidence that may be laid before him, he is satisfied is dangerous to the peace and good order of the Settlement.

He considered that the power of deportation consequent on the result of any legal investigation or trial would be wholly inoperative, owing to the difficulty or even impossibility of obtaining open, public evidence against the influential members of the Chinese secret societies. He realized that such absolute power was open to abuse, or, as he preferred to term it, 'erroneous administration', but pointed out that he would be acting under responsibility, and would minutely report his proceedings and the grounds of the exercise of his power. He was perhaps on more doubtful ground when he suggested that a possible error on his part would be considered less injurious than the existing immunity of those mischievous leaders of secret political societies who defied the law because they knew that they could not be convicted of any offence against it. He continued:

To be vested with such a power would be very far from being personally agreeable to me. It is without precedent and contrary to all principles of good Government, and its exercise would involve a most serious responsibility, but I believe that it is advisable to hold it. The Chinese of Singapore are not our Countrymen. They are separate from us in habits, ideas, and language. They belong to a foreign Country, whence their numbers are annually largely recruited and this most frequently by the worst and most turbulent of their class. All these people are bound to each other by oath, by sympathy and by education. They form a distinct community, disliking our laws and obeying them only so far as they may deem safe. There are exceptions, of course. There are many Chinese who are devoted to us and would willingly stand by and support us, but they have no influence and are cowed and rendered timid by the bold and unscrupulous. To such persons, vigorous measures on our part would be rejoiced at, but until relieved from their present dread of revenge and retaliation they will not move a finger in our favour.

With this despatch, the Governor enclosed a draft of an Act investing him with

the full and sufficient power to cause the apprehension of any member of a Hoey whom he may deem to be dangerous to the peace and good order of the Settlement, and to deport such person from the Station in which he may be residing to such place as he (the Governor) may appoint.

Any person so deported who returned was to be liable to transportation. The Governor was to report each case in detail to the Government of India, and his proceedings under the Act were not to be subject to review in any court of justice, nor was any writ of Habeas Corpus or any other writ from any court of justice to stay or impede the proceedings of the Governor under the Act.[3]

The *Singapore Free Press* (15 January 1857) considered the police to be far from blameless, and thought that illegal acts on their part very much conduced to excite the bad spirit which was recently displayed. It suggested that the levy of fees for permission to have processions at burials, etc., was a most illegal exercise of authority and created a great deal of bad feeling. It further hinted that power had probably been usurped in other matters 'with as little warrant for it'. It then referred to the various proposals which had from time to time been put forward, such as registration of the population and of associations, but was afraid that even if adopted the Government would not have adequate power to enforce

[3] SSR(R30); Gov., Lett. to Beng., 1856–7, pp. 218–34: No. 6, Sing., 10 Jan. 1857, with encl.

them, which would leave things worse than before. It doubted whether the Government could even make such a measure intelligible to the Chinese population, for it was a disgraceful fact that among all the officials who could be considered sufficiently trustworthy and intelligent to be entrusted with an important duty of this kind, there was not one who knew enough Chinese either to enable him to translate any measure correctly or even to give an intelligible verbal explanation of it. (The writer failed to add, what was probably true, that neither the gentlemen of the press nor the mercantile community were any more competent in this regard.)

The Grand Jury, with customary verve at the sessions held later in January, presented 'the Hoeys or Chinese Secret Societies as combinations formidable and dangerous to the peace of the Settlement and the safety of the lives and property of its inhabitants'. It recalled the former Grand Inquests which had repeatedly expressed the same opinion, deplored the apathy of the Bengal Legislative Council, and entered an emphatic protest against further procrastination. It considered that there were two plans which could be adopted, either of which if carried out with integrity would effect the purpose in view. The first was total repression; the second was to tolerate their existence on certain stringent conditions, which included the registration of all societies. The jurors considered that the second alternative was likely to prove the more productive of general good.[4]

In forwarding this Presentment to India, the Governor once more maintained that it was 'impracticable to contend by Legislative Enactments to be administered by English Courts, with the spirit of secret organization so congenial to the Chinese mind'. He admitted the evil of the Hoeys, and would much like to see them abolished, but he foresaw that if legislation were introduced, the Heads or Chiefs who registered would be men of straw, and the meetings held under licence would not be the meetings at which the real business was transacted. He reiterated the opinion he had already expressed that a really good police force was the first requisite, but to be really good and really efficient, something very different from the existing establishment was required. Secondly, he required the power of deportation 'as a powerful auxiliary'.

The knowledge that such power existed in the Governor's hands would be terrifying and tend to the superiority of the organisation of the police over that of the Secret Societies. I have always thought that if the Police could be raised to that degree of excellence as to recommend itself as the best protector of the injured and oppressed, the Hoeys would very soon decline into political insignificance though retaining all their powers for good in assisting the poor and needy.[5]

In reply, the Indian Government agreed that it would be inexpedient to try to suppress the Hoeys by a special law, but also thought that there were no grounds for vesting the local Government with the arbitrary power of deportation.

The ease with which the apprehensions of the Chinese shopkeepers were quieted shows that no such extraordinary measure is necessary, and that the most effectual means of preventing disaffection among the Chinese is to be found in a just application of the law.[6]

[4] *SFP*, 22 Jan. 1857.
[5] SSR(R30), Gov., Lett. to Beng., 1857, pp. 303–8: No. 31, Sing., 31 Jan. 1857.
[6] SSR(S25), Gov., Lett. fr. Beng., 1857, p. 70: No. 414, Ft William, 27 Mar. 1857.

Among the European community apprehension increased because the Governor, in response to a request from the British plenipotentiary in China, had sent a detachment of troops from the Straits to China in January, and the wrathful merchants informed him that they would hold him responsible for making good any losses which might be laid to his political acts.[7] In informing India of his decision to send the troops, the Governor felt no apprehension of any rising among the Chinese population, nor did his 'very able and experienced Assistant, Mr Dunman, the Magistrate', but he confessed that such an impression existed among the European community, and that the loss of a portion of the troops of the garrison would be 'anxiously felt'.[8] The local press published a letter which had been sent to *The Englishman* in Calcutta by a resident of Singapore which said: 'One fact speaks for itself. My pistols have been loaded for the last four weeks, but except during the Chinese riots in May, 1854 (and then Europeans were not at all menaced) they have not been loaded seven times in twice as many years.' He called for a firmer line in legislation backed by a force 'adequate to make Government and not the Secret Societies master here as they are at present'.[9]

A clash between the police and a crowd of Indian celebrants at the Telok Ayer mosque on 5 February made the situation worse. A police permit to celebrate a festival had been granted on condition that the festivities should cease at 10 p.m. But at 11 p.m. the Sub-Inspector of the District discovered that the celebration was still in progress, and that a strong fence of stakes across one of the side roads barred all entry. The Sub-Inspector ordered his peons to move the obstructions, whereupon they were furiously attacked by the crowd, driven back to the police station, and assailed with brick-bats and stones. The police opened fire, killing one man and wounding several others, two of whom died in hospital.

At the Coroner's inquest it was held that the police action was justified. With this the Governor disagreed, dismissed two Inspectors and one peon, and reduced in rank the other members of the force who were involved.

This caused intense indignation among the European community. Meetings were held and resolutions passed. The Governor, who had refused to see a delegation, was informed that 'the case under consideration forcibly illustrates the incompatibility of the union of the Commissioner of Police, Resident Councillor and Judge of the Court in one person'; and he was urged to place the management of the police in the hands of the ratepayers, failing independent magistrates, who might control it in Quarter Sessions.

But the Governor was not to be moved, and it is clear that he was no more popular in Commercial Square than was the Government of India.

Bad news from Sarawak then increased the tension. On 17 February the wave of anti-British resentment caused by the war in China resulted in a rising of Hakka gold-miners up-river from Kuching. Organized by a Triad society, the insurgents descended on the capital and sacked it; Raja Brooke and his staff narrowly escaped being murdered. In the end the Malays and Sea Dyaks annihilated the assailants, and Raja Brooke, in condemning the Chinese secret societies, said that the existing state of affairs in Singapore was a lesson to warn Sarawak.[10] In Singapore the Sheriff called a public meeting, at which a resolution

---

[7] SSR(R30), Gov., Lett. to Beng., 1857, pp. 299–300: No. 28, Sing., 27 Jan. 1857.
[8] Ibid. pp. 279–86: No. 22, 20 Jan. 1857.
[9] *SFP*, 2 Apr. 1857. Date of original, 28 Jan. 1857.   [10] Ibid. 19 Mar. 1857.

was passed drawing attention to the Sarawak outbreak and demanding from the Government of India 'those Acts which have been frequently called for, and without which it is impossible to control the turbulent and disaffected'.[11]

The Governor made use of the public perturbation resulting from the riot in Sarawak to press India yet again for the appointment of a whole-time Commissioner of Police. What had occurred at Sarawak might easily happen in Singapore,

when we take into consideration the immense preponderance of the Chinese portion of our population, that a very large proportion of them are from the neighbourhood of Canton, and that there they have evinced and are daily evincing their hatred of the English, and the unscrupulous means they will adopt for giving effect to that hatred.

Once again the Governor urged that the Settlement's protection lay in an efficient police force, which should ensure

not only the protection of person and property from ordinary thieves and plunderers, but the detection of what may, under the circumstances of a Chinese war be deemed political plots and conspiracies and the counteraction of Chinese secret societies.

He continued:

To this end, the Police should be under the management of an officer well adapted to the duty by previous training and who should devote his whole time and energies to that duty, not as at present under an officer not selected for his aptitude and having other avocations to distract his attention.

He considered the appointment of a Commisioner of Police so important that to provide funds he proposed abolishing the post of Resident Councillor, Singapore, his place to be taken by an assistant serving directly under the Governor.[12]

India had already decided that a separate head of the police was necessary at Singapore, and though refusing to pass a special law to suppress secret societies, or to grant the local Government arbitrary power to deportation, authorized the Governor to appoint a Commissioner of Police at a salary of 800 rupees a month.[13]

This must have been a matter of some satisfaction to the Governor, more particularly because he was faced with an outbreak of rioting in Penang, which added to his difficulties and unpopularity, and augmented the fears of an overwrought European community. As he wrote to Bengal on 27 April 1857:

It has been my misfortune throughout, to differ very considerably from the members of the European Mercantile community of Singapore in my estimate of the designs of the Chinese population in the Straits. Under the present circumstances of our being at war with their countrymen, it is necessary to show ourselves prepared to put down any outbreak or any rise against our authority; but, on the other hand, excessive precautions would show unnecessary fears and involve certain restrictions and impositions on the Chinese that might stimulate their resentment and drive them to inconsiderate hostility. My object has been to show that we are not to be taken unawares, without at the same time exhibiting any marked distrust of the designs of our Chinese population.[14]

[11] Ibid. 2 Apr. 1857.
[12] SSR(R31), Gov., Lett. to Beng., 1857, pp. 64–71: No. 55, 14 Mar. 1857.
[13] SSR(S25), Gov., Lett. fr, Beng., 1857, p. 70: No. 414, Ft William, 27 Mar. 1857.
[14] SSR(R31), Gov., Lett. to Beng., pp. 133–9: No. 79, Sing., 27 Apr. 1857.

He might have added, however, that the apprehensions of the European community were aroused not only by the riotous behaviour of the Chinese but by the outbreak of the Mutiny in India, and the knowledge that the garrisons in the Straits Settlements were largely manned by sepoy troops.

2. PENANG, 1857

Riots broke out at Penang on 14 March 1857 because of an attempt by the police to enforce the provisions of the new Act whereby theatrical performances on the public streets were only permitted under police licence. Chinese connected with a wayang which had been held in front of a temple refused to dismantle the wooden staging when the period of licence expired. A police officer thereupon ordered his peons to pull it down, and when they attempted to do so, they were violently and successfully resisted. Thus encouraged, the mob got out of hand, a police station was attacked, and shots were fired resulting in some deaths. Then next day all shops remained closed, persons bringing provisions into the town were stopped by the rioters, and a sepoy guard marching down the street was attacked, two muskets being taken from them. The garrison was under strength, but the European community enrolled as special constables, and the Resident Councillor appealed to the Malay community for help against the Chinese. The Malays apparently responded 'with alacrity and cheerfulness', and may even have convinced the Chinese of the folly of carrying their violence any further.

In later congratulating the Resident Councillor upon the measures taken to suppress the riot, the Governor nevertheless considered that the original action of the police in attempting to demolish the stage was unjustified and unlawful. Instead, they should have given notice that anyone opposing or violating the order to remove the stage was liable to a fine of 100 rupees. But he was so incensed at the carrying off of the two muskets that until these had been restored he refused to consider or redress any of the grievances of the population. One musket was forthcoming at once, but there was no sign of the second. He informed the Resident Councillor that it was 'necessary for the assertion of our superiority and for the vindication of our national honor that this musket should be restored'. He felt convinced that if it were not restored, it would be transmitted to Canton as a trophy, therefore from every point of view it was necessary to deprive the Chinese of such an object of exaltation.[15] A permit to hold a wayang on 28 March was revoked, and the leading Chinese residents of Penang, who had submitted representations on the whole sorry business, were curtly told, through the Resident Councillor, on the instructions of the Governor, that until they produced the musket no consideration would be given to their complaints.

To the Government of India, the Governor made it clear that the riot 'could not be construed into any design of rising against the Government or of seeking the lives of the Europeans' of Penang. The cause was 'the restriction of the licence hitherto accorded to the Chinese in regard to music, processions and festivals whereby the streets and roads of the place have been obstructed and rendered dangerous', possibly aggravated by 'national feelings' excited by recent occurrences at Canton, and probably by those at Sarawak. The intention was 'to intimidate the Local Government into the removal of the restrictions lately imposed on Chinese festivals, processions, etc., and the opposition was directed

[15] SSR(U33), Gov., Lett. to RCs, pp. 27–39: No. 137, 13 Apr. 1857.

solely against the Police, by whom the restrictions were enforced'.[16] Conceding that the action of the police was not fully justified, the Governor nevertheless stood firm on his stipulation that unless the musket was restored he would take no steps to hear the grievances of the Chinese.

But he received no support from the Governor-General. Instead he was informed that His Lordship in Council was of the opinion that even if the musket were not recovered, there ought not to be much delay in listening to the complaints of the 'respectable Chinese'. Furthermore, the Governor's assumption that the Chinese would have acted as they did even if they had not been unlawfully treated and annoyed by the police was unsupported, and did not appear to his Lordship in Council to be probable. In any case, it was the duty of the police to keep within the law. The Governor was accordingly requested to impress this more distinctly upon the local authorities, explaining to them that they must not only carefully avoid the illegal exercise of force (which was always an act of oppression), but that even when acting within the law in opposition to the feelings of a large mass of the population, whether Chinese or others, they should see that no cause of offence should be unnecessarily given, and that whatever must be done should be done 'with temper and consideration'.[17]

In this impasse, the 'respectable Chinese' of Penang approached the Governor-General of India direct. A memorial was drawn up on their behalf by J. R. Logan, the lawyer who had criticized Mr Garling's draft Act of 1843, and was accompanied by a skilful and persuasive letter. Mr Logan stated that he was acting as the legal adviser of the clans and open associations of the Chinese community of Penang, as contrasted with the five secret associations.[18] He assured the Governor-General that his clients were really desirous that the musket should be restored, but could not fairly be saddled with the responsibility of restoring it. They asked for an enquiry to be held into their grievances, and complained that licences for wayangs under the Police Act were being arbitrarily refused. These wayangs, he maintained, were an essential part of the homage paid to the different deities whose shrines were in the temple outside which the wayang was held.[19]

The memorial and Mr Logan's letter, together with covering letters from the Resident Councillor, Penang, and the Governor, were forwarded to India on 23 May 1857.[20] When these were acknowledged, the Resident Councillor was upbraided for the angry tone of his reply to the Chinese petition which was 'unnecessarily and injudiciously offensive', and the Governor was instructed to enquire into the complaints submitted—musket or no musket.

Take advantage of the opportunity offered by Mr Lewis's[21] assurance that the Petitioners really desire to have the musket restored to escape from the difficulty in which you have placed yourself and in accordance with the recommendation of that officer to enquire into their complaints.[22]

[16] SSR(R31), Gov., Lett. to Beng., pp. 85–87, 115–22: Nos 58 & 70, Sing. 21Mar. & 21 Apr. 1857.
[17] SSR(S25), Gov., Lett. fr. Beng., 1857: No. 817, Ft William, 9 June 1857.
[18] Presumably the Ghee Hin, Ho Seng, Hai San, Kien Tek, and Chin Chin.
[19] SSR(R32), Gov., Lett. to Beng., 1857, pp. 107–25: No. 173, Pg, 28 Sept. 1857.
[20] SSR(R31), Gov., Lett. to Beng., 1857, pp. 198–202: No. 96, Sing., 23 May 1857.
[21] W. T. Lewis, RC, Penang. Formerly the writer of a report on the secret societies in Penang, 1843, which was enclosed in Garling's despatch of that year.
[22] SSR(S25), Gov., Lett. fr. Beng., 1857, p. 177: No. 1059, Ft William, 14 July 1857.

Worse was to follow, for a few days later the Governor was required to inform the memorialists, through Mr Logan, 'in reply to his very temperate and proper letter', that the Governor-General in Council was satisfied that his clients were really desirous that the musket should be restored, and had already desired that enquiry should be held into their complaints. His Lordship in Council desired, too, 'that licences under the Police Act for the due celebration of religious festivals by the Chinese may not be arbitrarily refused even while the inquiry is pending, and it may be explained to the Chinese that such is not the intention of the Act'. Furthermore, arrangements were to be made for translating into Chinese Bills and Acts of the Legislative Council affecting the Straits Settlements.[23]

Condemned by European opinion, frustrated by the Chinese, and unsupported by India, the Governor was in an unhappy position. Fortunately for him, the musket was returned about the end of June, before the second letter from India arrived, so that he was able, without loss of prestige, to order an enquiry at once, and, what was more, to insist that he had been right all along, and that the leading Chinese could have produced the musket sooner had they been so minded.

He also had the opportunity of commenting on Logan's letter, a copy of which, together with a copy of the memorial, had been sent to him from India. He pointed out that Logan was a paid advocate, and claimed that he himself (Blundell) had a personal practical knowledge of the Chinese quite equal to that of Mr Logan. He continued:

> Throughout his letter, Mr Logan entirely ignores one remarkable characteristic of the Chinese . . . the well-known existence of secret Societies (Hoeys) among the Chinese whose power and influence among them is unbounded and by whom they are thoroughly organised for resistance to the governing Authority whenever it suits the views and purposes of the leaders of these Societies.

The Governor referred in particular to the thwarting of the administration of justice by these societies by means of intimidation and bribery. As to the claim that he represented the 'open' associations as distinct from these secret societies, the Governor remarked that Logan knew well that every Chinese who had signed the peitition, and every Chinese in the place, was enrolled as a member of one or other of these secret associations.[24]

He disagreed with the statement that wayangs were an essential part of the homage paid to the deities. Wayangs were plays performed by professional actors and were not confined to the precincts or neighbourhood of a temple but were performed indiscriminately wherever a vacant space could be found, without reference to religious ceremonies. At Malacca there were no wayangs, presumably because they unremunerative. At Singapore, with a larger Chinese population than at Penang, wayangs were prohibited after 6 p.m. But at Penang, over a period of many years, wayangs had been allowed to go on all night long, and during that period complaints of the inefficiency of the police had been loud and constant. In a town where the populace was allowed to attend open-air theatres all night no police could possibly be efficient and it was this consideration, together with the incessant din of gongs on these occasions, that had mainly induced him to introduce restrictions.

There is no doubt that in declaring that the wayangs were an essential part of

[23] SSR(S25), Gov., Lett. fr. Beng., 1857, p. 177: No. 1232, Ft William, 31 July 1857.
[24] SSR (R32), Gov., Lett. to Beng., 1857–8, pp. 107–25: Pg., 28 Sept. 1857.

a religious observance Logan had overstated the case. It is a fact that the wayangs are performed by professional troupes quite unconnected with the temples, and that the rites of the temples can proceed without recourse to wayangs. But, as a general rule, performances are sponsored by some organization, frequently a temple or a Clan or District Association, who build the stage and pay the fees of the troupe in order to give a free public performance in honour of the deity or ancestors. And frequently temples and Clan and District Association premises are built with a courtyard in which there is a permanent stage, so that on those festival days which they have traditionally adopted as their own, the organizations concerned can, without further ado, engage a troupe.

It is a fact, too, that the Chinese community, left to themselves on the occasion of a festival, will thoroughly enjoy a constant fusillade of firecrackers of deafening proportions continuing uninterruptedly for several days and nights on end, accompanied by unceasing play upon gongs by the orchestras of the open-air wayangs. Even today, when the firing of crackers at Chinese New Year is reputedly restricted to a few hours, it is possible to see a side street completely covered as with a red carpet by the burst cases of thousands of firecrackers. In the days of the horse-carriage, the indiscriminate tossing about of these crackers on the streets in the town, or, as was sometimes alleged, the purposeful throwing of crackers under the horses as they passed, was undoubtedly a dangerous proceeding. But as the majority of those using horses and carriages were Europeans, the Chinese were not affected by this danger.

Still dealing with the letter, the Governor said:

> From a perusal of Mr Logan's letter, a stranger to the Chinese of Penang would conclude that they were a patient, forbearing race, uncomplaining and obedient to the Laws, who have been ill-used and persecuted by the Police until they were driven to seek protection and redress by engaging his legal services. . . . There would be no difficulty in proving that the sole grievance of the Chinese was at the restrictions placed on their noisy ceremonies and plays and that they were determined to have these restrictions removed.

In that, too, there is no doubt that the Governor was right, and the solution, in the long run, was to find a middle way.

As to the instructions from India that he should have all Bills and Acts translated into Chinese, the Governor had already experienced the difficulty which this involved, both in Singapore and in Penang. During the riots a proclamation was issued in Penang similar to that which had formerly been issued in Singapore. But later on it transpired that the Chinese translation was to the effect that the new Acts had been withdrawn and that the former procedure would be reinstated. This was completely untrue. The English version of the proclamation was therefore sent to the Roman Catholic College at Pulau Tikus where it was translated by one of the professors into Latin, and with the aid of a well-educated Chinese pupil a translation was made from Latin into 'high Mandarin'. When this was ready for placarding,

> the Police Magistrates went round with it, verbally explaining its terms to various Chinese in different parts of the town. As there were doubts whether the high style not being generally understood might again enable the leading men to misinterpret it, some hundreds of copies were printed in *Malay* and circulated over the town and country.[25]

25 *SFP*, 9 Apr. 1857.

For many years this question of interpretation had exercised the minds of the authorities. As early as 1828, Governor Fullerton had tried to recruit interpreters from Macao to assist in the Courts of Judicature, but he was informed that there were two insuperable obstacles, first 'the venal and dishonest character of the Chinese . . . which alone must always form a sufficient obstacle to their employment in the highly responsible character of Interpreters', and, second,

the variety of dialects spoken by the inhabitants of the different provinces who compose the emigrants of the Straits, the greater part of whom are strangers to the dialect of Canton, the natives of which province alone are acquainted in any manner with the English language.[26]

The writers had referred the matter to Dr Morrison, the well-known Chinese linguist, who had agreed with their views, and whose letter they enclosed. He wrote:

The linguists, as they are commonly called, at Canton, do not understand the Fukien dialect . . . so generally necessary in the Straits. As to mere knowledge, I suppose some of the senior students of the Anglo-Chinese College (Malacca) are better qualified than any other natives, but in respect of integrity I feel all natives are much to be doubted in important cases, and require the check of European knowledge.[27]

The problem was no nearer to solution in Governor Blundell's time, and in replying to India on the subject of translations he suggested that the Right Honourable the Governor-General in Council had no idea of the difficulties.

Several efforts have been made to obtain such translations, and my predecessor sent an Act to Hongkong for the purpose, but the result was wholly unintelligible. . . . I am inclined to believe that owing to the peculiarity of the language, the undertaking is not practicable. To translate into hieroglyphic Chinese the technicalities of an English Legal Enactment seems utterly hopeless.[28]

Once again, the Governor was undoubtedly right in maintaining the impossibility of obtaining an accurate translation at that time, but the reason was not the fact that the Chinese language was 'hieroglyphic' but that there were so few people, either Chinese or English, who had a sufficient knowledge of both languages to be capable of producing such a translation. And even if it had been produced, its usefulness would have been very limited, for the vast illiterate mass of the Chinese population in the Straits would certainly not have been able to make head or tail of it.

A Commission of Enquiry into the March riots at Penang was appointed on 2 July 1857, and submitted a report three months later. It was not a very satisfactory document. The Chairman, T. Braddell, then Assistant to the Resident, Penang, and one member, F. S. Brown of Glugor, declined to comment on the evidence produced before them on the ground that they had been precluded from hearing any counter-statements, and consequently could not evaluate the statements made to them. The third member, P. E. Mathieu, did not confine himself to the evidence produced before the Commission but submitted a separate report, in which, the Governor said, he 'assumed to speak in the name of the

[26] SSR(N4), Sing., Resident's Diary, 1828, pp. 572–5: lett. fr. W. H. C. Plowden, Charles Millet, & W. Davis, to R. Fullerton, at the Presidency of Prince of Wales Is., Macao, 12 Aug. 1828.
[27] Ibid. p. 575: encl. fr. Robert Morrison to Pres. and Sel. Ctee (Macao), 14 July 1828.
[28] SSR(R32), Gov., Lett. to Beng., 1857–8, pp. 107–25: No. 173, Pg, 28 Sept. 1857.

general community which he was not entitled to do'.[29] The Resident Councillor, Penang, made the further comment that the 'separate report of Mr Mathieu could be presumed to have been drawn up at the suggestion of the Chinese legal adviser' (doubtless Logan).[30]

Nevertheless, despite certain shortcomings, the Commission made several recommendations which formed the basis of future policy. They advised that authentic lists should be prepared of all the periodic festivals for the information and guidance of the police, and that licences on the occasions of religious festivals, marriages, and burials should be given as a matter of course, the duty of the police being limited to seeing that general regulations for the conduct of processions were not infringed. They also recommended that the prohibition of the firing of crackers should be modified 'to allow of their being used on all necessary occasions' in their worship, but gave no hint of what these occasions might be. To obviate the risk of collision between the police and the Chinese at the temple, they suggested that the ground included in the grant to the temple should be enclosed, and the Chinese should be allowed to erect a permanent stage. Finally, they regretted that the Police and Conservancy Acts were not translated into Chinese, and recommended that a competent European inter- preter and translator should be permanently employed by the local government.[31]

Logan had submitted a valuable memorandum to the Commission, and the Governor instructed that this should be used by the Resident Councillor when deciding,

in concert with a few respectable Chinese . . . the several Associations who shall be entitled to form processions to carry the idols, the Festivals on which the firing of crackers may be allowed, and the extent to which they may be fired. Also in deter- mining the passages in the marriage ceremony at which crackers may be fired.

A final decision was not reached until 1858, and while the discussion continued, a long article dealing with the history of the Chinese at Penang and the legal sanction which had been accorded to their customs appeared in the *Singapore Free Press* of 10 December 1857, which, from its contents and its style, seems very likely to have come from Logan's pen. It maintained

that the public, religious, and social observances of the Chinese in Penang have now the double sanction of law and usage. Neither the local Police nor the Local Govern- ment has lawful authority to suppress any of them. They can only be restricted by the Legislature [i.e. in India] or by the Chinese themselves in deference to the wishes of the Europeans.

The article ended : 'The Chinaman is here by invitation and by right, as much as the private Englishman, or the Frenchman or the American. The European resident has no social privilege denied to the Asiatic.'

In the end, 27 distinct 'religious and friendly societies' and 10 distinct Clan Associations were recognized, and sanction was given to them to hold proces- sions on stated days. At the same time 19 periodic festivals were recognized.[32]

[29] SSR(U34), Gov. to RCs, 1857–8, pp. 55–72: No. 405, Gov. to RC Pg, Penang, 24 Oct. 1857.
[30] SSR(X), Gov's Diary (X14), 1857–8, p. 197: No. 355, RC, Pg, 7 Oct. 1857.
[31] *SFP*, 19 Nov. 1857.
[32] SSR(DD34), Pg, Lett. to Gov., 1861: No. 242, Prince of Wales Is., 24 June 1861, fr. RC (H.Man) to Sec. to Gov., SS. Covering lett. forwarding Police *AR*, 1860–1.

This recognition of particular societies and specific festivals was of the greatest importance to the Chinese of Penang. The same principle was not, it may be noted, applied to the Chinese in the other Settlements. But it did not affect the Hoeys, except in so far as they were connected with the other societies through mutual membership, or, at any particular time, through common aims.

In the Penang disturbances of March 1857 and those in Singapore at the beginning of January 1857, there is no hint of the machinations of particular secret societies, merely the general presumption, as stated by the Governor, that the Chinese community was 'thoroughly organized for resistance to the governing Authority whenever it suits the views and purposes of the leaders of these Societies'.

The fact that the Penang Chinese had won their case against the police and the Governor was evident by August 1857, when the decision of the Governor-General in Council to appoint a Commission of Enquiry became known, and it is likely that the knowledge of this 'victory' tended to heighten the mood of challenging truculence in the hearts of the leaders of the Hoeys, who were, in fact, the prime movers in the campaign of organized resistance. From then onwards a period of increasing turbulence began, caused not by protest movements against the Government but by open warfare between opposing Chinese Hoeys.

6

THE RISING TIDE

1. FURTHER MEASURES PROPOSED, 1857–67

No sooner had the excitement of the riot of March 1857 died down in Penang than a series of affrays began between two Hoeys, the Ghee Hin on the one side and the Kien Tek or Toh Peh Kong on the other. The first recorded collision took place on 15 September, followed by another on 6 October. In neither case was any person prepared to give evidence against the Ghee Hin members who were said to be the assailants, and it was left to several influential Chinese to arbitrate between the two sides.[1] There was no report of deaths on either side, though several persons were wounded, and these clashes were merely a prelude to what was to be a long-drawn-out battle for supremacy between two societies, which in due course was to cause the Government grave concern. Meanwhile the attention of the Governor was occupied in planning an increase in police and military strength.

During 1858 there was considerable discussion between the Governor and the Government of India over the question of strengthening the defences of the Straits Settlements against possible external aggression, and of improving means of withstanding the repeated internal riots brought about by the Chinese secret societies.

The Governor could only repeat that in his opinion a strong, well organized, and intelligent police was the most efficient instrument to deal with the societies, but it was difficult to form such a body. The Commissioner of Police urged the creation of a body of detectives, but the Governor thought this an impossibility. No Chinese would ever join the police force and no one without knowledge of the Chinese language could make a detective. If only funds were available to recruit a first-class police force there would, he thought, be a possibility of persuading responsible Chinese, in time, to rely upon the police and withdraw from the societies.[2] But in the meantime, he preferred the presence of a British regiment 'as a means of fully overawing the Chinese population'. It is interesting to note, however, that in 1865–6 four detectives were appointed at Penang, two Chinese on Penang Island, and two Malays or Indians in the Province. Of the Chinese detectives it was reported that though active in the detection of petty offenders, they had not proved so useful in tracing graver crimes where the guilty parties may have been connected with the secret societies.[3]

In November 1858 the European mercantile community of Singapore petitioned the Governor to introduce legislation to deal with the influence of the

---

[1] SSR(X14), Gov.'s Diary, 1857–8, p. 199: No. 373, note of lett. fr. RC, Pg, 16 Oct. 1857.
[2] SSR(R33), Govt, Lett. to GOI: No. 113, Sing., 4 Sept. 1858.
[3] SS *AR*, 1865–6.

secret societies in 'matters of contracts with skilled labour', but were advised that this was impracticable because of the almost impossible task of proving in court either that a secret society existed or that it had been used detrimentally. In forwarding the memorandum to India on 2 December, Blundell said that if he thought that the societies could be put down or their influence modified by legislation, he would recommend this, but he feared that the effect of such legislation 'would simply be to increase the means of influence possessed by these Societies and to embitter its nature'. This had always been his opinion, but it was solely his own individual opinion. It was evident that a large part of the European community thought otherwise and their opinion was entitled to respect and consideration.[4]

Shortly afterwards the Government of India, in a half-hearted attempt to meet the Governor's problem of devising a means to effect the removal of the headmen of the Hoeys without the use of extra-legal powers, suggested that an Act introduced in India in 1858—Act No. III of 1858—might be of use in dealing with these secret society leaders if it were extended to the Straits Settlements. This Act provided for the removal of 'State prisoners' confined under regulations operative in Bengal, Madras, and Bombay to any other place of confinement within the territories in the possession and under the government of the East India Company. 'State prisoners' were persons arrested and detained by order of the Governor in Council outside the normal operation of the law, and Blundell pointed out that unless the Act or the regulations were amended to include in this category the leaders of the Hoeys, and unless the Governor were given power to arrest and detain them, there would be no point in extending the operation of this law to the Straits.[5]

It was thus that Blundell's régime ended. In February 1859 the conflict between the Kien Tek and the Ghee Hin in Penang flared up again with renewed ferocity, accompanied by 'great violence and outrages of the most ruthless and revengeful nature'. Several fights took place in the town and at Jelutong where there was a strong body of the Kien Tek, and which was the focal point of the disturbances. Many shops in the town were closed for several days, the military were called out, and the members of the European community were enrolled as special constables. A warrant was issued for the arrest of Khoo T'ean Tek, the head of the Kien Tek Society, who was ordered by the magistrate to find sureties in 5,000 rupees to be of good behaviour for the space of two years. The sureties were soon forthcoming, but on 26 February, before the preparation of the bail bond had been completed, a curious incident occurred. From among those present at the court, twelve leading members of the Ghee Hin Society stood forward and offered to enter into similar recognizances, thinking, no doubt, that they would in this way absolve themselves from action by the authorities should there be further disorders. Not to be outdone, a similar number of the Kien Tek leaders made a similar offer, and in the end, twenty-four bonds were drawn up. When they were completed, 'three carriages that were in readiness, each containing two members of each of the two rival societies, started for the scenes of the disturbances, and open hostility ceased at once'.[6]

Although within twenty-four hours fighting was resumed at the two country

[4] SSR(R35), Gov., Lett. to Beng., 1858, pp. 30–32: No. 150, Sing. 2 Dec. 1858.
[5] Ibid. pp. 288–94: No. 78, Sing., 14 May 1859.
[6] Lett. fr. Mgte, PW (at the time also Mgte, Pg), 9 May 1860. Encl. in GD 108, 5 June 1860.

districts of Sungei Dua and Balik Pulau, the pact seems to have served its purpose of bringing hostilities to a close.[7]

In July 1859 the Governor was granted leave by the Government of India to proceed to Calcutta for one month preparatory to resigning from office. His last word on the subject of secret societies appears in his Annual Report for 1858–9, where he said again that there was no easy remedy for the evil of the secret societies and that legislation against them might increase it. Where the courts were open to all classes and lawyers were prepared to plead on any side, it was difficult to devise a remedy. As long as the Chinese were sufficiently rich and spirited to pay for the legal defence of their own Hoeys, 'the more the Legislature arrays itself against them, the more they will be cherished by the Chinese, and the more they will flourish'.

This was not well received by the local press,[8] which accused Blundell of having a mania on the subject of courts and lawyers, both of which he appeared to regard as 'public nuisances'.

The new Governor was Colonel Orfeur Cavenagh, who assumed office on 8 August 1859. Almost at once the problem of the Hoeys was forced upon his attention. In September, at Penang, a quarrel between the Kien Tek and the Ho Seng resulted in a week's rioting, and when Khoo T'ean Tek was again arrested and sent for trial members of the Kien Tek closed their shops in protest and all trade was brought to a standstill. There was a further complicating factor in that secret society activity appeared to be spreading among members of other races, and in acknowledging reports from the Resident Councillor and the police in Penang, the Governor asked for urgent information 'regarding the Secret Societies supposed to exist among the Klings and other Mohamedan residents, more especially as to their being affiliated or otherwise with the Chinese Hoeys'.[9]

As early as 1854 Vaughan had reported an extension of the influence of Chinese secret societies to non-Chinese. Details were given of the initiation of a Malay Haji[10] into the Ho Seng Society, and of Vaughan's own visit to a Malay village, where 'the Penghulu without hesitation admitted that some two or three years earlier all the Mohammedan male inhabitants had joined the Ho Seng, including himself'.[11]

In November 1859 a disturbing state of affairs was discovered at Malacca. Acting on information, the police visited the village of Parit Malana, and in the house of the Penghulu found a large meeting of nearly 100 Malays and Chinese assembled for the purpose of enrolling new members into the Ghee Hin Society. Within the house were seen 'from thirty to forty stands of arms and a quantity of powder, and in the back yard there was a Chinese altar and Joss lighted up, to which both Malays and Chinese indiscriminately made obeisance'. Two other Malay Penghulus from other villages were present, and the meeting was presided over by a Chinese who was described as 'a Malacca Chinese of respectable connections'.

[7] SSR(X16), Gov.'s Diary, 1858–9, pp. 287–90, 18 Mar. 1859: RC, Pg, 28 Feb. 1859, reports an outbreak of the Chinese Hoeys with great violence and outrage.
[8] *SFP*, 2 Aug. 1860.
[9] SSR(U39), Gov., Lett. to RCs, 1859–60: No. 420, 31 Oct. 1859, pp. 141–2.
[10] One who has performed the pilgrimage to Mecca.
[11] *JIA*, viii (1854).

Further investigation showed that the Parit Malana organization had ramifications further north in Malacca territory, in the region of Kendong, where
several Penghulus, with many of their followers, were said to have joined the
Ghee Hin or the Hai San societies, 'among them some known desperate characters'. Three of these Penghulus were known to have attended 'an open air
meeting in a retired spot'. Furthermore, a system of kidnapping Malay youths
of 20 and under was brought to light, whereby they were enticed to Parit Malana
and there, under threats of violence, compelled to join the society.

Three Penghulus from the Parit Malana area and three from the Kendong
area, in addition to the Chinese who presided at the meeting, were tried at the
Quarter Sessions and received sentences varying from three months' imprisonment and a fine of $50, to six months' and a fine of $100. Another Malay and
two Chinese headmen concerned with enticing young Malays to join the society
were sentenced to twelve months' imprisonment with hard labour.

It is recorded that throughout the trials, at which the Resident Councillor,
Captain Macpherson, presided, 'the Court was crowded with Malays who mani-
fested the deepest interest in the proceedings', and that 'the nature of the ceremonies gone through and the engagements entered into by the novices were
minutely detailed and exposed'. Only a summary survives which relates that on
entering the kongsi house the name of the novice was registered; he was stripped
almost naked and, if a Malay, forced to make obeisance to a Joss. He was then
instructed how to reply to questions to be put to him. After passing under
crossed swords or over a kind of bridge, he was made to kill a cock and jump
over a fire; then his finger was pricked and blood squeezed into a bowl containing arrack, from which all drank. He took a solemn oath of general brotherhood
and offensive and defensive alliance. Crime of every kind was to be screened,
the police resisted, and any fines imposed on a member by the Court of Justice
were to be paid from the public fund. 'In fact, it is a combination to set at
defiance the laws of the land, and well may the Malays of better feeling exclaim,
as they repeatedly do, that it is an evil which, if unchecked, will be the ruin of
Malacca.'[12]

Considerably perturbed, Cavenagh issued a proclamation warning the Malays
against being led by the 'false words of designing foreigners' who had no interest in the soil and no ties of attachment in the country, but who, in endeavouring
to persuade the Malays to join their societies, 'were merely seeking their own
advantage'. He further gave warning that the names of the headmen of the Ghee
Hin and Hai San societies were known to the authorities, who were exercising
strict surveillance, and legal penalties would undoubtedly be imposed for any
breach of the law.[13]

The proclamation was read aloud in open court and, according to the Resident Councillor, 'produced a startling effect. All order and propriety was for a
period forgotten in the rush and struggle made to obtain copies of it.' Thereafter
copies were distributed throughout the territory, with the result that a number
of people came forward with information, while about 200 others came forward
'to confess that they were enrolled as members but now desire a release from
their oath of brotherhood'. In his report to the Governor, the Resident Coun-

[12] Lett. fr. RC, Mal., to Gov., No. 153, 5 Dec. 1859, encl. in GD 203, 12 Dec. 1859.
[13] SSR(V21), Gov., Misc. Lett. Out, 1859: GD 191, 28 Nov. 1859. Copy of Procl. encl., Sing.,
24 Nov. 1859.

cillor mentioned that among those tried and punished for joining an unlawful assembly was one police peon, and that he had information that there were several other society members in the force. New Penghulus were elected to take the place of those imprisoned.

Many of the Malacca Malays openly stated that they 'dreaded the Hoeys more than the Law', and had joined for their own protection. In Penang the initiation of members of the Mohammedan Indian and Jawi-Pekan[14] communities into the Chinese Hoeys was confirmed, and faced with this spread of secret society influence the Governor decided to raise the question of legislative control with the Government of India, while he took immediate practical measures in Malacca by strengthening the local police force.[15]

The despatch he forwarded to India was far from convincing, and the enclosed Draft Act had been hastily prepared. In announcing the spread of secret society membership to other races, the Governor was forced to admit that one of the results of such an extension might be a weakening of the secrecy of the Hoeys, and the receipt of anonymous petitions already indicated that this secrecy was perhaps being breached. He found it difficult to believe that any bond could be found sufficiently strong as to 'unite in one brotherhood men of such different customs and ideas as Malays, Klings, and Chinese'. Nevertheless, he considered that legislative action was necessary, and hoped that it might establish a control, so that possibly, like mutual benefit societies in England, these dangerous associations might eventually be converted into instruments for good instead of evil.[16]

This well-intentioned endeavour received no encouragement from India. The Governor was referred to the previous correspondence on the subject, and was informed that the Governor-General in Council saw no reason for departing from the conclusion already reached that legislation would have no effect. Indeed, the fact that anonymous petitions had been received showed that the Government had already begun to benefit by the denationalization of the associations. The Governor was advised to apply himself to strengthening the police and military defences of the Settlement, to the more prompt administration of justice, and to grant himself the larger powers for the restraint of State prisoners which had already been suggested to his predecessor. As to his proclamation in Malacca, the Governor-General in Council doubted whether its issue was a judicious measure, and disapproved of its tone. 'Such language cannot but tend to alienate the Chinese from our Government, and to promote rather than to prevent the formation of secret societies.'[17]

This was not an encouraging beginning, but the Governor held his ground. He pointed out that although it was true that the societies far oftener displayed a feeling of bitter hostility to rival societies than to the Government, nevertheless two of the Straits Settlements had already been for days together the scene of anarchy and violence owing to their outbreaks, while only by calling in the aid of the Malay population had these outbreaks been quelled. Even with the aid thus afforded his predecessor, opposed though he was to severe measures, deemed it expedient to request that he be empowered summarily to deport any

[14] Of mixed Malay–Indian blood.
[15] SSR(R36), Gov. to GOI, 1859–60, pp. 1–4: No. 203, 12 Dec. 1859.
[16] SSR(V21), Gov., Misc. Lett. Out, 1859: No. 191, 28 Nov. 1859.
[17] SSR(S28), Gov., Lett. fr. Beng., 1860, pp. 3 ff.: No. 30, Ft William, 7 Jan. 1860.

member of a Hoey whose removal from the Settlements he might consider desirable.

As to the position of these societies in law, he said: 'The Law in force in the Straits Settlements being the Common Law of England, it requires a greater knowledge of it than I can at present pretend to possess, to discover how far it may be defective with respect to the suppression of secret societies.' He pointed out that a difference of opinion existed between the two Recorders, one holding that the common law was sufficiently comprehensive to enable the authorities to deal with these associations, while the other considered that a special enactment was required. He quoted a case where the police had raided an initiation ceremony and captured all the insignia and a copy of the rules, but the Recorder advised the Commissioner of Police to release those who had been arrested, 'because from ignorance of the language, no officer of the Police Force could swear that the oaths he heard administered in Chinese were unlawful, or the meeting an illegal assembly'. As to the Malacca proclamation, it had not been his intention to denounce the members of the Chinese community at large, but those persons who had been actually inducing the Malays to join the secret societies. He divided the Chinese population of Malacca into three classes, mercantile, agricultural, and mining. The two former chiefly consisted of native-born British subjects living in the town or its immediate vicinity. They were, so far as he could learn,

attached to our rule, and although from fear they may belong to the Hoeys, I have no reason to believe that they take any interest in their proceedings, whilst the most respectable of them . . . have expressed their gratification at the result of the measures taken towards checking their growing influence.

To these groups the terms used in the proclamation were certainly not applicable. The miners on the contrary, were 'a turbulent race'. They were unsettled in their habits, often remaining only a few months and then migrating to an adjoining native state. They worked mostly in the mines at Naning and Kesang, and as the road there went through several miles of dense jungle, it would be difficult to control an outbreak without the aid of the Malay population.

Among the miners, the Hoeys are in full operation, owing, I understand, to the machinations of worthless, idle characters who came down from China principally with the view of making a livelihood by means of their position as office-bearers in these Societies. They have no tie of attachment to the Settlement, can be only looked upon as Foreigners, and were, I have every reason to suppose, mainly instrumental in prevailing upon the Malay Penghooloos to betray their trust. To these men my denunciation most fully applied.[18]

The Governor's remarks about the unsatisfactory nature of the interpretation of the common law in its application to matters concerning societies appear to have made some impression on the Government of India, and Cavenagh was told that

if on mature consideration, and after taking the opinions of the Recorders and principal legal authorities and officers of Police in the Straits Settlements, you are still of opinion that legislation is necessary in respect of such Societies, the President in Council will be

---

[18] SSR(R36), Gov., Lett. to GOI, 1859–60, pp. 99–110: No. 18, 13 Feb. 1860.

prepared to consider the Draft of any law you may submit, with a view to its being laid before the Legislative Council.[19]

Thus primed, the Governor sought the views of the Recorders at Penang and Singapore, and of the Commissioners of Police and the Sitting Magistrates at each of the three Settlements as to the effect of the existing laws and the need for any legislative enactment for the purpose not of suppressing such associations but, by attaching responsibilities to office-bearers and others, depriving them 'of that element of secrecy in their operations which alone render them politically dangerous'.[20]

All but two of the replies advocated legislation of one sort or another, and from the suggestions received, a fresh draft Act was compiled, providing for the registration of all societies 'established for the management of Religious, Charitable or other Funds, or for the mutual benefit of its members'. Registration was to be by annual licence issued by the Commissioner of Police 'upon being satisfied that the Society had not been formed for any illegal purpose'. The names and addresses of office-bearers were to be registered, together with the place of meeting. Notice of meeting was to be given to the police, who were empowered to demand admission. A meeting of over twenty-four persons 'of the proceedings of which a satisfactory account cannot be afforded' was to be deemed to be an illegal assembly. Certain classes of societies might be exempted from the requirement of giving notice of meetings.[21]

The Draft Act was sent to India on 5 June 1860, but no further action was possible because on 16 July the India Office, London, informed the Governor-General that legislation on this subject 'should be deferred until the decision of the question, now under consideration, respecting the transfer of the Home Government of the Straits Settlements from the India to the Colonial office'.[22] This ruling was conveyed to Cavenagh, and for the time being, there the matter lay.

Meanwhile, in all three Settlements secret society disturbances continued. In August 1861 members of the two Hokkien societies, the Chin Chin and the Kien Tek, came to blows in Penang. Both societies had been given passes to hold wayangs at Ayer Hitam on the same day, and both had arranged with the local 'theatre' to hire planks for the erection of the stages. When each side claimed all the planks the battle began, and once the news had flashed from Ayer Hitam to Penang town the adherents of the two societies extended the fight.

Next day the leaders of both societies were warned that any further trouble would lead to refusal of permits for wayangs in future, but there was soon a fresh outburst. This time each side was required to name twelve men to arrange the matter under the chairmanship of an independent arbitrator. A settlement was reached, and one side paid a fine. But this was only a temporary and fragile truce, and shortly afterwards the passing of a Chin Chin funeral procession through a village mainly inhabited by Kien Tek members led to another clash.

---

[19] SSR(S28), Gov., Lett. fr. GOI, 1860, p. 63; No. 652 of 27 Mar. 1860.

[20] SSR(V31), Gov., Misc. Lett. Out, 1860, pp. 69–76: Nos. 180, 181, & 182, all dated 19 Apr. 1860.

[21] SSR(R37), Gov., Lett. to GOI, 1860, pp. 71–85: No. 108, Sing., 5 June 1860.

[22] SSR, Gov., Lett. fr. GOI, 1860: No. 1781, 25 Aug. 1860, encl. No. 80 (Judicial), London 16 July 1860.

By 25 August tension had increased to such an extent that fifty houses usually occupied by Chin Chin men had been deserted and the tenants had congregated at the Chin Chin Kongsi awaiting an attack.

The Resident Councillor, Captain Henry Man, sent for the headmen of both sides and had them sworn in as special constables. They were told that their services would be required as long as there appeared any danger of tumult. Divided into watches, equal numbers of each society were told off to accompany police parties under Inspectors who had orders in case of a riot to see that they occupied the front rank. The Resident noted that 'the new Specials found something ludicrous as well as disagreeable in their new office', and although they turned out in the middle of the night for a patrol, they were distinctly unpleasant, but this was 'preferable to parading the streets in mid-day, truncheon in hand, side by side with Peons'.[23]

There were no further disturbances, and before the end of a week the Resident was petitioned to intervene to end the dispute, as their own arbitrators had failed to reach agreement. A settlement was eventually reached, and each side bound itself to keep the peace, under penalty of $1,000. The document was signed by three leaders of each side, and deposited for safe custody with the Resident.

In commenting on this outbreak, the Resident drew attention to the readiness of the Hoeys to engage in affrays for the most insignificant causes, and to the power of the leaders to allay or foment the irritation. He felt that under existing circumstances the peace of Penang Island depended not so much on the efficiency of its constabulary as on the fiat of the Hoey leaders and their personal disposition and social standing.

Once again we have an example of the difference between the traditional Chinese and the British views of the place which the law should hold in the body politic. In their petition to the Resident, the contending parties agreed to a truce of six months on certain conditions. Such a state of affairs the Resident regarded as manifestly incompatible with the maintenance of good order and regular government, and at a meeting with the society leaders he pointed out that it was necessary to distinguish between complaints which mutual friends

---

[23] 'This power of requiring the known heads of the Societies to act as Special Constables and thus to bring the weight of their influence on the rioters proved to be a most useful agency in preserving the peace.' So wrote a later Governor, Sir Harry Ord, in 1868.

According to Captain Man, the idea was suggested by the Recorder, Sir Benson Maxwell, who recommended it to the magistrates when the alarming riots occurred in 1858, (possibly an incorrect dating for the riots of 1859 in Penang). In a letter to the Governor (Cavenagh), written in April 1860, Maxwell proposed that a law should be passed 'inflicting a short term of imprisonment for refusing to serve or disobeying orders during service, authorising the apprehension of persons neglecting to obey a Summons to serve, and perhaps also making continued absence from home after Summons in times of general disturbance presumptive evidence of being connected with the disturbances'.

Although such a law was not brought into force, and although the process was not sanctioned by law until 1867, it continued to be used not only in Penang but throughout the Settlements. In his Annual Report of 1861–2, Cavenagh referred to its success, and hoped that the swearing in of the acknowledged heads of the secret societies as special constables and attaching them to police stations, 'so as to induce them to take a warm personal interest in the preservation of peace might eventually result in the unseemly displays of resistance to the Law on the part of the Chinese being permanently suppressed'. (GD to S. of S., CO: No. 186, 11 Sept. 1868; SSR(DD34), Pg, Lett. to Gov., 1861: No. 374, Pg, 20 Sept. 1861, RC, Pg (Man), to Gov. (Cavenagh); Pg *AR*, 1861–2, p. 3, para. 6.)

are competent to settle, and what must be left to the courts of law. In his opinion, one of the most mischievous actions of the Hoeys was the manner in which the leaders constantly endeavoured to induce complainants to prefer their charges, including felonies, before the kongsi in place of the magistrates, and cases were known in which parties had been severely beaten for complaining to the magistrate.

He found that one of the surest symptoms of an impending crisis was the disappearance of the faction leaders from their usual haunts to some spot where, unobserved, they could direct the movements of their adherents through the medium of secret agents. This plan was checkmated when the most influential men of the Hoeys were appointed as special constables, and were made to serve so long as a fair reason existed for their being called into action. The chief factionists were thus made into active instruments in quelling affrays, and were assured of a fair chance of personal participation in a fight, 'a contingency of the greatest practical value in preventing its occurrence'.

Captain Man had previously served in both Malacca and Singapore, and found the societies in Penang more active than in the other Settlements. He noted that at Penang the societies had received a certain amount of official recognition which they had obtained nowhere else, and considered that 'this was in some measure brought about by the promulgation of new Police Regulations in 1857, which were rather injudiciously enforced, and a skilful use being made of the circumstance by their legal adviser, concessions were obtained unknown at the other Residencies'. Although not suggesting a sudden withdrawal of these privileges, he 'earnestly advocated their curtailment and the adoption of an uniform system throughout the three Settlements'. Finally, he wrote:

It is difficult for anyone at a distance rightly to appreciate a Hooey row. In its earlier stages it is chiefly signalized by a series of wanton assaults, each trying to outdo the other in increased brutality, but when once blood has been shed, nothing can exceed the reckless barbarity of their attacks. Without the slightest personal animosity but with a ferocity amounting to frenzy and simply at the call of their chiefs they will fall on an unoffending cooly and hack him to pieces. . . . These Societies are also serious obstacles to the Police in apprehending Offenders as the leaders are bound to give their men every assistance when flying from justice, this naturally ensures the hearty support of the dangerous classes.[24]

Although the swearing-in of secret society headmen as special constables continued to be an accepted routine on the outbreak of quarrels, it did not suffice to prevent the occurrence of riots, and the atmosphere of feud and intrigue between the Hoeys in Penang was intensified by open warfare in 1861 and 1865 between groups of Chinese miners on the mainland at Larut in Perak. This was a struggle for control of the mines waged between members of the Hai San and Ghee Hin societies, and it was feared that unrest between these two Hoeys might break out in Penang too. This was averted, but the Kien Tek made use of the climate of uncertainty to assert its power.

In December 1861 riots once more broke out between the Kien Tek and the Chin Chin, later embroiling the Ghee Hin also, and in May 1862 the headmen were sworn in once again as special constables because of the threatening

[24] SSR(DD34), Pg, Lett. to Gov., 1861: No. 374, 20 Sept. 1861.

situation in which the Kien Tek was arrayed against the Ghee Hin and the Ho Seng. There was further trouble in 1863, 1864, and 1865, and on most of these occasions the Kien Tek was involved either against the Ghee Hin or the Ho Seng or the Chin Chin. Matters reached a climax in February 1865 when a quarrel between the Kien Tek and the Ghee Hin led to extensive rioting which when checked in the town spread to the country districts. Jelutong, a Kien Tek stronghold, was burnt down and during the five days of the disturbance, twenty lives were lost. It was only with the help of the military and the Malay peasantry that the rioters were subdued, even though the headmen had been sworn in as usual.[25]

Resumed fighting in Larut in June 1865 affected the sensitive situation in Penang, and in October groups of Ghee Hins and Ho Sengs attacked one another as a result of a petty quarrel in a town brothel. The Ho Sengs were reinforced on 10 November by men of the Ho Hop Seah, a society of disreputable character formed a few years earlier, and described in 1865 as 'the smallest of the societies', its members mainly men from Sin Neng, being drawn from the 'lowest order of the Chinese' who had been collected from time to time from the other principal Hoeys, including the Ghee Hin.

Fortunately, both the Ho Seng and the Ho Hop Seah were concentrated in four streets of the town, and by placing strong groups of police in these areas the riot was prevented from spreading to the country. Once again the headmen were sworn in, and when the police steadfastly refused to be drawn away from their posts by rumours of trouble elsewhere the contestants, frustrated by inactivity, signed a treaty of peace.[26] The Ho Hop Seah, however, continued to give trouble, and in June 1866 twenty-six men were stabbed in George Town as a result of its fights with a rival society, the Choon Ghee (Chung Yi).

One outcome of the riots of February 1865 was the formulation by the Resident Councillor, Penang—Colonel Man—of proposals for legislation which differed from those which had previously been made by suggesting a new system of control through headmen, the 'headmen of the tribes'. He emphasized the importance of securing the services of these headmen as soon as possible. In this way, he maintained, 'the Civil officer can feel assured that, though peace may not immediately be restored, yet he has the means in his grasp of preventing the extension of disorder, and of ultimately putting a period to it altogether'.[27]

He pointed out that it was unfortunate that 'under our present system, a certain amount of violence and riot must have been committed before a Magistrate will consider himself justified in compelling persons as Specials', and during this period, retaliation grew and spread until possibly 20,000 people might be involved, in regularly organized factions with which the small regular police force had to attempt to deal. He proposed that this disability should be avoided by a system under which the town and country would be divided into districts, within which all householders would be registered as constables, of

[25] SSR(U50), Gov., Lett. to RCs, 1865: No. 58, 23 Feb. 1865; also SS *AR*, 1864–5. SSR(R44), Gov., Lett. to GOI (Judicial), 1862–7: No. 7, 23 Feb. 1865.

[26] SSR(DD42), Pg, Lett. to Gov., 1865: No. 484, 14 Dec. 1865. Encl. No. 78, 7 Dec. 1865, fr. Dy Commr of Police to RC, Prince of Wales Is.

[27] Sec. to Govt SS to Sec. to GOI, lett. No. 7, 23 Feb. 1865. Encl. No. 58, Minute of 17 Feb. 1865.

whom a certain proportion would be held available each year 'in the event of an outbreak occurring among the Kongsees'. In each district a Head Constable would be appointed who would receive the orders of the chief civil authority on such occasions, and arrange to warn and assemble his men. Failure to respond would be punishable 'by heavy fines and penalties'.

The effect of this proceeding [he suggested] would be to compel assistance in aid of the Police, of men who would either be actually engaged in fomenting disturbance and aiding the rioters, or, from the fact that their society was not concerned, sitting at home quietly indifferent, though murder and robbery were being openly committed by and upon their immediate neighbours.

He further suggested that sufferers from riots should be compensated not by making levies upon the societies involved, which would not only involve public recognition of these undesirable bodies but would also lead to great abuses, but by making the whole population of a district in which damage had been done responsible for reparations, in the same way as the English Acts provided 'compensation by the Hundred for malicious injury to property'. He also advocated that the police should have powers of summary arrest of 'armed bands patrolling districts with party flags and streamers'.

The press had its own suggestions for dealing with the situation. In a leading article which praised the efforts of Khoo T'ean Tek, the headman of the Kien Tek, 'perhaps the greatest sufferer from the riots', and Lee Ko Yin, the headman of the Ghee Hin, for their valiant attempts to help Colonel Man by restraining members of their Hoeys, the *Singapore Free Press* (9 March 1865) believed that if an Act were passed recognizing the existence of the Hoeys, and if the officers of Government did their best to direct the energies of members into proper channels they might become useful. With a little persuasion they might for instance be induced to erect almshouses. There was 'an important germ of good in the Hoeys'. If a Registry Act were passed, an influential man should be appointed Registrar of Friendly Societies, 'a sort of protector of Chinese, and he would, if possessing any tact, do an immense amount of good; and the Hoeys in a few years would be, instead of elements of discord, a source of strength and support for the Government'. This is the first suggestion in local documents of the appointment of an official 'protector of Chinese', foreshadowing the action taken by the Government twelve years later.

The Governor's former approach to India in 1860 had been rejected not on its merits but because of impending changes in administrative control. As almost five years had elapsed without the introduction of such changes, he decided to renew his request for legislation. Without enlarging on the topic of the more efficient supervision of secret societies, he merely reiterated that what was required was not suppression but control, so as to mould the societies into instruments of good instead of evil. He thought that this could be achieved by requiring their registration and by clearly defining the meaning of an illegal assembly. He added:

So long as the present uncertainty is allowed to exist as to the actual state of the law with regards to the proof required to convict members of illegal assemblies, all attempt on the part of the Police to control the Chinese societies must prove ineffectual, and the Stations in the Straits Settlements continue to be disgraced by being made constant scenes of bloodshed and violence by armed men, who, although they rarely if ever

openly oppose the constituted authorities, yet, by means of their numbers and organization are enabled, as in the present instance, to set them at defiance for days together
with almost perfect impunity.[28]

Despite this, he did not wish to incur the expenditure which would be involved
by a general registration, as proposed by Colonel Man, and suggested that the
draft regulations already submitted in June 1860, which could be introduced
whenever required, were suited to the conditions prevailing.

The Governor-General in Council sent in reply a review of the whole question. There had been three proposed methods of dealing with the Hoeys:
(1) dealing with them direct; (2) providing additional means of overawing them;
(3) attempting to undermine their influence by improving legal means of protection from crime and of obtaining justice. None of the plans proposed under (1)
could be carried out without legislation, and he doubted whether the time was
opportune when it was still undecided whether the Straits Settlements was to
remain a dependency of the Government of India; but if the Governor believed
that legislation was expedient, he should submit a draft law. Proposals under (2)
had in part been met by various arrangements sanctioned by Government from
time to time. The formation of a Volunteer Rifle Corps and the erection of
fortifications at Singapore, together an increase of the military force in the
Straits generally, had added to the strength of the local governments. The plan
of enlisting heads of Chinese societies as special constables had also proved
useful. It was possible that more could be done under (3). At one time it was
understood that Klings and Malays were joining the secret societies because
they believed them to be more effective in protecting life and property than the
Government, and it was probably in this direction that the influence of the
societies might be most easily and effectively met. The Governor was therefore
asked if he had any suggestions to make for improving the efficiency of the
courts or the character and powers of the police.[29]

Cavenagh felt compelled to adhere to his opinion that so long as the Singapore
Government was precluded from exercising control over the meetings of the
societies owing to the uncertainty of the law on the subject of what constituted
an illegal assembly, no additions to the strength either of the military or the
police force would prove of any avail in checking their pernicious influence.
He also referred to doubts about the transfer of the Settlement to the charge
of the Colonial Office and therefore proposed to submit drafts of two Bills, one
for regulating the meetings of societies, and the other for securing the general
preservation of the peace, 'without in any way infringing on the rational measure
of liberty which it must ever be the desire of the British Government to bestow
on all its subjects.'[30]

Let the Chinese clearly understand that whilst there is not the slightest objection to
their assembling for any lawful purpose, any Meeting, of which due notice may NOT
have been given to the Police, will be *ipso facto* illegal, and that no quibble of English
law will serve to relieve those present from the prescribed penalties and the leaders of
the Societies will rapidly lose their power, whilst the Societies themselves, in many
instances, may possibly become concerted into mere friendly brotherhoods susceptible

[28] SSR(R44), Gov., Lett. to GOI (Judicial) 1862–7, pp. 202–5: No. 7, 23 Feb. 1865.
[29] SSR(S33), Gov., Lett. fr. GOI, 1865, p. 162: No. 190, Simla, 17 July 1865.
[30] SSR(R44), Gov., Lett. to GOI (Judicial), 1862–7: No. 23, Pg, 12 Aug. 1865.

of being rendered, by the diffusion of their funds for charitable purposes, the instruments of incalculable benefit to the poorer classes of their fellow countrymen.

In due course, in October 1865, two draft Bills, one 'for the better regulation of Societies and the prevention of Illegal Assemblies' and the other 'for the better prevention of Riots and Unlawful Confederacies' were forwarded to India,[31] and the recent discovery of the 'combination among the natives of India living in Singapore for overriding legal authority' was urged as an added reason for early legislative action.

Towards the end of the year Colonel Man, in submitting an account of further serious secret society outbreaks in Penang and Province Wellesley, again pressed for legislative action, the more so, he said, because the 'evil example of the Chinese' had been followed by the Indians and was being taken up by the Malays, some of the worst of whom were already affiliated to the Chinese societies.

He was particularly anxious about a Malay society in Province Wellesley formed by one Syed Hussein from Kedah. This man by threats and promises had enlisted several hundred followers, terrorized the villages, and brought armed supporters from Kedah. When a warrant was issued for his arrest he took refuge over the border. It was feared that evidence against him would be very difficult to obtain because of the terror he inspired.

In an attempt to exert pressure on the Hoeys of Penang, Colonel Man called a meeting of a number of Chinese headmen in December 1865 and informed them that he had instructed the police that for a period of nine months no permits for processions, except simple marriage processions, were to be issued, and that this pressure would continue until they brought their moral influence to bear on their countrymen in support of order. The headmen professed themselves to be heartily sick of the Hoeys, and offered to petition the Government for their suppression, an offer which was accepted with alacrity, but the petition never arrived. After their interview, the headmen consulted their advocate, Logan, to enquire how best to extricate themselves from this dilemma. One of them later informed the Resident that Mr Logan did not hold out much hope that the Government would be able to help by suppressing the Hoeys, because their professed objects were, in the main, highly praiseworthy.

The headmen apparently agreed with the Resident that the punishment awarded to rioters by the courts was utterly inadequate. 'Indeed,' wrote Colonel Man, 'what possible deterring effect can a month's simple imprisonment have on a riotous coolie; it merely transfers him to the best house on the Island, where, while playing the martyr for his tribe, he has nothing to do but eat, drink, and sleep.'

A much simpler and more effective plan was proposed by the headmen who suggested that

men convicted of riot should be taken to the scene of the disturbance with a gong beaten before them, that the nature of the offence and the sentence awarded them should there be read out, and the culprit should then receive six stripes and be marched off to another locality where the same ceremony should be repeated, and so on until the whole punishment has been inflicted.

---

[31] Ibid. p. 254: No. 34, Sing., 23 Oct. 1865. Unfortunately it has not been possible to trace the text of these two Bills either in Singapore or in the records of the IOL.

The Resident had no doubt that this suggestion of the Chinese headmen would be far more likely to check outbreaks than the verdicts of the courts.[32]

Malacca

Malacca was reasonably free from secret society activities for a few years after 1859. The strengthening of the police force, and the holding of fortnightly courts in country districts seem to have restored Malay confidence. As for the Chinese, apart from a fight in 1863 at a funeral procession when members of the Hai San fought the Hok Beng and Hok Kin societies and which was quickly suppressed by the police, no record is to be found of society activities.

Singapore

In Singapore the Acting Commissioner of Police (C. B. Plunket) was one of those who, in 1860, had advised the Governor that legislation of the type proposed for the control of the Hoeys would have no practical value and might antagonize the Chinese population, and in submitting his memorandum he enclosed a list of the secret societies in existence in Singapore at the time. This shows fourteen societies in all, with a 'supposed strength' of 39,000 members.[33] The largest was the Hokkien Ghee Hin, believed to have 15,000 members, after which came the Hai San with 6,000; but the fact that these figures relate to 'supposed strength' is an indication of lack of reliability. In the light of statistics obtained when registration was later introduced, it would seem that Plunket's estimates were exaggerated.

But although there were fewer riots than at Penang, there was no lack of fights between members of rival societies. One particularly truculent society which made its first appearance in official records in Plunket's list with a 'supposed strength' of 800 was the Ghee Hok. It has been suggested above that this society may have been formed in 1854, and from now onwards it is constantly embroiled.

In 1861 it was concerned in the stabbing of a Christian Chinese who was seriously wounded. The culprit was finally arrested, and sentenced to fifteen years' transportation, and the Recorder, Sir R. B. McCausland, warned the inhabitants of Serangoon, where the crime had been committed, that such offenders would always meet with severe punishment.[34] In 1862–3 one of the reputed heads of the Ghee Hok was stabbed when within 100 yards of the central police station. The assailants were arrested, and one was sentenced to ten years' transportation, the remaining two to two years' imprisonment. Throughout the year, the heads of secret societies were sworn in as special constables, as at Penang, but even so there were no fewer than 230 cases of assault, mainly attributed to the disturbances between the members of the different Chinese Hoeys.[35]

The Ghee Hok was again prominent in 1863, when throughout the year secret society fights of growing ferocity took place between the Ghee Hin, the Ghee Hok, and the Hok Hin, the last-named being another newcomer to the scene. Contributory factors to these fights were the importation of women from China for prostitution, and the prevalence of gambling dens organized by the

[32] SSR(DD42), Pg, Lett. to Gov., 1865; No. 484, 14 Dec. 1865.
[33] See App. 3, p. 538 below.
[34] Sing. *AR*, 1861–2, p. 5, para 22.   [35] Ibid. 1862–3, pt 3, p. 3, para 2.

societies. The Ghee Hin was responsible for a particularly brutal attack on two men who were on their way to give evidence before the magistrate in a case in which the Ghee Hin was involved; one witness was murdered and the other severely wounded. The assailants escaped by leaving the island. In October 1863 a member of the Ghee Hin was murdered by several members belonging to the Hok Hin, and though four men were later apprehended, none were convicted owing to inconclusive evidence.[36]

Matters in Singapore were further complicated by the growing prominence of rival Indian elements of the underworld, organized in Red and White Flag societies. In 1861–2 there was a series of petty disturbances between two Indian factions, the one being composed of boatmen or Red Flag men, and the other of all the bad characters and prostitutes of Kampong Glam under the leadership of a time-expired convict.[37] The Governor in his Annual Report perhaps over-optimistically reported that the 'pretensions of the Kling societies had experienced a severe check' and their fraternities were consequently rapidly falling into disrepute and insignificance.[38]

In 1863–4 it was found necessary to discharge some of the members of the police force (presumably Indians) who were known to belong to secret societies,[39] and disturbances during the Moharram festival in 1864 led Cavenagh to decide that in future all processions in connexion with these celebrations should be prohibited.[40] In February 1865 the Red and White Flag societies were again at one another's throats, and in October of that year, the existence among the 'natives of India' residing in Singapore of a regular combination for overriding legal authority was proved in the courts, and six men were sentenced to two years' imprisonment each. Among them were two men of respectable standing in the community. They were proved to be members of a society which hired ruffians to assault their enemies. Exemption from punishment for the attackers was 'secured by disbursements from the funds of the society either in the way of payment of the fines inflicted for assault or that of bribery of the members of the police force whose duty it may have been to maintain the peace'.[41]

At the end of the year the Governor, when forwarding to India an account of the later secret society outbreaks in 1865, felt constrained to remark that

the evil effects of these societies, and the necessity for legislation to enable the local authorities to bring them under suitable control and neutralize their baneful influence has been so often urged upon the Supreme Government that he believes any further expression of his opinion upon that point to be unnecessary.

As to the Malay trouble in Province Wellesley, he reported that he had suspended the stipend of the Raja of Kedah until such time as Syed Hussein might be surrendered and a proper apology offered for the insult to British sovereignty. This action was approved by the Governor-General in Council, but no mention was made of the question of society legislation.[42]

In June 1866 a petition 'from a large number of respectable Chinese residents in Penang praying that suitable measures might be adopted in order to check the

[36] Ibid. 1863–4, pt 3, para. 23.   [37] Ibid. 1861–2, p. 5, para. 22.
[38] Ibid. p. 3, para. 7.   [39] Ibid. 1863–4, pt 3, p. 2, para. 1.
[40] SSR(U50), Gov. to RCs, 1864: No. 212, 25 June 1864, Sing.
[41] SSR(R44), Gov., Lett. to GOI (Judicial), 1862–7, p. 254: No. 34, 23 Oct. 1865.
[42] SSR(R41), Gov., Lett. to GOI, pp. 335–6: No. 31, 22 Dec. 1865. Reply from India at SSR(S35), Gov., Lett. fr. GOI: No. 99, 3 Feb. 1866.
I

pernicious influence exercised by the different Secret Societies' was received. Presumably this was the result of the consultation between the Penang headmen and Logan. This, too, was forwarded to India, and in the covering despatch the Governor expressed his agreement with Colonel Man 'in thinking that the infliction of corporal punishment upon persons concerned in street riots would have a beneficial effect'. He also considered that it was advisable

that persons appointed to act as special constables under the provisions of the Police Act, and declining to serve or neglecting to carry out any orders they receive, should be liable to summary punishment, either of fine or imprisonment by a Police Magistrate instead of, as at present, being indicted for the misdemeanour before a Court of Quarter Sessions.[43]

But, once again, as in 1860, no action was taken by the Government of India, for negotiations for the handing over of the Straits Settlements to the Colonial Office were now reaching their final stages. All that Cavenagh could do in a final review of his seven years' stewardship was to place at the head of a list of subjects upon which legislation was urgently required the better regulation of societies and the prevention of illegal assemblies, and the better prevention of riots and unlawful confederacies. He left on record his view that:

So long as the Local Government may remain unarmed with the necessary legal powers, not to suppress, but to exercise a salutary control over the Chinese Societies, so long will the Straits Settlements continue to be disgraced by their faction fights. No amount of vigilance or firmness on the part of the Police will check the evil.[44]

2. THE TINFIELDS OF THE MALAY STATES

From the middle of the nineteenth century the three main tinfields worked by Chinese labour in the Malay States were situated in the upper reaches of three rivers: the Linggi (Negri Sembilan), the Klang (Selangor), and the Larut (North Perak). The Linggi and the Klang fields used Malacca as their entrepot, while Penang was the base for Larut. Disturbances in these areas became a source of anxiety to the Government of the Straits Settlements because of financial repercussions and the threat to peace within the Colony caused by rival secret societies whose members at the mines were repeatedly in open conflict.

Linggi

Mention has already been made of fighting between Chinese miners and Malays at Lukut and Sungei Ujong during the period 1828–34. In 1844, in 1846, and again in 1848 the Chinese mining financiers of Malacca complained of injury to their trade caused by exactions levied by Malay chiefs at various points along the Linggi river, and in the last of these years the mines were destroyed during a war between local Malays and a group of Rawas (Sumatrans) who had settled in the area. After resumption of work there were again complaints, and in 1853 the Resident Councillor, Malacca (E. A. Blundell) intervened to try to reach a settlement, but though the principal chiefs, the Dato' Klana of Sungei Ujong and the Raja of Rembau, were amenable the main culprit, Lebai Kulup, was not, and the others had no means of bringing him to

[43] SSR(R44), Gov., Lett. to GOI (Judicial), 1862–7, pp. 277–8: No. 12, 22 June 1866.
[44] SS *AR*, 1864–5.

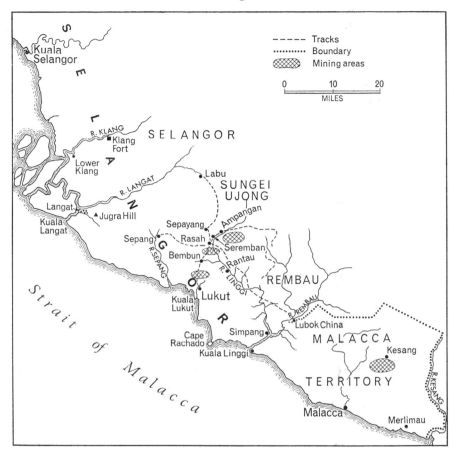

2. The Linggi river, 1875

heel. An inspection of the river by the Resident Commissioner, Malacca (W. T. Lewis) in 1855 revealed that Kulup was strongly established at Simpang where the river was joined by the Rembau tributary at the Malacca border, and that there were four more stockades upstream erected by interlopers who demanded tolls. The principal chiefs once more declared that they were powerless to interfere.[45] When Malacca was in Dutch hands, they said, they had looked to the Dutch for assistance, and now they looked to the British to resolve their difficulties by destroying the stockades and clearing the river.

The Government of India, to whom the matter was referred, sanctioned the use of a naval force from Singapore to clear the stockades of interlopers provided the chiefs would co-operate,[46] and at the end of 1857 HMS *Amethyst* destroyed a stockade and village on the Linggi river, and in May 1858 similar action was taken to clear the Rembau river.

But in August 1860 there was trouble at Sungei Ujong itself, where the major

[45] PP C.1320.   [46] SSR(S22), p. 205: No. 3914, 2 Nov. 1855.

chiefs (Klana and Rembau) tried to impose a levy of $4,000 on the Chinese community which numbered 14,000. When this was resisted they prohibited the import of rice and provisions up the river, which led to an attack on the Malays by the Chinese. In the end the miners were overborne and 200 were killed, many perished in the jungle, and others found their way to Malacca or Lukut.[47] To restore order in the area, and particularly along the river routes, the Governor (Cavenagh) proposed to erect a police station at Simpang, to station a British officer on the river at Linggi, and to send a gunboat up the river on occasional visits,[48] but while negotiations were in hand for the transfer to the Government of the site for the police station, he received instructions from India (in May 1861) that proposed expenditure should be postponed in view of the expected transfer of the Straits Settlements to the administration of the Colonial Office.[49]

The Governor had made it plain that with the exception of Raja Juma'at of Lukut, who was a progressive and helpful ruler, he thought little of the Malay chiefs, whose authority was so divided that it was impossible to get anything done. He found it 'very difficult to attempt to improve the governance of these states so that they should not continuously threaten the peace of the area without, at the same time, exercising undue influence'.[50]

Selangor

In Selangor there were two Chinese communities, each with its own supporting Triad society.

The Chinese mining camp at Lukut which started sometime before 1824 had, by the 1840s, developed greatly and was a valuable source of revenue to Raja Juma'at, who welcomed Chinese mining labour. This encouraged other Malay chiefs to prospect for tin in their own areas, and Sultan Muhammad and his son Raja Suleiman, both backed by Malacca merchants, tried their hands in the Klang river valley without success. But about 1844-5 Raja Abdul Samad (who was both nephew and son-in-law of the Sultan) pushed upstream to the watershed between the Klang and the Selangor rivers where he found a small settlement of Chinese miners, and before long several mines were opened. This was at Kanching, twelve miles north of what is now Kuala Lumpur, and the Chinese camp there was composed of Hakkas from the Ka Yin Chiu prefecture of Kwangtung Province. They had their Capitan and their secret society, the Ts'ung Paak (Pine and Cypress), which was the Hakka branch of the Singapore Ghee Hin. By the 1850s this was a flourishing community exporting its tin down the Selangor river to Kuala Selangor.

In 1857 another son-in-law of the Sultan, Raja Abdullah, with the help of his brother, Raja Juma'at, took Chinese miners from Lukut to the Klang valley to prospect, and despite the loss of 69 out of 87 men in the first month through fever and tigers, a camp was established at Ampang, and two years later export of tin from this field began.

Meantime, in 1857, Sultan Muhammad died, but it was not until 1859 that his successor, Abdul Samad (of Kanching) was elected. This was not a popular

[47] SSR(R38), Gov., Lett. to GOI, 1860, pp. 7–19: No. 195, 6 Oct. 1860.
[48] Ibid. pp. 38–44: No. 201, 13 Oct. 1860.
[49] IO Records, Range 204, vol. 49, p. 91: Memo. 1314, 22 July 1861.
[50] As n. 47 above.

choice and the new Sultan lived quietly at Langat at the mouth of the river of that name to the south of the Klang river, interested only in the prompt payment of his share of the State revenues and in his opium pipe, leaving the quarrelling chiefs throughout the State to their own devices.

Once the Ampang tinfield became established there was a rapid influx of Chinese labour, mostly Hakkas from the Fui Chiu (Waichow) prefecture of Kwangtung Province. They developed a trading centre, now known as Kuala Lumpur, on the bank of the Klang river, and in growth and importance it soon outstripped Kanching, and as a result, the Fui Chiu Capitan at Kuala Lumpur had greater power and prestige than his rival at the older settlement. For they were rivals. It is a mistake to suggest that because both were Hakkas they would normally be friends.[51] The Ka Yin Chius of Kanching and the Fui Chius of Ampang and Kuala Lumpur had their separate loyalties based on territorial origin in China and on immediate economic interests. This division was accentuated by their secret society allegiances, for whereas the Kanching group belonged to the Ghee Hin, the Ampang–Kuala Lumpur group belonged to the Hai San. It was fortunate that the channels of communication with the coast lay down separate rivers, otherwise there might well have been conflict in these early years. This was to be a later development.

The wealthiest man at Kanching, a friend of Sultan Abdul Samad and the holder of the gambling and cock-fighting farms, quarrelled with other leaders, probably over his non-election as Capitan. He sold out all his interests and went with his men to live at Ulu Langat where the Sultan had given him extensive mining rights. Thus a new Ka Yin Chiu settlement was started with outlet down the Langat river.

But at Kanching, the man who bought the interests thus disposed of was not a Ka Yin Chiu but a Fui Chiu named Yap Ah Sze, who had been one of the founders of Kuala Lumpur and was in partnership with the Capitan of the Fui Chius, one Hiu Siu. He was said to be the wealthiest trader in the state and was a leading figure in the Hai San Society. His purchase of the Kanching interests brought a new problem of balance of power in that village.

At Kuala Lumpur the Hai San Society had been strengthened by an influx of refugees from the Sungei Ujong massacre of 1860, including one Liu Ngim Kong, a fighter-leader. But by 1862 a branch of the Ghee Hin of Malacca was trying to extend its influence to the Klang valley and established a branch there and a kongsi-house at Ampang. Among the founders was Ungku Kit, the Malay ADC to the Sultan, doubtless brought in to give some appearance of official sanction to offset the power already held by the Hai San.[52]

About 1864 Hiu Siu died and Yap Ah Sze refused to accept the appointment of Capitan, which was then given to Liu Ngim Kong.[53] One of his first actions was to present a petition to the Sultan giving warning that the existence of two societies in the area—the Hai San and the Ghee Hin—would only lead to fighting, and asking for prohibition of the Ghee Hin. As a result, the kongsi-house was closed down. In the next year he invited the Capitan of Sungei

[51] The suggestion is made on p. 27 of S. M. Middlebrook and J. M. Gullick, 'Yap Ah Loy', *JMBRAS*, xxiv/2 (July 1951).
[52] Report by Chong Bun Sui, 1884, quoted by Wynne, pp. 411–12.
[53] Sources are confused as to date of death, but 1864 fits best with other dates that can be verified. Middlebrook (p. 20) seems to accept 1862.

Ujong, Yap Ah Loy, a Fui Chiu and a leader of the Hai San, to join him in Selangor to look after his mines which he did, and was eventually to succeed his master as the Capitan at Kuala Lumpur.

Just as, in 1860, fugitive Fui Chius from Sungei Ujong found refuge with their kinsmen in Selangor, so too in 1861 and 1865, when Fui Chiu miners were driven out of north Perak, some of these fugitives also made their way to the Klang valley and were helped in this by boats sent by their kinsmen to bring them. And here an anomaly arises, for the Fui Chius of north Perak had there been under the protection of the Ghee Hin Society. It may be that these refugees were responsible for the extension of the Ghee Hin to the Klang valley, but it is also possible that on reaching Selangor, where the Hai San composed of their kinsmen was in control, many of the fugitives were content to switch their allegiance to the society in whose hands the local power lay.

Meantime the increasing prosperity of the Klang valley attracted business men from Singapore, and in March 1866 the Sultan, unable to persuade the Malacca towkays to lend him any more money, farmed out the revenues of Klang district to Tan Kim Cheng and his partner W. H. Read, both of Singapore, under an agreement authorizing them to collect the taxes in the area, each retaining one-tenth of the total as commission. But civil war in the State during the year ruined the prospects of the syndicate, whose members then filed a suit against the Sultan for damages caused by these disturbances.

From now onwards the name of Tan Kim Cheng constantly recurs in connexion with the financial affairs of the western Malay States. He was the head of the Hokkien Hoey Kwan (Hokkien Association) in Singapore, and it is probable that he was also a power in the Hokkien branch of the Ghee Hin which had ramifications throughout the Settlements. His main interests were the revenue farms, and there is little doubt that when the glowing prospects in Selangor failed to materialize his influence was behind much of the pressure brought to bear by W. H. Read and others to persuade the British Government to intervene in the Malay States to restore peace, prosperity, and opportunities for financial transactions.

Larut

Further north, in the Larut valley of north Perak, the conflicting interests and traditional differences existing between two Chinese groups, each again backed by a Triad society, led not only to rivalry but to open hostilities.

Chinese miners were introduced into Larut by 'Che Long Ja'afar about 1848 and their numbers rapidly increased. The original mining hole was at Klian Pauh, close to the present site of Taiping gaol, and Long Ja'afar appointed one Low Sam, from Penang, to be his agent. With Low Sam was associated Chang Keng Kwee, a Hakka who hailed originally from the district of Chen Shang in the centre of the Province of Kwangtung.[54] He was responsible for the actual mining operations in areas obtained from Low Sam, and he introduced Hakka labourers from Chen Shang to work there. Both Low Sam and Chang Keng Kwee were headmen of the Hai San Society in Penang which Long Ja'afar also joined, and, naturally, the Chen Shang labourers who flocked to Klian Pauh were also members of this society.

[54] In contemporary documents the name Chen Shang is romanized in at least eleven different forms including Chen Sia, Tsang Sheng, Chan Sung, Tsen Shang, Tan Sian, etc.

Two miles north of Klian Pauh at Klian Bahru, later called Kamunting, another mining camp was set up composed of men connected with the Ghee Hin Society. Contemporary accounts do not say whether these men were Cantonese or Hakkas. It is known, however, that in 1865 Klian Bahru was a Fui Chiu village, which would imply that the inhabitants were Hakkas from Fui Chiu. This was most probably also true in 1861. They had their own head-man but held their mining rights from Low Sam.

Although thus settled in two camps, the division was not absolute. Some Ghee Hin men lived in the Hai San area and vice versa, and they worked adjacent plots of land. There is also a record of a Ghee Hin man employing Hai San labourers to work his land. Hai San men numbered about 3,000 as against 15,000 Ghee Hins.[55]

An indication of the prosperity brought by the mines is to be found in the refusal of the Sultan in 1861 to accept $10,000 annually as quit-rent though under the original agreement with Long Ja'afar the figure was fixed at $100. By this time Long Ja'afar had died and was succeeded by his son, Ngah Ibrahim. It was estimated that the revenue accruing to him was between $5,000 and $6,000 monthly, including income from the various 'Farms', the arrangements for the letting of which were also in the hands of Low Sam and were a further cause of dissension between the two Chinese groups.[56]

On 4 July 1861, at Klian Pauh, a miner of the Hai San Society quarrelled with a neighbour of the Ghee Hin Society over use of water from a stream and came to blows. At once the Hai San members at the camp attacked the minority Ghee Hins, one of whom was killed, and during the night and next day the Hai Sans attacked the Ghee Hin settlement at Klian Bahru, burning some houses and putting the inhabitants to flight. The refugees reached Permatang (Matang) where they were stranded without food or shelter. Two or three managed to get away by boat to Penang taking with them the corpse of the murdered man, and on their complaint the Deputy Commissioner of Police was sent to Larut in a gunboat, accompanied by headmen of both societies, to arrange a settlement On arrival it was discovered that the Malay chief temporarily in charge had hastily caused a document to be prepared in which the Hai San acknowledged their fault and agreed to pay compensation of $1,000, half of which was to go to men wounded and to relatives of the dead man. This settlement was said to have been accepted by local heads of the Ghee Hin, but one of the Penang Ghee Hin headmen, Lee Ko Yin, pointed out that apart from one signature of a man who signed under duress, the rest were forgeries, for the signatories were in Penang at the time. The Penang headmen of the two societies remained at Larut to negotiate a new settlement, but without success, for the victorious Hai Sans were in no mood to make further concessions. By the end of August Ghee Hin men to the number of about 1,000 abandoned Larut and reached Penang in a destitute condition.[57]

Soon there were complaints of assaults of Hai Sans by Ghee Hins in the streets of the town and there were clear indications that a staged fight in Penang was imminent. Two junks from Larut when searched were found to contain

---

[55] *ST*, 3 Aug. 1861.   [56] *Pinang Gazette*, 14 Apr. 1860.
[57] SSR(DD34), Pg, RC to Gov., 1861 (lett. fr. Dy Cmmr of Police to RC Pg, 12 July 1861). See also *ST*, 3 Aug. 1861 (art. of 13 July) and SSR(D34) 1861: Petitions by Hai San, 5 Aug., with RC's comments (lett. 343 of 1861, 26 Aug.).

an assortment of cannons, blunderbusses, swivel guns, spears, pistols, swords, powder, shot, and stink-pots, the seizure of which prevented the proposed outbreak.[58]

A number of the Ghee Hin mine operators were, by virtue of their birth in Penang, British subjects, and treaties of 1818 and 1826 with the Sultan had granted British subjects permission to trade unmolested throughout Perak. The Governor now called upon the Sultan to hold an enquiry and to award compensation for the losses incurred by British subjects in Larut where the Malay authorities had failed to maintain order.

By March 1862, as no progress had been made, and the Hai Sans were in full possession of all the mines, the Assistant Resident Councillor, Penang, Captain Smart, was sent on a mission to the Sultan to request an officer to accompany him to Larut to hold an enquiry, and in due course the Laxamana and Captain Smart arranged to hear the claims at Larut. Neither Muhammad Taib (who had been in charge during the trouble) nor the Hai San leaders put in an appearance, and the claim was heard *ex-parte*, a total compensation of £57,000 being awarded. Later, owing to complaints by Muhammad Taib that this was excessive, a further hearing was held with all parties present and the compensation to be paid to the Ghee Hin miners was scaled down to $17.447.04.[59] But despite the promulgation of the award, no one was prepared to pay, and the Laxamana was instructed that he must 'either enforce the award, or intimate in writing his inability to do so' and ask for British assistance.[60] This he did, and the steamers *Hoogly*, *Mohr*, and *Tonze*, in which guns had been mounted, were sent to the Larut and Sepatang rivers to ensure that no supplies should enter and that no tin should leave, and on 11 May Sultan Ja'afar informed the British that Ngah Ibrahim had agreed to pay the compensation due plus an additional $5,000 to cover the cost of the blockade.[61]

For Ngah Ibrahim this proved to be a profitable deal. On the one hand, he recouped the amount of compensation from the Hai San miners through his manager Low Sam, and on the other, he used the Sultan's predicament to extract from him confirmation of his authority over Larut, and the title of 'Orang Kaya Mentri'.[62]

But the most important result was that the Ghee Hins returned to Larut. They had petitioned the Resident Commissioner, Penang, to secure their reinstatement in their previous properties, but this was further than the Governor was prepared to go. He considered that some blame must attach to the society for the disturbances which led to their expulsion and stated that under no circumstances could the fraternity of an illegal and secret society have any claims upon the British Government for the redress of wrongs endured from a Native Chief.[63] Compensation had already been paid, and the allocation of

[58] SSR(DD34), 1861, Information and complaint of C. B. Plunket, 29 Aug.; ditto of Chan Ah Kew; Sworn Statement S. Smart, Magte of Police, 29 Aug. 1861.

[59] SSR(U5), CDPL, 1862–73: No. 2, 11 May 1862; SSR(R41), Gov., Lett. to GOI, 1862–7: Nos 31, 27 Mar. 1862; 45, 21 Apr. 1862; 54, 21 May 1862; 70, 6 June 1862.

[60] SSR(U44), Gov., Lett. to RCs, 1862, pp. 28–33: No. 95, to RC, Pg, 13 Apr. 1862.

[61] SSR(U44), Gov., Lett. to RCs, 1862: Nos 99, 25 Apr. 1862; 108, 27 Apr. 1862; 134, 21 May 1862; SSR(U5), CDPL, No. 128, 28 Apr. 1862, Gov. to Sultan of Perak.

[62] Doc. dated 23 Oct. 1863.

[63] The designation of the Ghee Hin as an 'illegal' society presumably referred to its status under the laws of Perak. In Penang it was not an illegal society.

mining land was a matter for the local chiefs.[64] In fact, Ngah Ibrahim had already promised that the Ghee Hin men could open fresh mines in an area distinctly demarcated and separate from the lands mined by the Hai Sans. In the end, practically the same pattern prevailed: Klian Pauh remained the stronghold of the Chen Shang Hakkas backed by the Hai San Society, while Klian Bahru became in the main a settlement of Fui Chiu Hakkas supported by the Ghee Hin Society.

But the segregation was by no means complete. An account of the area written in 1865 states that there were 7 Fui Chiu shops in Klian Pauh as against 70 or 80 belonging to Chen Shangs. At Klian Bahru all the shops were kept by Fui Chius, but although 16 mining holes in the area belonged to Fui Chius, 3 belonged to Chen Shangs. Furthermore, some Chen Shang men who held permits to mine but could not obtain labour had sublet their plots to Fui Chius who introduced their own labour, so that possibilities of friction were there, and on 9 June 1865 the smouldering embers flared up again.[65]

Trouble arose over a gambling quarrel between a Fui Chiu man and a Chen Shang man in a Fui Chiu shop at Klian Pauh. At once the Chen Shangs rallied round and looted all the Fui Chiu shops in the village. Those Fui Chius who lived there fled northwards to the protection of their fellows at Klian Bahru, but fourteen failed to escape. During the next day negotiations for a settlement began, but at night a meeting of the Hai San Lodge at Klian Pauh was held at which, after the flag had been honoured by offerings, thirteen of the prisoners were the victims of a brutal ritualistic murder. Into the neck of each man was thrust a sharpened bamboo, through which the blood spurted and was directed on to the flag as a sacrificial offering.

The fourteenth man escaped and made his way to Klian Bahru, where his story infuriated the Fui Chius. At once the two societies were embattled, the Ghee Hin supporting the Fui Chius and the Hai San backing the Chen Shangs. On 11 June 400 men from Klian Bahru marched to Klian Pauh, where a battle lasting for two hours was fought in which 30–40 men were killed and the village was put to the flames.

Ngah Ibrahim (referred to in documents of the period as Mentri of Larut) was away when the trouble started but returned on the night of 9 June. As things grew worse he decided that the only solution was to drive the Ghee Hins out of Larut. In this he was no doubt influenced by the fact that Low Sam, the 'farmer' of his mines, was a Hai San man and that he himself, like his father, was also a member. With the help of relatives he collected a force of Malays and at dawn on 18 June a joint Hai San–Malay army assembled at Klian Pauh. The main body of 1,000 Chinese and 100 Malays went up the road to Klian Bahru while a second party of 300 Malays went across country by footpath through Assam Kumbang. Klian Bahru was attacked and in two hours all was over. The Ghee Hins were put to flight and the village looted and burnt down. The tin stocks were removed to the Mentri's store at Klian Pauh.

Led by their headman, So Ah Chiang, the Fui Chius made their way northwards through the jungle heading for Kuala Kurau *en route* for Penang, but

[64] SSR(U46), Gov., Lett. to RCs, 1864, 20 May, pp. 95–99.
[65] SSR(DD42), Pg, Lett. to Gov. 1865, p. 99: No. 235. Encl. a petition from Loh Chong, an eyewitness, dated 26 June 1865.

the Mentri sent instructions to the local chief to intercept the fugitives and hold So Ah Chiang and some of the other leaders. These men had incensed the Mentri during the previous year by opposing the introduction of increased duties. Now that they were in his power he ordered them to be taken to Matang and sanctioned their execution at Telok Kertang. The main body of refugees was allowed to go through, and by 26 June over 1,000 had reached Penang in a very miserable and destitute condition. Many others had died in the jungle and on the roads in Province Wellesley.[66]

Once again the Ghee Hin headmen in Penang appealed to the Governor for redress. They were the financiers of the Fui Chiu mines and claimed that outstanding debts amounted to $49,573$\frac{1}{2}$ and that the tin slabs which should have been delivered to them had been taken by the Mentri. It might be thought that they had a better case for compensation on this occasion than in 1861, but the Governor refused to intervene, and the petitioners were informed that had they honestly exerted their influence to suppress the disgraceful feuds continually breaking out between the Chinese secret societies they would not, in all probability, have now to deplore the serious pecuniary injury from which they were suffering. The Chinese miners in Larut so greatly outnumbered the Malay defence force that it was probably necessary, he thought, for the Larut authorities to adopt stringent measures to restore peace.[67]

The reason for this change of attitude was that the Governor was unsure how the Government of India would view the matter. In November 1862 he had sent a naval force of three ships to Kuantan (Pahang) and Kemamam (Trengganu) to protect the interests of Chinese tin traders, and when, in due course, an account of this reached London, the Secretary of State commented that the Governor's action was 'characterised by undue precipitation', a criticism which Cavenagh resented. There was trouble in all the Malay States at this time, and the Governor was harassed by petitions from merchants, European and Chinese, in Singapore, Malacca, and Penang on the subject of the unjust treatment they received in their trading with the Native States. In August 1863 he had tried to get the Government of India to adopt 'some specific line of policy' in this matter. 'Were the Governor . . . empowered . . . to assure them [the Chiefs] that the British Government would not allow the general peace to be disturbed, there would be little difficulty in maintaining perfect tranquillity by inducing the Chiefs to refer all disputes to our arbitration and to acknowledge our permanent authority.'[68]

This plea received no encouragement from the Government of India, and Cavenagh was told that intervention in this way could not be countenanced. The Governor returned to the attack in December 1863 and reminded India that in 1862 trade with the Malay Peninsula had amounted to nearly £1 million, and that unless some semblance of order was restored to the Native States this trade would be seriously affected. But, trade apart, he thought that through treaty arrangements and by virtue of being the paramount power in the area, the British were already committed to some responsibility for keeping the peace, and this, he thought, would not be difficult once the intention was announced.

[66] SSR(D42), Lett. to Gov., 1865, p. 99: No. 235, 26 June. Also No. 42, 27 Oct., with statement by Oh Wee Kee, 18 Oct.
[67] SSR(V41), Gov., Misc. Lett. Out, 1864–6, pp. 280–2: No. 58, 28 June 1865.
[68] SSR(R41), Gov., Lett. to GOI, 1863, pp. 170–2: No. 156, 25 Aug. 1863.

But the Governor-General was not to be deflected, and Cavenagh was informed that the policy already laid down must be adhered to.[69]

In the light of these rebuffs it is not surprising that in 1865 the Governor was not disposed to intervene on behalf of the Ghee Hin financiers of Penang. There was also a practical difficulty, the Sultan of Perak, Ja'afar, had died, and it was not until the Governor had received a letter from the new Sultan, Ali, dated 25 January 1865, announcing his succession that it was certain who the new Sultan would be. In the meantime many further complaints were received about injustices perpetrated by the Mentri or suffered in his territory.

Although Cavenagh's attempts to secure a change of policy failed, he was authorized to send an officer to Larut to endeavour to adjust the complaints, but the imposition of a blockade, as suggested by the Governor, was considered to be of doubtful expediency.[70] The officer chosen for this task was a Deputy Commissioner of Police, P. W. Earl, and his mission was far from successful. Even the previous tenuous control of Larut by the Court of Perak was diminished through the disputed succession to the Sultanate. The Mentri was riding high, supported by his friends of the Hai San Society, and was in no mood to give way to representations on behalf of the Ghee Hin elements who had been eliminated from his province. Mr Earl, too, lacked the diplomatic skill to deal with such a situation, and his handling of the Mentri was later called by the Governor-General 'arrogant and offensive'. He stayed for three days only, and left with seven out of the original ten complaints unsettled. In reporting this failure to India the Governor again suggested a blockade but was told that this weapon must only be used in cases of murder or piracy on the high seas, when the offenders had taken refuge in Larut and were not surrendered on demand. The Government of India were also of the opinion that the majority of the cases put forward did not merit any intervention by the British Government and suggested that there might be 'a tendency among the authorities at Penang to push British interference with the neighbouring Native States further than was either necessary or desirable'.

It is clear from the correspondence which passed between the Governor and India that many of the people on whose behalf representations had been made to the Mentri were not British subjects at all but would merely 'seem to have acquired the right of domicile' which, the Governor asserted, 'earned a claim to protection'. In any case, he considered that in the interests of British commerce it was inadvisable to withdraw this protection.[71]

Whatever the legal position may have been, the Government of India were not prepared to sanction intervention on behalf of the Ghee Hin merchants of Penang, who were thus left without recompense. The feud between them and the Hai San Society remained unsettled.

[69] SSR(S31 & 32), Gov., Lett. fr. GOI, 1863: Despatch Nos 680, 16 Oct. 1863 & 232, 3 Mar. 1864; SSR(R41), Gov., Lett. to GOI, 1863, pp. 206–12: Despatch No. 243, 31 Dec. 1863.
[70] SSR(S33), Gov., Lett. fr. GOI, 1865, p. 241: lett. of 17 Oct. 1865.
[71] SSR(S35), Lett. fr. GOI: No. 436, 4 May 1866; (R41), No. 18, 10 Aug. 1866; (S35), No. 994, 28 Sept. 1866; (R41), No. 23, 23 Oct. 1866.

7

THE PENANG RIOTS, 1867[1]

THE transfer of the control of the Straits Settlements from the Government of India to the Colonial Office marked a turning point in Malaya's history. For many years the mercantile community, particularly that of Singapore, had urged that these Settlements should be removed from the control of the Government of India. They were irritated by the imposition of unpopular Indian legislative measures in the Settlements, as, for example, proposals for taxation at the ports, or for legalizing Indian currency. But they were even more incensed at the apparently intransigent attitude of the Indian Government towards their suggestions for the solution of certain urgent local problems. Refusal to legislate in regard to Chinese secret societies was one instance of this recalcitrance, but refusal to permit British intervention in the affairs of the Native States of the mainland was another of even greater moment.

There were good profits to be made from the tin and timber and other products of the Native States. There were various lucrative revenue farms. There was no difficulty in obtaining vast concessions on very favourable terms from impoverished rajas, but there was no guarantee that any enterprise which set itself up in these States would not be taxed out of existence by a swarm of petty chieftains each claiming a traditional right to levy his own tax. Nor was there any guarantee that the life and property of the traders and their employees would be reasonably safeguarded. In almost all the States, the turmoil caused by the rivalries and jealousies of the chiefs, the constant grouping and regrouping into opposed camps of the supporters of rival claimants to the thrones, and the fragmentation of responsibility among the various great and petty rajas were factors making for insecurity and chaos which varied only in degree between one state and another.

All observers were agreed that the only possible hope of restoring some semblance of rule in this anarchy was for the British to intervene in one way or another, not merely in the interests of the traders and the revenues of the Straits Settlements but to ensure that the internecine strife of the Malay States did not spread to Penang, Malacca, and Singapore, causing serious disorder and breaches of the peace in these areas also.

[1] The main source is the PRCR, produced on 14 July 1868 and published in the SSPLC, 1868. Other primary sources are:

(a) Contemporary reports by the Lt-Gov. of Penang, Col Anson, the Police Magistrate, C. B. Plunket, and the Dy Cmmr of Police, P. W. Earl, which are encl. in GD 143, 7 Dec. 1867 (PRO/CO 273/13, SS 1867, vol. 4, Dec.).

(b) SS Exec. Council Mins., 1867–9: 29 July, 12, 15, 16 & 22 Aug., 9 Sept. 1867 (PRO/CO 275/4).

(c) SSPLC, 1867–9.

(d) GD to S. of S., 1867–9, as indicated in references in the text and S. of S. replies, 1867–9 (PRO/CO 273). The most detailed secondary source is Wynne, chs. 10–16, esp. ch. 16.

To the inhabitants of these Settlements of whatever race, the problem was evident and the solution obvious, but nothing would persuade or induce the Government of India to see things in this light. It was well aware, from its own experience in India, of the heavy commitments and responsibilities, military, political, and administrative, that could result from intervention in the affairs of Native States. From the very beginning, when Francis Light had bargained with Kedah for Penang Island, the East India Company had set its face against entering into any undertaking which might develop into territorial responsibility. A trading station was permissible, a naval refitting station useful, but nothing more must be undertaken. As for Singapore, it was only the immediate prosperity of the new Settlement which enabled Raffles to maintain his hold on this territory in the face of the wrath and misgivings of the Directors. And as the years went by, as the Company's navy was abolished and as its monopoly of trade with China was lost, the Straits Settlements continued to be a financial liability, while the purposes for which they had come into being ceased to exist. To the Indian Government the Straits Settlements became a nuisance and an incubus of which they were only too glad to divest themselves.

As early as 1858 the European inhabitants of Singapore presented a petition to the House of Commons praying that the supervision of the Straits Settlements be transferred to the Colonial Office. It read:

. . . Your petitioners have long felt aggrieved by the manner in which Singapore is governed by the East India Company. Ignorant, apparently, of the many circumstances in which the Straits Settlements differ so widely from Continental India, the Supreme Government has almost invariably treated them from an exclusively Indian point of view, and shown a systematic disregard to the wants and wishes of their inhabitants, however earnestly and perseveringly made known. And only by appeals to the Imperial Government and Parliament have needful improvements desired by the inhabitants of the Straits Settlements been brought about, or redress obtained for injustice inflicted on them by the Government of the East India Company.

On various occasions when proceeding to deal with matters connected with these Settlements, the members of the Legislative Council have confessed their complete ignorance of Straits affairs, but this has not induced them to hesitate in their action or to take effectual means for acquiring the information acknowledged to be wanting. They have, on the contrary, passed Acts most detrimental to the interests of the Settlement in spite of the earnest remonstrances and prayers of the inhabitants.[2]

Official discussions between the Colonial Office and the Government of India on the subject of transfer began in 1859, but it was not until 1866 that all parties to the transaction, the Colonial Office, the Treasury, the War Office, and the Government of India, were able to reach agreement, and the formal transfer was arranged for 1 April 1867. On that date the Straits Settlements became a Crown Colony, under a new Governor, Colonel Harry St George Ord of the Royal Engineers. The Colony had its own official Executive Council, and a Legislative Council consisting of nine officials (including the Chief Justice, formerly known as the Recorder), and four unofficials nominated by the Governor. Three of the unofficial members, Messrs W. H. Read, T. Scott, and Dr R. Little, were from Singapore. Mr F. S. Brown was from Penang, and there was provision for a fifth unofficial member to represent Malacca. Before long a sixth unofficial member representing the Chinese community was appointed.

[2] GD 196, 16 Sept. 1869, para. 42 (Gov. to S. of S.).

No longer was the expression of public opinion restricted to Presentments of the Grand Jury, sheriff's meetings, and the press. There was now a forum where matters of public interest could be debated, and the mercantile community fully expected to make its opinions heard and its influence felt. It was believed that with its own legislature the Colony would be able to frame its own laws and direct its own policy. In particular, traders engaged in enterprises in the Native States would receive proper protection which had been denied by the unresponsive policy of the Indian Government. The business community was to discover, alas, that their new master, the Colonial Office, could be just as unsympathetic as the Indian Government had been, and in the unpopularity arising from this disappointment and frustration the first Governor of the Colony shared.

Colonel Ord, who had already held administrative posts in the West Indies and in West Africa, was a man of very forceful personality with decided ideas about his own capabilities. On the very day of the transfer he made himself extremely unpopular with the European community by pointing out that most of the revenue of the Colony, derived from the opium and spirit farms, came from the pockets of the Chinese population and not from the Europeans. At the end of the year, in reviewing the finances of the Colony, he further incensed the European community by stating that although there was every prospect of a more than adequate revenue to meet the proposed expenditure of the year, should more revenue be required it could best be obtained by import or similar duties or by direct taxation.[3]

This raised a storm of protest not only in Singapore but in London, and one result of the misgivings of the European merchants was the formation in London on 31 January 1868 of the Straits Settlements Association, whose members were, for the most part, the London heads of Singapore business firms. The object of the Association was declared to be:

> To guard against any legislation that might prejudicially affect the interests of the Settlements, and in particular that might be calculated to check or interfere with their commercial prosperity or prospects of trade; and to use means to prevent unnecessary expenditure by the local Government.

The Association, being in London, had direct access to the Secretary of State, and remained a constant and virulent critic of Ord's policies, despite the fact that the new Governor was an able administrator who, during his six-year term of office, put the finances of the Colony on a firm basis.

That he was unable to intervene in the Native States was entirely due to the restrictions placed upon him by the instructions of the Colonial Office. But at least where Chinese secret societies in the Colony were concerned he was able to introduce legislation which empowered the governing authorities to take more drastic and effective action against this menace to the peace and well-being of the community. In any case, once the preliminary official business connected with the establishment of the new Colony had been concluded, the subject of secret societies was the first to be raised by the unofficial members of Legislative Council.

At a meeting of the Council on 4 May 1867 a motion by an unofficial member, Thomas Scott, was unanimously adopted. It read: 'That the Executive Govern-

[3] GD 196, 16 Sept. 1869, paras 7–18; COD 88, 30 May 1868; GD 181, 27 Aug. 1869, paras 52–61.

ment be requested to publish in the requisite native tongues, and promulgate among the native inhabitants, either *in extenso* or in the form of an abstract, all Acts which ultimately or directly affect them.' On 18 May the same member introduced a Bill entitled 'An Act for the registration of the Officers and Members of Societies formed for certain purposes.' This he replaced at the meeting on 31 July by a 'Bill for the better regulation of Societies and Associations and for the prevention of Unlawful Assemblies', which was ordered to be printed, and which echoed Cavenagh's suggestions of 1865.

But for the time being no further action was taken on this Bill, for at this same meeting the Attorney-General, Thomas Braddell, asked for suspension of Standing Orders to enable the introduction of a 'Bill for the Better Preservation of the Peace', which was read a first time, and which, with amendments, was passed into law with all speed at the Governor's request on 12 August, as Act XX, 'An Act for the Better Preservation of the Peace'.

This measure provided that whenever it appeared to the Governor or Lieutenant-Governor that any tumult or riot had taken place or might be reasonably apprehended, authority might be given to any two JPs to summon before them any number of persons resident in the Settlement and appoint them to act as special constables, thus giving legal cover to the practice of swearing in the headmen of the secret societies at times of riots. There was also provision 'whenever any person shall be found unlawfully, riotously, or tumultuously assembled to the disturbances of the Peace and to the terror of Her Majesty's subjects' for a JP to require the assembly to disperse, failing which the persons assembled might be dispersed or arrested. Furthermore, the Governor in Council was empowered to order any person, not being a natural born subject of Her Majesty, to remove from the Colony, failing which he could be imprisoned 'until he shall be discharged by the Governor'. In order to deal with 'the assembling together of bodies of armed men for unlawful purposes' the Governor in Council was empowered to issue a proclamation in respect of any Settlement or part of a Settlement, whereupon it became an offence for any person to carry arms or instruments capable of being used as offensive arms. Penalties under this section included fine, imprisonment, and in addition 'not exceeding forty stripes with a rattan, or one hundred stripes with a cat-of-nine-tails'. During the life of a proclamation, the closing of shops and the discontinuance of the sale of food and other necessaries without reasonable excuse was made an offence. No writ of Habeas Corpus was issuable in respect of persons confined for offences under the Act, which was to continue in force for one year only. Thus, at one stroke, the Government obtained many of the powers, albeit of a temporary nature, and to be used only in an emergency, which had been frequently advocated in vain in the past, but powers to outlaw secret societies or to cause them to register were not included.

The Penang Riots

The reason for the exceptional urgency in passing this legislation was an ominous seething in Penang throughout June and July 1867, an outbreak of rioting in Singapore between the Ghee Hin (Cantonese) and the Hok Hin (Hokkien) societies, and the development of the Penang trouble during August into the worst riot in that Settlement's history, when for several days large areas of the town were in a state of siege, and the countryside, both on the island itself and in Province Wellesley, was ravaged by roving bands of rioters. In Penang these riots marked the culmination of the struggle between the Kien Tek and the Ghee Hin, and were at the same time an extension of the open warfare which broke out on 8 July on the mines at Bang Chiam, Tongkah, in Siam, where these two societies were strongly entrenched. There the Ghee Hin, though assisted by the Ho Seng, was worsted in the fight, and appealed to its brethren in Penang for help in arms and men. In response to a request from the Raja of Tongkah the Straits Government on 29 July forbade by proclamation the exportation of arms, ammunition, and warlike stores from the Colony to the Tongkah area.[4]

The rioting which broke out in Penang itself presented to the authorities an even more serious problem than usual in that the Red and White Flag societies were also embroiled, the former helping the Kien Tek and the latter supporting the Ghee Hin. The origins of the Flag societies are obscure, but it is known that in Penang and Singapore in 1867 they were largely composed of Indians (both Muslim and Hindu), together with Jawi-Pekans, and a few Malays. The two societies were mutually antagonistic and in Penang each had its zone of influence, that of the White Flag corresponding to the Ghee Hin area while the Red Flag covered approximately the same area as the Kien Tek, and each was allied to the Chinese society of its area. They were closely associated with the celebration of Moharram, which included a large element of buffoonery and carnival during the ten days in which processions surged through the town with increasing rowdiness. In India it was customary for the festival to end with a fight between supporters of the Shiah and the Sunni sects, but although no such sectarian division was evident in the Straits, the tradition of a public fight seems to have endured, and there was frequently serious trouble.

There can be little doubt that the growth of a resident criminal community of Indian and mixed Indian–Malay descent was an important factor in the degeneration of the Moharram festival in the Straits Settlements. It was not until 1873 that the last of the convicts from India and Ceylon were transferred to the Andaman Islands and the Straits were thus freed from periodic additions to their criminal population through this channel. Over the years, many of the convicts settled in the Straits on the expiry of their sentences, and the Jawi–Pekan or Peranakan community was the result of their intermarriage with the Malay women of the country, and was particularly numerous in Penang and Province Wellesley. Indians and Peranakans began to form their own secret protection societies on the Chinese model with which many of them were familiar, with the intention of safeguarding themselves, protecting their women, and avoiding unwelcome police attentions. Camouflaged as religious societies, they made use of the Moharram festival as a cloak to hide from the authorities more nefarious activities, and as an opportunity for the paying off of rival scores, such rivalry being due not to any religious or ideological differences, but to a struggle for power and for control of the activities of the underworld. By 1860 or soon afterwards they appear to have completed their alignment with rival Chinese secret societies, individuals even entering the Chinese societies by means of a special initiation ceremony. As corporate groups they appeared as the Red and White Flag societies, and as such were soon joined by criminal and rowdy elements among the Malays, though for many years the orgiastic displays of the Moharram

[4] PRCR, App. 7, Min. of Exec. Council, 29 July 1867 (PRO/CO 275(4)).

festival and the fights of the hooligan gangs had been viewed with distaste by the majority of that community.

At the time of the Moharram festival in May 1867, the feud between the Red and White Flag societies at Penang had resulted in the murder of a diamond merchant who was said to be a Malay, though it is possible that he was of Arab or Jawi–Pekan origin. He was found dead in Armenian Street, in the Red Flag sector of the town. At the same time, Khoo T'ean Tek, the leader of the Kien Tek, was preparing to take advantage of the explosive situation to involve the Chinese societies in the Malay quarrel, for he sought an opportunity to attack his rivals, the Ghee Hins, not only to avenge his society's previous defeat in 1865, but to forestall any retaliatory action which the Ghee Hins might try to take in response to the appeal for help from Tongkah.

On 1 July a Chinese member of the Kien Tek was insulted by a Malay member of the White Flag, and a series of attacks and reprisals by groups of members of these societies followed. Police intervention led to the holding of a conciliation meeting on 8 July at which headmen of the Kien Tek, Ghee Hin, Red Flag, and White Flag were present and a settlement was reached.

The agreement recording the settlement between the Flag societies was written in Tamil while that of the Chinese societies was in legally framed English and stipulated that neither side 'would join in any way with the Kling and Malay Congsees'.[5]

But despite these agreements, further outbreaks occurred involving some deaths. On 1 August Khoo T'ean Tek falsely alleged that Ghee Hin and White Flag men had stolen cloth from a Kien Tek dyer's shop, and as arbitration negotiations were unsuccessful the Kien Tek leaders that night decided to collect arms and attack the Ghee Hins. Orders to this effect was sent to Kien Tek street leaders in the town and to village leaders in the country. The timing of this attack was no doubt influenced by the fact that the battery of artillery which usually defended Penang had just left for Rangoon and its replacement had not yet arrived, while two men-of-war which had been in the harbour had left with fifty men of the sepoy garrison on an emergency expedition to the Nicobar Islands.[6]

Numerically, the Ghee Hin and White Flag societies were far superior to their opponents, the former counting some 25,000 members against the Kien Tek's 6,000, and the White Flag counting 3,000 against the Red Flag's 1,000. But the Kien Tek was fully prepared for a fight to the finish. In 1865, after the affray at Jelutong, regulations were drawn up covering the benefits to be paid to members injured, or to families of members killed, transported, or imprisoned by the Government while engaged in fighting the enemies of the society. These regulations had been applied to all subsequent fights, and were still in force. Moreover, the Kien Teks were much better armed than the Ghee Hins, partly because of the greater wealth of the members, and partly because the shops of the gunsmiths and dealers in ammunition were owned by members of this Hokkien society. From early July, arms had been distributed not only to Kien Tek members in the town of Penang but to the villages of Tanjong Tokong, Sungei Nibong, Dato Kramat, and Jelutong, on the pretext of being

[5] PRCR Evidence, Nos 1, 4, 10, 23, 37, and Apps 4 & 16.
[6] PRCR paras 41 & 43: Evidence Nos 44, 46, 51; GD 79, 19 Aug. 1867; GD 143, 17 Dec. 1867. Encl. by Anson, No. 286 of 17 Aug. PRO/CO 273(13), vol. 4.

prepared lest, in view of the trouble in Tongkah, the Ghee Hins should attack their rivals in Penang Island. Through their leaders, 'Che Long and Tuan Mahomed, the Red Flag members were also given muskets, and once hostilities had begun several small cannon were landed from armed junks lying in the harbour, and were used by the Kien Tek with considerable effect.[7]

The attack started about midday on Saturday, 3 August, when fierce fighting took place in Prangin Road and Pitt Street. Excited crowds of Chinese, Malays, and Indians waving flags, brandishing spears, swords, and sticks or armed with muskets thronged the streets as the Kien Tek and Red Flag societies fell upon any Ghee Hin and White Flag men who could be found. The Lieutenant-Governor, Colonel Anson, was living on Penang Hill but had authorized the Police Magistrate (C. B. Plunket) and the Deputy Commissioner of Police (P. W. Earl) to act in an emergency. They at once called in a detachment of sepoys, swore in members of the European community as special constables, and caused barricades to be erected and manned in the streets, so that a semblance of order was restored.[8]

But the Ghee Hin, having suffered losses and lost face, besieged the house of their headman, Lee Ko Yin, bringing with them the corpses of the victims and calling upon him to issue orders authorizing them to fight. At a meeting held later two of the Ghee Hin leaders, Lee Ko Yin and Oh Wee Kee, were in favour of petitioning the Government to arrest the Kien Tek leaders and thus stop the fight developing, but a third, Boey Yu Kong, the sinseh[9] of the society and the holder of its seal, was resolutely determined on revenge, and that night issued written orders 'to fight the Toh Peh Kongs wherever they were met; to kill, burn, and destroy'.[10] At the same time he sent word to Province Wellesley, Kedah, and Tongkah calling upon the brethren to help in the fight.

Next day (Sunday) Lee Ko Yin and Oh Wee Kee submitted their petition warning the Government that failure to arrest the Kien Tek headmen would undermine their own position and the Ghee Hin men would rise and take revenge. At 2 p.m. Ayer Hitam village was on fire and the headmen of both sides were ordered to report on the following morning. Boey Yu Kong slipped away into hiding, but the others duly reported and were confined to the Fort. But already by eight o'clock on Monday morning a furious fight was raging in the town with large bodies of men from both sides with flags flying marching and shooting and setting fire to premises.

Fighting continued throughout the day. In the evening Khoo T'ean Tek and Lee Ko Yin with a sepoy escort and the Police Magistrate toured the town ordering their respective members to keep quiet, but bitter fighting continued throughout the next day, and a European Government official who visited the Ghee Hin headquarters found 30 or 40 coffins occupied and 20 or 30 men lying upstairs dying. As he passed the Chinese temple in Pitt Street he saw several tiers of coffins awaiting burial.

There was fighting in the country districts too, with each side burning the houses of their opponents. More than 800 Ghee Hin supporters, Chinese and

[7] PRCR Evidence Nos 2, 28, 29, 35, 44. Also App. 3.
[8] The fortuitous arrival from the Dindings on 3 August of Colonel Man the former Resident Councillor enabled the Government to make use of his intimate experience of the Penang societies. He took an active part in all subsequent proceedings.
[9] Ritual expert at initiation ceremonies.   [10] PRCR, Evidence No. 36.

Malay, had landed in the Glugor area from Province Wellesley and were plundering and destroying. Jelutong village was burnt down on Thursday, 8 August, but Oh Wee Kee was persuaded to issue a written order to the men from the Province, whereupon they returned to their boats which were towed back across the strait by a government steamer.

Thereafter the first fury in the town abated and the headmen, still detained in the Fort, were able to bring their influence to bear so that negotiations for a settlement could begin. Sporadic assaults and robberies still continued, but the timely arrival of HMS *Wasp* from the Nicobars and the landing of her field guns and crew brought welcome relief to the weary troops, police, and civilians who for several days had prevented the rioters from capturing and destroying the town. HMS *Satellite* later arrived, and by 15 August all fighting had ceased. The losses sustained by the secret societies were never known for the rioters invariably carried off the bodies of their comrades.

Though the riot was a shocking and bitter experience for Penang it was not a seditious uprising but an internecine war between secret societies, and it is noteworthy that despite much indiscriminate firing the only government casualties were one sepoy corporal killed and one policeman wounded.

No news of the riots reached Singapore until the afternoon of Sunday, 11 August, when the Governor received a report from Colonel Anson and a petition signed by the leading inhabitants of the island, both European and Chinese, requesting that immediate steps should be taken to put a stop to these disturbances, and to secure for the future the peace of the Settlement. The Governor hastily summoned a Legislative Council meeting at which the Bill already introduced by the Attorney-General on 31 July was hurriedly passed through all stages. Then, armed with the powers under the new Act, the Governor embarked for Penang, arriving on 14 August.[11]

He was immediately deluged with petitions and memoranda from all communities, one demanding the immediate appointment of a Commission of Enquiry empowered to award compensation or damages to any sufferers from the riots should the secret societies be found to have 'caused, encouraged, or connived at the disturbances', such compensation to be levied on the property real or personal of the society. Others requested that a law might be passed empowering the Supreme Court, all magistrates and JPs to try all cases of assault, cutting and wounding, maiming, etc., and to sentence the offenders at their discretion to be flogged, either once or oftener, in addition to the punishment already authorized for the offences. Other petitions asked that the chiefs of the societies be made answerable criminally and civilly for the mischief perpetrated by them and their members. Even members of the secret societies themselves asked that the societies be suppressed by the Government, realizing that they themselves 'did not possess the power of compelling the numerous body of their followers to break up their organisation'.[12]

The Governor held Executive Council meetings in Penang on 15, 16, and 22 August, attended by himself, the Lieutenant-Governor of Penang, the Attorney-General, and as extraordinary members, Colonel Man and F. S. Brown, when the Governor was made fully aware of all that had happened. In

[11] Mins Exec. Council, 1867, 12 Aug. (PRO/CO 275(4)); SSPLC, 31 July & 12 Aug. 1867.
[12] GD 143, 7 Dec. 1867.

response to the demands of a public meeting held at the Chamber of Commerce, he issued an Order in Council proclaiming a state of emergency; and by a Police Notice of 17 August he ordered the disarmament of Penang Island, a measure not extended to Province Wellesley as the force at the disposal of the Government was quite insufficient should any attempt be made to resist it. The resolutions of the public meeting had included a request that the Governor should hold an enquiry, with power of examining witnesses, as to the societies in existence in Penang, 'with a view to suppressing those that are injurious, and regulating those that are not'. This request was not fully granted, but the Governor set up a Commission to enquire into the origin and causes of the recent riots, and to determine how far the secret societies had been concerned in instigating or fostering such riots. On 21 August a Bill 'to indemnify Officers of Government and other persons for proceedings during the recent riots at Penang' also passed through all stages.

The Commission of Enquiry began its deliberations on 26 August with Colonel Man as President. The other members included four British, three Chinese, and one Indian merchant. One of the Chinese members was Foo Tye Sin, whose services were frequently called for in arbitration proceedings between the societies.

Meantime, largely through the personal efforts of Colonel Man, the leaders of the Kien Tek and the Ghee Hin were induced to pledge themselves to pay a sum of $500 to the family of the soldier who was shot, $10,000 to defray the extraordinary expense incurred by the Government in repressing the riots, and $60,000 compensation to the people unconnected with the societies who had suffered damages to their houses and property from the rioters. But the society leaders decided, 'after consideration, that each party should compensate the other without (Government) interference for the losses they had mutually sustained'.[13] In the event, only $11,250 was honoured, the Kien Tek contributing $6,250 and the Ghee Hin $5,000.[14] Colonel Anson has stated in his book, published over fifty years later, that he himself persuaded the societies to make a 'voluntary contribution' with which the Government built four police stations in those parts of the town which were most likely to be centres of disturbances,[15] but no mention has been found in contemporary records of any contribution other than that arranged by Colonel Man while the secret society leaders were still confined in the Fort.

The climax in the attempt to achieve the pacification of Penang was reached when, on the recommendation of the JPs and with the advice and consent of Executive Council, the Governor ordered, under the powers conferred by Section 10 of the Peace Preservation Act, the deportation of two prominent leaders of the rival Chinese contestants, Khoo Poh, the leading Councillor of the Kien Tek and Boey Yu Kong, the sinseh of the Ghee Hin. As Khoo T'ean Tek was local-born, similar action could not be taken against him. As for the Ghee Hin leaders, it was plain that both Lee Ko Yin as president, and Oh Wee Kee, as vice-president, were overshadowed by Boey Yu Kong, whose violent temper had been an obstacle to any compromise, and who had taken upon himself the

[13] Pg Exec. Co. Mins, 15 Aug. 1867 & GD 79, 19 Aug. 1867.
[14] SSLCP, 1870, pp. 7 & 92, & App. 19, 'Return of Money received from Ghee Hin and Toh Peh Kong Societies at Penang in 1867', pp. 57–59.
[15] A. E. Anson, *About Others and Myself* (1920), pp. 278–83.

responsibility for authorizing hostilities on the part of his society, thus usurping the powers of his senior officers.

Khoo Poh, given a month in which to settle his affairs, made strenuous efforts to avoid his fate. Petitions on his behalf were immediately submitted not only personally but by his friends and his family, claiming that for several years he had played no part in society affairs, and in an attempt to bolster up this claim, his name was surreptitiously removed from the books of membership of the Kien Tek.[16] But from a report of the Attorney-General on the petitions presented to Executive Council on 22 August, together with the facts adduced by the Police Magistrate, the Council were of the opinion that so far from establishing the claim of non-participation, there could be no doubt that Khoo Poh had been a prominent instigator of the riots, and his deportation was strongly advised. Similar advice was tendered by Executive Council in Singapore on 9 September, despite the fact that Khoo Poh's status as a naturalized British subject had first to be withdrawn.[17] It was the Governor's view that nothing contributed more to the restoration of order and confidence than the removal of the two leaders.[18]

Finally, after it had been agreed to delegate to the Lieutenant-Governor the powers vested in the Governor by the Preservation of the Peace Act, 1867, Colonel Ord left Penang for Singapore, and the headmen of the Kien Tek and the Ghee Hin were released from the Fort.

In reporting to the Secretary of State the Governor made it clear that the riots were not directed against the local Government but were the results of rivalry and animosity between contending secret societies, the Chinese societies 'each having attached to itself the Mohammedan part of the population'. In commenting on the numerous petitions received by him in Penang asking for the suppression of the societies, he said that he considered this to be impossible. Apart from the large floating population there were about 90,000 Chinese in the Settlement of whom nearly all were members of one or other of the six principal societies.[19] Though formed for charitable or other beneficial purposes, they had degenerated into powerful combinations of armed men under the control of unscrupulous leaders who used them for their own purposes, and though never directed against the Government there was no reason why 'on any cause of offence being given by the Government they should not make common cause against it'. The association of Malays with the societies increased this fear. While the societies which were not engaged in the riot refrained from taking any part in the quarrel, 'although in some cases they suffered by the burning and plundering of their houses', he had little doubt that if the riot had not been contained and a battle had been fought in the town, all the societies would eventually have been involved.

The Governor then referred to the action already taken to strengthen the hands of the Government by passing the new Act, and mentioned a Bill which had been introduced to provide for the registration of the office-bearers and

[16] PRCR Evidence, Nos 27, 29, 32, 35, 44.

[17] Under Act VIII of 1867 the Governor in Council had power to cancel a Certificate of Naturalization 'if good cause shall otherwise appear thereof'.

[18] GD 128, 28 May 1869.

[19] Ghee Hin, Kien Tek, Ho Seng, Hai San, Chin Chin, and Ho Hop Seah.

members of all such societies and prohibiting their meeting without due notice. As to this, he proposed to await the report of the Commission before reaching a decision.

It is my impression [he said] that these societies will be more easily controlled in future by quiet measures of surveillance and by a vigilant enforcement of a moderate amount of restraint than by the application of any new law of a repressive and extreme character which might have the effect of arousing them to resistance.

After paying a particular tribute to Colonel Man, to whom the Government was indebted for very valuable assistance throughout the whole of the disturbances, the Governor ended with a plea for reconsideration of a decision recently made to reduce the garrison of the Settlements resulting in only 30 artillerymen and 180 Native troops being available for Penang. He suggested the raising of an armed police force but was convinced that the best protection the Settlement could have against a repetition of the riots would be a small force of European troops to provide a backing for the Native detachments.[20]

In giving general approval to the action taken by the Governor, the Secretary of State (the Duke of Buckingham and Chandos) asked for a further report from Colonel Anson himself, and expressed surprise that there was no indication that the principal actors in the outrages had been brought to justice. Furthermore, he doubted whether 'quiet measures of surveillance' would be sufficient in Penang or whether stronger action might not be necessary in the future. He wrote:

Although I am by no means blind to the imprudence of any measures which can be called extreme, yet it would be very unfortunate if the present favourable opportunity were lost of establishing the authority of Government and of combining in support of that authority as in opposition to those who attempt to defy it, the peaceable part of the Chinese population. It could only be considered a great misfortune if the Government on being appealed to by the body of the people to assume its proper position were to shew itself unable or unwilling to do so.

He asked to be informed whether any special machinery was in existence for the government of the Chinese; how far they were governed through authorities of their own; and how far their disputes were regulated and their conduct controlled by the direct action of the European Government. He fully approved of Ord's suggestion of forming an armed police force, and thought that Colonel Anson's previous experience in Mauritius in connexion with a similar force might be useful. Advice might also be available from Hong Kong.[21]

In a later despatch, written on 6 November 1867, the Secretary of State sounded a note of warning in regard to the Preservation of Peace Act. He disliked Clauses 10, 12, 15, under which the Governor had power to deport, sentence of 100 stripes with a cat-of-nine-tails could be passed, and a shopkeeper could be penalized for shutting up his shop. Since the Act had been passed under 'very peculiar circumstances' which rendered it necessary for the Straits Government to show that they were determined to put an end for the future to such riots as had recently broken out at Penang, and as, moreover, the measure was

[20] GDs 79, Pg, 19 Aug. 1869; 81 & 143 Sing., 28 Aug. & 7 Dec. 1867.
[21] COD/SS 80, 22 Oct. 1867.

only temporary, he had not thought it necessary to require any amendments in it, but he would hardly feel justified in advising Her Majesty to sanction any future Act of a similar kind without some modifications.[22]

In reply the Governor regretted that he had given the impression that 'an appeal had been made by the body of the people to the Government to assume its proper position which the Government shewed itself unable or unwilling to do'. He maintained that many of the measures suggested were impracticable and that, although a large proportion of the Chinese unconnected with the warring societies took no part in the riot, they could hardly be designated as peaceable on this account since very little would have involved them, and they resisted all efforts that were made to enlist them on the side of order. Under these circumstances he still felt that his policy of surveillance and moderate restraint was justified and, indeed, had been vindicated by the return of confidence shown in the new tenders for the Government opium and other farms in Singapore which were $80,000 higher than previous tenders.

He was still of the opinion that an armed police force would be very useful and could with advantage and economy be substituted for a portion of the force of Native troops with which it was proposed to garrison the Settlements, should Her Majesty's Government be pleased to sanction the appropriation of part of the military contribution then paid by the Colony towards this object, but he feared that very strong opposition would be aroused in the Settlements were it attempted to call upon them to incur additional expense for such a purpose.[23] The Governor's fears were well founded. He was to find that, on the one hand, the Colonial Office was not prepared to sanction the substitution of a local armed police force for part of the military force assigned to the Colony, and thus reduce the amount of the military contribution levied on the Straits, while, on the other hand, local opinion was not prepared to approve additional expenditure for this purpose lest increased taxation should result.

The Secretary of State approved the measures taken by Colonel Anson and the military and police authorities for 'preventing and when it became necessary for repressing the disturbances' but thought it unfortunate that the Lieutenant-Governor had not remained in the town on Sunday 4 August (he had come down the Hill on the Saturday afternoon and returned there the same evening, suffering from sunstroke), 'as the personal presence of an officer of his position and authority might have had an influence which no communications by others could exercise'.

As for Ord's defence of his policy, the Secretary of State disclaimed any intention to censure but added:

It is a fact for which you are by no means answerable that the Chinese secret societies are more independent of constituted authority than is consistent with good government.

You would, I doubt not, be the first to admit that no opportunity of restraining this independence should be neglected, and it is clear that a time of danger or of escape from danger is calculated to furnish such an opportunity. I desired to point out to you that it is your duty to make the most of every such opportunity, but I am quite ready to believe that under the circumstances which you describe you could do no more than you did.

[22] COD/SS 91, 6 Nov. 1867.
[23] GD143, 7 Dec. 1867, with encl. (PRO/CO 273(13), SS, 1867, vol. 4, Dec.).

The despatch ended with a final warning:

With regard to that part of your Despatch in which you express an opinion that an Armed Police Force might be with advantage substituted for a portion of the Force of Native Troops with which it is proposed to garrison the Settlements, you will remember that although at present it is intended to place in the Settlements a larger number of Troops than that on which the Military contribution is assessed, yet circumstances may at any moment require that the force should be reduced down to or even below that number.

The recent riot at Penang illustrates the danger to which, in the absence of a sufficient police force, the Settlements may be exposed either by such a reduction of force or by any temporary movement of Troops like that which took place in connection with the murders at the Nicobar Islands.

You will take care that the Council is fully impressed with the responsibility which the Government and Legislature of the Straits Settlements will incur in failing to provide for such means of protection as may be sufficient under any circumstances which may reasonably be expected to arise.[24]

While these despatches were passing between Singapore and London the police in Penang were taking action against such of the rioters as they could arrest and the Commission of Enquiry was examining the many witnesses summoned to give evidence before it as to the part played by the secret societies in the recent riots.

But although many thousands of secret society members had undoubtedly been concerned in the killing, looting, and burning which had taken place, so great was the difficulty of procuring evidence sufficiently reliable to warrant proceedings in court, and to secure convictions once proceedings had begun, that at the Criminal Sessions held in September and November 1867 and in February 1868 only 38 persons were found guilty on various counts. Of those convicted, 13 were Chinese, and 25 were 'Muslim Indians', a term which probably included Jawi–Pekans. Their crimes included the aiding and abetting of murder, arson, robbery and wounding, housebreaking, and unlawful possession of arms, and sentences ranged from death to transportation for 21, 10, or 7 years, or to imprisonment for 3 or 2 years, 1 year, or 6 months. Only 11 of these sentences were served in full, and of these, 6 were of 2 years' impsrionment or under. All other sentences were later commuted.

Those sentenced to death were Khoo T'ean Tek, president of the Kien Tek, and three other members, Khoo Mah Pean, clerk of the society, Yeow Seng, and Khoo Chye, all of whom were found guilty of aiding and abetting murder. 'Che Long, headman of the Red Flag Society, was sentenced to 21 years' transportation for arson. On the Ghee Hin side the only leader to face a charge seems to have been Lee Ko Yin, but the nature of the charge is unknown and he was not convicted.

The news of the death sentences caused strong reactions in Penang, members of the Ghee Hin were jubilant, those of the Kien Tek vengeful. Khoo T'ean Tek, undoubtedly the 'leading instigator of the outbreak',[25] was the acknowledged leader of the Hokkien community, a man of great power and personality. He had been a public problem since 1859, when he was arrested as a result of disturbances between his society and the Ho Seng, and the shopkeepers of the

---

[24] COD/SS 29, 18 Feb. 1868.
[25] GD 44, 23 Mar. 1868, and PRCR, paras 33, 43.

Kien Tek had forthwith shut up their shops, and trade had ceased. He aimed at being the virtual ruler of Penang, the Capitan China. He had been the opium farmer, and had the wealth and prestige which resulted from such a position, while as the 'Elder Brother' of the Kien Tek, the principal Hokkien society, to which post he had succeeded on the death of the founder, Khoo Teng Pang, he had a tremendous power to hand. Nor was he solely concerned with an increase of prestige for himself and for the society. During the period of the riots, when chaos reigned and revenue officials feared to visit the outlying parts of the island, he promoted opium smuggling on a large scale and thus recouped himself in some degree for the loss of the position of manager of the opium farm which he had held earlier, but which had changed hands on a recent call for fresh tenders.[26]

In a letter to the Governor dated 21 February 1868, Colonel Anson wrote that the sentence passed on T'ean Tek had taken everyone by surprise, and as it was anticipated that a rescue might be attempted during the prisoners' transit from the court to the gaol, he had sent them under the escort of a military guard. He added that should the sentence be carried out he would suggest that the execution take place on the seashore of the Esplanade, under cover of the Fort. The *Grasshopper* would be in by that time and might be lying off. Although Anson did not specifically state that he expected any disturbances, and indeed on 7 March expressed surprise that rumours to the contrary had reached Singapore, the naval authorities in the Straits scented trouble, and in London the Secretary of State was informed by the Admiralty that HMS *Perseus* was about to leave for Penang on 1 March, 'in consequence of the unsettled State of things there, arising out of the condemnation and expected execution of these Chinese', a report which, when forwarded to Governor Ord, called forth an angry denial of any 'unsettled' state of affairs.[27]

In Penang Khoo T'ean Tek boasted that the Government would not dare to carry out the sentence passed upon him. He proved to be right. There is ample evidence of the dilemma which presented itself to the authorities. On the one hand, the serious nature of the riots called for exemplary punishment of the instigators and participators, but on the other hand, there was a danger of causing resentment among the mass of the society members either by convictions secured through the evidence of partial witnesses, or by a lack of balance between the amount of punishment awarded to each side in the feud, which might easily lead to further disturbances. As the various sentences became known, numerous petitions on behalf of several of the convicted prisoners were received, praying for remission of sentence on various grounds, the general purport of which was that 'the evidence was false and the prisoners innocent'. The Governor referred these petitions to Sir William Hackett, the Judge who had tried the cases, who said that in most instances the evidence against the prisoners appeared at the time satisfactory; it was direct evidence, and the only question that arose was the credibility of the witnesses. He declared, however, that in one case circumstances which had come to his knowledge *after* the trial had considerably shaken his faith in the witness for the prosecution, and as a result he was disposed to recommend a very great, if not a total, remission of the prisoner's punishment. As the petitions continued to come in, Sir William

[26] PRCR Evidence, Nos 44, 46, 51.
[27] COD/SS 75, 16 May 1868, & GD 128, 24 June 1868.

agreed that most of the evidence against all the prisoners was that of 'pre-judicial witnesses', but he could not say that in any case it was insufficient to warrant a jury in convicting. Nor did he consider that the sentences were more severe than the circumstances of the case warranted, but should the Governor think it desirable to mitigate generally their severity, he would offer no objection to such a course, but if done in one case it should be done in all.[28]

It was in this atmosphere that in response to a further flood of petitions the death sentences passed upon Khoo T'ean Tek and his fellow prisoners were considered by the Governor at a meeting of Executive Council held on 18 March 1868, and attended not only by Sir William Hackett as a member of Council but by the Chief Justice, Sir Peter Benson Maxwell, who had recently returned from England, and who was specially asked by the Governor to attend. The Judge's notes of the trial having been read, the Council unanimously advised that sentence of death should not be carried out against any of the prisoners, advice with which the Governor was in full agreement. But there was consider-able diversity of opinion as to the nature of the punishment to be awarded in commutation of the death penalty. Some members, among whom was the Chief Justice, were in favour of a complete pardon; others advocated various terms of imprisonment and transportation. The majority, however, were against a pardon and were in favour of a limited term of imprisonment, which Sir William Hackett considered might with propriety be about two years. The Governor, feeling that to commute a sentence of death into one of two years' imprisonment could not fail to be 'misunderstood' by both the Kien Tek and the Ghee Hin, being construed as 'a concession made either from a desire to favour, or a fear of displeasing' the Kien Tek, decided to commute the death sentence to one of seven years' transportation, though he admitted that in the existing state of the law this could not be carried out. Khoo T'ean Tek, born in Penang, was a British subject to whom the penalty of transportation did not apply. But the Governor added that it was his intention, 'at no distant period, and when popular feeling should have subsided, to substitute a sentence of two years' imprisonment with Hard Labour'.[29] Meantime, the prisoners were transferred to Singapore gaol.

The Commission under Colonel Man had worked assiduously from August until October collecting a mass of documentary and verbal evidence, but his sudden departure on a posting abroad so angered and discouraged its members that nothing further was done until April 1868 when Colonel Anson, having been instructed by the Governor to produce a report from the evidence already available, called the Commission together and submitted a report on 14 July. Although little evidence was received about the organization and participation of the Flag societies, the report with the Minutes of Evidence and 24 appendices was a most valuable contribution to an understanding of secret society activity in Penang.[30]

Much of the information contained in the report has already been incor-

---

[28] GD 8, 6 Jan. 1869 (retrospective).

[29] GD 44, Sing., 23 Mar. 1868.

[30] GDs 71, 27 Apr. 1868 & 267, 20 Dec. 1870; SSPLC, 1868, app. A, p. ii, Gov's speech at opening of new sess. of Leg. Co., 6 May 1868; GN 58, Col. Sec's Office, 25 Nov. 1868 (PRCR, p. ii). The report is printed in SSPLC, 1868, inc. Act XXI of 1867, GNs, the Proc. of the Com-missioners (pp. i–xiv), List of Witnesses & Mins. of Evidence (pp. xv–xvi & 1–74), and app., pp. 75–134.

porated in the foregoing account of the riots, but the conclusions and the suggestions of the Commission remain to be considered. The Commissioners confirmed that the riots had their origin in a trifling quarrel between two rival Mohammedan societies during the Moharram festival, and that they were fostered by two other rival societies of Chinese, with one of which each of the former had joined in alliance. All these societies joined in the riots by the direction, and under the instigation of their respective headmen or office-bearers, who directed their principal movements, and who, from the funds of their societies, supplied them with provisions and arms, with rewards for the heads of their enemies, and with gratuities and pensions for the wounded and for the relations of those who were killed when fighting. The organization and discipline of the societies appeared to be as complete as that of any disciplined force of the Government, and the Commissioners therefore considered it evident that the secret societies were extremely dangerous to the peace and welfare of the community. Moreover, the combination of the Mohammedans and Hindus with the Chinese, with whose customs their religious prejudices were so much at variance, had rendered them more harmful.[31]

The Commissioners, though not so required in their original terms of reference, made several suggestions for future control. They recommended that the societies be entirely suppressed by legislation, as had been done in Hong Kong.[32] Failing this, all societies should be registered annually with the Commissioner of Police, registration including the names of the headmen of the society, its object, and number of members. All oaths should be prohibited. In case of riot, the headmen should be liable to prosecution and fine, and in default of payment, the property of the society should be forfeit to the Crown. Headmen and members should also be liable for damage or injury to property committed by the society, and heavy penalties should be imposed upon any person found guilty of preventing another from making complaint to the police. As a means of preventing opportunities of collision between rival societies or religious sects, processions in the streets of such societies or sects should not be authorized, but these ceremonies should be confined to the grounds or compounds of such societies or religious communities.[33] The report was placed before Legislative Council on 6 October, and a Select Committee appointed to consider the recommendations.

There was a good deal of prevarication by the office-bearers and members of the societies who gave evidence and who clearly found that the oaths of secrecy of their Brotherhoods were more potent than the court oath upon which they gave testimony. But the Commissioners were empowered to commit recalcitrant witnesses to the House of Correction for three months, and the imposition of this sentence went some way to redress the balance of fear. Oh Wee Kee of the Ghee Hin after a few days of incarceration told the Commission: 'I was afraid of my life. If I state the truth our people will kill me, if I don't you find fault with me, what am I to do? I want you to make an order to dissolve my connection with the Society. I dare not leave by my own will or act.'

The Kien Tek leaders were even more refractory, but eventually most of the plot was unravelled and Khoo T'can Tek exposed as the chief instigator, though

---

[31] PRCR, para. 45.
[32] Hong Kong Ord. of 1845, 'For the Suppression of Triad and other Secret Societies'.
[33] PRCR, para. 46.

he maintained an attitude of stubborn insolence and denied all accusations of complicity.

Evidence as to the relationship between the Flag societies and their Chinese associates was given. Lee Ko Yin of the Ghee Hin stated that the head of the White Flag, Tuan Chik, was also a member of the Ghee Hin and chief of the Ghee Hin Malays. The position of the Red Flag was not so clear. Two officials of the Kien Tek Society denied that the Red Flag men were admitted to membership of their society. 'They do not belong to our Society but they act with us. Che Long calls himself a Toh Pek Kong but he has not taken the oath of membership, nor does he attend the meetings of chiefs of the Toh Pek Kong at the Kongsee House'.[34] On the other hand another official said that he had heard that Malays had joined the society in great numbers. It would seem that they were affiliates rather than full members.

Some details of the composition of the Chinese societies also emerged. Although the majority of the members of the Ghee Hin were 'Macao men' (and it was estimated that seven-tenths of the Cantonese residents were members), there were also Hokkien members, apparently under the control of Oh Wee Kee, upon whose houlders the Ghee Hin sinseh, Boey Yu Kong, placed the blame for the provocations of which Kien Tek members so frequently complained. The Kien Tek, though composed mainly of Hokkiens, many of them Straits-born, also admitted some Hakkas, for there is mention of an office-bearer, Yeoh Hong Hin 'for Kay members [men speaking Kay dialect]'.[35]

The report of the Commission also contained accounts of initiation into the Ghee Hin of Oh Wee Kee in 1845, and of Shamoo, an Indian, in 1866.[36] Translations of ritual verses, regulations, and oaths of the society were also given in Appendices (Nos 17–23). Unfortunately no such detailed documents relating to the Kien Tek were procured, and a very brief description of initiation given unwillingly, revealed little of importance.[37]

The enquiry and the subsequent report were important in that the Commissioners ascertained and recorded the facts of the riots, and, as far as was reasonably possible, investigated the underlying causes of the outbreak. The enquiry itself also demonstrated to the people of Penang that the headmen of the secret societies could be called to account by the Government for the activities of the organizations under their leadership. Moreover, the veil of secrecy which shrouded the ceremonial of the societies was lifted, and authentic if incomplete data was placed on record concerning the ritual observed and the obligations undertaken by the members of the Ghee Hin and the Kien Tek. Perhaps most important of all, the report emphasized the threat presented to the community by the secret societies; and in advocating a policy either of complete suppression or at least of greater control, and in confirming the necessity for additional powers to deal with public upheavals of the nature of the recent riots, it strengthened the hands of the Government, and facilitated further legislative action by which such powers were granted and some control was made possible, though for many years to come the policy of suppression was not adopted.

By mid-July 1868 action had been taken in the courts and the Commissioners had produced their long-awaited report, but as the first anniversary of the riots

---

[34] Evidence No. 28.   [35] Evidence Nos 47, 35, & 22.
[36] Evidence Nos 15 & 36.   [37] Evidence No. 49.

of 1867 approached, the authorities became aware that a dangerous situation was again secretly developing in Penang. Early in August the Commissioner of Police reported that trouble was brewing between the Kien Tek and the Ghee Hin, allegedly because of the machinations of Khoo T'can Tek who, though still confined in the Singapore gaol, had been 'tampering' with his people in Penang, and 'urging them to measures which had alarmed and excited the Ghee Hins, and rendered it not at all improbable that there might be an outbreak'.[38]

The Act for the Better Preservation of the Peace was due to expire on 13 August 1868, and the Governor had not intended to take steps to continue its operation. But on receiving the disturbing news from Penang, a Bill was prepared to renew the Act for a further year, incorporating amendments to meet some of the objections of the Colonial Office, including the omission of the punishment of 100 stripes with the 'cat'. The Bill was hurriedly introduced into Legislative Council on 8 August, and with one exception all members voted in its favour.[39]

The Bill was opposed by the Chief Justice, Sir Benson Maxwell, who had been absent from the Colony when the original Act was passed. Incensed at the lack of notice of the introduction of the Bill, he addressed a long letter of protest to the Secretary of State, setting out his objections not only to the manner of renewal of the Act but to several of its provisions, particularly those which placed the power of imprisonment and deportation not only of aliens but of naturalized British subjects in the hands of the Governor, to be exercised at his absolute will and discretion, without any provisions requiring it to be shown that such deportation was necessary for the preservation of the peace, without the necessity of enquiry or even of written information, and with no right of bail, of appeal, or of Habeas Corpus. Nor did the Chief Justice consider that the 'faction fights' of the secret societies posed any real threat to British rule, and he felt that the powers granted to the Executive of firing on the mob, summoning the heads of societies to act as special constables, flogging for possession of arms, and allowing the magistrates to try riot cases, were excessive.[40]

In forwarding this protest to London, the Governor commented at some length upon Maxwell's criticisms. After enumerating a list of twelve riots which had occurred in Penang since March 1858, he contended that even if these riots were 'faction fights' it was altogether beside the point to dwell upon the origin of such outbreaks as evidence of their harmlessness. He continued:

It is impossible to deny that if large bodies of armed men traverse the country engaged in wrecking, plundering and burning, not only houses but whole villages, and killing and mutilating every opponent they meet, or if they occupy whole districts of a town for days together when similar scenes are enacted, and all the efforts of the authorities supported by the inhabitants are barely sufficient to preserve the town from destruction, it is immaterial what may have given rise to them, their existence is a serious menace to the power of the Government, and British rule is actually endangered.

Notwithstanding the trivial character with which the Chief Justice is anxious to invest these riots, I am satisfied from what I have heard and seen of them that they are

[38] GD 174, 12 Aug. 1868.   [39] Act X of 1868.
[40] This protest, dated 1 Sept. 1868, is published as app. B in SSPLC/1869.

highly dangerous to the peace, safety and prosperity of the Settlements, and that their existence is incompatible with anything aspiring to be called good Government.

Admitting that this is established, I think sufficient plea is made out for entrusting the Government with special powers for dealing with them, and on this ground the Preservation of the Peace Act of last year was passed and is now continued for another year.

The Governor contended that the power of deportation was nothing new, that the power of cancelling a certificate of naturalization was essential, and that the power of requiring the known heads of the societies to act as special constables and to bring the weight of their influence to bear on the rioters was one which, though not legalized until 1867, had been freely used by the former Government and had proved a most useful agency in preserving the peace. He considered that the Ordinance had not to be defended on a question of detail, but on the issue involved, namely the preservation of the public peace and the protection of property, a primary duty of any Government, and he felt that the Government had the right to demand that it be furnished with the means of carrying out these duties, and should not be hampered by the restriction that this right must always be exercised in conformity with the fundamental principles of English law.

The Chief Justice, who is known to entertain peculiar views as to the duties and powers of the Executive, and who states of himself that he is placed in a position independent of the Executive Government to stand between it and the people to shelter and protect the latter, clearly contends for the limitation I have alluded to, but I submit that this is altogether at variance with the principle on which the Government of countries such as the Straits is allowed to be carried on in the earlier stages of their occupation, and I have no hesitation in affirming that the application of this rule to the case of the three Settlements would make the task of governing them very difficult if not impossible.

Furthermore, owing to the difficulty of procuring trustworthy evidence, the convictions in the past had not been numerous nor the punishments inflicted severe, a result which had led the societies to believe that they might give effect to their feelings without fear of the Government. To remove this 'false impression' it was necessary that the Government should be furnished with more extensive powers than it had hitherto possessed, not necessarily that they should be put in force on every occasion, but rather that by their exercise in times of emergency the people should be made aware of their existence and of the readiness of the Government to use them if necessary.[41]

Fortunately, the threatened riot in Penang did not take place, and when proroguing the session of Legislative Council on 19 December, the Governor was pleased to note that during the year (1868) there had been no disturbance. On the contrary, 'he believed that a feeling of contentment and confidence prevailed generally, which was perhaps the best guarantee of the continuance of peace and order'.[42]

Possibly this feeling encouraged the Governor to choose this moment for carrying out his intention of a further remission of the sentences passed upon those found guilty of offences during the 1867 riots. Once again, Sir William Hackett and the Attorney-General considered the notes of evidence taken at the

[41] GD 186, Sept. 1868.   [42] SSPLC/1868/app. Z.

trials. No remission was granted to those offenders who had taken advantage of the outbreak to commit acts of plunder, but the remissions were in every case extended to those who, if their guilt was proved beyond doubt, might fairly have been considered to have been carried away by the excitement of the feud into actions of violence, not for the gratification of any personal feeling, but in obedience to what they looked upon as a duty to their society. Of the original 38 sentences, 3 had already been served, 8 remained unchanged, and 27 were commuted. In particular, Khoo T'ean Tek and his fellow prisoners, Yeow Seng, Khoo Chye, and Khoo Mah Pean, had their sentences reduced to two years' hard labour, and 'Che Long, leader of the Red Flag, served three years' hard labour in place of his original sentence of twenty-one years' transportation.

In forwarding a list of these remissions of sentences, the Governor told the Secretary of State that 'this clemency, shewn at the time of our Christmas and just before the Chinese New Year, when any such boon would be most suitably granted and most appreciated' had a good effect upon the population of the 'Settlements, and that the good effect would not soon pass away'.[43] The Secretary of State readily approved the mitigated sentences but was not entirely happy about the Preservation of Peace Ordinance which he returned 'with certain recommendations for its improvement'. A new Bill embodying these proposals was read a first time on 17 February 1869.[44]

The Secretary of State considered that the state of affairs existing in the Colony required the Executive to exercise the utmost vigilance for the public peace, and to be armed with such powers as would make that vigilance effective. He agreed with the Governor that the application of the ordinary law of England and of principles of procedure prescribed by that law were insufficient for such a purpose, and saw no reason for doubting that the Legislature had acted wisely in extending for a further period of twelve months the operation of the Act. Nevertheless, he considered that the law should not have been passed at a single sitting without notice, and that full opportunity should have been afforded for the objections of any member of the Council to be stated and discussed.

Furthermore, he felt that some of the objections of the Chief Justice were 'deserving of much attention', particularly in regard to the powers of removing or imprisoning foreigners. Though disagreeing with the Chief Justice in thinking that a person so removed or imprisoned should have a right to bail, or a recourse to a suit of 'Habeas Corpus', or a right to appeal, he felt that action for the banishment of any person should only be initiated upon written information against the person concerned. Thereafter, the accused should be summoned before the Executive Council. The information, the evidence, and the defence should be heard, and only after the Governor in Council had expressed an opinion in writing that removal from the Colony was required in the interests of public safety should an order of banishment be issued.

Redrafted along these lines, and with other minor amendments, including the reduction of punishment with the rattan from forty to thirty stripes, the Bill passed its second reading on 25 March, despite a motion by the Chief Justice, seconded by Mr Read, 'that the Bill be read a second time this day six months'. At the third reading on 17 May 1869 these two objectors submitted a written protest calling upon the Secretary of State to refuse his sanction of the Ordinance.

[43] GD 8, 6 Jan. 1869, encl. list of the remissions of sentences.
[44] COD/SS 31, 11 Feb. 1869 (PRO/CO 273(26)); 234, 18 Nov. 1868 (SSPLC/1869/app. B).

In the course of the debate, the Governor admitted that the main support for the Bill came from Penang. He quoted from a Penang petition sent during the early stages of the 1867 riots, urging that heavy flogging be introduced to punish the rioters. He also referred to yet another Penang petition signed not only by Europeans but 'by Chinese, Klings, and other natives' at the conclusion of the riots, expressing the opinion

that the means hitherto adopted by Government to prevent and suppress these outrages have been wholly inadequate, and that from the increasing number and wealth of the members of the societies, and the scale on which they now conduct their wars, for such they are, the peace of this Settlement cannot be preserved without some special provisions being made for that purpose. The ordinary Criminal Law is almost inoperative in the case of such conflicts.

As riots were less frequent in Singapore, it was understandable that unofficial members from that Settlement might not feel the necessity for the powers given to the Executive in the Bill, but with the support of two of the unofficials, Mr T. Scott, and Mr F. S. Brown, and the backing of the Secretary of State, the Governor felt justified in pressing the Bill, which became law as Ordinance VII of 1869, to remain in force until 30 June 1870. It repealed those sections of the 1867 Act which were now re-enacted in an amended form (in particular Clause 10 of Act XX of 1867, with its powers of deporting, and its punishments for the return of deported persons), and was forwarded to London, together with the protest signed by the Chief Justice and W. H. Read.[45]

In conveying Her Majesty's 'gracious confirmation and allowance' of this Ordinance the Secretary of State (now Lord Granville) expressed the hope that no serious emergency would arise to make necessary a continuance of a law of so special and unusual a character,[46] but even before he wrote these words an emergency, springing directly from the new Ordinances, had already arisen in Penang.

The drafting of the new Ordinance was faulty in that it did not provide for the continuance of the legality of action taken under the original section relating to deportation, so that, with the repeal of that section, persons who had been deported under the old Act could return to the Colony without suffering any penalty. The first to take advantage of this oversight was Boey Yu Kong, the sinseh of the Ghee Hin, deported in August 1867 for his part in the riots. His reappearance in Penang in July 1869 caused utter consternation. He was promptly arrested, fined by the Police Magistrate, and in default, committed to gaol. A writ of Habeas Corpus being issued, the Judge of Penang ruled that he was not legally in custody and ordered his release. The fine was not levied, the conviction being quashed, and it was at this stage that the serious omission in the law became apparent.[47]

The citizens of Penang were fearful and the JPs met together on 4 August and passed a resolution praying 'that the Governor be requested to take such steps as may appear to him to be necessary to avert the injurious consequences which the Meeting cannot but anticipate will ensue if the law is to be set at defiance with impunity', an odd form of expression considering that the law was not being set at defiance, but that the makers of the law had failed in their task. The fears of 'injurious consequences' were echoed by the Lieutenant-Governor, who believed that fresh disturbances among the Chinese would result.

[45] GD 130, 29 May 1869.   [46] COD/SS 132, 5 Aug. 1869.   [47] GD 202, 18 Sept. 1869.

The Governor hurried to Penang, and on 6 August held a meeting of Legislative Council, attended, as in August 1867, by himself, the Lieutenant-Governor, the Attorney-General, and Mr F. S. Brown. He explained that the defect in the law was a pure oversight, and to rectify this the Attorney-General introduced an amending Bill which was hurried through its first two readings. At a later meeting of the Council on 12 August, representations against the Bill, submitted by counsel for Boey Yu Kong (Mr R. C. Woods) in person, were received. The committee stage and third reading of the Bill were taken at a full meeting of the Legislative Council at Singapore on 28 August after the counsel for Khoo Poh, the second deportee, had been heard.

Once again the Chief Justice was the main opponent of the Bill, and, seconded by W. H. Read, moved its postponement. He felt that should the deportees return, and misbehave themselves, the Governor had ample powers to punish them. But he further maintained that the original orders of deportation and consequently the enforcement of punishment for the return of persons from deportation were illegal, and that the indemnity to the police and others for the apprehension of Boey Yu Kong was improper.[48] Nevertheless, he refused to specify why he considered that the deportations were illegal, and declined to take advantage of the recommittal of the Bill to move the rejection of the police indemnity. W. H. Read, in support of the Chief Justice, considered that the Government should have followed the example of Siam, Sarawak, and Java, and declared the secret societies illegal in the first place. As early as 1843 resolutions had been passed at a Sheriff's meeting calling upon the Government to pass a law for the suppression of these Brotherhoods, but no action had been taken, except to punish members with deportation. He considered that the present was a suitable time to pass a law to place such societies under control: 'You would then begin at the beginning; we are now beginning at the end. It is better to pass such a law than one such as this which crushes them after . . . patronising and encouraging them for years.'

But the remainder of the Council were quite persuaded of the advisability of retaining the powers provided by the Act, and after a very long debate the Bill was passed and became law as Ordinance No. IX of 1869, coming into force on 7 September. It ensured by its one operative section that any deportee ordered to leave the Colony under Clause 10 of Act XX of 1867 and thereafter returning might be arrested, and detained until such time as arrangements could be made for his further deportation.

Meantime, in consequence of a suggestion made by Counsel retained by the friends of the two deportees, Boey Yu Kong and Khoo Poh, the Governor caused enquiry to be made into the case of Khoo Poh, and was advised by the Attorney-General that the order for this man's deportation was, in fact, illegal. He had been naturalized under the provisions of the Indian Act, XXX of 1852, which conferred upon him all the privileges of a natural-born British subject, and there was no power under the Naturalization Act, VIII of 1867, to cancel this naturalization. This legal nicety had not previously been brought to the notice of the Governor in Council, and the order had been made in the belief that as Khoo Poh was not a 'natural-born' British subject he was liable to deportation. It now became necessary for the Governor in Council to cancel the order made against Khoo Poh, and at the same time it was considered to be

[48] Ibid., para. 9.

L

inexpedient to allow the order against Boey Yu Kong to continue in force. Both orders were thereupon cancelled.

This action was very unfavourably received in Penang, but the Governor hoped that as the law had now been made plain by the passing of the amending Ordinance, his action in cancelling the orders of deportation would be regarded as an act of clemency by the Chinese community.[49] In London, although Her Majesty was advised to confirm and allow Ordinance IX of 1869, 'An Ordinance to supply an omission in the Preservation of the Peace Ordinance 1869', the Secretary of State could not refrain from expressing his regret that more care was not taken at first to ascertain the status of Khoo Poh before he was arrested and deported, and that an oversight had rendered retrospective legislation necessary.[50]

And so, in the end, all the chief actors in the drama were back in Penang. Khoo T'ean Tek, Khoo Mah Pean, Khoo Chye, and Yeow Seng had been released after serving two years in gaol; Khoo Poh and Boey Yu Kong were now free from restraint; and Oh Wee Kee and Lee Ko Yin, leaders of the Ghee Hin who had not been sentenced at all, were still there. Boey Yu Kong discovered that during his period of deportation he had been replaced as sinseh of the Ghee Hin, and that his services were no longer desired by the leaders. He was given a small pension by the society, and moved over to the mainland to live at Kuala Muda in Kedah. A year later 'Che Long, head of the Red Flag, returned to Penang after completing his commuted sentence of three years' hard labour.

Khoo T'ean Tek once again took his place as head of his clan and of the Kien Tek Society, and as time passed became increasingly wealthy and powerful both in Penang and in Perak. But for a few years, until 1872, when once again the spotlight shone on Penang, the main centre of interest shifted to the Legislative Council, Singapore, where, for the first time, attempts were to be made to control secret societies by legislative action.

[49] GD 202, 18 Sept. 1869, para. 9.   [50] COD/SS 205, 29 Nov. 1869.

8

THE STRAITS SETTLEMENTS, 1869–73

1. ATTEMPTS AT CONTROL BY LEGISLATION

THE Peace Preservation Act had strengthened the hands of the Government by granting the Executive powers outside the ordinary law of England so that the riotous outbreaks caused by secret societies might be more effectively suppressed, but this procedure did not satisfy those who believed that the basic solution of the problem was to suppress the secret societies themselves, and to make their very existence unlawful. The petitions to this effect sent to the Governor on the outbreak of the Penang riots in August 1867, and the strong recommendation of the Riot Commission in 1868 that the secret societies be 'entirely suppressed', or alternatively 'that all societies, of whatever nature' should be registered annually with the Commissioner of Police, brought the problem into immediate prominence. But when, on 6 October 1868, the Riot Commission report was laid on the table of the House, a Select Committee of Legislative Council was appointed to bring in a Bill merely 'for regulating Chinese secret societies'.[1] There was no mention of any policy of suppression, nor were the terms of reference even as wide as the provisions of the Bill previously introduced by Thomas Scott on 31 July 1867, 'for the Better Regulation of Societies and Associations, and for the Prevention of unlawful Assemblies'.

The original Committee included the Attorney-General, the Treasurer, and three unofficials, W. H. Read, T. Scott, and Dr Little, but the Treasurer later withdrew, and Dr Little was replaced by Mr F. S. Brown of Penang, whose advice they were particularly anxious to obtain. They found great difficulty in reconciling the differing opinions of its members, and it was not until 22 July 1869, after a very pointed enquiry by the Governor, that a majority report signed by T. Braddell (the Attorney-General), W. H. Read, and T. Scott was eventually forthcoming, followed a month later by a minority report signed by F. S. Brown.

Between the date of the Committee's appointment and that of its report, the terms of reference had been considerably broadened, for the majority report stated that the Committee was appointed 'for the purpose of enquiring into the nature and objects of the secret societies . . . and of suggesting the measures to be adopted whether of total suppression or of restrictive regulation, in regard to the acknowledged evils which exist under their operation'.[2] The Governor, too, in a later despatch, said that the members of the Select Committee appointed on 6 October 1868, were directed to bring in a Bill

for regulating Chinese secret societies in accordance with the recommendations of the Penang Riot Commission, which comprehended the suppression, or if that were found

[1] SSPLC/1868/6 Oct.   [2] SSPLC/1869/app. Y, para. 1.

impossible, the registration of the societies, and the names etc. of their members; the prohibition of all oaths of membership or otherwise, with some penalties for intimidation; and the making the Societies and the headmen or managers thereof pecuniarily responsible for the good conduct of their members.[3]

After months of deliberation, during which they studied Schlegel's work,[4] read the Riot report and its Minutes of Evidence, circularized 'prominent Chinese gentlemen', consulted the Commissioner of Police, Singapore, (Mr Dunman), examined headmen and members of secret societies, and were given access to Colonel Cavenagh's despatches of 1860, the writers of the majority report merely echoed the opinion of the Riot Commissioners that many of 'the numerous secret societies in each of the Settlements . . . had degenerated into unlawful confederacies for objects altogether inconsistent with the public peace, and the due administration of Government by the constituted authorities', and required 'the most determined measures to be adopted for their control'. Their proposals, however, were considerably less rigorous than those suggested by the Commission. They recommended the registration of all secret societies (except Freemasons), to include details of membership and meetings. Headmen should be required to find sureties for their own and for their members' good conduct. Meetings should be open to the authorities. Delinquent societies should be suppressed.[5]

F. S. Brown, a strong supporter of the recommendations of the original Riot Commission, considered that the report now issued did not go far enough. The inter-society fights in Penang, Tongkah, and Larut had shown that they were both criminal and dangerous. They were criminal conspiracies under oath to help members to escape arrest; they concerned themselves with smuggling, gambling, and prostitution, and should be 'entirely suppressed'.[6]

The majority report suggested that secret society activity in Singapore and Malacca had decreased during recent years, but Brown stressed that in Penang not only had such activity increased but it was involving the large Malay population there and in Province Wellesley, particularly through the influence of the Indo-Malays and their societies, which were establishing a stranglehold along the coast opposite Penang Island. Legislation must include those Mohammedan societies, which though not themselves secret, had nevertheless joined with the Chinese secret societies in the riots of 1867, and which had added to the ferocity and destruction of the outbreak.

If the policy was to be confined to registration, then all societies, particularly all Chinese societies, should be made to register, as they all included in their membership numerous secret society members, and it would be comparatively easy for the secret societies to carry on their operations under cover of these other societies.

Finally, Brown objected to the majority report on the ground that it made no provision for the payment of compensation in the event of riots in which any society participated. He considered that leaders of societies cared little for their rank and file but would care a great deal if their own pockets were affected. He

[3] GD 267, 20 Dec. 1869, para. 3.
[4] Gustave Schlegel, *Thian Ti Hwi, the Hung League or Heaven and Earth League* (1866).
[5] SSPLC/1869/app. Y, para. 12.
[6] SSPLC/1869/app. Z, para. 18. While the minority report was submitted by Brown, its prolix legalistic style is probably that of Logan, who drafted it, as Brown himself admitted (SSPLC/1870/20 June, speech by F. S. Brown).

insisted that societies must be able to hold property and must be able to sue and be sued.

The majority report was tabled on 22 July 1869, and the minority report on 31 August, when at the suggestion of the Governor the Council resolved that the Attorney-General, the Auditor-General, and Mr T. Scott should form a committee of three, to prepare a Bill for the compulsory registration of all societies except those formed for trade and Freemasons; for authorizing the Government to require from the societies full information as to their objects, organization, rules, proceedings, etc.; for prohibiting all secret societies and secret meetings of societies.[7] He did not (at this stage) agree with Penang's proposal to make the societies pecuniarily liable for acts of violence committed by their members. But when the Draft Bill was read for the first time in Council on 14 September, Thomas Scott considered that it did not go far enough, and thought that headmen should be pecuniarily responsible and that members found guilty of engaging in street fights should be flogged, since corporal punishment was an effective deterrent to rioting.

The Bill was keenly debated during five Council meetings,[8] and at the second reading on 28 September, extremes of views ranged from Colonel Woolley, the Officer Commanding the Troops, who believed that nothing but suppression would be of any use, to Mr W. R. Scott, who thought that the societies should be allowed to have their riots openly in the streets rather than in secret. He added colour to the debate by suggesting that suppression might lead to secret poisoning and assassination instead of riots. The Governor, while agreeing that suppression would be most desirable, feared that a straightforward attempt would be dangerous. He urged acceptance of the Bill as 'but an instalment of measures by which it was hoped to deal successfully with these societies', and added that if it were passed, he would submit some modification of the Preservation of the Peace Act, which was considered by some whose opinions were entitled to great weight[9] to be unnecessary and unconstitutional, or at all events inexpedient.

The Bill passed its second reading, and was debated in Committee on 2 and 29 October. The chief obstacle to agreement remained the question of pecuniary responsibility. Without such a clause the Bill was considered by its critics to be incomplete and likely to be a dead letter, but the Governor still maintained that it would be impracticable. On 15 November, with Penang and Thomas Scott still holding out, the Governor again urged that the Bill should be passed, but he agreed to limit its operation to one year only. This concession seems to have won over the Chief Justice, for at a final meeting on 24 November, the Governor reported that with his assistance, clauses making the property of the society answerable for any damage which might take place from riots occasioned by the society, and conferring the right to transfer property, and to sue and be sued, had now been introduced.[10] The title of the Bill had been changed from 'secret' to 'dangerous' societies, and it was only to the dangerous societies that it was applicable. Even the Chief Justice now considered that the Bill was satisfactory, and it was passed without a division as Ordinance XIX of 1869, 'An Ordinance for the Suppression of Dangerous Societies'. The title was misleading, for it did not provide for the suppression of these societies but for the registration and

[7] SSPLC/1869/31 Aug.; also GD 267, 20 Dec. 1869, para. 6.
[8] 25 Sept., 2 & 29 Oct., 15 & 24 Nov.
[9] The Chief Justice and W. H. Read.   [10] GD 267, 20 Dec. 1869, para. 7.

control of all societies, whether dangerous or not. Although the original Bill had contained a provision empowering the Registering Officer to refuse to register a society whose objects as stated to him appeared to be of an illegal character, even this moderate form of suppression had not survived.[11]

All societies of ten or more persons other than joint-stock companies and Freemasons were required to register with the Commissioner of Police, giving details as to name, objects, place of business, and the names and addresses of the persons who were to act as managers of the society (s. 1). The Governor, on receipt of written information that any society, whether registered or not, had an illegal object, or that any of its proceedings were likely to prove dangerous to the public peace, could authorize the registering officer to call upon the manager to furnish further particulars as to office-bearers and members, accounts, rules, regulations, passwords, ceremonies, and insignia (s. 3). There was power to refuse registration of 'articles of a warlike or aggressive character or matters of an illegal character' (s. 4), and to call upon managers and office-bearers to enter into bond with two sureties not to infringe any of the provisions of the Ordinance (s. 5). Twenty-four hours' notice of meetings was to be given, and any magistrate, JP, or police officer could attend. Any meeting not complying with these requirements was an unlawful assembly (s. 7). If any riot took place between members of societies, the societies concerned were indictable for the riot and punishable with fine, which could be levied against the property of the manager, office-bearers, and members, and could include amounts ascertained as due in compensation for injury to person or property (s. 13). There were also provisions for the holding of property by registered societies and for them to sue and be sued (s. 26). The Ordinance was to continue in force until 31 December 1870, and not longer (s. 31).

In reporting to London the Governor stressed that his intention was not necessarily to take action under the new Ordinance, but to impress upon the Chinese that the Government was now armed with far greater powers. It would rest with them whether these powers were to be exercised or not. The Government had no intention of using the powers against any society formed for a legitimate object which conducted its affairs without prejudice to the public peace and welfare. Clearly, the Governor was playing for time. He hoped through a 'discreet exercise of these powers' to be able to control this dangerous element in the Straits society, although he knew that the powers were still inadequate to enforce total suppression, handicapped as he was by a weak and inadequate police force, a minimum of military strength, and an ever-growing Chinese population flooding into the Settlements.[12]

The Secretary of State, Lord Granville, in conveying Her Majesty's allowance of the Ordinance, said that he would view the effect and working of this measure with great interest, and asked to be informed from time to time about its operation and its effect on the Chinese.[13]

In fulfilment of his promise to amend the Peace Preservation Act should the Dangerous Societies Ordinance be passed, the Governor caused an Amendment Bill to be introduced immediately on 24 November 1869. But the Chief Justice

[11] SSGG, 1869, pp. 448 ff. (s. 3 of the Bill); ibid. 10 Dec. 1869, pp. 725–30, for Ordinance.
[12] GD 267, 20 Dec. 1869, paras 8–11; also SSPLC/1869/app. UU, Gov's speech at the closing of the sess. of the Leg. Co., Pg, 29 Dec. 1869.
[13] COD 42, 17 Mar. 1870.

strongly objected to any further continuation of an Ordinance which vested in the Executive extra-judicial powers, and sent a protest to the Secretary of State. The new session of Council did not open until 23 May 1870, and the Governor took advantage of the interim to correspond with the Colonial Office, and to incorporate the Secretary of State's subsequent recommendations in a revised draft which was presented to Council on 23 May.

The operation of the new Bill was limited to a period of three years. It confined the main powers conferred on the Government to times of danger and disturbance when part of the Settlement had been proclaimed. Several powers were abandoned altogether, including the suspension of Habeas Corpus, the punishment of a shopkeeper for closing his shop or discontinuing trade during a riot without reasonable excuse, and flogging or detention for illegal possession or keeping of arms. The power of banishment was to be exercised only in respect of persons arrested during the existence of a proclamation who were office-bearers of dangerous societies or had been implicated in riot or disturbance, and provision was made for suspending certificates of naturalization in such cases, subject to confirmation or disallowance by the Secretary of State. A further modification provided that, instead of being detained at the Governor's discretion, a banishee not leaving the Colony might be fined $500 or imprisoned (for not longer than a year) until he agreed to leave and did actually leave the Colony.

In introducing the Bill for its Second Reading on 14 June, the Governor repeated the arguments with which he had already convinced the Secretary of State, urging that the Dangerous Societies Ordinance and the Peace Preservation Act should be retained, at least for some time longer. He believed that the peace which had reigned in Penang during the past two and a half years was directly attributable to the societies' realization of the Government's powers of punishing them severely should they break the law, and any abandonment of these measures would be highly injudicious.[14]

But although the revised Bill went a long way towards meeting the objections of the opponents of the original Peace Preservation Act, particularly in regard to banishment procedure and by making it plain that the special powers could only be used in an emergency when civil disturbance was imminent, nevertheless the Chief Justice remained intransigent and opened the debate with an unprecedented and bitter personal attack on the Governor.

The Governor [he said] wants the *power*, and will look upon this Act much as he may regard the gold lace upon his coat, as only another ornament to his office. It is a sort of gaudy trapping that the Governor values as much as any other of his trappings. Now if that weighs with you, you must not be surprised that I as an English lawyer, refuse to contribute any of the constitutional principles which I respect to the gaudy trappings of His Excellency.

Stressing that what was needed was a stronger police force, he understood that there were objections to this on the score of finance, and again his wrath broke bounds:

Have you not spent, if report speaks truly, something like $200,000 upon the House,[15] and some $200,000 more upon Steamers, since the beginning of our sessions in 1867?

[14] GD 28, 8 Feb. 1870, para. 8; SSPLC/1870/14 June, Gov's speech.
[15] Government House, built 1867–9.

All this for the housing of the Governor and the travelling of a few officials? And yet will you say you would suspend the ordinary rights of the subject, and introduce these despotic principles into our law, to save the money required for a proper police force. . . .

He moved that the Bill be read 'this day six months'.

Surprised and angered at the personal nature of this attack, the Colonial Secretary, J. W. W. Birch, newly arrived from Ceylon and attending his first Council Meeting,[16] deprecated the tone which the Chief Justice had used in alluding to the legislation, pointing out that the laws were the acts of the Council by whom they were approved, not the personal acts of the Governor. He strongly supported the policy of the Government, and regretted only that the Secretary of State had prohibited the provision for flogging.

The debate was resumed on 20 June, when the Chief Justice was supported by three unofficials, W. H. Read, W. R. Scott, and W. Adamson; nevertheless his amendment was defeated. Colonel Woolley backed the Governor; F. S. Brown, speaking with the support of 'all respectable Chinese in Penang', felt that the Bill was necessary to prevent the recurrence of riots, and found particular reasons why the powers previously conferred on the Governor should be retained. In Penang, for instance, several of the secret society leaders who had taken part in the 1867 riots had now returned, and 'without a single exception' all the headmen of the dangerous societies had refused to come in and be registered. Another unofficial supporter of the Bill was the newly-appointed representative of the Chinese community in Singapore, Whampoa,[17] who claimed that he had the support of the 'respectable members' of his community, and confirmed that until recently no Chinese in Singapore had dared to live in the 'country' for fear of being kidnapped.

The Bill was eventually passed on 22 June 1870, as Ordinance III of 1870, and continued the operation of the Preservation of the Peace Ordinance until the end of June 1873. Before the vote was taken, the Chief Justice said that until the country had a strong police, secret societies would continue to flourish because men resorted to them for protection which they did not get from the police.

But although a strong police force and a simple and rapid judicial procedure were necessary ingredients in any plan for dealing with the secret societies, they did not provide the whole answer. For in addition to the protection which could be afforded by the police and the courts, the societies protected members engaged in extortion or those wanted by the police; they could arrange to defend members in court, and could also force their protection on anyone living in their area of control, a practice accepted by the victims because it accorded with the traditional way of life in China's thousands of villages whence they came.

Once the Peace Preservation Act had been extended to remain in force until 1873, steps were taken in like manner to extend the operation of the Dangerous Societies Ordinance until June 1873 by a Bill passed on 17 November 1870 as Ordinance XVI of 1870.

Three months later, on the eve of his departure for a year's leave in England, the Governor reported to the Secretary of State that since the law had been in

[16] The previous Colonial Secretary, Lt-Col. R. Macpherson, RA, had died with tragic suddenness in December 1869.

[17] Whampoa was Ho Ah Kay (see p. 67), who was appointed to Leg. Co. on 21 Dec. 1869 (SSGG, 249, 1869).

operation, no steps whatever had been taken under its provisions except to register societies in the manner required in Section 1. It had not been found necessary to enforce the powers given in Section 3 or in any other sections and there was no evidence to enable him to state with certainty what its effect had been. But he did not doubt that the freedom from riots enjoyed for some time past was largely due to the existence of this law, and the knowledge of the heads of the societies that the Government had the will and the power to enforce its rigorous provisions if necessary.[18]

2. RENEWAL OF SECRET SOCIETY OUTBREAKS, SINGAPORE

Almost as soon as the Governor had left, the Officer Administering the Government in his absence, Colonel Anson, was faced with a full-scale riot in Singapore between the Ghee Hin and another society,[19] during which the rioters fired on a strong body of police, military pickets were posted in the town, and many arrests were made. The societies settled their differences, but the outbreak had been aggravated by a number of bad characters, including several newly-arrived Chinese inhabiting a swamp near the town who took the opportunity to commit depredations at several places in the country.

The Government evidently found their powers too limited on this occasion, and on 13 May, at the first meeting of the new session of Legislative Council, Colonel Anson said that a Bill to amend the Peace Preservation Ordinance would be introduced in order to increase powers of the Executive in times of disturbance, but this was not done. He was hardly encouraged by the attitude of the unofficials, who advocated 'a prompt and conspicuous display of vigilance and energy at the very outset of these disturbances' and who were opposed to any measure encroaching on the liberty of the subject.[20] This implied some criticism of the police, whose incompetence to suppress riots had earlier earned the Chief Justice's strong condemnation. The police were suffering from weak leadership. When the Chief Commissioner, Thomas Dunman, went on a year's leave early in 1870, they were left in the hands of C. B. Waller, himself a sick man. Dunman might have been able to make a reality of the registration of secret societies under Section 1 of the new Ordinance, but Waller, lacking his superior's firm hand and closer knowledge of secret society personnel and activity, was less successful.

Early in June 1871 the Executive Council informed Colonel Anson that 'the public had lost all confidence in the Police'. Waller resigned, and was replaced by Speedy, recently arrived in Penang from Oudh.[21] Anson asked London for Dunman's immediate return and for permission to go on with the reorganization of the police as proposed by the Civil Establishment Committee in 1870.[22] This he was authorized to proceed with at once.[23] Dunman did not return, asking to

[18] COD 9, 16 Jan. 1871; GD 51, Pg, 2 Mar. 1871.
[19] In a despatch from the OAG to the S. of S. (GD 59, 25 Mar. 1871), Anson gives the names of the contending societies as the Ghee Hin and the Ho Seng, but as far as is known there is no other record that the Ho Seng ever existed at Singapore. It may be that Anson, who was normally stationed at Penang where the Ho Seng was very active, confused this society with the Hai San, which was very prominent in Singapore at this time.
[20] SSPLC/1871, 13 & 17 May.
[21] COD 12, 21 Jan. 1871; *SSGG*, 150, 22 June 1871.
[22] GDs 22, 2 Feb. 1871 & 141, 2 June 1871; COD 132, 26 June 1871.
[23] COD 123, 21 June 1871.

retire on grounds of health.[24] He recommended as his successor C. B. Plunket, who had served for four and a half years under him some time earlier, and who had since had experience as Police Magistrate in Penang and Singapore. This recommendation was supported by Ord and accepted by the Secretary of State, and Plunket was appointed in August.[25] Meantime, Speedy returned to Penang, and Waller went on a year's leave, being replaced by Captain S. Dunlop, RA, who had already won high praise for his work in police appointments in Penang and Province Wellesley since October 1870.[26]

In Legislative Council money was voted for the improvement of the police establishment, and on 17 October an Ordinance was passed (VI of 1871) providing for the appointment of an Inspector-General of Police for the Straits Settlements, with a Superintendent in each Settlement and another in Province Wellesley. The force was to be constituted as a single unit, and all officers were required to serve in any of the three Settlements, 'according to the exigencies of the Service'.[27] There was also provision for the regulation of assemblies and processions in public roads through general rules to be made by the IGP, subject to approval by the Governor in Council.

No sooner had this Ordinance been passed than the police were faced with renewed rioting, which broke out on 21 October, not between two societies but, as in 1854, between the Tiechiu and Hokkien elements in the island, who between them constituted the greater part of the population. Influential Hokkien and Tiechiu leaders, heads of the societies, kept aloof, and the disturbances were mainly confined to the 'lower and cooley classes', joined by criminals who took advantage of the opportunity for looting and rioting. Allegedly, fighting began when a Hokkien discovered a Tiechiu picking his pocket at a Chinese theatre, and raised a hue and cry. The trouble spread through town and country, arousing all the old tribal antagonisms. Naval and military forces were called in to assist the police, and on 23 October the Settlement was proclaimed under the Preservation of the Peace Ordinance.[28] All Europeans were sworn in as special constables, and additional magistrates were appointed, including five Chinese: Ho Ah Kay (Whampoa), Tan Kim Cheng, Seah Eu Chin, Tan Beng Swee, and Tan Seng Poh.[29]

Shops and offices closed. The heads of the Chinese societies were detained at police headquarters until the riot subsided and were used by the authorities to persuade the warring parties to desist. Even so, the disturbances lasted for several days, and 520 rioters were tried by the magistrates, 165 being publicly flogged and receiving from ten to thirty stripes each. For this public flogging there was now no legal sanction, and when the matter came to the notice of the Secretary of State through the columns of the *London and China Telegraph* of 26 December, he asked for an explanation.[30]

Once again the police made very poor showing. In his reports to the Secretary of State[31] Colonel Anson spoke warmly of the help he had received from govern-

[24] COD 126, 23 June 1871, with encl.
[25] COD 141, 10 July 1871 (*SSGG*, 181, 18 Aug. 1871); CDs 206 & 207, 6 Oct. 1871.
[26] Waller: *SSGG*, 188, 28 Aug. 1871; Dunlop: GDs 91, 20 Apr. 1871, & 153, 14 June 1871; *SSGG*, 194, 11 Sept. 1871.
[27] COD 131, 26 June 1871; *SSGG* (Extraord.), 224, 31 Oct. 1871.
[28] *SSGG* (Extraord.), 213, 23 Oct. 1871.
[29] *SSGG*, 216, 219 (Extraord.), & 220, 23 & 24 Oct. 1871.
[30] COD 10, 7 Jan. 1872.   [31] GDs 247 & 263, 24 Oct. & 8 Nov. 1871.

ment officers, magistrates, JPs, special constables, the Officer Commanding the Troops, and the Captain of HMS *Rinaldo* and his officers and men, but the police received a damning report:

Mr Plunket, the newly-appointed IGP exerted himself to the best of his abilities, but from what I myself saw and from the reports which reached me I am doubtful of his possessing the qualifications necessary for the reorganisation of the Police, the thorough disorganisation of which was only too apparent during the disturbances.

On the advice of his Executive Council, Anson brought the new Police Ordinance into immediate operation,[32] but repeated his misgivings in his speech at the end of the Legislative Council session, saying that neither legislation nor emolument could take the place of a competent head or of an able and willing staff of assistants.[33] Nor was Anson himself to escape criticism, for the Secretary of State, after receiving the first reports of the riots, echoed the earlier opinion of the unofficials, saying that if more vigorous measures had been taken at the outset, the disturbances might not have been so widespread.[34]

Meantime, in London the Governor had made a personal effort to solve the problem of interpretation in the courts. This problem was not new. As early as 1828 an abortive attempt had been made to obtain a person of standing from China to act as an interpreter.[35] Over the years, the difficulties of passing information to the Chinese community by means of the written word had been repeatedly evident in times of trouble. During the period of negotiations for the transfer to the Colonial Office, a memorandum prepared by former residents of the Straits Settlements included the proposal that 'a number of young men should be selected who, by becoming thoroughly conversant with the Chinese language, might qualify themselves to act as interpreters in the Courts of Justice',[36] and when the decision was taken to recruit Cadets for the Administrative Service in the new Colony, it was the intention of the Secretary of State that two out of the first three Cadets should be required to learn Chinese. Unfortunately, argument about the status of Cadets and Interpreters frustrated this intention, and in November 1869 Ord was advised to obtain the services of a Hong Kong Cadet. As no one suitable proved to be available, it was left to him to make further proposals, and there, for the time being, the matter rested.[37] The question was raised again in Legislative Council on 1 August 1871 by William Adamson, who gave notice that he would ask whether the attention of the Government had been called to the state of interpretation of the Malay, Chinese, and Tamil languages in the Supreme Court.[38]

About this time Ord made the acquaintance of William Alexander Pickering, home on leave from China. As a young man, Pickering had been third mate of a Liverpool tea-clipper, and had later joined the Chinese Maritime Customs Service as a tide-waiter, the most junior post occupied by Europeans, which entailed checking the loading and unloading of vessels. He applied himself to the study of Chinese and was transferred to Formosa where, after leaving the Service,

[32] *SSGG* (Extraord.), 224, 31 Oct. 1871.
[33] *SSGG* (Extraord.), 17 Nov. 1871.   [34] COD, 259, 19 Dec. 1871.
[35] See above, p. 98.   [36] COD 95, 1 June 1869, Encl.
[37] GDs 130 (27 June 1868), 58, 68, & 186 (5 & 15 Mar., 4 Sept. 1869), and 59 (14 Mar. 1870); CODs 233 (14 Nov. 1868), 102 & 191 (13 June & 13 Nov. 1869), and 71 (23 Apr. 1870).
[38] SSPLC, 1 Aug. 1871.

he took employment with a business firm. He was 31 years old and had lived for eight years in China when he met Ord in London, and was then said to have not only a knowledge of Hokkien but of Mandarin and other dialects, as well as written Chinese.

On 6 December 1871 Ord strongly recommended him to the Secretary of State for the post of Interpreter and Teacher of Chinese, asking that he be appointed Chief Interpreter with a salary of £500 a year, such salary to be reconsidered at the end of five years. His duties should include teaching Chinese to Cadets or others qualifying as Interpreters, interpreting in the courts and elsewhere, and drawing up proclamations or notices and translating documents. But Pickering also expressed his willingness to assist the police by keeping in personal touch with the influential men of the societies, generally making himself useful in any matters concerning the Chinese. He was appointed on 26 December 1871, and arrived in Singapore three months later, just as the Governor himself was returning from leave. While the lack of a European officer with a working knowledge of Chinese had been keenly felt, it is doubtful whether anyone realized how important Pickering would become in a very short time.[39]

In Singapore, once the riots of October 1871 had subsided, Plunket had turned his attention to the registration of secret societies which, to his consternation, he found had been most inefficiently carried out by his predecessors. Only one headman had been registered for each society, and in many cases the name given was not that of the real head of the society but had been entered from hearsay without even referring to the books of the society or to the person whose name was registered. He instituted a fresh registration, beginning with the Hokkien Ghee Hin, obtaining possession of all their books, entering the names of 94 of their managers, and calling the headmen to sign the register and to swear to the truth of their declarations before two Chinese JPs, Whampoa and Tan Kim Cheng. By September 1872, when Plunket submitted a report to the Governor, twelve secret societies had been so re-registered.[40] At the same time Dunlop had started training police in riot suppression until interrupted by his recall to his regiment at Hong Kong.

The secret society scene remained unsettled for, once the memory of the public floggings of October 1871 had faded a little, a series of disturbances began again which were a pale reflection of the earlier tribal rivalry. They did not amount to serious rioting, and were suppressed with comparative ease by the usual procedure of swearing in the society heads as special constables, but nevertheless they caused some anxiety to the more law-abiding sections of the public as being symptomatic of turbulent elements within the community liable to erupt.

The main disturbances resulted from an attempt by the Hai San and the clan association of the Lims to break up the Ghee Hok, which was weakened by internal dissensions. Outbreaks centred on the Ghee Hok headquarters in Carpenter Street and sometimes spread to New Bridge Road and Hong Kong Street, areas which were also the haunts of the hordes of 'samsengs' or professional thugs who hung around the brothels and the gambling dens and could be relied upon to assist in any street brawl. A brief outbreak on 6 December 1871

[39] COD 264, 27 Dec. 1871 (Encl.: Sir H. Ord to the Earl of Kimberley, London, 6 Dec. 1871); GD 52, 17 May 1872.
[40] Report of the IGP (C. B. Plunket) on the working of Ordinance No. XIX of 1869, the Dangerous Societies Suppression Ordinance, 24 Sept. 1872 (SSPLC/1872, app. 19).

was followed by a more lengthy one between the Lims and the Ghee Hok late in January 1872, when there was rioting and robbery. In March and April there was renewed trouble between the Hai San and the Ghee Hok, with sporadic fighting over a period of five days in each case.

Such was the state of affairs when the Governor returned to the Colony in March 1872. One of his first tasks was to reply to the Secretary of State's request for an explanation of the floggings the previous October, and he admitted that it was regrettable that punishment not sanctioned by law should be inflicted, but was convinced that no other course was open to the magistrates. He hoped that no censure would be passed upon them.[41] Speaking in the Legislative Council on 4 June, he regretted these disturbances and hoped that 'firm and judicious exercise of the powers with which the Government was furnished' would prevent further outbreaks. Then, as neither he nor the Secretary of State was satisfied with the Police Ordinance as passed in October 1871, a new Bill to repeal and re-enact that Ordinance was immediately introduced, and became law on 4 July as Ordinance I of 1872. It embodied suggestions made by Ord when in England and approved by the Secretary of State.

The debates on the Bill were particularly important in that the question of including Chinese in the police force was discussed. The suggestion was made by an unofficial member, Mr J. J. Greenshields, on 20 June, and was supported by another unofficial, Dr Little, who considered that if at least a third or a quarter of the constables were Chinese the whole force would be more efficient. The Colonial Secretary, J. W. W. Birch, seemed inclined to agree, though he pointed out the difficulty that Chinese members of the police would be members of their own secret societies. 'The whole system of secret societies', he said, 'is to be condemned, and it is doubtful whether the Government is right in tolerating them, or whether there will ever be order until they are put down.' He thought that there would be no difficulty in getting large numbers of respectable Chinese in the force if the right methods of recruitment were adopted, and he considered it 'extremely desirable' to make the attempt.

The Governor disagreed. He admitted that the employment of men who spoke the language was absolutely necessary for the detection of crime, but disapproved of their recruitment as uniformed police, and in this he was supported by Whampoa, and by other Chinese merchants.

Nevertheless, at the next meeting of Council on 27 June, Greenshields tabled a motion, seconded by Dr Little, 'That this Council considers that there should be a Chinese element in the Police Force and trusts the Government will see their way to introducing it.' The opposition was led by Thomas Shelford, who considered that Chinese police would be a failure. If it was thought desirable to appoint them, they should not be appointed without testimonials from two well-known and respectable Chinese inhabitants of the town, so as to avoid introducing the samseng and general blackguard element.

Referring to the danger of Chinese clan and tribal jealousies, he said that an Indian or a Malay constable could arrest a Chinese without arousing bitter feelings, but should a Hokkien constable arrest a Tiechiu, or vice versa, there would be far more chance of a serious breach of the peace than of the laws being respected. He also thought that the ramifications of clan and tribal loyalties were an added obstacle to appointing Chinese as constables. In China a man appointed

[41] GD 29, 2 May 1872.

as a Mandarin was moved to a distant part of the country as it was recognized that he could not administer the law with impartiality in his own district. In Singapore it was well known that the opium 'chintings' (outdoor officers) would sometimes refuse to search a house or watch a district because it was occupied by their friends.

But the employment of Chinese as detectives was a very different matter. Under European Inspectors they could doubtless often ferret out a crime of which a Malay or Kling constable might not have an inkling. The Government might have to adopt the old principle of setting a thief to catch a thief, and might take a lesson from 'the spying system at present pursued in connection with the gambling establishments'. He believed that an efficient police force might yet be created with an increased staff of Europeans, with increased pay and a gradual weeding out of useless men.

Greenshields' motion was not pressed to a division, and an amendment by the Attorney-General calling for an increase of the number of Chinese in the detective branch of the police was carried. But as the whole question was a matter which deserved more serious consideration, the Governor, although personally opposed to the admission of Chinese constables, appointed a Commission under the chairmanship of the Chief Justice, Sir Thomas Sidgreaves,[42] to enquire into the desirability of introducing Chinese as ordinary members of the police force. Those appointed included Greenshields, Shelford, and Little, together with W. H. Read (former member of Legislative Council), Thomas Dunman (former Commissioner of Police, and now retired in Singapore), and Tan Seng Poh. The Commission was gazetted on 19 July 1872,[43] but did not produce a report until June 1873.

Meantime, the information required concerning the flogging of October 1871 had reached London, and the Secretary of State, while not overlooking the fact that 'in the opinion of persons capable of judging' the action taken had stopped a dangerous riot, was by no means convinced that the riots could not have been suppressed without violating the law in this way. He again stressed that the infliction of punishment unauthorized by the law was a most grave act, never to be resorted to by the Government except under the pressure of extreme necessity and danger.[44] But he was sufficiently impressed with the 'peculiar circumstances of the Colony' to sanction an amendment of the Peace Preservation Ordinance so as to allow the punishment of whipping for offences committed during the continuance of a proclamation, though he still prohibited flogging for riot offences under the Penal Code.[45] The Governor decided to introduce the necessary amendment without delay and to take the opportunity of making the Peace Preservation Ordinance and the Dangerous Societies Ordinance permanent parts of the Colony's law. Bills to this effect were introduced into the Legislature on 15 August 1872.

It was at this stage that minor secret society disturbances began again. For nine days there was intermittent fighting between two societies of Straits-born Chinese, the Tong Soon and the Wah Kang. In September 'Macao' carpenters belonging to the Kong Fee Siew (Kwong Wai Shiu), a branch of the Ghee Hin,

[42] Thomas Sidgreaves was appointed to be Chief Justice on 12 Oct. 1871, in succession to Sir Peter Benson Maxwell who had retired (GN 211, 12 Oct. 1871).
[43] GN 133 of 19 July 1872.   [44] COD 132, 24 June 1872.
[45] Ibid.; GD 153, 4 Oct. 1872; SSPLC, 15 Aug. 1872 (Attorney-General's speech.)

and the Choong Hee (Chung Yi Tong), began to quarrel, then the Ghee Hok–Lim clan feud flared up once more, and finally there was a threatened disturbance between the Ghee Hin and another of its branches, the Ghee Sin (a Tiechiu affiliate) at Rochore. None of these outbreaks led the Government to call upon any of the societies involved to register full particulars under Section 3 of the Ordinance, with a view to placing them in the category of Dangerous Societies, and this was a basis of criticism by unofficial members when the proposal to make the Dangerous Societies Ordinance a permanent part of the laws of the Colony was brought before them.

Before this debate took place, there was a heated discussion in Council on 22 August in connexion with the prohibition of flogging for riot in the Penal Code. Thomas Shelford considered that the Secretary of State's decision was 'very much to be regretted'. He thought that 'all Eastern experience went to prove that whipping was a much more efficient punishment than imprisonment'. In Singapore it would be of great help in cases where a number of hooligans rushed out of a house to hound a few unfortunate victims in the streets. Rioters should be whipped on the spot in the presence of their associates. J. J. Greenshields and Dr Little also spoke in favour of whipping, and Colonel Woolley declared that he was certain that the riots of October 1871 would never have been quelled without firing on the mob unless flogging had been administered on the spot. The Governor, too, thought that if whipping could be introduced as a punishment for small riots of say a dozen men on each side, more serious developments might be prevented.

The debate on the Bills to amend and re-enact the Peace Preservation Ordinance and the Dangerous Societies Ordinance began on 19 September and while there was no opposition of any kind to these Ordinances being made permanent, there was very strong unofficial criticism of the Government's failure to use to the fullest extent the powers granted under the Dangerous Societies Ordinance. Shelford referred to that Ordinance as a 'semi-farce'. Greenshields asked why, when such an unusual display of force had been found necessary to deal with the riot, the Ordinance had not been brought into operation. The Colonial Secretary contended that the Peace Preservation Ordinance had provided the necessary sanction for the suppression of the riot, which had not in any case been a 'society' affair, but an outbreak by 'a large concourse of the rowdies of the place, who did not belong to the societies'. He claimed that the society leaders sworn in as special constables, even Chua Moh Choon (the notorious headman of the Ghee Hok society), had given the Government every assistance.

At the next meeting on 26 September, a report by the IGP on the registration of societies and on outbreaks since 6 December 1871 was laid on the table. Dr Little took the opportunity of reminding the Council that he had warned them that the societies would put forward men of straw as their headmen and so make registration useless. He declared that their influence was apparent not only in the riots but in every walk of life, to the extent that it was hardly possible to get an honest witness to come forward in the police court. 'It is boasted that they are the rulers of Singapore instead of the Government, and that is so well-known that I am only surprised that Your Excellency has not thought fit to show them who *is* the ruler of Singapore.' He regarded the law as a dead letter. The Chief Justice, in a quiet, firm speech, supported those who wished to see the Ordinance firmly implemented. 'What we are concerned to see is that the serious riots which have occurred shall not occur again.' He thought it very desirable that if there were a repetition of the riots, some of its provisions should be put into force, including pecuniary liability for damage.[46]

The Bill passed its third reading and became part of the permanent law as Ordinance V of 1872. Similarly, the Bill to amend and re-enact the Peace Preservation Ordinance became law as Ordinance VI of 1872. Its principal amendments were contained in Sections 11 and 12, which permitted the whipping of certain persons during the continuance of a proclamation. At such times, all persons remaining unlawfully, riotously, or tumultuously assembled after having been warned by a JP, and all persons carrying arms, were liable to whipping in place of or in addition to other penalties. The maximum number of strokes was to be fifty when ordered by the Supreme Court, forty when ordered by the Court of Quarter Sessions, and thirty when ordered by a magistrate. The instrument to be used was 'a rattan not exceeding half an inch in diameter'.

On 10 October, when the Council was faced with the bill for the landing of the naval brigade, the employment of the military for several days, and the turning out of all the European merchants and their clerks for more than a week as special constables, the sub-committee examining the various items of expenditure expressed the hope that such charges would be rendered unnecessary in future by the increased efficiency of the police force, which ought to be able to deal with riots without such aid.

There were further grounds for this criticism when on 29 October, during the absence of both the Governor and the Colonial Secretary on a visit to Selangor, a riot broke out in Singapore which once again had to be suppressed by the military. This riot, like that of 1857, was caused by an attempt to enforce the provisions of the Conservancy Act, by the removal of unauthorized stalls at the roadsides and on the pavements which impeded the work of town cleansing.

A police notice in Malay was issued announcing that this was to happen, but omitted to state that itinerant hawkers might continue to trade without interference provided they they kept on the move. The rumour soon spread that the police intended to prohibit all hawking, and once they began to remove the offending stalls they inevitably aroused the wrath of the hawkers who complained to Whampoa and other JPs. Although the IGP (Plunket) was warned by Whampoa on 26 October that discontent was rapidly rising, no action was taken to explain to the hawkers what was proposed, and by the 29th the samsengs of the town had taken advantage of their grievances to start a riot.

The riot was a demonstration against the police, and the mob gathered on the road between the Central Police Station and the magistrates' courts. Members of the force on the streets were stoned. Inside the courts and the police station were more than twenty magistrates and the chief officers of police, but the IGP was advised by some of the Chinese JPs to keep the police out of sight as much as possible to avoid inflaming the crowd. As a result no police action was taken and no arrests made.

The administration was equally impotent. In the absence of both the Governor and the Colonial Secretary the responsibility lay with an Assistant Colonial Secretary (E. A. Irving), a comparatively junior and inexperienced officer, to whom no powers under the Peace Preservation Ordinance had been delegated. He was not even empowered to summon a meeting of the Executive Council, and

[46] SSPLC/1872/26 Sept./Chief Justice/p. 107.

had to content himself with issuing a notice stating that the police order had been misunderstood, and then calling in the troops and the volunteers.

The Governor returned with all speed to Singapore, and found the town quiet, but was soon aware of the angry criticism of the manner in which the recent situation had been handled. He wrote immediately to the Secretary of State[47] lest press reports should precede his despatch, and admitted that his and the Colonial Secretary's absence had been a factor in the weakness which had been shown. A Commission was appointed to hold a public enquiry, and steps were taken to ensure that in future two JPs were permanently empowered to call out and swear special constables in the absence of the Governor, who also drew up a directive for the police and the administration for use in time of emergency. Later, from London, came added instructions.[48]

The Commission started its work at once, and the daily accounts of the evidence taken strengthened the Governor's conviction that changes were needed in the higher ranks of the police. He informed the Secretary of State that steps had clearly not been taken to organize and train the police to enable them to deal with even the smallest street riot. What was needed was military training, and he asked for the assistance of Captain Dunlop from Hong Kong. Dunlop arrived on 14 December and was appointed to act as IGP in the place of Plunket, who had applied for a year's leave.[49]

Two days later the Governor left for Penang to investigate the trouble caused by secret society antagonism at the Larut tinfields, and almost at once Dunlop was faced with the first of a series of society riots in Singapore, when the Ghee Khee (Tiechiu) and the Ghee Hin (Hokkien) fought in the streets. Under Dunlop's leadership the police acquitted themselves well, exhibiting 'a steadiness and determination very much greater than they had hitherto displayed',[50] but on 23 December there was another outbreak, this time between the Ghee Hok (Tiechiu) and the Ghee Hin (Hokkien) when there were several casualties. The Governor, still in Penang, authorized the issue of a proclamation under the Peace Preservation Ordinance, and instructed Dunlop to take action against the societies concerned. The police took possession of all the books and flags of the Ghee Hin, the Ghee Hok, and the Ghee Khee, the leaders of which were then called upon to register under the provisions of Section 3 of the Dangerous Societies Ordinance, giving full particulars of their membership and organization. In addition, the head of the Ghee Hin was required to find security against any further infringement.[51]

Cases of assault and occasional stabbings continued, and on 8 January 1873 there was a further disturbance between the Tiechiu and Hokkien communities. Gangs armed with spears, poles, and stones rushed into New Bridge Road intent on looting the rice shops. The police led by Dunlop were quickly on the scene; Dunlop himself entered the fray and seized two of the ringleaders, who the same afternoon were sentenced by the court to receive thirty stripes of the rattan and six months' imprisonment, thereafter to be bound over in two sureties to keep the peace for four months. Two men were sentenced to six months' rigorous imprisonment and five others ordered to find sureties. This quick and decisive action checked the riot, and for a few weeks there was comparative quiet.

[47] GD 178, 3 Nov. 1872.
[48] Ibid.; COD 72, 9 Apr. 1873 (printed as app. 23 of SSPLC/1873).
[49] GD 217, 14 Dec. 1872.   [50] GD 14, 18 Jan. 1873.   [51] GD 84, 27 Mar. 1873

M

But during the second half of February there was again trouble. The Ghee Hin came to blows with the Hai San, whose membership included Tiechius. The disturbance ceased after the flogging of five of the rioters at the police court had apparently filled the spectators with 'wholesome dread', and the Hai San was also called upon to register under Section 3 of the Dangerous Societies Ordinance. A few days later, a serious fight began at the Tanjong Pagar Wharf between Hokkien coal-heavers and 'Macao' carpenters, when one man was killed and several others seriously hurt. This was probably another manifestation of the Hokkien–Tiechiu feud. All work stopped, and the Macaos in particular seemed determined to continue hostilities. Eighteen ringleaders were arrested and sentenced to imprisonment, twelve of them receiving in addition corporal punishment with the rattan, whereupon peace was restored.[52]

The registration of the Ghee Hin, the Ghee Hok, the Ghee Khee, and the Hai San was carried out by Pickering, and from this time there began a partnership between Pickering and Dunlop which was to remain an important factor in the secret society world for many years to come. Reporting to London, the Governor acknowledged that Pickering's services had been 'of the greatest value to Government' in dealing both with individuals and with societies, 'about which we have at last obtained reliable information'.

It was against this background that the report of the Commission appointed to enquire into the hawkers' riot of October 1872 was laid before the House at the opening meeting of the new session on 11 March 1873, and was debated on 28 March and 4 April. The Governor had forwarded the report to London early in January, and had expressed his opinion that the neglect to have a correct notice to the hawkers translated into Chinese had been the primary cause of the outbreak. With this the Secretary of State agreed, but the matter had probably been oversimplified. Prolonged experience of such situations leads to the belief that hawkers do not as a rule abandon their positions on request. Instead, the police are invariably met with stubborn passive resistance, or are challenged to use force, and the point is inevitably reached when tact and persuasion are exhausted and physical removal is the only alternative. Then the trouble begins. The police in 1872 were not the highly-trained and disciplined force that they later became, but even today the hawker problem remains unsolved.

The Commission was highly critical not only of the manner in which the police rank and file had treated the hawkers when carrying out their original task of clearing the roads but of the subsequent failure of the higher command to take measures to contain the riot which followed. They considered that the riot was more than a fight between the hawkers and the police, and stressed that those principally engaged in the disturbances were samsengs and the rowdies of the town, who took advantage of the hawkers' grievances to create a riot for their own purposes of looting and theft. Over the past two years hordes of such rowdies and bad characters infesting the Tiechiu Prefecture of Kwangtung near Swatow had been driven out of China and had taken refuge in the Straits. According to the Commission (possibly primed by Pickering) these samsengs were attached to the various secret societies and implicitly obeyed the headmen's orders. They were brothel bullies, guarded illicit gaming houses, and were always ready to join a mob or create a riot, taking the opportunity of plundering and stealing. It was possible to assemble a group in a few minutes, and the Commission felt that

[52] GD 84; *Straits Daily Times*, 27 Feb. 1873.

unless this evil was suppressed firmly and without delay there would be 'most serious results to the peace and prosperity of the Settlements'.

The report stated that neither the Government nor the police had any knowledge of the movements of these immigrants, or any control over them, and the immigrants themselves knew of no authority but that of the secret societies to which they were soon affiliated. The Commission therefore recommended that all Chinese immigrants should be registered on arrival by a Registering Officer (with interpreters), and should be kept under proper supervision until they had found work. Each labourer should be given a numbered parchment ticket showing in Chinese the name of his employer, the place to which he was to be taken, and the terms on which he was to serve. The Commission even went a step further and suggested the introduction of a system similar to that in force in the French and Dutch possessions whereby the Settlements would be divided into districts, each of which would be under a Chinese headman responsible for the order of his district and the movements of the Chinese in it. The districts would be visited regularly by the Registrar, who would hear complaints, settle quarrels, and note any changes in the inhabitants as well as in the district itself.

Owing to a serious difference of opinion between the Secretary of State and the Governor as to the officer to be appointed as head of the police, and in an attempt to influence the Secretary of State in favour of Captain Dunlop, attention during debates in the House was concentrated *not* upon the recommendations concerning immigration but upon the 'amazing improvement' in the 'morale and general tone of the police' since the arrival of Dunlop. The Colonial Secretary referred to the subsequent riots of December 1872, which, though 'much more serious than the October riots', had been put down by the police without any outside help. Among the unofficials J. J. Greenshields considered that Dunlop was thoroughly capable and fitted in every way to be the head of the police. Shelford also supported his appointment, and these opinions reinforced that of the Colonial Secretary, who had already expressed to the Governor his belief that with Dunlop's aid the Government was quite able to cope with any future Chinese riots. But difficulty over finding an alternative post for Plunket delayed Dunlop's appointment as substantive IGP until 4 May 1875.[53]

Hard on the heels of the report on the riot of October 1872 came the report of the Commission appointed on 18 July 1872 to consider the desirability of admitting Chinese as ordinary members of the police force. All members of the Commission, with the exception of Dr Little, signed the main report. While they considered that, in view of the large Chinese population, it would be most desirable if practicable to employ Chinese as ordinary members of the force, they declared that they should only be employed as detectives, because of the powerful influence of the secret societies. The Commissioners claimed that this decision was supported by the most wealthy and influential proportion of the Chinese community, and by all the experienced witnesses examined before the Commission, with the exception of J. D. Vaughan, who believed that if a Chinese was sworn into the police and entered the service of the Government he would do his duty, and not regard the secret societies. Dr Little, who presented a minority report, asked how it was possible to prevent crime and keep the peace if the whole police force was as ignorant of the Chinese language as the Metropolitan Police in London. He thought that an earlier experiment had failed only because

[53] GN 132, 4 May 1875 (*SSGG*, 8 May 1875, p. 389).

Chinese had not been introduced in sufficient numbers. As for the influence of secret societies on Chinese police, the remedy he proposed was Government control of the societies by fining, imprisoning, and deporting the members who broke the law. When it had been demonstrated that the Government would not allow an *imperium in imperio*, it would be proved that the Chinese would do their duty 'faithfully and well', as they always had when employed by Europeans. He finally suggested that whenever a Chinese was involved in a prosecution, the Sitting Magistrate should be assisted by a respected, well-informed Chinese conversant with English, Malay, and either Hokkien or Tiechiu.

W. H. Read, in a memorandum attached to the main report, considered that the employment of Chinese in the police would lead to 'still further demoralisation', but offered an alternative solution based on the proceedings of a Commission which had sat at Hong Kong. This was to gain the co-operation of 'the respectable Chinese' by governing the Chinese community through 'Captains China'. He suggested that the Dutch system at Batavia should be studied, and referred to the 'somewhat similar arrangement' at Singapore when 'unrecognised by Government' the late Tan Tock Seng, Tan Kim Seng, and Tan Kim Cheng acted as Captains of the Chinese. He said that though they had no legal powers, they exercised considerable control over their countrymen, and he believed that without some such system the large sums it was proposed to spend on reorganizing the police would largely be thrown away.

The report was laid before Legislative Council on 16 June 1873 and was discussed on 7 July, when Thomas Scott urged the Government to suppress the societies, after which it would be possible to employ Chinese in the police. While agreeing that this was a very desirable policy, the Governor was clearly not prepared to adopt it. He pointed out that the societies had been individually brought under far greater control than ever before as a result of their re-registration, but he was forced to admit that in the Native States of the mainland they were causing serious trouble. Unfortunately, the Government was precluded from preventing this by the policy of non-interference in the Native States which had been laid down. The Council finally agreed that it was inadvisable to employ Chinese in the police force.[54]

The proposals for suppression and for including Chinese in the police had both proved to be unacceptable to the Government on the ground of impracticability, and attention was now turned to the suggestion made by the Commission on the riots of October 1872 that there should be some restriction of immigration, a suggestion that had aroused the interest of the Secretary of State.

From the earliest years of the British in Malaya, unrestricted immigration had been the accepted policy, and even the attempt made by Raffles to introduce a measure of protection of the immigrant labourers had little practical result. Nevertheless, suggestions for some form of restriction or registration of the immigrant population were repeatedly made by officials after periods of stress when the authorities had found difficulty in controlling alien communities of which virtually nothing was known.

Such a situation had arisen in Penang in May 1825, when the Governor, Robert Fullerton, feared an invasion by the forces of the Raja of Ligor with the help of Chinese on Penang Island. He at once asked whether enquiry was made of newcomers as to the object of their coming or their means of subsistence. He

[54] The report was printed as app. 27 in SSPLC/1873.

also asked whether there were any lists of the inhabitants showing their general character and conduct which might lead to the discovery and eventual apprehension of suspicious characters. Fullerton returned to the subject in January 1827 after investigation had been made into the activities of the Chinese Hoeys. Again he asked for details of the inhabitants of Penang, particularly the Chinese, 'to enable Government to judge of the expediency of removing from the Island all suspicious characters of that race who have no visible means of earning an honest livelihood'. He also issued instructions to refuse licences to newly-arrived Chinese unless some respectable inhabitant became responsible for their conduct for at least three years.

The arrival of three Portuguese ships from Macao in December 1826 and the fact that their passengers, both traders and labourers, landed without any enquiry being made and without the knowledge of the police, prompted the Governor to insist that in future the Master Attendant must require from all vessels arriving at Penang a list of passengers. Sanction to land was only to be granted after 'respectable Chinese' had guaranteed employment for two years.

Caunter, Superintendent of Police, realized that with his small staff it was impossible to carry out these instructions, for immigrants could be landed anywhere round the coast. Fullerton, who likened the current practices to 'slave dealing', undertook to inform the Governor of Macao that 'no passenger on a Portuguese ship would be allowed to land unless accompanied by a certificate that all passengers on such ships had voluntarily embarked, and that all found security for their good behaviour'. But, as Caunter foresaw, it needed more than instructions to control immigration, and it is unlikely that there was anything more than a token compliance with those issued by Fullerton.[55]

In 1830, in Singapore, Murchison's suggestion that immigrants be restricted in view of the unruly mob of Chinese in the interior of the island was hamstrung by the objection of the Land Office that 'so long as a hope exists of bringing about a cultivation of the lands in the interior it would be unwise to check the influx of Chinese settlers'.[56]

The objection raised by the European merchants in 1843 to the proposal that immigrants should not be allowed to land unless guaranteed by a householder to be of good behaviour has already been noted,[57] and again in 1850, when discussing the Census, the Governor, Butterworth, wrote to the Resident of Singapore saying that 'a system of registration has several times been mooted, and always recognized as desirable, if it could be introduced without interfering with the entire freedom of the Port, which is viewed with great jealousy by the Mercantile Community here, and in the Mother Country'.[58]

The Indian Government was willing to pass Acts preventing 'diseased and destitute persons' being landed on the shores of the Settlements,[59] but otherwise no action was taken, and vested interests, ship owners, junk owners, merchants, planters, and all others requiring cheap labour remained unalterably opposed to

[55] SSR(A20), Pg Cons, 1824–5, Council Mtg, 3 May 1825; SSR(A32), Pg Cons, 1826–7, Council Mtgs of 2 & 11 Jan. 1827, pp. 23–32, & p. 121.
[56] SSR(A68), Sing. Cons., 1830, Council Mtg of 2 Mar. 1830; Report dated 23 Feb. 1830, pp. 11–14. [57] Above, p. 65.
[58] SSR(U19), Gov. Lett. to RCs, 1849–50, No. 35, 26 Jan. 1850, pp. 230–2.
[59] SSR(U20), Gov. Lett. to RCs, 1850, No. 218, pp. 138–40 (4 June).

any restrictions on the flow of immigrants. As late as 1868 the unofficial members of Legislative Council objected to an attempt to introduce regulations for vessels bringing immigrants from China, and the law as eventually passed (Ordinance XXI of 1868) applied only to ships taking Chinese emigrants from Singapore.[60]

Over the years, suggestions for the restriction or registration of immigrants coming into the Settlements had all been made by the authorities themselves, mainly because of the threat to internal peace and security. But in March 1871 a proposal to regulate this traffic was made by prominent Chinese residents of Singapore on humanitarian grounds, though there were also economic implications. In their petition to the Governor they said that new arrivals were being kidnapped and transported to Sumatra where, because of the opening up of plantations by the Dutch, the demand for labour was great. Many of the 'piglets' suffered ill-treatment at the hands of brokers and agents, and even if not kidnapped were frequently kept below decks in the hulks in the Singapore Roads, and were then shipped off to Sumatra against their will. (Though not specifically stated in the petition, it may be assumed that as these practices drew labour away from Singapore, they tended to increase the difficulty and the price of getting labour locally.)

As the Governor was about to go on leave, he handed over the petition to Colonel Anson who was to administer the Government during his absence, but apparently assuming that no immediate action was intended, a further petition, signed by seventy Chinese merchants, was prepared, and through the agency of Thomas Scott was presented on 25 May to Anson and the Legislative Council.[61] It asked for a trustworthy officer to superintend all new arrivals, ascertaining from the newcomers themselves where they intended to go, and informing those who wished to stay that they were at liberty to act as free agents. Eventually a scheme should be drawn up to protect the immigrants and give them security.

A promise was given that the matter would have the early and earnest attention of the Government, but although Anson originally intended to take steps to deal with the complaints, he found that all members of the European mercantile community were opposed to any attempt to introduce regulations which might possibly interfere with the free flow of immigrants. Thomas Scott, who as the Chairman of the Tanjong Pagar Wharf Company was a big employer of labour, himself spoke of the 'difficulties and inconvenience' which would ensue from any system of control, and made it clear that although he had been induced to present the petition, he opposed it. Anson let the matter lie, nor did the Governor on his return from leave in March 1872 make any apparent move to satisfy the petitioners. But after the riots of October 1872 he took the opportunity to appoint the Commission of Enquiry (composed entirely of officials) who recommended that a system of registration of Chinese immigrants be adopted. This strengthened his hand, particularly when the Secretary of State considered the recommendation to be 'well worthy of consideration', and asked for details of the manner in which the proposal might be implemented.[62]

Meantime, a number of articles appeared in the press, both in Singapore and in Hong Kong, alleging shameful overcrowding of steamers engaged in the coolie traffic and drawing attention to other abuses connected with the system. The

[60] SSPLC/1873, p. 81, 2 July.   [61] SSPLC/1871/app. 13.
[62] SSPLC/1873/app. 23, reprinting the Despatch from the S. of S., COD 72, 9 Apr. 1873.

British Consul at Swatow and Foochow sent down a translation of a placard put up in the streets by Chinese labour brokers stating that the sinkhehs (newcomers) were confined on arrival at Singapore, were sent to Deli and other places, and had no protection. In London the attention of the Secretary of State was drawn to articles in the *China Mail* concerning the overcrowding of immigrant ships, and on 27 April 1873 he addressed a further despatch to the Governor in Singapore requesting him to introduce a Bill laying down minimum requirements of space per passenger and prohibiting the landing of immigrants before inspection by a Government officer.[63]

Ord consulted a number of the leading Europeans on the matter, receiving from them 'but little help or encouragement'. But the timely arrival of a further petition for submission to the Legislative Council, dated 30 May 1873 and signed by 250 of the leading Chinese firms dealing in gambier, pepper, and general trade, brought matters to a head. The petition begged for the introduction of legislation to prohibit the disgraceful kidnapping of sinkhehs, and suggested the establishment of depots where the immigrants might be lodged, fed, and registered, and where intending employers might engage their labourers, entering into registered contracts with the men before taking them away. The petition also asked for the appointment of labour inspectors to visit the sinkhehs at intervals after their engagement.[64] These suggestions clearly echoed the recommendations of the official Commission earlier in the year, and by command of the Governor the petition was laid before Legislative Council on 23 June.

Further delay was impossible, and after several consultations with leading Chinese a Bill was prepared which the latter agreed afforded a reasonable amount of protection to the immigrants without interfering with the importation of labour into the Colony or increasing its cost. Entitled 'A Bill to provide for the better protection of Chinese Immigrants', it was introduced and read a first time on 21 August, and was debated on 9, 16, and 22 September.

The Governor agreed with the petitioners that there were frequent cases of Chinese being kidnapped and taken away to other places by force. He realized that certain quarters would resent 'interference' as possibly increasing the price of labour, but asked the House whether members were willing to live in a Colony where a practice was carried out which was stigmatized as 'slavery'. Despite this appeal, the Bill was strongly opposed by all three European unofficial members of Council. Thomas Scott admitted that at the time of the first petition in 1871 there had been kidnapping, but declared that this abuse no longer existed. As for the complaint that the immigrants fell into the hands of the secret societies, he considered that the remedy lay in the suppression of the societies and not in any interference with the free entry of labour. Dr Little thought that existing arrangements were satisfactory, and he made no attempt to refute the very different statements made in the petitions of the Chinese themselves. Ramsay Scott contended that the coolies coming down to the Straits were perfectly free, but insisted that if they were not so it was the fault of the Chinese Government, and the Colony Government was not called upon and had no right to interfere. But Whampoa, the only other unofficial member, fully endorsed the statements of the petitioners, which, he said, he knew to be true. An unofficial motion to

[63] COD 81, 27 Apr. 1873 (*China Mail* extracts 19 Dec. 1872 & 7 Feb. 1873). Printed as app. 32 to SSPLC/1873.
[64] SSPLC/1873/app. 33, p. cxxiv.

appoint a committee to enquire into the allegations was defeated by the official majority, and the Bill passed its second reading. It was finally passed on 17 October with a suspending clause, but by this time Thomas and Ramsay Scott and Dr Little had all resigned, and Whampoa was the only remaining unofficial member of Council.

The Bill provided that every Chinese coming to the Straits for the first time to work as a labourer at an occupation not requiring skilled labour should be considered an immigrant. No provision was made for those who had been to the Colony before, or for artisans or persons of a superior class. Every ship bringing twenty or more 'immigrants' was to be boarded on her arrival by a Registering Officer who would record the name and occupation of every immigrant, where he came from, his destination, and the object of his coming, together with the particulars of any agreement to work he might have made. If the captain of the ship so desired, the immigrants would be landed and placed in large sheds where they would be registered. As soon as the necessary particulars were entered, such of them as it was considered necessary would be endorsed on a small ticket. If the coolie had not already indentured himself the ticket would be handed to him to keep and would serve for his identification at any time that he might require assistance. If the coolie had engaged himself to labour, the ticket would be handed to his employer who would be bound to report the circumstance to the Registrar who would enter the same in the Registry. The protection thus afforded to the immigrant was only to last for the first two years, when he might be expected to have learnt enough to be able to protect himself.

In writing to London, the Governor stated that in the event of complaint or even suspicion of unfair dealing or ill-treatment of a coolie, the police would be afforded facilities for tracing the man, and this fact alone would act as a very great check on abuses. The police would also be enabled to identify coolies who had run away from their employers and had become samsengs or rowdies. He criticized the European merchants whose opposition to the measure showed that 'more importance was attached to obtaining the coolie at a cheap rate than to the means by which his services were secured'.[65]

When reporting the resignation of the unofficials, who accused him of disregarding their unanimous protest in regard to the abolition of the Grand Jury, the Governor emphasized other contributory causes of their discontent, including the Municipal Bill which they found 'unpalatable', the closing of the port to shipping owing to an outbreak of cholera, which seriously affected the revenues of the Tanjong Pagar Dock Company of which Thomas Scott was Chairman, and finally, the Chinese Immigration Bill. He might have added other grounds for unofficial discontent—his own attempts to rush through legislation before the end of his term of office, due to expire in November 1873; the letting of the revenue farms for a period of three years in a manner to which they objected; the deterioration of the situation in Perak; and the six weeks of constant nightly processions accompanied by gong-beating and cracker-firing which had resulted from the cholera epidemic in Singapore, and which had frayed everyone's nerves.

The irritation of the European mercantile community had found vent at a public meeting on 15 September to protest against the abolition of the Grand Jury and the introduction of the Immigrants' Bill, and in forwarding to the

[65] GD 289, 30 Sept. 1873, para. 10.

Secretary of State the resolutions passed at this meeting the Governor made his final criticism, that the mercantile community were hardly interested in anything beyond their own immediate business, and many of them openly avowed that they came solely to make money; some of the important firms stipulated that their staffs in Singapore should not take part in public affairs.

Only let them be assured that their rights and privileges are being invaded and especially if it be trusted that it is only another instance of the tyrannical and despotic action of the Government under which they suffer, and there is not the least difficulty in rallying a public meeting to express its disapprobation of a public measure, even though the majority of those present may be entirely ignorant of or utterly indifferent to it.[66]

The breach between the Governor and the European community in Singapore was complete.

[66] GD 291, 1 Oct. 1873.

9

THE POLICY OF INTERVENTION

1. TURMOIL IN THE NATIVE STATES

WHILE there was a division of opinion between the leaders of the European and Chinese mercantile communities in 1872 on the question of regulating Chinese immigration, they were united in the desirability of British intervention on the mainland where the safety of their capital was threatened by increasing political chaos.

Representations about grave injury to trade in Selangor put forward in July on behalf of thirty-four Malacca merchants received the 'usual answer' from the Government disclaiming all responsibility for protection, and in May 1873 a Memorial signed by 248 leading Chinese merchants in the three Settlements was laid before the Legislative Council complaining of disorder in the Native States 'so that nearly the whole of the west coast . . . may be said to be in a state of anarchy, and anything like regular trade is altogether at an end'. It pointed out that the greater portion of the revenue of the Colony was obtained from the Chinese (through the opium and spirit farms) whose livelihood was thus imperilled, and asked for a change of policy to restore peace and order in the native states and to secure protection for legitimate traders.[1]

Unrest in Selangor

Raja Juma'at died in 1864, and the removal of his strong hand led to attempts by rival Malay chiefs to control the lucrative mining areas in the Selangor and Klang river valleys, resulting in civil war which raged intermittently from 1866 to 1873.

In 1866 one Raja Mahdi drove Raja Abdullah (brother of Raja Juma'at) from Klang, and despite counter-attacks remained in possession. He also discontinued the Sultan's share of the Klang revenues, and the latter, in need of a capable representative, arranged for the marriage of his daughter to Tunku Zia'u'd-din, the younger brother of the Sultan of Kedah, and brought him to Selangor as his 'wakil'.[2] In European documents he is referred to as the 'Viceroy' and his intrusion into local politics was deeply resented by the Selangor chiefs. And before long the Sultan, too, had quarrelled with him.[3]

The dislocation of control in the Klang valley was of great concern to the heads of the Chinese mining community who were uncertain which chief to support. The Capitan, Liu Ngim Kong, died in August 1868, having previously,

---

[1] The Memorial was dated 28 Mar. 1873 (C.1111. pp. 30-32).
[2] Agent or representative.
[3] 'Zia'u'd-din' is the modern romanization. In contemporary documents he appears as 'Dia Oodin', 'Dia Udin', or 'Kudin'.

with the Sultan's assent, nominated Yap Ah Loy to succeed him. The appointment was resented by the relatives of the former Capitan and by the Ka Yin Chius of Kanching, and Yap Ah Loy strengthened his position by introducing stringent laws, including the death penalty, and by recruiting a bodyguard. The spearhead of the opposition was one Chong Chong, a relative of the previous Capitan who, with twenty followers, arrived in Kuala Lumpur on the eve of Chinese New Year (February 1869) intending to cause a riot during the celebrations and to seize control, but timely precautions frustrated his plan. He thereupon left for Kanching and urged the Ka Yin Chius to rise against Yap Ah Loy and his clansman Yap Ah Sze. The latter, warned of his danger, tried to leave Kanching by night but was intercepted and killed by Chong Chong's men. Yap Ah Loy at once took a mixed Chinese–Malay force to Kanching to demand satisfaction, but the Ka Yin Chius professed ignorance of the plot, and Chong Chong, though tracked to Rawang, escaped.

In order to avoid further trouble, Raja Mahdi summoned the leaders of both Chinese communities to Klang and warned them to keep the peace. He arrested two of Chong Chong's supporters for sedition, and thereafter, on 14 June 1869, held a public installation of Yap Ah Loy in Malay style to impress upon both Chinese factions that the latter was the Capitan officially acknowledged by him.

In August 1869 a rival to Raja Mahdi appeared in the shape of Raja Ismail, the son of Raja Abdullah, who had died. He attempted to recover his father's possession of the Klang valley, and was joined in October by the Viceroy with 500 picked fighters from Kedah. After a siege lasting until March 1870 Klang capitulated and Mahdi fled. During the period of siege Yap Ah Loy was troubled lest his installation by the Mahdi be construed as reflecting disloyalty to the Sultan and his Viceroy, and in November he visited the Sultan at Langat to explain matters and to ask for help against the Ka Yin Chius of Kanching 'as a means of preventing further disturbance'. He was successful and received ammunition and cash. In the early part of 1870 an opportunity occurred to discipline the Ka Yin Chius, and a force of 200 Malays and 400 Chinese under Yap Ah Loy's fighter leaders attacked Kanching and massacred 136 of the inhabitants.

There still remained his enemy Chong Chong, who allied himself with Syed Mashor, a Malay warrior who was in revolt against the Sultan and the Viceroy, in planning an attack on Kuala Lumpur to overthrow the Capitan. Forewarned, Yap Ah Loy recruited fighting-men from Singapore and China, but although he had 2,000 men under arms when the attack took place on 7 September, he was hard put to it to defend the town against an army of 2,500 men including vindictive Ka Yin Chius. It was not until the end of October that, with the help of a Malay force, the attackers were driven off. A further attack in May 1871 was also unsuccessful, and Chong Chong again escaped though his force was cut to pieces. It was more than a year before he reappeared on the scene.

There was a lull in hostilities caused by the intervention of the British as the result of a particularly brutal piracy, in which thirty-four people were killed. The pirated junk was traced to Kuala Selangor where Raja Mahdi had installed himself, and HMS *Rinaldo* destroyed the fort there and several war prahus. Mahdi and his supporters fled to Sumatra, leaving Kuala Selangor to be occupied by the Viceroy's men. This naval action was followed by a visit to the Sultan by the Colonial Secretary (J. W. W. Birch), who demanded the surrender of all those connected with the piracy and the reinstatement of Zia'u'd-din as Viceroy with full authority over all Selangor.[4]

This was reluctantly conceded, and the Viceroy thereupon recruited a force of foreign mercenaries, including Europeans, Eurasians, Sikhs, and Indian sepoys, with whom he garrisoned Kuala Lumpur and Kuala Selangor, but despite this a further attack on Kuala Lumpur in August 1872 by the rebel chiefs and Chong Chong was successful.[5] Few of the garrison escaped and most of Yap Ah Loy's fighters were killed, though he himself escaped to Klang. With the Viceroy he recruited a fresh force and in March 1873 recaptured Kuala Lumpur. Determined to rid himself of the Ka Yin Chiu menace he also attacked Kanching and killed 300 of the villagers. He had now retrieved his position, and in May–June 1873 was officially reinstalled as Capitan China, this time by the Viceroy, 'according to Chinese rites and with Chinese robes, and not with Malay customs'.[6]

But it was not until the end of the year that most of Selangor was brought under the Viceroy's control. Mining (and therefore revenue) had virtually ceased, the countryside was devastated and deserted, and he was very heavily in debt. One of his creditors was a Singapore lawyer, James Guthrie Davidson, who for some time had provided both advice and finance. In return, in March 1873 he was given a concession to mine in Selangor territory, but the Selangor Tin Company, formed to exploit this concession, found difficulty in raising funds owing to the disturbed conditions in the State, and an approach was made by a representative of the company in London to the Secretary of State asking whether there was any possibility of protection being afforded, and, if not, whether the company might enlist its own armed force. As with many similar requests for protection forwarded by the Governor, the usual reply was given, and sanction for raising a private army refused.[7]

Undeterred, the company next suggested (September 1873) that as British help was not forthcoming, the Rulers might wish to approach another European power, perhaps Germany, to intervene to keep the peace.[8] This was a new form of pressure, and while the Secretary of State refused to be drawn into the net or allow any suggestion of support of the company by the Government, he did pass on the information that the new Governor had been instructed to make a careful enquiry into the state of affairs in Selangor, and until then he would express no further opinion.[9]

Unrest in Larut, 1866–73[10]

In Larut, after their victory in 1865, the Chen Shang Hakkas at Klian Pauh retained their supremacy under the leadership of Chang Keng Kwee supported

---

[4] PP C.465, containing GDs 172, 176, & 186 (14, 28, & 29 July 1871); COD 202, 26 Sept. 1871.

[5] R. O. Winstedt, 'History of Selangor', *JMBRAS* (1934), p. 27, gives the name as 'Teoh Ah Chong'. 'Teoh' is the Hokkien, and 'Chong' the Hakka version of the same surname.

[6] Middlebrook & Gullick *JMBRAS*, July 1951.

[7] COD 143, 8 July 1873 and encls.   [8] CD 197, 20 Sept. 1873. Encl. d. 18 July 1873.

[9] COD 259, 29 Nov. 1873 and encls.

[10] The main sources are GD 43, 24 Feb. 1874 (C. 1111, pp. 108–14). The basic source in Singapore is SSR (U5) which contains many of the original documents in manuscript, including some which were not later printed.

by the Mentri and backed by the Hai San Society. Associated with them were some Cantonese miners from an area in Kwangtung known as the Five Districts. Their leader was Low Sam, the Mentri's agent, and though Cantonese they worked amicably alongside the Chen Shang Hakkas whose home territory in China adjoined their own districts.[11]

The Ghee Hin faction, though defeated in 1865, once again took over the mines at Klian Bahru. Most of the earlier Fui Chiu Hakka labourers driven out in 1865 had dispersed and were replaced by Hakkas from the Sin Neng district of Kwangtung, though some Cantonese were also employed. The Sin Neng representative was Ho Ghi Siu, a mining promoter of Penang who had taken over at Klian Bahru after the murder of So Ah Chiang.

In China, Sin Neng was one of four contiguous districts to the south-west of Canton known as the 'Sz Yip' (See Yip) or 'Four District Cities' where, from 1854, a violent struggle had been taking place between the indigenous Cantonese population and a large Hakka community which had infiltrated into the area during the previous century. The struggle reached its peak in 1865-6, and most of the Hakkas were driven out, many taking refuge overseas. Hence the influx to Larut.

In Penang several of the Ghee Hin leaders were Sin Neng men, including Lee Ko Yin, Ho Ghi Siu, and Ch'in Ah Yam, and as early as 1853 there was also a powerful Sin Neng District Association which quarrelled with the Hai San Society. In addition, the Ho Hop Seah Society consisted mainly of Sin Neng Hakkas most of whom were dissidents from other societies, including the Ghee Hin. Indeed, in November 1865 it had joined the Ho Seng Society in its fight against the Ghee Hin, but in 1872 under the leadership of Ho Ghi Siu it was on friendly terms with the Ghee Hin.[12]

In describing the contestants in the Third Larut War most writers from Braddell (1874) onwards have followed the questionable arrangement used by Skinner in his 'Précis of Perak Affairs' (1874) of 'mostly Ghee Hins and Cantonese on the one side, and mostly Hai Sans and Khehs on the other', though he also said that the race divisions were much confused 'many siding with the Kongsee to which they belong rather than with their own people'.[13]

A close study of the relevant documents leads to some reappraisal. It is true that this war was a continuation of the struggle for paramountcy in the Larut tinfield which had been waged between two groups of Chinese financiers in Penang since 1861, one group backed by the Ghee Hin and the other by the Hai San. But it would seem that the mining labour of Larut was predominantly Hakka, and that the principal participants in the battles at the mines were, on both sides, Hakka, though coming from different districts in China.[14]

---

[11] See App. 6, p. 542.

[12] Vaughan, in *JIA*, viii (1854) & his *Manners and Customs of the Chinese*, p. 99; Irving's Memo. (C. 1111, p. 127, para. 4); SSR(DD42), Lett. to Gov., 1865, No. 484, 14 Dec. & encl. 78. The Ho Hop Seah was frequently referred to by the shortened forms of 'Hap Shah' or 'Habsya'.

[13] C.1111, pp. 114–25. Quotations from p. 121.

[14] Irving's Memo of 24 July 1872 (C. 1111, p. 127) says that at the time of the outbreak (Feb. 1872) there were 20,000–25,000 Chinese in Larut 'of whom about 2,000 or 3,000 were Macao men, the remainder being Khays who were divided into two branches the Chan Shiang and the Sin Heng' (i.e. Chen Shang and Sin Neng). See also ibid. p. 13, Statement of Ong Ah Yu to Speedy of 18 Oct. 1872, in which he refers to Ho Ghi Siu's men as 'Khay men'.

In the First and Second Larut Wars of 1861 and 1865 the contestants were, on the one side, Fui Chiu Hakkas based on Klian Bahru in the north, against Chen Shang Hakkas based on Klian Pauh in the south. In the struggle of 1872–3 Sin Neng Hakkas who had replaced the Fui Chius fought against the Chen Shang Hakkas, though before the end of this third war Cantonese were engaged on both sides, and Hokkiens and Tiechius were also involved.

The line of division lay between the secret society groups—the Ghee Hin and its ally the Ho Hop Seah on the one side, and the Hai San on the other, the latter being reinforced first by a group of Cantonese from the 'Five Districts' area of Kwangtung, and later by the Kien Tek and the Ho Seng societies. The following table summarizes the position.

Third Larut War

North (Klian Bahru)
Miners: Mostly Hakkas from the 'Four Districts' (Sz Yip), principally from the Sin Neng District, together with some Fui Chiu Hakkas and some Cantonese.
Leaders: Ho Ghi Siu. Later Ch'in Ah Yam. (Both Sin Nengs.)
Society Ghee Hin and Ho Hop Seah, with which societies the Penang financiers of
support: this group were associated.
Name: This side was known as the 'Four Districts' or (in the Hokkien dialect) 'See Kwan'.

South (Klian Pauh)
Miners: Mostly Hakkas from the Chen Shang District, together with some Cantonese from the 'Five Districts'.
Leaders: Chang Keng Kwee (Chen Shang Hakka), Low Sam.
Society The Hai San Society. From August 1872 it was actively assisted by 'Five
support: District' Cantonese. From early May 1873 it was joined by the Kien Tek Society (Toh Peh Kong) composed mostly of local-born Hokkiens, and by the Ho Seng Society of mixed membership, including Hokkiens. The Penang financiers of this group were chiefly local-born Hokkiens of whom Khoo Hong Chooi was prominent.
Name: From August 1872 (but not before) this side was known as the 'Five Districts' or (in the Hokkien dialect) 'Go Kwan'.

(*See Appendix 6, p. 542.*)

The trouble started in February 1872 when the Chen Shangs disputed the boundaries of some mining land claimed by the Sin Nengs. Lee Ko Yin represented the latter in an attempt to negotiate, but on 16 February he was murdered on the grounds of an alleged intrigue with a woman said to be a wife of a Chen Shang man. The culprits were carried round the village in pig-baskets and drowned in a mining pool. It is conceivable that the affair was engineered as a means of getting rid of an influential and tiresome opponent who had caused them to lose face in 1861.[15]

Although arbitrators agreed on a settlement, animosity was not abated, and on 24 February a gambling quarrel led to violence. The Chen Shangs brought out their weapons and unfurled their society flags. A proclamation signed by

[15] Versions of the pig-basket story are found (with discrepancies) in the following sources:
    C.1111, p. 16, Campbell's Memo, 24 Oct. 1872. Confused.
    CDPL, Encl. 96, Koh Boo An's account, 25 Aug. 1873.
    Swettenham's Journal, SSPLC, 1874, App. 26, p. 4. Confused.
    Wynne, p. 266.

their leaders urged an attack against the Sin Nengs and promised compensation to any who might be injured in the fight. Although they outnumbered their opponents by two to one the Chen Shangs were defeated, for the Sin Nengs were tough fighters. By 26 March the Chen Shangs had lost 1,000 men killed and the remainder had been driven out of Larut. About 10,000 reached Penang and others went to Kedah and Perak.

The Mentri had crossed to Larut from Penang on 22 February, but with only forty armed police at his command he was powerless to intervene, and once the Sin Nengs were in control he was obliged to come to terms with them.[16] As part of this accommodation he became a member of the Ho Hop Seah and made Ho Ghi Siu his agent in Penang. Low Sam was allowed to retain his position as the Mentri's agent in Larut. It was alleged that the Mentri shared in the loot, consisting mainly of tin stocks, and although this was denied it aroused bitter resentment among the dispossessed Chen Shang leaders.[17]

The victors entrenched themselves behind stockades at Matang, and the mouth of the Larut river was patrolled by junks to prevent the entry of unwanted vessels. This interference with normal trade caused protests from Chinese merchants in Penang, and on Ord's return from England late in March he sent a gunboat to the mouth of the river to discourage this form of blockade. He also sent C. J. Irving, the Auditor-General, to Penang for a quick discussion with the acting Lieutenant-Governor (A. N. Birch) who was about to return to London. The result was a disconcerting report on the powerlessness of the Malay Government in Larut to control the Chinese miners.

If ever the Chinese choose to combine and turn the Malays out altogether [said Irving] I do not see what is to prevent them. In such a case, there would be seen an entirely unprecedented political combination, groups of Chinese republics, with governments of secret societies tempered by faction fights.[18]

Meanwhile dissension between Malay chiefs arising from the disputed succession to the throne of Perak threatened to add fuel to the flames, and Ord again sent Irving on a tour of investigation up the west coast to visit Selangor, Larut, and Penang. He was to inform the Mentri who, under pressure from the Ghee Hin–Ho Hop Seah combination, had asked for the arrest of the Hai San leaders in Penang to prevent a possible invasion of Larut, that this could not be done but that no one would be permitted to organize 'any hostile expedition' against his country.[19] Irving was also to urge the rival Malay chiefs to lay aside their differences and unite their efforts to restore peace and order.

The Malay trouble arose from the position of Raja Abdullah who, after the death of Sultan Ali in May 1871, was the heir-apparent but was not elected by the Council of Chiefs ostensibly because of his non-attendance at the late Sultan's funeral. Instead, in June 1871, Raja Ismail, the Bendahara, was elected

---

[16] Skinner's Précis gives 12 Feb. but this must be a miscopying. A letter from the Mentri (CDPL, Encl. 6) gives 13 Dhulkajah as 22 Feb. This date is confirmed by Koh Boo An's report (CDPL, Encl. 96).

[17] C.1111: p. 16 (Campbell's Memo.), p. 127 (Irving's Memo.), pp. 148–50 (Mentri's Statement); SSR(F7), Gov., Lett. fr. Native Rulers, 1865–74, p. 372, No. 150, 24 June 1873; CDPL, Encl. 10, Petition fr. Four Chinese, 8 Apr. 1872; Encl. 21, Petition fr. Chang Keng Kwee, 26 Sept. 1872.

[18] CDPL, Encl. 10, 13 Apr. 1872.

[19] SSR(G7), p. 22, Minute by Ord, 18 Apr. 1872.

and for several months thereafter there was no overt sign of dissatisfaction. But in January 1872, having received some support from the chiefs of lower Perak, Abdullah appealed to Tunku Zia'u'd-din of Selangor to address the British Government in support of his claim to the throne. He also sent a letter to the Governor signed by himself and four minor chiefs, but Irving, though he visited Larut again in May and June was unable to get the Council of Chiefs to meet to discuss the matter and the *status quo* continued, with Ismail as the elected Sultan and Abdullah as the discontented, disinherited claimant.[20]

Having discovered that repeated appeals to the Penang Government for redress merely elicited the 'usual reply' the Chen Shangs, backed by the strength of the Hai San Society and by the wealth of some of the richest merchants in Penang, took matters into their own hands and began to make plans to fight their way back into Larut.[21]

The first sign of a gathering storm came in June 1872 when Ho Ghi Siu's house in Penang was blown up though he escaped injury. In August he was stabbed in the back and fired at by a Malay in a crowded street but survived. The Chen Shangs and their backers recruited fighting-men and war junks from China and induced the 'Five District' Cantonese to align themselves against the Sin Nengs. At the same time the Mentri asked the Lieutenant-Governor, Penang, for help first against Abdullah whose agents were attempting to collect revenue in Larut, and also against 'all the Chinese who had left Larut during the late riots, and who were now collecting together and intending to come to damage Larut again'. In reply he was assured that action would be taken to prevent measures being concerted in Penang for causing disturbance in Larut.[22]

On 14 October Captain Speedy, the Deputy Commissioner of Police at Penang, boarded a Hai San junk in the harbour belonging to Khoo Hong Chooi and found 200 muskets and bayonets, 8 pieces of small ordnance with shot, 400 spear-heads, and 100 fighting-men. As her papers showed that she was bound for the Perak river and not for Larut she was allowed to leave, but it later transpired that she did, in fact, go to Larut and was the last of several such vessels taking men and arms for the support of the Chen Shangs. Ho Ghi Siu as the Mentri's agent complained that within the previous four days 2,000 muskets and over 10,000 lb. of gunpowder had been sent in this way and that over 1,000 fighting-men had secretly gone from Penang to Larut and were already burning and slaying. He named Khoo Hong Chooi as the instigator.[23]

Campbell and Speedy hurried over to the Larut river and found three heavily-armed Hai San junks, but all that Speedy could do was to obtain the release of two bound and terrified prisoners found in one of them.[24]

[20] C.1111, pp. 1–4: GD 189, 6 Nov. 1872, paras 7–11; pp. 117–20 (Skinner's Précis); pp. 128–36 (Irving's Memo).

[21] CDPL: Encl. 7 (A. N. Birch to Col. Sec. S'pore, 18 Mar. 1872); Encl. 10 (Petitions 6 & 8 Apr.); Encl. 12 (Petition 11 June); Encl. 13 (Reply to Encl. 12, 24 June); C.1111, p. 121 (Skinner's Précis), footnote.

[22] G. W. R. Campbell, Commissioner of Police, Ceylon, had succeeded A. N. Birch as acting Lt-Governor, Penang. CDPL: Encl. 17 (Campbell to Col. Sec., 6 Sept. 1872), Encl. 16 (Letter from Mentri, 27 Aug., reply 30 Aug.).

[23] C.1111, pp. 11–12.

[24] A statement made to Speedy by one of these men, Ong Ah Yu, on 18 Oct. contains the first reference that has been traced to the participation of the Five District men. He mentions 7 or 8,000 'Goh Tay Kwan' men of whom 2,000 were fighting-men and all armed. 'Goh Tay Kwan' = Goh Tai Kwan or Five Large Districts. (See App. 6.)

The attack had begun on the 14th when armed bands of Five District men led by Hai San headmen and reinforced by heavily-armed fighters from the junks made five simultaneous surprise attacks at the mining settlements which were overrun with great slaughter. Fugitives making their way overland through Krian were killed by local Malays under instructions from the Mentri. Three or four hundred women and children were taken captive and either sold as slaves or divided among the victors and their Malay supporters. At least 1,000 men were killed and over 2,000, including 100 wounded, reached Penang and lay about the streets exhausted and destitute.[25]

Once again the Chen Shang faction with its Hai San backing was in complete control of Larut, but Ho Ghi Siu lost no time in planning a counter-attack. He appealed to the Singapore Ghee Hin for help in arms, money, and men. From China he brought war junks and recruited fresh reinforcements of fighters whom he assembled near Nibong Tebal in Province Wellesley, arming them once they were across the Krian border in Perak territory. In Larut he intrigued with two discontented rajas at Trong who allowed him to fit out and arm his junks in their creeks. This was necessary because a proclamation had been issued prohibiting the export of arms from Penang. Seven weeks after the Hai San victory Ho Ghi Siu, with the full support of the Ghee Hin and the Ho Hop Seah, launched his attack on 12 December.

A force of about 1,000 advanced overland from Krian, and others from Trong landed at the mouth of the Limau river on the south side of the Larut estuary. Despite strong opposition, before midday the port of Matang was in Ghee Hin hands together with the vital road to the mines as far as Simpang where, later, a strong stockade was built. The river channel was staked and a chain boom thrown across it, while eleven armed junks from Trong took up positions at the mouth.

The Mentri at Matang was in a precarious position. His house was besieged for two days, ten of his police killed, and all his tin stocks looted. He managed to get away to Bukit Gantang and his fort was occupied by the Ghee Hins.

Thereafter the war on land reached stalemate. The Ghee Hins, though retaining Matang and continuing their blockade of the Larut river, were unable to drive the Hai Sans from the mines, while the Hai Sans, though in possession of a fort at Kota, were unable to recover their main supply route. At sea, however, there was considerable activity. During February Ho Ghi Siu's junks attacked every vessel which was in the remotest degree connected with their enemies, but an arms embargo imposed by an Order in Council on 21 February, backed up by a patrol of the Royal Navy at the mouth of the Larut river, caused the Ghee Hins to disperse their junks. Thereafter they used light-draught row-boats which by taking to the innumerable shallow creeks along the coast could easily evade the deep-draught gunboats and steam launches sent to pursue them. Alternative landing places were also established along the coast by the Ghee Hins, at Sungei Gula, Selinsing, and Klumpang, while the Hai Sans, having obtained fighting junks from China, and anxious to avoid any entanglement with the Penang

---

[25] C.1111, pp. 10, 14–15, 146–7; CDPL, Encl. 96. Sources vary greatly as to the number of casualties. The Sz Yip petition (C.111, p. 146) says that of 8,000 men at the mines 2,000 were killed there and 3,000 perished on the way out. Campbell reported that of 4,000 half had been killed. Speedy's report was 'over 1,000'. Koh Boo An said 500–600 killed and 200–300 starved to death, with 300–400 women and children abducted (CDPL, Encl. 96).

N

authorities, armed many of them in the creeks of the Sembilan Islands off the Perak river. Kuala Kurau, a Hokkien village, became a Hai San base for supplying the mines at Klian Pauh and Klian Bahru by an overland route.

The Mentri, on 19 February, alleging that both sides were being helped from Penang, appealed to the Colony Government for help 'against the Chinese who were fighting in Larut' and whom, he admitted, he was unable to control. His request was supported by Campbell, fearful that the war would spread to Penang, and who had previously suggested that the appointment of a British officer as Resident in Larut would probably bring peace to the area. But the Governor, mindful of his strict instructions from the Colonial Office, was not prepared to take any action beyond the introduction of an arms embargo and the provision of the naval patrol, and the Mentri was told, on Ord's instructions, that he was always siding with the victors without indicating which side he really favoured. This drew the response that he was on the side of the Hai San, and he accused the Government of failing to honour its treaty obligations with Perak which was 'as it were, under the shelter of Our Friend in Penang or any other of the Straits Settlements. Because of this we do not appeal to other Powers for help.'[26]

Abdullah continued to press his claim to the throne, and on 28 February signed an agreement with the Ghee Hin promising that if they would drive the Mentri and the Hai San from Larut and support his installation as Sultan, he would farm out the mines at Larut to them and repay half their war costs. Later (28 April) he sent to the Governor a list of the 'Chief Men of Perak' who supported him and asked for help to put a stop to the fighting in Larut on the grounds that British subjects were implicated. In reply the Governor offered no assistance until he and the Mentri had decided which was the rightful Chinese faction.[27]

It was then suggested by an intermediary, Nakhoda Trang, that Tan Kim Cheng of Singapore should be asked to mediate between the Ghee Hins and the Hai Sans. To this Abdullah readily agreed, but the Mentri was lukewarm. Despite his diplomatic shifts he was on the side of the Hai Sans and could see no chance of coming to terms with the Sin Nengs who were, he said, 'exceptionally violent'.[28]

But any prospects of a settlement were ruled out when the Mentri learned that Abdullah had offered Tan Kim Cheng five-elevenths of the revenue received by the Mentri (which he affirmed was rightly his) for ten years if he could obtain the formal recognition of Abdullah as Sultan. The Mentri thereupon refused to have any further dealings with Abdullah, and in reporting this to the Governor, the latter asked for support for his claim to the Sultanate and that the Mentri be ordered to obey him. The Governor's reply was that until Abdullah was installed with proper ceremony it was useless bothering the Colony Government. Although Tan Kim Cheng received the consent and encouragement of the Governor to mediate, nothing came of the proposal, and on 4 July Colonel Anson, who had resumed duties in Penang, reported that Abdullah had openly declared in favour of the Ghee Hins and handed over his seal to Ho Ghi Siu

[26] CDPL, Encls 26, 29, 50 (with attachment).
[27] SSR(F7), Lett. fr. Native Rulers, p. 368; GD 43, 24 Feb. 1874, para. 32 (C. 1111, pp. 108–14).
[28] CDPL, Encl. 43, 23 Apr. 1873.

as his agent. He added that he had little confidence in anything being satisfactorily arranged by Tan Kim Cheng.[29]

It was at this juncture that Ord, after long delay during which he had hoped that some solution would emerge, forwarded to London the Chinese Memorial of 28 March and reported that there seemed no likelihood of a change for the better in Larut affairs, and no prospect of a solution being found.[30]

Before these despatches reached London Campbell had already arrived there and had submitted a report to Lord Kimberley emphasizing the seriousness of the situation, urging that 'friendly intervention' would end this, and that a 'resident political officer' would prevent its recurrence.[31]

Meanwhile hostilities along the coast had been intensified. The Hai Sans turned their attention to the Ghee Hin bases north of the Larut estuary. On 7 May 1873 a force of junks and fishing boats, flying the flags of the Mentri (yellow), of the Kien Tek Society (red with black edges), and of the Ho Seng Society (black with white edges), raided Sungei Gula, a settlement of about 2,000 Tiechius, and massacred the inhabitants.[32] This combined fleet operating from Kuala Kurau later attacked Klumpang and Selinsing, both Tiechiu settlements, while Sepatang (also Tiechiu) was attacked by Malays in the Mentri's employ, and a further raid on Sungei Gula took place on 12 June 'by Malays and Hokkien Chinese'.[33] Many Tiechius fled to Province Wellesley, where there was a large Tiechiu community, and from now on the Tiechius aligned themselves with the Ghee Hins.

The attack on Gula was the first evidence that the Kien Tek and Ho Seng societies were openly taking part in the Larut war on the side of the Hai Sans and the Five Districts, against the Ghee Hins and the Ho Hop Seah.[34] As these societies between them included nearly the whole Chinese male population of Penang, Anson became increasingly afraid of an outbreak within the Settlement. Furthermore, his Superintendent of Police, Captain Speedy, had suddenly resigned in July and was rumoured to be in India recruiting discharged sepoys for service with the Mentri.[35] Contemporary records do not support the assertion that both Anson and Ord were aware of, and even encouraged, Speedy's venture.[36]

Anson arranged a meeting of the Chinese leaders of each side at which the Mentri and Abdullah were also present,[37] and after five hours of argument induced the two latter to agree to refer outstanding disputes to him for arbitration. Hostilities were to cease on land and sea, and the whole party would go to

[29] PEP, vol. ii, Statement of Nakhoda Trang, 1 Sept. 1876; CDPL, Encls. 49, 50, 54, 56.

[30] GDs 188 & 216 of 10 & 24 July 1873 (C.111, pp. 28–30 & 32–33).

[31] Campbell's Report, dated London 28 June 1873, received 3 July (CO 273/74). Also quoted in D. MacIntyre, 'British Intervention in Malaya, the Origin of Lord Kimberley's Instructions to Sir Andrew Clarke in 1873', *JSEAH*, Oct. 1961.

[32] CDPL, Encl. 48, 27 June 1873.

[33] Ibid. Encl. 96, Koh Boo An's account, 25 Aug. 1873; Encls 59 & 48.

[34] SSR(G7), 20 May 1873. The first official mention of the Ho Seng joining the group is in a report by the Supt. of Police of 20 Aug. 1873 (CDPL, Encl. 89).

[35] Reports of the terms of Speedy's engagement by the Mentri vary widely. See GD 246, 14 Aug. 1873. Also PEP, ii, Penghulu Mat Ali; L. Wray, *The Tin Mines and Mining Industries of Perak* (Taiping, 1894); GD Conf., 18 Oct. 1876.

[36] GD 246, 14 Aug. 1873; COD 143, 8 July 1873 (CO 273/69).

[37] Abdullah was accompanied by the Viceroy of Selangor, and once again the suggestion was made that if the British were unwilling to assist, help might be sought from other powers.

Larut to announce the decision and order compliance. But at the last moment Ho Ghi Siu, who had strongly opposed this proposal, refused to go, and instead sent a messenger by fast boat to instruct his men to ignore the proposed armistice, so that when the party reached Larut on the morning of 11 August, a proclamation issued reluctantly by Abdullah calling upon the headmen of the Sin Neng, Tiechiu, and Fui Chiu factions to lay down their arms was ignored and the mission was a failure. On its return to Penang, Anson ordered the arrest of Ho Ghi Siu and informed Abdullah that he should never, so long as he (Anson) had any influence, become Sultan of Perak.[38]

From then onwards, with both Anson and Ord, the star of the Mentri was in the ascendant. Anson approved his scheme to recruit sepoys but was worried by a rumour that Tiechius from Province Wellesley with the support of Ghee Hin junks intended to attack Kuala Kurau (a Hokkien village under the protection of the Ho Seng Society) as a reprisal for the massacre of Tiechius in the coastal villages of Krian.[39] In Penang the Ho Sengs threatened that if this happened they would take revenge on the Ghee Hins, and Anson, mindful of the riots of 1867, ordered the arrest of several society headmen while informing the Governor that unless the disturbances in Larut were stopped, it was certain that within a few days there would be riots in Penang.[40]

Ord, accompanied by Pickering, immediately left for Penang. The latter was sent to Larut and a naval patrol instructed to clear the creeks. On 3 September, Ord, advised by Anson, recognized the Mentri not only as the lawful but as the independent ruler of Larut, and two days later the embargo on shipments of arms was waived in his favour.[41] To help in the control of coastal waters a Marine Police Station was to be established on Pulau Kra, north of the mouth of the Krian river in Province Wellesley. On his return to Singapore the Governor reported the change of policy to the Legislative Council, adding that 'all apprehension of danger being removed, the traders and fishermen have resumed their avocations under the protection of HMS *Midge*'.[42]

He was soon disillusioned for the Ghee Hins, incensed at this official recognition of the Mentri, redoubled their efforts to assert themselves. On 16 September an attempt was made to blow up the Mentri's house in Penang, and a similar attempt was later made on Chang Keng Kwee's house.[43] The Mentri, encouraged by the Government's change of front, offered Tan Kim Cheng $16,000 if he would arrange for the Ghee Hins to be driven from Larut and ensure that Abdullah would not be recognized as Sultan, but Kim Cheng replied that he would not on any account intervene to drive out the Ghee Hins, but only to mediate between the two factions, so nothing came of this.[44]

Piratical attacks on shipping increased, and the gig of the *Midge* patrolling the Larut river was fired on from the first stockade. A retaliatory expedition sent up the river on 20 September destroyed this stockade and cleared away the boom. On reaching Matang, 4,000 Ghee Hins who had taken refuge there

[38] CDPL, Encls 74, 75, 78, 80, 88; Anson, p. 322.
[39] CDPL, Encl. 80; C.1111, p. 45.
[40] SSR(G7), p. 185, 19 Aug. 1873; CDPL, Encls 89, 97; GD 248, 21 Aug. 1873 (C.1111, p. 43).
[41] GD 253, 5 Sept. 1873 (C.1111, pp. 43–44); COD 208, 22 Oct. 1873; CDPL, Encls 90–95.
[42] SSPLC, 9 Sept. 1873, p. 151.
[43] GD 271, 19 Sept. 1873 (C.1111, p. 46).
[44] PEP, ii, Statement of Nakhoda Trang, 1 Sept. 1876.

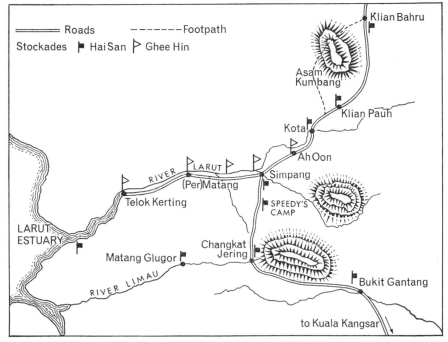

3. Larut, end of 1873

offered to surrender unconditionally to the British but begged for protection from the vengeance of the Mentri. This was not part of the programme, and the boats withdrew to resume the patrol.[45]

In the meantime there was news from Calcutta of Speedy, who had arrived there with a party of men enlisted for service with the Mentri. There was a flurry of official telegrams and correspondence ending by no objection being raised by Ord to their embarkation. They reached Penang harbour on 27–28 September—110 sepoys with some Krupp guns—and after assembling supply craft left for Larut on the 29th and landed to the south of the Larut estuary. From there they pressed inland to Bukit Gantang where they were joined by a party of Mandilings sent by Ismail from the mines at Kinta to help the Mentri.[46]

Speedy managed to get arms and supplies through to Hai San men at Kota, but the key point was the road junction at Simpang, strongly fortified and defended by the Ghee Hins, and it was a month before he moved against this, without success, and built a stockade 400 yards away. An attack on Ghee Hin stockades threatening Kota was more successful, and the Hai Sans also took possession of the lower stockade and small fort at the mouth of the river, thus cutting the supply lines of the main Ghee Hin body at Matang, with their outpost at Simpang.

At this juncture the Ghee Hins at Penang, led by Ch'in Ah Yam, who had replaced the discredited Ho Ghi Siu, appealed to Anson to intervene in Larut,

[45] C.1111, pp. 46–50.
[46] Estimates of the size of this force vary from 100 to 1,000. See PEP, iii. 48; Gullick. 'Captain Speedy of Larut', *JMBRAS*, Nov. 1953; C.1111, p. 43.

only to be told that nothing could be done until they withdrew completely from the area. Faced with this deadlock they increased their attacks on shipping to disrupt the Hai San supply lines.[47] Prospects of a settlement seemed as distant as ever. On 3 October Abdullah, concerned about the official recognition of the Mentri and the support implied, visited Singapore hoping, through Tan Kim Cheng, to see the Governor. In this he was unsuccessful, and he was advised by W. H. Read and other members of the Legislative Council to await the arrival of the new Governor, Sir Andrew Clarke, whose appointment had been notified. Abdullah renewed his agreement with Tan Kim Cheng to appoint him as Collector of Revenue, Larut, with entitlement to five-elevenths of the revenue, once Abdullah was recognized as Sultan. After three weeks of riotous living at Tan Kim Cheng's expense, Abdullah and his followers, about twenty in all, returned to Perak to await developments.[48]

2. INTERVENTION

Sir Harry Ord left Singapore on retirement on 2 November 1873, and the *Straits Daily Times* in a farewell leader on 1 November heaped upon his luckless head all the disabilities which appeared to arise from the rule of the Colonial Office, including the policy of non-interference in the Malay States which clearly was not of his contriving.

He was succeeded by Sir Andrew Clarke, who reached Singapore on 4 November and who, before leaving London, had been made aware of Lord Kimberley's views on future policy. The latter had discussed Larut with Campbell, and had been greatly impressed by his report in which he recommended the appointment of a political officer there. On 7 July he minuted that he thought an endeavour should be made to put a stop to the Larut disturbances but also thought it 'very undesirable' to interfere directly in Perak.

The conversations between the Selangor Tin Company and the Colonial Office started on 25 June and continued by letter and interview through July. The Memorial from the Chinese merchants reached the Colonial Office on 21 August, but it is clear from the files that the conclusion had already been reached that the policy of rigid non-interference should be re-examined and perhaps replaced by an extension of existing treaties and the appointment of British officers in such of the States as were prepared to accept them. It is also clear that the main factor leading to this change of front was the suggestion put forward through the Selangor Tin Company that if Britain was unwilling to provide protection, Germany might be asked to do so. There is no reason to suppose that the Chinese Memorial standing alone would have had any more influence than had the numerous pleas for intervention previously made.[49]

The possibility of a change of policy was envisaged in the new Governor's instructions, which required him to examine and report what steps could properly be taken to restore peace and order, and especially to consider

---

[47] C.1111, pp. 70–73, 124–5.

[48] PEP, ii. 39–42, Statement of Nakhoda Trang, 1 Sept. 1876; iii. 26–27, Statement of Haji Mahomed Syed, 16–18 Dec. 1876.

[49] CO 273/67; C.1111, pp. 28–32, 39–42. The main file is CO 273/74. For detailed documentary studies, see C. D. Cowan, *Nineteenth Century Malaya* (1961), ch. 4, and MacIntyre, *JSEAH*, Oct. 1961.

whether it would be advisable to appoint a British officer to reside in any of the States.[50]

Intervention in Perak

On arrival in Singapore Clarke consulted Dunlop and Pickering as well as W. H. Read and other leaders of the mercantile community, including Tan Kim Cheng,[51] and early in December received a report from Anson, who had recently visited Larut, in which he declared that without some intervention nothing but anarchy and riot could be foreseen.[52] There was further deterioration during December culminating in an attack by the Ghee Hin faction on the police station at Pulau Kra on 2 January 1874. Clarke decided to act and sent Pickering to Penang bearing a letter from Tan Kim Cheng to the leaders of the See Kwan faction, as a result of which they agreed to surrender their weapons and war-boats and to place all their Larut affairs in the Governor's hands provided that Speedy was instructed to hold back. A document to this effect was signed by twenty-four See Kwan leaders on 6 January.[53]

As far as the records show, Pickering had not as yet made any approach to the Hai Sans and their allies, nor did he make any report upon their attitude. But, encouraged by the success so quickly achieved with the See Kwans, Clarke decided not only to enforce arbitration between both Chinese factions but to seize the opportunity to settle the disputed succession to the throne of Perak.[54] He instructed Anson by telegram to send Frank Swettenham to Larut to see the Mentri and Speedy 'about the surrender of the Hai Sans' and to request an armistice. He was also to summon the Malay chiefs of Upper and Lower Perak to a proposed conference with the Governor at Pangkor on the 14th, where the Chinese leaders were also to be assembled.

Swettenham left Penang for Larut on 8 January in HMS *Avon*, taking with him ten of the principal men of the Go Kwan faction, and landed at Matang. From there, accompanied by the commander and three marines, he walked the thirteen miles to Speedy and the Mentri at Bukit Gantang, calling at the stockades along the road to inform the Chinese of both factions that an armistice was proposed. Both the stockades at Simpang were still manned. Having obtained the Mentri's promise to attend the conference, Swettenham returned to the coast, sailed to Pangkor, and leaving the *Avon* there with the Go Kwan headmen on board went up the Perak river in the *Fair Malacca* to make contact with the Malay chiefs.[55]

Meanwhile, in Singapore, Clarke on 9 January received a letter from Abdullah which had been drafted by W. H. Read after a talk with the Governor on

[50] COD 197, 20 Sept. 1873 (C.1111, pp. 38–39).
[51] PEP, ii. Nakhoda Trang.   [52] C.1111, pp. 142–4.
[53] Ibid. pp. 74–75, 153–4. The negotiations were conducted not with the headmen of the Ghee Hin Society as such but with the 'Four District' leaders (who were also officers of the Ghee Hin or the Ho Hop Seah) and the form 'See Kwan' is therefore used in this account. The Chinese date on the document corresponds to 6 January 1874 and not, as in the printed version, 16 January.
[54] In his despatch (CD 14, C.1111, pp. 70–73), Clarke gave the impression that Pickering had obtained the consent of both Chinese factions. It was not until 13 January that Chang Keng Kwee on behalf of the Chen Shangs agreed, and not until 15 January that the rest of his faction followed suit.
[55] F. A. Swettenham, *Footprints in Malaya* (1941), pp. 32–33; C.1111, pp. 157–9, report by J. C. Patterson (HMS *Avon*); PEP, iii. 48, Statement by Kulop Rhee, 29 June 1877.

13 December. Abdullah wrote as Sultan, suggesting that a new treaty be made with 'the English Government', and asking for 'a man of sufficient abilities to live with us in Perak . . . and show us a good system of government . . .'. This was so much in keeping with what the Colonial Office had in mind that it is not unreasonable to assume that Read had been prompted by the Governor to include these proposals in the letter.[56]

Major McNair and Captain Dunlop, sent by the Governor to arrange the conference, reached Penang on the evening of 10 January and next morning obtained confirmation from the See Kwan headmen of their agreement with Pickering. Such Go Kwan headmen as were still left in Penang merely said that they would accept whatever their other headmen agreed to. When, next morning, these three officers reached the Larut river in the *Johore* they were told by the Go Kwans manning the first stockade that they had strict orders not to allow any vessels to enter or leave, and they had no instructions about an armistice or about handing over their boats. A boom was lowered and nine junks loaded their guns in readiness to fire. The *Johore* withdrew and sailed for Pangkor, arriving on the morning of the 13th to find that the *Pluto* with the Governor on board was already there. As Swettenham had not yet returned from the Perak river, Dunlop and McNair were sent off in the *Johore* to help in collecting the chiefs. They were again accompanied by Pickering, who took with him not only Ch'in Ah Yam, the leader of the See Kwans, but Chang Keng Kwee, the representative of the Go Kwan faction who had been brought to Pangkor by the *Avon* and had not yet acquiesced in the proposed arbitration. After several hours' discussion he was persuaded to sign an agreement relying, as the See Kwan leaders had done, on the Governor's 'just, righteous, and impartial judgment'. But he signed only as the 'Chen Shang man', though he promised that on return to Pangkor he would try to persuade the other headmen of the faction to agree.[57] On arrival there on the 15th he spent the morning discussing the matter with his colleagues, and in the afternoon the Governor saw the headmen of both Chinese factions with Pickering as interpreter. Both sides were prepared to forego all claims to compensation so long as they were permitted to return to the mines. Those whose women and children had been taken asked for them to be restored. After a long conference terms were agreed upon to be embodied in a document which all were to sign on the 20th.[58] On the appointed day the agreement was signed by twenty-six headmen belonging to both factions. The 27th whose name appeared in the agreement was Ho Ghi Siu, who was not present but who signed on 10 February.[59]

Both the contending parties were to be disarmed and their stockades destroyed, and both factions were to be at liberty to return to their work in Larut. One or more officers of the Colony Government with one Chinese from each side were to form a Commission with power to settle all claims as to mines occupied and business conducted. All future arrangements as to water supply were to be subject to the orders of a British Resident to be stationed at Larut whose decision would be final. At last, for the Chinese, there was a basis for peaceful resumption

[56] Read, pp. 25–26; C.1111, p. 85, Abdullah's letter, 30 Dec. 1873.
[57] C.1111, p. 78 (Report by McNair & Dunlop); p. 156 (Chang Keng Kwee's Agreement); p. 166, para. 53 (Braddell's report).
[58] C.1111, p. 167 (Braddell's report).
[59] Swettenham's Journal, 11 Feb.

of their mining activities with a neutral arbitrator to settle disputes and with recourse to an appeal to the Governor if necessary.[60]

As for the Malay problem, Clarke disposed of this summarily by humiliating the Mentri and dragooning the other chiefs into acceptance of his proposals. Abdullah was to be recognized as Sultan and Ismail pensioned off. The Mentri, though Governor of Larut, was to be subordinate to the Sultan, in whose name all revenue was to be collected and all appointments made. A British Resident for Perak and an Assistant Resident for Larut were to be appointed, and all expenses incurred in the intervention and the restoration of peace and trade were to be borne by the Mentri. Some territory in Krian and the Dindings was to be ceded to Britain to facilitate control of piracy.[61] The Malay agreement was signed by the chiefs on the afternoon of 20 January, but it was with the greatest reluctance that the Mentri affixed his seal. For him this was a sorry end to the battle of wits in which Abdullah and the Ghee Hin faction through their associates in Singapore were victorious, while he and the Hai Sans were subjugated. He returned to Larut embittered and powerless. Speedy was appointed by the Governor as Assistant Resident and at once took control.[62]

Action for the pacification of Larut was begun without delay. The commissioners appointed were Dunlop, Swettenham, and Pickering, together with Chang Keng Kwee and Ch'in Ah Yam. With the See Kwan men at the mines and stockades they had no difficulty; they at once handed over their arms and demolished their defences, even at Simpang and Ah Oon where they had been strongly entrenched. But the Hai Sans were very recalcitrant and obstructive. Only after the arrest of eleven of their leaders and with the help of Speedy's sepoys were they eventually prevailed upon to dismantle the forts, and not until a public flogging had been administered were the whereabouts of the missing Ghee Hin women revealed. Of these, in all, fifty-three were recovered. The Mentri was equally obstructive, but firm handling by Dunlop and his partners persuaded him that resistance to the Commission's requirements was useless. By 19 February all the stockades had been destroyed, arms surrendered, and the missing women either rescued or their whereabouts traced. As it was impossible to determine the ownership of about 150 mines to which both factions laid claim, the Commission decided to stake a line across Larut, the mines to the north being handed over to the See Kwans, those to the south being retained by the Go Kwans. The Assistant Resident was to issue leases for all the mines clearly specifying the boundaries and annual rental, and the opening of new mines would need his sanction.

These decisions were announced to a meeting of both factions at Kota on 20 February by Swettenham who, on the Governor's instructions, had already taken the precaution of obtaining Ho Ghi Siu's signature to the Chinese Pangkor agreement while in Penang ten days previously. The Mentri was present at the meeting, but Chang Keng Kwee, who had not accompanied the Commission to the end, was unable to bear the loss of face entailed in being publicly associated with a decision which gave the See Kwans equal rights with his own faction.

---

[60] C.1111, pp. 174–5.

[61] For the text of the Pangkor Engagement, see C. Northcote Parkinson, *British Intervention in Malaya (1960)*, App. A.

[62] GDs 14 & 15, 26 Jan. 1874 (C.1111, pp. 70–73, 85–86); GD 43, 24 Feb. 1874 (C.1111, pp. 108–14); COD 14, 6 Mar. (C.1111, p. 88).

He pleaded illness and went to Penang. The See Kwan headmen were happy to accept the arrangements, but the Go Kwans, protesting that they must consult Chang Keng Kwee, walked off. In the end, however, the settlement was never challenged, but from Swettenham's Journal it is clear that both Chang Keng Kwee and the Mentri had hoped that the agreements signed unwillingly at Pangkor would be frustrated by their supporters on the ground, and it needed all the firmness which the other commissioners possessed to overcome this obstacle and to restore peace to Larut.[63]

The post of British Resident, Perak, remained unfilled, however, until November because the conduct of J. W. W. Birch, the Governor's nominee, was under enquiry, and this delay in introducing the new administrative structure was to have serious results.[64]

Intervention in Selangor and Sungei Ujong

Having, as he believed, settled the affairs of Perak at Pangkor, Sir Andrew Clarke turned his attention to the other west-coast mining States. A piracy committed in Selangor waters in November 1873 gave him the opportunity in February 1874 to send a naval force and to insist on the holding of an enquiry with British representatives present, and after another piracy in July he was able to persuade the Sultan to receive F. A. Swettenham as an unofficial adviser (August). So well did the latter play his part that in October the Sultan offered to pay $1,000 monthly to defray the expenses of a British officer resident with him, and agreed that he should be in charge of the import and export duties.[65]

To this post Clarke, at the end of 1874, appointed the Viceroy's friend and adviser Davidson, to which the Colonial Office raised strong objection, and, in the absence of another suitable candidate, agreed only with great reluctance as a temporary measure and after he had transferred his financial interests in the State. He was attached to the Viceroy at Klang while Swettenham remained with the Sultan at Langat.[66]

In 1874 all the factors making for disruption in the tinfields were present in full measure in Sungei Ujong.[67] Jealousy existed between the young Dato' Klana who had been elected in 1873, and the old Dato' Bandar who claimed equal status with the Klana and who, since his election in 1849, had exercised the traditional right to collect customs, harbour, and port dues on the Linggi river, the main artery of trade.

In the adjacent State of Rembau two contestants were fighting for the succession and levying illegal tolls on part of the Linggi river, to the annoyance of the Chinese miners and their financiers in Malacca and Singapore. At the mines there was rivalry between the Hai San and the Ghee Hin societies, and an ever-

---

[63] C.1111: pp. 229–30, Report and Journal; p. 240, Gov. to Earl of Carnarvon, 27 June 1874; pp. 241–2, Carnarvon to Gov. 4 Sept.; also SSPLC, 1874, Papers laid on the table 15 Sept.

[64] Birch was heavily in debt, and had accepted a loan from the Chinese Opium Farmers in Singapore at a time when tenders for the farm were being received in 1873 (CO 273/76, ff. 95–105, Clarke to Carnarvon, private letter, 13 July 1874).

[65] GD, 27 June 1874 (C.1111, pp. 240–1); GD 319, 3 Oct. 1874 (C.1320, p. 5).

[66] GD 357, 30 Dec. 1874 (C.1320, p. 55).

[67] The main sources are: GD, 8 May 1874 (C.1111, pp. 232–4); GD, 29 Dec. 1874 (C.1320, pp. 7–11) with 24 encls, the most important being: Encl. 1, Braddell's Report; Encl. 17, Pickering's Report, 23 Dec. 1874. Pickering's Journals, though printed and sent with the Despatch, are not in C.1320. Encl. 18, Dunlop's Report, 18 Dec.; Tatham's Report, 18 Dec.

present tendency for the rival Chinese groups to ally themselves with rival Malay chiefs.

During 1873 and early 1874 petitions from traders and discussions with the chiefs came to nothing, but in April 1874 Sir Andrew Clarke, seeking once again a strong central government, decided to recognize the Dato' Klana as the major chief and give him British support. The claim of the Dato' Bandar to equal status, if indeed it was known, was disregarded, and early in May the Governor, relying on an agreement reached with the Klana and some minor chiefs, visited the Linggi river and cleared away some stockades.[68]

The Bandar, incensed by this interference in Sungei Ujong affairs, declined to subordinate himself to the Klana, and when the latter reported his intransigence to the Governor, Pickering was sent to Sungei Ujong to warn the Bandar not to disturb the peace, and to instruct the Chinese not to participate in any dispute that might arise. He found that there were over 10,000 Chinese living in the area in large stockaded villages, and that they far outnumbered the Malays. Many had come from the Klang valley in 1872 as refugees. The Hai San Society controlled by far the greater number, including both Cantonese and Fui Chiu Hakkas, the former under Capitan Wong Ying, the most powerful of the leaders, who had been in the State for over thirty years, and the Hakkas under their own Capitan, Hiu Sam.[69] The Ghee Hin Society, whose members appear to have been Hakkas (possibly, as in Selangor, Ka Yin Chius) were under Capitan Ng K'im.[70]

Pickering found the Bandar utterly recalcitrant. He refused to admit that the Klana had any precedence and objected to any intervention by the British. With the Chinese Pickering appeared to have more success by threatening to banish any who interfered to oppose the Klana, and Ng K'im, who had been on the Bandar's side, thereupon withdrew his support. Representations by the Bandar to the Governor on the 'fashion of Sungei Ujong' were of no avail, and on 15 November the Klana called a meeting of all the chiefs (which the Bandar refused to attend) at which he obtained their consent to the removal of the Bandar from his office and the election of the Panglima Besar, Ahmad, in his place. A document to this effect was prepared, and Pickering witnessed the signatures of all present.[71]

Hostilities began the next day, and Pickering soon found himself in charge of operations on the Klana's side. With the help of military and naval reinforcements from Malacca and Singapore, the fighting was over by the end of November when the old Bandar withdrew to the jungle and eventually reached Singapore.[72] But during the fighting a Chinese document had been found signed by Wong Ying urging all his men to assist the old Bandar at any time and in any way, and further evidence of his sympathies and those of Ng K'im was obtained when a cache of the Bandar's tin was found to be guarded by their men. There

[68] C.1320, pp. 40–42, Agreement of 21 Apr.; C.1111, pp. 232–8, GD 142, 8 May 1874.

[69] This is the Hakka pronunciation. In many contemporary documents he is referred to by the Hokkien pronunciation 'Khoo' Sam.

[70] Or Ng Li K'im. Also spelt Ngo Khim, Gnoh Khim, and Ugoli Khim.

[71] The English date on the document is indistinct owing to an ink-blot, and has been misread as 10 November. But the Malay date corresponds to 15 November, and this is confirmed by Pickering's Journal, p. 15.

[72] For detailed accounts of negotiations and fighting see Parkinson, ch. VII, and R. N. Jackson, *Pickering, Protector of Chinese* (1965), ch. III.

had also been serious Chinese disorders at Rasah where Hiu Sam had allowed his Fui Chiu Hakkas (Hai San Society) to attack Ng K'im's men (Ghee Hin Society) and burn down the village. Several were killed and many wounded, and only the arrest of Hiu Sam and his headmen had stopped the fighting.

Captain Dunlop, who had come from Singapore in charge of the relief force, fined each of the Capitans $3,000: Hiu Sam for disturbing the peace, and the other two for helping the Bandar to escape. In default of payment they were to suffer twenty strokes of a rattan, deportation, and confiscation of property. Ng K'im was the only one to default and he was flogged, but thereafter agreed to pay. All the Chinese in the area were disarmed, and on 9 December the three Capitans entered into an agreement with a bond of $10,000, to forget their old quarrels, live in harmony, and return to the mines. All prisoners were released, and the Klana provided a buffalo for a feast.

Regulations were promulgated covering the leasing of mines, the control of water supplies, and taxation. The unpopular poll-tax was abolished and the duty on tin reduced to one-fifteenth. The carrying of arms was forbidden except under permit from the Klana. The opium, spirit, and gambling farms were let to the three Capitans in syndicate for a monthly payment of $1,500, and each of them was allowed to run a gambling farm in one locality on payment of $200 monthly. Captain Tatham, who was part of the relief force, was appointed Assistant Resident, attached to the Klana, and Pickering received 'much credit' for the gallantry and initiative which had undoubtedly saved a very difficult and dangerous situation.

Thus, in the space of thirteen months, Sir Andrew Clarke had apparently transformed the gloomy picture of the Malay States as described in the Chinese Memorial of 1873 into one of hope and expectancy. He had appointed a Resident and an Assistant Resident both in Perak and in Selangor, and an Assistant Resident in Sungei Ujong, and had, in addition, created the appointment of 'Secretary for Native Affairs' to which he nominated Thomas Braddell. The framework of intervention was established.

Failure in Perak

Birch reached Perak on 4 November 1874 to administer a State divided in political loyalties between two Sultans, where individual chiefs were all-powerful in their respective areas, and where those who had signed the Treaty of Pangkor were still unaware how much it would affect their independence. Moreover, whereas they had surrendered the right to collect revenue themselves, the delay in appointing a Resident had meant delay in setting up a new system of collection; consequently no funds existed from which the allowances promised to them could be paid. The Mentri was already deeply embittered; by comparison with his former revenue he now received a mere pittance, and other chiefs soon joined him in resisting British control.[73]

An exception to the general picture was Larut, where Speedy had at once organized the framework of government. Work was resumed at the mines, and

[73] The main source here is the material collected by the Commission appointed in 1876 to enquire into the complicity of the chiefs in the 'Perak Outrages' (EPO). It consists of a Précis of Evidence, an Abridgement of Evidence, and a large number of appendices of letters produced at the enquiry. Other sources are three unpublished volumes of Perak Enquiry Papers, 1876–7, in the Singapore Archives, and C.1505 & 1506, which contain despatches and other important material.

during 1874 the population rose from 4,000 Chinese fighters to 33,000 miners and traders, 26,000 of whom were Chinese.[74] From the first Speedy decided to prohibit secret societies, with the approval, he claimed, of the Chinese headmen. This diplomatic acceptance can hardly, however, have caused the swarm of miners entering Larut to discard a deeply-rooted social habit which provided them with personal protection, death benefits, and a pleasurable feeling of importance and strength. Nevertheless this ban enabled Speedy to take action against those promoting secret society activities, and on two occasions attempts to form societies were frustrated; but both the Ghee Hin and the Hai San societies continued to exist surreptitiously, though without open conflict.[75]

There was, however, evident rivalry among Chinese businessmen and secret societies over revenue farms during the period of transition from Malay to British control. The chiefs, who after all had no other source of income, maintained their customary tax-raising procedure as long as they could. Regardless of his previous promise to Tan Kim Cheng, Abdullah farmed out his revenues to a Penang Chinese, almost certainly Ch'in Ah Yam of the Ghee Hin. Foreseeing that it might be more profitable to be associated with the British than with Abdullah, Tan Kim Cheng had offered to hand over his own agreement, signed by Abdullah, to the Governor, but he was not prepared to sit idly by while Abdullah disposed of his revenues to others. His brother-in-law Lee Cheng Tee visited Abdullah, who thereupon discarded the Penang agreement and, on receipt of $24,000, gave him the farm, despite a warning from the Governor that no revenue concessions must be granted. Birch, on arrival, told Lee Cheng Tee that his farm could not be approved, but eventually granted him a revenue farm at the mouth of the Perak river for five years at an annual rental of $84,000.

One of Birch's proposals was that there should be one all-Perak chandu farm on the lines of the farm in the Colony, and despite strong opposition from local interests who had previously held their own farms, accepted a tender for $96,000 from a Singapore syndicate headed by Lee Cheng Tee. This caused great local resentment not only from the holders of the Penang farm (which, since 1873, had been in the hands of a Hokkien group headed by Khoo T'ean Tek of the Kien Tek Society) but even more from the mining contractors in Larut. Previously these contractors had paid a tax on raw opium imported, and had then cooked the drug to make chandu as used for smoking. This was then retailed at a considerable profit, enhanced by the universal practice of adulteration. Under the new system only the farmer had the right to import opium and to prepare chandu. So great was the objection to the new system that after the settlement of wages at Chinese New Year (5 February 1875) labour began to drift steadily from the mines. Between 3,000 and 5,000 left for Klang and other areas; tin production dropped sharply, and the opium revenue fell from $3,500 in March to $1,500 in April. Birch's hand was forced and the panic exodus was halted, but the damage had been done, and tin production in 1875 reached only 40 per cent of Speedy's original estimate.[76]

The failure of this comprehensive farm was a serious setback to Birch's

[74] C.1111, pp. 238–40, report by Swettenham and Birch.
[75] Speedy's *AR* on Larut; *SSGG*, 3 Apr. 1875.
[76] Swettenham, Memo. on the Financial Condition of the Native States, 8 Feb. 1877 (SSPLC, 1877, App. 4); Speedy's *AR* on Larut, 1874, para 86; Gullick, *JMBRAS*, Nov. 1953, pp. 48–49.

financial schemes. The Governor, already destined to leave for a post in India, was very disturbed by Birch's 'head-over-heels' methods and the 'regular mull of the farms', but the issue by Birch with the Governor's sanction of regulations concerning new revenue arrangements only served to increase the opposition of the chiefs in Lower Perak. The new Governor, Sir William Jervois, reached Singapore on 10 May, and early in July visited Larut and the Perak river, but came away convinced that the only solution was for the government of Perak to be taken over by British officials, a proposal which was later rejected by the Secretary of State. Feeling the increase of pressure, Abdullah turned for help to Tan Kim Cheng, and at the same time corresponded with the Penang Ghee Hin who were offering help in exchange for a revenue farm, but nothing came of these moves. Tan Kim Cheng chided Abdullah for not adhering to the Pangkor engagement which, after all, had placed him on the throne, and persuaded him to sign certain decrees required by Birch as well as acknowledging a debt of $16,000 to Tan Kim Cheng which was endorsed by Birch for payment from revenues.[77]

But Abdullah and the chiefs had already decided that the only way to safeguard their rights was to kill Birch. Ismail's supporters who approached the Hai San and Kien Tek leaders in Penang received no encouragement, but agents of both Abdullah and the Mentri bought arms there from Chinese merchants. Birch was murdered on 2 November while on a trip up the Perak river posting proclamations announcing his powers. The military force which thereafter was sent to Perak, however, met with no determined resistance for the Malays were disunited through their own intrigues.[78] After trial, three of the conspirators closely concerned with the murders were hanged and six sentenced to life imprisonment. As a result of the findings of a commission of enquiry into the complicity of the chiefs, Abdullah, the Mentri, and two others were exiled to the Seychelles, while Ismail was allowed to live in Johore under the care of the Maharaja.

The Chinese took no part in the hostilities; Speedy reported that those in Larut were 'to a man favourably inclined to the British rule' and they offered to supply fighters or labour as required. As a result of the troubles, Lee Cheng Tee threw up his tax farm in despair, and Tan Kim Cheng withdrew from Perak politics, leaving the field of revenue farms open for the old rivals, grouped round the Ghee Hin, Hai San, and Kien Tek societies, whose protagonists, Ch'in Ah Yam, Chang Keng Kwee, and Khoo T'ean Tek, were not slow to enter the lists once peace had been restored.

Success in Selangor and Sungei Ujong

On Davidson's appointment as Resident in Selangor the desolation of civil war still lay upon the land. Kuala Lumpur was in ruins, much of the mining labour had left the State, and there was a rumour, put about no doubt by Yap Ah Loy and his Hai San supporters, that no Chinese who had supported Chong Chong would be allowed to return. This affected, in particular, the Ka Yin Chiu community formerly occupying Kanching and the valley of the Selangor river, and one of Davidson's first duties, on instructions from Singapore, was to make it known that all labourers, no matter whom they had supported, would

---

[77] EPO, Apps. XVIII, XXII–XXVII.
[78] For details of the expedition, see Parkinson, ch. X.

be welcome to return to their homes and occupations, and a special effort was made to induce the Ka Yin Chius to return by offering transport and free rice until work was found.[79] In February 1875 an influx of Chinese labour began, and thereafter continued. Hundreds of miners who had left Larut because of the unpopular chandu farm sought work in the Klang valley; others, including Ka Yin Chius, returned from Sungei Ujong. Thus, as in Larut, members of both Hai San and Ghee Hin societies returned and became established.

A police force recruited from Malacca under an army officer, Captain Syers, was formed with stations at each of the river mouths and in the mining areas, and Yap Ah Loy was able to prevent the intrusion of other secret societies in the Klang valley by the simple method of passing on all information about their activities to Captain Syers. He was also of help to Davidson by providing 200 Chinese fighters to suppress a threatened movement to reinstate Raja Mahdi, in which the Sultan, dissatisfied with the meagre revenue from the Langat valley, was implicated. Thereafter the Governor ordered the introduction of a system of uniform taxation and central collection of revenue with allowances to chiefs. Warned by the example of Perak, care was taken to convince the chiefs beforehand that they would not lose by the change.[80]

Yap Ah Loy was energetically involved in all measures of rehabilitation. He was encouraged in his development schemes by loans from government funds, and was granted the opium, spirit, and gambling farms in Kuala Lumpur. During 1876 and 1877 when the price of tin was low, he was saved from financial difficulties by permission to levy a tax on all tin exported from Klang. Until the seat of government was moved to Kuala Lumpur in 1880, the administration of justice was largely in his hands and in those of Yap Ah Shak the other Hai San headman. As magistrates for the Chinese community they wielded not only the powers derived from the Government, but also those, far more drastic, arising from their position in the society. Even after the British took over the town administration, Yap Ah Loy levied an annual 'voluntary contribution' upon Chinese merchants towards his public expenses, and continued his magisterial control. It is understandable that some found the yoke of this autocrat hard to bear. Cantonese and Hokkiens took umbrage because he and not they had the ear of the Resident; Ka Yin Chius and other Ghee Hin members were inevitably in the opposing camp, and members of other societies, such as the Hock Beng of Malacca, who attempted to establish themselves within his bailiwick and were promptly reported to the Chief of Police, naturally regarded him with animosity. Illiterate, energetic, persistent, and ruthless, he was an outstanding example of the Capitan China of his day, and until his death in 1885 was undoubtedly the true ruler of the district.

Sungei Ujong. The settlement made by Dunlop and Pickering was successful. Work at the mines was quickly resumed, at Rasah a new village was built, a police station opened, and a road traced to the river down which the tin went to Malacca unimpeded. But the attitude of the Dato' Klana, now a man of wealth with the prestige of British support, irritated his fellow chiefs to such a degree

[79] C.1512 pp. 7–24; GD, 10 Feb. 1876.

[80] C.1111, pp. 269–71, Swettenham's report, 18 Dec. 1874; C.1320, pp. 94–96, Davidson's report, 16 Mar. 1875; pp. 97–103, Swettenham's report, 8 April 1875; pp. 105–11, Skinner's report on the West Coast States, 22 Mar. 1875; C.1505, pp. 59, 93, 95, 100, 107, 165; Swettenham's Memo., 8 Feb. 1877 (SSPLC, 1877, App. 4).

that they proposed to curb his power by filling the office of Yam Tuan Besar (Great Sovereign Chief) which had been vacant since 1869. The quarrel over this proposal led to a local war in which British troops took part on the Klana's side. A political settlement was reached in November 1876, and thereafter resistance ceased.

As in the Perak war, the Chinese in Sungei Ujong took no part in the fighting. Though the two societies, the Ghee Hin and the Hai San, continued to exist side by side, the Capitans, having learnt their lesson in 1874, refrained from lending their support to any of the combatants, and relied upon a satisfactory outcome from British intervention.[81]

Conclusion

As was to be expected, British intervention was welcomed by Chinese traders and miners throughout the country, even though in Larut it meant a temporary loss of face for one side, for settled conditions were a prerequisite for profitable enterprise. Among the Malays, reactions were mixed. Clarke's impetuosity combined with Birch's clumsiness produced resentment, suspicion, and resistance among the chiefs, though those who co-operated profited in power and prestige. And the removal from Perak of Abdullah, Ismail, the Mentri, and other leading chiefs meant that the new Resident necessarily had the appearance of a ruler rather than an adviser.

[81] Wynne, p. 412, Chong Bun Sui's report; C.1505, pp. 193–6, GD, 17 Dec. 1875; C.1709, pp. 84–86, GD, 13 Dec. 1876; pp. 128–9, COD, 27 Feb. 1877. For a detailed account of hostilities see Parkinson.

Part 2

ATTEMPTS AT SUPPRESSION

10

THE APPROACH TO SUPPRESSION

1. THE STRAITS SETTLEMENTS, 1873–6

ON his arrival in Singapore in November 1873, one of Sir Andrew Clarke's first tasks was the reconstitution of the Legislative Council from which the three European unofficial members had resigned the previous September. After Ord's departure the Secretary of State sent a tactful despatch which was read to the disgruntled gentlemen by the new Governor, and at his suggestion they agreed to resume their seats and were reappointed.

Meantime, although the Chinese Immigration Ordinance which had passed its third reading during the absence of these members appeared in the law books as Ordinance X of 1873, it was passed with a suspending clause, and was not brought into force. Clarke, anxious to appease, decided to review the proposal, and called for opinions from the Chambers of Commerce in Singapore and Penang, from the IGP, and from the two Chinese Interpreters, Pickering and Karl (Penang). Thereafter, until March 1877, the immigration problem was the subject of constant discussion.

In December 1874 the European merchants and bankers of Singapore petitioned the Legislative Council urging 'the inexpediency' of proceeding with a Chinese Immigration Bill. They stressed that the best way to prevent the immigrant from coming under the control of the secret societies was to abolish the societies, which were at the root of every serious disturbance which occurred. They supported the control of emigration from Singapore, but pressed for absolute freedom of immigration, on the grounds that prosperity depended more than ever upon an abundant supply of labour, which could only be obtained through immigration.[1]

The Governor, despite the opinions of the IGP and the Chinese Interpreters that the proposed law would not impede immigration, informed the Secretary of State in April 1875 that he saw no chance of bringing the Ordinance into force with any hope of success, and was preparing another Bill granting additional powers to the police, and introducing a modified form of the Hong Kong system of registration to be worked by the Municipal Commissioners and not by the Central Government.[2] This plan was based on suggestions made by Pickering to divide Singapore into wards with a wardmaster in charge of each, responsible to the Government for the conduct of those within his area.[3] But before the Bill could be framed, Clarke had been transferred and a new Governor, Sir William Jervois, had been appointed who had yet different ideas.[4]

---

[1] SSPLC/1874/app. 33. [2] GD 127, 29 Apr. 1875.
[3] W. A. Pickering, 'The Chinese in the Straits of Malacca', *Fraser's Magazine*, Oct. 1876, pp. 443–4. [4] GD 256, 31 Aug. 1875.

Meanwhile, both Dunlop and Pickering were endeavouring to persuade the Government to make full use of the powers they already possessed to control the societies. Pickering's first comments were contained in a 'Report on the General Condition of the Chinese in the Straits Settlements, 1873',[5] in which he referred to the absence of serious quarrels during 1873 between rival secret societies in Singapore, and attributed this improvement to the registration of all such societies under Section 3 of the Dangerous Societies Ordinance, and to the enforcement of the Preservation of the Peace Act by means of a proclamation under the Ordinance. For the proclamation issued in December 1872 had not been lifted (and was not, indeed, lifted until 1885) and its existence ensured that the Government had power, after suitable enquiry, to banish any person (other than a natural-born British subject) who was implicated in riots or disturbances or was an office-bearer of a registered society so implicated. It also ensured that any persons forming part of a riotous assembly who did not disperse after being warned could be sentenced to whipping.

Both Dunlop and Pickering recommended the extension of these measures to Penang and Malacca. Both these Settlements were affected by the troubles on the adjacent mainland, Penang by the Larut disturbances, Malacca by those in Sungei Ujong, Rembau, and Selangor. Stricter registration of the more prominent Hoeys was carried out in Penang during the first half of 1873, but both the Chinese and the Red and White Flag Societies continued to be active. In June 1874 Dunlop recommended the issue of a proclamation in Penang, and as an alternative even proposed that secret societies be abolished, but when no action was taken upon either recommendation, he was forced to rely upon registration. The situation further deteriorated in 1875, when a branch of the Singapore Ghee Hok was started both in Penang and in Province Wellesley, and at the end of the year the Superintendent of Police attributed most of the crime in the Settlement to the secret societies, which, he said, were daily becoming more powerful. He urged that they should be broken up, being given two years' notice, during which time they could wind up their accounts.

In December 1875 at Malacca there were severe inter-society clashes originating in a trivial incident at a Malay 'joget' performance, and involving the Hok Beng and Ghee Boo societies. At the time, the acting Lieutenant-Governor of Malacca (C. B. Plunket) was absent in Sungei Ujong where a Malay rising had begun, and the officer officiating in his place was persuaded that the Malays of Sungei Ujong intended to attack Malacca territory and would be joined in revolt by the Malacca Malays. He sent for 100 Gurkhas from Penang, but Plunket when he returned to the Settlement discounted the rumours, though he asked for a larger force of troops to be stationed permanently at Malacca. Meantime, negotiations between the Hok Beng and the Ghee Boo were protracted, and the Ghee Hin society joined in on the side of the Ghee Boo. The headman of the Hok Beng, Boon Swee, who held the post of official government interpreter, was instructed to reach a settlement, but it was found necessary to issue a proclamation before order was restored through the co-operation of police, troops, and the Malays. Over 130 men were charged, of whom two were sentenced to death and 63 others to varying terms of imprisonment.[6]

[5] Dated Oct. 1874, laid before Leg. Co. 4 May 1875.
[6] The Ghee Hin, comprising Hokkiens, Cantonese, and Hainanese, used a white flag. The Hok Beng comprised Hoi Luk Fung Hakkas and used a red flag. Boon Swee was a local-born

As a result of the riots four of the Malacca societies, the Ghee Hin, the Hok Beng, the Ghee Boo, and the Hai San, were required to register under Section 3 of the Dangerous Societies Ordinance, and the police found that many rich planters and traders belonged to these societies.[7] When all was over, Plunket was able to report to the Governor that the riots had no connexion whatever with any Malay movement objectionable to Government in Malacca or in the Native States; on the contrary, the Malays had, generally speaking, rendered every assistance in putting them down.[8]

Writing in June 1876, and surveying the Chinese scene as a whole, Dunlop was not prepared to advocate the suppression of the Dangerous Societies Ordinance without something to take its place. In the light of subsequent events it may be presumed that he originally had in mind the complete prohibition of secret societies (as he had previously recommended) but that discussion with Pickering had led him to the conclusion that if they were abolished there would be no medium of contact between the Government and the Chinese masses. He found the Chinese as a community very ignorant of the laws of the Colony, unaware of the British desire to treat the immigrants justly, and only too glad to join societies where their interests were looked after by powerful headmen. He considered that what was wanted was not so much new or amended laws as 'a strong personal Government in which the administrators were brought into intimate relations with the people' and he recommended that in each Settlement a system of registration of Chinese should be instituted, and a Protector of Chinese appointed who should be a thoroughly trustworthy European conversant with some dialect of Chinese and able to write the language. This officer should be assisted by influential Chinese selected from the several tribes represented in the Settlement, and he should have an office in the centre of population to which ready access could be had at all times by anyone requiring his assistance or advice. All Chinese notices published by the Government should pass through his hands, all Chinese publications issued by private 'chops' or persons should be submitted to and stamped by him before publication, under a penalty, and all Chinese mercantile firms, associations, charitable and secret societies should be registered by him.[9] (It seems possible that this was Pickering talking through Dunlop, who shortly afterwards had the opportunity of pressing these views more forcefully.)

Sir William Jervois had become Governor on 10 May 1875, and on 7 October held his first Legislative Council meeting. In his opening address he stated that in his view the Hong Kong system of registration was unsuited to Singapore, and he was in favour of a measure based on the Ceylon Master and Servants Act, adapted to apply to all communities. But by June 1876 further consideration led him to appoint a Committee 'to consider and take evidence upon the condition of Chinese labourers in the Colony, as to whether any legislation was necessary with a view to their protection'. The Committee was composed entirely of officials: the Colonial Secretary (John Douglas), the Treasurer

---

Hakka. The main sources for the Malacca riot are: GD 371, 29 Dec. 1875, printed at PP C.1505, p. 236, with encl. to p. 243. Other relevant parts of C.1505 are serials numbered 65, 66, 67, 87, 93, 105 (with encls), and C.1709, p. 31 & serial no. 17.

[7] IGP *AR*, 1876.   [8] PP C.1505, p. 243.

[9] IGP *AR*, 1875. See SSPLC/1876/app. 19.

(W. W. Willans), and the IGP (Samuel Dunlop). Its report, completed in September, and laid before the Legislative Council on 3 November 1876, clearly reflected Dunlop's influence.[10] It contained a most instructive picture of the position of the immigrant and of the lack of contact between the Government and the Chinese community.

The Government knows little or nothing of the Chinese who are the industrial backbone of these Settlements, and the immense majority of them know still less of the Government. We know that a certain number of Chinese arrive every year and that a certain number go away, but how long they stay, how many come back a second time, what they think about and desire, as to all this we know nothing. With the exception of two interpreters, Messrs Pickering and Karl, there is no other officer of any standing in the Public Service who can hold the most ordinary conversation with the Chinese in their own language.

It is not surprising, therefore, that the mass of our Chinese population bringing with them as they do from their own country the leading idea that the main function of Government is to squeeze money by fair means or foul, know even less of our Government than it does of them. An immigrant arrives, is landed by his Kay Tow [importing agent] and carried off straight to the place where he is to work. While he is at work he is, unless he commits a crime and is found out, never brought into contact with any officer of Government, and we believe that the vast majority of Chinamen who come to work in these Settlements return to their country not knowing clearly whether there is a Government in them or not.

Soon after his arrival, the immigrant becomes, in all probability, a member of a Secret Society—supposing him not to have been a member already. If he gets into any trouble, he goes to the Secretary of his Society. Failing redress through him, he goes to some influential Chinese gentleman and asks for help from him. If he does not get what he wants from him, possibly he may hear of some old European resident who is known to be kind to the Chinese, and he applies to him, but it never enters his head to apply to a Government Officer.

The Committee had come to the conclusion that the Dangerous Societies Ordinance (XIX of 1869) taken in conjunction with the Peace Preservation Act of 1872 appeared to deal with the secret societies as effectively as the laws of a free country could do, and added that anything further could only be effected by the officers of Government obtaining influence over and winning the confidence of the Chinese population by being brought gradually more and more into contact with them, or by a law rendering membership of these societies penal, a measure the Committee was not at that moment prepared to advocate.

The Committee first recommended that Protectors of Chinese should be appointed in Singapore and Penang (possibly later at Malacca), who should be European gentlemen conversant with Chinese dialects, and who should be assisted by respectable Chinese belonging to the different nationalities who resorted to the Settlements. It was also recommended that a certain proportion of the Cadets sent out for the public service of the Settlements should be sent first to China to learn to read Chinese and to speak one, or if possible two, of the dialects.

As for the control of immigrants, coolie-brokers and their recruiting agents should be licensed, and depots provided for the reception of immigrants who would be taken before the Protector for scrutiny of the terms of their engagements. Similarly, labourers recruited in the Colony for service in other territories

[10] SSPLC/1876/app. 22.

would be brought before the Protector for a like purpose. The Ordinance should be simple, because it was essential to obtain the confidence and co-operation of the responsible portion of the Chinese community for whatever was done, and any great and sudden interference with their habits and customs would only provoke evasion and would increase the influence of the secret societies.

2. THE POST OFFICE RIOTS, SINGAPORE, 1876

Hardly had the report of the Committee been made public when the peace of Singapore which had persisted since 1873 was rudely disturbed by the 'Post Office Riots', which demonstrated that the existence of a proclamation under the Peace Preservation Ordinance and the detailed registration of certain societies under Section 3 of the Dangerous Societies Ordinance were insufficient guarantees that no riot would take place, a fact already recognized by Dunlop when he gave warning that should discontent arise among the Chinese population, the Hoeys, because of the great influence possessed by their headmen, would assuredly prove a source of great trouble and danger to the Settlement.[11]

The Post Office riots broke out in Singapore on 15 December 1876. They were not an inter-society quarrel, but were directed against the Singapore Government which was attempting to introduce a new system of sending letters and remitting money to China to the families or business contacts of the Chinese in Singapore who had hitherto relied on letter-shops.[12] These shops shipped letters and remittances in the same way as merchandise to the appropriate port in South China, where an agent forwarded them to his representatives in main towns, who in turn passed them on to sub-agents in smaller towns and villages. The system offered limitless opportunities, which were fully exploited, for exchange manipulation, and the remitter had no real redress. To give the Chinese better postal facilities, Sir Andrew Clarke proposed to grant to a Penang Chinese firm a monopoly of collecting and forwarding letters and remittances to China from the Colony, levying a charge of 6 cents on each letter and 10 per cent on each remittance. For this privilege they were to pay the Government $7,000 annually. Jervois succeeded Clarke before the arrangements were completed and feared that the scheme might be open to abuse. Instead, it was agreed that the firm should be appointed as sub-postmasters at a small monthly salary, making them legally public servants. They would be allowed to undertake, at fixed rates, a money-order business, the profits from which would belong to them, but this was not to be a monopoly—they would compete with the letter-shops. These latter would be required to have all letters handled by them stamped and sent through the Chinese sub-post-office or through the General Post Office, and not, as formerly, as merchandise paying no stamp fee. The letter-shops would receive their fees from their clients as usual, and the letters would be delivered by the Government postal system to the agents of the letter-shops at Amoy or Swatow.[13]

About ten days before the new system was to come into force, there were

[11] IGP *AR*, 1875.
[12] Argument about a proposed postal 'Farm' will be found at GDs 285 (9 Oct. 1874) & 72 (17 Mar. 1875); COD 10 (19 Jan. 1875) & COD(AI)28 (11 Feb. 1875).
[13] GD 46, 4 Feb. 1876; CODs 75 & 87, 29 Mar., & 11 Apr. 1876.

rumours that the Government had farmed out the monopoly of sending remittances to China to a firm belonging to two Hokkien 'Babas'. If this were true, it would put the Tiechius, who ran most of the letter-shops, out of business. Though the real version was conveyed by Pickering not only to the leading letter-shopkeepers but to their supporters, the headmen of the Ghee Hok and the Tiechiu branch of the Ghee Hin, there could be no disguising the fact that the new scheme, whether a monopoly or not, would have detrimental effects on the business of the letter-shops. Here was a Government-sponsored organization with the security which that implied offering to remit money to China at lower rates than those customarily charged. The letter-shopkeepers refused the offer of the Chinese sub-postmasters to co-operate in the working of the scheme.

Matters were made worse because a draft notice prepared by the sub-postmasters firm giving details of the scheme erroneously stated that the firm was to have a monopoly of the business, and although Pickering had this clause deleted, the letter-shopkeepers had already obtained a copy, and placards appeared inciting the mobs to attack the new Chinese post office and to kill the sub-postmasters.

In the ensuing riots on 15 December 1876, the police who arrested some of those attacking the post office were surrounded and stoned; another mob released prisoners being taken to the police station; and when the police station itself was attacked, the sergeant ordered his men to fire, killing three or four of the rioters and wounding several more. There was a similar outbreak at Rochore. Shops and markets closed and posters appeared telling them to stay closed. One market that dared to open was closed by a gang of Tiechiu Ghee Hin and Hai San fighting-men, three of whose members had earlier been killed in the assault on the police station. The Government ordered troops to stand by at Fort Canning, and the headmen of the two societies were arrested, but no other societies became involved. Eventually, ten of the most troublesome letter-shopkeepers, together with the headmen of the two societies, were put on board the Government steamer *Pluto*, which had orders to steam away but to keep within signalling reach. That evening the town returned to normal.

The headman of the Tiechiu Ghee Hin, Lim Ah T'ai, who had long been a thorn in the flesh, was banished; the headman of the Hai San was charged with rioting, and the ten shopkeepers, after spending two days upon the stormy waters outside the harbour, were thankful to enter into bonds of $3,000 each to keep the peace, while others found security of $1,000 each. The Chinese post office was formally opened on 18 December and attracted a steadily increasing business.[14]

The Secretary of State later impressed upon the Governor the importance of fully informing the people concerned in their own language of any new law or regulation, but Pickering, in reporting on the riot, considered that the letter-shopkeepers 'in instigating a riot simply tried a remedy which had been known to prove successful before with the Straits authorities, and a longer notice would only have given them time to plan a more serious riot.'

Instigating a riot was, indeed, not only a customary method of protest of the Chinese in the Straits, it was the method used from time immemorial in

[14] GDs 444, 27 Dec. 1876, & 3, 4 Jan. 1877; COD 43, 5 Mar. SSPLC/1876/app. 31, Reports by R. W. Maxwell & W. A. Pickering.

China whenever the local magistrate or other official introduced new measures to which vested interests objected. Each side measured the strength of the other and acted accordingly. The riot in Singapore was of precisely this nature. The letter-shopkeepers used the machinery of their own secret societies to rouse the mob. The rest of the community immediately recognized the signs, and until it was evident which side was going to win refrained from any action which would bring the wrath of the dissidents upon them. In this particular instance, had the matter affected the whole Chinese community, the Government might well have found, as the IGP had previously suggested, that the whole of the secret society organization was mobilized against them.

Once the excitement of the Post Office riots had died away, the attention of the Government was again focused on the problem of the protection of Chinese immigrants by a report submitted on 17 February 1877 by Pickering. This concerned the kidnapping of sinkhehs which had taken place at Singapore within the previous fortnight.

A respectable Chinese had gone to see the IGP, Major Dunlop, to ask him to sanction a contract of employment under which he proposed to engage some sinkhehs to work in his bakery. The period of indenture was 360 days, for which each labourer was to be paid $30, of which, according to the contract, he had already received $24 in respect of passage-money and expenses. If the man refused to work his employer was at liberty to punish him, and if he ran away, to issue notices for his arrest. When told that such a document was unlawful the applicant expressed surprise and said that these terms were better than those on which many sinkhehs were engaged. As for the $24, it had not been paid to the sinkhehs but to the broker, who, after paying the captain of the junk $5 or $6 for passage-money kept the balance to cover his expenses and profit.

Going deeper into the system of importing sinkhehs, Pickering visited a fleet of 20 or 30 junks in the harbour recently arrived from China. Each of these vessels had brought from 50 to 120 coolies, many of whom were from the interior province of Kwangsi, 6 or 7 days' journey from any seaport. Several of the sinkhehs were cooped up on the junks and were not being allowed to leave until the various immigration agents had found a market for them and had paid their passage money. The Supercargo was not to be found, but through the head of his secret society he was eventually brought to the police station. Some of the secret societies were known to be heavily involved in this business of the detention of sinkhehs and their shipment to Sumatra, certainly the Ghee Hok (Tiechiu) and the Ts'ung Paak (Hakka). On the morning of the very day that Pickering wrote his report there was a minor riot. A posse of fighting-men of the Ts'ung Paak Society conducted a party of sinkhehs to the water-front to embark them on tongkangs[15] for transportation to junks in the roads which were to take them to Sumatra. The sinkhehs, who had been landed from Hailam junks a day or two previously and had been confined in a house in Telok Ayer, refused to embark, saying that they had been told on leaving China that they were to work in Singapore. The brokers and secret society bullies then tried to force them to embark and a fight started. The brokers complained to the police that the sinkhehs had assaulted them, the police turned out in vigorous support of the brokers, and over twenty sinkhehs, some of whom were wounded, were

[15] Large cargo lighters.

taken to the police station. Pickering and Dunlop then visited the tongkangs and released a further fifteen men who had been forced on board.

In reporting this incident to the Government, Pickering recommended that immediate steps be taken before the season of arrival of junks reached its height to require the names of all employers of sinkhehs to be registered, and to prohibit the engagement of coolies for work outside the Colony unless they had first been taken to the police office and the terms of their engagement explained to them. This report was laid before the Legislative Council on 23 February 1877, and added urgency to the introduction the same day of a Bill for the protection of Chinese immigrants.

Another document which, though not generally available, had a bearing on immigration and on secret societies was the report, signed on 19 February 1877, of a Committee appointed in November 1876 to enquire into the working of the Contagious Diseases Ordinance. In discussing prostitution, this report referred to the 'highly objectionable influence' of the secret societies and the samsengs in connexion with the brothels. Not only were brothel owners members of the societies, but both they and the inmates paid monthly subscriptions to the societies and blackmail to the samsengs. One example was given of a brothel-keeper who paid an annual fee of $100 to the Ghee Hok, plus a head-tax on each prostitute of 20 cents monthly. In addition, the brothel-keeper had to pay for the support of a number of samsengs of the society, who lived in the brothel as 'guardians', and part of whose duty it was to see that no girl was taken away.

These complaints were not new. As early as 1863 (the year in which a small but steady flow of Chinese women immigrants began) the *Singapore Free Press* noted that towards the end of the year, many Chinese women had been imported by the secret societies for prostitution. Articles on the subject continued to appear in 1865, and by 1877 the system was well established.[16]

On 23 February 1877, when the Bill for the protection of Chinese immigrants came before Legislative Council, Mr W. H. Read, an unofficial member who had been a member of the Committee on the Contagious Diseases Ordinance and was therefore aware of the contents of its report, gave notice that at the next meeting of Council he would move a resolution that before proceeding further with the Immigrants' Bill, a measure should be introduced for the suppression of Chinese secret societies. In due course, he did so, but after discussion the resolution was withdrawn and the Chinese Immigrants' Bill went forward. It became law on 23 March as the Chinese Immigrants' Ordinance (II of 1877), and provided for the appointment of a Protector of Chinese Immigrants at each or any of the Settlements, for the examination of sinkhehs, the establishment of depots for their reception, and the registration of their labour engagements. No period of contract was laid down. In conveying Her Majesty's Gracious Confirmation and Allowance of the Chinese Immigrants' Ordinance, the Secretary of State (Lord Carnarvon) remarked:

I should fail in my duty if I did not express my opinion that the abuses connected with Chinese Immigrants in the Straits Settlements which are disclosed in the Reports

---

[16] A few Hokkien wives and families had been brought from Amoy towards the end of 1853 to escape the wrath of the Imperial troops when the Triad occupation of the city ended. There were a few single women among the immigrants of that year, but thereafter there was no further female immigration of note until 1863.

accompanying Sir William Jervois's Despatch are little creditable to the legislation of the community. It is humiliating that it should be possible in a British Colony for free persons having committed no offence to be imprisoned and confined in large numbers against their will, and that special legislation should have been found necessary for their protection.[17]

A second Bill became law on 23 March 1877 as the Crimping Ordinance (III of 1877). This provided for the appointment of Protectors of Chinese Emigrants, for the establishment of depots for the accommodation of emigrants, the annual licensing of recruiters, the signing before a Protector of engagements for service outside the Colony, with penalties for inducing any person to enter such engagement by fraud, deceit, intimidation, false pretences, and so on. The Crimping Ordinance was brought into force first (on 14 May 1877), and the office of the Protector was opened on 1 June. Pickering had been appointed on 4 May to be Protector of Emigrants, Singapore, and E. Karl to a similar appointment in Penang. In addition, Dr Dennys, a Chinese scholar from Hong Kong, was appointed to be an Assistant Protector of Chinese at Singapore, and arrived at the end of May.[18]

The Chinese Immigrants' Ordinance was not brought into force until later in the year in order to allow time for notification or the proposed changes to be distributed at ports in China. Nine sections came into force in September 1877 and two more on 1 December, but the sections concerning the provision of depots, about which the Secretary of State expressed considerable doubt, were not brought into operation until April 1878, by which time, under the requirements of the Crimping Ordinance, licensed agents had already provided suitable new houses which were licensed as depots and used for the purposes of both ordinances.[19] Pickering and Karl were also appointed to be Protectors of Chinese Immigrants. In September 1877 the Protectors were made Registrars of Societies and took over this work from the police. One more step had been taken to weaken the power of the Hoeys, though certain unofficial members would have preferred complete prohibition.

Pickering's first move as Registrar of Societies was to undertake a re-registration of all members and office-bearers, entering the members' names under the headmen in charge of each district, so that a member could always be found through his headman. The Hokkien branch of the Ghee Hin, whose principal headmen were Straits-born Chinese, objected to this re-registration, but on being summoned before the magistrate apologized and complied.

There was, in fact, very little society trouble in 1877. In Penang and Province Wellesley the Indian–Malay societies (the Red and White Flags), most of whose members were said to belong also to the Chinese societies, continued to be a nuisance at each Muslim religious festival, with the result that permission to hold a procession for Moharram was refused. There was also some friction between the two old Penang rivals, the Ghee Hin and the Kien Tek (Toh Peh Kong), because the opium farm had passed from the hands of Kien Tek members to those of the Ghee Hin when it was relet by tender in 1877, but no serious outbreak occurred. In Malacca there was a typical secret society fracas

[17] GD 99, 29 Mar. 1877; COD 146, 5 July 1877.
[18] GDs 99 & 100, 29 Mar. 1877, & 168, 18 May 1877.
[19] GDs 300, 356, & 378 (12 Oct., 28 Nov., & 24 Dec. 1877); 25 (24 Jan. 1878) & 47 (3 Feb. 1879); CODs 258 (27 Nov. 1877) & 31 (13 Mar. 1878).

during a Chinese funeral procession in October, when the eldest son of the deceased, a headman of the Ghee Hin, refused to allow the Hok Beng Society to participate in the procession, although his brother was a Hok Beng member. In Singapore, late in December, there was an outbreak at Bedok and Mata Ikan between members of the Ghee Hok and Ghee Sin societies, which was prevented from spreading into the town by the prompt arrest of 100 rioters and a warning from the Colonial Secretary that if the trouble spread they would be deported.

Deportation, or 'banishment' as it came to be called, was more feared than imprisonment. The scope of the provisions of the banishment law was widened in March 1877 at the same meeting of Council at which the Chinese Immigrants' Ordinance was passed. Previously the power could only be used against persons arrested during the period of a proclamation under the Preservation of the Peace Act who were office-bearers of Dangerous Societies or had been actively engaged as instigators or participators in a riot or disturbance. The amendment authorized the Governor in Council after enquiry to banish any person whose removal from the Colony was necessary for the public safety, provided that the person was not a natural-born British subject.[20] This power, however, could still only be used during the existence of a proclamation, and no action for banishment could be started until the Chief Police Officer had laid a written information that the person's removal was necessary.

According to Pickering, in his Annual Report for 1877, banishment had proved effectual in Malacca and had had a very salutary effect on the chiefs of other societies, who now saw plainly that they would no longer be allowed with impunity to presume on the mildness of British rule. Not only was the deportee cut off from the source of his power and his profit, but there was also a risk that an enemy might betray him to the authorities in China where membership of a Triad society was a capital offence. Pickering also quoted the case of Lim Ah T'ai, the headman of the Tiechiu Ghee Hin, who had been deported at the time of the Post Office riots in 1876 but had returned to Singapore in December 1877. The headmen of his society at once brought him before Pickering, lest all the members should be implicated in his unlawful return, and when he was again deported they raised no objection.

This was satisfactory as far as it went, but Pickering was concerned about the increasing number of Straits-born Chinese who were joining these societies and who were beyond the scope of the banishment law. He recommended that it be made a penal offence for any such person to join a secret society, and believed that if this were done the Hoeys would in the course of a few years 'lapse into the same harmless if not beneficial status as Masonry or Forestry in Great Britain', surely a remarkable underestimate of the power latent in the increasing flow of immigrants from China to keep the secret society tradition alive.

It is unlikely that the Governor or anyone else regarded the appointment of 'Protectors' as a historic occasion, yet such it was, for it marked the establishment of a government department, the Chinese Protectorate, whose officers became the trusted intermediaries of the Chinese in their relations with the Government, not merely on matters relating to immigration and emigration but on all matters which in any way affected the Chinese community. The Pro-

[20] Ord. V of 1877.

tectorate became, too, a department upon which the Government relied for the governance of the Chinese. Once the Protectors were appointed, there began a close connexion between the common people and the Government to the benefit of all concerned. Cases of petty dispute could be taken before an official who understood, to some degree at least, Chinese language and customs, but who, having no affinity of clan or district or province with either party, was impartial. Moreover, this service was free, and the Governor (Weld) when addressing the Secretary of State a few years later (1882) on the outrageous charges made by some members of the legal profession, which even a report of the Judges had considered to be unreasonable and exorbitant, remarked that one of the great advantages arising from the strengthening of the Chinese Protectorate was that by means of that office every individual member of the Chinese community who did not know sufficient English to address the Colonial Secretary could be assured of having any representation he might wish to make being submitted to the Government.[21]

The Protectors, too, rapidly became possessed of a fund of knowledge about the various sections of the Chinese population, their disputes, intrigues, and differences, their reactions to proposed legislation and the like, which was of the greatest use to the Government. The Chinese Protectorate proved to be a cushion absorbing some of the shock of impact between the cultures of China and the West in the Straits Settlements.

3. THE STRAITS SETTLEMENTS, 1878–87

One result of the establishment of the Chinese Protectorate was that each year the Protectors produced a report, and these documents provide more detailed information about the Chinese community and in particular the secret societies than had previously been available.

The re-registration of the Dangerous Societies in Singapore was completed in January 1878, and the report for that year shows a total membership of 17,906, of whom 3,862 had joined during the year. The numbers continued to increase, and in 1879 there were 23,858 members. This is the first year for which official figures are available for the Malacca societies, and the position at each of the three Settlements is set out in the table overleaf.

Of the Singapore societies, nine were affiliates of the Ghee Hin, the only exception being the Hai San. We know that in the early days of the T'in Tei Wui (which became the Ghee Hin) in Singapore there were four sections each of a different tribal composition, and Major Low, writing in 1840–1, gave the names of the tribes as Hokkien, Hakka, Tiechiu, and Cantonese, with a total membership of 5,000–6,000. From later documentary evidence it is known that the Hakka section was known as the 'Ts'ung Paak Kwun' or 'Pine and Cypress Hall', and the Cantonese section had the title 'Kwong Wai Shiu', meaning that the members were drawn from the three main prefectures of Kwantung Province: *Kwong* Chau, *Wai* Chau, and *Shiu* Hing. The fifth tribal section, that of the Hailams (Hainanese), is first officially mentioned in 1860.[22] Its date of formation is unknown.

---

[21] GD 168, 1 May 1882.

[22] 'List of the different Secret Societies in the Island of Singapore', prepared by C. B. Plunket, actg Comm. of Police, 1 May 1860 (see App. 3, p. 538). It is an encl. to GD 108 of 5 June 1860.

Why, in addition to the five tribal sections, four more sections or affiliates of the Ghee Hin were formed in Singapore is not clear, nor is there any certain evidence of the dates of their foundation. Their titles were: Hok Hin, Ghee Khee, Ghee Sin, and Ghee Hok. None of them is mentioned either in Garling's list of societies in 1843, or in the *Singapore Free Press* of 18 March 1846, and it may therefore be assumed that they did not come into existence until after the latter date. All except the Hok Hin appear in a list of societies prepared by Plunket, the acting Commissioner of Police, dated 1 May 1860. The first official mention of the Hok Hin appears to be in a report for the year 1861–2.[23]

Chinese Secret Societies registered under Section 3 of the Dangerous Societies Ordinance in 1879

Singapore		Penang		Malacca	
Society	Members	Society	Members	Society	Members
Ghee Hin (Hokkien)	4,291	Ghee Hin	22,939	Ghee Hin	1,380
Ghee Hin (Tiechiu)	1,453	Kien Tek		Ghee Hin (Macao)	282
Ghee Hin (Hailam)	1,576	(Toh Peh Kong)	8,116	Ghee Boo	556
Ghee Hok	4,728	Ho Seng	4,623	Hok Beng	1,126
Ghee Sin	1,212	Ghee Hok	1,725	Hai San	156
Ghee Khee Kwang		Tsun Sim	1,830		
Hok	2,331	Hai San	394		
Hok Hin	3,109				
Kong Fooy Sew					
(Kwong Wai Shiu)	1,576				
Song Peh Kwan					
(Ts'ung Paak Kwun)	2,224				
Hai San	821				
Totals:	23,858		39,627		3,500

Source: CP *AR*, 1879, app., gives figures for Singapore and Penang; figures for Malacca are from Mal. *AR*, 1881.

The figures for Penang include membership in Province Wellesley, and it is noteworthy that although there were only six Dangerous Societies in Penang as compared with ten in Singapore, there were far more members in the former Settlement.

According to Plunket, the Ghee Khee was composed of Hakkas and Tiechius, and the Ghee Sin of Tiechius. The full title of the Ghee Khee appears to have been 'Ghee Khee Kwang Hok', from which it may be assumed that its members were drawn from both Kwangtung and Fukien. It was under this title that it was called upon to register as a Dangerous Society in 1873.

Finally there was the Ghee Hok, the most untameable of the Singapore societies and one which frequently engaged in feuds with sister societies in the Ghee Hin group. No official mention of its existence has been found before 1860, and its origin is conjectural. W. H. Read, in *Play and Politics*, says that it existed in 1841, but this is believed to be unreliable. It would seem that he confused the Ghee Hok with the earlier rival of the Ghee Hin, the Kwan Tec. The first reliable mention of this society refers to 1854, in Song Ong Siang's *One Hundred Years' History of the Chinese in Singapore*. Speaking of the death

[23] SS *AR*, 1861–2.

in 1880 of the leader of the Ghee Hok, Chua Moh Choon, he says that he was prominent as its headman as early as 1854. This we know to be the year in which the Triad refugee rebels from Amoy came to Singapore, and were the cause of the Singapore riots of that year because the local Hokkien community refused to contribute to the support of the Tiechiu section of the rebels. According to Plunket's list of 1860, the Ghee Hok was a Tiechiu society, and it is possible that it was formed by these recalcitrant Tiechiu rebels from Amoy, already organized as a Triad society, which, like an 'Old Comrades' Association', retained its identity under the title 'Ghee Hok', indicating that it had come from Fukien province. But in deference to the powerful existing mother-lodge of Triad at Singapore, this interloper became affiliated to it, and was thereafter in the same position as the other sections of the Ghee Hin, except that it was regarded as a reprobate cousin composed of ruffians and vagabonds. This, at least, is a possible theory of origin which might account for the Ghee Hok's turbulent nature and for the fact that it is found so frequently at war with the other affiliates of the Ghee Hin.

The only Singapore society shown in the above list for 1879 which was not an affiliate of the Ghee Hin was the Hai San, which would appear to have come to Singapore sometime between 1846 and 1860. It was registered as Dangerous in 1873.[24]

There was, indeed, general agreement that the re-registration in Singapore had resulted in a lessening of tension and a decrease of incidents, but a contributory factor to this improvement was the close co-operation which had existed between Pickering and the police ever since his appointment as Chinese Interpreter in 1871. In Penang things were not so peaceful. There the Hoeys were numerically stronger than in Singapore, due, in some measure, to the proximity of the tin mines of Perak. On 16 August 1878 a disturbance occurred between the Ghee Hin and the Ghee Hok societies at Nibong Tebal in Province Wellesley. The latter society, an offshoot of the Singapore society of the same name, had only been established among the Tiechius of the northern Settlement for about three years, and in the Province, where there was a considerable population of Tiechiu agriculturalists, it was the natural enemy of the Ghee Hin Society which was of long standing there. Already in May 1877 there had been trouble, and only the fact that the Settlement had not been proclaimed under the terms of the Preservation of the Peace Ordinance prevented the deportation of the local Ghee Hin leader who had repeatedly been guilty of riotous conduct. The issue of a proclamation on 22 June 1877 removed this disability.

The disturbance in 1878 would appear to have been premeditated. A week previously the Ghee Hin headman had applied for permission to hold a sacrificial feast on this day but this had been refused. Nevertheless, between 200 and 400 Ghee Hins congregated together at an hour when the majority of the local Ghee Hok members were away fishing. Sacrificial tables were set up, and the opportunity was taken by a Ghee Hin man to start a quarrel with a passing Ghee Hok man who owed him a debt. At once a riot flared up, the Ghee Hins moving on to the Ghee Hok headquarters and pillaging it. The small force of police was overwhelmed, and the sergeant in charge appealed to a Mr Piltert, a former member of the Colony's police force who lived at Nibong Tebal, to quieten the Chinese.

[24] It appears in Plunket's list of 1860 with a membership of 6,000.

Unfortunately the Ghee Hoks returned from fishing just as Mr Pilfert arrived on the scene, and a general fight ensued. The sergeant's right hand was broken by a blow, and fearing that the whole police party might be overborne and killed Pilfert fired at his attackers, killing the leader of the Ghee Hoks, upon which the crowd dispersed. The immediate result was that two Ghee Hin leaders, including the previous trouble-maker, were banished.

In justifying his action to the Secretary of State, the Governor, Sir William Robinson (who had succeeded Jervois on 29 October 1877), referred to 'the improbability, amounting to almost an impossibility of procuring a verdict against the present and similar offenders in the regular Court' and added:

The difficulty in procuring sufficient evidence to secure the conviction of the Head of a wealthy and numerous Chinese Society is almost insuperable where testimony has to be sought from Chinese sources, and I believe it was principally to meet this difficulty that the Ordinance under which I have now acted was passed.[25]

Despite this outbreak it was agreed that the appointment of Protectors had produced good results and that there was a growing disposition on the part of the Chinese to take their disputes to the Protector rather than to the secret societies for settlement. But as Pickering pointed out, this very trend was leading to a weakening of the authority of the headmen, and this undermining of the fabric meant that it would be increasingly difficult for the Government to hold the headmen responsible for acts of violence committed by the members. Clearly he was still anxious to introduce a system of control which would take the place of the societies.

More of the headmen, too, were banished; two of the Singapore Ghee Sin leaders in 1879 because of a quarrel between that society and the Ghee Khee in which one man was killed, and a Ho Seng leader from Penang in the same year for participation in a serious disturbance between his society and the Ghee Hok.[26] But the Secretary of State (Sir Michael Hicks-Beach) in approving this action gave a warning that this power should be used very sparingly and only in exceptional instances.[27]

Pickering also recommended that powers should be taken to deal not only with the leaders but with the society as a whole by suspending or cancelling its registration if it should show itself not to be amenable to control by milder measures, presumably the persuasion of the Protector.

It is unjust to the European community and to the well-disposed and really respectable portion of the Chinese that the public peace should be disturbed, life endangered, and law set at defiance by semi-savages whom hunger, poverty and the punishment due to crime committed in their own country have forced to seek the protection and immunity afforded by our too lenient rule.[28]

This outburst appears to have been caused by the riot in Province Wellesley in 1878 and the murder at Pangkor in October of the same year of Captain Lloyd, the Superintendent of the Dindings, which was attributed to members of the Ho Seng Society.[29]

It is all very well [he continued] to call the Chinese 'the backbone of the Colony', but it must be recollected that the flag made the Settlements and that the Chinese flock to

[25] GD 281, 28 Sept. 1878.   [26] GD 330, 26 Sept. 1879.   [27] COD 157, 9 July 1879.
[28] CP *AR*, 1878.   [29] See below, pp. 252–3.

them only for their own advantage. Take away our Government and there would be a state of anarchy of which Larut has afforded an expensive example. Singapore and Penang have but few natural resources, and being for the most part mere entrepots for European trade would relapse into a state of jungle inhabited only by piratical fishermen, and the mines of the Malay States under similar conditions would be worked only by a population of Chinese adventurers subject to periodical diminution by massacre.

Pickering acknowledged that things were not as bad as they had been, but he attributed this to the personal efforts and influence of the heads of police and the Chinese Protectors. This, he thought, was an unsound foundation and should not be accepted with complacency. He advised that 'our own too liberal code of law' was not adapted to the control of the Chinese population, and urged the Government to consider introducing a more suitable system. Otherwise, despite the apparently quiet state of affairs, it was his opinion that the problem would, 'at some future and no distant time, force itself to notice in an unpleasant manner'. Even if the Hoeys were abolished, the difficulty would still remain, for there were several of the large Clan Associations which would readily take the place of the secret societies and would cause, perhaps, even more trouble.[30]

Nevertheless, conditions continued to improve for a year or two. Although there were many minor disputes between the Hoeys which in former years would have led to serious conflagrations, the authorities were now better informed and were able to intervene before things got out of hand.

Not only was the influence of the headmen being undermined by the policy of the Government but a number of the old chiefs died in 1880, including the most colourful of them all, Chua Moh Choon, who since 1854 had been the head of the Ghee Hok Society, and whose name had figured more than once in debates in the Legislative Council. Pickering referred to his 'long career of intrigue' and declared that he was much feared by his countrymen, although in fact for some years before his death he had found that the best policy was to be on the side of the Government, and great use was made of him in keeping the peace not only among members of his own society but also between other societies and clans. To the Chinese of Singapore, Chua Moh Choon was the embodiment of power. His word was law because he had the means to enforce it. Not only was he the unchallenged head of the largest and most unscrupulous Hoey in the town but he was also in the confidence of the principal officers of the Government and was thus in a position to blacken the name of anyone who failed to do his bidding.

The successors of these old headmen were of a different stamp. They had neither the prestige nor the personality of their predecessors and had little influence over the disorderly elements of their societies, nor, apparently, were they able to enforce the payment of subscriptions, all of which added to Pickering's uneasiness. There was also no lack of new members: each year there were between 4,000 and 5,000 in Singapore, rather more in Penang, and 1,500 or more at Malacca. A disturbing feature was that a proportion of these new members were local-born Chinese, not subject to the law of banishment.

The problem of the secret societies also received public attention through the Annual Reports of the Protectors and the police and through the report of a Commission appointed to examine the state of the police force.[31] The Chairman of this Commission was Cecil Clementi Smith, who in 1878 came to Singapore

[30] CP *AR*, 1879. [31] SSPLC/1879/app. 32.

P

as Colonial Secretary from Hong Kong, where Triad societies were prohibited and where the ranks of the police force were, for the most part, Chinese. The other members of the Commission were W. W. Willans (the Colonial Treasurer) and three unofficials: Read, Shelford, and Walter Scott.

The Commission reported in August 1879, and it commented unfavourably on the liaison existing between the police and secret societies, particularly on the practice of relying on the headmen of the societies to effect the arrest of 'wanted' persons. There was, it said, no other channel of communication between the police and the mass of the Chinese population. When a Chinese interpreter was required at a police station, the head of one of the societies was called in, and Chinese complainants unable to speak Malay often preferred to go to their own societies for assistance.

The Commission was informed that Chinese had been tried as regular members of the force, but the scheme failed because they entered the secret societies and devoted themselves to their interests which paid them best. It was agreed that with very few exceptions the weight of evidence was wholly against the employment of Chinese as constables. Instead, to bridge the gap between the police and the public, the Commission recommended that at the principal police stations there should be a Chinese Station Officer speaking the dialect of the majority of those about him as well as Malay. Despite the objections of the IGP (Dunlop), the Commission recommended that about one-half of the detective force should be Chinese and that this force should be considerably increased.

The IGP and the Protector of Chinese, both of whom gave evidence before the Commission, were opposed to destroying the influence of the societies further than had already been done by the existing law, but the Commission considered that instead of bolstering up the waning influence of the headmen it would be better in the end to adopt all other possible means to detect and suppress crime.

The stage had thus been reached at which there was a difference of opinion even within government circles as to the policy which should be followed. All were agreed that the secret societies were bad and that it would be a good thing if they did not exist, but whereas Dunlop and Pickering were afraid that a further weakening of the influence of the headmen without providing some alternative system of controlling the Chinese population would result in disaster, Clementi Smith was in favour of either suppressing the secret societies altogether or of continuing the process of gradually undermining the position of the headmen.

The question was raised again in a debate in June 1880 on a new Chinese Immigrants' Bill which, like its predecessor, was opposed by some of the unofficial members, partly on the ground that it was 'restrictive' and partly, as had previously been argued, because the Government had never squarely faced the necessity of suppressing the secret societies, but instead had tinkered with palliatives such as the Immigrants' Bill. 'It appears to me,' said Mr Shelford, 'that the Government is always lopping off the branches and never reaching the roots. Ever since the passing of the Ordinance of 1869 [the Dangerous Societies Ordinance], you have been attacking the outworks, and surely you may now assail the citadel itself.'

To the first of these criticisms—that the Bill was 'restrictive'—the Colonial Secretary gave the spirited reply that it was the duty of every civilized Government 'no matter at what cost, to ensure that natives of any kind coming within our jurisdiction should receive the fullest measure of support to prevent their being down-trodden, as they frequently are, by their own people'. He was speaking from knowledge of the subject gained in Hong Kong. As to the societies, he made it clear that he, for one, would be only too pleased to advocate their abolition, but, as he was a comparative newcomer, he deferred to the advice of the experienced officials of Singapore, and thought that in the circumstances the best course to be followed was to let them disintegrate.

That the new Colonial Secretary was thus persuaded against his better judgement is not altogether surprising when, in the same debate, we find the Attorney-General (T. Braddell) maintaining in forceful language that in his view the day of the secret society was over, and that it would be injudicious and useless for the Government to take what he called 'rash measures' against them. But despite his confident and somewhat arrogant assurance, and the acceptance on all sides that the societies were not as bad as they had been, it was soon found advisable to introduce some amendments to the Dangerous Societies Ordinance, partly to attempt to control the undesirable developments pointed out by Pickering in his Annual Reports, and also to deal with the increasing threat presented by the Red and White Flag societies among the Malays at Malacca and the Indian–Malay community at Penang.

At Malacca these societies seem to have started about 1878 when they first came to notice through a fracas in the town. Next year men belonging to the White Flag attacked a party of Red Flag men as they were returning from the mosque, causing one death. The excitement was so great that the trial of eight Malays was transferred to Singapore. All were convicted, two being sentenced to seven years' rigorous imprisonment. At Penang, too, there was from 1879 onwards a resurgence of the power of these Flag societies.

The Bill brought before Council in 1882 embodied three separate changes. The first prohibited by name the Red and White Flag societies and all similar associations by whatever name they might be known which had among their members persons not born in China of Chinese parentage. Also prohibited were secret societies which had among their members any British-born or naturalized British subjects. Finally, the law was amended to give power to the Governor in Council, on the joint written information of the Registering Officer and the Chief Police Officer that a society, whether registered or not, was dangerous to the public peace, to call upon the society to show cause why it should not be suppressed. After hearing the case put forward, the Governor in Council, if satisfied that the society was a danger to the public peace, could order that it be suppressed. Thereafter, any person acting as a manager of the society was liable to a fine of $1,000 or to imprisonment for twelve months, while any person found to be a member of a suppressed society was liable to a fine of $500 or to imprisonment for six months. The Bill became law on 7 March 1882 as Ordinance IV of 1882. So that, at last, the Ordinance passed in 1869 as the 'Dangerous Societies Suppression Ordinance' came, in 1882, to bear some resemblance to its title, and for the first time machinery was provided for the suppression of dangerous societies.

When forwarding the Ordinance to the Secretary of State, the Governor (Weld) remarked that some non-official members of the Council thought that all Chinese secret societies should be suppressed, but, after hearing the opinions of the IGP and the Protector of Chinese, he believed it better to work gradually towards ultimate suppression.[32] In reply the Secretary of State, while approving the Ordinance in principle, made it clear that he would have preferred it to have been more simply constructed, to ensure that all 'dangerous societies', whether composed of Chinese or non-Chinese, were unlawful and would be suppressed.[33] But no amendment was introduced, and the Ordinance remained in force without change for the next three years.

Nevertheless, it is clear from Pickering's report for 1882 that he was not happy about the future. This report was never made public, probably because it was mainly concerned with presenting a very uncomplimentary and controversial picture of the trade in Chinese prostitutes in the Colony, which he described as 'a system of slavery compared with which the debt-slavery of the Malay States is innocent and just'.[34]

In his remarks about the governance of the Chinese it is obvious that he was still worried because of the precarious nature of the machinery of control. Though there had been no incidents in Singapore during the year, he felt it necessary to say that he believed 'that in default of legislation suitable to the condition of the Chinese in the Straits, strong societies are really a help to the Government. Under the present circumstances it is indeed difficult to imagine how the large Chinese population could be kept in order without their assistance.' He did not advocate the rigid control exercised by the Dutch but a system of ruling through headmen. He was anxious, too, that officials of all government departments should learn Chinese. Were this done, the Protectorate could be abolished and the security of Singapore placed on a more solid foundation.

The new provisions of the Dangerous Societies Suppression Ordinance came into force in March 1882, and before the end of the year action was taken to have the Hai San Society in Singapore suppressed, as it was 'an incorrigible nuisance and danger to the peace of the Colony'.[35] This was the smallest of the 'Dangerous' societies and the only one which was not an affiliate of the Ghee Hin group. It had been troublesome for some time, and two of its headmen were banished in 1881 (but returned clandestinely in 1883). Even after its dissolution the former members continued to give trouble, for the ways to which they were accustomed were not at once discarded.

This was the next problem to be faced. When a society was suppressed, its members joined another society so that they could continue their protection and extortion activities under the shield of a registered society. There was another development, too: the weakening of the power of the Dangerous Societies by the deportation of headmen and the suppression of the societies themselves encouraged other societies which had registered as Friendly Societies to take over their activities, such as brothel protection which had previously been the monopoly of the Dangerous Societies. In some instances these Friendly Societies were merely reorganizations of the old members of Dangerous Societies which had been suppressed. In 1885 two such societies, only recently established, were suppressed, and another three were called upon to register as Dangerous

---

[32] GD 108, 14 May 1882.   [33] CODs 115, 15 May 1882, and 288, 13 Nov. 1882.
[34] T. Shelford, during the debate on the Societies Bill on 7 Feb. 1899, revealed that the report for 1882 had never been made public. Copies were sent to the S. of S. by the Governor (Weld) on 27 June 1883 (GD 274. Filed at PRO in CO 273/121). The report was dated 12 Apr. 1883.
[35] GN 1 of 1883; GD 272, 27 June 1883.

Societies.[36] In the same year two of the nine affiliates of the Ghee Hin group, the Teo Kun Ghee Hin (the Tiechiu section) and the Ghee Sin, were also suppressed, 'having yearly become more dangerous to the public peace through disorganization and the incompetence of their managers and office-bearers'.[37]

In other Settlements, too, the new powers were used. In Malacca, the two old rivals, the Ghee Boo and the Hok Beng societies, were again the cause of disturbances and were suppressed.[38] At Penang the Ghee Hok Society ever since its foundation about 1875 had been a cause of violence, particularly in disputes with the Ghee Hin Society which naturally resented the intrusion of this new power-bloc. In September 1885 the Ghee Hok of Penang was suppressed.[39]

Earlier in the year in April two Bills were introduced, one to amend the Dangerous Societies Ordinance and one to amend the Preservation of the Peace Ordinance. The first was originally drafted to incorporate the suggestion of the Secretary of State that it should provide 'for the suppression of all societies (whether Chinese, Mohamedan, or otherwise) which are shown to the satisfaction of the Governor in Council to be dangerous to the public peace', but although Clementi Smith, who was administering the Government, was in favour of this policy, the fears of Pickering and Dunlop, supported unanimously by the members of the Executive Council, prevailed.

These two officers, together with the other 'Registering Officers' (R. W. Maxwell, acting IGP, H. Riccard, acting Chief Police Officer, Penang, and E. Karl, Assistant Protector of Chinese, Penang), had submitted a lengthy memorandum protesting against the proposal to suppress all Dangerous Societies. It was their view that experience proved that the existing system of registration and supervision could prevent the Triad from being dangerous, and also render it serviceable towards governing the Chinese in a British Colony 'where legislation existing in French, Spanish and Dutch Colonies would not readily be approved by the Home Government'.[40]

When forwarding this memorandum to the Secretary of State, Clementi Smith remarked that although he personally was anxious to get rid of the Dangerous Societies as soon as possible, he refrained from recommending their general suppression in deference to the opinion of the Protector of Chinese and the heads of the police. He was, however, in favour of bringing them under increasingly rigorous control. The second Bill introduced to the Legislative Council in April sought to remove the provision of the law under which the banishment of aliens could only take place during the existence of a proclamation under the Ordinance. Pickering in his Annual Report for 1884 had expressed his conviction that the powers of banishment were

unduly restricted, and might advantageously be extended towards the banishment of habitual criminals, alien Chinese who merely made use of our Colony as a scene for

---

[36] The societies suppressed were the Kwang Kit Tong and the Ng Fuk Tong. (GNs 354 & 355 of 1885, publ. on 26 June. The date of the orders was 19 June 1885.) Those called upon to register were the Li Seng Hong, the Hong Ghee Tong, and the Yuet Tong Kun (CP *AR*, 1885).

[37] GNs 352 & 353 of 1885, publ. 26 June; orders dated 19 June. Wynne (pp. 392 & 399) cites GN 353 as suppressing the Ghee Hin Society. This is incorrect; it was the Ghee Sin Society.

[38] GNs 411 & 412 of 24 July 1885, publ. 31 July.

[39] GN 508 of 1885.

[40] GD 502, 17 Nov. 1884, encl. 2, 11 Nov. 1884 (PRO 273/130).

their lawless exploits. At present these men overflow our gaols and are for long periods fed at the public expense, but though they are well known as dangerous to the peace of the Colony it is impossible to banish them unless they are found guilty of what may be called a semi-political offence.

It may be that Clementi Smith considered that this declaration from an officer whose views on matters affecting the Chinese were listened to with respect by members of the legislature strengthened his hand in reopening the question of powers of banishment. During the debate on the Bill it was admitted that there had been a proclamation in force in Singapore for twelve years (actually since 24 December 1872) not because there had during all this time been apprehension of disturbances, but so that the Government would not lose the power of banishing aliens whose presence was 'inconsistent with the public safety', a power which, said the Attorney-General, had been found most useful at different times, enabling the Government to cope promptly and effectually with illegal combinations for which the ordinary machinery of the Penal Code was found to be insufficient. At the same time the Government thought that the Settlement should not be kept under proclamation as if it were an unusual or abnormal condition.

The proposed amendment met with some opposition, and an unofficial member moved a postponement, a proposal which was seconded by the Chief Justice (Sir Thomas Sidgreaves) who thought that to place such power in the hands of the Executive, unless guarded as it had been in previous years by a proviso that it should only be exceptionally used, was open to grave objection.

It was at this point that Mr Read, who was again a member of the Council, declared that this legislation was aimed at the secret societies. As always, he attacked the Government for having failed to suppress the societies. He pointed to the fact that since 1881, that is in four years, 15,000 members had joined the societies in Singapore and 16,000 in Penang. He counselled strong action to suppress them, and thought that this would not be difficult, for the headmen were men of straw with very little power. The Attorney-General remarked that Mr Read had, in fact, produced strong arguments in support of the Bill. He emphasized the care with which the powers of banishment were used, and it is surprising to find that in the previous five years only three Chinese had been banished.

One unofficial member, Shelford, considered that it would be mischievous if the Government were to relax any of the extraordinary powers which it possessed over its foreign population. He added that he thought it was time that the Council got rid of

that mythical monster, the future Governor of these Settlements. I think we ought to look on any gentleman who comes to administer the government of this Colony, to credit him with the amount of good sense, fairness and ability which is possessed by previous Governors and by His Excellency the Officer Administering the Government [Clementi Smith] at the present moment.

This is a far cry from the attitude of unofficial members in the time when Ord was Governor, and there is no reason to suppose that his colleagues shared this feeling. Nevertheless, Shelford was deeply concerned about the power which the societies still wielded, and remarked:

After all your legislation, your labour laws, the Chinese Protectorate, it is humiliating that we should have such influence in our midst, but it is so. We have, in fact, a large alien population, recruited year by year, last year by some 120,000 of the very lowest classes in China. They are ignorant of our laws, of our customs, of our language. They recognize no authority but that of their clans and societies.

In reply, Clementi Smith undertook to endeavour to prepare the way for the suppression of the societies altogether, and meanwhile to minimize their operation and effects. The Bill was finally passed, though four unofficial members and the Chief Justice voted against it. It became Ordinance VI of 1885.

In his report for that year Pickering, having in mind this debate, and anxious to ensure that the banishment procedure would be used to remove objectionable gaming promoters from the Colony, referred to the seeming existence of a 'sensitiveness towards and a shrinking from this form of punishment' and argued that it was not too much to expect from the Chinese that in return for the protection and assistance which they received so freely in the Settlements they should be obliged to obey the laws and live peaceably and quietly. In particular, he declared that however much long experience, acquaintance with the headmen or knowledge of the Chinese dialects might have assisted the heads of the police and the Protectorate in their control of societies, they had to confess that the most powerful weapon on which they had relied was that of deportation, which though applied sparingly had always proved a specific.

There was one other Bill introduced in 1885 which had relevance to secret societies. It was a measure designed to prohibit public flogging. This proposal when put forward by the Secretary of State in 1872 had been strongly opposed by the Legislature, and it received a similar reception on this occasion. Once again the suggestion had emanated from the Secretary of State who, on 18 January 1883, sent a Circular Despatch to all Colonial Governors requiring public flogging to be prohibited by law. It would seem that this instruction evoked no immediate response, for on 22 October 1884 a further Circular Despatch was issued calling for a report on the position. In replying to this in January 1885, Clementi Smith enclosed a draft Ordinance providing for the prohibition of public flogging, but, in the light of what had earlier been said in Legislative Council and of his own experience of twenty-five years in the East, he ventured to suggest that provision be made for an exception to the general rule if thought advisable by the Governor. He had in mind the possibility of serious riot, when, it was generally agreed in Singapore, the infliction on rioters of public flogging was a potent deterrent.[41] This suggestion merely drew from the Secretary of State (Lord Derby) the reply that he was of the opinion that the practice should be entirely forbidden and that no discretion should be left to the authorities in the matter.[42]

The Bill was thereupon introduced on 16 April 1885, and came up for its second reading on 18 May. It was at once attacked by Mr Read, who considered that it took away 'the only deterrent punishment we have, short of shooting men down in the streets, which has been done once and which I do not wish to see done again, but which must be done unless you have some punishment to deter rioters'. He gave instances of seven serious riots in Singapore, at all of which he had been present, and called attention in particular to the riot of 1871 which, he considered, had been put down because of the free use of public flogging

41 GD 13, 12 Jan. 1885.   42 COD 42, 18 Feb. 1885.

of rioters by order of the magistrates. He pointed out that though deportation was a useful weapon in the hands of the Government it could not be used against British-born Chinese; moreover, what was wanted at such times was a punishment which could be applied on the spot for all to see, and for this reason he objected even to the suggested reservation to the Governor alone of the power to order flogging. He would leave it in the hands of the magistrates, and he moved that the Bill be read a second time 'this day six months'.

Other unofficial members supported Mr Read, not only because they believed that experience in Singapore had shown that flogging in public was a deterrent but also because they strongly objected to being ordered by the Secretary of State, who had no personal knowledge of conditions in the Colony, to pass legislation which they considered to be entirely unsuited to the Colony's needs. Mr Shelford doubted whether there was any point in debating the question at all. The Secretary of State had interfered before, and he referred to the debate on the Penal Code Amendment Bill in 1872, when, although the principal official members had spoken against the abolition of whipping for rioting, all had voted in favour of abolition. He referred to the excellent effect of whipping during the riot of 1871: 'Rioters taken red-handed were whipped and sent back with the marks upon them to their comrades, and the effect upon them was much better than had those men being marched off in gangs to fill our gaols.' As far as the unofficial members were concerned, he declared that they attached little honour to a seat on the Legislative Council if they were to be employed 'only to register the parochial decrees of the Colonial Office'.

Two official members addressed the Council in support of Read's delaying motion, and the Chief Justice, too, considered that the Executive would be put in almost a humiliating position if the Bill were passed. It was his view that it rested with the Executive and not with the magistrate who imposed the sentence of whipping to decide whether it was to be inflicted publicly or privately, He went on to say that a certain gentleman during the 1871 riot 'had the happy audacity to break the law, . . . and had the rioters whipped in public and with very excellent effect, for it stopped the riot'. Strange words indeed from the principal officer of the Judiciary whose business it was to see that the provisions of the law should not be set at nought.

But the most peculiar feature of the debate was that Clementi Smith, stung, perhaps, by the scornful references by Shelford to the official attitude at the previous debate, did not instruct the official members to vote for the Bill. Had he done so, it could have been passed by his casting vote; as things went, it was thrown out, the only members voting in its favour being the Officer Administering the Government, the acting Colonial Secretary, and the Attorney-General.

As might be expected, the Secretary of State (now Lord Stanley) was incensed at this turn of events, and did not hesitate to express his displeasure, but although he was not able to have public whipping forbidden by law without reintroducing the Bill and ordering the official votes to be used, which, under the circumstances was clearly inadvisable, a similar result was achieved by the issue of a standing instruction to the Governor to the effect that public flogging was not to be allowed, so that whenever whipping was ordered by the magistrate and it fell to the Executive to decide where it was to take place, the Governor would give such instructions as would ensure that it would not take place in public. And there the matter rested.[43]

The legislation which aimed at preventing local-born Chinese from joining the Hoeys was thought to have had a measure of success, though it was admitted that appearances might be illusory; but the problem was not solved, for many of the 'Friendly Societies' which were springing up were said to be formed from the worst elements among the Straits-born Chinese, and they very quickly tended to usurp the position of the Hoeys as trouble-raisers. Indeed, the heads of the Hoeys complained that whereas they themselves were kept under strict supervision and were held responsible for the behaviour of their members, the Friendly Societies had no such restraint or responsibility, and carried on their intrigues with impunity. Five of these newly-formed societies, called upon to furnish particulars as being dangerous to the public peace, took legal advice, and rather than face the risk of being suppressed or called upon to register as Dangerous Societies, they dissolved themselves, so that their promoters were free to start again.[44] And even when one of the registered Dangerous Societies was suppressed, there was the danger that it would survive or be revived under the leadership of its more turbulent elements in disregard of the requirements of the law. This happened to the Tiechiu section of the Ghee Hin, which was suppressed in June 1885, but was still functioning illegally under disreputable headmen at the end of 1886.

Another matter of concern in which the societies were involved was public gaming. Attempts to subdue what Light had described as the Chinese 'excessive fondness for gambling' had never been successful, and many of the local administrative officers would have agreed with the Lieutenant-Governor of Malacca (Cairns) when he said in 1868: 'A passion for gambling pervades all classes of the Chinese; it may be said to be the national pastime, and the only results of our efforts to make it criminal is a thorough demoralisation of the Police who extort large amounts as hush money from the players and then become their confederates and scouts.'[45]

In Singapore, from 1882 onwards, Pickering had drawn the attention of the Government to the open existence of over 100 gaming houses, 'causing great danger to the welfare and good order of the Chinese, and . . . certainly demoralising the native portion of the Police Force'. His proposed remedy, however, was not to remove the prohibition but to introduce more severe measures to stamp out the practice. 'Nothing,' he said, 'is more likely to create quarrels and jealousy between the secret societies than the emulation which is aroused to share in the great profits accruing from the establishment of gaming houses in the various sections of the Settlement.'[46] That Pickering was correct in this assessment of the interaction between gaming and secret society warfare would be endorsed by any police or Protectorate officer of experience, and its relevance in modern times can be gauged from the detailed account of the gambling nexus given in Chapter 20 below. In Pickering's day, the Ordinance under which control of gaming houses was supposed to be exercised was the Common Gaming Houses Ordinance of 1879, but it was plain that this legislation had

[43] COD 22, 10 July 1885.
[44] They were the Tung Meng, Kim Hok, Hok Tek Choon, Ghee Lan Tong, and Eng Chuan Tong. They dissolved themselves in 1886.
[45] COD 241, 26 Nov. 1868: Report on Malacca, para. 53.   [46] CP *AR*, 1885.

not achieved its purpose. At the time of its introduction it was characterized by the outspoken unofficial member, Mr Read, as 'an Act to still further corrupt the already corrupt Police', and as the years went by this prognosis was increasingly justified.

A Commission, of which Pickering was a very active member, was appointed in April 1886 to enquire into the question of public gaming and lotteries, and concluded that both in Singapore and in Penang there had been a systematic arrangement for corrupting the police. The system in Singapore was that two or three kongsis levied subscriptions from the gaming houses to bribe the police. One of the societies most involved in gaming promotion and protection was the Ghee Hok, and its activities extended to the adjacent Dutch islands, the Karimuns, where in April 1887 the 'Lieutenant China' was murdered.

In the course of his duties Pickering was naturally concerned with investigating the ramifications of the professional promotion of gaming, and predicted that the Ghee Hok would revenge itself on the headmen of societies who had given evidence against them before the Gaming Commission. Instead of this, on 18 July 1887 a Tiechiu carpenter named Chua Ah Siok walked into Pickering's office as though to present a petition, suddenly produced an axe-head and threw it, severely wounding Pickering in the forehead.

The whole populace was shaken by this attack, the Chinese no less than the Europeans, for the Protector had come to be regarded as a most useful member of the body politic for whom the Chinese had not only respect but something akin to reverence. A Commission set up to enquire into the reasons for the attack concluded that it was a conspiracy planned 'if not by the Ghee Hok Kongsi at all events by certain of its headmen' in revenge for Pickering's action in connexion with gaming.[47] The assailant who had been hired to assassinate him received a sentence of seven years' rigorous imprisonment, but though it was not possible to bring home proof of abetment against any of the Ghee Hok headmen or anyone else, five headmen of the Ghee Hok were banished; the case against them rested on their complicity in the murder of the Lieutenant China of the Karimuns.

In order to mark the displeasure of the Government, the Governor issued a proclamation suspending the usual granting of passes for the use of the streets for processions for the forthcoming Seventh Moon Festival. Although some inflammatory posters of protest were published, this restriction seems to have been accepted on the whole with good grace, for at a meeting of the Legislative Council on 13 October Shelford expressed his admiration of the attitude adopted by the Chinese 'when they were deprived of a privilege which they had enjoyed for years, and which touched their deepest and dearest feelings'. At the same time he called for a review of the Government's policy towards the Hoeys, despite the fact that both the Protector and the IGP had been of opinion that they should be retained for the purpose of repressing and discovering crime.

Pickering recommended that the Ghee Hok Society should be suppressed as a warning to others, adding that the reasons for so doing were far graver than those submitted in respect of societies which had been suppressed during the previous seven years. At the same time he said he believed that the time had arrived when the Government should take serious measures for the gradual abolition of all the existing Dangerous Societies, and to forbid under severest

[47] GD 445, 17 Oct. 1887.

penalties their revival, or the establishment of any new societies of a similar nature. In his Annual Report for 1887 he gave the reasons which led him to a conclusion which was at variance with the opinion expressed by him in 1879. He wrote:

I have always been of the opinion that the existence of the Thien Te Hoe in our dominions is an anomaly and a reproach, yet considering that they had been allowed to flourish here unchecked since the establishment of the Colony, and that by cordial cooperation between the heads of the Police and the Chinese Protectorate Departments we have not only been able for some years to keep them in order but also in many ways to make them useful to the Government, I have not, since 1878, urged their suppression. Late experience has shown me that, in the absence of the above-mentioned cooperation these societies would soon become as dangerous as ever, and for this reason I am obliged to recommend their suppression.

He was, however, still bothered about what the result would be, and could not recommend abolition. The result would be that the societies would be only nominally suppressed and that their control would impose an intolerable burden on the Chinese Protectorate. Once more, though not stated in the same terms, we find an expression of the conviction that English legal principles are inadequate to ensure the control of Chinese societies, for Pickering, in addition to recommending severe penalties—long terms of imprisonment, fines, and banishment—for those who kept up a suppressed society or started a new one, also required: 'that the onus of proof of innocence must rest on the defendants'.

Not only Pickering, but Dunlop, too, found it necessary to make a reappraisal of the position in the light of the attempt on the life of the Protector and of the latter's changed opinion. In commenting upon his suggestions for the abolition of the Dangerous Societies, Dunlop stated that he believed the time had come for Government to suppress the societies, and he thought it would be better 'to make a bold stroke and suppress all the existing dangerous societies at once'. If the Ghee Hok branch of the Ghee Hin Society were suppressed, as proposed by the Protector of Chinese, he feared this would greatly strengthen the remaining branches of the society. There was nothing to choose between these societies. They were all equally dangerous, and all engaged in the management and protection of gaming houses and brothels. 'If Government is satisfied that the Ghee Hok has perpetrated the crimes laid to its charge in this letter, I feel satisfied no better opportunity could be found for suppressing it and the other societies with which it is affiliated.'[48]

[48] GD 292, 20 June 1888, para. 7.

11

THE POLICY OF SUPPRESSION, 1887–90

THE attack on Pickering marked a turning point in the Government's policy towards the Hoeys. There had always been a strong though not unanimous body of European unofficial opinion which opposed the policy of toleration in the Legislative Council and in the press. On the other hand there was in Government circles in the early years of the Settlements a disinclination to introduce restrictions on the liberty of the subject contrary to English practice. Emphasis was upon improvement of the police force and of the processes of law. Later, when it became evident that something more than this was needed, the secret societies had become so powerful that the Government feared the consequences of facing the challenge directly, and temporized by introducing legislation in 1869 to provide only for the registration of societies in the hope that gradually control would be achieved. But twenty years after the introduction of registration their power was still so extensive that it deterred the Protector of Chinese and the IGP from supporting any policy of outlawing them.

The tide was beginning to turn when Sir Cecil Clementi Smith was appointed as Governor in 1887. As we have seen, he had always believed that suppression was the only right policy, and his arrival doubtless influenced both Pickering and Dunlop, even though they differed as to the method of procedure.

The report of the Commission on Public Gaming of November 1886 gave added reason for taking action against the societies. It was improbable that the position would improve, for the flood of immigration from China showed no signs of abating; in 1887 there were no fewer than 167,906 new arrivals at Singapore and 70,109 at Penang. Membership of the Dangerous Societies increased during the year by 6,136 in Singapore, and by the astonishing number of 14,536 in Penang. The total number of members shown in the registers was 62,326 in Singapore and 92,581 in Penang, but there was no means of checking how many of these had left the country or died.[1]

Although there was no inter-society rioting during the year, apart from one clash between the Ghee Hin and the Ho Seng societies at Penang in January, the annual accession of new members showed the potential seriousness of the position.[2] Early in 1888 two events occurred in Singapore which strengthened the Governor's determination to remove the secret society menace from the life of the Colony.

The first of these arose from the coming into force on 1 January 1888 of a new Ordinance providing for the registration of domestic servants, which had been passed in 1886 to provide means of identification of domestic servants so

[1] CP *AR*, 1887, app.

[2] It is amusing to find that these societies and the Kien Tek jointly presented an Address to the Queen on the occasion of her Jubilee in 1887 (GD, 5 Oct. 1887).

as to check the time-honoured habit of passing testimonials from one to the other. Naturally, the servants were strongly averse to such a restriction. A large proportion of them belonged to the Hainanese community, and were members of the Hailam Ghee Hin Society which became the organizing body for resistance to the law. It incited attacks on servants who registered, and forced them to leave their employment. It also organized a boycott of employers who insisted on complying with the terms of the Ordinance. Because of these activities the society was suppressed in January 1888 and Banishment Orders were issued in respect of nine of its members.[3]

In reporting this, the Governor said that he had been opposed to the introduction of such a law because experience of the operation of similar laws in Hong Kong and Ceylon showed that they failed to achieve their objects. In March 1888 he was instructed by the Secretary of State to consult his Executive Council on the desirability of repealing the Ordinance, and a Bill to repeal it was passed in October, the Governor declaring that it had been found 'unsuitable, unworkable, and not desirable to be kept on the statute book'.[4]

The second disturbance took place between 20 and 22 February 1888, and though not originally organized by the secret societies, it was necessary to warn their headmen to use their influence to prevent their members joining the rioters. It occurred through an attempt to enforce Section 129 of the Municipal Ordinance, which prohibited the blocking of open arcades or verandas abutting on public streets with goods or stalls, and the riot is known as the 'Veranda Riot'.

Some Chinese and European members of the Municipal Commission who let out the space under the verandas on the public way outside their premises to stall-keepers were opposed to the enforcement of the law.[5] The existence of this opposition was well known to the shopkeepers who hired out the veranda space in front of their premises, and when the Municipal Inspectors, led by the President of the Commission (to ensure that no needless harshness should be employed) instructed the keepers to clear their verandas, they met with resistance.

In the zone affected, on 21 February shopkeepers who were instructed to clear their verandas closed their shops. The Commissioners held a meeting at which it was decided to compromise by requiring that only three feet in width of the veranda need be cleared. Despite this, on the following day shops and markets were closed, and the mob took to the streets, stoning Europeans, Malays, and Indians. Gangs of samsengs also stoned the police. Here, once more, was the familiar gesture of non-compliance: the closing of shops with the mob roaming the streets.

At a further meeting of the Commission, attended by the Protector of Chinese and by several of the leading Chinese, it was arranged that more publicity should be given to the compromise measure. During the morning of the 23rd there was some further rioting, but by noon this had died down and the shops were open again. Three Chinese rioters had been wounded by the police, and one of the men died;[6] four were publicly flogged.

While it might appear that had the authorities in the first instance required

---

[3] GN 115/1888; Order dated 24 Jan., published 24 Feb. The premises of the society were at 31 Malabar Street. The register showed 62 office-bearers and 4,763 members of whom 2,200 were subscribers in 1887.

[4] GD 79, 20 Feb. 1888; COD 92, 28 Mar. 1888.

[5] One of the principal opponents was Thomas Scott.   [6] GD 83, 27 Feb. 1888.

that only three feet need be cleared, there would have been no trouble, this would be entirely to misunderstand the position. The compromise measure meant the frustration of the attempt to keep a way clear for pedestrians, for while making a pretence of complying with the requirements, encroachment would continue, and the result would once again be the blockage of the verandas. The vested interests had proved to be stronger than municipal zeal.

The flogging of four of the rioters on the orders of the Superintendent of Police caused the Secretary of State to ask for an explanation for this disregard of the instruction of his predecessor; he remarked that public flogging should never be permitted without the Governor's direct instructions.[7] This in itself was a relaxation of the absolute prohibition imposed previously, and Clementi Smith at once issued instructions to the police in this sense. It would seem that this form of punishment was never again inflicted in the Colony.

Early in 1888 the Government introduced a Bill designed to remove the section relating to banishment from the Peace Preservation Ordinance and make it a separate Ordinance, and at the same time an amendment removing the requirement that before action could be started a written information signed by the Chief Police Officer must be laid, and, in replying to the debate, the Governor pointed out that in banishment proceedings he considered not only the statements and reports of the IGP but also particularly those of the Protector of Chinese 'who in 99 cases out of every hundred knows more, or may know more about the case'.

There was one other small though important amendment. In the old Ordinance, banishment proceedings were to be used against persons whose removal from the Colony 'was necessary for the public safety'. To this clause were added the words 'or welfare', an alteration which called forth no adverse comments, but which did significantly enlarge the scope of the banishment provisions. Step by step these provisions had been removed from their original context, which was the disturbance of the peace by riotous or tumultuous assemblies of such a nature as to call for the issue of a proclamation introducing particularly stringent laws not generally in use. Now persons who had not caused a breach of the peace could be banished, provided that their removal from the Colony was deemed to be necessary by the Governor in Council in the interests of the welfare of the Colony. This is not to imply that this power was used without proper discrimination. It was still, of course, applicable only to aliens, and it was still necessary for the Governor in Council to hold an enquiry, after which the papers of each case were forwarded to the Secretary of State who looked most carefully into all the circumstances. But in fact banishment could now be used against such undesirable persons as gambling promoters and traffickers in women and girls, and also against secret society members whose activities, while not necessarily leading to an imminent breach of the peace, were detrimental to the welfare of the community. The new Banishment Ordinance came into force on 1 March 1888 as Ordinance IV of 1888.

1. THE SOCIETIES ORDINANCE, 1889

By June the Governor, after consultations with Pickering and with his Executive Council, was satisfied that the time had come to abandon the policy

[7] COD 99, 9 Apr. 1888.

of tolerating the secret societies. Before bringing a draft Bill to this effect before the Legislative Council, he consulted the Secretary of State in a despatch which set out very clearly the case for the suppression of the Hoeys and for the control of the formation of societies generally.[8] In this he described the extent and character of the Chinese secret societies in the Colony, their evil effects upon the peace of the community and the administration of justice, and the failure of existing legislation to control them. He had always, he said, regretted the policy adopted by the Government, which he considered to be weak and detrimental to the public interests. As for the argument that the Government had no machinery to put in place of the secret societies if they were suppressed, he pointed out that the position had changed considerably since Pickering's appointment. With the growth of his department and the increase in the number of government officers trained in the Chinese language, the Government was now much better informed on Chinese affairs, and the Chinese inhabitants were becoming increasingly aware that they could obtain from the Government a real and honest protection in lieu of that which they sought from the societies. But even if it should prove that the removal of the small degree of help which the authorities obtained from the headmen resulted in some lessening of control of the Chinese mob, he would still unhesitatingly advise that the societies should be suppressed. 'The Government must be the paramount power, and it is not so in the eyes of many thousands of the Chinese in the Straits Settlements.'

He admitted that the introduction of the Bill would create considerable commotion among a large number of Chinese.

There will probably be disturbances, because the headmen of the societies who have for years been living and fattening on the gambling houses and brothels, and on the money they have been able to squeeze out of their ignorant and superstitious countrymen . . . will not give up their influential position without a struggle.

He gave an assurance that plenty of time would be given to enable the object and intention of the Government to be well understood, and all possible means of publicity would be used. 'Happily,' he said in conclusion, 'the Government will have on its side the great strength arising from the support of the respectable and law-abiding portion of the community, and I have no fear of a successful issue of the policy which I have advocated, should it be adopted.' He was confident that the longer the complete suppression of the secret societies was delayed, the more difficult it would be to suppress them.

This despatch, together with a copy of the Bill, was sent to London on 20 June 1888, and copies of the Bill were given to Dunlop and Pickering who, on 9 July, jointly signed a letter to the Governor objecting to its introduction. They believed the Government would lose all control over the 165,000 registered members of the Chinese Dangerous Societies, and the managers of between 200 and 300 Chinese Friendly Societies. They pointed out that the Bill provided nothing to take the place of the control already existing, and declared that though they wished to see these Dangerous Societies dissolved as soon as practicable, something must be provided to take their place, otherwise mere legal dissolution would not dispose of the problem. They recommended that a full enquiry be held before deciding on the nature of the legislation required, and believed that special legislation would always be required where Chinese

[8] GD 292, 20 June 1888.

were concerned, thus giving expression once again to the conviction that the principles of law as conceived in England were inadequate for the control of the Chinese population of the Straits Settlements.

This was an unexpected development. Both Pickering and Dunlop had now reverted to the position which they had taken up in 1879 when giving evidence before the Commission on the Police Force of which Clementi Smith was the Chairman. When asked by the Governor to explain his attitude, Dunlop maintained that when he counselled suppression he had in mind that before taking such a step the Government would take into consideration 'the whole question of the efficient control of the Chinese element in our population'.[9] Pickering, when he too was asked to explain, gave his opinion that

instead of hastily repealing legislation which has done much good, and which is . . . the strongest check we possess over the disorderly classes of the Chinese, it would be wise to appoint a Commission . . . to enquire into and report upon the whole subject of the abolition of Secret Societies, and of the best method for controlling the Chinese in the absence of the power which we now undoubtedly possess under Ordinance XIX of 1869 as amended by Ordinance IV of 1885.

He recommended that the heads of the Police and Chinese Protectorate Departments should give evidence before the Commission, as well as Chinese of all classes, and suggested that the Government should obtain and place before the Commission full information as to the special legislation for the control of the Chinese in force in Netherlands India, Indo-China, and Hong Kong. Such a Commission, he believed, would be able to recommend some system by which the Government could control the Chinese and abolish the Dangerous Societies which, he said, 'in default of better means have for some time been made useful towards preserving the peace of the Colony'. He continued:

Unless such system can be prepared, if the Ordinance . . . should come into force, I can only look to the future with most serious apprehension, as likely to produce nothing but disorder and confusion; its provisions take away nearly every check and restraint now possessed by the Government.

He concluded:

The turbulent, conceited, and alien masses of the Chinese inhabiting and entering the Straits Settlements and Native States are understood by at most four or five officials of the Colony, and are seldom taken into consideration by the Government except when they cause trouble by their unruly and intriguing dispositions, these will, if the Ordinance . . . be sanctioned, be left with no other laws to overcome and control them than are applicable to the civilized and law-abiding Anglo-Saxon race.[10]

The Governor, though he forwarded copies of the letters to the Colonial Office, was not prepared to modify the opinions set out in his despatch. 'No Commission or Committee of enquiry that could be formed,' he said, 'could give the Government one iota more of useful information than it at present possesses.' He was completely averse to the adoption of the methods in vogue in the Dutch and French colonies for dealing with the native population.[11]

The strain thrown upon Pickering by the consideration of this proposed upheaval was too much for him. Since the attempt on his life he had never been

[9] GD 347, 30 July 1888, encl. 2: lett. dated 20 July 1888.
[10] Ibid. encl. 3: lett. dated 20 July 1888.   [11] Ibid.

the same man, and now his condition was such that he was granted leave on 19 July, from which he never returned, for he did not recover sufficiently.

The Secretary of State in response to the proposed change of policy was very encouraging;[12] he agreed that the danger to the peace arising from the secret societies had been recognized for many years, and that those best qualified to judge had agreed that their suppression was very much to be desired. It was to be regretted that steps in this direction had not been taken earlier, but he was glad to hear that the Governor believed that the Government was now strong enough to deal with the danger. Although he regarded the criticisms of Pickering and Dunlop as being directed more to the proposed mode of suppression rather than to the suppression itself, he made it clear that the Governor would be responsible for taking these criticisms into account, and that before taking action he would decide how best to control the Chinese population after the suppression of the societies.

Consultations were held in London between the Secretary of State, the Attorney-General of the Colony (Mr Bonsor), and the acting Colonial Secretary (Mr Skinner) as to whether it would not be advisable to introduce an Ordinance similar to that in force in Hong Kong rather than the draft prepared in Singapore. The Secretary of State favoured the Hong Kong Ordinance (VIII of 1887), the principal provision of which was:

The Society known by the name of the Triad Society or Samhopui [Sam Hop Wui] and other societies by whatever name known formed for an unlawful purpose, or having among their objects purposes incompatible with the peace and good order of the Colony, are hereby declared to be unlawful Societies. . . .

The Attorney-General pointed out that it was doubtful whether it would be found possible to prove the character and objects of a society so as to secure a conviction under this provision. 'Long experience of these societies has shown that they may, on paper, have the most unexceptionable objects and yet by their actions prove to be a constant danger to the peace of the community.' The Governor was instructed to consider with his Executive Council which mode of proceeding would be best calculated to effect the desired object with the least friction and danger of opposition. Should the decision be against the Hong Kong type, then he was authorized to introduce his draft Bill as amended by the Secretary of State after consultation with Mr Bonsor.

On the whole, the despatch from the Secretary of State is an excellent example of the Whitehall art of keeping oneself covered at all points in all possible circumstances, but nevertheless it did give the signal to go ahead, and Clementi Smith at once caused the correspondence between him and the Secretary of State to be laid on the table of the Legislative Council. This was on 12 December 1888, and a week later the Attorney-General moved the first reading of the Bill, 'to amend the law relating to Societies'.

He warned the Council that the importance of the matter, 'dealing as it does with the most cherished institutions of a large portion of our foreign population', could hardly be exaggerated. References to 'cherished institutions' were to recur more than once in the ensuing debate. He explained the objections to an Ordinance of the Hong Kong type and set out the main features of the Bill. Every society of more than ten persons, with certain exceptions (registered

[12] COD 342, 22 Oct. 1888.

Q

companies, chartered companies, Freemasons), was to be unlawful unless registered under the Ordinance, and no society could be so registered without the previous approval of the Governor in Council. Existing societies registered under the old law were required to obtain approval and register afresh within three months from the commencement of the Ordinance. Power was taken to dissolve and thereby render unlawful a registered society if at any time it appeared necessary for the public safety or welfare to do so. The Governor in Council was also empowered to exempt any society from registration. In prosecutions for membership of an unlawful society, once it was established that a society of some sort existed, the onus was on the accused to show that it did not consist of ten members, or that it fell within the other specified categories of exemptions. The punishment for managing or assisting in the management of an unlawful society was imprisonment which might extend to three years, and for membership of an unlawful society, a fine of $500 or imprisonment up to six months, or both fine and imprisonment.

One immediate result of the introduction and publication of the Bill was a Memorial to the Governor and the members of the Legislature from the office-bearers of the Ghee Hin Society, Penang, who declared that their society had no political object but was established for laudable and charitable purposes somewhat allied to those of Freemasonry. It was not conducted on the same lines as the Triad society in China but was a distinct and separate body founded in the Colony. Before 1885 membership was not restricted to Chinese, but since the amending legislation of that year it was restricted to Chinese born in China. They gave examples of charities they endowed and supported: land given to the Government for a pauper hospital, land set aside for vegetable cultivation by poor Chinese, donation to the Leper Hospital at Pulau Jerejak. They had acquired land and drawn up plans for an international pauper hospital in Penang road which they would build and maintain; they always provided coffins gratis for the burial of the poor of the Colony and they listed a number of appeals to which they had subscribed.[13] In the light of this record, the memorialists prayed that the society might be refused registration.

The next meeting of the Legislative Council was held on 7 February, and the second reading of the Bill was then moved. It might be thought that in the climate of opinion then existing in Singapore and the oft-repeated chastisement of the Government for failing to deal with the menace, this Bill would have passed its second reading with acclaim. On the contrary, it led to one of the most spirited debates in the history of the Council, with the extraordinary result that every unofficial member (seven in all) voted against the Bill, while every official member (eight in all) voted for it.

The basis of the opposition was summarized in the opening words of the first unofficial member to speak on the motion—Mr Shelford—who said that no question brought before the Council had received more consideration than this Bill. While there was an 'earnest desire to aid the Government in the suppression of those societies which are dangerous to the public peace', the Bill was 'so objectionable in its form, and so sweeping in its provisions' that it was impossible to accept it. The sentiments embodied in his long speech were very different from many he had previously expressed. While he had formerly

---

[13] A stone commemorating the gift of the land for the Pauper Hospital is still to be found built into the corner of a wall outside what is now the Penang General Hospital.

ridiculed the idea that the Governor could not be entrusted with powers, he now took the contrary view and even quoted some of the scathing indictment of a Governor's powers made by a former Chief Justice, Sir Benson Maxwell, in the famous debate of 1870. By quoting passages from successive Annual Reports of Pickering and Dunlop, he maintained that there had been a gradual improvement in keeping the peace and that there was no need for any stringent measures at that time. He found that, despite the tremendous influx of immigrants, increase in crime had been astonishingly slight. Whereas in July 1874 there were 810 prisoners in gaol, the daily average for 1884 was 834. In February 1888 the figure for inmates of the criminal prison was the same as it was ten years earlier —982. These were remarkable figures bearing in mind that the population increase in Singapore in the period 1871–81 was estimated at 115,400 persons. His arguments followed the same lines as Pickering's objections to the Bill. The societies were a form of organization to which the Chinese were accustomed, and the Government had recognized them and worked through them with some success. The Protectorate was now better informed on Chinese matters than previously, and the police were in some ways stronger, but these were no sufficient substitute for the society organization. There was not a single police officer who could converse with the Chinese in their own language. There was a European constabulary, there was a Sikh contingent, chiefly employed on guard and not in the streets, but as regards the rank and file the position, according to the report of the IGP, was worse than ever before.

Shelford reproved the Government for ignoring Pickering's suggestion of a full enquiry before legislation was introduced. In a matter which touched 'the most cherished institutions' of the Chinese, it had not been thought necessary to obtain information from the departments most concerned. He supported the proposal for gradual abolition and advocated strengthening the police, increasing Chinese-speaking civil servants, and improving interpretation in the courts. This he believed, 'in the course of time, and not a lengthy time', would eliminate what was dangerous in the societies, and it should be possible in some future period to look forward to the time when the Government would be able, in some degree, to relax restrictive measures 'repugnant to our ideas of a liberal and popular Government even though it be over an Eastern people'.

Each of the unofficial members, including the Chinese member Seah Liang Seah, spoke against the Bill, but not all for the same reasons. The oldest and most experienced member (Mr Adamson) differed entirely from Shelford's assessment of the comparative harmlessness of the societies. He quoted passages from the Annual Reports of the Protector and the IGP illustrating the constant challenge to good government presented by the societies. He considered that the time had come to interfere, but he opposed the provision in the Bill giving the Governor in Council the power to refuse registration of a society thereby causing it to be unlawful, and the clause declaring that any person convicted of managing or assisting in the management of an unlawful society was liable to banishment. As drafted, this clause applied equally to British subjects and to aliens, and he would have none of it. He agreed with the Secretary of State that the Hong Kong Ordinance was preferable. The other unofficial members covered much the same ground as Shelford and Adamson, one of them again referring to 'the most cherished institutions of the people concerned'.

The debate continued through 7 and 8 February, and was wound up by the

Governor in a long and vigorous speech in which he was particularly scathing about Shelford's attempt to whitewash the societies. Knowing that they had a most disastrous effect upon the large and ignorant classes of Chinese who came to the Settlements and that there was nothing to be said for them, he nevertheless spoke of them as 'cherished institutions'. (It would seem that the Governor had failed to notice the use of this phrase by the Attorney-General when introducing the Bill in the previous December.) 'Cherished institutions,' declared the Governor rhetorically, 'cherished institutions of whom? Of a lot of scoundrels and blackguards who force them upon the Straits Settlements; and whatever their cherished institutions maybe we ought to suppress them with a strong hand.'

As for the crime figures, the Governor pointed out that the speaker had made no mention of the crimes which were never brought to light because of the jurisdiction of the societies, and he referred to the inconsistency of Shelford who, in 1880, had accused the Government of 'always lopping at the branches and never reaching the roots', while now his arguments were directed to preventing the eradication of the evil, and asking for a continuance of the policy of gradual elimination. The usefulness of the societies to the Government was regarded by the Governor as a rotten reed,

because the Police, instead of performing their proper functions, rely upon the headmen of the societies to detect and arrest criminals . . .; they receive such a measure of assistance as the headmen, with reference to their own interests, choose to give, and the Force suffers in consequence in its training, efficiency, and morale.

On the subject of banishment, the Governor remarked that though members had been quick to quote Pickering and Dunlop when it suited their argument, they had omitted to mention that both had frequently declared that banishment was the only effective means of keeping the societies in order. In saying this, however, he would appear to have been dodging the point at issue. As far as can be ascertained, neither Pickering nor Dunlop had advocated the banishment of British subjects, though they would, no doubt, have welcomed such a proposal. Still, the Governor promised that if, in Committee, there was a majority of opinion in favour of removing the banishment clause, he would agree to its withdrawal.

The Governor then addressed himself to the question which had repeatedly recurred throughout the debate—'what is the Government going to put in place of these organizations?' On this he believed that when the societies had been suppressed, friendly societies would emerge to perform the charitable functions of the old societies. This could never happen so long as the entrenched power of the secret societies existed. The Governor also declared that it was part of his policy to increase the number of Chinese-speaking officers not only in the Protectorate but in all government departments.

Earlier, when writing to the Secretary of State, the Governor had stated that there would probably be disturbances arising from the introduction of this legislation, and during the debate members had commented on this. It was indeed this fear that was at the bottom of Shelford's, as of Pickering and Dunlop's, opposition, but the Governor now declared that he believed that there would be no disturbances. The Government was not proposing to confiscate the property of the suppressed societies and this, he thought, was the only point on which trouble might have arisen. Finally, he gave the reasons why he was anxious to deal with this matter at once. Firstly, as Adamson had said, times were prosperous and quiet and therefore propitious, and secondly, he himself hoped to stay in Singapore to see the policy carried out, and not leave what might be considered *damnosa hereditas* to his successors. Nevertheless, he was not able to win over a single unofficial. Adamson, it is true, at the end of his speech asked to be excused from voting because he supported the Government's policy but dissented from the terms of the Bill, but the Governor ruled that under the Standing Orders, no member could abstain. He therefore voted against the Bill, which nevertheless passed its second reading by virtue of the official votes.

The Committee stage of the Bill was postponed to the next meeting of the Council: in the meantime the Governor had to inform the Secretary of State that he had failed to secure a single unofficial vote. In doing so he said that he nevertheless proposed to proceed with the Bill, but the Secretary of State telegraphed on 14 February suggesting an adjournment till objections had been discussed and if possible removed by amendments. He was too late, for on the same day the Council met again to consider the Bill in Committee with the most astonishing result, for with the cordial assistance of the unofficial members, amendments were framed which were accepted by all.

In the Preamble was included the phrase (taken from the Ordinance of 1869): 'Whereas great danger has arisen from the existence of Societies having among their objects purposes incompatible with the peace and good order of the Colony, and it is expedient to provide against such danger . . .' To the list of societies exempt from registration was added: 'Any company association or partnership consisting of not more than twenty persons formed for the purpose of carrying on any lawful business other than that of banking', and the Governor in Council instead of being empowered to exempt 'any society' could exempt 'any society or class of societies'.

The period within which the registration of existing societies must be completed was extended to six months or such further period as might be allowed in a particular case by the Governor in Council, and approval of registration of such a society was not to be withheld unless it were deemed that it had among its objects purposes incompatible with the peace and good order of the Colony. A presumption was added to the Bill, that a person found in possession of banners, insignia, or writings of a society was a member thereof unless the contrary was proved. This was adopted from the Ordinance of 1885. Regulations framed by the Governor in Council prescribing the manner of registering societies were to be laid on the table of the Legislative Council and could be rescinded by a resolution of that Council. The clause concerning banishment was withdrawn by the Attorney-General, and the only objection to the withdrawal came from the Resident Councillor, Malacca (D. F. A. Hervey), who would have liked the power introduced because he thought that this was the only way to get at the Red and White Flag societies, all of whose members were British subjects.

Under the original Bill, upon the dissolution of a society its assets were to vest in the Official Assignee who was to distribute them among members after paying all just debts and charges. If such a division was not possible he was to submit a scheme for the disposal of the assets for the approval of a Judge of the Supreme Court. To these provisions was now added a further sub-section empowering the Governor in Council to suspend their operation to enable the society to wind up its own affairs, thus making it clear that there was no question of the seizure of the assets of a society by the Government.

As a result of this very satisfactory consideration of the Bill in Committee, the Governor was able to reply to the Secretary of State informing him that the Bill had passed through without any division and that there was nothing to be gained by postponement. A clause had been incorporated suspending its coming into operation so that the Secretary of State would have the opportunity to consider it. The third reading of the Bill was taken on 21 February, and it was passed without dissent, but it was not until August 1889 that the Secretary of State was able to inform the Governor that he had advised the Queen to sanction the Ordinance, and that the royal assent had been received.[14] In the intervening period he had considered the representations made to him by the Straits Settlements Association, and a Memorial sent to him by the Ghee Hin Society at Penang which followed much the same lines as the previous Memorial. It gave the number of the affiliated members in Penang and Province Wellesley as 45,000 and in the Straits Settlements as 80,000. The society owned property to the value of $300,000 in Penang. The various charities to which it contributed were set out, and it was emphasized that not only had it not been repressed, but it had been a registered and recognized institution. The Memorial suggested that if more control were desired this could easily be provided, for if necessary the head of the Chinese Protectorate could be made Chairman of the society, and it could be made illegal to hold meetings in his absence. It very strongly supported all the objections to the Ordinance that Pickering and Dunlop had mentioned in their joint letter which had been published and laid on the table of Council.

A copy of this Memorial was sent to the local press, and the *Pinang Gazette* had no hesitation in saying that it was unlikely that it would have any effect. One of its leaders (on 16 April 1889) summarized the position in the following terms:

They give large sums of money to charity; they assist their helpless members; they bury the poor dead; their headmen arrange disputes, and when it suits them prevent disturbances: but on the other hand they are monstrous tyrannies, inflicting under fearful oaths of secrecy penalties that the law would not allow, instigating crimes, shielding criminals, and forming by their wonderful organization and far-reaching machinations a constant source of danger to the peace and welfare of the Colony.

In forwarding the Memorial the Governor, while not underrating the value of their charitable work, considered that it was wholly incommensurate with the wealth of the society, and that the greater part of the funds were spent on illegitimate objects, and formed the means of carrying on a series of outrages and providing for the protection of criminals. He quoted some of the oaths of the society, including one requiring all members to use all their power to deliver a fellow member arrested by the police, and others requiring all members to harbour a fellow member who through crime or misfortune was in difficulty. Finally, he declared that of all the societies the Ghee Hin was the most dangerous

[14] COD 255, 17 Aug. 1889.

to the welfare of the Colony, and that the Memorial was wholly undeserving of any favourable consideration.[15]

Nothing came of this attempt by the Ghee Hin to establish its respectability, but it is of interest as showing that this society felt that it might persuade the Secretary of State that it was an important part of the social fabric of Penang, and that its position as dispenser of charitable funds might enable it to escape suppression under the new law.

This new law, the Societies Ordinance 1889, became Ordinance I of 1889, but the Secretary of State desired that it should not come into operation until 1 January 1890 so that there would be abundant time to warn the societies and no excuse for non-compliance on the grounds of ignorance. But the battle for a change of policy had been won by the vigour and perseverance of Sir Cecil Clementi Smith, whose long experience of governing the Chinese persuaded him that the fears felt and expressed by Pickering and Dunlop could largely be discounted. Never again was it suggested that the secret societies should be permitted to continue as part of the essential social organization of the Chinese, and only once—during the period immediately after the Japanese occupation—has there been any relaxation of the ban on them.

Pending the coming into force of the Ordinance, consideration was given to the setting up of a Chinese Advisory Board. On 19 December 1888 a letter had appeared in the *Straits Times* from a Chinese suggesting that a Board of Chinese should be appointed to advise the Government and to be a medium of communication with the Chinese generally.[16] This idea at once met with the approval of the Secretary of State, who in January 1889 asked the Governor to consider it, at the same time suggesting that it might be advantageous if some leading European merchants were also added to the Board.[17] A deputation from the Straits Settlements Association in London which interviewed the Secretary of State on the subject of the Ordinance also suggested that the setting up of a Consultative Board to include the leading Chinese and possibly some Europeans would be a good move,[18] and in due course the Governor submitted a scheme for a Chinese Advisory Board for Singapore. Regulations governing the formation and duties of this Board were published on 20 December 1889,[19] and the names of the members were gazetted on 31 January 1890, so that there was a Board in being almost as soon as the new Societies Ordinance came into force.[20]

The Advisory Board was to consist of a maximum of 18 members to be nominated by the Governor, including not more than 6 Hokkiens, 5 Tiechius, 2 Cantonese, 2 Khehs (Hakkas), 2 Hailams, and the Protector of Chinese. Ordinary meetings were to be held monthly and there was provision for special meetings. Minutes were to be transmitted to the Governor. The subjects to be discussed included matters of legislation specially affecting the Chinese community, rites and ceremonies, Chinese education, schemes for the relief of the poor and sick Chinese, and cases of hardship which should be brought to the attention of the Government. The Board was also empowered to conduct

---

[15] The oaths quoted were, in fact, taken from the 36 oaths of the Ghee Hok Society at pp. 115–19 of Vaughan's *Manners and Customs*. They do not differ in any essential from those of the Ghee Hin Society as published in the PRCR, 1868, app. 22.

[16] The writer was Tan Kong Saik (GD Conf., 6 Mar. 1889).

[17] COD Conf., 25 Jan. 1889. [18] COD 255, 17 Aug. 1889.

[19] GN 745. [20] GN 79, 1890 (publ. 31 Jan. 1890).

arbitrations between members of the Chinese community. In this way it was hoped that a channel of communication would be opened and a body of respectable and representative Chinese brought into being, capable of handling Chinese charities and settling disputes. It is to be noted that apart from the Protector of Chinese there was no European member of the Board.

It may seem surprising that no attempt had been made to form such a body years earlier, but while the Hoeys exercised the tremendous powers which through tradition had fallen into their hands, and while they were to some degree recognized by the Government as the arbitrators of Chinese disputes, no Chinese of standing would dare to be a member of a body which might well reach decisions unacceptable to one or other of these vested interests. Only when these societies had been declared to be unlawful was the way clear for the establishment of a non-partisan tribunal of this sort.

A similar Advisory Board was appointed in March 1890 for Penang, consisting of the Assistant Protector of Chinese, 8 Hokkien members, 3 Tiechiu, 4 Cantonese, and 2 Kheh (Hakka).[21]

From the outset these Boards were a great success. Membership was regarded as an official indication of status, and recommendations received the serious consideration of the Government. They were invaluable as forums at which, on the one hand, representative Chinese could put forward their views, and on the other the Protector could explain the policy of the Government on any particular matter, and hear objections or suggested variations. Knowing the Government's point of view, members were able to discuss proposals in their respective District Associations and thus come to meetings with a good claim to represent the opinion of the Chinese community.

Neither of the officials who for so long had exercised control over the societies and who objected to the Governor's proposals for dealing with the problem—Pickering and Dunlop—was called upon to take any part in the administration of the new law, for both retired from the service for health reasons. Pickering while on leave in England had, in January 1889, written to the Secretary of State setting out at length his objections, and stating that what he and Dunlop had wanted was a law enabling the Governor in Council to dissolve any society which became dangerous or a nuisance, to refuse the registration of any society, and punish headmen by deportation or imprisonment.[22] But his letter put forward no fresh arguments and nothing of importance that had not already been covered by the Governor in his original despatch of 20 June 1888. Pickering was clearly annoyed because he had not seen the draft of the Bill until the day on which it was sent home, and felt that he should have been more closely consulted, but the Governor, in a marginal note on this letter, refers to the many conversations he had had with Pickering on the subject, and there is no reason to suppose that the Governor was not well informed of his views, fears, and objections, many of which it was found necessary to override. As time went by Pickering's general health improved, but his leave was repeatedly extended because of mental and nervous disturbance. He retired from the service with a specially enhanced pension of $3,500 yearly.[23] Although

---

[21] GN 187 of 27 Mar. 1890.

[22] 16 Jan. 1889, encl. to S. of S. Conf. despatch of 25 Jan. 1889.

[23] GD 338, 17 July 1889. The computation included an extra five years for special qualifications and an extra ten years as compensation for injury.

Pickering lived in Singapore for less than seventeen years and left at the comparatively early age of 48, he made an enduring mark on the administration of the Colony and of the Malay States too, for the Chinese Protectorate spread to include those states where there were large numbers of Chinese.

Colonel Dunlop, the IGP, had also reached the end of his tether. There had been differences between him and the Government at the time of the Commission on Public Gaming, when he took strong objection to the allegation that the police were involved, and because of this reluctance to face the facts, the Secretary of State in 1887 called for a report on the manner in which he discharged the duties of his office.[24] To this the Governor, Clementi Smith, was able to reply that although Dunlop had this undoubted defect which had been apparent at the time of the Police Commission of 1879, he had an excellent record, possessed valuable experience, and exhibited great tact in the management of the mixed races of which the police force was formed. Though he could see no prospect of Dunlop becoming a better head of the police than he then was, he did not think that the public interests would be promoted by causing him to retire.[25] But in October, when agreeing to the introduction of the new societies legislation, the Secretary of State again asked for an assurance that Dunlop would exhibit the requisite vigour, firmness, and resource in putting down any disturbance which might occur in consequence of the suppression of the societies.[26] By now the Governor thought that the time had come for Dunlop to go. He was then acting as president of the Municipal Commission. His health was failing and it was thought that if after a period of leave he returned as IGP, he was unlikely efficiently to perform the very onerous and responsible duties of the post. Arrangements were made for him to leave in June 1890 on the termination of his municipal appointment. He was then 52 years old and had been IGP for 17 years, but although his retirement did not take place until after the new Societies Ordinance had come into operation, he had no part in its enforcement because of his secondment to the post of Municipal President.[27]

Attention was given to the suggestion that the police should be strengthened by the appointment of a Commission to enquire into the efficiency of the force. Among its recommendations was one calling for the recruitment of a Chinese contingent from Hong Kong. It may be that the Governor, who had considerable experience of handling a Chinese force at Hong Kong, prompted this recommendation, which was acted upon with speed. Twenty-five constables were recruited in 1890, and this number was later increased, but by the end of 1891 the contingent was reported to be 'not entirely satisfactory', and in the following year the IGP remarked that he could say 'but little in favour' of it. Only a sergeant, 2 corporals, and 27 constables remained, and he did not propose to fill the vacancies. It had been found that many of the n.c.o.s and men had been 'more or less connected with persons of bad character'. He therefore regretted to have to acknowledge that the experiment of a Chinese contingent had been a failure. The last members were discharged on the termination of their agreements in 1894. The sergeant had already been dismissed after

[24] S. of S. Conf., 2 Nov. 1887.   [25] GD Conf. of 20 Jan. 1888.
[26] S. of S. Conf. despatch of 22 Oct. 1888.
[27] He retired on 3 Sept. 1890, and received a pension of $2,142 yearly (GD 230, 31 May 1890; COD 262, 30 Aug. 1890).

serving a sentence of two months' imprisonment for assault with intent of wrongful detention. This well-intentioned proposal to effect a closer contact between the police and the Chinese public therefore failed.

The question of training more officers in Chinese was again raised in October 1889 by Adamson, who asked that Cadets who had been sent to China for language training should, on their return, be posted to the Protectorate and not put in the ordinary service of the Colony. In reply the Governor gave an assurance that no opportunity would be lost of increasing the strength of the Protectorate, but said that men were being educated not just for the Chinese Protectorate, for they were needed in all government departments. Despite this declaration of policy, it was many years before a serious attempt was made to reach this goal, which, indeed, was never remotely approached. Always the 'exigencies of the service' in a country of rapidly-expanding development tended to work against the drafting of officers for a study period of two years in China when they might usefully be employed to relieve the heavy pressure on officers in the Colony, and, later, in the Malay States.

2. IMPLEMENTATION

The new Societies Ordinance came into operation on 1 January 1890, but some months earlier proclamations were widely issued throughout the Settlements to prepare the Chinese community for the abolition of the secret societies, and special notices were given to those societies registered as Dangerous under the old Ordinance that they would not be registered under the new law. They were given until 30 June to wind up their affairs. At this time the Dangerous Societies still on the register in Singapore were as follows:[28]

Ghee Hin group
(1) Hokkien Ghee Hin; (2) Hok Hin; (3) Song Peh Kwan (Ts'ung Paak Kwun); (4) Kong Fee Siew (Kwong Wai Shiu); (5) Kwang Hok Ghee Kee; (6) Ghee Hok.

Others
(1) Hong Ghee Thong; (2) Lee Seng Hong; (3) Yuet Tong Kun; (4) Heng Sun.

Of these, the first six were the surviving affiliates of the Ghee Hin group. Previously there had been nine of these branches, but three—the Tiechiu Ghee Hin, the Hailam Ghee Hin, and the Ghee Sin—had already been suppressed in 1885. The four societies not in the Ghee Hin group had originally been registered as Friendly Societies, but became so unfriendly that in 1885 and 1886 they were registered as Dangerous Societies.

Between all ten societies there were, in 1889, 1,321 office-bearers and 68,316 members on the register, though the number of these surviving in Singapore was unknown. In February 1890 all these societies delivered their seals and insignia to the Protector of Chinese, together with their books and registers which, at the request of the societies, were destroyed. The headmen of those societies belonging to the Ghee Hin group asked that these items belonging to their societies should be destroyed at the central Ghee Hin temple at Rochore,

---

[28] For details, see App. 4, p. 539.

and this was done at a ceremony attended by the Protector and the Assistant Protector as well as by members of the societies concerned.[29] At this ceremony, the headmen of the six societies burned the original diplomas of affiliation 'which constituted them part of the mother-organization, the Ghee Hin'.[30]

The Governor in reporting this to the Legislative Council stated that this action was tantamount to the formal renunciation of any connexion with the famous 'or rather infamous' societies in China. From this it might be thought that the diplomas were derived from an organization in China, but this is very improbable for the title was one used for one of the Triad organizations overseas, not in China. As the Ghee Hin petitioners had said, it was 'a distinct and separate body founded in the Colony'. Moreover, the Singapore Ghee Hin was organized as a system of branches or affiliates with a central temple at Rochore where this final ceremony took place, and it seems likely that the diplomas which were then destroyed were originally issued from this central 'Lodge' as Cowan called it. This central body itself was never registered as a society, but it constituted the nearest thing to a central controlling body that had, at that time, been known in Triad history either in China or abroad. It managed the central temple, and probably issued a diploma of membership to each branch entitling it to use the facilities of the temple. By the destruction of these documents, the links between the branches and the 'mother Lodge' in Singapore were severed. This public burning of the documents by the headmen was also a personal renunciation, making it plain that they could no longer be held responsible for the actions of those who had been members. Furthermore, this act proclaimed that in future anyone claiming to use the insignia, diplomas, or 'chops' of these societies would be an impostor. It was a dramatic climax to the relationship which had for so long existed between the Hoeys and the Government.

The winding-up of the Singapore societies was completed before the expiry of the six months' grace which had been granted. One of them was singled out for special treatment, the Ghee Hok, which Pickering in 1887 had recommended should be suppressed. On 20 June 1890 an Order of Dissolution was issued by the Governor in Council on the grounds that such action was necessary for the public safety or welfare.[31] The other nine societies were not subject to Orders of Dissolution, but a notification was published in the *Government Gazette* informing the public that from and after 1 July 1890 these societies and the Ghee Hok Society became unlawful.[32]

Action at Penang followed similar lines. There was no public renunciation, but this may be accounted for by the fact that there was in Penang no group of affiliated societies with a central 'mother Lodge' as existed at Singapore. Each society was an independent foundation. They were: (1) Ghee Hin; (2) Kien Tek (Toh Peh Kong); (3) Ho Sing; (4) Tsun Sim (Chun Sim); (5) Hai San. Between them, in 1889, they mustered 409 office-bearers and 113,300 members, though, as in Singapore, the number of members surviving was unknown.[33]

[29] F. Powell acted as P. of C. after Pickering's departure. G. T. Hare was Assist. Protector. The wood blocks from which their membership diplomas and other documents were printed, and their seals were still kept in the office of the Chinese Protectorate, Singapore, up to the time of its occupation by the Japanese in 1924, but were not to be found after the war.

[30] Address by Gov. to Leg. Co., 13 Mar. 1890; Cowan's Wall Sheet 1897; GD 111, 14 Mar. 1890; CP *AR*, 1890.   [31] GN 373 of 27 June 1890.

[32] GN 381 of 4 July 1890.   [33] For details, see App. 4, p. 539.

Innumerable meetings were held between the Assistant Protector, Penang, and the headmen to clarify the procedure of dissolution, and considerable recalcitrance was encountered. The Ghee Hin in particular was an extremely powerful organization with a great deal of property and did not relish the prospect of disintegrating. There was, as it turned out, a further reason for the disinclination of the headmen to agree to dissolution—they had made use of the funds of the society for private purposes, and the winding-up of the society would reveal their culpability. There was talk of further petitioning against the threatened dissolution, but the headmen were assured that this would be useless. Within the society there was dissension due to accusations of embezzlement of funds and to differences of opinion as to the objects to which the proceeds of the disposal of the society's property should be put, but before the middle of March all the Penang societies had handed over their seals to the Assistant Protector and closed their doors, though the disposal of funds was not finally settled.[34]

On 21 August these five societies, like the Ghee Hok in Singapore, were dissolved by Order of the Governor in Council.[35] Why this procedure was used is not disclosed. It may be that the deep-rooted position of the societies in the life of Penang and the great strength of the Penang Ghee Hin led to the conclusion that it would be wise to make positive orders of suppression rather than to allow them to become unlawful by default of registration.

In addition to the dissolution of these five Dangerous Societies, two other Penang societies which had been registered as Friendly Societies were declared to be unlawful. They were the Ho Hop Seah and the Tsuan Ghee Seah.[36] Why the former of these two had not been registered as Dangerous is again a mystery, for in the 1870s it had an evil reputation, and Vaughan, writing in 1878, mentioned that both these societies were registered as Dangerous.[37] As the records are no longer available, one can only surmise that if he was right, their aggressiveness must at a later date have diminished.

At Malacca in 1888, the last year for which figures are available, there were three societies registered as Dangerous, the Ghee Hin, the Macao Ghee Hin, and the Hai San. Between them they had over 7,000 members, the Ghee Hin being much the biggest with 6,487, the other two having only 500-odd each. There is no record as to how there came to be two Ghee Hin societies. The original one was in existence as early as 1835. It was registered in 1876 along with the other three societies then existing, the Hok Beng, the Ghee Boo, and the Hai San, of which the first two were suppressed in 1885.

By 1879 the Macao Ghee Hin had come into being. This may have been a result of the Triad war in Malacca in 1875, and it is possible that the Cantonese members then broke away to form their own Ghee Hin. In 1879 the Macao Ghee Hin had only 282 members compared with 1,380 in the old society. The two continued to exist side by side until 1889 when a new name, the Sin Ghee Hin, or 'New' Ghee Hin, appeared in place of the old Ghee Hin, while the Macao Ghee Hin continued. From this it would appear that the old Ghee

[34] GD 111 of 14 Mar. 1890.
[35] GN 472 of 22 Aug. In this Notification the Kien Tek Society appears under its proper name (romanized as Kean Tek) instead of under the name 'Toh Peh Kong' which appears in so many documents of the period.
[36] GN 473 of 22 Aug. 1890.   [37] Vaughan, *Manners and Customs*, p. 99.

Hin was reorganized in 1889, possibly in the hope that with a changed con-stitution and a different name it might be permitted to register under the new Ordinance. Nothing is known for certain except that in that year a fight took place in Malacca between the Sin Ghee Hin and the Macao Ghee Hin, and that at the time of suppression the societies dealt with at Malacca were the Macao Ghee Hin, the Sin Ghee Hin, and the Hai San.

The first of these, like the Singapore Ghee Hok and the Penang societies, was dissolved by an Order dated 5 August 1890, while on the same day it was notified that in addition the Sin Ghee Hin and the Hai San societies had become unlawful.[38] Again, one is led to presume that the reason for this differential treatment was that the Macao Ghee Hin was regarded as more dangerous than the others, but the Sin Ghee Hin which, if it was, as suggested above, a reorgani-zation of the old Ghee Hin, was far the most powerful of the three, seems to have ignored the milder treatment of merely being declared unlawful, for later in the year the Governor in Council found it necessary to issue an Order dis-solving the society.[39]

In this way was the formal suppression of the Hoeys carried out in all three Settlements. As early as 13 March 1890 the Governor announced in Legislative Council the successful closure of the Singapore and the Penang societies, and on the following day sent a similar report to the Secretary of State.[40] He paid great tribute to the work of the acting Protector in Singapore (Powell) and to the Assistant Protector in Penang (Wray), who had 'performed the duty entrusted to them with great tact, discretion, and energy'. Through their agency the operation of the law for suppressing the Dangerous Societies has been satis-factorily carried into effect, and the Colony had thus got rid of all 'the secret Associations connected with the Chinese which have been for so very many years fraught with evil to the public welfare'.

The Governor was naturally overjoyed with the immediate results of the policy he had so warmly advocated, and he set off for England on leave on 8 April before the completion of the legal formalities of suppression, with every confidence in the successful outcome of his policy.

In Singapore and Malacca, no difficulty had been encountered in persuading the societies to dispose of their property and to distribute their funds. Only the property of the Singapore Ghee Hok Society was taken over by the Official Assignee in accordance with the terms of dissolution. But in Penang things were different. Both the Ghee Hin and the Kien Tek possessed a great deal of property, and though the sales were just completed within the six months ending 30 June, as prescribed by the notices which were served at the beginning of the year, the distribution of assets took much longer owing to conflicting claims.

The affairs of the Ghee Hin were not settled until after four years of suits in the Supreme Court, from which the lawyers reaped a rich harvest. A member of the Penang Bar was for a time acting as Registrar of the Court, and, according to reports by his successor and by the Attorney-General, allowed exorbitant fees to be paid out of the estate to the legal firms concerned in the winding-up. In addition, the trustees did not pay out the money in accordance with the list submitted to the court, some items of which were said to be fictitious. Some of the money was paid out not in satisfaction of just debts but 'rather as a

[38] GNs 444 & 445 of 8 Aug. 1890.
[39] GN 1 of 9 Jan. 1891.   [40] GD 111 of 14 Mar. 1890.

present'.[41] By order of the court, two houses belonging to the Ghee Hin were permitted to be devoted to the housing of the 'tablets' of deceased members, and the sum of $3,000 was put aside in trust from the funds to provide for the performance of worship to these tablets. The houses with the tablets installed are still in existence, and the fund is managed by four trustees, all Sin Neng men. Similarly the altar gods of the Kien Tek Society remained in the premises of the society and are still there, three small figures representing the Toa Pek Kong. They are looked after by a body formed for the purpose on the dissolution of the Kien Tek, known as the Po Hok Seah, which is responsible for the necessary ceremonies. The Ho Seng Society, too, was permitted to retain its tablets in a house in King Street where its headquarters had been.[42] Although no mention is made of similar action in Singapore, the altar tablets of the Ghee Hin are still in existence in a small temple in Lavender Street not far from the site of the old Central Temple. In this way are the ancestral sacrifices perpetuated.

The Assistant Protector at Penang was disturbed by the allocation of premises for the continuance of the worship of the Ghee Hin tablets, and remarked in his report 'These houses will require attention in the future'. Similarly, in reporting the closure of the Kien Tek, he remarked:

It is of the utmost importance that no society (religious, charitable or otherwise) be ever allowed to occupy the Kien Tek Kongsi-house which is, owing to the semi-religious, semi-party character of the society, an object of peculiar interest and reverence to a large and influential class of Chinese, Straits-born and others, and it is almost certain that an attempt will be made to revive this society under a new name in the old haunts.

He also warned the Government that although all five Dangerous Societies had apparently ceased, the members had not given up their membership tickets and that at the earliest opportunity revivals would be attempted.

He was bothered, too, because the insignia of the Ghee Hin had been sent by the Penang society to Kedah, and recommended that the Kedah authorities should proscribe the societies. The Officer Administering the Government (Sir Frederick Dickson) passed on the recommendation to the Raja of Kedah, only to receive the tart reply that Kedah would have suppressed the societies long ago were it not for their continued existence in the Colony. A new Kedah Ordinance was passed announcing that 'heretofore the law did not allow these kinds of kongsees being established for they hindered and menaced the laws of the country and further they are forbidden by Mahommedan law because they resist and endeavour to undermine the laws and customs of the country'. There were also specific suppressions: 'The Chinese Secret Societies such as the Ghee Hin, the To Pe Kong, the Ho San (Hai San) and the Ho Seng, and all Kongsees other than Chinese are forbidden.'[43] Warning was given that the property of the societies must be distributed among the members by 2 August, and, as this was not done, it was sold by auction on 16 August and all the flags and other articles removed.

Johore was to Singapore what Kedah was to Penang, and as early as March 1890 the Chinese Advisory Board, Singapore, passed a resolution asking the

[41] Report by G. T. Hare, Act. P. of C., Penang, 6 June 1893; SSPLC/1893/app. 30; CP *AR*, 1894, p. 8.

[42] GD 340, 21 Aug. 1890, encl. report by G. E. Wray, 10 July 1890.

[43] GD 392, 6 Oct. 1890, encl. 25 Sept. 1890.

Governor to invite the co-operation of the Johore Government. Dickson thereupon wrote to the Pemangku Raja, as the Sultan was away in Europe, asking him to take steps to suppress any such societies existing in Johore. The Raja replied that the only secret society that had ever been recognized by the Government of Johore was the Ghee Hin Society, and that he was not aware of any other. This society had been recognized for so many years that he could not take the responsibility of suppression without consulting the Sultan, to whom he would refer the matter.[44]

In commenting on this reply Powell, in a memorandum of 22 April, threw some light on the ramifications of the Ghee Hin. The Johore society, he said, was a branch of the Ghee Hin in Singapore and received its original diploma from the central Lodge in Lavender Street. It was correct that it was the only society allowed in the State. Some ten or fifteen years previously the Ghee Hok had tried to establish itself there but was repressed by the 'Maharaja' on the grounds that if two secret societies existed they would fight. The Ghee Hin influence extended to Muar, and it was connected with the Ghee Hin societies in Malacca to the extent that a member of either could apply to the other for assistance when in the other's district. He urged its suppression.

The Singapore Ghee Hin with its original nine branches here, its tributary societies in Malacca and Johore, and its cognate associations in Penang, Sumatra, Borneo, and Rangoon, was a combination which played a large part in the life of the Chinese in this quarter of the world, and there are many who foster the spirit which led the originators to form an *imperium in imperio* first of all in China for the purpose of overthrowing the present dynasty and afterwards in European Colonies to manage their own affairs in their own way and to protect their members guilty of whatsoever crime against the Executive, Police, or other opposing force which endeavoured to bring them to justice.

There was nothing to prevent the Johore Ghee Hin from enlisting all the Triad members of Singapore and Malacca under its own banner provided that meetings were held openly only in Johore. Penang societies had in this way been able to control a multitude of members in Perak and Sumatra, and Singapore societies in Selangor and Sungei Ujong, in spite of the severe penalties attaching to membership in those countries.

Powell suggested that one reason why Johore might be reluctant to suppress the Ghee Hin was that, according to a former secretary of the Ghee Hok, the 'Maharaja' had himself been initiated as a member, though Powell had on several occasions heard this contradicted. Nevertheless, despite repeated attempts by Dickson to have the Johore society suppressed, no action was taken by the Johore Government, and it was not, in fact, until 1915 that a law for the control of societies was introduced in Johore, by which time Sultan Abu Bakar had been dead for twenty years.

At the same time as the policy of suppression was enforced in the Colony in 1890, the registration and exemption of societies under the new Ordinance began, and by August of that year 30 Chinese societies had been permitted to register in Singapore, and 81 in Penang; 52 societies were exempted in Singapore, 18 in Penang, and 6 in Malacca.[45] The classes of societies which would be considered for exemption had been set out in a Gazette notification in

[44] GD 340, 21 Aug. 1890, encl. 5 Apr. 1890.
[45] GD 340, 21 Aug. 1890.

December 1889.[46] They were societies formed for recreation, charity, religion, or literature. It is perhaps not surprising to find that the Straits Settlements Association did not fall within any of these categories. It was the first of the Registered Societies under the new Ordinance.

3. SUPPRESSION OR SUBMERGENCE, 1890–9

The Societies Suppression Ordinance of 1889 was no magic wand to transform the Chinese passion for secret associations and intrigue into a humble acceptance of a governmental prohibition, and over the succeeding years it was only the constant vigilance of the Chinese Protectorate and the police, and prompt action under the Societies and Banishment Ordinances, which checked the rise of many new societies from the ashes of the old.

The Government faced many problems. The atmosphere was embittered by the insistence of the British Government on the payment of £100,000 annually to cover the cost of British forces in the Colony. Trade suffered from fluctuations in the price of silver, and official salaries based on silver were affected. The British Government strove to introduce reforms on the English pattern covering prison conditions, treatment of prostitutes, gambling, and the sale of drugs, overriding the protests of the Colonial Government which found flogging the greatest deterrent in riots, maintained that control of prostitutes was the means of minimizing the spread of venereal disease in a preponderantly male population, recognized gambling to be an inherent passion throughout the Chinese community, and derived from its opium farm the major portion of its revenue.

During these years, too, an attempt was being made from China to influence the Straits-born Chinese through the Chinese consuls to render loyalty to Peking. In addition, revolutionary movements were afoot in China, and the wealthy Chinese communities overseas were obvious targets for propaganda and requests for financial support. It was at the turn of the century that Sun Yat-sen in Hong Kong called together leaders of the Elder Brother and Triad fraternities of north and south China respectively, to seek their support against the Manchu Government, a development which caused officials in the Straits Settlements to foresee the possibility of political complications in what had previously been essentially a problem of law and order. The suppression of Triad societies in the Straits remained, therefore, of paramount importance.

As early as August 1890 Sir Frederick Dickson, the Officer Administering the Government, who had disagreed with the Governor's policy but claimed that he had, nevertheless, loyally carried it out, ventured to inform the Secretary of State of the 'almost suspicious quietness' with which the headmen of the societies had accepted the decree of the Government. He believed that it would require the utmost vigilance to ensure that the societies had really been suppressed and had not gone underground. And the Protector of Chinese, Powell, in his Annual Report for 1890, observed that he was not prepared to say that societies which had lasted as long as these, with their extended organizations, were no longer a danger to the peace, and might not at any future dates show themselves again and again.[47]

A few relics of the old societies did, in fact, reappear. The Tong Beng,

---

[46] GN 735 of 18 Dec. 1889.   [47] CP *AR*, 1890, para. 5.

formerly a 'Dangerous Society' of 4,000 members, had dissolved itself in 1886 to evade prosecution, and attempted to re-form the same year as a mixed China-born and Straits-born society. Prosecution of its leaders halted this move, but in June 1891 it reappeared and caused disturbances through attempts to recruit rickshaw pullers. Eleven members were convicted in court and two headmen banished.[48]

Another society found to be continuing under disreputable leaders was the Ghee Hok, conducting extortion, promoting gaming, and engaging in street brawls. A raid on its premises in March 1892 produced sufficient evidence to justify the banishment of some of the leaders, including one who had been implicated in the murder of the Lieutenant China of the Karimuns in 1887 and in the attack on Pickering. He was arrested when he unwisely returned to Singapore from Johore.[49]

For the most part, the old suppressed societies did not attempt to reconstitute their organizations, but in their absence the lure of profitable exploitation of 'protection' of brothels, wayangs, shops, and hawkers, and of the promotion of gambling led to the formation of many smaller groups whose members had belonged to the old societies and were alive to the economic prospects. By 1891 these gangs were described as being a real menace.[50]

In Penang there was a similar pattern, the vacuum left by the dissolution of the Hoeys being partially filled by the newly-formed unlawful societies, in particular two powerful groups of Hokkien fishermen and rickshaw pullers of Jelutong known as the Tian Thien Sia and the Tai Te Ia.

In a slightly different category was an important society with the title Shui Luk P'eng On, or 'Peace on Water and Land', popularly known as the P'au Kwun Ts'oi or Coffin Breakers.[51] This was an organization operating on board ships between China, the Straits, and Burma. Theft, robbery, confidence tricks, drugging of passengers, blackmail, cheating, control of deck space, fraudulent gambling, and such like were the sources of income of its members. Possibly the title 'Coffin Breakers' came from the long pillow-box with a rounded top in which every Chinese immigrant of those days carried his few possessions. It is said to have been founded in China or Hong Kong in 1885 by a Cantonese named Kwan Fan, and by 1888 a branch was established at Penang by headmen flushed from Hong Kong by police action. There was no ritual and no flags or other paraphernalia, but the membership token was a silver coin in the shape of a copper cash and bearing the characters 'P'eng On' (Peace) and the membership number. At weddings and funerals the ceremonial lanterns of the society bore the words 'Wa Kei' (Chinese Record) which were also used on its seal. Investigations by the Protectorate in 1890 revealed that there were about 400 members operating on the steamers with confederates on shore at all the main ports, thus

---

[48] CP *AR*, 1889, para. 6 & 1891, para. 6; Police *AR*, 1891, para. 63; GD 340, 24 Aug. 1891. Reply: COD 365, 30 Nov. 1891. Wynne (p. 402) suggests that this society was the foundation of the T'ung Meng Hui of Sun Yat-sen. Although the characters are the same it seems improbable that they were connected. Sun's party was copied from the Domeikai of Japan.

[49] CP *AR*, 1892, para. 3; Police *AR*, 1892, paras 13, 14; GDs 193 (30 Apr.), 305 (14 July), 396 (6 Oct. 1892).

[50] CP *AR*, 1890, paras 7–11 & 1891, paras 3–5; GD 234, 2 June 1890.

[51] Contemporary documents call it the Broken Coffin Society. 'Coffin Breakers' is closer to the Chinese title, and is used by W. G. Stirling, 'The Coffin-Breakers' Society', *JRASMB*, iv/1 (1926), pp. 129–32.

affecting both Singapore and Penang. Banishment warrants were issued against 17 of the headmen, 11 of whom were arrested and deported.

The emergence of the crop of small protection societies called for drastic action by the Protectorate and the police if the policy of suppression of the Hoeys was to be demonstrably justifiable. In Penang, in 1892, warrants were issued against 42 of the headmen of the two Hokkien societies which thereupon dispersed. In Singapore the three chief groups were the Gi Tiong Heng, the Gi Tek Chhun, and the Gi Hong Chhun. Warrants against 16 headmen were issued, and 150 of their members were listed in the Protectorate's black book after being photographed and warned. There were also many prosecutions.

The number of banishments aroused some anxiety in London lest the policy was failing and the societies were being renewed and gaining strength, but the Governor assured the Secretary of State, Lord Knutsford, that the really powerful organizations had been effectually suppressed. If the policy of banishing promoters continued, he felt confident that the Colony would be freed from the most dangerous element which had for so many years affected its welfare.[52]

In his Budget Speech in October 1892 he asserted that not only were the old powerful societies practically institutions of the past but the Government had been enabled to break up all, or nearly all the societies of a dangerous character, and the Colony was more free from this tyranny than it had been for many years past. This had been achieved solely through the use of the powers in the Banishment and Societies Ordinances, and a further result had been a drop in serious crime.[53]

There can be no doubt that the vigorous implementation of the policy of suppression was a great relief to the Chinese community, and commendation was expressed in a farewell address presented to Sir Cecil Clementi Smith by the unofficial members of the Legislature in August 1893 shortly before his retirement, which read:

> The knowledge which your long official connection with Hong Kong and the Straits Settlements has given you of the native races who inhabit these Settlements, has enabled you to deal successfully with a subject which might have presented insuperable difficulties to a Governor not possessed of that experience. We refer to the suppressing of Secret Societies. That this measure has been carried out, not only without disorder, but with the cooperation and good will of the respectable and industrious classes, that its beneficent operation has been generally recognized by the Chinese, and that crimes of violence have, as one of its results, diminished in number, must be exceptionally gratifying to Your Excellency, for in this matter you have been justly regarded, not merely as the Governor responsible for the change of the law, but as the actual author and originator of the measure.[54]

At this time, too, a further restriction was included in the Societies Ordinance to make it clear that a registered society could only operate in the Settlement in which it was registered, and not elsewhere in the Colony.[55]

The greatest vigilance continued to be necessary. Apart from the smaller societies promoting local gambling, big syndicates also operated through the medium of 'Wai Seng' lotteries in which the public were invited to stake upon the candidates in the periodic examinations in China. To evade the Singapore gaming law a central office was set up in Johore with secret ticket agencies in

[52] COD 180, 3 June 1892; GD 303, 13 July 1892.   [53] SSPLC/1892/app. 8, 20 Oct.
[54] SSPLC/17 Aug. 1893.   [55] Ord. VII, 23 Nov. 1893.

Singapore, and the scheme was so successful that the remittance of large sums to Johore (estimated at $100,000 monthly) prejudicially affected Chinese trade. Documents found on ticket-sellers were often so obscure that their connexion with a lottery was difficult to prove, and a special fund created by the Singapore promoters, some of whom were businessmen of good standing, was available for the payment of lawyers for the defence. A personal appeal by the Governor to the Sultan of Johore to suppress the lotteries was ineffective, but eventually the Chinese Protectorate obtained details of the Singapore promoters, and action taken under the Common Gaming House Ordinance led to the banishment of five of them in 1893 out of twelve against whom warrants had been issued. The remaining seven fled to Johore, and operations continued on a smaller scale from places in that State and from the Rhio islands. In Penang similar lotteries were operated from a headquarters in Kedah with a turnover of $1 million yearly. A number of agents uncovered in Penang were prosecuted, and in 1895 eight banishment warrants were issued against the principal promoters, but the system was still working in 1898. A small form of gambling, known as the Hua Hoey, a 50-character lottery, was also rife in Penang, operating twice daily.[56]

While action against the Wai Seng lotteries was in hand, a new form of gambling appeared called the Chap Ji Ki or 12-card lottery. It became very popular among Straits-born women, leading to domestic strife, and Dr Lim Boon Keng drew the attention of the Government to its widespread effects throughout the Colony. The usual action was taken against promoters when discovered, namely, prosecution when possible and banishment when applicable.

With this extensive public gaming went an increase in crime figures and 'great activity amongst brothel bullies'. This latter development was attributed by the Colonial Secretary to the abolition in 1894 of the registration of brothels and prostitutes which 'had hitherto been supervised by the Chinese Protectorate with good effect'.[57] This removal of Government control was the result of direct instructions from the Secretary of State despite intense opposition in the Straits, and the immediate result was an upsurge of brothel-protection societies in all the Settlements and an increase in street fights between rival gangs contending for the right to collect levies from brothels, shops, and hawkers.[58]

Once again the Secretary of State enquired whether there had been a renewal in the vitality of the secret societies, and was told by the Governor (Sir Charles Mitchell) that there had, and that gambling had increased, but that action taken during 1895 and 1896 was taking effect.[59]

The Protectorate also discovered a complicated nexus of secret societies and registered 'friendly' societies in Singapore. The old Tong Beng was again revived in Geylang and allied itself with two registered societies, the Ho Keng Sia, entirely restricted to Straits-born members, and the Bun Heng, restricted to Hainanese. Between them they recruited a large membership in Kampong Bencoolen and Kampong Glam, and were later joined by another registered society of Straits-born Chinese, the Sun Tek Ho. At the same time a new unlawful society known as the Gi Leng (Two Dragons) composed of Hokkiens

---

[56] CP *AR*, 1895, paras 13–15, & 1898, paras 23–26.
[57] Col Sec's Report 1894 (J. A. Swettenham).
[58] CP *AR*, 1895, paras 6–12. Ord. XII of 1894 amending the Women and Girls Protection Ord., 1888.   [59] CP *AR*, 1895, para. 25; COD 355, 4 Sept. 1896. GD 461, 4 Oct. 1896.

and Tiechius, mostly surnamed Tan, was found to be operating in Kampong Saigon and Havelock Road. A feud developed between the two groups leading to breaches of the peace. Local-born leaders were charged in court and convicted, four China-born headmen were banished, and the three registered societies were dissolved. In Malacca an unlawful society, the Chiau Eng Si, was broken up, as was one in Penang.[60]

A weakness in the banishment procedure which permitted banishees from the Colony to reside 'undisturbed in a neighbouring Malay state' was remedied in 1896 by a reciprocal arrangement between the Colony and the various Protected States. In pursuance of this a law was passed prohibiting 'all persons banished from Johore or from any Native State and not being natural-born subjects of Her Majesty' from residing in the Colony. Orders in Council with reciprocal effect were passed in the Protected States.[61]

But in addition to society fights and gambling enterprises there was another matter of concern which threatened the public peace—the enforcement of new provisions in the Municipal Ordinance in January 1897, resulting in a strike of 16,000 rickshaw pullers, fomented by the rickshaw owners who objected to the more stringent controls being introduced. This was a dangerous situation, and a proclamation was at once issued under the Preservation of the Peace Ordinance, with copies in Chinese posted throughout the town, and the chief instigator, a Foochow rickshaw owner, was arrested. Little actual rioting took place though there were many crowds to disperse, and after three days the town returned to normal.

But at the end of September similar trouble threatened when the tax on rickshaws was increased and certain polluted wells in lodging houses in the town were ordered to be closed. Notices in Chinese were found posted in the streets calling on the population to rise up on the ninth of the ninth moon (4 October) and promising a reward of $500 for the head of each official or member of Council. There was trepidation among the shopkeepers as the day approached, but a show of force was made by the police with the military and volunteers standing by, while Protectorate officers counselled the masses to ignore the threat, and the day passed without incident.[62]

A challenge to the powers of the Government was made in 1899 when it was proposed to banish seven headmen of the unlawful Panglong Society (Timber Yard Society), Penang. This Tiechiu society was discovered late in 1898, and when its leaders were arrested a petition on behalf of the principal headman was sent to the Secretary of State criticizing the use of powers under the Banishment Ordinance in this instance, and suggesting changes in the law. The Governor was disturbed at this possible threat to the banishment powers and drew attention to the Secretary of State's agreement with the Governor in 1868 that the application of the ordinary law of England and of principles of procedure prescribed by that law were insufficient to ensure the preservation of the public peace in the Settlements, and had considered it essential that the Executive in exercising the utmost vigilance for the public peace should 'be

[60] CP *AR*, 1896, paras 4–6, 7, 9, 12; GDs 291 (24 June), 339 (26 July), 422 (12 Sept.), & 461 (4 Oct. 1896).
[61] Ords II & XIV of 1896; SSPLC/1896; COD 239, 15 June 1896; GD 373, 19 Aug. 1896.
[62] CP *AR*, 1897, paras 1–8; Col. Sec's *AR*, 1897, para. 21; GDs 55 & 381, 1 Mar. & Nov. 1897; Song Ong Siang, pp. 294–301.

armed with such powers as will make that vigilance effective'. He pointed out that it was only because of these powers that reasonable quiet existed, and that the prevalence of quiet was no reason for abrogating the powers. The Secretary of State (J. Chamberlain) supported the Governor and declined to concur in the alteration of the Banishment law as suggested in the petition. It was 'necessary as affording effective protection to the community', and he saw no reason to interfere. When the decision to banish the headmen was sent to him he raised no objection.[63]

Other difficulties had arisen in the administration of the Banishment Ordinance from claims to local birth by banishees, and the frequent lack of proof of place of birth. As the law stood, an application to the Supreme Court for a writ of Habeas Corpus might be made by any person dissatisfied with the issue of an Order of Banishment against him, and if he could prove to the satisfaction of the court that he was a natural-born British subject, the court would be bound to quash the Order, for the Ordinance applied only to those '*not* being natural-born subjects of Her Majesty'. By 1899 false claims to local birth were frequently made by secret society members when arrested, and the ease with which witnesses could be suborned caused the Governor grave concern lest the only effective weapon in the armoury of the Executive should be blunted by fraudulent cases brought before the Supreme Court in this way.

The point at issue was whether the Supreme Court or the Executive should decide whether or not a person was local-born. To avoid this dilemma Sir Charles Mitchell suggested to the Secretary of State that the Banishment Ordinance might be amended so as to include within its scope all persons who, though born on British soil or in Her Majesty's dominions, were yet regarded by any foreign power with the general assent of Her Majesty's Government as subjects of that power. He pointed out that the Chinese Government did not regard Straits-born Chinese as having lost their Chinese nationality until the third generation, and remarked that there was a growing tendency for persons involved in banishment proceedings to plead British nationality without surporting the plea by any testimony whatsoever.

The Governor's proposed solution did not commend itself to the Law Officers in London. They thought it neither desirable nor practicable. They agreed, however, that it was advisable to provide against the interference of the courts with the action of the Executive in this matter, and suggested that the law should be amended to provide that the Order of Banishment should be conclusive in all courts and for all purposes that the person named was not a natural-born British subject. With this the Secretary of State agreed, but advised the Governor that if, after an Order of Banishment had been issued, it should be proved to the satisfaction of the Governor in Council that such person was a natural-born British subject, then the Order should be revoked.[64]

The sequel to this correspondence was the introduction to Legislative Council on 29 August 1899 of a Bill to amend the Banishment Ordinance to make the decision of the Governor in Council as to the nationality of a person to be banished from the Colony final. At the second reading on 5 September, Dr Lim Boon Keng opposed the motion but was informed by the Attorney-General

[63] CP *AR*, 1899, paras 1, 2, 4, 9, 19; GDs 115 & 136, 23 Mar. & 13 Apr. 1899; CODs 127 & 147, 10 & 25 May 1899.
[64] GD 190, 17 May 1899. Reply: COD 208, 15 July 1899.

that the Bill was not to be taken as a measure for ousting the criminal jurisdiction of the courts but was an Ordinance which enabled the Government to get rid of persons who were undesirable subjects. It was entirely an administrative matter, and, he added, 'all of us with experience of this place must be aware of what exceptional benefit this piece of legislation has been to us'.

There was further opposition to the terms of the Bill in Committee on 12 September, this time by Burkinshaw, the leader of the local Bar. He admitted that he was thoroughly in favour of the Government taking, within proper limits, the fullest powers of controlling the mixed population of the Settlements. 'In dealing with people who are the most perfect adepts at conspiracy and vile machinations of all kinds,' he said, 'exceptional powers must undoubtedly be vested in the hands of the Government, without the necessity of the matters which are dealt with being brought before the courts of the Colony.' But he thought that the Governor's powers should be limited by certain safeguards. The Governor in reply admitted that theoretically he could not defend the Banishment Ordinance at all. 'But,' he said, 'I put aside theory and take practice as to what will prove the greatest benefit to the inhabitants of this Colony with the sort of community we have here.' In his view the responsibility should not lie partly with the Supreme Court and partly with the Executive Council but should continue to be vested in the body which was primarily responsible for the safety of the Colony.

When the Colonial Secretary (Sir Alexander Swettenham) spoke about the consequences of the unscrupulous use of their power by the headmen of secret societies for the purpose of misleading the Supreme Court, Burkinshaw retorted that

the Government must have gone back very much during the last three or four years, because from the assurances that we have had from time to time in this Council we have had reason to believe that the Secret Societies Suppression Ordinance has been working, and is now working, very successfully, and that dangerous societies were a thing of the past. We must have been very much mistaken, because the Colonial Secretary indicates that they are rampant still.

In fact, the records show that the control exercised was effective. The old, formidable Triad organizations had been broken up and their threat to the community removed, while the smaller emergent groups were unremittingly harassed. But this was achieved entirely through the exercise of the exceptional powers placed in the hands of the Government through the Societies Ordinance and the Banishment Ordinance, and the Government were well aware that if any loophole were found through which the efficacy of these powers could be nullified, the menace of the secret societies would grow again. The final words of the Governor when the Bill was passed into law on 26 October as Ordinance XVII of 1899 were no more than the truth: 'We do this unpleasant duty,' he said, 'in view of the exceptional circumstances of the Colony, and because the safety of the Colony depends to a very large extent upon these powers that have been given to the Governor-in-Council.'[65]

[65] SSPLC/1899/29 Aug. and 5, 12, & 26 Sept.; GD 367, 29 Sept. 1899, & COD 315, 27 Oct. 1899.

12

THE MALAY STATES, 1875–1900

1. CHINESE SOCIETIES

THE pacification of the west coast Malay States through British intervention led to further increases in the Chinese population. Already in these mining States the Chinese exceeded, and sometimes greatly exceeded, the Malays in numbers, and Sir William Jervois in 1875 believed that this would 'compel us sooner or later to interfere'.[1] Pickering, writing in *Fraser's Magazine* in October 1876, voiced the same opinion:

We cannot shut our eyes to the fact that peace in the Malay States means a large influx of Chinese; this involves our interference to keep the peace. The men who find the capital for mining or agricultural purposes are, for the most part, born or naturalized British subjects, and the labourers are all connected with our colonies by the secret societies, so that any disturbance in the Native States injures the trade of our people, and endangers the good order and tranquillity of our Settlements. Furthermore, we have a moral duty to protect the Malays from majorities of Chinese, and to protect the turbulent Chinese from massacring each other.

Certainly the introduction of the Residential system led to the adoption of an increasingly British administration throughout these States.

Perak

At the end of the Perak war there was difficulty in finding a suitably experienced officer to fill the post of British Resident. Davidson (from Selangor) and W. E. Maxwell[2] temporarily filled the gap until the appointment in April 1877 of Hugh Low, originally a botanist who had been for thirty years in Borneo and had there held various administrative posts. He is was who, by his knowledge of Malay ways, his sound policy, firm character, application to detail, and devotion to the welfare of the people, laid the foundation of a peaceful and prosperous Perak and set the pattern for other States.[3]

The removal of Sultan Abdullah and the rest of the conspiratorial chiefs after the Perak war effectively reduced Malay opposition to the extension of British influence, but Abdullah's successor, Yusuf, was not popular. He was appointed first as Raja Muda in 1877, and later (from 1 September 1878) as Regent. In order to broaden the basis of the Government, Low set up a State Council consisting of the Raja Muda, three Malay chiefs, the Resident and Assistant Resident (Speedy),[4] and two Chinese members, 'Capitan' Ah Kwee and 'Capitan'

[1] GD 335, 2 Dec. 1875.   [2] Son of Sir P. B. Maxwell, the former Chief Justice.
[3] Emily Sadka, ed., 'Journal of Sir Hugh Low', *JMBRAS*, Nov. 1954, covers the period 19 Apr.–15 June 1877.
[4] Speedy resigned his post late in 1877. Maxwell, Low, and Jervois were all critical of his capabilities. He was succeeded by Maxwell.

Ah Yam. Thus were the protagonists of the rival Chinese factions in the Larut war, Chang Keng Kwee and Ch'in Ah Yam, brought into the official administrative framework with acknowledgement of their status.

Secret Societies and the Revenue Farms

The interest of secret society leaders in the revenue farms throughout the Malay States becomes clearer after the appointment of British Residents. The successful tenderer for a farm had the monopoly for the supply of opium or spirits or tobacco for a certain area, but the protection of his interests against smuggling was primarily a matter for him and not for the Government, though investigations would be made if he complained. To protect his monopoly the members of a secret society were invaluable. They were the eyes and ears of the underworld and were quick with information to protect their own group and to collect the resultant reward. They formed a force ready to hand for policing the area on the farmer's behalf. Without the support of such a force the farmer was likely to fail, for his rivals would undermine his business by smuggling, conducted by members of their own societies.

Only two months before the arrival of Hugh Low the Perak Government had let a series of farms in the Krian and Kurau area and in south Larut (not the mining area) to Oh Wee Kee, a Hokkien, who, at the time of the Penang riots was the 'Second Brother' of the Penang Ghee Hin. The farms included the import of opium and the preparation and sale of chandu, the import of spirits and tobacco, the licensing of pawnbroking and gambling shops, and duties from the sale of timber, ataps, and salt fish. The possession of these farms by a Ghee Hin man was of prime importance to the opium farmers in Penang who, for the period January 1877 to December 1879, were also Ghee Hin men, and the likelihood of smuggling into Penang against their interests was thus reduced.

In addition to letting this new series of coastal farms, the Government had established a police post at the village of Tanjong Piandang to maintain order in this turbulent zone. This was a Tiechiu village under the control of the Ho Seng Society, and the introduction of the farm and the presence of police in their midst were found to be resented by the villagers who had hitherto looked after their own interests. In May the farmer complained of the smuggling of opium to the detriment of his revenue, and Maxwell, accompanying Low on a visit to the coastal villages, with a party of police made a search in Tanjong Piandang for smuggled opium. The discovery of some of this contraband in the house of the village headman caused an uproar among the villagers who attacked Maxwell's party with spears, tridents, and other weapons. It extricated itself by firing on the crowd, killing two and wounding others.[5] As a result of this incident, Low ordered all the villages along the Kurau coast to be disarmed.[6]

It was Low's policy not only to maintain the prosperity of the Larut mining area but also to develop the rich mining field in the Kinta valley in Perak proper. Tin had long been mined there by Malays and a few Chinese, and from early 1874 there had been an influx of mining labour from Larut, for, in addition to the discontent caused by the proposal to introduce a Larut chandu farm, the Larut field had been worked over by thousands of Chinese miners for more than twenty years, whereas Kinta was merely scratched. But the difficulty of

[5] GD 174, 26 May 1877.   [6] Sadka, p. 39 n. 36 & p. 60.

access, the long haul down the rivers from the foothills to the sea, and the consequent repetitive payment of tolls to Malay chiefs all along the line had been discouraging factors.

Already the toll system of remunerating the chiefs had been replaced by regular payments from the central treasury, and in 1879 Low arranged for work to be carried out in the clearance of snags and log-jams in the Kinta river and the lower reaches of the Perak river. Thereafter roads and tracks were constructed connecting the mining areas to the rivers where collection ports were established. Late in 1880, the site for Telok Anson, sixteen miles up the Perak river, was chosen for the accommodation of sea-going vessels.

In order to attract capital for the development of this field, Low proposed to establish revenue farms for the three-year period January 1880 to December 1882, and in announcing this to the State Council in November 1879 he said:

I was induced to devise this liberal measure in my great desire to do something to open up our neglected rich deposits of tin-ore in that district, and to assist in the further development of others. The Perak River has hitherto been much neglected, but by interesting the Penang Opium Farmers in its prosperity I am inclined to hope that they will assist in the introduction of labourers and capital which, while increasing their income from opium, will increase that of the Government from the export of tin.

The Penang farmers to whom Low referred were represented by Khoo T'ean Tek, the strong man of the Kien Tek Society who, as he had predicted, had survived the death penalty passed upon him in 1867. He was now, once again, the leading figure in the Hokkien community of Penang, and his syndicate had recently ousted that of the Ghee Hins which had held the Penang opium farm for the period 1877–9.

Low's intention was to combine all the farms in the State into one comprehensive unit to include opium, chandu, spirits, gaming, pawnbroking, tobacco, ataps, and the collection of duty on tin. For this he expected to receive an average of $50,000 monthly, starting with $42,000 monthly for the first year. He was urged by Khoo T'ean Tek not to pursue this plan for it involved too great an outlay for any one syndicate, but tenders were, nevertheless, invited.

It was part of the scheme that the farmer, in addition to being empowered to sell ball opium to other persons who would be licensed to prepare and sell chandu, would himself also be authorized to prepare and sell chandu. In Low's view such a system would not only produce a higher revenue than the simple tax on ball opium but would also benefit the labourers by providing cheaper chandu of better quality.[7]

Once again, as in 1874, the miners of Larut strongly objected to this interference with the existing system and demanded free trade in the preparation and selling of chandu. If more revenue was needed they were willing to agree to an increase in the duty on ball opium so long as no restrictions were placed on chandu.

On 3 October 1879 Low and Maxwell arrived at Taiping where, in the presence of Capitan Ah Kwee and others, it was proposed to explain to the labourers the benefits to be expected from the new system. But during the morning a crowd of 1,500 miners swarmed up the hill to the residency and surrounded it, demanding the withdrawal of the chandu farm proposals, and

[7] A similar system was in operation on Oh Wee Kee's farms (Sadka, p. 52 n. 82).

Low's attempts to parley were unavailing. The Indian police,[8] when called in, dispersed the crowd, but later, in the town, a fracas occurred in which the police opened fire, killing twenty-eight and wounding many more.[9]

During the next two days Low held conferences with the Chinese leaders including both Capitans and Khoo T'ean Tek who, in turn, consulted their own groups among the miners, but in the end it was clear that nothing would shake the determination of the men not to accept the chandu farm. Both the Capitans advocated the abandonment of the proposal and advised an increase of the duty on opium to $5 a ball.

The plan to introduce a comprehensive farm had failed, and Low contented himself with letting regional farms for specific items. The Krian–Kurau farms and those in south Larut formerly held by Oh Wee Kee (Ghee Hin) were let to Khoo T'ean Tek (Kien Tek) 'on behalf of the Penang opium farmers', as were two new farms on the Perak river for the collection of duty on opium ($5 a ball) and on tobacco ($3 a pikul) imported up the Perak river.

In the mining area of Larut, the system of importing ball opium with direct taxation was continued, but for other items—spirits, tobacco, gambling, and pawnbroking—Capitan Chang Keng Kwee had long held the farm licence and was allowed to keep it. There were no offers for the gambling, pawnbroking, and spirit farms for the Perak river, and Low was informed by a Singapore man (Koh Sew Swee) who had formerly held farms in Perak that the Chinese miners at Gopeng and Batang Padang would never allow them to be introduced.

Thus the allied Kien Tek–Hai San financial group represented by Khoo T'ean Tek and Chang Keng Kwee was, for this three-year period, paramount not only in Penang but throughout most of Perak, to the discomfiture of the Ghee Hin syndicate.

The early development of south Perak was not without its society troubles. In Kinta both the Ghee Hin and the Hai San were represented in the labour forces, and during 1878 there were two occasions on which mining kongsis were fined collectively for affrays. In the same year, the Ho Seng Society again showed its power in the coastal zone by the murder of Captain Lloyd, the first Superintendent of the Dindings, appointed after its cession to Britain by the Treaty of Pangkor.

Lloyd, with his wife and three young children, lived in an atap bungalow on Pangkor Island, and although a twelve-man Malay police guard lived only twenty yards away with one man on sentry-go, the house was attacked by a band of men in the early hours of 26 October. Lloyd was killed with a hatchet, and his wife and a visiting friend stunned with the same weapon. The children escaped with the ayah to the jungle. Firearms and money were removed by the marauders and the place was set on fire, but the Penghulu arrived in time to rescue the two women.

It would seem to have been an organized operation with one junk landing men from Penang and another from Lumut on the mainland opposite Pangkor, and suspicion fell on the Ho Seng Society of which the Malay in charge of the guard was an active member and who was found to be in possession of Lloyd's revolver. The leader of the Ho Seng at Lumut, a Chinese labour contractor, was

---

[8] These were Speedy's sepoys embodied in an armed police force under Lt Walker.

[9] Sir Frank Swettenham, *Malay Sketches*. Low's Reports and Diary encl. in GD Conf., 18 Oct. 1879, & GD 357.

arrested, and though he denied complicity he implicated other contractors. They were all part of a Chinese labour force of about 1,000 engaged to open up a European-owned sugar estate at Lumut, when the scheme was suddenly stopped. All except about 200 returned to Penang, but those contractors who remained had lost money on the deal through paying advances to the labourers and were incensed and vengeful.

In February 1879 a man who had confessed to the murder was hanged in Penang, but it was rumoured that he was a scapegoat put forward by the Ho eng Society to screen the real culprit. In reporting the results of his enquiries, Low said:

> The whole coast of Perak is in possession of the Ho Seng Society, from the Krian to the mouth of the Bernam River, and they have an idea that having established themselves as they allege without the assistance of Government, the Government has no right to tax them or impose regulations for their guidance. The Government of Perak was defied by two of these communities in 1877, but successfully vindicated its authority, and the belief is current in Larut that discontent at the dues charged at Pangkor has engendered a feeling of resentment which has encouraged the perpetration of the crime.[10]

The Pangkor murder emphasized the lack of supervision of the rapidly increasing groups of Chinese in the coastal swamps as distinct from the mining camps. Most of this labour was employed in cutting firewood for use in Penang, and the lawless tendencies of these groups south of the Larut river were such that in March 1879 the State Council introduced regulations for the registration and licensing of all Chinese along the coast from the Larut river southwards to the Bruas river. In this area, 'every woodcutter's, sawyer's, or fisherman's kongsi or other establishment of any kind' was to be registered. The headman of each house or kongsi-house was responsible for furnishing full particulars about the work of the kongsi, including the number and names of the labourers, and he was required to report any changes that took place. A licence was to be issued to each man on payment of $1 yearly, but no licence would be issued to anyone whose employer was unwilling to give security for his good and peaceable behaviour. Persons found unlicensed were liable to a fine of $100 or to imprisonment for six months. There was one further security provision which read: 'No Chinese will be permitted to reside at any place which cannot easily be reached either by land or else by water at all states of the tide.'

The implementation of these regulations was only possible because of the existence of the armed police force brought to a high standard of efficiency by the Commandant, Lieutenant R. S. F. Walker. Each kongsi in the area was visited by him, and the registration was carried out without any disturbance.[11]

During 1880 and 1881 this system of registration was extended throughout Perak. Every Chinese male of over 16 years of age was required to register annually and pay a fee of $1. The sum obtained from this poll-tax was applied to a Chinese Hospitals Fund (the Yeng Wah Hospitals) established for the treatment of sick Chinese labourers.[12] One of the objects of the introduction of the registration was said to be 'to facilitate the apprehension of contract labourers

[10] Principal sources for the Pangkor Murder are: GDs 301, 304 & 348 (27 Oct., 30 Oct., & 12 Dec. 1878): reports by Low at SSPLC, 1878, app. 45, & 1879, app. 2.
[11] State Council Mtg., 1 Mar. 1879, & Report on Revenue and Expenditure, Perak, 1879.
[12] Diary, 29 Sept. 1879; mtgs 3 Nov. & 30 Dec. 1879.

who escape from Larut to Perak proper and *vice versa*'. It is difficult to believe that without photographs or fingerprints individual identification could be ensured, but perhaps the visits of the police to the various kongsi-houses to carry out the registration and the knowledge that there was some surveillance by the authorities may have discouraged violence. On the other hand, there were near-riots at Taiping and Parit Buntar in 1882 by objectors to the poll-tax. At the end of 1885 the tax was abolished (it had produced $48,675 in 1884) and a new system of registration of Chinese mining labourers without tax was introduced. The loss in revenue was made up by an additional tax of $1 a ball on opium.[13]

The early British Residents in the other west coast states were, like Low, anxious to attract outside capital to develop the mines. In Sungei Ujong the Resident (Paul), in 1882 and 1883, bemoaned the fact that there was no one with sufficient capital or enterprise to develop the industry, and that Malacca Chinese did not care for speculating in mines. One can only assume that they found the areas concerned insufficiently rich in tin. Later on, the Resident of Negri Sembilan (Lister) let the opium and other farms to Singapore and Malacca tenderers hoping to get them to invest in mining. That was in 1888, but the attempt failed, and during the next two years he ruefully reflected that the holding of the farms by uninterested outsiders instead of by local mining advancers had had a very bad effect.

A similar attempt made in 1884 by the Resident, Selangor (Rodger) to infuse greater life into the mining industry by letting the farms to Penang traders was also unsuccessful and caused much ill-feeling.

In all such cases the attitude of the local secret society was of major importance to any intruding financier tendering for the farms. Invariably the existing holders of these monopolies (usually the local mining advancers) were the leaders of the local secret society and relied upon it to protect their interests. Unless the outsider could come to terms with these men he faced the opposition of the society with all the intrigue and smuggling which that implied. In most of these States the days of the opium farmer were numbered. In 1892 the opium farmer in Negri Sembilan went bankrupt and thereafter the Resident decided to collect the government tax on ball opium direct and was very successful. This example was followed in turn by Selangor in 1894 and Perak in 1895, though the farms for spirits, gambling, and pawnshops remained.

The Chinese Protectorate in the Malay States

Low was very conscious of the need for a better means of contact with the rapidly-increasing Chinese community and appointed a 'Protector', Captain Schultz, who started work at the beginning of 1884. What his qualifications for the post were is not known, but he set about his work zealously, and on 20 January recommended that all Friendly Societies in Larut should be registered at his office, and this was approved.

Soon afterwards a controversy arose as to whether secret societies still existed in Perak and Selangor. Powell, who was acting for Pickering in Singapore during the latter's absence on leave, referred in his Annual Report for 1883 to the existence of such societies in the Malay States. That an acting Protector in Singapore should presume to comment on affairs in the Malay States was too

[13] Perak *AR*, 1884, 1885.

much for Swettenham, who had been Resident, Selangor and was then acting in Perak in Low's absence. He referred Powell's report to Schultz, who wrote:

> Secret societies are not allowed to exist in the State; it is however more than probable that there are a good many members of such societies here who have been initiated in Penang or elsewhere, and it is also possible that these members hold secret meetings in the jungle, although none have ever been discovered by the police. As far as I have been able to ascertain, no serious disturbance or riot has taken place here that could be put down directly to the influence of these societies.[14]

It must be assumed that Schultz was referring only to the very recent past, and Swettenham went rather further by commenting: 'It appears that there are no Chinese secret societies in Perak, and, as far as I am aware, the existence of such societies is prohibited.' He continued: 'In Selangor where there are no such societies, I believe certain clans have in Kuala Lumpur what they call a kongsi-house which corresponds to our Rest House, and they assist each other in making temples and burying the dead.'[15]

Similarly Rodger, the acting Resident of Selangor, denied even more out-spokenly the existence of such societies in Selangor. Thus challenged, Powell consulted an interpreter of the Supreme Court, Singapore, named Chong Bun Sui, a Malacca-born Chinese of Hakka descent who had been employed in the government service in Perak, Selangor, and Sungei Ujong and thus had, according to Powell, 'special opportunities of obtaining a knowledge of the subject'. If, as seems highly probable, this interpreter was the same as 'Boon Swee', the Malacca interpreter who accompanied Pickering to Sungei Ujong and who during the Malacca riots of 1875 was the head of the Hok Beng Society, he certainly had had 'special opportunities' to discover the truth about the organiza-tion of these societies in these States.

He confirmed Powell's opinion, and gave detailed information, from which Powell was able to report that the headmen in Larut and Selangor were appointed by the societies in Penang, Malacca, or Singapore. Because of the government prohibition there were no recognized kongsi-houses but meetings were, never-theless, held. New arrivals often had their entrance fees paid by their employer who debited the amount to their accounts. Both the Ghee Hin and the Hai San were established in all three States. In Larut the Ghee Hin headman was Capitan Ch'in Ah Yam, and the Hai San headman Capitan Chang Keng Kwee. In Kinta there was a Ghee Hin headman at Papan and a Hai San headman at Gopeng. In Selangor there were Ghee Hin headmen and Hai San headmen, the latter being Yap Ah Shak and Capitan Yap Ah Loy, so that when these two sat as magistrates they were, in effect, a court of the Hai San Society. At Kan-ching the Ghee Hin was mostly composed of Ka Yin Chiu Hakkas who were members of the Ts'ung Paak Society, the Hakka section of the Singapore Ghee Hin. The headman of the Hai San at Kanching was a clansman of Yap Ah Loy. Both the Ghee Hin and the Hai San also existed at Semuntan. In Sungei Ujong both societies had been established for many years and the names of the head-men were given.[16]

From the details given in the report it is clear that these two societies were not rigidly confined each to one language group. There were both Cantonese and

---

[14] Wynne, p. 409.   [15] Ibid. p. 410.
[16] The report is given in full by Wynne, pp. 411–12.

Hakka headmen in each society, and it must be assumed that each of these two groups had a mixed membership, though the Cantonese appear to have predominated in the Ghee Hin and the Hakkas in the Hai San.

Faced with this document, the Chief Police Officer, Selangor (Syers), still maintained that there was no evidence of the existence of any society organization in his state. It was true that members of the Hai San appealed to Yap Ah Shak in any difficulty, but they had (openly) no kongsi-house, and Syers had reason to believe that the Capitan was not a member, but the reason was not disclosed. He agreed that in 1884 an attempt was made to establish the Hok Beng Society of Malacca in Selangor (as Bun Sui had reported to Powell), and admitted that 2,000 men had been recruited before the police were aware of it. On this occasion the Capitan evidently played his cards well; he gave all the information available about this possible rival in order to ensure that the authorities would suppress it.

There can be no doubt that the interpreter's report was correct, and that throughout the whole trouble between the Chinese communities in Selangor the hand of Triad moved, unseen and unknown to European observers, even to those closely connected with the administration of the State.

In Perak Captain Schultz was equally disinclined to admit that there was any society organization in that State. He ingenuously approached the Capitans and the other leaders named in the report, all of whom denied ever having been headmen. Ch'in Ah Yam admitted having been a member of the Ghee Hin for over twenty years but said that the society had no need of headmen in Perak where there was no branch or kongsi-house. He had often told the society in Penang that it was unlawful to start a branch in Perak. Chang Keng Kwee told a similar story and added that he had resigned his membership of the Hai San in the beginning of the year, 'a fact which is known to me', said Schultz.

Pickering on his return from leave supported Powell. Though he did not enter into the argument as to whether there were State organizations of the societies, he was satisfied that their influence was still there, and it was understandable that the leaders would not wish to compromise themselves by admitting that they were involved.

During the next three years, indeed, Schultz was able to dig deeper and discover the existence of widespread ramifications of the Triad root system. In his report for 1887 he referred to several riots which took place, all of which were 'due to the pernicious influence of secret societies which through their perfect organisation for evil have caused petty quarrels and jealousy between individual members of rival societies to develop into serious breaches of the peace resulting in murder, arson, and destruction of valuable property'. Of these riots the most important were at Salak near Kuala Kangsar in April, and at Papan in the Kinta district in November. Both started as brothel quarrels. At Salak the fight was between men of the Ho Seng and the Ghee Hin. The leaders of both societies were banished and others sentenced to terms of imprisonment. It transpired that the Ho Seng leader had been elected a few months earlier as the President (Elder Brother) of the Ho Seng Society in Penang, but continued to live in Perak where his ardour in recruiting new members had incensed the Ghee Hin leaders. At Papan the riot was between members of the Hai San and the Ghee Hin.[17]

[17] Low's *AR*, 1877, says 'Ho Seng' and Ghee Hin, but Schultz's and Pickering's reports give 'Hai San', as does the Resident's report, 1888.

The two sides were distinguished by the wearing of red and white badges. The Ghee Hin wore red bands round their waists, the Hai San had white bands round their wrists and heads. About 500 Ghee Hins arrived from Lahat in the early morning and at once attacked and looted two Hai San kongsis, seriously wounding six men, one of whom later died. On arrival of the magistrate, rioters taken with arms in their hands were flogged on the spot while the leaders were arrested. After trial before the Sultan, the Resident, and the Chief of Kinta, two men were sentenced to death for culpable homicide and were executed at Taiping. Others received prison sentences varying from six months to two years and twelve stripes with a rattan. Twelve kongsis were fined sums varying from $36 to $5,000, and the Resident tendered his thanks to the magistrate and the police for restoring public confidence in the district 'the peace of which had been shaken to an alarming extent'.

Schultz wrote:

> These secret societies consider the Native States, especially Perak, as a happy hunting ground from which they derive a very considerable portion of their exceedingly large income; so tempting is this to them that notwithstanding the considerable risk to their emissaries and agents in carrying on their work here, any number of these latter over-run the State secretly inducing their countrymen to join their societies. Not content with doing this, in order to increase their numbers and their revenue, they have lately, I understand, relaxed their own rules with this object in view, by not making it a condition any more that the candidates from the Native States who are willing to enter the Societies must come over to Penang to be initiated. Their travelling agents or Secret Masters have power to hold lodges in the State and there to make the candidates acquainted with the necessary signs and take the oath from them.[18]

This is a very different picture from that given by Schultz to Swettenham three years earlier. He contended that the difficulties faced in the States in dealing with the societies were enhanced by the fact that they were recognized by the Government of the Colony, and regretted that the Government of Perak had not adopted his suggestion that the carrying of the 'ticket' of one of the societies should be made an offence. He was opposed to the Colony system of recognition which, though supposed to place them under better control, left them as powerful as they were before and gave them the right to collect fees from their members, making them still more powerful.

During the year, three men were tried by the Sultan and the Resident for being active agents of the Ghee Hin Society and were sentenced to death, but this was later commuted to twenty-four years' penal servitude on the grounds, as Low stated in his Annual Report, that the full sentence had not recently been carried out, though it was in accordance with the laws of Perak. A proclamation was issued informing the public that in future the death penalty would be enforced.

This, in turn, led to a question in the Legislative Council of the Colony on 14 November 1888 pointing to the inconsistency between the laws of the Colony and those of Perak where the death penalty could be imposed for something which was openly permissible in the Colony. The result of this was that in August 1889 the laws of Perak were amended, and the penalties for organizing Chinese secret societies were prescribed as: (a) fine up to $1,000; (b) imprison

[18] GD 347, 30 July 1888, Encl. (PRO).

ment up to 5 years; (*c*) flogging up to 30 strokes; (*d*) deportation; (*e*) confiscation of all property. Persons joining such societies were liable to similar penalties of a lesser degree of severity, and the use of flags, insignia, tickets, or documents of such societies was prohibited.[19]

In 1887 the Protectorate in Perak was strengthened by the appointment of a second officer (W. Young) stationed at Telok Anson, the gateway to the Kinta valley. A sudden outbreak of disturbance in November of that year caused the authorities to be on the alert, and in the following September there were further disquieting reports from the same area—Papan. Major Walker, Commandant of the 'Perak Sikhs', as the armed police force was now known, made a show of force by visiting the mining areas and making an inspection of the kongsis in which the men lived. At each place he tried to assess the number of labourers likely to belong to either the Ghee Hin or the Hai San. How he was able to gauge these sympathies is not disclosed, but it might be done with reasonable approximation through an experienced interpreter.

It is noteworthy that in seven out of the eight areas visited there were both Ghee Hin and Hai San supporters. In all, 246 kongsis were visited and frequently there were kongsis of Ghee Hin men and kongsis of Hai San men in the same area. At five places the Ghee Hin predominated, and at three the Hai San. At one place which had only six kongsis and 222 miners all were Hai Sans. Walker estimated that in the whole area visited there were 9,447 miners of Ghee Hin and 5,394 of Hai San sympathies.

A further check on mining labour had been introduced by Schultz in the form of a system under which all labourers were required to obtain a certificate of discharge when leaving employment, and no employer might engage a labourer who was not in possession of such a document. The primary reason for this experiment was the draining away of indentured labourers whenever better prospects offered elsewhere. The scheme was introduced in 1885 and originally applied to mining labour only. Later it was extended to contract labourers employed in agricultural and mechanical occupations. A register of indebted immigrants with their photographs was kept by the Protector. At the end of 1888 William Cowan, who had succeeded Schultz, reported that the system was working satisfactorily in Larut but was not so successful in Kinta. The Resident was not so sure of its success even in Larut. Men were reported to be exceedingly dexterous in forging the necessary entries, and imitated the 'chop' of the kongsi by carving it on a piece of sweet potato with which impressions were then made—a typical example of the difficulties encountered by such a system of registration and identification. By 1891 it was recognized that the system effected little if any good.

Difficulties were encountered in applying the law introduced in 1889 when the death penalty was abolished, and it was amended in 1892, after which 18 prosecutions in that year resulted in 17 convictions. In 1895 legislation for the registration of societies in Perak was adopted similar to that introduced in the Colony in 1889.

During the final years of the century there were no more spectacular society troubles in Perak, though in 1896 the Assistant Protector, Kinta, believed that about 70 per cent of the Chinese population of Kinta were members of secret

[19] CODs 42, 130, & 336 (9 Feb., 10 May, & 18 Oct. 1889); GDs 146, 261, & 433 (2 Apr., 5 June, & 5 Sept. 1889): Perak State Council Mins., 5 Aug. 1889 (Perak GG, 30 Aug. 1889).

societies, mainly of the Ghee Hin. Owing to the arrests of members for being in possession of membership tickets, they were becoming more crafty in the concealment of such evidence. Among recommendations made by him for closer control were: (*a*) a system of night-passes on the lines already adopted in Hong Kong, and (*b*) the photographing of bad characters. He also suggested that the Protector should have at his disposal a secret service fund from which to pay rewards for valuable information.

In 1897 an attempt to set up a Hai San society at Tronoh was discovered, and in 1899 there were two attempts to start new societies, one in Kinta and one in Larut, but the names of these interlopers are not on record.

In Selangor during the period from 1885 to the end of the century there were several attempts to establish secret societies. One such occurred in 1887, and in the following year Chinese secret societies were formally prohibited by an Order in Council of 24 May. A proclamation set out the penalties which were similar to those introduced later in Perak. Despite this, in the same year, an attempt was made by men from Deli (Sumatra) and Penang to start a society at Serendah. They were Hai San men and their activities caused a disturbance. They were fined and ordered to leave the State.

Once again the Chief of Police congratulated the Capitan on his help, and the Resident (Swettenham) wrote that this proved 'that there are no dangerous societies; the most respectable and intelligent members of the Chinese community possess a valuable influence over their countrymen and exert it to support the Government which they regard as the cause of law and order'. There was certainly no doubt about the 'valuable influence' that could be exerted by Yap Ah Loy and Yap Ah Shak through the organization of their society.

Again, in 1891, the Resident (W. E. Maxwell) wrote:

Efforts are made from time to time by secret societies outside the state to extend their influence among the miners in Selangor . . . There is a marked antipathy on the part of the leading Chinese . . . to the establishment of secret societies in the State, and information given to the police in 1891 led to the arrest of a headman of the Ghee Hin Society with books and papers in his possession which clearly showed what his occupation was.

Later on he remarked: 'In the population, one nationality (the Kheh or Hakka) preponderates, a fact which contributes to the maintenance of order in the mines.'[20] He would probably have been nearer the mark had he said that one secret society, the Hai San, predominated.

In 1892 branches of the Ghee Hin were opened at Serendah and Sungei Besi, the ringleaders being arrested and convicted. There were rumours of branches at Rawang and Sepang, but no proof was forthcoming. In the following year a Chinese Secretariat was formed under a Chinese-speaking officer, H. G. Ridges, who, though appointed as Chinese Secretary in 1890, had been organizing the Mines Department. Regulations for the control of secret societies were drafted, and in 1894 legislation for the registration of societies and for the prohibition of those unregistered was passed.[21]

With the federation in 1896 of the four States of Perak, Selangor, Negri Sembilan, and Pahang, an officer of the Straits Settlements Civil Service was appointed to be the Secretary for Chinese Affairs in the Federated Malay States,

---

[20] Sel. *AR*, 1891.   [21] Reg. X of 1894 (26 Sept.); in force fr. 1 Jan. 1895.

with headquarters at Kuala Lumpur. This was G. T. Hare, who eventually achieved a reputation second only to that of Pickering. In 1898 he surprisingly reported that there was no secret society of any power or influence in Selangor, and that only a small percentage of the Chinese living in the State were members of such societies elsewhere. This statement is so at variance with the known history of Chinese mining groups wherever and whenever found (including Selangor) that it is difficult to accept it as a correct conclusion. As Schultz had discovered in Perak, it took time even for a Protectorate officer to penetrate the façade of an apparently well-conducted community and find the hidden web of Triad organization.

The year 1899 was noteworthy for the passing of three laws: the Secretary for Chinese Affairs Enactment (VIII) under which powers were given to this officer to arbitrate in disputes between Chinese; the Banishment Enactment (XIII), and the Societies Enactment (XXIX), this last being along the lines of the Societies Ordinance in the Colony.

Reports from Negri Sembilan from 1884 onwards add little to our knowledge of society organization. An Ordinance for the prevention of secret societies was passed in 1889 on the Colony pattern That societies did exist may be inferred from a report by the District Officer,. Jelebu, in 1892 that the appointment of a local Capitan was a failure because the man appointed, the oldest and most popular Chinese in the District, was always in pecuniary trouble, and was believed to be much under the influence of a secret society 'who made use of him for an extension of its power'. There was difficulty in dealing with Chinese crime because the Chinese said that they dared not give information. In 1896 the Resident (E. W. Birch, acting) was disturbed at the lack of a Chinese-speaking officer in the State, and noted that the Chinese population was increasing; there were 3,000 mining labourers at Broga. One secret society murder was reported. The victim would appear to have been a police informer who was gagged, beaten, and buried alive. The body was three times removed to different graves and a dog was buried in the first grave to deceive the police.

In Pahang a proclamation similar to that in force in Selangor was passed by the State Council in January 1890 prohibiting the formation of Chinese secret societies, and shortly afterwards three men were prosecuted at Kuantan for infringement. The Chinese population at Bentong, in west Pahang, did not begin to develop until 1897 when land was granted on special terms to 'Mr Lok Yew, one of the principal Chinese capitalists of the neighbouring State of Selangor'. As it is known that in 1884 Lok Yew (Loke Yew) was a leader of the Ghee Hin in Larut, it is reasonable to assume that his employees at Bentong were also of this society. By April 1898 he had 700 men there. In 1899 a Banishment Enactment was passed (XI) and a Chinese-speaking officer (W. D. Barnes) appointed.

It is clear that in all four of these Malay States legislative action for the prohibition of Chinese secret societies was taken before the Societies Bill was put forward in the Colony, but after the Bill became law in the Colony in 1889, the four States, one by one, adopted similar legislation.

The introduction of prohibition in these States had very much the same effect as in the Colony. The existing recognized secret societies, such as the Ghee Hin and the Hai San (and in Perak the Ho Seng), obeyed the law to the extent that they maintained no outward appearance of an organized lodge, but membership continued and the influence was still there, though it was unwise to flaunt it for the authorities to see. There can be little doubt that prohibition did help to curb the vicious outbreaks between rival societies, for any arrogant demonstration of power or overt exertion of pressure was liable to bring official retribution. That it did not induce the Chinese population to abandon this deep-rooted manifestation of their cultural heritage should not be allowed to obscure the very real benefits to the community which derived from the power of partial control which prohibition placed in the hands of the Governments.

2. MALAY SOCIETIES

Evidence of the formation of Flag societies by Malays in Perak first occurs in the early years of Low's administration. At a meeting of the State Council on 20 October 1879 the Resident drew the Regent's attention to a report from the Superintendent of the Krian and Kurau Districts (Denison) stating that these societies were a threat to the peace of the area. Since in origin the Flag societies mainly consisted of southern Indians, later joined by Jawi–Pekans,[22] and the true Malays tended to shun them, it is not surprising to find the earliest notices of their existence in Perak coming from the coastal areas in close contact with Penang. But the exact date of their introduction is unknown. Though Wynne believed that they existed throughout the Larut troubles, there is no supporting evidence. Since the Flag societies in Penang were well known to the authorities, they would almost certainly have known of similar societies in Perak had they existed. Moreover, there is no mention of their existence in careful notes taken from a large number of Malay witnesses in an attempt to elucidate the circumstances of the murder of Birch, though other combinations were freely revealed. This evidence was given in private by individuals of all groups, many of whom were only too anxious to implicate their rivals, so that it is highly improbable that if the Flag societies had been in existence, they would not have been mentioned.

When the Resident raised the matter in October 1879, the Regent stated that these societies were illegal by the laws of the country, which punished members by banishment. This doubtless referred to religious law in Perak, which prohibited unorthodox sects. The next reference to the societies occurred at a meeting of the State Council on 20 February 1880, when the Resident laid on the table a ticket book of the Red Flag Society which had been seized near Kuala Kurau from a man reported to have 'recently established a lodge of the society at that place during the absence of the Penghulu'. The minutes stated that Mr Denison had frequently complained of the trouble caused by these societies and that the Council had on former occasions declared them illegal. It is not known if this refers to the Regent's comment in 1879 or to a decision the record of which has not been traced.

Off the coast of Lower Perak lies the island of Pangkor, which formed part of the Straits Settlements and was therefore subject to the Ordinance of March 1882 amending the Dangerous Societies Ordinance, under which the Red and White Flag societies were specifically prohibited by name. In May 1882 the Inspector of Police, Penang (R. W. Maxwell), under whose jurisdiction Pangkor came, called on the headmen of the two societies there to dissolve the societies and hand over their books, which they did in June.[23]

[22] See above, p. 105.
[23] IOP to Lt. Gov., Pg, 11 Sept. 1882 (quoted by Wynne, pp. 346–7).

In August 1882 a link between the societies of Pangkor and Penang was found in Lower Perak, when three headmen, two of the White Flag and one of the Red, were arrested and in September tried before a court in Perak. All three were sentenced to rigorous imprisonment. The record of the trial stated: 'These societies have their head offices in the Colony, but have recently ramified into Lower Perak.' The principal White Flag leader was 'Che Sarib, the village head-man of Bagan Nakhoda Omar, and he stated that about four years earlier his son had given evidence in a stabbing case in which the accused was another Malay, a member of the White Flag Society. As a result, when the son next visited Pangkor he was severely beaten by members of the Ghee Hin Society there. In order to secure protection the youth had gone to Penang and had there joined the White Flag Society, and was advised to persuade his father to join too, with the prospect of being given official rank. The beating of the son by Ghee Hin men and not by men of the White Flag, coupled with the fact that he had to go to Penang for initiation, suggests that at that time (1878) there may have been no branch of the White Flag in his area.

A search of 'Che Sarib's house revealed no books, but several persons in the village surrendered membership tickets which they said they had got from him. There were also four houses at which white flags were flying. Two undated letters were found from Pawang Wahab, one of the Pangkor or White Flag 'Twah Kohs' (Elder Brothers), giving instructions to 'Che Sarib and two others 'to flog, fine, and disgrace some people who have committed offences against their Jema'ah'.[24] It is not possible to say whether the letters were written before or after the dissolution of the Pangkor societies in May–June 1882. In later years the development of these societies throughout Perak was to prove a serious embarrassment to the Administration, not only because of the crimes they committed but because of the suborning of the Malay police and subordinate officials.

No record has been found of the existence at this time of such societies in other Malay States, and, indeed, no further mention of them in Perak till 1901–2 when a White Flag society was discovered at Telok Anson, in the lower reaches of the Perak river, extending some ten miles upstream as far as Kampong Pasir Panjang. It was said to have a large membership and to be dangerous because it coerced non-members to join. A similar society, also called White Flag, was found in Krian. This, too, was said to have a large membership and to be threatening non-members. Enquiries were made in each area, and revealed that the Malay police force was affected. In Lower Perak four men were arrested, but the British Resident decided that the evidence against them did not justify banishment. Of the Krian Malays, six were banished, some to Penang and some to Kedah, depending on their place of birth, and four others who evaded arrest were proclaimed.

The investigations revealed that these societies were, once again, linked with Penang where both Red and White Flag societies still existed, the former based on Acheen Street and the latter on Jelutong. Unfortunately there is insufficient information to establish the initiation ritual employed, nor is there any indication of local Chinese interest. The principal result was the issue of a proclama-

[24] 'Journal of Mr J. B. M. Leech, Magistrate and Collector, Sabak Bernam, Aug. 1882 (quoted by Wynne, p. 346). Instead of 'Twah Kohs' Wynne has 'Terah Kolis', but this obviously derives from miscopying. Jema'ah = Assembly, usually of a religious group.

tion by the Sultan on 24 March 1903 giving warning that membership of a Jema'ah was strictly forbidden and would be punished with banishment, imprisonment, and fine. It added that this prohibition was in force under the former Malay rule and would be strictly enforced under the present ruler.

Twelve years elapsed before there is record of a police report, in September 1915,[25] stating that a Triad society existed at Sitiawan with Chinese and Malay members, known locally as the 'Red Flag'. Enquiries by the Protectorate revealed that there was, in fact, a Triad society in this area with Hainanese leaders, and that an initiation ceremony at which 100 people were present was held on the last day of the year. It would appear that this was another instance of Malays being admitted to a Chinese society, and this pattern extended further north through the kampongs along the Perak river which were almost entirely inhabited by Malays, on which some light was thrown by investigations in 1917.

In January of that year, the British Resident, Perak (W. G. Maxwell), wrote a minute stating that he had it from a high Malay authority that there was considerable activity in pushing Flag societies, and that, as in 1902, the headquarters was in Penang. Enquiry made by the Protector of Chinese (W. T. Chapman), disclosed that there was a considerable Chinese influence in these societies, and the Assistant District Officer (Jervois), who had been in charge of the Perak river area since 1915, submitted a report on what he had gleaned about these societies during that period.

From this we learn that he had information about four Malay societies which he believed to be distinct, though covering largely the same area, i.e. from Kampong Pulau Tiga in the south, northwards to Kampong Layang-Layang with ramifications to Parit and Bruas. Only one of these was specifically stated to have Chinese members, who lived at Tronoh and Telok Anson and numbered 300 or more. It may be assumed that this particular society was a section of a Chinese one, and from the slight information about the secret signs employed by the Malays, it would appear that they were based on Triad usage. This Malay society was active in the southern part, around Lambor (Kiri and Kanan) and Pulau Tiga. Its entrance fee was $5 and the monthly subscription 50 cents.

One other society at Layang-Layang was said to have connexions with Telok Anson, and though nothing is said about Chinese, it seems likely that this, too, would be a Malay section of a Telok Anson-based Chinese society. Its entrance fee was $2.50 and the monthly subscription 25 cents. This group was hostile to another society, with a $5 entrance fee and the same monthly subscription, which seems to have been the biggest of these groups, centred on Lambor Kanan but extending northwards to Layang-Layang. It was of purely Malay membership with no Chinese connexions, and had several hundred members. At the initiation ceremony a large sword was used with a crescent and a sun on the handle. The initiate stood with a copy of the Koran balanced on his head while he swore the oath, after which he drank water. Such secret signs as are described do not seem to be of Triad origin. A cover was provided by the formation of a Rubber Estate Company whose shareholders included members and non-members. The purpose of the society was to provide legal assistance for its members when necessary and to settle cases out of court. It may be

[25] Details of the report and court cases mentioned in this chapter will be found in Wynne, chs 23–25.

regarded as the Malay response to the penetration of their community by the Chinese societies.

There was one other of these allegedly purely Malay societies at Bota, but details are lacking. The Assistant District Officer in reporting on these societies stated that he had no proof that they fostered crime beyond assisting criminals and the fact that one society bred another for self-protection. He admitted, however, that the assistance given by the Malay police in providing information and investigating suspicious circumstances was negligible, which suggests that the influence of the societies was such that the police were not disposed to interfere, the more so because the report says that many of the leaders were young men of good family, and therefore influential in the world of the Malay policeman.

As to the suggestion that these were Flag societies and that they were linked with Penang, Jervois was unable to trace any connexion between them and the Red and White Flag societies of early Perak days. Unlike them, these 'Perak River Societies' as he called them, were, in general, 'purely local Malay'; on only one occasion had he heard of a Penang Malay being mixed up with them. They were mutual benefit and protection societies; there were provisions usual with Malay clubs for mutual visits in the event of illness, marriages, etc. He had the impression that as there had been doubt about the outcome of the Larut war, the people thought it wise to make provision against contingencies in this way.

This was a quite reasonable suggestion, for if there were any possibility of British control being removed, it was to societies such as these that the Malay would need to look for protection both against the Chinese and against other Malays. It would seem, however, that although Jervois obtained a certain amount of information, particularly lists of members, from informers and occasionally from Penghulus, he was unable, because of the atmosphere of secrecy and fear, to dig to the root of the matter. As far as can be ascertained, no suppressive action of any consequence was taken.

Nothing further is heard about Malay secret societies until 1920, when information came to hand that two societies, Red and White, existed in the Bruas area. Each had a Malay headman, but apparently once again these groups constituted Malay membership of Chinese Triad societies, said to be the Toh Peh Kong (Red) and the Yi Hing (White). Each had a local Chinese headman, and Chinese emissaries from Penang used to visit. Malays who were admitted went through a form of initiation which, from the scanty information available, would appear to be of Triad type. One member of the Red society mentioned cutting a fowl before the altar (To Kong), swearing brotherhood, and eating the fowl. Another Malay who was used as an informer by the Protector went through the ceremony of the White society when the middle finger of the left hand was pricked, and while looking towards the sky the Chinese headman repeated the oath. In both these cases, the oath of brotherhood was spoken by the Chinese headman in their own language, which was not understood by the Malays. They were told that the penalty for betrayal was death.

One initiation ceremony held on June 1921 was raided by the police, and 12 Chinese and 11 Malays were arrested. In the police records and the court proceedings in this case there was no mention of either Red or White Flag, but it is clear from the exhibits produced in court that the ceremony was Triad.

Indeed it would appear to have been an 'umbrella' Triad ceremony for the initiation of members of different societies. This is shown by the 'Foundation Numbers' which appear after each name in the list of people present, which indicate that people were admitted to three separate societies of the Brotherhood. Ten out of the fourteen initiates carried the Third Lodge numbers 4–9 after their names, so that it may be assumed that the Hoi San (Hai San) Society, or a derivative from it, was more numerous in the area than the others.[26]

One document contained the Triad secret language form of showing the number of new and old members present at the ceremony. The form is as follows:

Flesh. 1 Tahil, 4 Chis.
Bones. 6 Tahils, 9 Chis.
Total. 8 Tahils, 3 Chis.[27]

The interpretation of this is: new members 14; old members 69; total 83. The same form has been found on other Triad documents used in Perak about this time.

In the resultant court proceedings, two Chinese were sentenced to imprisonment and later banished. Fifteen others, Chinese and Malays, were bound over. Five days after the ceremony, the body of the Chinese agent who had told the police the time and place of the initiation was found. His skull was fractured and he was stabbed in the neck, the knife being left in the wound. It is probable that he was murdered on the same night as the ceremony took place.

One of the principal Chinese leaders of this society at Bruas who was arrested was among those bound over, and later in the year he is mentioned in a report from Lenggong in Upper Perak which had connexions with the Bruas society through the Penghulu who came from Blanja on the Perak river east of Bruas. The Chinese leader had been busy enrolling recruits in the Lenggong area, and correspondence seized in September 1921 mentioned that the 'Superintendent' of the society was a Chinese living in Penang.

Other indications of Malay interest about this time (1921) are to be found in information covering the formation of a Malay society by the Penghulu of Layang-Layang (Perak river) and the existence of a Triad society in north Krian composed of Malays and Banjarese, the headman of which also lived in Penang. Many Kedah Malays were joining, including Kedah police. Among the leaders were 3 Malays, 2 Banjarese, and 1 Chinese.

An attempt to assess the scope of the Malay societies in the Perak river area was made by the Protector of Chinese, Perak (A. M. Goodman), in 1922. In a report dated 3 July he said that as a result of the uncovering of the Bruas society in 1921, members had burnt their books, receipts, and membership tickets, but since then the societies had re-formed. They were of mixed membership having both Chinese and Malays, and existed for the purpose of mutual protection. He specifically referred to the societies as 'Red Flag' and 'White Flag' and gave their distribution as follows:

White Flag: down-river from Parit to Telok Bakong (i.e. about half-way to Telok Anson); thereafter a mixture of Red and White. Red Flag: from Parit to Simpang Ampat (Sitiawan). He added that practically all the small agriculturalists in the area had to belong, and it was practically impossible for an outsider to live in any of the river villages unless he subscribed to them.

[26] See App. 1, p. 532.   [27] The tahil and the chi are measures of weight.

Among the Malays, subscriptions were raised under the guise of contributions for religious purposes. Practically all the Penghulus and Assistant Penghulus were members. The report included a list of headmen in the Parit area belonging to the White Flag, which is also called the Sa Tiam (Three Dots). Apart from Parit itself, where the names of two Chinese headmen were given, eight Malay villages, the most southerly being Lambor, were listed, at each of which there was a Malay society headman. These headmen included three Assistant Penghulus, a Ketua Kampong (head of a small village), and a teacher in a Malay school. There were Kwangsais to the east of the river in the Bota Kanan area who were members of the society, and the headquarters were said to be in this area.

Unfortunately the only name given of the Chinese society is 'Three Dots', which was likely to be applied to any Chinese secret society. It was, perhaps, the Cantonese descendant of the Ghee Hin—the San Yi Hing—but there is evidence that there was also a Hai San Society in the area to the north-east of Parit along the valley to Ipoh. Nor is any information given about the Red Flag nexus in the areas nearer to the coast, though it is reasonable to suppose that it was descended either from the Hokkien Toh Peh Kong or from the coastal Ho Seng composed of Hokkiens and Tiechius, both of which societies would attract to themselves the Malays in the zones which they controlled.

In March 1923 an unusual document was discovered in the possession of a Malay at Bagan Datoh at the mouth of the Perak river. It purported to be issued by a Penang society with the title 'Kwong Lung Hing', and was written in Chinese in the form of a notification to the Malay members of the society at Bagan Datoh, empowering three Malays, whose names were given, to conduct the affairs of the society with justice and reason in accordance with the principles of the 36 Oaths, and instructing members to submit all matters arising between them, whether large or small, to the three persons named for decision. It was clear from terms used in the document that it referred to a Triad society. The 'chop' contained the name of the society in Chinese and in Arabic script. The Protector reported that this was the only case in recent years in which documents of undoubted Triad origin had been found in the possession of Malays. Its importance, however, was not merely that it was a Triad document but that it was a form of commission issued by a Chinese society in Penang to Malays in Perak appointing them to be agents of the society among the Malays in their district, indicating a high degree of organized fraternization for the extension of the society's interests.

The next glimpse of Malay involvement is in 1925 when some investigation by the CID took place. It was reported that the most important society in this area was composed of Chinese and Malays and was centred on Bagan Pasir, south of Bagan Datoh. There were two Malay and one Chinese headmen at this place, and a Chinese headman at Penang. The entrance fee had been raised to $30 to ensure that members would regard the society seriously. Many Malays of good standing were members. An initiation ceremony was held in December, and a description of what took place was given to the police by a Malay who had heard that there was to be this ceremony near his house and was sufficiently interested to make his way there and remain in hiding while the initiations took place.

The ceremony was arranged in a clearing of the undergrowth where several lamps had been placed on the ground, and it continued from about midnight until 4.30 a.m. There was an altar with a red candle upon it, and candidates stood in front of this with both hands together as in prayer. A fowl was cut and the blood collected in a cup. While this was taking place, the man (a Malay) who cut the fowl said: 'Whoever reveals secrets or betrays his brethren shall suffer the fate of this fowl.' The candidates passed under the altar and a man pricked their fingers and squeezed their blood into the cup. Then holding the cup of blood he threw it down on to a piece of wood on the ground, and as it broke said: 'We are of one mother and one father. Let anyone who deceives or betrays suffer the fate of this cup.' Then each candidate stood forward and said: 'I truly swear,' and each was ordered to dip his finger in the blood and drink it.

There is no reference to the presence of Chinese among the hundred or so people present, who were referred to as 'a crowd of Malays'. It would seem that the ceremony was of the Chinese type but was conducted by Malays. Four of the people present were arrested in the following June for complicity in a robbery. The police investigations and a number of arrests in connexion with this robbery damped down the activities of the society for a period.

Also in 1925 there was news of a Malay society away to the east in the Tapah area. There were said to be no Chinese members, and the society had a Malay headman in Penang. The nature of this connexion of Malay societies in Perak with Penang was not at the time understood, but at a later date it was discovered that a Malay club in Penang known as the Darul Ma'amur Football Club had been carrying out a recruiting campaign among Malays in Perak. This club, which was founded in 1920, carried on the tradition of the old White Flag Society with a Triad type of initiation, but it was not until 1925–6 that it attracted attention.

About this time some of the members in Penang broke away and formed the Jelutong Football Club, whereupon the Darul Ma'amur reorganized, introduced an attractive benefit scheme and a club badge, and pressed recruitment in Kedah, Perlis, Perak, and Selangor, drawing into its membership many members of the Malay police. The president of the club in Penang was Chah bin Idris, alias Mohamed Isa, a cloth-seller with a criminal record dating back to 1905, who was also on record as having been present at an initiation ceremony of a Malay society at Layang-Layang in 1917. The recruiting campaign by the Darul Ma'amur in 1926 resulted in a membership of some 1,300 and an income of $7,000–8,000 a year by 1927, but in December of that year the attention of the authorities was drawn to the secret society nature of the club by an affray between one of its canvassers and another Malay who was recruiting members for the Jelutong Football Club in the same village. The intervention of the police prevented a large-scale clash between partisans of the two clubs, and in March 1928 the Darul Ma'amur Club was dissolved by order of the Government. It was not until 1935 that the Jelutong Club was gazetted as having ceased to exist.[28]

These recruiting campaigns for the Penang 'Football Clubs' infused new life into the Malay societies along the Perak river. From 1925 onwards the head of the Detective Branch in Perak (Morrish) was busy collecting information about these societies and trying to unravel the ramification of society influence, and from 1927 this investigation was helped forward by the keen and painstaking

[28] Darul Ma'amur Club (GN 569, 31 July 1928); Jelutong Club (GN 2461, 20 Sept. 1935).

work of a succession of police officers stationed at Kuala Kangsar: Hussey, Duthie, Dalley, and Kemp. But it was slow work: each officer in turn was confronted by a curtain of non-co-operation by the general public due to the complicity of Penghulus, subordinate police officers, and wealthy Malays in the affairs of the secret groups, and the fear of reprisals at the hands of these repositories of power.

There was, apparently, one large Brotherhood extending from Lenggong in the north to the mouth of the river, with a branch at each of the kampongs along its length. The principal leader, Latif, lived at Telok Anson and moved along the river as the link between the village branches. He was also the link with Penang, where Syed Alwi was the head of the group descended from the old White Flag Society. There is evidence that there was a Malay ceremony of initiation (Wayang Melayu) for admission into what was known as the 'Ugama Melayu'. This was distinct from the 'Wayang China' which was the ceremony of admission to the 'Ugama China'.[29] For the Malay ceremony the chief constituents were a copy of the Koran, a cup of milk, and a knife. The Koran was placed on the head of the candidate, the knife was used to stir the milk in which, according to some accounts, a verse of the Koran (the 'Heart' of the Koran) written on paper had been placed. According to others, the paper was speared with the knife.[30] The recruit swore that he would not betray any member or reveal the secrets of the society. He then drank from the milk, as did the officer presiding at the initiation, and was shown a few of the secret signs. Various sources said that the entrance fee was $21 and the monthly subscription 50 cents.

There is clear evidence that this Malay Brotherhood was linked not only with the Malay secret society in Penang but also with a parallel Chinese Brotherhood in Perak which, too, had its headquarters in Penang. Along the Perak river most of the Malay landowners employed Kwangsai tappers on their smallholdings, and these men were invariably members of the Ts'ung Paak branch of the Ghee Hin Society which was strong in the Bruas area. From Bruas there was road communication eastwards to the mining villages on the west side of the Kinta valley: Siputeh, Pusing, Papan, etc., where, as has already been noted, there was a traditional residue of the Ghee Hin and of the Hai San societies among the Cantonese, Kwangsais, and Hakkas. There is no certainty as to the identity of the Chinese society to which the Malay Brotherhood was linked, but it seems probable that it was the Ghee Hin (in its Cantonese form 'Yi Hing'). Whatever it was, there was a procedure by which Malay members, after probation in the Ugama Melayu, and on payment of additional fees, could go through the Chinese ceremony including the cutting of a cock and the drinking of blood, and thus become full members of the Ugama China.

This was the position as far as could be ascertained at the end of 1925, though it is probable that this picture is oversimplified and that in the lower reaches of the river at least there were rival societies. But about that time, or perhaps earlier, there was a quarrel between a leader of the Malay society in the Kuala Kangsar area, Hashim bin Abdullah, and a man from Kota Lama Kiri named Megat Ibrahim. Both were wealthy landowners, and the cause of the quarrel lay in the marriage of Megat to Hashim's stepmother, a woman of property.

[29] Ugama = religion, sect.
[30] Wynne, p. 537, gives the verses of the Koran used as follows: 36: 1–38, 50–59, & 79–83; 18: 19.

Sometime after the marriage, Megat managed to get possession of his wife's property, to the discomfiture of Hashim. The result of the quarrel was that Megat with a number of adherents started his own society, known as the Orang Dua-belas (Twelve Men). They persuaded Latif, the Perak–Penang link, to accompany them to Penang where they underwent the Chinese ceremony, doubtless with the intention of showing that they were officially recognized and backed by the headquarters of the Chinese parent society in Penang—a warning to anyone who was disposed to cause trouble.

Once again, it is not known which society this was, but as Megat was accompanied by Latif, and as it is on record that Latif told 'Penang' that from then on the district would have to be treated as two branches instead of as one, it may be surmised that the Chinese society was the same one to which Hashim's society was already linked. Nevertheless, Hashim refused to recognize the Penang initiation and was very angry when Megat and his group arranged for a Chinese initiator to hold ceremonies in the area. From this time forward there was strife between the two groups, and in February 1927 an attempt was made to shoot Megat. It was commonly believed that this was organized by Hashim and his followers, but police investigations failed to produce any evidence worthy of being produced in court.

The rivalry between the old society, usually known as the 'Kaum Tua' or 'Old Sect', and the Orang Dua-belas, known as the 'Kaum Muda' or 'New Sect', continued, and their influence among the Malays of the area became paramount. In March 1928 an anonymous letter was received by the Sultan concerning the activities of the old society at Kota Lama Kanan, and giving the names of sixteen members, but the District Officer reporting on his investigation of the allegations was unable to give any information about the society. 'The Penghulus say vaguely that there is a society but state that no overt act had been done by it. . . . My impression was that there was little more than small mutual benefit societies.'

Meanwhile police enquiries continued. Hussey in June 1929 submitted a report in which were listed headmen of the old society in fourteen villages from Manong in the south, said to be the most active centre, to Lenggong in the north, and extending westwards to Bukit Gantang, in addition to District headmen at Kuala Kangsar. They included landowners, some of them wealthy, Assistant Penghulus, and motor-car drivers. According to his information, candidates at initiation had their fingers pricked, drank blood, and swore loyalty on the Koran. This would appear to be a fusion of the Chinese and Malay ceremonies, though it is possible that his informant was including items from both ceremonies. Members were known as 'Adek beradek', i.e. 'Brothers'. There is no mention of any connexion with a Chinese society, though it is known from later evidence that this connexion existed.

In March 1930 the police received information from a man who had been assaulted because he had not paid his entrance fee. Hashim bin Abdullah and two others were arrested, and one of these was convicted on the only charge which was applicable, that of assault. From January to April 1931 several gang robberies were carried out by a Chinese gang in the region of Kuala Kangsar, the victims in each case being Malays. It was believed that the robberies had been done in conjunction with members of the Malay society who acted as informers to the gang as to the possession of property and the movements of the owners. Petitions against Hashim were frequent. He was the possessor of fire-arms which were properly licensed, and it was alleged that he was in the habit of loaning these to the Chinese robber gang. In September 1931 the influence of the society was felt at Kampong Cheh where a man was murdered as a result of his misconduct with another man's wife. But coupled with this was the fact that the victim was a member of the Kaum Muda while his assailants were of the Kaum Tua. Furthermore, the headman of the village was the local leader of the Kaum Tua and organized a collection for the defence of the accused and actively suborned the witnesses for the prosecution. This was the third murder in three years at this village, and on each occasion police enquiries were thwarted by the reluctance of the headman or the villagers to help.

The persistence of police investigations into the activities of the societies was rewarded in September, when Dalley searched the house of a Malay at Kuala Kangsar and found a register of the members of the Orang Dua-belas dating back to January 1926, showing 224 enrolments in the Kuala Kangsar District, to which this society was apparently restricted. There was provision in the rules for non-Malay membership, but no Chinese names were on the register, and it may be assumed that any Chinese were catered for by the related Chinese society. There were, however, Indian names: the treasurer was a Chettiar, and two of the committee members were Sikhs who owned rubber estates in the district. The immediate result of this find was that 119 members who could be traced were summoned to appear before the Protector of Chinese, in his capacity as Registrar of Societies. All denied membership, and their photographs and fingerprints were taken under the provisions of the Societies Enactment.

The proved existence of the society also led to a discussion of the subject by a special committee of the State Council which was of the opinion that known leaders of Malay societies should be banished. This presented legal difficulties because most if not all of the people concerned were Perak-born and there was the problem of where to send them. The authorities unsuccessfully cast about for other suitable measures of control. In May, after consultation with the Government of the Colony, the legal objections were surmounted and warrants of arrest were issued under the Banishment Enactment against four leaders of the Orang Dua-belas, including Megat Ibrahim. The enquiry was held in June by the District Officer, Larut, who recommended that all four men be banished. Legal objections to the form of procedure at the enquiry were raised, and a further enquiry ordered, this time conducted by the District Officer, Lower Perak (N. K. Bain). He concluded that there existed in Kuala Kangsar District and in other parts of Perak a widespread, influential, and dangerous secret society and that the four prisoners were leaders. He recommended banishment, and this was eventually done after an application for Habeas Corpus had been dismissed by the Supreme Court and by the Court of Appeal. The four men were sent to Labuan, with the sanction of the Government of the Straits Settlements of which Labuan was a part. Each man was given a monthly allowance of $25.

The evidence given at this enquiry contains some details of activities and initiation ceremonies of the Kaum Tua and the Kaum Muda societies, though these titles are not used in the report. Neither is there any reference to these societies being either Red or White Flag: the Enquiry Officer merely said: 'It is . . . clear . . . that . . . there are two opposing branches of the society.' This seems to support the statement made earlier, that both were sections of the same society.

One interesting feature was that on the arrest of the four leaders of the Orang Dua-belas, three of the leaders of the old society, obviously fearing a similar fate, absconded and could not be traced. They included Hashim bin Abdullah. From the evidence given it is obvious that the ordinary processes of law were ineffective throughout the area. One Penghulu who gave evidence in secret declared that he never travelled at night without a pistol and torchlight, and never without a companion. He could not trust the village headmen, who kept him in the dark about society matters.

At the same time as action was taken against the four leaders, the Sultan of Perak undertook a royal progress down the Perak river 'for the purpose of showing his concern at the attitude of his subjects towards the secret society'. At every stage there were general expressions of loyalty and regret. The Sultan made it clear that all who confessed their membership and renounced future dealings with the society would receive his pardon.[31] The only recorded result was that eight penitents from the Parit area went to the Malay Assistant District Officer and made confessions to him.

There was one further outcome of the interest taken by the Government at this time. Because of the difficulties encountered in applying the provisions of the Banishment Enactment to local-born Malays, a new law was passed early in 1933 known as the 'Restricted Residence Enactment', under which such persons might be restricted to residence in any particular place in the State and could thus be removed from the area in which they had exerted a malign influence.

Despite these measures and a police campaign of increasing vigour against the Perak River Society (Perisoc) it was discovered that an initiation ceremony had taken place in March 1933 near Kuala Kangsar, and that the society still exerted influence in suppressing information about crimes, the number of which, particularly housebreaking and thefts, was rising. At last, in July 1933, the police were able to break through the wall of silence as a result of a housebreaking at the home of the Penghulu of Kota Lama Kanan, when the robber stole, among other things, a shotgun and a revolver. The arrest of a member of Perisoc in possession of some of the stolen property led to a round-up of 30 members, 7 of whom had previously been convicted, usually in connexion with housebreaking and theft; 27 of these men were charged in court as suspected persons and bound over on sureties of good behaviour. Seven were dealt with under the Restricted Residence Enactment. This was the first occasion that the power of the society had been seriously challenged, and this was followed by the cancellation of the arms licences of 14 known bad characters and the confiscation of their arms.

Further south, a keen Malay Inspector of Police, Raja Yahya, was stationed at Tronoh in April to ferret out the society ramifications in the area south of Parit. By collecting information and bringing suspected persons before the court to be bound over, he succeeded in a few months in reducing the incidence of crime in that region to a degree described as 'phenomenal'. In July he arrested a well-known leader named Hitam Samad who was concerned with rubber smuggling from the Dindings via Sitiawan. The society held a 'ronggeng' at a

[31] History of 'Perisoc', quoted by Wynne, p. 513.

lonely jungle spot to collect funds for his defence. This performance, at which a professional Malay dancing-girl danced, was attended by some 400 Malays and Banjarese who bought coloured paper badges, the proceeds of the sale of which went to the defence fund. Hitam was nevertheless convicted, and the arrest of some of the men who attended the ronggeng revealed further information about the society, not only in this district but southwards to Telok Anson and beyond, confirming police suspicions of its grip on the whole population. Similar rounding-up of bad characters throughout the region was undertaken. Along the southern reaches of the river, and particularly below Telok Anson where there was a mixed Malay–Boyanese population, many Banjarese were found to be active leaders of the society.

As in 1931, the Sultan was again brought into the picture, and on 28 September 1933 issued a memorandum to all Penghulus calling upon all members of the secret society (kongsi gelap) to appear before him to perform the Tobat (a public confession) under threat of banishment should they fail to do so. The result was astonishing: more than 3,000 Tobats were made by the end of the year. Thereafter it was ordained that future Tobats should be made by Statutory Declaration sworn before District Magistrates. In all, by the end of 1934, about 5,000 persons had performed the Tobat, of whom 2,000 came from the Tronoh area alone.

In part, at least, this mass urge to confess must be attributed to the increased police pressure on the society and the demonstration that the authorities were not powerless to bring the leaders to book. The Tobat gave to the people the opportunity to escape from the trammels of the society and to point to the religious authority of the Sultan as the mandatory reason for abandoning the oath they had taken. In addition, some of the leaders, foreseeing the probability of falling into the hands of the police now that information was being more freely given, undoubtedly used the Tobat as an insurance, not to be regarded as a serious renunciation, but providing a defence should they later be accused of secret society activities. Finally, it is possible that some who were not members of the society made the Tobat, partly because all their neighbours were doing so and partly as an instrument on which to rely should they be badgered to join the society in the future. Nevertheless, the response was remarkable and it affected people along the whole length of the Perak river.

One other event helped the Tobat: the arrest of Hashim bin Abdullah, the Kuala Kangsar leader, who had absconded in 1930. A warrant under the Restricted Residence Enactment was also issued against his brother, Sahari, in July. The latter, hearing of this warrant through society channels, also bolted before it could be executed, but returned in September to make his Tobat to the Sultan and then hastily left the district again. He returned in November with his brother Hashim, who also intended to make the Tobat before the Sultan to whom he had made a personal application. Before this could happen, both brothers were arrested, and after statutory enquiry Hashim was banished to Labuan for ten years while his brother was restricted to residence in Kuala Kangsar under police supervision.

Confessions of those making the Tobat made it plain that the influence of the society had not been overestimated. Several initiators were brought to light, against one of whom, Lassam bin Mat of Telok Anson, twenty-eight witnesses were prepared to appear to give evidence of having been initiated by him. He pleaded guilty to the charge of assisting in the management of an unlawful society. Seventy-five persons claimed to have been initiated by another man, Haji Hussain, who pleaded not guilty but was convicted. Yet another Malay, Mat Zin, was said to have initiated no fewer than 350 members, though no charge could be laid against him in court. One Master of Ceremonies who had initiated many Malay members by the Malay form of oath was a Chinese *ma'alaf* (convert to Islam) known as Lebai Ibrahim.

Among the statements made by those who passed through the hands of the police was one which gave the Malay terms for some of the ranks of the Malay society. They seem to be taken direct from Triad usage:

Tembaga (copper): Probably referring to the Incense Pot in the Chinese ceremony and meaning 'Master of Incense' or 'Initiator'.

Kipas (fan): Equivalent to the 'White Fan' of Triad.

Kasut (shoe): Equivalent to 'Straw Sandals'.

Tongkat (rod, staff): Equivalent to the 'Red Rod'.

During 1934 applicants for Tobat were still coming forward, and police prosecutions continued, but in May 1935 an initiation ceremony was held on a small island in the Perak river above Chenderoh Dam. The police were now better informed, and had, indeed, known for two months that the ceremony was in prospect. When the date was finally fixed, an ambush was laid and twelve Malays were arrested as the ceremony which was of Malay pattern, was about to begin. This was not at night time but at ten o'clock in the morning. The two leaders were sentenced by a Malay magistrate to twelve months' rigorous imprisonment.

Such was the improvement in the general atmosphere by this time that three Malay peasants were willing to give evidence in court, if required, as to the method of their initiation six years previously, though this did not implicate the accused in this case. One of the leaders, Ngah Latif, admitted that he had taken the Tobat before the Sultan in 1933. The other ten Malays arrested at the ceremony were bound over to be of good behaviour. Most of them belonged to a group known as the Sunlight Club of Taiping, an area from which less information had been obtained than from any other.

In addition to the sentence, the two leaders were ordered to be banished for life on its completion. The announcement of this decision was made by the Sultan himself in a proclamation once more warning all his subjects that anyone, including Rajas and Chiefs, and particularly those who had made the Tobat, who joined a secret society would be banished for life. The date of this proclamation was 7 August 1935, yet in the same month another initiation ceremony was discovered, this time at Kuala Kangsar in the house of a leader. Two men were arrested of whom six were identified from reports made in 1933 as having been members then. Four of them admitted having made the Tobat, but claimed that they had participated in the initiation ceremony under duress. As they were prepared to give evidence against the promoter, they were not charged in court. Once again the leading figure received a sentence of twelve months' rigorous imprisonment.

Yet another initiation ceremony of the Perak River Society took place in April 1936, five miles from Lumut in the Dindings. Five Malays were arrested, one of whom had made the Tobat, and all were convicted. Thereupon the Sultan called upon all members of the society in this area to make the Tobat, and some 300 did so.

At this point information about the Perak River Society ceases. It is not mentioned in the Annual Reports of the Police Department for 1937 or 1938, the last year before the war for which such reports were printed, and no departmental records survived the Japanese occupation. Had it not been for the devoted labour of Mervyn Llewelyn Wynne, who in 1933 was the Chief Police Officer, Perak, and directed the police offensive, and who later collected and placed on record all available material relating to this society, its history would not have been known at all. Even with this material the picture is far from clear, particularly as regards the possible connexion between the society and the traditional Red and White Flags. Wynne found himself in difficulty over this and said: 'We are nevertheless impelled to presume for what is now known as the Perak River Society a separate existence or at least a separate origin from the flag associations with which it is today inextricably mixed up.' Despite this, after reviewing the evidence available, he maintained that it was clear that throughout its history the line of cleavage between members of the White and Red Flag remained constant. In accordance with this concept he regarded the original society as White Flag and the Orang Dua-belas as Red Flag.

That the original society was a manifestation of the White Flag survival seems very probable, but the placing of the Orang Dua-belas in the Red Flag camp can only be regarded as not proven, and, as has been said above, there are good reasons for surmising that although opposed to the original society it was in the same camp. But in the southern reaches of the river there can be little doubt that there were adherents of both White and Red Flags, the former linked with a Chinese Triad society of 'Macao' background (Cantonese, Kwangsais, Hakkas), which may have been the Ghee Hin (Yi Hing) or the Hoi San, and the Red Flag linked with a Triad society of Hokkien (plus Tiechiu) background, which may have been the Ho Seng but might also be the Toh Peh Kong. It would also seem that the White Flag influence was more widespread than the Red, particularly in the middle and upper reaches of the river.

But leaving these conjectures aside, some things can be said with reasonable certainty. The first is that during the period 1900–7 secret societies were a powerful influence among the Malays in Perak, and that they existed in or near to zones where Chinese secret societies were influential. It is a reasonable assumption that in forming these societies the Malays were following the Chinese example, or even that they were instigated by the Chinese. It is clear that there was a special form of initiation ceremony for the Malay societies, but that the oaths of loyalty and secrecy were akin to those of the Triad societies. It is possible that in some places the Malay societies were not connected with the Chinese societies, but the evidence goes to show that usually they were so connected, and that they were, in fact, Malay sections of Chinese societies. But the evidence also shows that Malays were permitted to go through the Chinese form of initiation and become members of the Chinese societies. It is also possible that a ceremony combining elements of both rituals was practised by some. Next there is evidence that both the Malay and the Chinese societies in Perak regarded Penang as the headquarters of their Brotherhoods, thus following the pattern which existed in earlier years.

As to the part played by the societies in the life of the people, although there was apparently no direct interference with government measures such as the payment of land rents, it is plain that matters which should properly have been dealt with by the legal processes of the Government were settled instead by the societies using their own sanctions of power. There is evidence, too, that the societies included criminal elements, engaged, in particular, in robbery, who could rely on the protection of the society to avoid the legal consequences of their acts. The life of the village was largely under the control of the society headman. In addition to the official head of the village or area—the Penghulu, appointed by the Government and frequently from a different locality—there was an unofficial head, the leader of the secret society, normally the most important resident, often a wealthy landowner. At times the two heads coincided, and Penghulu and society leader were the same person particularly when the Penghulu was a local man appointed because of his prestige in the village or area. In such a case, loyalty to the society came first, for that is where the immediate power lay. If the Penghulu were not the society leader, then his official powers were undermined and his loyalty sapped by the pressures exerted locally and the fears which they engendered.

Attention must be drawn, too, to the religious content of these societies. The fact that the terms 'Ugama Melayu' and 'Ugama China' were used for the societies is an indication of the religious concept, and there is evidence that during the 1930s many 'Madrasahs' or religious meeting houses were built along the Perak river, and that these places were used for meetings of the societies. Collections for society purposes were also frequently made under the cloak of religious donations. The use of the Koran in the Malay ceremony, and the term 'Kaum' to designate sections of the Brotherhood, are further indications of religious associations. It is not suggested that these societies were developments of Islam, but, on the contrary, that their promoters made use of the religious practices and sentiments of the people to ensure the secrecy of society affairs, just as the Chinese Triad societies had harnessed their native religious practices to the use of the Brotherhood.

It seems likely that the attempts of the Government of Perak (including the spiritual-temporal influence of the Sultan) to suppress these societies met with considerable success, and lifted the weight of oppression from the people, though it is clear that promoters were not easily discouraged, and that the persistency which marked the Triad weed was also to be found in the Malay counterparts.

As for the rest of the country, apart from the State of Perak, there is no factual information available, merely the suggestion that Malay societies did exist in parts of Kedah, Selangor, Negri Sembilan, and Johore, but there is no reliable evidence, so that this review of the connexion of the Malays with secret societies must remain incomplete. Nevertheless, the story of Perak is of some value in revealing the potential importance of society influence in the life of the Malay population.

There is only one later note to be added. In 1949 there were reports that the Malay ceremony of initiation was being used at places along the lower reaches of the Perak river to form a Malay organization to support the Communist revolt, but apparently this did not develop, and the United Malay National Party (UMNO) had a greater appeal to the Malay peasantry than did the Chinese-organized Communist movement which, in any case, was not Triad in sympathy and frequently found that the Triad and similar societies were its most forceful opponents.

T

Part 3

TWENTIETH-CENTURY MALAYA

13

THE NEW CENTURY IN MALAYA

1. THE RISE OF CHINESE POLITICAL PARTIES

THE ferment of political change at work among Chinese students in China and overseas at the end of the nineteenth century had its repercussions in Malaya where extensions of some of the political parties made their appearance. As some of these parties later became involved with secret societies, it is advisable here to give a short sketch of their origins.

K'ang Yu-wei, the leader of the reformist movement in China, who escaped from the wrath of the Empress Dowager in 1898, had supporters in Singapore, where he took refuge in February 1900. After founding a branch of his Protect the Emperor Party he moved to Penang. The death of the Emperor in 1908 left K'ang and his party without a cause, but his presence, and his articles on reform in China in the local Chinese press had done much to develop a new political awareness in the Straits.

The second politically-inspired movement was the Chung Woh T'ong whose founder, Yau Lit, arrived in Singapore in 1901. Under the guise of reading rooms, lecture halls, book shops, and schools he established Chung Woh associations, first at Singapore and later in Kuala Lumpur and Ipoh, but his activities in the collection of funds for these projects led to his being accused of swindling, and he was banished in 1909 and went to Siam.

Sun Yat-sen, passing through Singapore in July 1905, was welcomed by Yau Lit, who introduced him to three local supporters of the revolution, Tan Cho Lam, Teo Eng Hock, and Lim Nee Soon. In February 1906, after founding the T'ung Meng Hui in Japan, Sun returned to Singapore where he started a branch of the League with Yau Lit's three friends as the leading figures. The Chung Woh T'ong joined this new organization *en masse*. Other branches of the League were formed at Seremban, Kuala Lumpur, and Penang, where there was great enthusiasm for the revolution.

From then onwards, Sun used Singapore increasingly as his base for the planning of revolts in China. Funds were solicited by offering for sale printed bonds of $100 and $1,000 face value, promising that the 'Chinese Revolutionary Government' would pay these amounts one year after its establishment. Loke Yew, the mining magnate of Selangor, was offered the rights to all the mineral resources of Yunnan for ten years in return for a contribution of $100,000 but he was too astute to be caught by this fly. For the smaller man there were 'protection passes' at $2 each, guaranteeing protection for the holder should he be in China at the time of a rising.

During 1908 about 350 Triad rebels who had participated in anti-Manchu risings in southern Yunnan on the borders of Indo-China were deported by the

French authorities to Singapore, and were looked after by the T'ung Meng Hui. They soon became a nuisance through their involvement in gang robberies and were eventually dispersed, some going up-country to Johore, Malacca, and Selangor. Apart from the Chung Woh T'ong, which was of Triad membership, there was no contemporary evidence of any organizational connexion between the revolutionary movement and the Triad societies in Malaya, though it is beyond doubt that there were many Triad members in the ranks of the T'ung Meng Hui. The only hint of such a link appeared as late as 1934 in a document prepared by the Chinese Secretariat, Singapore, which recorded that from 1909 to 1911 a Triad society in Malacca carried out a large number of gang robberies, the proceeds of which were sent to China to aid the revolutionary cause.[1] It is possible that the refugees from Indo-China were responsible.

Local disappointment at Sun Yat-sen's failure to stage a successful rising, coupled with accusations in the *Union Times* of embezzlement of party funds, caused him to move to Penang in 1909, where in the previous year the Philomathic Union had been founded by ardent supporters of the revolution, with the enthusiastic encouragement of Wang Ching-wei. During this period of political fervour, other centres of revolutionary zeal were active, such as the Chinese YMCA in Singapore and Kuala Lumpur, the Chinese Commercial School and the Chinese Free Dispensary in Perak, in addition to Chung Woh groups, usually organized as clubs.[2]

The success of the Wuchang Rising of October 1911 and the subsequent founding of the Republic caused a rush for membership of the T'ung Meng Hui. Party officials, alive to the situation, introduced a minimum entrance fee of $5, shopkeepers, traders, and property owners being expected to pay much more.

One element of importance to the political future of the Chinese in Malaya and elsewhere emerged from the ferment of propaganda and the eventual foundation of the Republic of China. The concept of a nation-state of China received great impetus. Hitherto there had been but little focus of national loyalties. Men had felt the pull of local ties, of the family, the clan, the language group, and the district or province from which they or their ancestors had come; there was a constant awareness of the superiority of the Chinese ethnic stock, and an allegiance to the cultural heritage, but little to the state as a political entity. Because of this, the Straits Chinese of the nineteenth century were able to declare themselves to be loyal subjects of Her Majesty the Queen of England, and there can be no doubt of the genuineness of their declarations. But once the Republic came into being, governed by men of Chinese stock and traditions and taking its place alongside other nations, a process of reorientation for Chinese everywhere began.

The Kuomintang

From the fusion of the T'ung Meng Hui with other parties, the KMT was formed in China in August 1912. A branch was formed in Singapore and registered under the Societies Ordinance on 12 December of the same year. It followed the Triad tradition by calling itself a 'Lodge', and was to be the head

---

[1] 'Historical Notes on Chinese Political Societies', *Monthly Review of Chinese Affairs*, May 1934.

[2] e.g. Man Wah Club, Ampang; Man Hon Club, Sungei Besi; Yi Man Club, Kuala Kubu; Man Wui Club, Tronoh; Man Min Reading Room, Ipoh.

Lodge in Malaya. Of the 8 principal office-bearers in 1913, 7 were British subjects, as were 9 other office-bearers. Among the leaders were the three stalwarts of Yau Lit's day, together with Dr Lim Boon Keng, who earlier had been a supporter of the Reform movement rather than of Sun Yat-sen. Another branch was registered at Malacca in July 1913, but registration of a branch at Penang was refused because of the highly inflammable local political temper. The Philomathic Union clandestinely took its place.

In the FMS four subsidiaries of the Peking Lodge were set up at Kuala Lumpur, Ipoh, Chemor, and Papan, while twenty other branches under the Singapore Lodge were registered in other parts of the Federation, mainly in Perak. In November 1913 the Peking Lodge was dissolved by Yuan Shih-k'ai, and this setback to Sun Yat-sen's fortunes was reflected in Malaya, where the Singapore and Malacca branches dissolved, as did five of the Perak branches. At the same time many members of the KMT in China fled to Singapore as political refugees, and in 1915 Teo Eng Hock informed the Protector of Chinese that about 200 persons 'wanted' in China for political offences against the new régime were then in Singapore, many having become schoolteachers. In this way the germ of political thinking was spread throughout the Chinese vernacular schools of Malaya.

During the First World War, there was little political activity among the Chinese in Malaya except for an anti-Japanese boycott movement in March–April 1915, when the Twenty-one Demands were presented to China by Japan. The KMT was in the doldrums, and the Chung Woh T'ong, whose total membership throughout the country was only about 1,000, was becoming identified with hooliganism. There was a gang robbery at Kuala Kubu in 1913, a fight with the Sin Ghee Hin (New Ghee Hin) at Sungei Besi in 1914, and fights with the Ghee Hin at Tanjong Malim in 1917 and 1919. As a result, many members were banished during the years 1915–19, though the Chung Woh T'ong was never wholly eradicated.

Opposition by China to the Versailles Treaty in 1919 led to a quickening of political interest, strengthened by the reorganization of the KMT and the proclamation of Sun Yat-sen in 1920 as the President of the 'National Government' formed at Canton. Emissaries were sent to Malaya to collect funds, and the local Chinese press reported that during the year $400,000 was remitted. A recruitment drive for the KMT in the Federation was very successful. The entrance fee was $10, and applicants were required to swear an oath of secrecy, obedience, and loyalty, which concluded: 'From this moment, I will abide by this oath for ever, and will not depart from it even in death. If I change my mind I will willingly accept the severest punishment.' The membership certificate, like the Triad diploma, recorded details of the member, his introducer, and the administrator of the oath, and the applicant was required to affix the print of the middle finger of the left hand, analogous to the pricking of this finger in the Triad ritual. Members were forbidden to join another society or to resign.

A tremendous pressure of propaganda was brought to bear through KMT branches, vernacular schools, and labour organizations. No one dared to refuse to join the KMT if approached or to pay the special subscriptions whenever called for. The Malayan Governments were embarrassed by these activities connected with a régime in China which was not the recognized Government, and were conscious, too, of the impropriety of allowing this propaganda full play among the 'Straits Chinese' whose representatives asked for protection from these pressures.

But the admission of Communists to the KMT in China, and the evident weakness of Sun's position from 1921 onwards, caused a cooling of enthusiasm among Chinese businessmen in Malaya, and in 1922 fourteen of the branches in Perak voluntarily dissolved. Also, the Hakka–Triad political association, the World Chi Kung Tong, supporting General Ch'en Chiung-ming against Sun, was founded in Hong Kong in 1923, and its propaganda influenced the Fui Chiu Hakka community in the Federation, still further weakening the KMT position. In 1925 sanction was given by the Secretary of State to outlaw the KMT in the Federation, and on 21 September the headmen were informed that all registered branches must disband within a month, as the Government had reached the conclusion that the existence of the society was prejudicial to the peace, good order, and welfare of the country. By 26 October, all these branches had closed down, and orders of dissolution had been issued.

In Singapore no new branch of the KMT had been registered since the dissolution of 1913, but various subterfuges had been adopted to keep the party in existence. By 1925 the principal channel for left-wing KMT propaganda was the 'Main School' movement, operating chiefly through Hainanese night schools for adults. From these schools a stream of anti-British, anti-Dutch, anti-Japanese, anti-imperialist, anti-capitalist, and Communist propaganda flowed, addressed mainly to the workers, who were to be organized in just the same way as the workers in Shanghai and other cities in China were being mobilized by the Communists. The field was promising, for the troubled conditions in China had led to an unprecedented wave of emigration of disgruntled vagabonds to Malaya.[3]

Action taken against sixteen of these Hainanese night schools in 1926, over forty arrests, and the banishment of leaders disrupted the organization, but a Nanyang General Labour Union was formed, also under Hainanese leadership, which, on Sun Yat-sen's birthday in March 1927, staged a riotous demonstration and attacked a police station, losing six men killed.

The purge of the Communists from the KMT in China in 1927 and the success of Chiang Kai-shek put new life into the dormant right-wing KMT groups in Malaya which separated completely from the left-wing groups. The National Government at Nanking proposed a comprehensive registration system to include all Chinese abroad and all their schools and organizations, to be carried out through KMT branches, and officially approached the British Government to permit the re-establishment of KMT branches throughout Malaya. The Malayan Governments remained firmly opposed. Even without recognition the spate of propaganda and the pressures exerted on Chinese in Malaya had again become embarrassing, and the arrival in February 1930 of a new Governor, Sir Cecil Clementi (from Hong Kong where the KMT had been banned), was the signal for action to suppress the unlawful branches in Malaya. Although the Nanyang General Branch, on instructions from the Governor, closed its premises and issued a circular to all branches announcing the dissolution of party organizations in Malaya, the General Branch continued

---

[3] Immigration from China was as follows: 1925; 214,696; 1926, 348,593; 1927, 359,262. The highest figure previously recorded was 269,854 in 1911. The figure for 1927 was the highest ever recorded, either before or since.

surreptitiously to perform its function and to convey instructions to other branches, and as a result, two of its leaders were banished.

There were diplomatic repercussions in China, and in February 1931 the British Minister, Sir Miles Lampson, visited Singapore for discussions. These resulted in the amendment of the Societies legislation permitting Chinese in Malaya to be members of organizations in China, but prohibiting the formation of branches of such organizations in Malaya. In response to this action, the Chinese Minister for Foreign Affairs (Dr C. T. Wang) informed the British Minister on 2 April that it was not proposed to establish party offices in Malaya. Yet on the same day a meeting of the standing committee of the KMT was held, at which Dr Wang and Chiang Kai-shek were present, to approve a recommendation to establish eight direct branches of the party in Malaya to take the place of the General Branch. Such are the vagaries of diplomacy. But although the activities of the branches continued, they remained unlawful.

At all times, the KMT in Malaya possessed the potentiality of becoming the supreme influence over the Chinese community. Nevertheless, it never quite achieved complete control, partly because of the action taken against it from time to time by the Malayan Governments, but also because of divisive influences within the community and the party itself. Some of these sprang from tribal jealousies, others from the fluctuations in power of the various leaders in China and from personal attachments, quite apart from the rift caused by the association of the left wing with the Communists.

The Malayan Communist Party

The Communist organizations which had developed within the KMT by 1927 continued to harass the Malayan Governments, particularly in Singapore where, in 1928, an attempt was made on the life of Dr C. C. Wu, a distinguished Cantonese statesman who was visiting the city. Later in the year Communists were concerned in a number of murders, and in the aggravation of a strike when bombs were placed in the shops of employers. The police seized 25 pistols and 2,000 rounds of ammunition intended for this group, and most of the known leaders were banished.

In 1930 a reorganization took place, and the MCP was formed under the Southern Bureau (Hong Kong) of the Far Eastern Bureau of the Comintern at Shanghai, and at the same time a Malayan Labour Union was formed as the Communist labour organ. The discovery in Singapore in 1931 of Serge Lefranc, an agent of the Far Eastern Bureau, uncovered the various ramifications, and for a time disrupted the party's functions.

From being (even as late as 1935) mainly a Hainanese movement, Communism spread to the Hakka, Hokkien, and Cantonese communities, among teachers, journalists, and workers. The anti-Japanese boycott movement provided an excellent patriotic theme for propaganda, and when, in 1937, a National Front of KMT and Communists was formed in China, and 'National Salvation' became the slogan of all patriotic Chinese, the scope and influence of the MCP, working through Relief Funds, Anti-enemy Backing-up Societies, and labourers' Mutual Aid Associations, was greatly enlarged. Through these labour associations, dozens of which were formed, large numbers of workers on mines and rubber estates who had not previously been organized apart from their secret society ties, were brought into the fold.

With all these national salvation projects KMT supporters were also involved, until they found themselves being dragged into an anti-British movement (following Moscow's policy of alignment with Germany) and into a series of politically-motivated industrial disturbances.

These troubles reached their peak in the middle of 1940, and then suddenly ceased, for Germany had attacked Russia, and the Communist Party ordered an anti-German, pro-British policy. When, in December 1941, the Japanese attacked Malaya, the MCP offered recruits for training in guerrilla warfare, an offer which was accepted by the Government, and these men later formed the nucleus of the Chinese guerrilla forces in the jungle under the title of the Malayan People's Anti-Japanese Army (MPAJA). This was, in fact, an 'army' of Chinese Communists, and in no sense representative of the people of Malaya, as its title would imply.

Later, when the Japanese forces reached Johore Bahru and the attack on Singapore was imminent, the Government sanctioned the formation of a Chinese Mobilization Council consisting of representatives of the KMT, the MCP, the Chinese Chamber of Commerce, and the Chinese Relief Fund Committee. Thus at this time of crisis the two main Chinese political parties, though still unregistered and therefore unlawful, were given official recognition.

2 THE TRADITIONAL SECRET SOCIETIES: STRAITS SETTLEMENTS, 1900–19

During the first two decades of the twentieth century three factors affected the Malayan scene and modified the immigration pattern—the emergence of rubber as a main crop, the revolution in China, and the First World War.

The cultivation of rubber was introduced experimentally to Malaya in 1877. Expansion on a commercial scale dated from 1895, but it was not until 1905 that rubber became a main crop. This meant an increase in the area cultivated and in the demand for labour which was still (as in the 1870s) more readily satisfied through the channel of unrestricted immigration from China than through the limited flow of individually-recruited labour from India. On the other hand, in 1908 the average tin price fell from $88.28 to $66.78 a pikul, with a consequent reduction in the labour forces at the mines and a serious increase in crimes of violence. In 1910 world demand for rubber produced a sharp rise in price, leading to further expansion and the increase in immigration to the record figure of 269,854 in 1911. This increased flow was also stimulated by conditions in China —floods, poor harvests, rising rice costs, and political disturbances and revolts in the early stages of the revolution.

The imminence of war in Europe in mid-1914 caused a sharp setback to the production of both rubber and tin. The smelting companies could not continue indefinitely to buy ore while the European market was closed or restricted, and the tin industry directly employed over 200,000 labourers. On 3 August immigration from south China and the Coromandel Coast was prohibited, and free passages to their own homes were offered to all destitute and unemployed labourers who wished to be repatriated. But whereas the number applying for repatriation totalled about 22,000, the labour force on mines in Perak alone decreased by nearly 30,000. An arrangement between the Government of the Colony and that of the FMS, whereby the former agreed to finance the purchase of tin and promised help to the rubber industry, prevented complete collapse. Nevertheless, at the end of 1914 and early in 1915 there was much un-employment. Total prohibition of immigration was maintained until the end of March 1915; thereafter there was gradual modification until the end of July when all restrictions were removed. By that time the shock of the declaration of war had passed, and tin and rubber were both in good demand. In the second half of the year the unemployed were reabsorbed.

From 1900 onwards the secret society pattern continued, on the whole, to reproduce that of the last decade of the previous century—recurrent emergence of local groups and constant pressure by the authorities to break them up and prevent their enlargement. Fluctuations of labour influenced the pattern, in-crease of immigrants revivifying the tradition, and unemployment encouraging the formation of criminal gangs.

Among the new societies in Penang were two which continued to plague the authorities for years, the Ban An T'ai and the Khien Khoon. The former took its title from a theatre of that name in Rope Walk and was of mixed Hokkien-Tiechiu membership. It had branches in the Tiechiu agricultural area of south Province Wellesley where opium smuggling through the creeks was a source of much profit. The Ban An T'ai was repeatedly in conflict with the Tiechiu Panglong Society which reappeared in the Province in 1904, and until the Japanese Occupation these two societies were the cause of trouble both in the Province and on Penang Island.

The Khien Khoon (Heaven and Earth) Society (from the characters used for the Heaven and Earth Hoop in the Triad ceremony) was based on Penang, with branches in the Province. It was disorganized by the banishment of its headman in 1901, but re-emerged from time to time. Two other Penang societies which were never entirely uprooted were the Ke Iau San and the Kampong Lai, the first of which became the enemy of the Khien Khoon.[4] In 1906 a revival of the Coffin Breakers came to light.

In Malacca, too, there were new formations—the Tong Hing Kongsi dis-covered in 1903, and a Hainanese society, the Tong Nam Heng, in 1908.

In Singapore five unlawful societies were uncovered by Hare in 1904, two of which, the Ch'ung Sun and the Chung Yi T'ong, had assumed the names and ritual of Triad societies. This would appear to be the first occasion since the introduction of suppression in 1890 that evidence of the survival of the Triad ritual was discovered, but Hare did not believe that the old dangerous societies were reviving. Thirty men were banished for their connexion with these five societies, and a Hainanese registered society, the Sin Nam Hop, was dissolved for complicity with one of them.

With the increase in immigration in 1905 (when more than 200,000 Chinese arrived during the year) it would seem that a decision was taken to use the power of banishment more freely against habitual or dangerous criminals. There were 50 banishments in 1903 and 65 in 1904, but in 1905 there were 394, and thereafter figures of this order and greater were usual. Among the immigrants at this period were many Hokchius and Hokch'ias from the region of Foochow, who swarmed into the Colony and became rickshaw pullers. Their speech differed so widely from that of other Hokkiens that they formed a community

---

[4] Ke Iau San (fowl's claws mountain) was a local name for Mount Erskine, Kampong Lai (Carnarvon Lane) was a street in Penang.

apart with a reputation for turbulence. In 1906 the Protectorate uncovered an unlawful Hokchiu society managed by men 'of the samseng class', the leader of which, when arrested, claimed local birth, and produced a Singapore birth certificate. Enquiries established that he had been brought from China as a small child, and that the certificate was that of someone else of the very common surname of Lim. The prisoner's father had died in Singapore, and in order to support his claim the son had hired a stone-mason to add to his father's tomb-stone the name of the father appearing in the birth certificate. An application for a writ of Habeas Corpus and a petition to the Secretary of State were un-availing, and he was banished.[5]

A new element in the field of Chinese relationships in Singapore came into existence in 1906 in the shape of the Chinese Chamber of Commerce, which was exempted from registration on 14 April. The Chamber was composed of leading members of the various language groups. In common with other Chinese Chambers which were to be established throughout Malaya, it was not con-cerned merely with commerce. The Chinese Advisory Board, set up when the Hoeys were suppressed, was a body of government nominees, and lacked the possibilities for intrigue in elections and discussion implicit in organizations set up by the people themselves. It was this lack of a socio-political representative group which the Chamber of Commerce supplied, and it became the leading representative body of the Chinese community. Thus in some degree, for ex-ample in maintaining contact with the people and in the settlement of disputes, it was the natural inheritor of the Triad nexus, and although it did not possess the disciplinary powers of a Triad tribunal, pressure could, at times, be exerted by it and through it to calm the people and restrain the mob.

An instance of this occurred in November 1906 when Singapore was threat-ened with a repetition of the Hokkien–Tiechiu riots of 1854. The trouble started on the 13th with a dispute between boat-coolies of the two tribes over the use of a mooring berth in the river, but soon spread throughout the town with mobs looting, assaulting, and robbing. The Chinese Consul-General in official robes tried to restore order but with no effect. A proclamation under the Preservation of the Peace Ordinance was issued, and the Chinese Chamber of Commerce was asked to warn the rioters of the serious consequences of continued rioting. The town returned to normal on the 17th after the arrest of 300 persons and a march through the town by the Sherwood Foresters which restored confidence, but it was acknowledged that the assistance of the Chamber was of great value. The Protectorate considered that no society, secret or not, had taken part in the disturbances, but the Commissioner of Police significantly criticized his Chinese detectives for failing to provide information about the riot, and Song Ong Siang suggests that the crowds were gathering 'apparently at the instigation of secret society headmen'. While this was not an inter-society fight, it is hardly credible that the hooligan elements of the Hokkien and Tiechiu secret societies would refrain from exacerbating the trouble.[6]

The tendency noted by Hare in 1904 for the small societies to use Triad ritual and titles was evident in subsequent years. A San Yi Hing (Cantonese form of New Ghee Hin) was discovered in 1905 among Cantonese blacksmiths and fitters in Singapore and also at Prai Dock, Penang, in 1906. In the same year

[5] GD 297, 27 July 1906; CO 273/318.
[6] CP *AR*, 1906; Police *AR*, 1906; SOS, 402–3.

the 72 Friends Association, the 36 Friends Society, and the Thung Yi Thong (probably meant to be the Chung Yi T'ong) were found in Singapore, and in 1909 there were Triad initiation ceremonies both at Penang and at Malacca. That at Penang took place in a house in Rope Walk (where the Ghee Hin ancestral tablets were housed). It was interrupted by the police and those present were prosecuted. Seventeen men were later banished. At Malacca the ceremony was rounded up by the Malay inhabitants of Paya Lebar who, tired of the depredations of Chinese gang robbers, became suspicious of numbers of Chinese going into a coconut plantation. They surrounded the place and captured twenty-two men who were sentenced by the court to six months' imprisonment for attending a Triad meeting. Seventeen were banished.

In Singapore the police report for 1907 remarked that there was little use in suppressing secret societies when the 'Seh Theam Whai' and other dangerous societies were allowed to flourish in Johore, and two years later it was found that there was also a brisk trade in Triad society membership tickets brought into the Colony from nearby places in Dutch territory such as Rhio and Muntok.[7] (Seh Theam Whai probably meant Sa Tiam Hui or Three Dots Society, a generic term for a Triad society.)

Apart from these indications of Triad survival and penetration, a White Flag society was found at Ayer Hitam, Penang, in 1908, and for the first time there was mention of a society with the title Wa Kei in Singapore. This was referred to as a development of the Coffin Breakers' Society which used the characters 'Wa Kei' on its seal, but whether this was a correct assumption or not, it was from about this time that the ritualistic Wa Kei Society developed an identity of its own, and began to spread throughout the Cantonese community in Malaya.

One of the old sources of secret society intrigue was removed at the end of 1909 when the excise farms in the Colony were abolished. A Government Monopolies Department was formed to take over not only the preparation and sale of chandu but also the collection of duty on liquors.

The increased immigration from 1910 to 1912[8] stimulated society activity, and during these three years Protectorate and police action against the gangs and unregistered societies was intensified. Of 1,267 banishees during this period, 247 were banished because of their connexion with unlawful societies, but it is a reasonable presumption that most of the others, banished for criminal activities, were also members of such societies.

Between 1910 and 1914 action was taken against forty-seven unlawful societies or gangs in Singapore and the pattern in Penang and Malacca was similar though on a smaller scale, and there is a hint in the police report for 1912 that there were active society members within the force. One registered society was dissolved in 1913 on the grounds that it was being used for purposes incompatible with the good order of the Colony and inconsistent with its approved rules. This was the Pineapple Cutters' Association which had been formed in 1908 among labourers employed in Singapore canning factories. Its original membership comprised men from the three tribes—Hokkiens, Tiechius, and Hainanese, and its first application for registration was under the title Sam Hop (Three in accord). This, however, was considered to be too close to the name of the Triad Brotherhood, Sam Hop Wui, and the promoters were prevailed upon

[7] SSPLC/19 Nov. 1909.
[8] Deck passengers from China: 1910, 216,321; 1911, 269,854; 1912, 251,644.

to change the title to 'Hok Tio Kheng' signifying a union of Hokkiens, Tiechius, and Hainanese. At the time of its dissolution most of its members were not pineapple cutters, and the society had been involved in a number of serious disturbances with unlawful societies. Though dissolved it continued for many years to be a power in the underworld.

In Penang the banishment of twenty-four ringleaders of the Khien Khoon, the Ke Iau San, and the Kampong Lai societies in 1911 checked a run of intersociety affrays, though the organizations still persisted.

In Malacca a Triad society composed of men from the Lui Chiu Islands was discovered with the title of Dong I Kongsi (i.e. Chung Yi Society). The leader and six of the members were banished in 1910, but this did not cause any abatement of the widespread assaults and robberies which continued into 1911, and led to the appointment of a Protectorate officer in April. The districts of Alor Gajah and Jasin were proclaimed under the Prevention of Crimes Ordinance,[9] and many of the atap dormitories in which Chinese labourers were housed were searched. On one occasion twenty-seven men were arrested, all armed with revolvers or pistols. After three months' imprisonment they were banished. It seems likely that they were remnants of a batch of Triad rebels deported from Indo-China in 1908 who had wandered up-country from Singapore, and who engaged in gang robberies. On the outbreak of the First World War in 1914, the Government were armed with additional emergency powers which were used to arrest a large number of known bad characters in Singapore who were subsequently banished, and in Malacca the Protector in 1915 helped the police to 'induce' 200 Chinese undesirables to leave the Settlement. It is noteworthy that during the anxious days of the Singapore Mutiny of the 5th Madras Light Infantry in February 1915, the Chinese underworld made no attempt to take advantage of the situation. According to an official report 'there was amongst the Chinese in particular all through the town and country districts an imperturbability which amounted to unconcern'.

A further step in the control of the spread of Triad influence was taken in 1915 when the Protector of Chinese, Straits Settlements, was given advisory powers in connexion with the Chinese Protectorate, Johore, which had been set up as a result of the acceptance by the Sultan in May 1914 of a British General Adviser. A Societies Enactment was introduced in Johore in 1915 bringing this state at last into line with the Colony and the FMS. On 1 July 1916 the Ghee Hin Society of Johore, the last remaining lawful Triad society in Malaya, was dissolved, to the relief of both Singapore and Malacca.[10] A

---

[9] The Prevention of Crimes Ordinance (XVI of 1902) empowered the Governor in Council to issue a proclamation whenever it appeared to be expedient for the prevention of crime in any Settlement or part thereof. Thereupon it was an offence for any person to be abroad in possession of any 'gun, pistol . . . or other offensive weapon' without lawful excuse. Penalty $100 or six months or both. It was also an offence to be abroad between 9 p.m. and 5 a.m. without carrying a lighted lantern or to loiter abroad or in the grounds of any dwelling house.

[10] Johore Enactment 2 of 1915. The terms were similar to those of the SS Ordinance. It came into force on 1 May 1915. The Order of Dissolution was dated 14 June 1916, but the procedure adopted was to register it on 1 July 1916 and to dissolve it on the same day for being used for purposes prejudicial to the State (GNs 75 & 76 of 1 July 1916). The assets of the society were used to buy property the income from which goes towards the support of local Chinese schools. An enormous token tomb was built in 1921 (called the Ming Tomb) in the Chinese cemetery at Johore Bahru (itself a Ghee Hin foundation) at which festivals of sacrifice are held in spring and autumn when Chinese schoolchildren are present *en masse*.

further development was the closing down of the gambling farm in Johore which for many years had provided great attraction for inhabitants of Singapore.

For the years 1916–18 detailed information is scanty for owing to a shortage of paper due to the war the annual reports of the Protector of Chinese were not printed. But it would seem that the pattern of small society fights continued. There was a spate of a dozen clan fights in Singapore, while in Penang eight secret societies were known to exist in 1918, including the old five—Panglong, Ban An T'ai, Khien Khoon, Ke Iau San, and Kampong Lai, engaged in their usual affrays.

With the end of the war came a collapse in the price of rubber and a fall in the price of tin, while the price of rice remained high. There was, too, bitter feeling against Japan as a result of the proposed provisions of the Versailles Treaty, leading to rioting in Singapore in May 1919, and in Penang and Province Wellesley in June. Mobs forced shopkeepers and householders to destroy goods of Japanese origin, and there was widespread looting and attacks on the police when they intervened. Order was restored in Singapore with the help of military patrols and naval parties landed from HMAS *Sydney*, while in Penang the Volunteers were called out, and HMAS *Sydney* again landed parties. The organization behind these riots called itself the 'Patriotic League', published inflammatory articles in the Chinese press, and posted up notices inciting to riot. It included members of the hooligan gangs who found through this channel a medium of expression. The anti-Japanese boycott lasted throughout 1919 and on several occasions bombs were exploded in Singapore at the doors of shop-keepers who showed a tendency to be defiant.

Legislation affecting both the Societies and the Banishment Ordinances was passed during the period under review. The Societies Ordinance was strengthened in several respects. In November 1909 an amending Ordinance (XX of 1909) was passed empowering the Registrar to order photographs and fingerprints to be taken of persons connected with secret societies, and to search any place where there was reasonable cause to suspect that documents relating to an un-lawful society might be found. In order to deal with cases when men were found in possession of membership tickets of Triad societies existing outside the Colony, a presumption was introduced that such a person was a member of such a society, and if the society was a Triad society it was presumed to be unlawful. There were other minor amendments including a fee for registration or exemption of a society, provision for the regular publication of lists of societies actually in existence, and the procedure for ascertaining whether a society was still in existence, and the right to initiate a prosecution with the sanction of the Registrar instead of the Deputy Public Prosecutor.

In December 1911 a further amending Ordinance (XXII of 1911) was passed in which it was specifically declared that 'every society whether it be exempted or registered or not which uses a Triad ritual shall be deemed an unlawful society', and persons found in possession of documents, etc., of a Triad society were guilty of an offence. Penalty was a fine of up to $500 or six months or both.

Another legislative venture concerned the Banishment Ordinance. As the law stood, a banishee returning from banishment faced a mandatory sentence of penal servitude for life upon conviction for this offence. The Secretary of State proposed to substitute for a first return, imprisonment for five years, for a second return, fifteen years, and for a third, penal servitude for life. When the

Bill came before the Legislature the unofficials, led by Sir Evelyn Ellis, unexpectedly objected to these proposals because they would weaken the deterrent to the return of banishees. Mr Tan Jiak Kim supported the opposition, protesting that the Chinese community had no sympathy with banishees, and, once banished, did not wish to see them come back. The second reading of the Bill (December 1914) was thereupon postponed, and no further action was taken. Later a consolidating Bill was introduced to combine, with some minor amendments, the various laws relating to banishment and the detention of banishees from the Malay States. It passed into law as Ordinance XVIII of 1915 on 27 August.[11]

3. THE TRADITIONAL SECRET SOCIETIES, FEDERATED MALAY STATES, 1900–19

Administrative reports for the FMS during the early years of the twentieth century contain few references to secret societies, which 'gave no trouble' in Perak in 1900, were apparently non-existent in Pahang in 1903, and in 1904 gave 'little or no trouble' in Selangor. Intermittently, there were reports of the banishment of individuals connected with Triad societies, and recognition by the British Residents of the efficacy of the use of the power of banishment.

In December 1901 Chang Keng Kwee, the last of the two 'Capitans' of Larut, died at his home in Penang, and in the following month Yap Kwan Seng, the 'Capitan' of Selangor, also died. On each occasion it was announced that the appointment of 'Capitan China' was no longer necessary, and these appointments were allowed to lapse. They were the last reminders of the former official policy of attempting to rule the mass of Chinese immigrants by delegating responsibility and authority to the men thrown up as leaders and representatives by the interplay of forces inherent in the Chinese social pattern. Throughout the years their executive powers had been whittled away as legislation on the western model had transferred to the courts or to the Protectorate the duty of assessing the rights and wrongs in both criminal and civil cases. But the leaders of the various Chinese communities, though no longer officially recognized as 'Capitans', still retained, until the 1930s, a high measure of prestige and were known unofficially by their old title. They continued to be the arbitrators of disputes within their communities, and were constantly consulted by the Protectorate in cases involving members of these groups.[12]

Nevertheless, although unlawful societies appeared to be well under control, there were occasions when they suddenly came into prominence in particular areas. A typical instance occurred near Kuantan, Pahang, in 1905, only two years after the opinion had been expressed that no secret societies existed in the state. The Belat valley, close to Gambang village, was a tin-mining area, and in 1905 a large number of labourers were brought to the mine to expand production. Before the end of the year a secret society formed by the newcomers

[11] GN 932, 10 Sept. 1915.

[12] In 1921 the Sultan of Perak appointed Towkay Chung Thye Phin, MSC, JP, to be Capitan China, Perak. This was the son of the former Capitan Chang Keng Kwee, but it was stated that the honour was conferred upon him at the personal wish of the Sultan in recognition of services rendered to the royal family of Perak, believed to have been of a financial nature (*FMSGG*, 24 Mar. 1921, p. 370; GN 1147).

was a cause of serious trouble, and continued to be so through 1906 until a series of banishment proceedings had removed seventeen of the important members.

It is clear, too, that in other mining areas secret society activity was taking place. In Perak a Hainanese 'dangerous society', the Hui Lan Kui, was discovered at Gopeng in 1907. In the Kinta valley a Cantonese society known as the Sam Pak Luk (360) came to notice in 1908 and reappeared frequently in subsequent years. By 1912 it was found that the Ghee Hin tradition was continuing in a Cantonese New Ghee Hin (San Yi Hing), the Hai San Society was operating among Hakka miners, while towards the coast Hokkiens at Kamunting (Larut) had formed a Toh Peh Kong Society.

In Selangor, too, there was evidence of the continuance of Triad. Three members were banished in 1906, and in 1908 fourteen men were convicted for the possession of Triad documents. In that same year a new Triad society, formed of Hainanese domestic servants, recruited about 600 members in the Kuala Lumpur area before being interrupted by police action. In 1911 the village of Gemas on the borders of Negri Sembilan and Johore was the scene of a night attack in March by a large gang of armed Chinese reported to be members of a secret society operating in Johore and Malacca territory. Carbines and ammunition were taken from the police station, and shops and houses were looted. But the most interesting development of this early period was the penetration of the Cantonese areas of the Federation by the Wa Kei Society. As in Singapore and Penang this society was also known as the Shui Luk P'eng On (Peace on Water and Land) from which it got the title of 'Four Character Society', of which there was a shortened form, Shui Luk P'iu (Land and Water ticket).

The Wa Kei did not come to notice in the Federation until 1912. Early that year the Protector of Chinese, Penang, reported that he was informed that all the detectives in Perak were mixed up with this society, and this, no doubt, explains why its activities were concealed from the authorities for so long. Investigations revealed that it was already a highly-organized Brotherhood operating throughout the Federation and neighbouring countries, with many thousands of members. Certain it is that from that time until the present day there has always been the closest connexion between Cantonese detectives (and their informers) and this society, and considerable skill and persistence have been required on the part of police and Protectorate officers to pierce this protective cloak.

Whereas its forerunner, the Coffin Breakers' Society, had been mainly concerned with thefts and swindles on board ships, the Wa Kei was particularly noted for the promotion and protection of gambling, with the usual additions of protection of 'sly' brothels, gang robberies, and blackmail. Throughout its history it has been a predominantly Cantonese society, and though some Hakkas have been admitted, Hokkien or Tiechiu members have been very rare. But among its members have always been numbered the actors in the touring Cantonese theatrical troupes who thus secured protection for themselves and their performances from interference by other gangs.

In 1913 a concerted attempt was made by the authorities to cripple the Wa Kei organization by making simultaneous raids in Perak, Selangor, and Negri Sembilan on places used by its members. Of the men arrested in this sweep, 121 were banished, 46 being from Kampar, Perak.

U

During the same year suppressive action was also taken against other societies, in Perak against the San Yi Hing, the 360, and the Hai San, and in Selangor against the Ek Sam Hui and the Hua Ju Ki, among others. This action is reflected in the banishment figures, for whereas the number of Chinese banished from the Federation during the years 1909–12 had averaged under 200 annually, in 1913 the number was 486, of whom 187 were accused of secret society activities, 76 in Perak and 71 in Selangor. But despite this repressive action the secret societies continued to exist.

During the second half of 1914 the dislocation of labour and the unemployment in the early stages of the war led to an outbreak of serious crime, particularly gang robberies, in the mining areas of Perak, Selangor, and Pahang, and parts of Selangor were proclaimed under the Prevention of Crimes Enactment. In 1915 the situation improved except in Kinta, where a gang of 20–30 Cantonese from the Ch'ing Yuen district of China carried out a series of armed raids on villages. Police stations were attacked and arms seized. Chenderiang was held up in October, and Menglembu in December, and under the leadership of Ch'an Lun or his comrades, Lung Wing and Lee Fong, who soon acquired locally something of the status of the traditional heroes of Liang Shan in China, these raids were continued in the area for several years.

Ch'an Lun was an old member of the Brotherhood, and some of the extortion demands issued by him followed the Triad pattern. From time to time information was received alleging that in a particular area the robbers had the support of a local society, the San Yi Hing, or the '360', or (less frequently) the Wa Kei (the '360', like the robber band, had a high proportion of Ch'ing Yuen Cantonese among its members). It was also suggested that from time to time small groups of these society members imitated the exploits of the main gang.

In 1916 the gangsters were responsible for raids at Kampar, Tronoh, Chemor, and Gopeng, and gang-robberies on a considerable scale continued, involving several murders of policemen and others. But in September 1918 Ch'an Lun and Lung Wing quarrelled and the band divided, Ch'an Lun and his men keeping in the main to the north of Kinta, based on the Chemor Hills, while Lung Wing's band operated from the hills behind Kampar in the south. During the early months of 1919, intensification of the collection of information by the Protectorate and scouring of the hills and swamps by the police led to the capture of some of the bandits from whom further information was obtained. Ch'an Lun was captured, armed, while taking part in the extortion of money from a shopkeeper. Though responsible for several murders it was not possible to prove this in court, and on charges of attempted murder and gang robbery he was sentenced to 15 years' imprisonment and 12 lashes. In all, 25 of his gang were arrested during the year. Lung Wing, finding himself hard pressed, fled to Selangor and thence to China, and with his departure and the capture of 22 of his group the menace of the Kinta valley gangs was, for the time being, removed.

It was the opinion of the Protectorate that the success of these gangs over a long period had encouraged Triad societies throughout the State, and there is evidence of this expansion in some Perak Chinese Protectorate files which survived destruction during the Second World War, and which reveal that while the secret societies did not constitute a major threat to the Federation or to the maintenance of order in general, they increased their control over the Chinese population, particularly in the mining areas which comprised most of the Chinese aggregations in Perak.

In 1914, at Tronoh, where the local Hai San had its headquarters in the Decrepit Ward (Lo Yan Yuen) for old Chinese miners, there was a two-day battle between the Hai San (mainly Hakkas from Chen Shang and Shek Lung) and the San Yi Hing (mainly Cantonese from Sz Yip). In the spring the '360' at Kampar and Ipoh gave trouble, and several of their members were banished. On the Perak coast, in the Kuala Kurau area, in addition to the activities of groups of Ban An T'ai and Panglong societies flushed from Penang by police action, there were three local societies, the Kwan Teh Yeh, originally founded about 1899 among local Tiechius on the north side of the Kurau estuary, the Kwan Sui Yeh, formed in 1914 by Hokkiens on the south side to withstand the pressure exerted by the Kwan Teh Yeh, and a Three Dots Society which in 1917 amalgamated with the Ban An T'ai group, while the two other local societies aligned themselves with the Panglong.

Meantime, in 1915 the Yi Woh T'ong, comprising Hakkas and Kwangsais, was discovered at Tronoh, and another Hakka group, belonging to the Ts'ung Paak Society (the Hakka component of the Singapore Ghee Hin) was found at Asam Kumbang, near Taiping. Between the Perak river and the coast a Triad initiation ceremony was held on the last day of the year near Bruas at which 100 men were said to be present. On the Krian coast the Panglong Society held sway at Parit Buntar, where all the employees of the existing four sawmills were members. They called themselves the Hok Hing Ho, and printed their membership diplomas on yellow silk which purported to be delivery orders of a Swatow firm of vegetable importers. Their rivals, the Ban An T'ai, remained very strong at Kuala Kurau, where the rice-mill labourers were members, and there was almost daily fighting between members of the two societies at this village. During the year 36 members of the Panglong were sentenced in court and 7 were banished. In all the police discovered 16 societies in the State, and the courts convicted 54 persons of membership.

In 1916 repressive action in Perak was directly mainly against the Tiechiu society in Krian, the Ban An T'ai, and against the Cantonese '360' in Ipoh, in each case resulting in several convictions and some banishments. The '360' had held an initiation ceremony in October at Silibin, five miles from Ipoh, and in the course of subsequent investigations it became known that there were several thousand members of the San Yi Hing in Ipoh town, with formations of the same society in existence at the surrounding mining centres of Kampar, Tronoh, and Chemor. At Gopeng there was a Hai San Society which was said to be teaching the cult of invulnerability, and it was reported that there were 300 members of the Wa Kei at Menglembu, which was, and still remains, the main Wa Kei centre in Perak.

In April 1917 a Triad initiation ceremony held at Kuala Kangsar was raided by the police while the ceremony was in progress, and 16 men were arrested, of whom 13 were convicted and later banished. During the same year a reorganization of societies took place among the Tiechius on the Krian coast, resulting in an amalgamation of the Three Dots Society with those remnants of the Ban An T'ai which had escaped the police net, and the Kwan Teh Yeh (Tiechiu) absorbing the Kwan Sui Yeh (Hokkien) and then joining up with the remaining fragments of the Panglong, thus forming two main camps. In March

1918 a drive by the police against these two groups took place, and many members were arrested, resulting in the temporary relaxation of the grip of the societies in this area.

Details of Triad activities in other states of the Federation are very meagre. In Selangor a Hokkien society known as the Ghi Ho Hin (or Heap Ho Hin) was discovered in the Klang district in 1914, and during the following year a Triad society at Kuala Kubu engaged in gang robberies and dealings in arms was brought to book through temporarily stationing a Protectorate officer in the town. There were frequent discoveries of Triad documents, and many convictions for Triad membership, and blackmailing gangs operating in the State in 1919 were also believed to be Triad organizations. In April 1914 an Assistant Protector of Chinese was appointed for the first time in Negri Sembilan, and was very successful in obtaining evidence of Triad activity. The highlight of the period in this State was the raiding of an initiation ceremony at Kuala Pilah in July 1917 which resulted in 93 arrests, 72 convictions, and 5 banishments.

According to the report of the Secretary of Chinese Affairs at the end of 1919, Triad societies existed in all the states of the Federation, and evidence had been obtained of the close connexion between Triad societies and gang robbery and other organized crime. Links between societies in north Perak and Kedah had also been found.

In addition to Triad societies proper, it was known that there were branches of the Chung Woh T'ong and the Wa Kei societies throughout the Cantonese communities of the Federation. The former, the politico-secret brotherhood originally formed by Yau Lit, was invariably found under the guise of reading rooms, literary institutes, or libraries, a subterfuge which at times enabled branches to obtain registration under the Societies Enactment. They differed little from other hooligan and Triad societies with which they frequently clashed. They protected their members, fought their battles, and exerted their influence on the populace through the traditional secret society channels. A raid on the premises of the branch at Sungei Besi (Selangor) in 1919 resulted in the conviction of 24 members and the banishment of 15. The Wa Kei was reported to be more widespread and powerful than ever.

In the legislative field, the first Federal Societies Enactment, based on the Colony Ordinances of 1909 and 1911, was passed in 1913 (No. 20 of 1913) and came into force on 13 February 1914. An amendment to the Banishment Enactment was also passed in 1914 providing for a maximum term of five years' imprisonment for returning from banishment for the first time. (In the Colony a similar amendment was opposed by all the unofficial members and was not adopted.)

Although little is said in the brief official reports, there can be no doubt that during the years of the First World War there was a serious recrudescence of unlawful societies throughout the Federation, and that the use of Triad ritual was widespread, and it was some considerable time before the strenuous efforts of police and Protectorate aided by extraneous political influences reduced the Triad threat to reasonable proportions. One result of the all-pervading Triad influence in Perak was the re-emergence of Malay societies and mixed Chinese–Malay societies using the Triad ritual, as already recounted.

14

RESURGENCE AND REPRESSION, 1920–38

DURING the period 1920–9 the impact of secret societies became decidedly greater, at least in Singapore, and an important factor in this resurgence was a trend towards the amalgamation of the scattered societies into fewer larger groups. The most notorious of these were the Sin Ghee Hin (New Ghee Hin) and the Sin Kongsi among the Hokkiens, and the Hok Tio Kheng (commonly known as the Sa Ji or 'Three Characters') which after its dissolution in 1913 had developed as a Tiechiu secret society. The Cantonese societies never coalesced to the same extent, but among them the Heng Alliance, the Khwan Yi, and the San Wui Khwan were all of considerable size. Moreover, it became apparent that these larger groups tended to belong to one or other of two types: those which used the Triad ritual and those which did not. This placed the Sin Ghee Hin (ritualistic) facing its rival the Sin Kongsi among the Hokkiens, and the Sin Tong Hua (ritualistic) facing the Hok Tio Kheng among the Tiechius. Among the Cantonese, the Heng Alliance (ritualistic) faced the Khwan Yee and/or the San Wui Khwan.

The revival of the Triad ritual with its oaths and mystic symbolism undoubtedly gave an added prestige and sense of unity and cohesion to those societies which used it, but the risk of arrest at a ceremony or in possession of easily-identifiable Triad diplomas of membership was ever present, and after seven initiation ceremonies had been raided by the police in 1929 the urge to revive the use of the ritual seems to have weakened. But in the meantime the struggle for power between the Sin Ghee Hin and the Sin Kongsi, and between the Sin Tong Hua and the Hok Tio Kheng, convulsed Singapore through many turbulent years, and when at last a measure of peace was restored, the Sin Ghee Hin started fresh activities in Penang and Malacca.

The power of the societies reached two peaks of aggression in 1922 and 1927, when recourse was had to the settlement of disputes within the Chinese community by leaders of the Hoey Kwans or the Chinese Chamber of Commerce, at the request and with the support of the Chinese Protectorate, a situation analogous to the days of Pickering, except that the Hokkien Hoey Kwan and the Chinese Chamber of Commerce had taken the place of the heads of the Hoeys in the arbitration of disputes.

The threat presented by the upsurge was met first by amendments to certain Colony laws which increased penalties and gave the Protectorate and police added powers. But these measures were insufficient and were followed by a complete reorganization of the police during 1927–30, along the lines recommended by Mr G. C. Denham, formerly of the Ceylon Police, who was the IGP from 1923 to 1925, and who had been appointed specifically to advise on reorganization. When this was complete, the Protectorate gradually handed over the work of detection and suppression of secret societies to specialized branches of the CID equipped with modern techniques of crime detection, and staffed by officers, detectives, and translators conversant with the Chinese language. The 'dual control' ended in 1933.

A further measure in another sphere, namely the introduction of a law to provide for the restriction of Chinese immigration with effect from August 1930, enabled the Government to vary the volume of new immigrants in accordance with the needs of Malaya's main industries—tin and rubber—and the lessening of the flood of new arrivals year by year was a positive contribution to the control of secret societies.

As Singapore dominates the scene in the police and Protectorate reports of the 1920s, Penang and Malacca are treated here in separate sections. In addition to the Annual Reports, two special Protectorate reports on Chinese secret societies in Singapore were printed in 1929 and 1930: *Tio Chiu and Hokkien Unlawful Societies in Singapore* (Dec. 1929); *Cantonese Secret Societies in Singapore* (1930). These two reports reveal the extreme complexity of secret society relations in Singapore. They are also evidence of the difficult problem faced by Protectorate and police officers in attempting to elucidate the dark channels and of the painstaking care required to fit the pieces of the puzzle together.[1]

1. SINGAPORE, 1920-9

The decade 1920-9 opened quietly enough with nothing more serious than a few society, tribal, or clan fights in any of the Settlements. In Singapore early in the year there was some street fighting the responsibility for which, the police suspected, lay with the Sin Ghee Hin. In addition there were two disturbing clan fights, one between the Tans and the Gohs in Hokkien Street, and the other between the Seahs and the Lows in and around Boat Quay, in both of which several people were injured and in the first of which one man was killed. The raiding of a Triad initiation ceremony sponsored by the Sin Ghee Hin in November gave further evidence of the revival of this society.[2]

Owing to the world depression economic storm clouds were gathering. Fortunately the rice shortage had ended so that one cause of discontent had been removed, but from the early autumn of 1920 the prices of both tin and rubber fell seriously. Depression in trade was a dominant feature of 1921, and all communities suffered. There was some Chinese unemployment chiefly among up-country labourers formerly employed in mines or on railway construction, but nevertheless tens of thousands of new immigrants from China were added to the population.[3]

Lack of employment led to an increase in gang robbery and other crimes of violence. Singapore was subjected to an influx from adjacent areas of men in search of work, lacking which they turned to crime. Arms were easily obtainable,

---

[1] The Singapore Reports were by J. A. Black (1929) and S. E. King (1930) respectively. A third report, *Hokkien and Tiechiu Secret Societies in Penang*, was prepared in 1930 by R. Ingham, Protector of Chinese, but no copy appears to have survived.

[2] CP *AR*, 1920, paras 15, 38; SS Police *AR*, 1920, paras 80–81.

[3] During 1921, 191,043 arrived by sea; 98,986 Chinese deck passengers left Singapore for China. Excess of immigrants over emigrants: 92,057 (CP *AR*, 1921, paras 1, 6).

for automatic pistols of German manufacture were being smuggled into most Eastern countries by the crews of vessels trading with Northern Europe, and though many seizures were made, enough escaped the net to cause the police anxiety.[4] It is not therefore surprising to find that during 1921 secret society activities increased. There was much street fighting, one serious outbreak occurring in March among Tiechius as a result of a gambling quarrel at Chinese New Year. In August there were brawls between gangs from Bali Lane and two Surname Tan gangs from Hokkien Street. But the Sin Ghee Hin were the worst offenders, and in November they fought a combination of all the Hokkien Surname Tan gangs, and then the Sin Kongsi gangs. Many arrests were made, and in all 360 men were banished.[5]

The situation continued to deteriorate during 1922. It became a common occurrence for Cantonese hooligans belonging to rival gangs to engage in gun duels in the streets. After one man had been sentenced to death and executed, this form of fighting became less popular. These gangs lived largely by organizing gambling and by gang robbery, and a series of combined raids by the Protectorate and the police on Cantonese gaming centres, particularly at the Harbour Board lines where 113 men were arrested and later convicted, helped to dislocate their activities. This was followed by the round-up of a dangerous gang at Sin Koh Street in November when a determined fight resulted in 1 gangster being shot dead, 3 wounded, and 23 arrested, 1 constable and 2 detectives were wounded. Several of those arrested were banished.

Fighting of a less serious nature between Tiechiu pangkengs[6] and gangs in the Kampong Malacca district also continued sporadically until August, when three men were sentenced to death for murder and two were executed. Two of these men had taken refuge at Pulau Minyak, the island hiding-place of the Hok Tio Kheng, and were discovered during a combined raid of the Protectorate and the police. The gambling promoted by the Tiechiu gangs in Kampong Malacca was suppressed, and constant visits to the pangkengs by the Protectorate and the police kept down the fighting until the end of the year, when yet another secret society murder was committed.

The feud between the Sin Ghee Hin and the Sin Kongsi increased in intensity during 1922 as the former society tried to extend the sphere of its operations at the expense of its rivals. Of these, the Sin Kongsi became allied with the surname Tan pangkengs against the Sin Ghee Hin, and both sides resorted to forcible recruitment and widespread extortion. Many murders were committed but none was brought home, and both sides were thus encouraged to commit further acts of violence. Although arrests and prosecutions were numerous, the violence continued.

[4] *Statistics of Serious Crime, 1919–21*

	1919	*1920*	*1921*
Murder	31	46	70
Attempted murder	13	8	19
Gang robbery	24	65	106
Robbery	96	122	172

(SS Police *AR*, 1921, para. 114.)

[5] CP *AR*, 1921, para. 14; SS Police *AR*, 1921 & SS *AR*, 1921.

[6] A pangkeng is a room hired by a group for the use of its members as a dormitory, meeting-place, and depository for baggage.

The first clash came early in January when there was a serious fight between the Sin Ghee Hin and the Hok Tio Kheng, its Tiechiu rival. At the end of the same month the Sin Ghee Hin made an apparently unprovoked attack with knives and poles on the spectators of a wayang in Upper Circular Road, when four men were killed and several wounded. On 9 February the same society held an initiation ceremony off Serangoon Road. This was raided by the police who had advance information, and 26 men and 1 woman were arrested and convicted. Shortly afterwards, when the Sin Kongsi marched armed through the streets on their way to avenge insults by the Sin Ghee Hin, 17 men were arrested and later convicted.

The raid on the initiation ceremony and the arrest and banishment of some of the leaders of the Sin Ghee Hin, the Sin Kongsi, and the Hokkien surname Tan pangkengs brought a lull in these disturbances, but there was a recrudescence in July though with a change of tactics. In addition to the street clashes, deliberate attacks were made by small groups on individuals belonging to the rival party, and in the succeeding three months no fewer than 38 cases of stabbing and 2 of shooting were reported to the Protectorate, including 7 murders. The attacks were so carefully planned that the assailants escaped without difficulty on each occasion. Apparently undeterred by any fear of the authorities, another initiation ceremony was held by the Sin Ghee Hin on 21 August near Jervois Road, and the police, again forewarned, arrested 15 of those present.

Responsible Chinese began to take alarm at the repeated street assaults, and a meeting of the Chinese Advisory Board in October discussed the lawlessness of the Hokkien unlawful societies. In November the president and Committee of the Hokkien Hoey Kwan and the heads of the Hokkien clans, with the encouragement of the Protectorate, formed an arbitration board which quickly proved its usefulness by taking up quarrels and settling them before too much damage had been done. This was a new development. In the days before the suppression, the Hoey Kwans had kept out of secret society disputes. Gradually, as further banishments took effect, the number of affrays began to diminish. During the year 339 aliens were banished, and 99 persons were convicted for offences against the Societies Ordinance, of whom 62 were Triad members. Cases against 22 others were pending at the end of the year.

The Protectorate, in referring to this 'exceptional lawlessness', attributed it to three main causes: the slump which had thrown many able-bodied men out of work, wholly or partly; the struggle to take possession of areas of extortion by the Sin Ghee Hin and the resistance of their established rivals; and the influence of unsettled conditions in China and of communistic ideas brought in from China.

The work of the arbitration board continued into 1923 and contributed to a reduction in the number of outbreaks of violence between the Sin Ghee Hin and the Sin Kongsi, but there were, nevertheless, two periods of serious disturbance, one in February and March, and the other in July and August, while organized extortion and robbery by the hooligans of both sides increased throughout the year, and spread to the country areas as well as in the town. Tongkangs in the river about to sail were also targets for organized robbery.

The trouble in February and March took the form of a series of stabbings by small groups of men, with several murders. The feud was eventually settled by the Hokkien Hoey Kwan. But the outbreak at the end of July was far more serious. It originated in a quarrel between the Sin Tong Hwa and the Hok Tio Kheng, both Tiechiu societies, but it eventually involved the whole of the Sin Ghee Hin and the Sin Kongsi with their supporters.

The Sin Tong Hwa had been formed in 1921 as the Tiechiu branch of the Sin Ghee Hin and had recruited many members. In 1922 the large unlawful Tiechiu society, the Hok Tio Kheng, became affiliated to it, but the two societies quarrelled as to the right to 'collect' in the country districts of the islands for the Seventh Moon Festival, and the Hok Tio Kheng thereupon dissolved the alliance, and became the inveterate enemy of the Sin Tong Hwa. In the next move, the Hok Tio Kheng was joined by another unlawful society, the Chiau An Hop Soon Hin (a society of Hokkiens from Chiau An), which nursed a grudge against the Sin Ghee Hin for the murder of one of their members earlier in the year. The Sin Kongsi was also drawn in as an ally, whereupon the whole of the Sin Ghee Hin took up the struggle in support of the Sin Tong Hwa, and what had been a minor inter-society quarrel became a struggle between the two main rival camps in the secret society underworld. The order of battle was thus:

Sin Ghee Hin (Hokkien) versus
Sin Tong Hwa (Tiechiu)

Sin Kongsi (Hokkien)
Hok Tio Kheng (Tiechiu)
Hop Soon Hin (Hokkien)

Fighting began on 3 August in River Valley Road and Boat Quay; on 8 August the Sin Ghee Hin attacked the Sin Kongsi people with spears and knives at Macpherson Road, and on the 11th two members of the Hop Soon Hin were murdered in broad daylight by a large body of armed men who marched down Geylang Road to the scene of the murder. On the 17th the fighting at River Valley Road and Boat Quay flared up again. Arrests by the police brought a lull, and two men, one of whom was of the so-called 'inner council' of the Sin Ghee Hin, were convicted and executed for the murder of the Hop Soon Hin men at Geylang.

Another street fight, of a 'tribal' nature and unrelated to the secret society complex, took place when the Hokch'ia and Hinghwa rickshaw pullers quarrelled over the right to occupy the rickshaw stands outside the large hotels, but this did not develop any further.

There was considerable public uneasiness voiced in the press and in the Legislative Council over the prevalence of crimes of violence, and at a meeting of the Council in October an unofficial member, Mr Tan Cheng Lock,[7] proposed that a Committee be formed consisting of 'trustworthy and energetic representatives of the Chinese community . . . to be chosen from all over the city of Singapore so that each section of the city, each street, perhaps, or group of streets, will have one representative'. In that way, he thought, the criminals would be brought to book, and information would be obtained of the persons who caused the trouble. This was exactly the same suggestion as had been made in 1854 after the Singapore Riots, but nothing came of it on either occasion. It was a cumbrous device, and one which would have been attended with the same tendencies to abuse and corruption as was the system of working through the heads of the secret societies before their proscription.

In December a Bill was introduced by the Government to amend the criminal law by increasing the penalties for offences under the Arms and Explosives

[7] Later Dato' Sir Cheng Lock Tan, KBE, DPMJ, JP.

Ordinance, and adding thereto the penalty of flogging which was also prescribed for various forms of extortion. During the debate Mr Tan Cheng Lock, while admitting that a condition of unprecedented lawlessness existed, regarded it as a temporary phase and considered that flogging was unnecessary. Another member, Mr Lowther Kemp, referred to a report of a recent case in Singapore: 'Men marching with flags flying and bands playing and murdering a compatriot in his own house.' In such a situation he considered that an extremely drastic remedy was required. The Bill duly passed into law.

Meanwhile the Protectorate and police had the good fortune once more to arrest a large gang returning from another initiation ceremony at Seletar, of whom eighteen were convicted, and every effort was being made to round up all the known headmen and leading samsengs belonging to the Sin Ghee Hin and the Sin Kongsi. The arrest and banishment of many of these caused some of their companions to leave the Settlement, at least temporarily, and to transfer their activities to Penang, Malacca, and the Malay States. The police strengthened and increased their patrols in the bad areas and rewards for information were greatly increased. It was also proposed to recruit from India a Special Armed Police of picked men to deal with street battles. During the year 76 persons were convicted of offences under the Societies Ordinance.[8]

The efforts of the authorities and the removal of society leaders appear to have had some effect, aided, perhaps, by improved employment conditions resulting from the introduction of the rubber restriction scheme in November 1922. A few isolated cases of assault and extortion occurred among the Chinese hooligan gangs; reports of extortion and robbery by the Sin Ghee Hin and the Sin Kongsi were much fewer than usual; rivalry between Hainanese hooligan gangs (the Kheng Hoa and others) led to some small affrays, and there were internal brawls among the Hokch'ia and Hinghwa branches of the Sin Ghee Hin and the Sin Kongsi, possibly an echo of the rickshaw fight of the previous year. The only serious outbreak of the year was a fight between the Tiechiu Sin Tong Hwa and a combination of several pangkengs of the Tiechiu surname Tan clan. It began in August in the Kampong Malacca district arising from a petty dispute between two labourers who took the quarrel to their respective societies. According to the Protectorate report:

> After a few small affrays it was evident that operations on a larger scale were contemplated, but these were frustrated by the removal of collections of fighting poles from pangkengs by the Police and the Protectorate, and by other Police precautions, and both sides then engaged in a series of stabbings, assaults and robberies committed by small armed parties on single individuals, under such carefully chosen circumstances as to make prosecution very difficult. Several persons were murdered in and near Kampong Malacca, including one man shot with a revolver, and others seriously wounded.

Once again, however, close co-operation between the police and the Protectorate resulted in the arrest and banishment of many known headmen and fighters of both sides, and the disturbances subsided at the end of September.

In the meantime the reorganization and strengthening of the police force was continuing, strong patrols were maintained in the bad areas, and particular attention was paid to the thieving on the Singapore river and on immigrant steamers.

[8] CP *AR*, 1923; SS Police *AR*, 1923.

But by 1925 the underworld had regained its impetus, and trouble broke out again with frequent use of firearms. At intervals throughout the year the Cantonese gangs made vicious attacks upon one another, usually for some trivial cause, and in the Hokkien and Tiechiu world the old rivalry between the two camps burst into flame once more. In May tongkang and twakow[9] men of the Hokkien branches of the Sin Ghee Hin and the Sin Kongsi came to blows on several occasions and the Hokkien river traffic which handled the rice trade came to a standstill. The Protectorate and police were able to get sufficient incriminating evidence to arrest twelve of the fighters and leaders on banishment warrants, and the dispute died down. A deputation of twakow owners and rice merchants then asked for the warrants to be withdrawn on the ground that a settlement of the 'temporary differences' between the two sides was about to be reached but was being jeopardized by the arrests. The request was refused and the deputation in their turn refused to give any information as to how these negotiations were taking place. Whatever they were, the 'peace' was disrupted again in September and recourse was had once more to action under the Banishment Ordinance.

And then in December came the worst outbreak of the year, this time between the two Tiechiu societies, the Sin Tong Hwa and the Hok Tio Kheng, once again through trouble on the river. The Hok Tio Kheng attacked the Sin Tong Hwa and a series of shootings and stabbings ensued in the Boat Quay area and at Pulau Minyak, the hideout of the Hok Tio Kheng. Two deliberate murders were committed and at least twenty-two men were wounded. New and unknown fighting-men were employed for isolated attacks on individuals and were difficult to trace. Very little information was forthcoming, and the outbreak continued for several weeks. In the midst of the trouble, overtures were made through the Protectorate to establish an agency for the collection of intelligence against the two opposing parties provided that, should the informers become known to the police, no action would be taken against them. This offer was rejected by the police, but towards the end of January 1926 the societies settled their differences, just as a large number of banishment warrants had been issued against men of both sides. The police believed that the Chinese Chamber of Commerce had arranged the settlement and that a sum of money had been paid over by the traders whose livelihood was affected by the stoppage of the river traffic, as the price of peace. The police also believed that the arbitrators had the support of the Protectorate.[10]

The tally of convictions under the Societies Ordinance in 1925 was 43, of whom four were juveniles found attending an initiation ceremony. In the Legislature, the Police Force Ordinance became law as No. 9 of 1925 and provided for an Armed Police Reserve. Attempts to stop the importation of arms resulted in the seizure of 86 small arms from ships passing through the port, and of 53 from places or individuals in the Settlement, together with thousands of rounds of ammunition. A closer look was also taken at immigrants on their arrival from China, and during the year nearly 400 who were regarded as undesirables were refused permission to land.

The settlement of January 1926 gave a period of peace among the Tiechiu societies, but the Cantonese gangs now took the centre of the stage, with a characteristic indiscriminate use of firearms. An old feud was rekindled in April

[9] Cargo ship.
[10] Wynne, unpublished ch. 27, p. 76, quoting Encl. 7 in CSO Conf. 351/1927, 2 Dec.

and a series of fights ensued which only ceased in June after a gunman had been shot dead in Sago Street during a fight with a detective patrol. The Heng group and the Woh Kei Society added to public alarm by a series of armed gang robberies including murder, but by August it was believed that nearly half of the culprits were arrested and the tension decreased.

It was at the September meeting of the Legislative Council that reference was made to 'the recent outbreak of abnormal violent crime' in a reply to a question from Mr Song Ong Siang, who was anxious to ensure that the families of policemen and civilians 'who sacrifice their lives in suppressing the present crime wave' were adequately compensated. Later, in his speech on the adjournment, this member suggested that the Banishment Ordinance should be used 'not only in the case of notorious criminals but also in the case of habitual offenders and all bad characters whose names are in the black lists of the Police Department or the Chinese Protectorate'. He followed this with the unique suggestion that Judges should be given the power to order that a man be flogged, not only once but repetitively, once a year, so that those banished would be deterred from returning through fear of being periodically flogged.

The number of immigrants from China reached a record total of 348,593 during the year, including the unprecedented number of 225,834 from Amoy, many of whom were Tiechius from the district behind Swatow who had reached Amoy by coastal steamer. The police prevented the landing of 554 undesirables at Singapore and 217 at Penang, and from two vessels in transit seized 86 automatics and 8,500 rounds of ammunition. An even greater wave of Chinese immigration engulfed Singapore in 1927 totalling 359,262, a number which has never been equalled. In this year, too, secret society and gangster turbulence reached its peak for the decade.

Early in the year the feud between the Heng and the Khwan Yi Cantonese gangs was resumed with renewed fury, because of a dispute over the 'protection' of sly brothels, and not only members of the gangs but innocent passers by were shot in the affrays in the public streets. These gangs were also responsible for so many armed robberies that in the middle of the year the police proposed a general round-up of all known Cantonese suspects under the Banishment Ordinance, 220 warrants were issued, and the city was thus freed of a large number of notorious bad characters. Two large-scale raids in July and September brought in 40 leading members of the Khwan Yi and the Heng groups, and a further raid on the Heng in October virtually reduced this group to impotence.

At the Legislative Council meeting in July Mr Song Ong Siang had again counselled stern measures to quell the gang warfare and the robberies, and remarked that if the Government dealt with the situation 'with a strong hand and in a drastic manner, even to the extent of reviving the practice of public flogging which many of us had been willing to condemn as brutalising', he was convinced that it would have the unanimous approval and support of the law-abiding citizens of the Settlement. To which the Colonial Secretary replied that public opinion all over the world had reached the stage where such a proposal would never be tolerated.

In the meantime, the turbulence in the town was increased by a recurrence of the feud between the Tiechiu societies—the Sin Tong Hwa and the Hok Tio Kheng. In June there was a quarrel between members of these societies, once again on the Singapore river, and funds were collected to finance a fight which should have started in August but was postponed until September. The police were forewarned, but hostilities began in an unexpected quarter at a wayang in Balestier Road on 2 September, and on the following day, but for the prompt appearance of armed patrols, would have spread to Boat Quay. Frustrated in this, the Hok Tio Kheng mob scattered, and from then until the 14th, when the disturbances ended, the affray took the form of attacks by small parties armed with knives or guns on individual members of the rival society. During the first few days sixteen men were stabbed, three fatally. Most of them were street stall-holders, and not one of them was able or willing to give any idea of who assaulted him or why.

On 6 September the Protectorate advised the police that the Chinese Chamber of Commerce was holding meetings and it was hoped that as a result the trouble would die down, but police information pointed rather to an extension of the conflict by the entrance of the Sin Ghee Hin into the arena.

On the next day a deputation of rice-dealers saw the Protector and asked for a police guard to be provided from 7 a.m. to 4 p.m. daily to ensure that there was no stoppage of work on the Singapore river. This deputation, which included two members of the Chinese Chamber of Commerce Committee, then saw the Chief Police Officer, and informed him that the Chamber could settle the dispute, but when asked for particulars of the channels of communication with the society leaders, they went away, ostensibly to enquire, but did not return.

Thereafter the disturbances intensified. At daybreak on the 9th two Tiechiu fishermen were shot while unloading their catch near the Ellenborough Market, and their assailants escaped in the crowd that thronged the wharf for the fish auctions. On the next day a Tiechiu was stabbed at Pulau Saigon and another at Geylang, when five assailants were seen to escape into the mangrove swamps of Pulau Minyak. Five more Tiechius were shot that night, and a poster purporting to be issued by the Sin Ghee Hin was found in Clyde Terrace warning people to stay at home lest they be mistaken for Hok Tio Kheng members.

On the 13th three more Tiechius were stabbed in the early dawn while taking down the shutters of their shops, and next day another was shot in Serangoon Road, but two of his three assailants were overpowered and arrested by a Malay lance-corporal with the help of some Malays and Tamils. It was not until late on the night of the 14th that rumours of a settlement began to spread, and these confirmed next morning when handbills published by the Chinese Chamber of Commerce were distributed in the streets exhorting people to stop fighting. The handbills were dated 10 September, and it seemed probable that a settlement negotiated at this earlier date had broken down at the last moment.

On the Hokkien side, there was a quarrel later in September at Telok Ayer involving twakow and tongkang labourers which, though a minor affair, resulted in two murders. Its significance lay in the fact that the traders affected by the quarrel promptly appealed to the Twakow Association to mediate, and that assistance from the Protectorate or the police was not sought either by the sufferers or by the Association.[11]

This lawlessness deriving from secret society conflicts had deeply undermined public confidence. Reporting at length on the Tiechiu disturbances, the Protectorate emphasized that there had been a greater disinclination than usual on

[11] Encl. 7, dated 2 Dec. 1927, in CSO Conf. 351/1927, quoted by Wynne, pp. 75–76.

the part of those who suffered, either by direct violence or by extortion, to report to the police or to the Protectorate, what they knew of their assailants. The police were even more explicit and referred to an almost total lack of information either to them or to the Protectorate. Indirectly, the police had heard that certain Chinese had been held as hostages for short periods, and that in at least one case of kidnapping $3,000 had been paid as ransom, but no reports were made in any instance. The Protectorate report also referred to the similar secrecy about the terms of settlement and the manner in which it had been brought about, and gave the following account of what was known to the Department:

The big Tiechiu rice importers whose business was held up by the dislocation of the twakow traffic in the river, approached the Chinese Chamber of Commerce with a view to getting the quarrel settled. The Chamber appointed a sub-committee of their number, of whom only one took any share in the subsequent negotiations. He called a meeting of thirteen twakow owners who appointed five so-called 'arbitrators' to deal with the headmen of the societies. Three of the arbitrators were Hokkiens, the other two were Tiechius. (Among them were a twakow owner and two Straits-born Hokkien bad characters who had been arrested on banishment warrants in connection with society disturbances and released on proving local birth.) . . .

The terms of settlement were that each side should present the other with a pair of candles and red cloth, no money passing except a nominal 'ang pau'.[12] There is reason to believe that the presentation to the Hok Tio Kheng was made in the temple of the Orchard Road Chinese Cemetery, and that to the Sin Tong Hwa at Pulau Ubin. It is not definitely known to whom the presentations were made or with whom the arbitrators dealt on behalf of the two societies. The arbitrators must, of course, know these facts, but it appears to have been a condition of their accepting their position as arbitrators that they would not be asked to disclose this information to Government. . . .

The report considered that the existing methods of the police and the Protectorate had done little or nothing to check the growth of these unlawful societies, which about twice a year developed a 'big burst' with its train of murders, attempted murders, and kidnappings. It also averred that there was a conspiracy among the detectives, and such respectable Chinese as were from time to time involved, to keep the authorities in the dark as to the details of the 'arbitrations' and the inner workings of the societies generally.

As in 1923, Mr Tan Cheng Lock had his own solution to offer to bring the populace into closer touch with the Government. This time his scheme comprised:

1. Registration of every individual of every nationality resident in Singapore.
2. A systematic distribution of well-armed, uniformed policemen on patrol duty daily and nightly throughout the whole of the streets of Singapore, particularly on those where the criminals were liable to operate.
3. By way of enlisting the co-operation of the public, Chinatown should be divided into a number of sections or groups of streets, over each of which is a headman assisted by a detective, and to a certain extent held responsible for its good order.

In the last of these suggestions we find an echo of the system practised with wide unpopularity in China centuries ago, and advocated by Pickering in 1889 as an alternative to the suppression of the secret societies. It was far too drastic a regimentation to be acceptable either to the Government or to the people of Singapore, and, in addition, it would have been open to the same abuses and

---

[12] 'Ang Pau' ('Hung Pau') = 'Red Packet', the red paper packet in which gifts of money are customarily made.

corruption as beset the 'Capitan' system and the practice of controlling the public through headmen, whether 'Capitans' or secret society leaders.

In commenting upon the action taken under the Banishment and Societies Ordinances since the beginning of 1923, the Protectorate emphasized the importance of the banishment weapon but again drew attention to its inadequacy in that it could not touch those who were local-born. Of 1,007 banishment warrants issued from the beginning of 1923 (four and a half years), 663 were confirmed; the balance of 344 were ineffective, almost entirely because the prisoners proved local birth. As for the Societies Ordinance, the number of prosecutions in the previous four years were 29, 20, 17, and 27, and the report remarked that owing to lack of information, action taken under this Ordinance was insignificant compared with the number of members, even with the number of headmen and samsengs of the different societies. As the Chinese Chamber of Commerce believed that in 1923 there were 12,000 members in the Sin Ghee Hin alone, the term 'insignificant' seems well justified. The report closed with the following description of a typical secret society in Singapore in 1927:

> The typical secret society consists of a number of pangkengs or coolies' lodging-houses. The pangkeng is rented by a number of Chinese of the same tribe and engaged in the same kind of work. Each subscribes $1.50 or $2.00 per mensem towards the rent. Some of the members sleep in the pangkeng; others sleep out, e.g. twakowmen if they are working an early tide, house-building coolies in the suburbs, and those who prefer the fresh air of the five-foot way or the all-night smoking shops,—these keep their belongings there and use the place as a sort of club. Round this harmless nucleus gather a crowd of professional hooligans who run the gambling and chandu and do the extortion, and, when necessary, the fighting.

> Above them are the police-court and police-station touts, the informers, the professional arbitrators and bailors, ticket brokers, lawyers' clerks and so forth. A large proportion of this type are young Straits-born wasters, who are exempt from the provisions of the Banishment Ordinance. At the top of all are the mysterious 'headmen'. The cash to support this gang of unemployed hangers-on is derived from extortion. Each pangkeng has its area, more or less rigidly defined, from which it collects $3.00 or $4.00 per mensem from every shop. In return for this the pangkeng gives 'protection', i.e. guarantees that no other society will practice further extortion in the same area. Most of the big quarrels between the societies in the past have arisen over this right to 'protect'.

> How far the various pangkengs of the same society are affiliated to each other is uncertain. In all probability there is no 'inner council' of (say) the Sin Ghee Hin with its office-bearers and its own finance. The headmen of the pangkengs are, of course, known to each other, and in moments of crisis when the society wishes to act as a whole such headmen will naturally confer together.

> It is probable that some sort of mutual benefit or co-operative society is bound to arise in any community of Chinese. The type of society that has arisen in Singapore is due to the special conditions which obtain in the town. Among these special conditions are the gross overcrowding of many districts; the ramifications of unlawful gambling and unlawful dealing in Chandu; the corruption of the subordinate officers of Government and the Municipality; and the lack of confidence among the respectable inhabitants that the Authorities are able to protect them against society hooligans.

One further contemporary comment is of interest. It occurs in a police report written in December 1927, and reads:

> ... It will be a wrong and dangerous policy to continue, any longer than is absolutely necessary, to permit or to encourage arbitration by private persons or by associations,

especially if the arbitrators deem it necessary to enter into a bond of confidence with the offenders. It should be plainly recognised that matters such as the suppression of these society feuds which so seriously affect the peace and safety of large portions of the city are primarily the duty of the Police, and that Police officers must be properly equipped and trained to perform this duty.

This, no doubt, was meant to be a challenge to the policy which had been adopted by the Protectorate of calling in the Chinese Chamber of Commerce and other associations in an attempt to bring some measure of peace to the town, and as a statement of what ought to be it is unexceptionable. But the reason why such a policy had been tried was clearly that neither the police nor, apparently, the Protectorate had found themselves capable of fulfilling the duty of maintaining the peace of or keeping the unlawful societies under control. The Protectorate, too, was far from satisfied with the way the experiment was developing, with secret agreements and hidden commitments while the criminals went unpunished, and it was discontinued.

Over the next six years (1928–33) the dual control of secret societies by Protectorate and police which dated back to the days of Pickering and Dunlop was gradually replaced by a unitary control exercised by the police. During the interim period the closest co-operation existed between the Protectorate and the secret society section of the CID, particularly in the exchange of information, and at the end of 1933 the Protectorate handed over its secret society records to the police, who thereafter became primarily responsible for the discovery and control of the activities of unlawful societies, though the Protector remained the Registrar of Societies and therefore exercised the powers vested in the Registrar by the Societies Ordinance.

This, however, was in the future. In 1928 it was recorded that there was a very considerable abatement in the disturbances. The arrest and banishment of so many Cantonese suspects had crippled the two big Cantonese groups, the Heng and the Khwan Yi, and although spasmodic attempts were made at revival they were promptly dealt with. Isolated affrays in April and June resulted in still further arrests of Khwan Yi men. The Tiechiu societies were also kept under close surveillance, and better regulation of the river traffic removed some of the causes of minor quarrels which had previously so frequently resulted in serious faction fights. Among the Hokkiens, the Sin Ghee Hin and the Sin Kongsi quarrelled throughout the year but the peace of Singapore was never seriously menaced. Nevertheless, although the gang affrays were regarded as 'minor', they resulted in no fewer than twelve murders and six attempted murders. In addition there was considerable disorder caused through the activities of Hainanese groups who were the forerunners of the MCP.[13]

Within the police force reorganization was already taking place. Chinese translators were appointed to the office of the CPO, to the CID, and to the Detective Branch. Information was more readily forthcoming and more expeditiously dealt with, enabling action to be taken early when trouble threatened. Some changes were made, too, in the composition of the Chinese Advisory Board by giving the Chinese Chamber of Commerce and the Straits Chinese British Association the right to nominate one member each, and the Chinese member of the Legislative Council was also made an *ex-officio* member of the Board. It was hoped that these appointments would help to produce greater coherence between represent-

[13] See above, p. 282.

atives of the Chinese community, and closer co-operation between them and the Government.

The year 1929 was again free from any prolonged outbreak of lawlessness, although gang squabbles entailing a number of shootings and stabbings occurred. Heng Yi gangs were rounded up in January, and Khwan Yi gangs in June after a series of gang robberies. In March there was a threat of a more serious quarrel within the Sin Ghee Hin when members of the Gi Hong San pangkeng came to blows and one man was murdered. Police investigation of this case revealed the varied membership of the Sin Ghee Hin, including 'Hokkiens, Chiau Ans, Hokch'ias, Tiechius, and Hainanese'. Prompt action against the pangkeng prevented any further development. The Tiechiu societies were quiet throughout the year, and the continued freedom from the bloodthirsty feuds of previous years was noted by the police as a 'great relief'. Under certain heads, the state of crime showed a 'remarkable improvement', and, according to the police report:

Robberies of all kinds were little more than one half and one third of the 1928 and 1927 figures, and form a low record for at least six years past. Under murder and attempted murder there is a large decrease from the high figures of the previous 2 years. Of the 55 murders, 11 were classed as faction or society feuds.

One factor which may have made some contribution to the comparative calm was the abolition of the system of 'tolerated' brothels. It had been customary since 1894, when the system of registration of brothels ceased, for the authorities to permit brothels to exist provided that their inmates had been interrogated by the Protector of Chinese, assured by him of their freedom, and given a 'Protection Ticket' containing a printed version in Chinese of this assurance. At the same time, particulars of the prostitutes in each brothel were kept at the Protectorate. When the Protection Ticket system in turn was abolished, toleration was no longer extended to these brothels and they closed down, thus reducing appreciably, for the time being at least, an obvious field of 'protection' by society agents, with a corresponding diminution in the number of disputes arising therefrom.

The picture given in the police report quoted above appears most encouraging as to the reduction in crime, but perhaps the most disturbing feature of the year was that the police found occasion to raid no fewer than seven initiation ceremonies at various places on the island. Despite all the action taken against them, the secret societies were still recruiting new members and performing their ritualistic initiations.

This account of the activities of the societies in Singapore during the decade 1920–9 may fittingly be brought to a close by summarizing the two Protectorate reports mentioned on p. 296 above.

The organizational pattern of the Tiechiu and Hokkien gangs at this time was set out in the report prepared by the Protector of Chinese (J. A. Black) in December 1929. Of the Tiechiu societies, the Hok Tio Kheng or Sa Ji, which did not use the Triad ritual, had ten branches in Singapore and was also very powerful in south Johore. Its rival, the Sin Tong Hwa, formed of Tiechius who in 1921 seceded from the Sin Ghee Hin, used the Triad ritual and had only four branches, each of which had a number of subsidiary pangkengs. Disputes between branches within the society were not uncommon, and this was true of all the societies. Other Tiechiu societies were the Seh Ho Lim, and the Seh Tang,

x

both clan societies, the former with five pangkengs and the latter with six branches, three of which were moribund. Another Tiechiu clan society was the Lau Kuang Tiun, a small society for men of these three surnames.[14]

On the Hokkien side, there were two main societies, also at rivalry, the Sin Guan Seng or Sin Kongsi, and the Sin Ghee Hin, this latter being the more powerful. Among the less important Hokkien societies were the Seh Ah Long and the Hop Soon Hin—two rival groups of men from Chiau An—, the Ia Kha or Ghee Chuan Seng, the Ji-tsap (20) Kongsi, and the Poeh-Si (84).

The Sin Kongsi was an amalgamation (1921) of two older societies, the Guan Seng with 21 pangkengs, and the Sin Kongsi with 12 affiliated gangs. By the end of 1929, only 7 branches of the Sin Kongsi were known to exist. It did not use the Triad ritual, and had rules for the settlement of disputes between member pangkengs, and for financial support of any pangkeng which fought against the rival Ghee Hin, with compensation for members wounded or banished.

Of the Sin Ghee Hin Society, the biggest of them all, the report noted that it was the descendant of the old Ghee Hin Society, officially dissolved in 1890, and that it occurred in the FMS and in the Dutch East Indies as well as in Singapore. It was a Triad society, using its initiation ritual and issuing Triad-type certificates. It had grown steadily since the beginning of the century and as early as 1923 was the biggest and strongest society in Singapore. Since then, with the decline of its main rival, the Sin Kongsi, and the reabsorption of its Tiechiu branches from the Sin Tong Hwa, it had become bigger but, through internal dissensions, no longer had the same unity of purpose. The report continued:

It is misleading to refer to the Sin Ghee Hin as a society. Probably at no time since the dissolution of the old Ghee Hin have there been common headmen or any central organization embracing all the branches of the so-called society. In recent times, certainly, the society has always consisted of a number of loosely-affiliated pangkengs often at enmity with each other and combining for joint action only in times of stress.

During the last five or six years these various pangkengs have more or less definitely assorted themselves among a number of groups, known as the 8, the 18, the 24, the 36, the 72, and the 108. Of these, the 72 existed only for a short time and is no longer heard of. The 8 is a distinctive group, being composed entirely of Chuan Chiu pangkengs. The 18 and the 108 are allied if not identical; similarly with the 24 and the 36. In the cases of the 8 and the 24, the numbers were chosen because at the time of their formation the groups consisted of eight and twenty-four pangkengs respectively; the other numbers are mystic numbers from the Triad ritual.

After enumerating sixty pangkengs in Singapore known to the Protectorate, the report continued:

It must not be supposed that the sixty pangkengs mentioned above represent a complete list of the Sin Ghee Hin branches, or that they all exist today or even that they all did exist at any one time. Old names are constantly dropping out and new ones being added: branches too, with the exception of those of the 8, are not infrequently reported as changing from one group to another. The disappearance of a pangkeng may be due to prosecution by the authorities or eviction by the landlord or voluntary disbandment for some reason or other. Or a pangkeng may change its chop and reappear with the same personnel at the same or another address, or, finally, it may cease to take part in any illegal activities and, while retaining its name and corporate existence, avoid the attention of the Protectorate and the Police.

[14] The Tiechiu forms of the surnames of the Peach Garden Trio: Liu, Kuan, and Chang.

The report drew attention to the fine distinction that might exist between a kuli-keng[15] and a branch of the Sin Ghee Hin, and gave an example of one of the former which apparently had no unlawful purpose. It continued:

It is easy to see how an association like this might be forced through some petty quarrel to seek alliance with a hooligan gang of the same surname or the same occupation or from the same village in China, or might be led by bad influence to practice extortion from hawkers and others in the neighbourhood of its kuli-keng. The use of Triad ritual for initiation might or might not follow, but it would not be long before it was reported as a pangkeng of the Sin Ghee Hin. The converse is equally true. A society at one time dangerous and a menace to the public peace might reform and become nothing more than an association for mutual benefit. . . .

The report on the Cantonese gangs by the Assistant Protector (S. E. King), dated March 1930, revealed an even less closely integrated structure. Starting as mutual protection and assistance societies for men in the same trades, they had degenerated into loosely connected gangs of criminals with little or no organization. The self-styled office-bearers and collectors were invariably unemployed hooligans who battened on the members, coercing them to join with the promise of protection and the implied threat of trouble for refusal. Entrance fees were $3.60, $7.20, $10.80, or more, and monthly subscriptions 50 cents or $1. Receipts were rarely given. Most of the members were not actively criminal and merely paid up to protect themselves.

The report continued:

They are not societies in the true sense of the word. They are merely bands of unemployed criminals who use the various titles Khwan Yi, San Wui Khwan, etc. as labels under which they commit their crimes. . . . The history of Cantonese societies has been one long tale of armed gang-robbery, extortion, protection of brothels and gaming houses, and inter-gang fighting, generally from the most trivial causes such as an argument over the protection of a certain brothel, the collection of a gaming tax, or even an insulting remark passed by a member of one gang against a member of another gang.

Cantonese gangs have been responsible for nearly all the armed gang-robberies which reached such alarming proportions in the years 1926 and 1927. Inter-gang fighting with the use of pistols, even in daylight and in the main streets of the town, became so frequent that about the middle of 1927 the Detective Branch applied for Banishment Warrants against 220 of the best known Cantonese society samsengs. A large proportion of these warrants were executed, and as a result the end of 1927 saw an enormous diminution in the activity of Cantonese gangs. With the exception of isolated shooting cases and gang-robberies, coupled with numerous reports of the pettier types of crime such as pickpocketing, hawker and brothel extortion, no noticeable renewal of activity has occurred during the years 1928 and 1929.

After listing nineteen Cantonese 'so-called societies' known to the Protectorate, of which the most important and dangerous were the Khwan Yi, the San Wui Khwan, the Heng Alliance (consisting of five societies: Heng Kee, Heng Yi, Heng Wah, Heng Yau, Heng Kiu),[16] the Woh Kei, and the Wa Khiu, and

---

[15] A room where, in return for a monthly subscription, labourers usually of one type of employment and often of one tribe and surname, stored their baggage and slept on the floor.

[16] There had also been other components of the Heng Alliance: the Heng Fat and the Heng Woh.

describing the incidents in which they were known to have been involved, the report concluded:

> With present conditions in Singapore it is difficult to see how crime of this sporadic nature can be stamped out. Banishment is a powerful weapon. This has been clearly shown by the inactivity, except for isolated cases, of gunmen since the issue of 220 banishment warrants in 1927. But banishment is only a palliative and not a cure. Unrestricted immigration and the consequent presence of a large unemployed population in the town, over-populated areas, and a noticeable lack of public spirit assist the gunmen and hamper the methods of the Police. Periods of inactivity are invariably succeeded by a recrudescence of crime. With the above conditions prevailing, it is essential that a generous use of the powers under the Banishment Ordinance should be allowed.

Useful as these reports are in delineating the structure of the gang and society organization, they unfortunately throw no light on the agencies or organizations which arranged and conducted Triad initiation ceremonies, or on the relationship between such agencies and those societies and gangs which made use of Triad ritual.

2. SINGAPORE, 1930–41

The main feature of interest in the 1930s was the decline of the more powerful societies and the further fragmentation of the secret society world. Something of the organization of the Ghee Hin remained in the numbered groups to which many gangs belonged, but there was no apparent control by any hierarchy of Sin Ghee Hin leaders. The police, with improved organization, better intelligence, and more detailed recording, were gradually able to obtain a more comprehensive view of the secret society mosaic. In this they were assisted by restricted Chinese immigration and by the return to China of hundreds of thousands during the early years of the decade owing to slump conditions in Malaya. Moreover, a close watch was maintained by the Special Branch upon all political societies and their ramifications, which prevented any extensive exploitation of the secret society underworld in support of political projects until the Second World War began. It is probably true to say that the influence of secret societies in Malaya was never less pronounced, though it never entirely disappeared.

The background for 1930 was given in the Annual Report of the Protectorate. There were more labour troubles than usual because of a trade depression which particularly affected rubber factories. During the summer over 1,000 coolies became unemployed in this one industry alone. Several attempts to create disturbances were made by Hailam workers, but there was no serious outbreak. Wholesale dismissals and a general lowering of wages had also occurred in sawmills, timber yards, and pineapple factories, and here too the Communist element had unsuccessfully attempted to foment strikes. In the engineering trades, except for one big undertaking in Singapore, the depression was met by putting men on short time rather than dismissing them. During the second half of the year 500 shops shut down.[17]

The economic distress appears to have worked to the detriment of the secret societies, for not only were large numbers returning to China but those who

[17] CP *AR*, 1930, para. 16.

remained were no longer able to make their usual financial contributions. Apart from a number of armed robberies during the first three months of the year for which a Cantonese gang, the Ha Heng Yi, was responsible, and a certain amount of extortion and minor robbery by small Hokkien groups, there was no secret society crime worthy of comment. Troubles which threatened between Tiechiu societies were scotched by prompt intervention, but the Triad tradition still lived, for one initiation ceremony was raided by the police, and 14 Tiechius arrested there were convicted.

The year 1931 was not quite so peaceful, though there were no major outbreaks. During the first three months there was disturbance within the Tiechiu Sin Tong Hwa resulting in a number of street fights between two branches, the Gi Sio Hwa and the Gi Tong Hwa. Two members were convicted of murder and hanged and many banished before the dispute was settled. There was also an inter-society fight between a branch of the Sin Tong Hwa and the Hokkien '24' Society, the most powerful of the Hokkien groups, in which one man on each side was killed by stabbing, and a further 29 fights were recorded between Hokkien society members over trivial matters in one of which one man was shot.

The Cantonese gangs were so harassed by the police that many of their members moved over to Johore and the FMS, whither they were followed by Colony detectives who identified them for the local police. There were three important seizures of documents belonging to two of the most dangerous Cantonese societies, and a further eight seizures of other society records, all of which gave useful information as to membership and internal economy.

The police were very pleased with the measure of control which they now appeared to exercise, and attributed this success to the preventive effect of a specialized headquarters and detective staff able to investigate and advise on this form of crime, and to set in motion large bodies of detectives and police when necessary. There was also an economic factor: unemployment and poverty severely affected the flow of contributions to societies and gangs, and lowered the level of extortion. The abolition of tolerated brothels was also thought to have restricted the field for extortion, and prostitutes and other payers of protection money seemed increasingly inclined to report to the police. Though there were many disturbances and threats of disturbance, the police had been able to maintain reasonable order.[18]

By the end of 1932, only five groups of Hokkien societies comprising some seventy pangkengs remained, and of these half could hardly keep going. There were about twenty fights between members of these Hokkien pangkengs, but on only four occasions were whole gangs involved. On three other occasions, Hokkien gangs fought Cantonese or Tiechiu gangs. The Tiechiu societies seemed to be weakening; two which had been active in 1931 ceased to exist, and the once fearsome Hok Tio Kheng gave no trouble. There were eight minor affrays between Tiechiu gang members and one with a gang of the Hokkien '24', but no firearms were used. Cantonese gangs were also reasonably quiet. Four men were stabbed, one fatally, when two sub-branches of the Khwan Yi came to blows, and there was one stabbing affray between the Khwan Yi and the Heng. It was noticed that arms were sometimes carried and occasionally fired, but apparently for intimidation. A former branch of the Heng—the Heng Yau—made an attempt at revival, but another branch was weakened by the conviction

[18] C *AR*, 1931, para. 8; SS Police *AR*, 1931, paras 97–101.

of four of its members. At the end of the year the police report was able to say: 'For the first time for several decades the actual damage done by society and gang activity has been almost negligible.' It attributed this to the 'constant drudgery' of keeping information up to date, to attacks on known leaders and prompt punishment or expulsion of those whose doings threatened the peace of the town, which factors enabled the police to break up combinations before they became too well established.[19]

As far as the Hokkien and Tiechiu societies were concerned, the picture for 1933 is similar to that of the previous year. Apart from one fight between the Sin Kongsi and the Tiechiu surname Ho Lim, which might have become serious had not the police intervened promptly, there were only minor brawls. But the Cantonese societies, as though challenged by the police report, began to revive and to grow stronger, and by the end of the year had become a menace to the continuance of the peace. This revival was in part due to a fresh set of circumstances which had arisen originally in 1932 when, early in the year, unemployed Chinese seamen had established a Seamen's Union. 'Wearied of the extortionate demands of ghaut serangs and boarding-house keepers, and faced with increasing difficulty in securing employment, these men established an informal seamen's boarding house on union lines in a genuine attempt to redress part, at any rate, of their grievances.'

A police raid on the premises revealed a large membership, and the matter was referred to the Chinese Protectorate. With the co-operation of the leading shipping companies an attempt was made by the Protectorate to establish a working organization through the Union. The intricacies of the problem would have made it difficult to reach a satisfactory method under the best of circumstances, but the scheme was bedevilled from the start by two inimical factors. The first was the penetration of the Union by Communist agents who used it to increase their contact with local labour forces and to establish connexions, with Red organizations outside Malaya through seamen-couriers. The other was the use made by both sides (the Union and the Ghaut serangs) of secret societies. The Union called on the Cantonese Luen Yi Society, to which it paid a monthly subsidy for protection of its members, and the Ghaut serangs turned to the Heng Woh for similar support. There was great bitterness on both sides and several vicious assaults took place, referred to by the police as 'a long tale of assault, intimidation and even kidnapping from ships'. Special police precautions were taken and protection frequently given. Apart from these direct effects, the morale of the Cantonese societies was bolstered up by this employment, and a large number of cases of armed robbery with a general increase in extortion were noticeable.[20]

The pattern in 1934 was much the same. Between 20 and 30 Hokkien inter-gang fights took place, in three of which firearms were used. On two occasions Hokkien gangs were supported by Cantonese. Among the Tiechius there were thirteen gang fights, one of which was against a Hokkien gang. No firearms were used in these. The Cantonese gangs were reported to be 'more fluid than ever' with members and even office-bearers frequently changing their allegiance; 4 murders, 1 attempted murder, and 13 robberies were known to have been committed by these gangs. One of the murders was the shooting of Inspector

[19] SS Police *AR*, 1932, paras 114–15.
[20] Ibid. 1933, paras 97–101, 117; 1935, para. 138.

Popejoy by a member of the Khwan group as the Inspector was about to enter a pawnshop on a routine inspection in broad daylight. Although the shooting took place in full view of the staff of the shop, and the gangster escaped along a populous thoroughfare, evidence of identity, even after arrest, was extremely difficult to obtain.

Repressive action by the police against known Cantonese gangsters after this murder resulted in imprisonment or banishment of 27 leaders and 40 other members. Nevertheless, in the following year there were two Cantonese gang murders arising from the usual protection disputes, and there were at least seven other instances in which shots were fired during Cantonese affrays. There were also twenty robberies, some with arms, attributed to the Cantonese gangs. An attempt was made to establish a branch of the Heng Wah Society among the labourers of the Phosphate Company on Christmas Island, but was discovered and foiled.

Among the Hokkien groups, the '24' the '18', and the '108' of the Sin Ghee Hin were active in protection squabbles, often against the Sin Kongsi gangs. One of the main items in dispute was the protection of waitresses in coffee-shops, a form of employment which had become very popular after the closure of the recognized brothels. Many of the waitresses were clandestine prostitutes and offered a field of exploitation for the gangs, to such an extent that serious consideration was given by the authorities to banning this form of employment for women.

Among the Tiechiu societies there were several cases of stabbing, though none was fatal, and the Seventh Moon festival produced the usual crop of cases of minor extortion resulting in the conviction of five notorious headmen and their eventual banishment. An improvement in employment conditions, particularly in Johore, led to the emptying of some of the Tiechiu pangkengs, whose members crossed to Johore and found work.

The police report drew attention, as it had done in the previous year, to the increasing prominence of Straits-born Chinese in the Hokkien societies. Several office-bearers within the Sin Ghee Hin complex were found to be local-born. And once again the report stressed that only because of the ceaseless vigilance of the police was the Colony kept free from serious riots or affrays resulting from the activities of unlawful societies.[21]

The year 1936 was enlivened by gang clashes between Hokkiens and Tiechius, Hokkiens and Cantonese, and Tiechius and Cantonese, as well as fights between rival Cantonese societies in which two men were killed. On one occasion firearms were used, and the four men arrested and convicted (two of whom were local-born) were sentenced to long terms of imprisonment and to flogging. In the following year there were only minor ripples to vary the comparative calm. Hokkien twakow-men engaged in a series of fights, but police raids on the societies concerned prevented serious developments, and there was one shooting affray by the '108' in July. The Tiechiu societies were exceptionally quiet, and for the first time for ten years there were no Cantonese society murders, but during the last three months of the year these societies committed more robberies than during the whole of 1936.

There seems to be no doubt that severe police action over the decade which followed the formation of the special secret society sub-branches of the Detective

[21] Ibid. 1935, paras 122–39.

Branch had been effective in reducing crime. Society murders, for instance, decreased from 26 in 1927 to 6 in 1934, 3 in 1935, and 2 in 1937. A police report remarked that it was a long time since Singapore citizens had been unable to use a certain thoroughfare on account of the thick carpet of broken bottles that used to cover the streets after a serious Tiechiu society fight. Moreover, the Triad nature of the societies had apparently declined. Seven initiation ceremonies were raided in 1929, but after 1930 when only one came to light in Singapore, no more such ceremonies are heard of during this period.

Although at the end of the 1930s the main groups still existed: the Sin Ghee Hin and the Sin Kongsi, the Sin Tong Hwa and the Hok Tio Kheng, the Heng Alliance and the Khwan group, their component units were all very independent and evidence of effective affiliation was rare.

Even so, it must be admitted that the threat still existed, and that should leaders arise, or opportunities offer, or police vigilance be relaxed, the power was likely to erupt. Once the Japanese invasion of China began, and the war in Europe got under way, some of this latent power was diverted into political and industrial channels, into anti-Japanese boycott movements and into industrial disturbances intended by the Communists to hamper the war effort of Britain, an aspect of the utilization of secret society collaboration to which reference has been made in a previous chapter.

3. PENANG, 1920–41[22]

There are only brief references to Penang in official reports for 1920–8. It appears that, as in Singapore, the decade opened peacefully after the anti-Japanese rioting of 1919, and of the eight known societies (Ban An T'ai, Panglong, Kong Kang Ngo, Kampong Lai, Seow Ke Iau San, Khien Khoon, Sin Kow Teo, and Low Kow Teo), only the Kampong Lai and the Kong Kang Ngo gave trouble. An affray between these two societies in Cintra Street in which a member of the latter was killed, led to the arrest of four members of the Kampong Lai who were sentenced to five years' rigorous imprisonment. Three of them were members of the Municipal Fire Brigade. During the year, a new society, the Ghi Lu Siah, managed by women, was discovered and broken up. It is possible that this was a tontine society, which are very frequently formed by Chinese women.

There was also very little trouble in 1921. Two gangs, the Toa Ke Iau San and the Seow Ke Iau San (the Large and the Small Mount Erskine societies), came to blows, and in the Relau and Balik Pulau districts there were some fights between the Malay Red and White Flag societies leading to several arrests.

The same two Chinese gangs were again active in the following year, and though a number of the leading members were convicted in court, there was trouble again between them in 1923, a year which also witnessed an extraordinary increase in public gaming, due probably to an influx of gangsters from Singapore anxious to escape the attentions of the police there.

From 1924 to 1926 nothing disturbed the peace of the Settlement, but in 1927, which was a year of crisis in Singapore, there were signs of an increase in

[22] The only sources are: P. of C. *ARs*; SS Police *AR*; Report by E. V. Fowler, Asst Cmmr, Detective Branch, Pg, 22 May 1930 (quoted by Wynne, ch. 27—unpubl.).

society activity in Penang and by the end of the year the murder rate had risen from 5 in 1926 to 15 in 1927. The reason for the disturbances was the arrival of several Sin Ghee Hin headmen who had fled from Singapore and started to form a branch in Penang, composed of Hokkiens: building labourers, stone-masons, and rickshaw pullers. On 1 October a gang of fifteen of the members, mainly stone-masons from the quarries in Waterfall Road, murdered the pro-prietor of a stone-mason's shop because he refused to join the society or to allow his labourers to do so. Thereafter a number of initiation ceremonies were known to have been held, and there was evidence, too, that the two local societies, the Seow Ke Iau San and the Kampong Lai, were associated with the newly-formed Sin Ghee Hin. An initiation ceremony held on 6 March 1928 by a well-known secret society headman in a house in Kedah Road was interrupted by the police, who arrested eleven men and seized all the paraphernalia.

Nothing further was heard of the Sin Ghee Hin until late in September when a Hokkien who had reported another stall-holder to the Market Inspector at Chowrasta Market was murdered at the instance of his rival. Four days later a Detective Branch informer who had given information leading to the arrest of those concerned in this crime was the victim of a ritual murder carried out on Penang Hill.

By this time twelve pangkengs of the Sin Ghee Hin had become known to the police. One was a shop at Pulau Tikus (a strongly Triad area), another was a shop in Kinta Lane, but the rest consisted of single rooms rented for the society in Kimberley Street, Prangin Road, Macalister Lane, and elsewhere. Two days after the ritual murder on Penang Hill the police simultaneously raided all the known pangkengs and arrested 103 Hokkiens of whom 55 were subsequently banished. Many of those arrested had recently arrived from China and protested that unless they joined the society it would be impossible for them to obtain work, particularly in the house-building trade. During the year there were 7 prosecutions (18 men) for possession of Triad documents compared with 3 cases (6 men) in 1927.

In February 1929 a serious stabbing affray took place in Cintra Street between members of the Sin Ghee Hin and the Khien Khoon societies, after which nine more Sin Ghee Hin members were banished. In all, 77 Sin Ghee Hin members were banished between October 1928 and March 1929, and though the society continued to exist, its activities were curtailed.

It is not clear why the two local societies, the Seow Ke Iau San and the Kampong Lai, which were usually found in opposition to the local Triad society (the Khien Khoon), should ally themselves to the Sin Ghee Hin, which was also Triad, but the explanation probably is that they hoped to strengthen the opposition to their enemy the local Triad society. The fight between the two Triad societies, the Sin Ghee Hin and the Khien Khoon, is explicable on the ground that the Khien Khoon was an established Triad society in Penang and resented the intrusion of a rival society from Singapore. It is also possible that they represented different Lodges of Triad. The Sin Ghee Hin was certainly Second Lodge; the Khien Khoon may have been First Lodge—a descendant of the old Ho Seng of Penang.

There is some information in police reports as to the composition of some of the societies at that time. That of the Sin Ghee Hin has already been given. All the pangkengs were of the '108' group and used the Triad ritual. The entrance fee was $10.80, plus an initiation fee of $1.36 and a monthly subscription of $1.00. The Seow Ke Iau San had a membership of hire-car drivers and gambling touts. The Kampong Lai consisted mainly of hawkers, harbour coolies, and pig-rearers from the outskirts. The Khien Khoon drew its membership mainly from labourers in the Eastern Smelting Works, but also included Hokkien rickshaw pullers from the districts of T'aupak, Hinghwa, and Sinyiu in China, vegetable sellers in the Central Market, and coolies from nine coolie-houses. The Toa Ke Iau San, which maintained its independence from both sides, included rubber-factory labourers from Bridge Street, and fishermen.

There was no further society trouble during 1929 after the fight in February, and the police turned their attention to the suppression of gambling in Penang, Province Wellesley, and the Dindings; 1930 was also quiet, but the Sin Ghee Hin held an initiation ceremony in November which was raided by the police. Twenty-four Hokkiens were arrested and were successfully prosecuted in 1931, a year in which there was also considerable Sino-Japanese tension owing to political events in China, culminating in 1932 in the Japanese invasion of Manchuria and the attack on Shanghai. Thereafter the tension and ill-feeling were exacerbated in Penang by inflammatory reports in the local Chinese press, and a mob attacked the Central Police Station on 5 March. Later, in August, a home-made bomb was thrown into the Penang Bazaar with the intention of intimidating stall-holders selling Japanese cloth, but there were no reports of secret society activities either in 1932 or 1933, and the only items recorded in 1934 were disputes between the Sin Ghee Hin and the Ke Iau San societies during July and August, leading to prosecutions of some members.

In 1935 three societies were active at intervals: the Sin Ghee Hin, the Ji Tiau Loh and a society whose name is given as 'Sin Khien Khoon', i.e. New Khien Khoon, from which it would appear that the old Khien Khoon had in some way been reorganized. The Sin Ghee Hin and the Sin Khien Khoon fought in January, and the headman of the former society was arrested and convicted. Another leader of the same society was sentenced to six months for criminal intimidation in March, and then banished. An ex-member of the Sin Ghee Hin was assaulted for acting as an informer to the Customs Department, and in December a bus-owner of Butterworth was murdered for giving information leading to the seizure of Triad documents.

The only record of society activity in 1936 and 1937 relates to two cases in the latter year. In one a Cantonese was stabbed to death and a Hokkien severely wounded by Sin Ghee Hin men, and in the other a minor riot occurred involving the Sin Khien Khoon and some Boyanese (immigrants from the Celebes, usually car drivers).

Nothing further is known until after the Japanese occupation, when, as will later be seen, the same secret society pattern emerged in Penang, with the Sin Ghee Hin playing a very active part.

4. MALACCA, 1920–41[23]

There is even less information about Malacca during this period than there is about Penang. There were affrays between Hakkas and Hokkiens during January and June 1920, but no secret society activity whatever was recorded in

[23] Sources are: Mal. *AR.*, P. of C. *AR*; SS Police *AR*; Wynne, ch. 27 (unpublished).

1921. Next year there was information that Malays in the countryside were joining secret societies in order to obtain immunity from their unwelcome attentions rather than for any unlawful end, and a large number of anonymous petitions were received by the Protectorate relating to an alleged Triad society on the Muar boundary of Malacca. One unlawful society was discovered, named the Han Ghi Koan, and 19 persons were convicted under the Societies Ordinance and were bound over to be of good behaviour, from which it would seem that but little danger was apprehended. It was later to become plain that the undercurrent of uneasiness in Malacca territory was due to the activities of secret societies based on Segamat and Muar in Johore.

As in Penang, refugees from the police sweep of gangsters in Singapore began to arrive in Malacca after August 1923. Some of them were soon in gaol, and others left for the FMS. Other newcomers came from south China where parts of Fukien and the whole of Kwangtung were distracted by civil war. These included not only refugees from the turbulence of their own districts but also agents of one or other of the parties in China who were seeking funds in Malaya for their military and political campaigns. In particular, supporters of the Hakka General Ch'en Chiung-ming arrived at Malacca and founded a branch of the Chi Kung Tong in touch with the Hakkas of north Johore.

According to the official reports, the Settlement was free from any serious disturbances from 1924 to 1929, and during that period only 9 men were convicted of membership of unlawful societies, 6 in 1927 and 3 in 1928. There was a noticeable increase in crime in 1929, particularly in housebreakings, but this was attributed to the deteriorating economic conditions. In 1930 there were a few minor assaults due to society intrigue, but the main trouble came from societies which were described as having 'communistic connexions' and which made their influence felt in labour disputes.

From then onwards, interest centred upon anti-Japanese activities. A Hainanese schoolmaster was convicted in 1931 for promoting an anti-Japanese boycott society and there was a minor disturbance when a small Chinese mob clashed with the police who were attempting to protect the shop of a Chinese trader suspected of dealing in Japanese goods. As the anti-Japanese boycott fever rose in response to the feeling in China in 1932, there were further incidents, including the slicing of an ear from a Chinese trader and the throwing of acid on several occasions. Unemployment was evident in Malacca as elsewhere, and there were clashes between bands of loafers. A considerable number of destitute labourers were repatriated to China, and apart from an affray between two gangs of Hokkien fishermen in 1935 there is no further record of disturbance of the peace in prewar reports. While there can be no doubt that secret societies continued to exist, their activities were evidently not sufficiently disruptive to warrant mention in the official reports of the period.

5. FEDERATED MALAY STATES, 1920–41

During the period from 1920 to the invasion of Malaya by the Japanese the information available about Chinese secret societies in the FMS is very scant indeed. It is clear, however, that they continued to exist and that the Triad ritual was used.

Perak, as usual, provided more scope than the other States for the Triad adventurer to organize societies, and some information about these is available from some relics of the Protectorate files for this State up to 1930 which survived the Japanese Occupation, during which most government records were destroyed.

In the Bruas area, and stretching down towards Sitiawan, there was competition from 1919 to 1922 between the Ts'ung Paak, a Ghee Hin (Yi Hing) society, with Kwangsai and Kochau (Cantonese) members, and a Hokkien society said, once again, to be a Toh Peh Kong formation. Each of these local societies was said to be organized by people from Penang, and each sponsored a Malay society, the Yi Hing having as of old a White Flag subsidiary, and the Toh Peh Kong a Red Flag. In this area two police informers were murdered, one in 1921 and another in 1922.

In the Sitiawan area, round Kampong Koh, Ayer Tawar, Sungei Wangi, and Simpang Ampat, a society known as the Hok Ho Seng was discovered, members being Hokchius and Sin Yius.[24] It is probable that this society took its name from the original coastal Ho Seng, adding the prefix 'Hok' to indicate the Hokkien (Fukien) origins of its members. The banishment of eleven of its brethren in 1919–20, including an old Hokchiu plantation owner who was a prominent member of the Hokchiu Christian Mission, led to a period of quiet, but by 1922 it was on its feet again, and in the following year some membership diplomas written on red cloth were found in possession of an office-bearer at Ayer Tawar. These documents contained references to the flag, base-number, and watchword of the first of the five original Triad Lodges, an additional reason for believing that this society was a descendant of the old Ho Seng, which we know purported to belong to the First Lodge.[25] There were also lists of names of recruits to be presented at an initiation ceremony, so that clearly Triad practices were still in use.

The Ban An T'ai, from Penang and Province Wellesley, had a branch among the Hokkiens at Pantai, and the Wa Kei (Cantonese) was also reported to be still operating in Perak, promoting gambling at Papan, Bekor, and Chemor.

Further south, at Telok Anson, there had for years been quarrels between two groups of Sin Yiu Hokkiens, one group of surname Ng, mostly employed at a brick-kiln belonging to one of the clan, and the other of surname Ong, mainly rickshaw pullers. There was a riot caused by the antagonism of these groups in 1922, and thereafter those of surname Ng joined up with a branch of the Sin Ghee Hin with headquarters on the coast at Sungei Blukang and branches at Bagan Pasir and Telok Anson. Attempts were made to absorb into this branch members of other surname-groups (Tans, Lims and Chius) in opposition to the Ongs. The Sin Ghee Hin of this area also called itself the Si Ji Sa Tiam or 'Four, two, three dots' and issued membership diplomas of yellow silk.[26] On their side, the Ongs were formed into a society calling itself Si Tiam or 'Four Dots', and in 1923 there was a battle between the two sides as a result of which many leaders were banished,[27] whereupon a new society came into being known as the Goh Kongsi having as its object the uniting of the Ongs and the Ngs

[24] From the district around Sin Yiu, midway between Amoy and Foochow.

[25] See above, p. 55.

[26] 'Four, two, three dots' a title derived from reading backwards the Triad cipher for 'Hall of Obedience to Hung'.

[27] 'Four Dots' possibly because of the four strokes in the character for 'Ong'.

against everyone else, but nothing further is known of this proposed shift in the balance of power.

At Ipoh there was another area of rivalry between two societies of Sin Yiu Hokkiens, one of Chung Woh origin and one of basic Triad origin calling itself the Three Virtues Society (San Tek Kongsi), and purporting to be a branch of a 'newly-formed Ghee Hin'—presumably the Sin Ghee Hin. Action taken in court and under the Banishment Enactment in 1923 removed a number of its leaders.

Yet another society mentioned in 1923 was the Kwong Kung Hing, established at Bagan Datoh at the mouth of the Perak river by Chinese from Penang. Membership included Chinese and Malays, and a document found on a Malay proved to be a commission appointing three Malays to be headmen of the society in the district. The document was in Chinese and was plainly Triad, while the 'seal' bore both Chinese and Arabic script.

In 1928 an attempt was made to organize a Triad society at Port Weld by men from Penang, and at least two initiation ceremonies were held. The intention was to enlist all the fishermen and to control the fish market by restricting sales to members only. It was not long before it fell foul of the society already existing at Matang, which appears to have been a survival of the coastal Ho Seng, and a battle took place in which the newcomers were defeated. Eight of their headmen were arrested, of whom four were banished. The only name given to this intruding society is 'Three Dots'. It is known, however, from postwar evidence that some time before the war there was a battle in this area between the existing society and a branch of the Toh Peh Kong which tried to establish itself, and this may well have been the occasion.

Memories of the robber bands of Kinta were revived when the redoubtable leader Lung Wing who had fled from Kinta in 1919 reappeared in 1925, but was arrested before he could get a gang together. No one was prepared to give evidence in open court as to his previous crimes, and he was merely charged with being a bad character. There was, however, sufficient evidence in the files to justify his banishment, and he was duly sent off to China. Four years later he was in Siam with Lee Fong, one of his former associates, and there formed a gang which carried out raids in Kedah and gradually worked south to Kinta again. After several small robberies, Lung Wing succeeded in tracing the man who had given him away in 1925 and murdered him. For two years the gang managed to evade capture while engaging in extortion and kidnapping, but in 1931 the leader was stabbed with a spear by one of his victims and died. The remainder of the gang under Lee Fong were rounded up.

There is little more factual information about societies in the period immediately preceding the Japanese war. Sungei Blukang was again the scene of trouble in 1930 with fights between two Hokkien societies, and in 1932 a Sin Ghee Hin society was discovered at Kuala Kangsar composed of Sin Yiu rickshaw pullers, and a 'Three Dots' Society at Grik. In March 1933 the murder of a Malay Outdoor Customs Officer in Krian led to the uncovering of a smuggling gang, eleven in number, at Kuala Kurau. They, too, were members of a 'Three Dots' Society, and had as their leader one of the leading Hokkiens of the village who was President of the local Chinese school and had, apparently, successfully carried on a brisk trade in smuggling for some twenty years. All members of the gang, including the leader, were banished.

Recent interrogation of Protectorate and police officers and of old society members makes it clear that, although the records no longer exist, the same pattern of inter-society intrigue continued throughout the country up to the time of the Japanese invasion, with new societies constantly springing up whenever there seemed to be a chance of exploiting any set of circumstances. This led invariably to clashes with societies already established in the area. An unending battle of wits between the Protectorate and police on the one hand and the promotors of secret societies on the other was in constant progress.

6. SUMMARY

The position of the Chinese societies at the time of the invasion of Malaya by the Japanese at the end of 1941 may be summarized as follows:

In the urban areas both of the Colony and of the Malay States there were gang organizations engaged in protection–extortion activities. Their composition varied, but frequently they were formed of men of one dialect-group and/or of one type of occupation if they were in employment. Some of these gangs purported to trace their organization from older Triad societies and used Triad nomenclature, but although all were imbued with the Triad spirit, the use of the ritual of initiation, though well in evidence as late as 1929 in Singapore, diminished, due largely to the severe measures taken by the authorities, notably at Singapore and Penang.

Outside the main towns, the use of Triad initiation was more common because of the more tenuous nature of governmental supervision. In particular, Triad was rampant in the traditional coastal belt from Kedah to Klang among the fishing communities of the bagans[28] and near-by towns and villages such as Port Weld, Matang, Taiping, Klang and Port Swettenham, all of which had largely Hokkien populations. This coastal group was at all times in close contact with Penang and would appear to have developed from the old Ho Seng Society which in the 1870s was paramount in this area and represented the First Lodge of the five which, according to the Traditional History of the Brotherhood, were formed in China as the basic organization. From time to time, however, there were intrusions of other groups from Penang, the Ghee Hin in its new form the 'Sin Ghee Hin' (representing the Second Triad Lodge) and the Toh Peh Kong.

In the inland agricultural and mining areas of Perak and Selangor there was also a strong Triad strain among the Cantonese–Kwangsai–Hakka population. In Perak, along the Kinta valley, it owed its origin to two old Penang roots: the Ghee Hin (Yi Hing) and the Hai San (Hoi San), the latter representing the Third Triad Lodge. In Selangor the origin lay in the Hai San and the Ts'ung Paak (Ghee Hin) societies of the nineteenth-century mining days.

In general, the pattern which had developed among the early immigrants remained, with the influence of Penang origins affecting the whole of the north of the Peninsula—Kedah, Perak, and the coast of Selangor—while Singapore influence extended northwards through Johore and Malacca to Negri Sembilan and Selangor. There was, however, no rigid division between the two zones, for the greater mobility of labour had tended to blur the picture.

In particular it is to be noted that it was not until 1916 that the Triad hege-

[28] Jetties. Bagan is also applied to estuarine fishing villages.

mony of the Ghee Hin was declared to be unlawful in Johore, and that until then this immunity permitted the Ghee Hin in that State to retain its organization and its influence.

While there is evidence of a considerable recrudescence of Triad activity in the period from 1910 to about 1927, its growth thereafter would appear to have been held in check. Though not eradicated, it did not seriously disturb the Administration but remained under cover, making use of whatever opportunities offered. Initiation ceremonies did take place, but either they were not of frequent occurrence or the system of intelligence of the Protectorate and the police was inadequate to detect them.

In addition to Triad proper, there was throughout the Cantonese community, and including some Hakkas, a widespread network of Wa Kei societies with a notable flair for promotion of gaming. These societies were alleged to have had their origin in the old Peace on Water and Land or Coffin Breakers' Society of the early years of the century. Though in many respects modelled on the Triad Brotherhood, the Wa Kei fraternity had its own distinctive ritual.[29]

Finally, among Cantonese, Kwangsai, and Hakka labourers there were Chung Woh societies which were descended from the poor man's politico-Triad association of Yau Lit, but having lost almost all their political significance were on much the same level as any other of the secret societies, except that they did, as a rule, provide 'reading rooms' or some such club facilities.

Two events of importance to our study occurred in the 1920s and 1930s: the reorganization of the police force of the Colony, particularly in Singapore, and the control of immigration.

With the arrival from Ceylon in 1923 of Mr G. C. Denham as IGP, a beginning was made with the reorganization of the Colony police force, a process which was continued with increasing momentum from 1925 onwards under his successor Mr H. Fairbairn. The recruitment of an Armed Police Reserve direct from India began in 1924 to form what was later known as the 'Sikh Contingent' whose function was to deal with riots and public disturbances. Once again an attempt was made to recruit a Chinese contingent, and, once again, the attempt failed. In reporting this in 1927, the IGP remarked:

Men of a poor coolie type with low morality are the only applicants so far, and they are not worth spending money on. It is doubtful even if the new Depot and the sight of fine town barracks will bring sufficient material of the type required. An examination of conditions in Hong Kong and Shanghai has not provided any solution, and in view of establishing at an early date an adequate Chinese contingent the problem is at present receiving special consideration.

Despite the special consideration, no success was achieved.

There was, however, a considerable increase in the numbers of Chinese detectives, clerks, and interpreters who were distributed throughout the various police divisions. The greater efficiency achieved throughout the force by the many improvements introduced, in particular by the greater specialization within the Criminal Investigation Department, made it possible in 1933 for the police to take over from the Chinese Protectorate the full responsibility for detecting and investigating secret society matters. The files and records relating to these societies and their members were transferred from the Protectorate to the CID,

---

[29] See below, p. 544.

but the registration of lawful societies still remained a function of the Protector-ate. Furthermore, the sanction of the Protector was still required before any prosecution under the Societies Ordinance for membership of an unlawful society or for the possession of Triad documents or for any other offence under the Ordinance could be instituted. The Protector had therefore to be satisfied that there was sufficient evidence, documentary or verbal, to establish a *prima facie* case before sanction to prosecute was issued. Invariably, too, when expert evidence as to Triad documents was required by the court, it was given by an officer of the Protectorate.

The advisability of controlling the flood of Chinese immigration to Malaya had, as has been seen, repeatedly been suggested at various times since the first expression of opinion by Governor Fullerton in 1825, but always the business community, both European and Chinese, had opposed any interference with the free flow of labour.

At the outbreak of war in 1914, immigration from both China and India was prohibited to alleviate the distress caused by the sudden temporary closure of markets for tin and rubber. Before this, immigrants from China since the beginning of the century had, with few exceptions, numbered over 200,000 a year, reaching a peak of 269,864 in 1911. Although the wartime prohibition was later modified and finally abandoned, it was not until 1925 that the number of immigrants from China again reached this figure. From 214,692 in 1925, the figure jumped in the next year to 348,593, and in 1927 a new peak was reached with 359,262, a reflection of the disordered state of southern China. Although the numbers fell in 1928 and 1929 to 295,700 and 293,167, due to depression in the rubber industry, there had been a considerable migrational gain to Malaya, and when in 1930 a serious slump in both the rubber and tin industries occurred, the results of which affected all trades and occupations, widespread unemploy-ment rapidly developed. Large numbers of Chinese left the country for China, a movement which was encouraged by the repatriation at government expense of any decrepit labourers who wished to leave. In addition, relief camps were opened to house and feed unemployed labourers left in the Malay States without resources.

Faced with this problem, the Government of the Colony, with the concurrence of that of the FMS, introduced a system of restriction of immigration which came into operation on 1 August 1930. The immediate effect of this measure may be gauged by the following table which shows the number of adult males arriving from China:

1928	Unrestricted	192,809
1929	,,	195,613
1930	Five months' restriction	151,693
1931	Full year's restriction	50,120
1932	,, ,, ,,	18,741
1933	,, ,, ,,	13,535

In the three years 1931–3, the total migrational loss of Chinese to Malaya amounted to over half a million persons, men, women, and children.

One of the side effects of this limitation of entry of male Chinese (for no restriction was placed on the entry of women until 1938) was that there was a significant reduction in the renewal of Triad fervour by the insurge of members fresh from China, a large proportion of whom had frequently been the offcasts of wars and distress. The police were thus able to concentrate on dealing with the residuum of secret society members already in the country.

Limitation of immigration has continued ever since. A special Ordinance was brought into force on 1 January 1933 (The Aliens' Ordinance) under which persons already in Malaya might apply for Certificates of Admission which would allow them to return to Malaya outside the restrictive quota, thus strengthening the tendency for such persons to return to Malaya and settle there. One unlooked-for result of the exemption of women from restriction was the influx of swarms of women from China in search of employment. This was a very different picture from that presented by the early Chinese immigrants who, as has been seen, were almost without exception males. Apart from some Hokkien families, refugees from Amoy at the end of the Triad occupation of that city in 1853, there had been practically no female immigrants until 1863. Thereafter they continued to arrive in a steady stream, small at first but later increasing, the rise in numbers being particularly noticeable from 1911 onwards. Even so, it is surprising to relate that it was not until 1924 that the authorities of Hainan Island allowed their women to emigrate, and the arrival of the first batch of these women at Malacca in that year caused a near-riot in the streets by members of the Hainanese community who objected to the lifting of the ban, many of them having married wives locally in addition to having wives in Hainan.

By 1938 the flood of Chinese women arriving threatened to upset the policy of restricting immigrant labour to the numbers required to satisfy the needs of industry throughout Malaya, in so far as these could be judged, and restriction by quota was extended to include women. Nevertheless the trend towards reduction in the disparity of the sex-ratio among the Chinese community was already well-established, and by the time that the Japanese war broke out it was clear that there were sufficient Chinese children being born in Malaya to satisfy all future labour needs without recourse to immigration from China. The Chinese were increasingly becoming a settled community in their Malayan habitat.

Part 4
POSTWAR MALAYA

15

POSTWAR REACTIONS

1. THE JAPANESE OCCUPATION AND THE TRIAD SOCIETIES

WHEN, in December 1941, the Japanese armies began to sweep southwards through Malaya, members of Chinese secret societies were among the categories who received particular attention. For the Japanese were not only familiar with secret society techniques as practised in Japan itself, but since their invasion of Manchuria had become well versed in the uses and abuses of secret societies in China. They were alive to the fact that all Triad societies were centres for the development of Chinese patriotism, and knew that in Malaya Chinese secret society members had participated in the anti-Japanese activities of the Anti-Enemy Backing Up Society and other patriotic organizations. Secret societies in Malaya were, therefore, to be ruthlessly suppressed. Nevertheless, just as certain of the society members had been used as instruments for the spread of Japanese propaganda and influence in China, so the Japanese were prepared to use these members in Malaya, provided that their leaders, through fear, were first brought under Japanese control. With the surrender of the British on 15 February 1942, the rule of fear began.

The male Chinese population of every town and village was rounded up into areas surrounded by barbed wire and guarded by sentries. One by one the captives filed out for interrogation and for inspection by hooded informers, and members of the KMT, the MCP, schoolteachers, and members of secret societies were among those whom the Japanese sought. Society hooligans who before the war had obtained prestige in the underworld by being able to display three or five dots tattooed in the web of the hand between thumb and forefinger now found that this adornment was often a fatal liability. Thousands of suspected secret society members together with other 'antagonistic' categories were taken off and executed out of hand. Others, if they were more fortunate, were detained, often tortured and released if someone of substance would stand surety for them, or if they themselves would promise to work as intelligence agents for the Japanese in the underworld they knew so well. As certain Triad members had been detained by the British but had been released from the gaols immediately before the surrender, it was a comparatively easy task for detectives and others wishing to gain favour with the Japanese to point out such individuals, who were then forced to co-operate.

In a desperate effort to avoid recognition, many secret society leaders fled from their usual haunts and all members generally tried to efface themselves. But with the whole country in Japanese hands concealment became more and more hazardous. Many threw in their lot with the Chinese Resistance Forces which were beginning to form, and joined either the MPAJA under the flag of the MCP (MPAJA or Three-Star Army), or the KMT resistance group, the Overseas Chinese Anti-Japanese Army (OCAJA or Two-Star Army). Others left the main centres of population and lived among the village folk near the jungle edge and helped with the supply of foodstuffs to the 'hill-men'. The OCAJA was centred in the hills of Upper Perak, beyond the villages of Grik and Lenggong, but the hills bordering the Kinta valley in Perak became the main MPAJA stronghold, with Communist guerrilla influence spreading south-westwards towards Pangkor, Sitiawan, and the Dindings. Other MPAJA resistance groups based in Selangor and Johore were linked to Perak through a system of secret couriers who used the jungle paths, and towns and villages near the guerrilla units were secretly organized through the Malayan People's Anti-Japanese Union (MPAJU) for intelligence and supplies.

At the end of December 1943 an important agreement was signed between a representative of South-East Asia Command (SEAC) and the Secretary-General of the MCP, whereby the MPAJA units were to be provided with arms, money, and supplies by parachute, and were to receive officers of Force 136, a special unit organized by SEAC to assist resistance movements in areas occupied by the Japanese, who would be landed by submarine or dropped in by parachute. In return, the MPAJA agreed to give all assistance to the SEAC forces, not only during actual hostilities, but during a period of military occupation which would follow the defeat of the enemy. This agreement added greatly to the morale and strength of the MPAJA and increased their confidence. Nevertheless, this movement was never pro-British, it was essentially anti-Japanese and pro-Communist. Once the Japanese had been driven out of Malaya by the MPAJA assisted by Allied troops, then the MCP, at the appropriate time, would use its newly-equipped and trained armed force to defeat the British and establish a Communist State in Malaya. This, however, was not common knowledge. Meantime, the resistance groups received the admiration and secret assistance of the Chinese population of Malaya, and earned in equal measure the enmity and ruthless persecution of the Japanese.

But those Triad members who had neither escaped Japanese detection nor got away to the hills found themselves for the most part committed to working in some capacity for the Japanese. On the whole, this afforded the collaborator some protection and ensured him enough food to sustain life. Moreover, on occasion his close contact with the Japanese enabled him to do profitable business through his protector. This was especially true of the traditionally Triad-controlled area of the coast of North Perak, the need for intelligence agents being particularly important to the Japanese down the west coast of Malaya, where Allied submarine landings were feared. There are allegations that co-operation with the Japanese had begun during the early weeks of their attack on Malaya, and that Japanese troops were guided to Taiping by an unusual route, enabling them to cut off part of the rear of the retreating British forces. Later, as elsewhere throughout Malaya, both Malay and Chinese leaders were obliged to co-operate in setting up units of the Peace Preservation Corps, to ensure that any Allied activity was immediately reported to the Japanese. In Kuala Kurau itself a headquarters of this Corps was established on the premises of a local trader. Naturally, the people who really knew the coastline of this area and the intricacies of its innumerable tidal creeks and mangrove swamps were the Chinese fishermen, all of whom were Triad society members, skilled in using these creeks for opium smuggling, and so the Triad fraternity, under pressure from Kuala Kurau, was drawn into the Japanese intelligence network. But as the Japanese in their turn were notorious for participation in any racket which promised a profit, it was not long before a brisk trade developed among these coastal dwellers, under the shelter of their Japanese protectors, in the smuggling of rice, foodstuffs, copra, opium, and tobacco, with some piracy when opportunity offered. Gradually this trade expanded not only along the coast but across to Sumatra and north to Siam, while internally a secret network which included Taiping, Ipoh, and Telok Anson enabled smuggled goods to be widely distributed in the State. Japanese military police, suitably entertained, bribed, and rewarded, gave their full protection and co-operation. As a result, some small Chinese traders in the Krian area so benefited from these operations that they became men of wealth and standing in the community. But though openly working in close contact with the Japanese, they were careful to propitiate the guerrillas in the hills by secretly providing food supplies. In this way, for example, contacts were maintained between Kuala Kurau and some Communist sympathizers centred on Selama (possibly a unit of the 5th Independent Regiment of the MPAJA) some thirty miles away in the hills on the Kedah border. For many people, to remain alive it was often necessary to serve two masters, the Japanese and the resistance leaders.

In Penang Triad groups were even more completely at the mercy of the Japanese, and at a round-up of the Chinese male population held on 6 April 1942 large numbers were incarcerated and either executed, died from ill-treatment, or agreed to co-operate, and all societies were rigorously suppressed. It is, however, alleged that the Sin Ghee Hin agreed to work for the Japanese Intelligence, and that others worked for the Military Police, but although a few individuals appear to have prospered financially through questionable trading operations, or through being granted small monopoly permits, the benefits of co-operation were scarcely on the Perak scale. Perak, however, gave sanctuary to the many Penang members of the Brotherhood who fled from Japanese persecution, and throughout the Occupation the closest relations were maintained between the two areas.

There is information that in Penang itself four initiation ceremonies were held during the Occupation, and that the sponsors were a group of prewar Sin Ghee Hin members who were attempting during a period of great stress to hold together the survivors of the Triad groups on the island, and at the same time to provide some form of protection for themselves. The first of these initiation ceremonies apparently took place late in 1942 in the hills at Ayer Itam, when the sinseh was said to be Ooi Ah Soh, of the Penang Sin Ghee Hin, and the 'Promoter' a Triad member from Perak, Yeoh Ah Geow, then living in Penang. This partnership broke up when the two men quarrelled, and at three further initiation ceremonies in 1943, 1944, and 1945, another sinseh, Yeoh Ah Teik, officiated as sinseh, though again Yeoh Ah Geow was the 'Promoter'. In all, some 300 initiates were admitted into the Brotherhood. On the Perak mainland, also, there is information from another source that some six initiation ceremonies were held in the fishing bagans during the Occupation, all of them, it would appear, of the Yen Hai or 'Coastal' group of the Sin Ghee Hin. Apparently, the first initiation of this series was held in the Gula swamps 'in the year of the Japanese invasion', with Ooi Ah Soh as the sinseh, and Yeoh Ah Bah, the Elder Brother of Port Weld and Matang as the 'Promoter', and there were nearly 100 initiates from Port Weld, Kuala Kurau, and Kuala Sangga. A month later a further ceremony was held, with an even greater number of initiates, coming from the coastal villages as far South as Pasir Hitam and as far north as Penang. Once again, the 'Promoter' is said to be Yeoh Ah Bah, but the sinseh was Lim Ah Hah, a famous Triad figure from Taiping. Details of the next three ceremonies are not available, but it is said that the sixth ceremony was held after the surrender of the Japanese and before the arrival of the British forces in 1945. In 1942 the motive for joining the society was fear of the chaos which ensued upon the Japanese invasion, but by 1945 the motive was self-protection from the vengeance meted out by the MPAJA to collaborators, and a determination to maintain control of the coastal area. As was stated by a fisherman from Pasir Hitam, 'When I entered the Ang Bin Hoey we were gathered together and invited to save ourselves against the invasion of communists. There were no prayers. There were joss sticks, and we took our oaths that we would be punished by Heaven if we did wrong.'

There is similar evidence of initiation ceremonies in the Kinta valley of Perak, and the picture is probably true of all areas in which Triad societies had existed secretly in 1941.

The end of the Japanese war came with unexpected suddenness. Rumours of Japan's possible surrender had filtered through Malaya from the evening of 10 August, but although confirmed on the 15th, relief on the part of the general population changed to apprehension as it became known that the Japanese commander, General Itagaki, intended to continue the struggle, a decision only altered by the arrival from Tokyo of the Emperor's personal envoy with the Imperial command to surrender. Thereafter, owing to the difficulty of an immediate switch of emphasis at SEAC headquarters in Ceylon from the requirements of an invasion force to those of a British Military Administration, together with the necessity for extensive mine-sweeping operations in the Straits of Malacca, it was several days before British forces arrived in Malaya in any numbers. British landings were made at Penang on 3 September, at Singapore on the 5th, and at Morib, the gateway to Kuala Lumpur, on the 11th. British Military Administration officers reached Kuala Lumpur on the 12th, Kelantan on the 17th, Taiping and Ipoh on the 18th, and Kedah on the 19th, but it was later still before Pahang was taken over, and months before the resources of the Government permitted resumption of control of coastal swamps or remote areas which had always been on the fringe of administrative capacity. The formal signing of the surrender terms took place in Singapore on 12 September, and in Kuala Lumpur on the 13th.

During the interregnum between the Japanese surrender and the arrival of the British forces, the MPAJA emerged from the jungle, in accordance with SEAC instructions issued on 20 August, and together with the Malayan Communist Party assumed control of the countryside, the MPAJA taking over the police stations, and the MCP setting up People's Committees as ruling bodies in many of the villages, particularly in Johore, Negri Sembilan, Selangor, and Perak, where the resistance movement had been most highly organized. This action, though resented and feared by the Malays, was accomplished without immediate untoward incident except in North Johore, where Malays attacked the MPAJA who were assuming control of the Muar–Batu Pahat areas. Everywhere the MPAJA units were greeted by the Chinese population with enthusiasm and admiration for their endurance in facing the rigours of jungle life and the dangers of torture and death if captured. The MPAJA were Chinese in uniform, and besides representing local Chinese resistance to the Japanese, were also symbolic of the new-found might of China herself, whose prowess in Burma and the homeland, it was widely believed, had been mainly responsible for the downfall of Japan. Both at the surrender parade in Singapore and the official entry into Ipoh, it was not the British troops but the MPAJA which received the roars of acclamation from the crowds.

But this enthusiasm waned as the new 'liberators', though posing as the leaders of democracy for Malaya, exercised their power in an arrogant and ruthless fashion, requisitioning supplies and buildings, paying off old scores, and eliminating not only so-called collaborators but all who had the temerity to oppose their demands. Even the arrival of British troops and the setting up of the British Military Administration did not, for some considerable time, remove the threat of terror which menaced the population. A general shortage of food and consumer goods led to ever-increasing looting, smuggling, and black-marketing, and a crime-wave of unprecedented dimensions swept the country as groups of armed hooligans found that a pistol was the easiest way to secure a livelihood, to enforce an extortion demand, or to eliminate an enemy. The police force was in a sorry state. It had been used by the Japanese as an instrument for the oppression and humiliation of the Chinese and had thus earned the hatred of this community. Accused of graft and corruption, its ranks depleted by desertions and eliminations, it was utterly demoralized and in no state to maintain order. Growing tension between rival political groups of Chinese, and communal tension between Malays and Chinese added their quota to the disquietening scene, and it is therefore not surprising that the various groups in the community began to take steps to protect themselves from the many dangers which beset them. It was in these circumstances that the traditional Triad societies began to emerge as a refuge in the storm, not only for those who had immediate reason to fear the vengeance of the MPAJA, or who were politically opposed to a Communist régime, but for all who sought protection from physical harm and extortion in the chaotic conditions which prevailed.

The renaissance of the Triad Brotherhood began in August 1945, with the formation of the Ang Bin Hoey ('Society of the Ang or "Hung" People')[1] in the village of Kuala Kurau in North Perak. Mention has already been made of the holding of initiation ceremonies in the swamps of the Perak coastal area during the Japanese occupation. With rumours of a Japanese surrender more immediate factors contributed to the society's resurgence, the first and most urgent being the instinct of self-preservation. Always notorious as a focus of Triad activity, and throughout the Occupation the centre of a profitable import and smuggling concern under Japanese protection, the local fishermen and traders, with reason, feared the retribution of the MPAJA, and shortly before the Japanese surrender, when such retribution seemed imminent, are said to have received secret permission from the Japanese officer in charge of the district to organize all Triad elements in the area for mutual protection. Thus the Ang Bin Hoey, financed by Kuala Kurau and sponsored by the Triad leaders from the seven bagans—Kuala Kurau, Kuala Gula, Port Weld, Pasir Hitam

[1] Ang Bin Hoey is the Hokkien form, Hung Man Wui the Cantonese.

('Big Trong'), Bagan Jaha ('Little Trong'), Bagan Kuala Larut, and Pantai Remis—came into being. This combination of all Triad elements along the coast was intended to be a headquarters organization, the Ang Bun Tua Kongsi (Ang Headquarters) covering and controlling the whole area from Province Wellesley to Pantai Remis, and it is significant that new members joining the Ang Bin Hoey at this time were informed that the purpose of the society was protection from 'invasion' by the Communists. It is believed that in addition to Chinese, some hundred Malays, mainly Banjarese who have a reputation for belligerency, were recruited from the district between Kuala Kurau and Tanjong Piandang, and were sworn in on the Koran at a special ceremony. Support came, too, from Penang Triad members who had taken refuge in Krian and Larut during the Occupation, and from the Kwangsai gangs in the Kuala Kangsar hills. Arms were obtained (possibly at Simpang) from the Japanese stocks which were being rapidly collected in view of the surrender, and were distributed to Triad groups in every coastal village. Some, however, also filtered through to the near-by Communist sympathizers at Selama from their contact in Kuala Kurau.

When the Japanese surrender was confirmed and the MPAJA units surged out of the jungle to take over control during the interregnum, MPAJA forces from Sitiawan took over Taiping as the centre of control for Larut, and other troops from Selama made Bagan Serai their headquarters for the control of Krian. These operations were accomplished without difficulty, but the MPAJA were not alone in the field, for their rivals, the OCAJA guerrillas, also came swiftly down from Lenggong and established themselves in Kuala Kangsar, where they were reinforced by those Kwangsai gangs who had spent the occupation in the hills of the district. There are some indications of armed clashes between the two groups, as the MPAJA attempted unsuccessfully to disarm the OCAJA. Moreover, when the MPAJA attempted to extend their control to the fishing bagans of the Perak coast they were met with armed opposition from the Ang Bin Hoey. At Kuala Kurau, where their suggestion that the society should co-operate in the setting up of a Communist government was repudiated, and where the Triads refused to hand over their arms, the leading Chinese trader of the village and his brother were arrested, taken to Bagan Serai, and their shop was looted. Their prosperity under the Japanese made them an obvious target, and they were fortunate to be released in exchange for a prominent MPAJA leader who had been captured by the Ang Bin Hoey near Trong.

Both sides began an armed fight for control. Several severe clashes took place at Kuala Kurau, in one of which some ten MPAJA men were killed, and alarmed at probable retribution both from the MPAJA and the returning British, about 100 Triad members, including many who had taken refuge during the occupation, fled to Penang, where in any case equally gainful opportunities were expected. But the Yen Hai (Coastal Triad Group) continued the struggle on the Perak coast. At Kuala Gula a young leader, Tan Leng Lay, proved a fierce fighter, and from Port Weld the Triad veteran, Yeoh Ah Bah, drove the Communists out of Matang and back to Taiping. Further south again fierce fighting took place in the Trong area, where some of the MPAJU are said to have been attacked by Triad members armed with nibong spears. Eventually, however, the MPAJA groups prevailed, and the Triad fighters took refuge in the inaccessible swamps of Pasir Hitam, where they were joined by KMT guerrillas. Throughout September the struggle continued, and as late as the 28th two boat-loads of wounded Triad men sailed across to Penang Island to seek succour from their Brethren. Only the arrival of the British, some widespread arrests, and the disarming of the MPAJA units eventually stopped the fighting, and the Triad gangs began to return to their bagans. Before long they had re-established their traditional pattern of control. Within a very short time there was not a single declared Communist in Kuala Gula or Kuala Kurau: they had either left the area or been otherwise disposed of. The Triads had returned to power, and piracies and smuggling, gambling and protection rackets once more became general.

2. THE PLANNING OF POSTWAR MALAYA

Once Britain had recovered from the shock of the Japanese conquest of Malaya a Planning Unit was appointed to consider the policy to be adopted after the Japanese defeat, and by the time British forces returned to Malaya in September 1945 it had been decided to make important constitutional changes, with the intention of moving as rapidly as possible towards representative government.

Before the war the pattern of administration in Malaya had been the subject of constant criticism on the grounds of its fragmentation. In addition to the Straits Settlements there were nine separate States, each empowered in some degree to legislate, and each with some claim to independent administration. The connecting link was the Governor of the Straits Settlements, who was con-currently the High Commissioner for the Malay States, but while this arrange-ment made for a fair degree of uniformity of policy, it could not overcome the constitutional barriers which prevented the whole of Malaya from being treated as a single administrative unit. In a country whose area was only slightly larger than England without Wales, this diversity was a hindrance to common develop-ment and a vexation to traders.

It was therefore proposed that a Malayan Union should be created, formed from all nine Malay States combined with the Settlements of Penang and Malacca. The constitutional position of the Sultans was to be changed, and the Malayan Union placed under a Governor. Singapore was not to be included in the Union, but was to be a Colony under a separate Governor. The constitu-tional pattern was to be completed by the appointment of a Governor-General above the Governors of the Malayan Union and Singapore.

The reasons for the severance of Singapore from the rest of Malaya were never adequately explained. The White Paper on Postwar Policy in Malaya merely stated:

> In considering the need for a closer political integration in Malaya, His Majesty's Government consider that, at least for the time being, Singapore requires separate treatment. It is a centre of entrepot trade on a very large scale and has economic interests distinct from those of the mainland.[2]

It has been left to later writers to assume that as the addition of the massive Chinese population of Singapore to the Chinese population in the Malayan

[2] Cmd. 6724, Jan. 1946.

Union would make the Chinese the numerically preponderant race in the country, this factor would increase the difficulty of obtaining the agreement of the Malays to the new proposals.

The position to be accorded to the Chinese community under the new constitution undoubtedly presented a problem. No longer were the Chinese merely transitory migrants, staying for a few years and then returning to their homeland. This practice still continued on a large scale, but an increasing number of families remained permanently settled in Malaya, their contacts with China becoming more tenuous with each succeeding generation. Furthermore, the part played by the Chinese in resisting the Japanese both before the fall of Singapore and during the occupation of Malaya could not be ignored, and although Sino-Malay relations had deteriorated during this period, this deterioration had been deliberately fostered by the Japanese for their own ends.

The aim of British postwar policy was to erase, as far as possible, the dividing lines between the different racial communities and to offer, through broad-based institutions in which the whole community could participate, the means and prospect of developing Malaya's capacity in the direction of responsible self-government. 'In this development,' continued the White Paper, 'all those who have made the country their homeland should have an opportunity of a due share in the country's political and cultural institutions.'

One immediate result of the new policy was the abolition of the Chinese Protectorate which, according to a somewhat cryptic announcement made by the British Military Administration soon after its arrival in Malaya, had 'fulfilled its historic mission'. Although there was still to be a Secretary for Chinese Affairs as an Adviser to the Government, it was intended that the expression of Chinese opinion should, in future, come through elected representatives of the people and not through a government department. A further concomitant of the new approach was the necessity to review the legislation concerning the registration of societies, in order to ensure that there would be no hindrance to the formation of political parties which, it was hoped, would emerge to form the basis of a new electoral system of government.

In the event, the Constitution of the Malayan Union which came into being on 1 April 1946 on the resumption of civil government was never acceptable to the Malays, and the inaugural ceremonies were boycotted by the Sultans. It was objected that instead of being a congeries of sovereign States, each under its Sultan who by treaty arrangement accepted the advice of a British Adviser, the new Constitution virtually made a Colony of these States under the direction of a Governor. Not only so, but it gave equal political status to all persons born in the country. This was very acceptable to the Chinese community, who very wisely made no comment on the new constitution except to suggest that they would have preferred to see Singapore included in the Malayan Union. But to the Malays, acceptance of this principle of equal political status meant eventual political submergence and the loss of the right of the Malays to govern the country, for the local-born Chinese population was increasing at such a rate that the local-born Malays foresaw that they would be rapidly outnumbered. It is true that the proposals on which the new constitution was based had received the consent of the Sultans, but the consent was obtained by a rapid visit of a British emissary to each ruler in turn during the early weeks of the British Military Administration, with little opportunity of consultation between the

Sultans themselves. And the manner of presentation of the emissary's proposals was little short of coercive.

Widespread Malay opposition resulted in the formation of the United Malay Nationalist Organization (UMNO), created to oppose the new Constitution and to demand the re-establishment of the position of the Sultans, together with an acknowledgement of the paramountcy of the Malays in the Government. Faced with this situation, the British Government set up a Commission of Review, and before the end of 1946 fresh proposals for the constitution of a Federation of Malaya were published which acceded in large measure to the Malay demands.

This in turn resulted in the emergence in December 1946 of a political body under the chairmanship of Mr Tan Cheng Lock, CBE, which called itself the Pan-Malayan Council of Joint Action. Its object was opposition to the new Federation proposals, and it made the extravagant claim of being the sole mouthpiece of the peoples of Malaya. It based its opposition on the grounds that the new proposals provided insufficient representation of Chinese interests on the Councils (in particular, on the proposed Federal Legislative Council), that the residential and language qualifications for citizenship were too strict, and that Singapore was not be included in the Federation. In January 1947 a Consultative Committee was set up by the Government to invite the opinions of the public, and as a result of its recommendations alterations were made in the proposed constitution which increased the proportion of Chinese representation on Legislative Council and modified the citizenship qualifications.

But these amendments satisfied neither the Chinese members of the Committee, who submitted a minority report, nor the Chinese community at large. From the outset, the Council of Joint Action boycotted the Consultative Committee, and staged mass meetings throughout the country in opposition to the proposed Constitution. Moreover, it became increasingly the mouthpiece of the Chinese, Indian, and even Malay leftist groups, who saw in it a means of embarrassing the British Administration.

With this development the main body of Chinese traders was by no means happy, the more so since they preferred to express their opposition to the new constitutional proposals through the Associated Chinese Chambers of Commerce. Nevertheless, all groups (including the Associated Chinese Chambers of Commerce) joined in a One-Day Hartal (cessation of business) on 20 October 1947, as a mark of dissatisfaction with the constitutional proposals, and markets, shops, amusement parks, cinemas, factories, and street stalls went out of business for the day, with consequent financial loss to all concerned. But from then onwards the star of the leftist groups waned, and the Chinese community in general, while still opposed to the new Constitution on certain issues, co-operated in its working by serving as members of the State, Settlements, and Federal Councils, in the hope that outstanding differences might be composed through closer association rather than continued opposition.

On 1 February 1948 the Malayan Union ceased to exist, and the Federation of Malaya came into being. Through successive constitutional developments the Federation became an independent country on 31 August 1957, and chose to remain a member of the British Commonwealth.

The change in policy regarding the Societies Ordinance was destined to have important consequences. It was intended to introduce a new Ordinance on the

Hong Kong model, under which all societies should be permitted to exist without being required to register, subject only to the restriction that the Governor in Council should be empowered to declare unlawful any society whose activities were a threat to peace and good order. Pending the introduction of such amending legislation, the old Societies Ordinance was to remain in abeyance. In this way the field would be left clear for the formation of political parties, the problem of the recognition of the MCP and the KMT would be overcome, and there would be the administrative advantage of avoiding the registration of thousands of societies whose objects and activities were innocuous.

In the difficult and chaotic conditions which prevailed in Malaya during the early days of the new Civil Government in 1946 there was a tendency to regard this change of policy as a generous but impolitic gesture of the Labour Government which came into power in the United Kingdom in the middle of 1945, but this was not so. The decision was taken in August 1944, during the term of office of the National Government, and it is probable that no government in power at the time when the decision had to be made would have reached a different conclusion. For whatever the critics of colonialism may say, freedom of association is very much part of the British tradition, and as the history of British rule in the early years of the Straits Settlements amply shows, it was only with great reluctance and after experience over a long period had demonstrated the necessity for some control in the interests of the public that any legislative steps were taken to limit this freedom. In any case, the legislative control introduced in 1890 was aimed at the criminal activities of Chinese Triad societies, but for some years before the Second World War the impact of ritualistic Triad on the Chinese community had, to all appearances, been slight, and the possibility of its re-emergence as a serious menace to the Government seemed remote. Moreover, with the spread of Chinese and Western education, and with a growing proportion of Chinese among the population who had either been born in Malaya or had spent a large part of their adult lives there, it was to be expected that the Chinese would be more familiar with and amenable to the legal system and the administrative routine of the Government, and less likely to feel the need of the support of secret societies.

On the return of the British to Malaya in September 1945 the announcement that freedom of association was to be permitted led to the formation of a spate of Chinese, Indian, and Malay societies. Chinese Communist groups were well to the fore, apparently taking as their platform an 'Eight-Point Programme' issued by the MCP in August 1945 as the basis for a new democratic form of government in Malaya. These groups included not only the MCP itself, but the New Democratic Youth League (NDYL), the Women's Association, the General Labour Union, and, on the disbandment of the MPAJA army in December 1945, the MPAJA Ex-Service Comrades' Association. As British control spread, Chinese Nationalist (KMT) Associations emerged, and rapidly increased, being supported by Chinese businessmen and merchants already sickened by Communist excesses, and fearful of the economic effects of a Communist régime. In addition to the KMT, which established branches throughout the country, the San Min Chu Yi Youth Corps (SMCYYC) was particularly active. Allied to the KMT, but working to a separate headquarters in China, this Corps aimed at the indoctrination of Chinese youth with the principles of the KMT party, and was organized on the lines of the Hitler Youth Corps. Wherever a branch of the NDYL was set up, there too appeared a branch of the SMCYYC, in premises as close as possible to those of its Communist rivals, whose influence the Corps endeavoured to undermine.

The attempt of the KMT groups to capture the allegiance of the local Chinese population was greatly strengthened by the visit in October 1946 of the Vice-Minister of the Chinese Overseas Affairs Department, Tai Kwee Sheng, who spent six weeks in the Malayan Union and four in Singapore rallying the ranks of KMT sympathizers. He had been preceded as early as January 1946 by an 'Inspector of Chinese Education Overseas', who had arrived by air from Chung-king and had spent three months touring the country, holding conferences of school committees and teachers, and arranging for the registration of Chinese schools and teachers with the Ministry of Education in China. A very detailed code of rules and regulations governing the internal management and curri-culum of the Chinese schools, issued jointly by the Chinese Ministry of Educa-tion and the Overseas Affairs Commission, was published in the local Chinese vernacular press.

In these ways the KMT endeavoured to secure the allegiance of the Chinese in Malaya and to frustrate the efforts of the Communists, thus reproducing in Malaya the KMT–Communist struggle already being waged in China. Even so, as in China, other political groups also sprang up, some, like the Chi Kung Tong and the Chung Woh Tong, being revivals of old prewar organizations which had been moribund, while others were branches of middle-of-the-road parties which had already been established in China, such as the CDL, the KMT Revolutionary Committee, and the Society for the Promotion of Demo-cracy in China.

This division of the Chinese political field into right, left, and centre, though valid for China, cut deeply across the new policy laid down by the British Government, which aimed at the establishment of a system of government in Malaya based upon the enfranchisement of its inhabitants. Viewed from this standpoint—the creation of a Malayan community with a Malayan outlook—any organization which had its roots in and was directed from China, whether right, left, or centre, was a menace, and any movement of independent Malayan origin, no matter what its political colour, was of value in promoting local loyalties. Whereas the KMT groups were patently tied to China, and blatantly proclaimed the intention of organizing all Chinese overseas under the wing of the Chinese Government, the Communist groups constantly averred, and with some justification, that they were not instruments of the CCP but affiliates of the MCP, a body quite independent of any organization in China, whose aim was, as shown by the Eight-Point Programme, to establish a democratic form of government and a self-governing Malaya. This contention it was impossible at that time to refute.

But apart from the vociferous political groups among the Chinese in Malaya, and despite their vigorous propaganda, there was still a large body of Chinese merchants, shopkeepers, and small traders who, while acutely aware of their own interests, had no political axe to grind. Lacking the fire of ideological devotion to any group they were politically inert, but were unfortunately liable through intimidation and underground pressure to become at once the tools and the victims of unscrupulous minority groups.

In a category by itself and of paramount importance to this study was the early revival of Triad societies throughout Malaya, which is described in considerable detail below.

A further embarrassment to the Government was the emergence of scores of small criminal gangs, some bearing extravagant titles such as Exterminate Traitors Corps, or Blood and Iron Corps, or Dare to Die Corps, ostensibly occupied in the elimination of those who had collaborated with the Japanese, but in fact using this plea as a cover for extortion. Some of these gangs were linked with ritualistic Triad societies, while others were independent hooligan gangs taking advantage of the unsettled times and of the new freedom to organize. As a rule these gangs were composed of Chinese youths, sometimes joined in urban areas by Indian members. In Kedah similar gangs of Malay youths became prominent.

The rapid emergence of this spate of societies, political, Triad, and criminal, immediately after liberation and the establishment of the British Military Administration, and the power which these societies exerted upon the population, once again caused those responsible for the administration to wonder whether complete freedom of association was compatible with the maintenance of order, and led to yet further attempts at legislative control.

3. THE ANG BIN HOEY IN PENANG[3]

Although the origins of the postwar revival of Triad are to be found in the Ang Bin Hoey of North Perak, the greatest development of Triad power and control took place in Penang, where a few senior surviving members of the prewar pangkengs of the Sin Ghee Hin, led by their prewar sinseh, Ooi Ah Soh, and reinforced by other Penang Triad refugees who rapidly returned to Penang from Perak, followed the example of their Brethren in Kuala Kurau, and set up a parallel organization which they also called the Ang Bin Hoey.

Among the participants in this revival were some who before the war had been initiated into the '108' Society of Singapore, while others were members of the Sin Ghee Hin of Penang. All were alleged to have collaborated with the Japanese, though such of them as later came under official enquiry denied this. Whatever the truth, this group was certainly afraid at the time of the Japanese surrender, and wished to revive the Triad society as a means of protection for themselves, in view of possible reprisals by the Communists for their alleged pro-Japanese activities during the Occupation. Among them were businessmen who had prospered during the Occupation, Chinese detectives who had been forced to work for the Japanese, and some alleged Communists who had co-operated with the enemy.

But in addition, there were prewar members of the Sin Ghee Hin who were interested in such Triad activities as illicent trading, the promotion of gambling, and the money to be made by the smuggling of opium and tobacco, particularly in co-operation with the Triad groups of Perak. And the Perak illicit traders,

[3] *Note on sources for postwar chapters.* Material for the postwar story came mainly from police and secretariat files made available to the author for the purpose of this study. During the period 1946–8 all material concerned with the prosecution of Triad members (documents, statements, etc.) passed through his hands as Secretary for Chinese Affairs in the Federation. Then and later (1955–8) further information was obtained by questioning many persons connected with the story. It has not, therefore, been possible to quote references for specific items except when they derive from the press or from government publications.

smugglers, and pirates of Kuala Kurau, Port Weld, and Matang welcomed the opportunity to continue the collaboration between Penang and Perak which had existed during the Occupation, and which had already paid dividends. They were completely in favour of a strong Triad organization in Penang, and were backed, particularly in Jelutong, by Yeoh Ah Geow, the promoter of the Penang initiation ceremonies of the Occupation period, and his friend, Yeoh Chin Geok, a waterfront labourer who had become reasonably prosperous by looting in 1941 during the chaos preceding the arrival of the Japanese. On the waterfront, however, the situation was complicated by the presence of the pre-war Ji Tiau Loh gang, a rival of the Sin Ghee Hin, which was also hoping for profits from smuggling and looting. Inland, in the Dato Kramat, Burma Road area, the Sin Khien Khoon still existed as a rival in the 'protection' of gambling and prostitution. Finally, there was the sinister figure of Ooi Ah Soh, who had been forced to spend the Occupation on the Perak coast owing to his quarrel with Yeoh Ah Geow in 1942, but who now returned post-haste to Penang, determined to re-establish himself as the ritual head of a large Triad society, with all the power and financial advantages which such a position would entail. Though challenged by Yeoh Ah Geow, he was the driving force behind the scenes.

The first signs of Triad revival began with the Sin Ghee Hin, and centred in a coffee-shop in Jelutong, frequented by Sin Ghee Hin groups before the war. It was kept by Khor Khum, a Triad member of White Fan[4] (415) rank and a gangster who had spent much of the Occupation in jail. At the beginning of the Interregnum, when the MPAJA on the mainland were beginning to tyrannize in the villages, Khor Khum rapidly formed a group of gunmen who acted as a protection gang for Triad members who sought his aid in Penang. Shortly afterwards Ooi Ah Soh arrived from Perak after the fight with the MPAJA at Kuala Kurau, and on 1 September 1945, the anniversary of the Feast of the Five Ancestors (the 25th day of the Seventh Moon), an auspicious day for a Triad revival, the Ang Bin Club was secretly formed as a nucleus for the development of the society, and began its operations on the waterfront in Jelutong under Khor Khum's leadership. Khor Khum was readily won over to the support of Ooi Ah Soh by the promise of the lucrative position of Incense Master at forth-coming initiation ceremonies at which Ooi Ah Soh intended to officiate as sinseh, while the prowess of Khor Khum's gunmen soon added to the prestige of the society in the underworld, and facilitated recruitment by intimidation.

The arrival of the British forces in Penang on 3 September, and the subsequent announcement that the Societies Ordinance would not be implemented, gave a tremendous impetus to every type of society. Freed, as they believed, from the necessity of operating any longer in secret, members of the Ang Bin Club called a meeting on 7 September at a club in McNair Street, to discuss the formation of a much more ambitious all-society union, on the model of the Ang Bin Hoey of Perak. This suggestion was strongly approved by Ooi Ah Soh and Khor Khum, but when the latter further suggested that the gangs of the Sin Khien Khoon and the Ji Tiau Loh should be invited to become members, some Sin Ghee Hin members demurred, only to be overruled by Ooi Ah Soh, whose main concern was the increased profits which would accrue to him from the fees of these new initiates. It was decided to form the Ang Bin Hoey Club

[4] See below, App. 1, p. 530.

z

with Khor Khum as secretary, to invite all Triad societies to a joint meeting, and to keep in close touch with the Perak Ang Bin Hoey.

Life in Penang at the time, despite the return of the British, was far from pleasant. On the waterfront, the Ji Tiau Loh gangs were looting and thieving. In the town, Communist groups of the Three Stars and the NDYL, together with extortion gangs with blood-curdling names of the Iron Blood Traitors' Eradication Corps and the Racial Traitors' Eradication Corps roamed the streets, eliminating alleged 'traitors', and extorting from shopkeepers. The Ang Bin Club sent out patrols ostensibly to keep order in the town, but their main activity was robbery and looting. By the end of September, after being joined by a number of wounded from Perak who had brought with them a machine-gun and some hand-grenades, the society was said to have over 400 members and 100 pistols, with influence in the country districts of Bayan Lepas, Sungei Ara, Sungei Dua, Relau, and Glugor, and strong control on the waterfront.

It was in these circumstances that on 2 October, in response to invitations issued in the name of the Ang Bin Club to Triad members (including all those who had belonged to the Sin Ghee Hin, the Sin Khien Khoon, and the Ji Tiau Loh) a meeting was held at the Builders' Associations' premises in Macalister Road, with the object of forming an Ang Bin Hoey and setting up a sub-committee to arrange for the new society's participation in the celebrations of China's National Day, on 10 October. There was a representative gathering of shopkeepers, petty tradesmen, hawkers, and labourers; estimates of the numbers present vary from forty to more than 100. The decision to form an Ang Bin Hoey as the central organization of Triad Brethren was unanimous, but there was serious dissension on the question of whether it should be 'open' or 'secret'. The Perak group, headed by Yeoh Ah Geow, supported the continuance of a secret organization in keeping with Triad tradition. He pointed out, with a combination of realism and naïveté, that in an 'open' organization, the president, who presumably would be a respectable businessman, would be blamed by the authorities for the misdeeds of the members, and so an innocent man would be made to suffer. Quite clearly he had no illusions about the future activities of the Brotherhood. Those supporting the formation of an 'open' association main-tained that the Brotherhood throughout its history had of necessity been forced to work in secret, but that the time had now come for it to exist openly and take its rightful place in the community. There was now no reason why it should not do so, since the British were permitting freedom of association. An acri-monious debate developed in which the personal rivalry between Yeoh Ah Geow and Ooi Ah Soh was clearly evident to the invited representatives of the Sin Khien Khoon and the Ji Tiau Loh. In the end, the supporters of the 'open' policy won the day. It was also decided to have no truck with the MCP, and that the society would not accept the Communists' 'Eight-Point Programme'. This was in line with the anti-Communist policy of the Perak Ang Bin Hoey, but the decision was ignored by Ooi Ah Soh, who admitted to the society anyone who was willing to pay the entrance fee. The meeting elected as president of the new society Teoh Teik Chye, the proprietor of a small Tiechiu remittance shop who had prospered by association with the Japanese during the Occupa-tion. He was a Triad member of several years' standing with KMT sympathies. The reason for this choice is obscure. Presumably, as Yeoh Ah Geow had suggested, an 'open' organization required a respectable businessman as its nominal head. Khor Khum was appointed secretary and treasurer, and Ooi Ah Soh as the sinseh to conduct initiation ceremonies. This again aroused the antagonism of Yeoh Ah Geow who had put forward a clansman Yeoh Ah Teik, and left the meeting breathing defiance.

A temporary headquarters was established in Sandilands Street, and recruitment was pushed forward. When the society took part in the Double Tenth procession, it was said to have more than 2,000 members (in addition to a great many members from Perak) and had established three branches.

Meantime, for all to whom honest labour was anathema, and for those members of the Brotherhood who all their lives had lived by their wits, by petty extortion, theft, intimidation, opium peddling, smuggling, and the whole intricate ganglia of underworld rackets here was a real opportunity to operate under the protection of the society. Even its own organization was a paying proposition, for every new member meant not only an initiation fee for Ooi Ah Soh but profit for all concerned with the ceremony, and pressure could always be used to make non-members join. From the outset, there were evident signs of criminal activities by some of the members as well as by others using its name. Teoh Teik Chye soon realized that there were dangers ahead, and on 15 October published an announcement in the *Modern Daily News*, a Chinese-language newspaper, referring to 'unscrupulous persons posing as members of our society to extort money and threaten people with death', and advised the public to report such occurrences to the society or to the police. He declared that the society's objects were to 'foster mutual friendship among members, and to avoid discussion of political matters', but robbery and extortion continued, for few people would report to the police, and none would identify their assailants, whether Ang Bin Hoey or not, for fear of the inevitable reprisals.

On 1 November three Hokchiu members of the society were arrested in possession of the proceeds of a robbery. Four days later one of the detectives investigating the case was shot dead by Yeoh Ah Geow, and the same evening Yeoh Ah Geow himself was shot dead. The strongest suspicion fell on his rival, Ooi Ah Soh, who was at the scene of the shooting with a group of friends and who had the reputation of being a crack shot. Later Ooi Ah Soh commented that Yeoh Ah Geow had caused the death of many innocent people in North Perak, but all members of the Ang Bin Hoey knew that he had died because he was attempting to oust Ooi Ah Soh from his position in the society.

As a result of these two murders, a combined force of police and troops raided the headquarters of the society on 6 November, took away its books and seals, and closed down the 'open' organization of the society. Ooi Ah Soh and Khor Khum went into hiding in Jelutong, and Yeoh Ah Teik, the sinseh who had been favoured by Yeoh Ah Geow, fled to Kuala Kurau, where he informed the Perak Ang Bin Hoey of the circumstances of the shooting. Never again were Ooi Ah Soh or Khor Khum able to set foot in North Perak.

The suspension of the Societies Ordinance had faced the police with a dilemma. They had no authority to take action against any society, but only against individuals who could be shown, by evidence in court, to have committed crimes. In addition, it was known that the Government were averse to using the Banishment Ordinance. The position had reverted to that existing in the early years of the nineteenth century, and the police responded, as did their predecessors, by trying to use the Ang Bin Hoey to assist in the control of crime. Three weeks after the raid on the society's premises, the articles seized were returned to Teoh Teik Chye who was told that the society would be permitted to function provided that it would assist the authorities in the maintenance of order, and this was agreed. The consequences, however, were disastrous, for the public now believed that the society had government support, while the Ang Bin Hoey did little to give the assistance promised.

Teoh Teik Chye spent the next few weeks drafting rules and regulations for the society, and gathered a group of respectable small businessmen whom he persuaded to act as a temporary committee. His right-hand man was a fellow member of the '108' Society of Singapore, Ong Keng Hooi, a strong and ruthless character who was soon to dominate the society's central committee just as Ooi Ah Soh and Khor Khum dominated in ritualistic matters. On 8 January 1946 notification of the reorganization was given to the Chinese press in the following terms:

> Unscrupulous persons have wrongly used the name of this society, the Ang Bin Hoey, and undermined its reputation. The public are informed that with the kind permission of the Government this association is being resuscitated, and in future every official document of the association must have the official seal. All former members are asked to re-register, and their applications must be passed at a meeting of the Committee before they can be regarded as full members.

In February the society established its headquarters at 55 Maxwell Road in premises formerly occupied by the MPAJA which, in accordance with their agreement with the British authorities, had voluntarily disbanded in December. For this transfer $3,000 was paid to the MPAJA. At a general meeting held on 27 February, office-bearers were elected under the new rules, and their names were published in the press.[5]

But already the shadow of the murdered Yeoh Ah Geow was falling across the scene. At Jelutong a clansman, Yeoh Chin Geok, who headed a group of fishermen promised to co-operate with the police in maintaining order. Ooi Ah Soh and Khor Khum, in hiding from the police who wished to investigate the murder of Yeoh Ah Geow, saw this as a threat to their security and surrounded themselves with a group of hooligans. Within a week Yeoh Chin Geok had been shot dead. Further allies were found in the Sin Khien Khoon gangs at the Eastern Smelting Works, Dato Kramat Road, and the Ji Tiau Loh gangs of the waterfront led by a ruthless gangster Lim Oh Yeoh, and his young henchman Chew Kit Ling, half-Chinese, half-Tamil, who were among the worst of the looters of cargo. From such types Ooi Ah Soh recruited his gang of 'killers' ('Tiger' Generals) and his personal bodyguard, all of whom were initiated by him.

During the decade preceding the Occupation the Ji Tiau Loh gangs had been the bitter enemies of the Sin Ghee Hin, but they were now willing to join the Ang Bin Hoey since that society was apparently operating with official approval and might be expected to become very powerful. Once admitted as members, they hoped to be able to take control. In any case, they would be able to retain control of their own area. Months later, Teoh Teik Chye was to tell the police that 'the root of all the trouble of the Ang Bin Hoey in Penang was the unwise acceptance of the Ji Tiau Loh to membership'.

When originally started in October 1945 the Ang Bin Hoey was a single unit,

[5] *Northern Star*, 1 Mar. 1946.

but in the reorganization which began to function in December 1945, each of the sixteen original pangkengs of the Sin Ghee Hin recruited as individual units, new units being added as the need arose. Each unit adopted the title of 'division' or 'cell' as being more appropriate to sections of a combined organization. The character used was *Ch'u*, the same as is used by the Communists for 'cell'. By the end of February 1946 there were in all twenty-two cells, numbered 1–22. Cell numbers were not allocated by the headquarters committee to specific territorial divisions of the island, but each cell crystallized round the acknowledged leader in his own area. Some of the cells had both town and rural members.

By far the most powerful were Cell 12, led by Tan Keng San, and Cell 4, controlled by Khor Khum, though with others as official area supervisors. Cell 12, in addition to a strong town membership in Bridge Street and along the waterfront from Magazine Lane to Katz Street, embraced the pirate lair of Batu Maung to the south, and also included in an associate membership men from the seven coastal bagans of North Perak, all of which had originally been included in the Ang Bin Hoey formed at Kuala Kurau. Close co-operation between Perak and Penang for illicit trading, smuggling, and piracy had always been intended, but this associate membership developed because of the ill-feeling which had arisen between Perak members and Ooi Ah Soh through the murder of Yeoh Ah Geow, for on their frequent visits to Penang, Perak men were afraid of attack by Ooi Ah Soh's supporters, and appealed to Tan Keng San for protection. He proclaimed them members of Cell 12, and thereafter they were safe, for even Ooi Ah Soh and Khor Khum feared Tan Keng San, who not only had plenty of guns but a reputation for using them whenever necessary. By maintaining membership of this one cell of the Penang Ang Bin Hoey, the link between Penang and North Perak was strengthened, and Cell 12 became the most powerful of all, with the greatest number of firearms. It was soon notorious for the participation of its members in piracies in the narrow water between Malaya and Sumatra, which spread eventually down to the Selangor coast.

Cell 4's main operational area was Jelutong, between Perak Lane and Jelutong Road, where its headquarters was situated, but it also controlled the village of Sungei Nibong, on the coast in the rural area further south, which, like Batu Maung, was soon a centre of smuggling and piracy. In the Dato Kramat and Burmah Road areas it was given added strength by the Sin Khien Khoon gangs. But in Penang town, backed by Lim Oh Yeoh's formidable gang, it became deeply involved in waterfront robberies and looting cargoes. Cell 4, too, was heavily armed, and earned much prestige in the underworld from the personality of its leaders.

The secret society group the Ji Tiau Loh, which penetrated the structure of the Ang Bin Hoey, was an important factor in its evil reputation and eventually led to its dissolution. This was the group originally known as the Ke Iau San, operating in the vicinity of Noordin Street Ghaut, the second road leading from the sea-front to the town, and known to the Chinese as 'Road No. 2', in Hokkien, Ji Tiau Loh. This waterfront area was one of the toughest zones of the town, and contained a number of gang groups, subsidiaries, as it were, of the Ji Tiau Loh, and composed, as a rule, of workers of a particular calling. All these subsidiaries were represented in the Ang Bin Hoey, though in different cells.

The Impact of Chinese Secret Societies in Malaya

The wharf labour at Noordin Street Ghaut, the tough core of the Ji Tiau Loh, dominated by gangsters under Lim Oh Yeoh, joined Cell 4, as did the workers in the sampan-building yard (Choon Long). Labourers belonging to the Rubber Workers' group (Chu Nin Ka) were divided, some 80 per cent joining Cell 12, the rest joining Cell 4 or Cell 2. Each of the four jetties between Noordin Street Ghaut and the railway pier was inhabited by sampan men of a single surname, and two of these belonged to Cells 12 and 13 respectively. The rickshaw pullers (trishaw pedallers) of the area were mostly T'au P'ak Hokkiens of surname Tan, and formed their own cell, No. 18, while a group of gambling promoters working under the protection of the Ji Tiau Loh became the new Cell 21. Distinct from the Ji Tiau Loh groups were the workers at the Eastern Smelting works, members of the Sin Khien Khoon, who first joined Cell 4 but later formed their own cell, No. 20.

When, early in January 1946, initiation ceremonies were resumed, each cell strove to expand, since more members meant greater power and increased income for cell leaders. Theoretically the initiation fee of $10.80 was equally divided between the sinseh (Ooi Ah Soh), the cell leader, and the society headquarters. Also theoretically, applications for membership were made through the committee, and were sanctioned before initiation, but such restrictions were ignored by Ooi Ah Soh and Khor Khum, who recruited candidates direct and retained the bulk of the fees involved. In fact men were press-ganged in the streets, hustled into lorries in broad daylight, and taken off to initiation ceremonies without daring to protest. 'Entrance tickets' were sold by canvassers round the town, using the usual pressure techniques, and lorries went along the streets, picking up ticket-holders with cries of 'This way for the Show!' 'Any more for the hills?'

Most of the ceremonies were held in the Relau Hills, some miles to the south-west of Penang, up the Ayer Itam valley, and reached a scale unprecedented in the history of Triad in Malaya. Ooi Ah Soh admitted that by the end of March 1946 twenty ceremonies with full Triad ritual had been held. Numbers of initiates at any single ceremony rose from 300 or 400 after the Occupation to over 1,000 at each of the nineteenth and twentieth ceremonies held on 26 and 31 March 1946. At the twentieth ceremony, besides new initiates, over 1,000 ranks were confirmed or conferred, and some twenty groups from villages along the Perak coast were initiated. The ceremony lasted through the night, but when at dawn the police intercepted those coming away, they missed their target; Ooi Ah Soh got away unrecognized. Some of those interrogated estimated that at least 3,000 people were present, and from later information it would appear that this was intended to be the last initiation ceremony held on Penang Island, as Ooi Ah Soh meant to move away from police attentions and to hold future ceremonies in Province Wellesley. He and Khor Khum fled to the mainland on 1 April.

With the increase in the membership crime, too, increased, for very little had resulted from Teoh Teik Chye's promise of co-operation with the police. He paid no attention to the misdeeds of society members but was willing to take action against non-members, particularly Communists who, in addition to being rivals for the control of the masses, were the declared enemies of collaborators who had joined the Ang Bin Hoey for protection. There was in any case a basis of political antipathy since Teoh Teik Chye and many other members were long-standing members of the KMT, and this antipathy had shown itself in the society's decision not to endorse the MCP's Eight-Point Programme.

Undoubtedly, however, there were many Communist sympathizers in the Ang Bin Hoey at this time. Some had been collaborators and had joined for protection against the revenge of their own party. Others had been admitted by Ooi Ah Soh, who was unconcerned with political alignments when money was at stake. Some had deliberately penetrated the society in an attempt to win it over to Communism. Others, again, attracted by its rapid progress and growing power, found it more profitable or expedient to belong to the society, despite the fact that politically they were inclined to favour the Communist Party.

At the time of the Ang Bin Hoey's resuscitation in December 1945, the Communist front included the MCP, the NDYL, the Women's Union, the General Labour Union, and the MPAJA Ex-Service Comrades' Association, all of which were conducting vigorous and indeed violent propaganda against the British Military Administration, powerfully aided by the Chinese vernacular press. A few weeks later the Communist groups attempted to hold mass rallies throughout Malaya on 15 February 1946, the anniversary of the fall of Singapore in 1942, to celebrate the defeat of the British. Despite prohibition by the Supreme Allied Commander, Admiral Mountbatten, of processions or meetings on that day, some meetings were held and were dispersed by the police. This resulted in a great loss of prestige for the Communists, especially since the Ang Bin Hoey, which had been invited to take part in this rally, had warned its members not to do so. Moreover, on 18 February, the Ang Bin Hoey showed, for the first time, a few signs of being of practical assistance to the police in their battle against widespread extortion and robbery, when a group of members arrested several persons suspected of having carried out extortion in the society's name and handed them over to the police. The society received the personal thanks of the officer in charge, Detective Branch, and were commended by the press on the following day for their 'valuable help' in the 'arms drive'. But one of the men they arrested was not handed over to the police. He was Teh Aik Seng, nicknamed Chap It Chye or 'Eleven Toes', and it was not until some days later after a complaint laid by this man's wife and the subsequent discovery of his corpse tied up in a sack in the sea, that investigations were started which left no doubt that Teh Aik Seng had been taken to Ang Bin Hoey headquarters, and there 'charged' with having informed against the society. He was sentenced to death by an official of the society. Pressed by the police, Teoh Teik Chye produced two of the four members of the Ang Bin Hoey suspected of being concerned with this murder, but at the same time made a statement to the press in which he sought to enhance the reputation of the society by criticizing the police who, he said, had detained members of the society and accused them of robbery, extortion, piracy, and murder despite the help recently given by the society.[6]

The police now realized the true nature of the Ang Bin Hoey, but the society was so powerful and exerted such a terrorizing influence over the general public that information which might lead to the arrest of its criminals was unobtainable except from detectives and informers, and of these, by the middle of April 1946, six had been shot dead, two were missing, one had been drowned,

[6] *Kwong Wah Jit Poh*, 7 Mar. 1946.

and one shot and wounded. One of those killed was the informer whose information had led to the raid on the initiation ceremony in the Relau Hills on 31 March 1946.

Meantime, on 9 April differences between the ex-MPAJA and the Ang Bin Hoey in Penang came to a head when one of the men, 'arrested' by the Ang Bin Hoey and handed over to the police, was sentenced to five years' rigorous imprisonment for being in illegal possession of a pistol. He had tried to extort money in the name of the society, and several members gave evidence at the trial. In retaliation, three members of the Ang Bin Hoey were murdered between the 10th and 13th, two MPAJA members being wounded in this last affray. The MCP concentrated on the feud with great intensity because desertions from their organizations to the Ang Bin Hoey had been increasing. For some time the public regarded this as merely a feud between two equally undesirable criminal groups, but later in April there was such an obvious extension of the grip of the Ang Bin Hoey on all sections of the community that there was widespread alarm. In addition to the usual 'protection' imposed on hawkers, prostitutes, and stall-keepers by each of the twenty-two cells, every bale of goods entering or leaving the harbour paid tribute, whole tongkangs loaded with cargo were frequently boarded, their crews turned off, and the goods taken away for disposal. Along the sea coast there were frequent piracies by the pirate groups associated with Cell 12 and based on Kuala Kurau and Port Weld in North Perak. Throughout Penang Island there were innumerable cases of extortion, armed robbery, and assault, the victims usually being too terrified to report. One complainant in a case of armed gang robbery by some of the Ji Tiau Loh was shot dead in the street on 25 April, the day before the trial of three of the gang, all Ang Bin Hoey members, whom he had dared to identify. Twelve days later a Sikh watchman was shot dead in his hut because he had been a witness of the shooting on 25 April.

On 28 April the society held its official opening ceremony at 55 Maxwell Road. The Chinese Consul in Penang was invited, but after discussing the matter with the police, said he was unable to send a representative because of illness. Determined to obtain public recognition, two members of the society went to the Consulate and, under threat of future difficulties that would ensue from 'lack of co-operation', they forced a representative to attend.

About a week later a group of Chinese merchants belonging to the Importers' and Exporters' Association offered to pay for the services of twenty members of the Ang Bin Hoey to police the harbour and prevent robberies of their cargoes on the waterfront, payment to be $15 per head per day, a total of $300 per day. The agreement eventually reached was that twice the number of men should be engaged at the same rate, making a total of $600 daily, or $18,000 monthly; $5,000 was paid in advance, but on the sixth day of the working of the scheme a cargo belonging to one of the merchants was robbed and the arrangement came to an end. This failure was largely due to the inability of the committee to control the Ji Tiau Loh and its waterfront gang leader, Lim Oh Yeoh. At the same time it was believed that those 'policing' the harbour were not paid the amounts they had been promised, but that the money was retained by Ong Keng Hooi.

Police pressure was now increasing. On the night of 14–15 May 1946 a search of the society's premises at Maxwell Road was made, during which a punishment room was discovered, containing ropes, sticks, and sacks. This confirmed the stories of two victims who said that they had been taken to the punishment room for 'trial', allegedly because they had falsely used the name of the Ang Bin Hoey for extortion, which they denied. They were tied up, beaten, and threatened with drowning in sacks unless they confessed. They were eventually released at a price, through the pleading of a member of the society. Minute books and account books also found gave the police further proof of the society's activities and raids were made on the houses of Teoh Teik Chye and Ong Keng Hooi. Nevertheless, on 15 May the Ang Bin Hoey officially entertained the Chinese Consul-General, Dr Wu Paak Sheng, who was visiting Penang during a tour of the peninsula, when Teoh Teik Chye publicly stated that the object of the society was to assist the British Government in the maintenance of peace and order in Malaya, and to strive for the welfare of China and the Chinese, and the promotion of national unity in China.

Next morning he was told by the police to close the Ang Bin Hoey within three days. That night (16 May) police raided the house of Tan Keng San, the leader of Cell 12, and arrested him in possession of two firearms. On 18 May Teoh Teik Chye closed down the headquarters, and on the 20th notifications to this effect (dated the 18th) appeared in the Chinese and the English press, signed by Teoh Teik Chye as president.

Membership at the time of dissolution was variously estimated to be between 20,000 and 40,000, of which about 90 per cent were Hokkiens, the balance being a mixture of Cantonese, Hakkas, Tiechius, and Hainanese. Most of the harbour labourers, lorry drivers, and rubber factory workers were members although they had their own labour organizations which were linked with the MCP. The same was true of the members of the General Labour Union. Indeed, contemporary report stated that most of the Penang labourers were either members or were connected with the society in some way.

The Decline

But the disruption of the central organization of the Ang Bin Hoey in Penang had little immediate effect upon the criminal activities of the members, and even when empowered to take limited banishment action, it was some considerable time before the police were able to bring the situation on Penang Island under control.

Despite Teoh Teik Chye's public announcement of the dissolution, he had informed only a few members of the executive committee, who were told to pass on his decision to the cell leaders. Angered by his action, and unwilling to disband, the cells continued to operate underground as individual units. Protection and extortion rackets continued unabated, as did the looting of cargoes and piracy. Furthermore, jealousy between cells and disputes concerning areas of influence frequently caused serious gang fights which added a further element of unrest. In addition, the partial vacuum caused by the removal of the control centre not only caused internal strains but attracted the attention of various outside political groups, all of which saw in the leaderless and fragmented Ang Bin Hoey a potential source of backing and power.

Police attention was first turned to the waterfront, and the arrest of Lim Oh Yeoh in May 1946, and of his henchman, Chew Kit Leng, in June removed these two 'terrors' of Cell 4 from the scene and disorganized the main gang operating at Noordin Street Ghaut in the wholesale looting of cargoes and extortion from merchants. Lim Oh Yeoh jumped bail and fled to the Perak coast for refuge, and it was almost two years before he returned to Penang, where he was rearrested in February 1948 and banished. Chew Kit Leng, acquitted in July 1946, was rearrested in August on a charge of possessing arms, sentenced to imprisonment, and banished in September 1949. These two arrests marked the turning-point in the harbour situation. Not only did they remove the most feared leaders from the scene but they caused several other gangsters to flee to the mainland, and within a few weeks the conditions in the harbour had so much improved that for the first time the Importers' and Exporters' Association reported that cargoes were being loaded and unloaded unmolested.

The disruption of the intricate network of smuggling and piracy on the high seas was more difficult. Smuggling was endemic, but piracy had developed along the three main trade routes linking Penang with (*a*) Sumatra, (*b*) the Perak ports, and (*c*) the Siamese ports and Rangoon, and although temporarily dislocated on the northern route during the early weeks of 1946 by British troops and local Volunteer units it had again reared its ugly head.[7] The normal route to Sumatra ran south from George Town to Pulau Jerejak, thence to Pulau Rimau passing close in-shore, and then proceeding S.S.W. for Sumatra ports. Traders making for the Perak ports also sailed south to Pulau Jerejak, then went S.S.E. passing within five miles of Pulau Rimau, and thereafter sailed south within three miles of the mainland coast. Vessels bound for Siam and Rangoon sailed north from George Town to Pulau Bidan, thence north-west to Langkawi, leaving this island to the east. The same three routes were used for the return journeys.

The Ang Bin Hoey was primarily concerned with the first two routes. Piracy was based upon Batu Maung in the far south-east of Penang Island, and on Kuala Kurau, Kuala Gula, and Matang on the North Perak coast. It was believed by the authorities that the master brain of all the smuggling and piracy centred in Kuala Kurau, that the gangster operatives were mainly members of Cell 12, and that the closest co-operation existed between Kuala Kurau and Batu Maung.

The pirated craft were almost invariably Chinese and Indian wooden sailing junks, exceedingly clumsy to handle. The pirate craft consisted of sailing sampans, Chinese-type motor junks (used extensively on the Penang–Sumatra run because of their long range), fishing sampans, and even on occasions a Japanese landing-craft. It was later discovered that piracy on the northern route was operated from Pulau Teratau, an island off the coast of Siam close to Pulau Langkawi.

Pirate gangs on Penang Island existed at Batu Maung, Batu Uban, Sungei Nibong, Permatang Damar Laut, and Telok Kumbar, but they were all controlled from the headquarters at Batu Maung, and no gang worked independently. In the event of lesser fry making an attack they were always accompanied by at least one representative from Batu Maung, who received a share of the 'profits'.

Ninety per cent of all piracy in Penang waters was carried out by the Batu Maung gang. Their usual method of operation was to put out from their base

[7] *Straits Echo*, 5 July 1946.

in two or more sampans and intercept junks inward and outward bound off Pulau Rimau, Pulau Jerejak, or Pulau Kra. Most members of the gang were armed, and a few shots into the air were usually sufficient to make junk crews obey the order to drop sail and heave to. The pirates then boarded their prize, confined the crew, navigated the junk to some convenient place near their headquarters, and removed the cargo by a systematic sampan ferry service from ship to shore. This job frequently took some hours to complete. The loot was taken over by a buying agent, who either purchased the goods himself or arranged sale to certain receivers in Penang, whither it was taken by road. This part of the proceedings was exceedingly well organized, and the disposal of cargoes was always completed within a few hours of goods being landed. Once the vessel had been emptied, the junk crew was released and threatened with death if the matter were reported. Usually the threat had the desired effect, and if the police ever got to know of the incident it was through agents, days or even weeks too late to take any action.

The Kuala Kurau and Kuala Gula gangs frequently used the same system, but with motor junks they were able to operate about ten miles from their base. On such occasions they either transferred valuable cargoes to their own vessel, and allowed the pirated junk to continue on her way, or they towed the victim to their own headquarters. Like the Batu Maung gang, the Perak gangs were heavily armed, and no attempts were made by the pirated craft to defend themselves.

In June 1946 the Penang police went into action. Two large buried petrol dumps were discovered at Sungei Nibong, one of them close to the beach. They were believed to provide fuel for taxis and lorries on shore and for motor tongkangs at sea connected with smuggling activities. They were said to have been bought by Teh Boon Hoon (leader of Cell 11 at Sungei Nibong) during the Interregnum. These dumps were destroyed, and the police made several raids in adjacent areas during July.[8] Nevertheless, during the six weeks between August and mid-September 1946 there were more than twenty piracies in the area south of Penang Island and off the north-west coast of Perak from Matang northwards, and although the total loss to traders was more than $1,000,000, only two incidents were reported. It was believed that in general the cargoes were being smuggled across from Sumatra, and the pirates were 'high-jacking' the smugglers. With only one harbour launch, the police were able to do little at sea, but during the early hours of 20 September, supported by naval and military units, they raided Batu Maung, captured a large quantity of ammunition, and detained six men for questioning.[9] As a result, several gangsters fled to Kuala Kurau, but not before they had attempted to pirate a junk belonging to Cell 20 off Pulau Rimau on the night of 22–23 September. The junk was armed and in the gun battle which ensued two of the attackers, members of Cell 12, were killed. Thereafter, with increased military and police patrols, piracies ceased at Batu Maung, though smuggling continued.

The Perak coast remained as bad as ever, and in November there was a great increase in piracy on the northern route, which caused an outcry in the press and among traders.[10] In January 1947 the police, after making an anti-piracy

---

[8] *Sunday Gazette* (Penang), 21 July 1946.   [9] *Straits Echo* (Penang), 25 Sept. 1946.
[10] Ibid. 5, 6, 7 Nov. 1946 & 4 Apr. 1947; *Sing Pin Yih Pao & Modern Daily News*, 11 Nov. 1946.

patrol to the Langkawi and the Butang Islands (Siamese), discovered that the piracies in this northern area had nothing to do with the Ang Bin Hoey but were based on Siam, the operators being Siamese officials from the convict settlement on Terutau Island.

On 27 May 1947 a Siamese motor tongkang laden with pigs and fowls for Penang was stopped one-quarter mile east of Pulau Paya off Kuala Kedah by a former Japanese landing-craft which bore down upon them from the north. Shots were fired at the tongkang, which was ordered, in Siamese, to stop her engines; the crew were confined in the cabin and an hour later were called on deck in pairs, shot, and thrown overboard. Unknown to the pirates, one of the third pair escaped, swam towards the Kedah coast, and after tying himself at dusk to a fishing stake was rescued at dawn on the 28th by two Malay fishermen. He made a preliminary report at Sungei Limau (Kedah), and reached Penang late on the 29th. The non-arrival of the junk had been reported, and during the night of the 29–30th the police arrested five Siamese in a Penang hotel and the Malay captain of the pirate craft in a house. Four were identified by the man who had escaped being murdered. The pigs were traced to the slaughterers.

It was then found that the landing-craft had been sub-chartered to a Penang Chinese said to be the leader of the six accused. He was arrested early in June, and this murder and piracy led not only to heavy sentences upon the gangsters and to a fifteen-year sentence by a Siamese court on the Superintendent of Prisons, Terutau, but to combined Malaya–Siam anti-piracy operations. There-after piracies on this northern route ceased.

Meantime a watchful eye was being kept upon Sungei Nibong, where the petrol dumps had earlier been discovered. Every shop paid protection money and every villager became a member of the Ang Bin Hoey. A path through the rice-fields led to the waterfront, where smuggled goods were loaded on to a lorry for transport to town for sale. Alternatively arrangements were made to reload cargoes on to small ships and to take them to Sumatra for sale. The Ang Bin Hoey headman became rich and opened an import–export firm in Penang.

In April 1947 two lorry loads of textiles and tyres, worth $40,000, were seized by the police near Sungei Nibong; the headman, who was present, was arrested, charged, and fined $500 or eight months' imprisonment. Three months later his younger brother (an active pirate) and seven others, members of the crew of a motor tongkang were arrested by the Dutch and their vessel seized off the Asahan river, for robbery on the high seas. They returned to Penang in January 1948, took refuge in Sungei Nibong, and were soon involved in another piracy at Pulau Rimau. At this stage the police recommended that the headman of Sungei Nibong be banished. He was arrested on 24 March and with his removal both smuggling and piracy at Sungei Nibong were disrupted.

But in addition to countering the Ang Bin Hoey's criminal activities, the police were faced with a political problem, for from June 1946 an intensification of the struggle between right, centre, and left Chinese political groups for the control of the Chinese population in Malaya led to attempts by several oppor-tunists to utilize the influence of the Hung Brotherhood by reconstituting a central Triad organization to operate openly as a political party in Malaya under the title Hung Mun Chi Kung Tong. This followed the example already being set in China,[11] where the Min Chi Tang was being formed as the political manifestation of the Hung Mun Chi Kung Tong.

The first attempt in Penang was made by Ch'ng Beng Lee, well known in the island before the war as a member of the Committee of the China Distress Relief Fund, a prominent leader of the Anti-Enemy Backing-up Society, responsible for much of the agitation for an intensive boycott of Japanese goods, and the organizer of two mechanized Chinese volunteer units (drivers and mechanics) who left for active service in China in 1939. In 1941 he found it advisable to leave Malaya. He returned in May 1946, as a representative of the CDL, charged with establishing a branch of that society in Penang. Two other representatives who had accompanied him were to form branches in Singapore and in Perak. The Penang branch of the CDL was duly formed in August at 33 Farquhar Street, and in September another branch appeared in Alor Star, Kedah.[12]

Ch'ng Beng Lee had reached Penang on 8 June, only three weeks after the dissolution of the Ang Bin Hoey, and had found a leaderless Triad organization which might be won over to his support. As the CDL in China and Hong Kong at this time was already competing with the KMT for control of the Triads, Ch'ng Beng Lee adopted a similar policy. He made contact with old friends in the Lorry Drivers' Association and with three left-wing members of the Ang Bin Hoey, one of whom was an official of the New Democratic Youth Corps, the second a committee member of the Penang Harbour Labour Union, and the third a member of the Penang Rubber Workers' Association. He aimed at winning the support of the General Labour Union, which was strongly Communist, and hoped to make himself not only the head of the Triads but the supreme controller and arbiter in labour matters in Penang, as T'u Yueh-sheng ruled the Triad and labour world in Shanghai. To this end, besides forming a branch of the CDL he began to form what he called the Preparatory Headquarters of the China Hung Mun Chi Kung Tong/Malaya.

Early in August (1946) pamphlets purporting to be issued by this Preparatory Headquarters were secretly distributed in Penang. They contained a brief history of the Triad movement, alluded to the opposition of members of the Hung Brotherhood to the Japanese both in China and in Malaya, referred to the formation of the Ang Bin Hoey in Penang and its 'suppression' by the authorities, and urged the Hung Brethren of the three northern States of Malaya to respond to the call of the China Hung Mun Chi Kung Tong by forming a Malayan branch. A nine point policy was then enumerated which followed in every particular the Manifesto issued on New Year's Day, 1946, by the Hung Brethren in the United States and Canada (and which was being adopted in China), including the cessation of civil war in China, and the abolition of one-party government. A newly-added section was specially applicable to Malaya:

At present, large numbers of people are still living an inhuman life in hunger and starvation, unemployment, sickness, and their civil rights are not protected at all. We, brothers of the Hung Family, should, in conjunction with the democratic movement in Malaya, unite all factions to struggle for the realisation of the democratic system in Malaya, so as to enable the five million brethren of various races to live a blessed life of freedom.

---

[11] See above, p. 33.   [12] *Sing Pin Yih Pao*, 12 Sept. 1946.

Ch'ng Beng Lee had received some assistance in his propaganda efforts from left-wing elements in Jelutong, and under cover of the Farmers' Association had spread his influence in the rural areas around Balik Pulau. About the middle of August two Triad initiation ceremonies were held, at which twenty Tiechius introduced by Cell 21 of the Ang Bing Hoey were admitted to membership of the Hung Mun Chi Tung Tong.

But Ch'ng Beng Lee made no further progress. The headman of Sungei Nibong, who in addition to being leader of Cell 11 had taken charge of Cell 4 on Khor Khum's earlier flight to the mainland and had arrogated to himself considerable authority among the few remaining Ang Bin Hoey committee members, questioned the validity of the initiation ceremonies, refused to recognize the new initiates as Triad Brethren, and threatened reprisals. He was supported by other cell leaders who foresaw that their own financial position would be adversely affected by this new rival, the Chi Kung Tong, and refused their support.

But the intervention of the KMT was the deciding factor. Determined, as in China, that no other political party should in any way control the Triad groups, and already secretly planning to enlist Triad aid in its struggle for power against the Chinese Communists in Malaya, the KMT leaders took steps to counteract the influence of Ch'ng Beng Lee and the CDL, and encouraged Teoh Teik Chye in his refuge in Singapore to reconstitute the Ang Bin Hoey as a political organization, knowing that they could rely upon his loyalty to use his influence to bring the Brotherhood on to their side.

In August, ostensibly on business, Teoh Teik Chye went to Alor Star in Kedah, an area already notorious for Triad activities sponsored by Ooi Ah Soh, and within a few weeks of this visit there were signs of increased activity in near-by Penang. Several cell leaders and a few committee members returned to the island from 'exile', and the collection of subscriptions began again. Co-operation between the society and the KMT became closer. Already in June an important Ang Bin Hoey leader in Jelutong had been made head of the newly-formed local branch of the SMCYYC in order to combat Communist influence in that area. In September an Ang Bin Hoey leader who was concurrently Vice-President of the KMT in the Balik Pulau rural area, where Ch'ng Beng Lee had been operating, offered to bring 400 members of the Ang Bin Hoey into the KMT. It was well known that several members in that district held official positions in both organizations. Further afield, during October and November, Penang Triad officials and rank and file actively assisted their KMT brethren in the Dindings against Communist interference. Meantime, at the end of October, Ch'ng Beng Lee, who was a member of the KMT as well as the CDL, was expelled from the former for alleged 'Communist activity'.

On 1 September the inauguration of the China Hung Men Min Chi Tang was officially announced in Shanghai by Szeto Mei-tang, and this proposed entry of Triad into China politics received considerable publicity in the Malayan press. The *Northern Star* (in which the Penang Ang Bin Hoey had shares) published a series of articles on 'Malaya's Five Political Societies', enumerating the KMT, the Communist Party, the SMCYYC, the CDL, and the Hung Mun Chi Kung Tong, the last-named 'not, as yet, openly established'.[13] In November official instructions were received from China by the KMT in Malaya to cultivate

[13] *Northern Star*, 30 Sept. 1 & 2 Oct. 1946.

good relations with the newly-formed political Triad party in China, the Min Chi Tang, and two KMT officials from Penang and Butterworth (both of them Ang Bin Hoey leaders) left for China to enquire about the possible formation of the Min Chi Tang in Malaya.

It was at this stage that Ooi Ah Soh, still operating in Kedah and in touch not only with local KMT and Chinese consular personnel but with the visiting Vice-Minister of the Overseas Department of the KMT, Tai Kwee Sheng, called together all Ang Bin Hoey cell leaders from Kedah, Province Wellesley, and Penang (although omitting Cell 12), to discuss the raising of funds and support for Teoh Teik Chye's proposed reorganization of the society on a political basis. At this meeting a minority of the Penang cell leaders expressed resentment at the manner in which the society had previously been dissolved without their being consulted, and as they believed that both Teoh Teik Chye and Ong Keng Hooi had already misappropriated the society's funds when they fled from Penang, resisted the suggestion that more money should be raised. There was no opportunity to pursue the question further, for these plans for the revival of the Ang Bin Hoey in a new guise collapsed with the arrest and banishment of both Teoh Teik Chye and Ooi Ah Soh.

Certain members of the old central committee made strenuous efforts to hold the Ang Bin Hoey together as an organization, and small initiation ceremonies continued to be held under the code name of Sam Chuan & Co (Ang Bin Hoey, Penang), by an important sinseh from Perak, Lim Ah Hah. But other sections also held initiation ceremonies, and a string of so-called sinsehs sprang up, some of them scarcely able to recite the chants but unscrupulously looking for monetary gains derived from the initiation fees.

In September 1946 the Government came to the conclusion that the prohibition of Triad societies (as contained in the prewar Societies law which had been suspended) must again be enforced, and thereafter the police were empowered to charge in court persons against whom there was evidence of membership of such a society. In October it was further agreed that applications for banishment of persons directly connected with criminal activities would be considered.[14] By the end of the year twenty men, arrested while attending two initiation ceremonies, had been convicted in Penang, but many initiation ceremonies escaped detection, and the police began to concentrate upon the arrest of sinsehs, without whose services no initiation could be held. Many of these men were on record, and they were invariably China-born. Several were arrested during 1947, usually on the grounds of possession of Triad documents, and were banished in 1948; others went into hiding. This policy was sufficiently successful for the claim to be made that during 1948, within the area covered by the jurisdiction of the Penang police, no initiation ceremony had been held.[15]

Meantime, the authority of all the Triad leaders in Penang was threatened by a new and grave challenge from within the Brotherhood itself. As early as January 1946 the piracy gangs on the Perak coast were known to be out of control, and even before the dissolution of the Ang Bin Hoey in May 1946 the committee of that society had been disturbed by the notorious criminal activities of 'the brother across the water'. This was Tan Leng Lay, the young leader of Kuala Gula, who, to evade the police, first sought refuge with Cell 12 in Penang, accompanied by his gang of thugs, and then, returning to the Perak

---

[14] See below, pp. 358–9.   [15] Pg CID *AR*, 1948.

coast, presumed to set himself up as overlord of all Triad societies in North Malaya. Tan Leng Lay operated first from a headquarters in the Perak coastal swamps, and then, after August 1947, from Bagan Si Api Api in Sumatra.

The full story of his exploits illustrates Triad tyranny at its worst,[16] and although Ooi Ah Soh had deliberately omitted Cell 12 from the conference of cell representatives which he held in Kedah on 30 November 1946, no other Triad leaders dared to oppose the upstart's demands. Only an unexpected gun-battle in January 1948 at Bagan Si Api Api in which Tan Leng Lay and his gang were eliminated removed this menace. But even after his death, his example encouraged the younger members of the Ang Bin Hoey to repudiate the authority of their elders and to form units of their own. In March 1948 an extortion and protection gang called the Tiap Piat Gi Hong Khoon was formed by a White Fan of Cell 8, together with a young Hokkien member of Cell 12. The latter took refuge in Bagan Si Api Api when the police began to notice his activities, but the idea had attracted attention, and in May a prewar member of the Sin Ghee Hin formed the Lian Hup Khoo, embracing members from several cells and areas with the object of assisting any affiliated member or cell in the event of trouble from a rival party. Again police action broke up the organization.

In August, when gangs of Ang Bin Hoey hooligans were forming in the town area, Ayer Itam, and Jelutong, the leader of the Jelutong group attempted to merge the six Ang Bin Hoey Cells, Nos 4, 7, 8, 19, 20, and 21, into the Lok Kak Tong. He enrolled 100 members, basing his gang on the earlier Tiap Piat and Lian Hup Khoo, and was strongly supported by Cells 4 and 7. A month later the Sin Ang Bin Hoey (New Ang Bin Hoey) made its appearance, once again with the intention of settling disputes between cells, but after ten satellite members had been warned by the police, development was checked. In December 1947 there had even been a further unsuccessful attempt to form a Chi Kung Tong branch in Penang, this time by members of the China Chi Kung Tong from Sultan Street, Kuala Lumpur.[17]

Despite these various manifestations, nothing dangerous developed during 1948. The use of powers under the Banishment and the Societies Ordinances, heavy sentences for extortion, and the introduction of the death sentence for the illegal possession of arms, together with the strengthening of the police in personnel, equipment, and morale, and finally the introduction of the Emergency Regulations in June 1948 as a result of the outbreak of the Communist revolt were effective elements in the anti-Triad campaign, and by the end of 1948 the greatest existing problem lay in the extent to which MCP influence might capture the Triad societies.[18]

4. RECONSIDERATION OF OFFICIAL POLICY

It was the appalling crime record of the Ang Bin Hoey in Penang which caused the Governor of the Malayan Union, Sir Edward Gent, to order an official enquiry into the criminal activities of members of the committee and eventually with his advisers to reconsider the whole question of societies and unrestricted freedom of association. According to an official police report, the following crimes were known to have been committed by members of the society in Penang and Province Wellesley during the period September 1945–13 June 1946:

[16] See below, pp. 371–8.   [17] See below, pp. 432–3.   [18] See below, pp. 421–8.

Murders of members of the public	30
Murders of members of the police force	5
Murders of police informers (also 1 detective missing, believed murdered)	6
Attempted murders: members of the public	7
„ „ members of the police	1
Armed gang-robberies	46
Armed robberies	59

In addition there were innumerable cases of extortion, and because of the reluctance of the public to report to the police it was believed that the real figure for robberies was very much higher than that given above. There was widespread organization of gambling and lotteries, and cases of wrongful arrest and confinement with physical punishment carried out by the disciplinary committee of the society at the Maxwell Road headquarters. The empire of the Ang Bin Hoey extended throughout the area, and in Penang alone membership was estimated to be 20,000.

As early as 1 March 1946 the State and Settlement Civil Affairs Officers of the British Military Administration, alarmed by the proliferation of societies of evil intent throughout the Malayan Union, had held a meeting to discuss the matter. They came to the conclusion that some form of control was essential, and recommended that every society should submit to a Registrar a true and complete copy of its constitution, rules, and objects, a list of its officers and their addresses, and the name and address of the person to whom any notices might be sent or served. Any society failing to supply such particulars would be declared unlawful. At the same time it was suggested that power was needed to control public collections and subscriptions, which had degenerated into extortion, but pending information as to the legislation in force in the United Kingdom governing public collections, the whole question was postponed, and by 1 April 1946 when the British Military Administration handed over to the Civil Government no further action had been taken.

With the resumption of Civil Government there was widespread expectation that the Societies Ordinance would again be enforced, but instead the policy of freedom of association as laid down by the British Government continued to be implemented, on the grounds that owing to the abnormal conditions which had obtained since the liberation, the new policy had not yet been given a fair trial. Furthermore, it was considered inadvisable to hamper in any way the possible formation of political parties which it was the policy of the Government to encourage, and there was in addition some doubt whether the policy of complete freedom of association had not been communicated to the MCP through the officers of Force 136 during the period of the Japanese Occupation, in which case any restriction might be regarded by the MCP as a breach of faith and might provide a stick with which to belabour the Administration.

Although no one society had reached the formidable proportions of the Ang Bin Hoey in Penang, the Colony of Singapore was faced with similar problems of criminal extortion gangs, and in prevailing conditions had no faith in the practicability of free association and wished to revert to prewar legislation. But after consultations between the two Governments, Singapore agreed to await the publication of a Bill which was being prepared by the Malayan Union before taking any independent action.

AA

The Bill was published on 27 July 1946, and provided for a system whereby societies could register voluntarily, such registration carrying with it the prewar benefits of a legal status, the capacity to hold property, and to sue and be sued. The Registrar was empowered to call upon any registered society to furnish him with a copy of its constitution and rules, and a list of officers and a statement of the number of members, together with such other particulars as by rule under the Ordinance might be prescribed. For societies which chose not to register there were no such controls. As for Triad societies, these were once more specifically outlawed. Every society which used a Triad ritual was deemed to be an unlawful society, and any person found to be in possession of any Triad writings thereby committed an offence and was in addition presumed to be a member of an unlawful society.[19]

Apart from Triad societies, the procedure for declaring a society to be unlawful was indirect. If the Registrar had reason to suspect that an unregistered society was being used, or was likely to be used, for unlawful purposes or for purposes incompatible with the peace, good order, or welfare of the Malayan Union or any part thereof, or if it was being used for purposes at variance with its professed aims or objects, he was empowered to call upon it to register. If, after registration, he had reasonable cause to suspect that it was being used for any of these purposes, the Registrar, with the approval of the Governor in Council, might declare the society to be dissolved.

The Bill did not find acceptance either in the Malayan Union or in Singapore. The Malayan Union Advisory Council took the view that legislation should be at least as drastic as before the war.[20] The Singapore Government quickly reached the conclusion that it would be a mistake to introduce legislation along the lines of the Draft Bill, and considered that conditions in respect of the need for the registration of societies had not changed materially since 1888, when Sir Cecil Clementi Smith sent home his despatch on 'The Case for Suppression'.[21] It regarded the proposed procedure for calling upon a society to register before it could be dissolved and thus become unlawful, as an ineffective method of dealing with hooligan societies. Nor did the Bill appear to take into account the very real fear of intimidation which existed among the Chinese, and the consequent necessity for dealing in rapid and direct fashion with societies which employed intimidation. Some sort of compulsory legislation was believed to be essential, though the machinery of the prewar Ordinance might well be simplified.

Sir Edward Gent did not share this view. He was not prepared to abandon so readily a policy which had been adopted only after the most careful consideration as being in the best long-term interests of Malaya, and which had not been fully tried. He considered that the correct way to deal with extortioners, kidnappers, and protection racketeers was by police action, and that with the increasing efficiency of the police force and the energetic pursuit of these criminals there was reason to believe that they would be brought to book. In this he was re-echoing (though doubtless unconsciously) the sentiments of the early Governors of the Straits Settlements and the convictions of the Government of

---

[19] The wording ran: 'Triad books, accounts, writings, seals, banners, or insignia.'

[20] Both in the Malayan Union and in Singapore, Advisory Councils of unofficials were appointed as an interim measure. They were, in due course, superseded by Legislative and Executive Councils. As their title implies, the Advisory Councils were purely advisory. Decisions lay with the Governor.   [21] See above, p. 225.

India, who, during the first sixty years of the nineteenth century, were convinced that an efficient police force and not special legislation was the answer to the threat of the criminal societies. In 1946 those who took the opposite view could point to the fact that both prewar and postwar experience demonstrated that Triad societies and extortion gangs were organizations for the furtherance of criminal intent and not merely innocuous associations, some of whose members happened to be criminals. Admittedly, before the war, despite the existence of the Societies legislation, it had not been possible to prevent the illegal existence of such 'societies' as the KMT and the Communist Party, and the object of suppression had not been fully achieved. On the other hand, the fact that the existence of these societies was unlawful meant that the police could take action against their members whenever opportunity offered. Even if this did not result in their eradication, it was preferable to permitting them, with the sanction of law, openly to extend their influence over the whole population by threats and intimidation which the victims would never report.

So the pendulum of argument swung. Eventually the Malayan Union Bill was amended by including in the category of societies which the Governor could declare unlawful any society which was being used or which was likely to be used for intimidation, extortion, or any other unlawful purpose. At the same time (September 1946) it was agreed that as far as Triad societies were concerned there was no need to wait for the introduction of the new law, and permission was given for the implementation of those sections of the existing legislation which declared that Triad societies were unlawful.

But even these revisions failed to satisfy the Singapore Government, whose Advisory Council expressed strong and unanimous dissatisfaction with the Bill. Consultations by the Governor-General with both Governors failed to break the deadlock, and eventually the consent of the Secretary of State was obtained to a divergence. The Malayan Union was to introduce the Bill, while Singapore was to retain the old Societies Ordinance with some amendment to provide for political parties. In the Malayan Union the Bill became law as Ordinance 11 of 1947, and came into force on 1 April of that year. In Singapore registration was resumed under the old Ordinance on 15 April 1947, and on 29 May an amendment was passed excluding from the operation of the Ordinance 'any association which the Governor in Council may by order declare to be a political association'.

That membership of a Triad society was once again a criminal offence, and that possession of documents relating to such a society raised a presumption of membership, was something that the Chinese public could understand. Previously confusion had reigned in their minds. These societies had always, in their experience, been clandestine and prohibited by law. Yet since the war, despite the crimes that could be laid at their door, not only had no action been taken to suppress them but the Chinese Consul had publicly praised the Triad Brotherhood as a righteous organization which deserved full recognition by the Government. In general, the Chinese community as a whole considered that when evil threatened the welfare of the people it was the duty of the Government to take action to remedy the situation. Specifically, the secret societies which terrorized and victimized the community and which were known to be evil should be outlawed and suppressed. By the end of 1946 the knowledge that Triad societies were again unlawful and that promoters of Triad activities operated at their own peril had brought some consolation to law-abiding citizens, and in May 1947 confidence increased when the Government of the Malayan Union gave a further indication of its intention to take a firm line with societies connected with crime, and proscribed nine societies by name, all of them being either Triad societies or gangs with Triad associations operating at different places throughout the Union.[22]

5. RECOURSE TO BANISHMENT

The magnitude of the threat which the Ang Bin Hoey of Penang offered to the Government as the guardian of public order, and the argument which had ensued about criminal societies, led not only to the implementation of the Triad clauses of the Societies Ordinance pending the introduction of the new law by the Malayan Union Government but also to consideration of the use of the powers vested in the Governor in Council by the banishment legislation.

Once again, as so often in the past, it was recognized that normal legal processes could no longer control the situation. Despite the widespread incidence of serious crime in which members of the Ang Bin Hoey were known to be involved, both victims and witnesses were deterred by the general climate of intimidation from reporting to the police or giving evidence in court, with the result that criminals could not be convicted and made to pay the penalty for their crimes.

On the return of the British to Malaya it was the intention to avoid as far as possible the use of powers under the Banishment Ordinance, although no public pronouncement on the matter was made. That the leaders of the Ang Bin Hoey expected banishment action to be taken against them is proved by the minutes of a joint committee meeting held at Maxwell Road headquarters on 3 April 1946, three days after the police raid on the initiation ceremony at Relau Hills and two days after the resumption of Civil Government. At this meeting the second item on the agenda read: 'To discuss measures in case members of the Executive Committee and Supervisory Committee are banished by the Government. Resolved: Every member to participate in the "One Dollar Movement".' At a second joint meeting held on 16 April the matter was again discussed, and it was resolved that each section (cell) 'should get the subscription ready'.

On 30 April the police reported that the situation in Penang was serious, and recommended that the Societies Ordinance should be reintroduced. On 20 May, when the president, Teoh Teik Chye, publicly announced in the press that the Ang Bin Hoey had dissolved, it was further recommended that banishment proceedings should be taken against twenty-five named members. Four days later an investigation into the activities of the society was begun by a police officer specially appointed for the task. He was joined later by a member of the Attorney-General's Department, who was to examine all the available information and to report to the Government on the criminal activities attributed to the Ang Bin Hoey, and upon the personal responsibility of its leaders for these activities. His report, dated 28 August, disclosed that there were reasonable

[22] The Ang Bin Hoey, the Bunga Raya Boys, the Chung Yee Tong, the Harvard Estate Youth Corps, the Land and Sea Gangs, the Three Dots Society, the San Ji Thoan (= Sa Ji or '32'), the Thik Leng Thoan (= Thit Leng or Iron Dragon). (*MUGG*, Suppl., 8 May 1947; GN 3028.)

grounds for believing that some of the leaders were personally inculpated in criminal acts. He confirmed that members of the public were terrified of the society, that there was no prospect of witnesses giving evidence against its leaders or members in court, and that banishment appeared to be the only practicable means of checking the sinister activities of the organization. The institution of proceedings under the Banishment Ordinance against eight members of the committee and against the two ritual heads, Ooi Ah Soh and Khor Khum, was recommended.

Meantime, despite police efforts, the crime wave had continued in Penang and had spread to Province Wellesley, Kedah, and Perak. The English press in Penang urged banishment action,[23] and questions were asked in the House of Commons concerning 'organized crime' in North Malaya. Nevertheless, it was not until the middle of October that the Government of the Malayan Union decided to proceed against ten named persons, not on the ground of membership of a Triad society but as individual cases whose banishment was necessary in the public interest—a course which was sanctioned by the Secretary of State.

Several of those against whom warrants were issued had already left Penang, but by the end of 1946 five had been arrested and the whereabouts of a sixth, Ooi Ah Soh, had been discovered. A Banishment Enquiry Officer was appointed, and on 7 January 1947 an enquiry opened at Penang gaol. Ooi Ah Soh was arrested on the morning of 6 January in a remote kampong in Kedah. The enquiry ended on 18 January, and the report submitted on 29 January recommended that three of the prisoners, Teoh Teik Chye (president of the Ang Bin Hoey), Thor Boon Huan (supervisor of Cell 22 and controller of the rural areas), and Ooi Ah Soh (the Kwun Lam),[24] should be banished, and that the other three prisoners (the vice-president, the assistant secretary, and a leader of Cell 4), should be released. This recommendation was accepted. Those who were not recommended for banishment were released early in March, and on 4 May the three banishees sailed for China.

Although Teoh Teik Chye's personal participation in any criminal act was not proved, it was clear that as chairman of the Ang Bin Hoey and an old Triad member he could not have been unaware of the criminal activities of the society, and of the demoralizing and intimidating effect these activities had on the general community. Furthermore, documentary evidence found in his possession at the time of his arrest in Singapore disclosed his continued interest in the affairs of the society after its dissolution in May 1946, and his determination to revive it when opportunity offered. This made him a potential danger, and his continued residence in Malaya was held to be undesirable.

In his own defence Teoh Teik Chye attributed the evil reputation of the society to the admission to membership by Ooi Ah Soh of hooligan elements,

[23] *Straits Echo*, 24 June 1946: 'In Singapore, the Governor has sought and obtained from Whitehall full powers to take the necessary measures to deal with the crime wave. It may be presumed that among the measures contemplated is the exercise of the provisions of the Banishment Ordinance whereby a person can be banished without trial. We have advocated in this column the use of this very same measure to deal with "bad hats" in the country, for it is an instrument which should prove a more effective deterrent than a term of R.I. It is unlikely that the application of the Ordinance will give rise to political repercussions as Malaya would merely be exercising her rights to rid the country of undesirable aliens who have hurled defiance at the law and terrorised peaceful inhabitants by the ruthlessness of their evil deeds.' See also ibid. 5 July 1946.   [24] A senior Triad ritual officer.

particularly the Ji Tiau Loh, which, he said, had always been the bitter enemy of the Hung organization. He maintained that he himself had tried throughout to conduct the society's affairs along proper lines, but that the gangster element had been too strong.[25]

The second banishee, Thor Boon Huan, superintendent of Cell 22 in the Balik Pulau area of Penang Island, was a tough, middle-aged, China-born Chau An Hokkien, a fisherman by trade. He lived at Kuala Jalan Bahru, and not only directed the robberies in the area, which were particularly numerous in May, June, and July 1946, but allowed his village to be used by the notorious sea-pirates of Kuala Kurau Cell 12, as a rendezvous with the local gangs and a hideout when necessary. There was documentary proof that he had attended a meeting called by Ong Keng Hooi on 6 May 1946 to discuss the question of 'assistance' to the Importers' and Exporters' Association whose cargoes were being robbed both at the waterfront and in the sea approaches.

Widespread police raids in the hills round Balik Pulau in July helped to restore confidence in that area, but even so there was the greatest difficulty in persuading anyone to come forward to give evidence.

At the banishment enquiry it was considered that Thor Boon Huan must be held as partly if not mainly instrumental in the creation of the atmosphere of terror which existed among the general public in the Balik Pulau area, and his banishment was therefore recommended.

Ooi Ah Soh, the Kwun Lam and 'the evil genius behind the scenes', was connected with the Ang Bin Hoey from its earliest days, although he denied such connexion before the society was established in the Maxwell Road head-quarters. A typical member of the Brotherhood in the tradition of the 'Heroes of Liang Shan', he was ruthless, avaricious, and jealous, with the reputation of a 'killer', prepared to shoot at sight any rival who might attempt to challenge his position or who interfered with his activities. At the enquiry it was accepted that he was personally connected with the shooting of three persons. He exerted a powerful influence on the society and was held in great fear by its members. As Kwun Lam he had powers of punishment extending even to death, and through his five 'Tiger' Generals, bound under oath to obey his commands, wreaked vengeance upon those who betrayed the society and upon members of the police who tried to bring Triad criminals to justice. He took pride in the fact that he had held many initiation ceremonies, and admitted that he had initiated thousands of recruits and had conferred innumerable ranks. But he claimed that the general secretary, Ong Keng Hooi, had defrauded him of the traditional and agreed rates of payment, paying only 'what he thought fit and pocketing the rest'. Recommended for banishment as 'a thoroughly dangerous character', Ooi Ah Soh created a scene on the wharf at Singapore as he boarded the ship for China, shaking his fists in the air and calling upon the onlookers to witness that his only crime had been that he had tried to forward the interests of the Brotherhood.

Of the four 'wanted' leaders who were still at large, Khor Khum, Ooi Ah Soh's henchman, escaped to Siam, whence he was eventually banished to China for extortion. The treasurer, Tan Teik Eng, also fled the country, but on 23 October 1947 Poh Teng San, superintendent of Cell 11, was arrested in Perak,

---

[25] He was killed in a motor accident in Sumatra in March 1953, and messages of condolence to his family appeared in the Penang Chinese press.

and in May 1948 Ong Keng Hooi, the elusive general secretary, was arrested in Singapore.

Poh Teng San, who described himself as a trade-seller of Chinese medicines and a magician, was a prewar Triad member, convicted for rioting at the time of the anti-Japanese boycott in 1938. In 1945-6 he operated Cell 11 of the Ang Bin Hoey under cover of the Sungei Dua Benevolent Society. He held the Triad rank of Straw Sandals (432), and was energetic in recruiting new members. Unemployed, he was said to live on the proceeds of Hua Hoey lotteries, and on protection money levied on non-members of the society. He admitted that after fleeing from Penang in December 1946 he organized Hua Hoey lotteries in Selama, and eventually ended up as caretaker of a gambling den run by the Ang Bin Hoey at the Fishermen's Club, Tanjong Piandang. Described by a witness at the enquiry as being 'not a man of violence but a worm living on the easy money got through influence of the Ang Bin Hoey' he was recommended for banishment on 21 January 1948 and sailed for China five months later.

Ong Keng Hooi did not figure prominently in the earliest records of the Ang Bin Hoey, although he worked with Teoh Teik Chye for the resuscitation of the society after it had been closed down in November 1945, and soon became the president's right-hand man and the brains of the organization. When the society began to function again, he became a member of a small committee entrusted with the negotiations for 55 Maxwell Road as a headquarters, was elected a member of the Disciplinary Committee empowered to carry out 'civil' and 'military' action against those who endangered the name and status of the society, and finally was elected general secretary, or, as he preferred to call himself, general affairs officer. Although he denied that he ever held any Triad rank other than that of an ordinary member (49), he is believed to have been a White Fan (415).

Far more forceful and ruthless than Teoh Teik Chye, he soon dominated the executive committee, and even when Teoh Teik Chye was present at meetings, Ong Keng Hooi, a far more fluent speaker than the president, often presided and monopolized the proceedings. He certainly acted for Teoh Teik Chye when the latter was away, kept the key of the safe, and together with the president and the treasurer signed all cheques. Ooi Ah Soh alleged that Ong Keng Hooi controlled the square seal of the society, given to him by Teoh Teik Chye, which enabled him to demand obedience to any instructions stamped with this seal. As presiding-officer and chief investigator of the disciplinary committee he conducted trials at the Ang Bin Hoey headquarters, and ordered the punishments meted out to offenders against the society. In this capacity he was mainly responsible in February 1946 for the flogging and murder by drowning in a sack of Teh Aik Seng, alias Chap It Chye, believed by him to be a police informer. When his house was raided by the police on the night of 14-15 May 1946 a document was discovered which proved to be a prepared statement on this murder drawn up for the instruction of suspects who were arrested by the police early in March.

His ruthlessness as a disciplinary inquisitor brought him great power, and earned for him the admiration and support of the thugs of Cell 12, whose piracy and robbery he secretly encouraged though outwardly condemning their activities in committee. He was able to demand a share of the proceeds of the robberies committed on the waterfront, could negotiate between the owners of cargoes and the piracy gangs, and could enlist members of the Ang Bin Hoey cells in protection rackets such as that negotiated with the Importers' and Exporters' Association in May 1946. In the last case he was betrayed by the non-co-operation of Lim Oh Yeoh, the waterfront leader of Cell 4, and his own avarice which led him to pocket the proceeds without paying his subordinates. Even Ooi Ah Soh with the killers of Cell 4 behind him had hesitated to provoke an open breach with Ong Keng Hooi.

After the police raid on his house, Ong Keng Hooi fled to Kuala Kurau and took refuge with the Perak members of Cell 12. Later, in Singapore, he was in touch with Teoh Teik Chye, but on the latter's arrest in December 1946 he again fled northwards, and in 1947 succeeded in getting away to Amoy, where he met both Teoh Teik Chye and Ooi Ah Soh after their banishment. When he thought that police vigilance had abated he returned to Malaya via Siam and reached Singapore unobserved. For some time he was interested in a suggestion that he might organize a political party of Triad Brethren, the Hung Mun Chi Kung Tong, and endeavoured to obtain a Singapore birth certificate to enable him to claim local birth and avoid being banished should the police catch up with him. When he was eventually run to earth and arrested in May 1948, the application for a renewal of a Singapore birth certificate was found among his papers.

After a banishment enquiry held in March 1949, and based upon the evidence already produced in the big enquiry of January 1947, his banishment was recommended and confirmed. His claim to local birth was disallowed. Faced with the mass of evidence accumulated in 1946 he himself called no witnesses but merely asked for a swift expulsion. Owing to the difficulties of the times, it was 1951 before he left Malayan shores for China, and as far as is known disappeared from the Malayan scene.

16

TRIAD ACTIVITY ON THE MALAYAN
MAINLAND, 1945–8, I

1. INTRODUCTION

THE flight of the ritual leaders of the Penang Ang Bin Hoey, Ooi Ah Soh and Khor Khum, to the mainland early in April 1946 led to an immediate acceleration of Triad activity in Province Wellesley, Kedah, and Perlis, for which they were, in the main, personally responsible. A few weeks after the Penang society had been ordered to close down, considerable numbers of its rank and file also sought refuge on the mainland. Many of them went to Perak, for the affiliation of Cell 12 of the Penang society with the Triad members from the fishing bagans of North Perak were an obvious inducement for members 'on the run' from Penang to cross over to Kuala Kurau, and thence make their way southwards down the coast to Pangkor, Port Swettenham, Pulau Ketam, Malacca, Singapore, or even Bagan Si Api Api in Sumatra. As it happened, many fugitives decided to remain in Perak, and stimulated Triad activity throughout the State.

With this influx of members of the Penang society to the mainland the name Ang Bin Hoey, or simply ABH, came to be used in police circles to refer to all Triad societies, in much the same way as such societies before the war were commonly known as Sa Tiam Hui (Hokkien), Sam Tim Wui (Cantonese), or Three Dots Society. This led to some confusion, for although the Kuala Kurau Triad organization retained the title Ang Bin Hoey which had been adopted at the time of the reorganization at the end of the Japanese period, and although the fugitives from the Penang Ang Bin Hoey influenced a number of Triad societies which revived or were established not only in Perak but throughout Malaya, these societies were not normally branches of the Ang Bin Hoey of Penang (or of Kuala Kurau), but were separate manifestations of the Triad Brotherhood, most of which had their origins in the prewar societies of their particular areas.

2. PROVINCE WELLESLEY

In August 1945, when news of the imminence of the Japanese surrender became known, Triad began to revive in Province Wellesley, to afford protection for minor collaborators against the MPAJA. The leader, an ex-detective who had been in Japanese employ, was a prewar Triad member, and operated from Bukit Mertajam in the centre of the province.

In the beginning the society was far from strong, and many collaborators were killed by the MPAJA. Later on, when the MPAJA had been disbanded and its members were looking for a means of livelihood, some were believed to have joined the Triad groups in the province to participate in the extortion and protection rackets, and several were said to be 'killers'. The society was also joined by another group, which worked under the protection of the General Labour Union. It consisted of about 100 labourers, originally brought into the province by the Japanese to build ships. At Chinese New Year (February 1946), despite police prohibition, these men held a Dragon Procession in Kedah at Kulim, Sungei Patani, and Alor Star, when they collected money from shops by 'pressure', and forty of them were arrested.

Little was known about Triad activities in the province during these early months, but from April 1946, when Ooi Ah Soh and Khor Khum arrived, it became increasingly evident that developments were taking place.

On 7 May the police received information that a joint meeting of some 200 Sin Ghee Hin members from Kedah, Penang, Kuala Kurau, and Province Wellesley had been held two days previously on the hillside at Bukit Mertajam. On 22 May a club known as the Band of Heroes Mutual Aid Association was opened at Bukit Mertajam and was soon found to be a cover for Triad activities. It appeared that Bukit Mertajam was to be the operations centre for the whole of north Malaya, to replace the headquarters in Penang which had been closed down on 18 May. In June, a fortnight after the event, the police received information that an initiation ceremony had been held on 9 June at Matang Tinggi, attended by 860 initiates, while information later gathered from persons arrested showed that other such ceremonies had been held at the mouth of the Krian river, one as early as April 1946, at which Ooi Ah Soh had been the sinseh.

Meantime, robberies, extortion, kidnappings, and 'protection' spread over the countryside, the '36' and '50' Character lottery (Hua Hoey) appeared, and the statistics for serious crime rose steadily. Anonymous letters from Nibong Tebal at this time complained bitterly of the pressure under which an estimated 90 per cent of the male population had been forced to join the society, paying not only an entrance fee of $13.80 and a monthly subscription of $1.00 but also contributing to special collections, shopkeepers being assessed at anything from $50 to $1,000. The society's influence was described as being 'as high as the sky', and to have spread in this area to every kampong, estate, and by-road. The same was true throughout the Province.

Police action against Triad members began. The Mutual Aid Association closed its doors, and as a result of frequent raids and arrests many of the local leaders went into hiding or fled to join Khor Khum and Ooi Ah Soh who, after the meeting at Bukit Mertajam on 5 May, had moved northwards to Kedah, Perlis, and the Siamese border. Thirteen leaders from Butterworth alone went to Padang Besar, where the railway enters Siamese territory, and which at this time was the Mecca of gangsters and smugglers. During a boom which began in September 1945 and did not end until early 1947 when conditions returned to normal, the population of this border town increased from its prewar figure of about 700 to 10,000, all engaged in smuggling, or in the gambling and extortion rackets which abounded.

By September 1946 a comprehensive list compiled by the Province Wellesley police from information given by arrested Triad members included 34 leaders in Butterworth, 34 in Bukit Mertajam, 22 in Nibong Tebal, and 12 in Kapala Batas. The knowledge that the police were taking an active interest in their movements proved to be a restraining influence. This remained true during

1947, for the banishment of the Penang leaders in May, and the gazetting of the Ang Bin Hoey as an illegal society, also had a deterrent effect, while the outbreak of the Emergency in mid-1948, and the Emergency powers given to the police to arrest undesirables likely to be a menace to the peace, caused Triad gangsters to lie low.

Meantime, during the second half of 1946, the Triad societies of Northern Malaya (as in Penang) became politically important as the struggle between the KMT and the Communists grew in intensity. In November (1946) the chairman of the KMT, Province Wellesley, frankly admitted that Triad members were being recruited into their ranks, but stated that this drive had only recently become effective as, previously, there had been great pressure on the Triad groups from the Communists, who had been trying to swing them to the left. He alleged that the former chairman of the General Labour Union in the Province, a Communist-dominated society, had joined the Ang Bin Hoey with the specific purpose of introducing Communist control. Nevertheless, he was convinced that the KMT had won the struggle and estimated that out of a total of 10,000 members of the Ang Bin Hoey in Penang and the Province, 80 per cent had been recruited into the KMT. (The police estimate of Ang Bin Hoey membership at this time was 30,000–40,000.) He also claimed that the Ang Bin Hoey had ceased to be a criminal association and that in origin it was essentially anti-Communist, but that in a misguided attempt to increase its power it had recruited gangster elements who had brought disgrace upon the society. He was particularly interested in the recent formation (September 1946) of the Min Chi Tang in China, as a Triad political party to participate in the Government of China, and believed that should such a society be started in Malaya it would receive the full support of all Triad members. Meanwhile, the position in China was being closely watched, and the return of two KMT emissaries who had been sent from Penang and the Province to China was awaited.

3. KEDAH AND PERLIS

From Province Wellesley the influence of the Ang Bin Hoey spread rapidly among the Chinese throughout Kedah, making its first appearance in the south, near Kulim, where it was active in extortion, and working northwards through Sungei Patani and Alor Star to Padang Besar in Perlis. Along the sea-coast it spread from Tanjong Dawai northwards to Kuala Kedah, while to the north on the turbulent Siamese border remnants of ex-KMT guerrilla bands joined forces with the Ang Bin Hoey refugees from Penang, particularly at Padang Besar. Further north still, Haadyai in Siam became a refuge for Ang Bin Hoey members fleeing from police attention in Malaya, and an 'accommodation centre' in that town provided them with food and protection.

It was noteworthy that throughout Kedah, though particularly around Sungei Patani, the Ang Bin Hoey appeared to be on good terms not only with the KMT guerrillas but also with such leftist organizations as the People's Peace Preservation Society, the Farmers' Union, the NDYL, and the Workers' Union. There was even information that in the Baling Hills the Ang Bin Hoey, ex-MPAJA, and some Japanese had joined together and had established a headquarters, with a branch in the Gurun Hills.

It has been suggested that Sino-Malay friction, a relic of the Japanese Occupation, may have played a part in the rapid development of the Ang Bin Hoey in Kedah. Kedah is a predominantly Malay State, and a political movement of 'Malaya for the Malays' caused some apprehension among members of the local Chinese community. Therefore not only certain KMT members welcomed the reinforcements of guns and personnel from the Penang Ang Bin Hoey, but Chinese leftist organizations, all of which were indirectly sponsored by the MCP, came to some sort of a working agreement with left-wing elements among the Triad groups.

The driving force behind the advance of the Ang Bin Hoey in Kedah, as in the Province, was the formidable Penang sinseh, Ooi Ah Soh, assisted by Khor Khum. Within a matter of weeks the rising crime statistics for extortion, kidnapping, armed robbery, and intimidation testified to the sinister presence of Triad gangsters. In Kulim swift police action held up development for a time, and the earliest initiation ceremonies were reported from the Sungei Patani area, where on 14 and 15 May 1946, in a rubber estate, some 150–200 initiates were admitted to the society at each of the two ceremonies. On 24 May, at a lonely place in Semiling, a few miles further north, a third ceremony was held, and on the night of 6–7 June, at the 16th mile on the Sungei Patani–Alor Star road, there was a fourth. Two old Triad members, backed by Cell 4 members from Penang, became the leaders at Sungei Patani, and Ang Bin Hoey influence soon spread to Kuala Muda, Sungei Lallang, Bukit Selambu, Bedong, Gurun, and Yen.

At Alor Star more than one Ang Bin Hoey group attempted to stake a claim. Early in May a notice was found stuck to a pillar in the town announcing that the Ang Bin Hoey would be organized to knit the people together. The poster, bearing the seal of the Ang Bin Hoey, Kedah, gave warning that 'bad elements' were using the name Ang Bin Hoey and thus bringing discredit on the society. After an outbreak of armed robberies in the district, the police arrested five suspects who, on arrival at the Central Police Station, Alor Star, decided to shoot it out, and in the affray one gangster was killed (17 May). On 12 June, the police arrested another four armed gangsters, two of whom were from Penang. Four days later an initiation ceremony was held at Kuala Kedah a lonely fishing village in the swamps only a few miles from Alor Star. The police stopped two car-loads of Chinese returning from the ceremony, but the evidence was insufficient to warrant court proceedings. Reports of extortion in the area were increasing, and it was clear that Kuala Kedah was becoming an important Ang Bin Hoey centre, including Alor Star in its jurisdiction. One shopkeeper who was ordered to join the society at Kuala Kedah was told to pay $3,008 for the privilege. A carpenter from the same village, a member of the General Labour Union, disappeared after refusing to join, and rumour had it that his body, weighted with stones, would only be found on the sea bottom.

In an attempt to avoid competition, one Triad leader paid $2,000 to Ooi Ah Soh as the price of the independence of this area. It became Cell 9, and paid a percentage of its revenue to the mother Cell 9 in Penang, but in return had the power to refuse to allow any other Triad interlopers to operate in the area. The leader in Sungei Patani paid a like sum for the independence of his district, which included Sungei Patani, Bukit, Selambu, Gurun, and Tanjong Dawai. It became Cell 4.

In August 1946 four Triad members in the Sungei Patani area were arrested and charged with intimidation and extortion, and in December an important police operation resulted in the arrest of thirty-eight persons as they were leaving an initiation ceremony at Kulim. This time there was adequate evidence, and each was sentenced to six months' rigorous imprisonment.

Early in January 1947 Ooi Ah Soh was arrested at Tanjong Dawai, and the removal of his powerful influence discouraged further development, though Triad groups continued to exist. In particular, arrangements for the exclusive control of any particular area were ignored, and rivalry increased between Triad groups endeavouring to become established. At Gurun, in July 1947, a leading member of the MPAJA was kidnapped by Triad members, three of whom were later murdered by the Communists. A Triad leader of Kuala Kedah found in possession of Triad documents in October was sentenced to six months' imprisonment, and shortly afterwards a small initiation ceremony was held only ten miles from Alor Star. But Triad activity was noticeably on a smaller scale.

In Kedah, as elsewhere in north Malaya, the KMT was interested in the Ang Bin Hoey development, and, at the same time, some of the Ang Bin Hoey leaders were considering the possibility of operating under a KMT label, particularly after it became known that Triad societies were no longer free to operate without penalty. When Ooi Ah Soh was arrested he had in his possession a certificate issued by the Executive Committee of the Kedah branch of the KMT stating that he was an honest and trustworthy man, and that he had been instructed to link together party affairs in the State of Kedah. The certificate called upon all members to give whatever assistance was required to facilitate this work. The document, issued officially by the KMT, was dated 18 November 1946, and may well have been obtained as a cloak for his Triad activities.

In a letter sent to the former president of the Penang Ang Bin Hoey (Teoh Teik Chye), found when he was arrested in hiding in Singapore, Ooi Ah Soh recounted some details of a meeting which he had with the Chinese Vice-Minister, Tai Kwee Sheng, on 1 December 1946. This meeting took place at an assembly of members of the various KMT branches in Kedah, 'who are mostly Hung [i.e. Triad] people'. Ooi Ah Soh was introduced to the Chinese Consul, Penang, and privately reported the story of the Ang Bin Hoey to the Consul and the Vice-Minister, asking them to approach the authorities on the society's behalf. According to the letter, the Vice-Minister declared that the history of the Hung People was a glory to China, and that if members did not break the law, there was nothing to fear. The Consul was instructed to look into the matter.

But here Ooi Ah Soh appears to have been in some doubt as to whether he was not perhaps becoming too deeply involved with the KMT, for he wrote that the KMT executives wished to accompany him on his visit to the Penang Consulate, but that he had not yet given them a definite answer. He would have to consider this invitation. However, he apparently visited the Consulate, for he had in his possession at the time of his arrest a document in English and Chinese, issued by the Chinese Consul, Penang, on 25 December 1946, in which reference was made to him as a KMT member. The Chinese version called him 'dependable in loyalty and honesty', the English version referred to him as being 'of good character'. Clearly the intention was to keep him aligned with the KMT.

One result of the approbation accorded to the Ang Bin Hoey by the Chinese

Vice-Minister and the Consular officials was that in March 1947, after a number
of the leaders of the Penang society had been arrested on banishment warrants,
official representations were made to the Government citing the terms of a
Sino-British pact which was signed in 1943, which, it was claimed, these arrests
violated. This interpretation was not accepted.

Throughout his period in Kedah and Perlis, Ooi Ah Soh was in close touch
with Siam. He was in possession of a Siamese passport under the name of
Tan Kiong Yiu, and operating as a cigar merchant, using the name Tan Khim
Gek, had unrestricted passage between Haadyai in Siam and Bagan Serai in
South Kedah.

At Padang Besar on the Malaya–Siam border, he had as allies a small group
of Kwangsai guerrillas who came from Sungei Golok in Kelantan, where they
had been part of the anti-Japanese resistance movement. They joined him in
the gambling, extortion, and protection rackets established by Triad groups, and
assisted in squeezing out certain MPAJA elements who had taken early possession of the field at the time of the Japanese surrender. They operated also in
Siam, moving between Patani, Haadyai, and Padang Besar, and when that
town's temporary glory departed early in 1947 they set up their headquarters
at Kaki Bukit. There they resisted attempts by the MCP to persuade them to
join forces. As 'opium smokers and gentlemen of adventure' they found Communist discipline irksome.

It was not until after Ooi Ah Soh was banished that the full significance of
the part to be played by the main body of the Kwangsai guerrillas in Perak in
the plan of the KMT to overthrow the Communists in Malaya was realized by
the authorities.[1]

4. PERAK

At the time of the influx of Penang Ang Bin Hoey members, three groups of
Triad societies were already operating in Perak. In Krian, the Ang Bin Hoey
of Kuala Kurau, with strong Hokkien and some Tiechiu membership, was the
centre of Triad activity, and was linked with inland societies at Bagan Serai,
Parit Buntar, Selama, Kamunting, Taiping, Kuala Kangsar, and Ipoh, and
with coastal organizations at Tanjong Piandang, Port Weld, Pangkor, Lumut,
and Telok Anson. Down the Perak coast societies of the fishing bagans, known
collectively as the Yen Hai or 'Coastal Organization' (the modern successor of
the old Ho Seng), were co-operating with the Ang Bin Hoey, of which they were
affiliates. Their membership was exclusively Hokkien, and their main centre
was Pasir Hitam. In the Kinta valley survivals of the old Hai San and Ghee
Hin societies among the Cantonese and Hakka mining labourers formed the
third group, centred on Pusing, and among the Cantonese there were also many
branches of the Wa Kei Society.

North Perak

By the middle of 1946 the districts of Krian, Matang, and Larut were already
the scene of activity of a closely-linked Triad organization based upon Kuala
Kurau, Port Weld, and Taiping, members of which, as in the Japanese Occupation, were engaged in smuggling and piracy on the coast and the disposal of

[1] See pp. 388–91 below.

looted cargoes throughout the State, as well as in the usual blackmail, kidnapping, protection, opium, and gambling rackets common to all secret societies.

The smuggling at Kuala Kurau was planned upon a large scale and had ramifications which extended to Siam, Burma, and Indonesia. It was backed to the full by the local Triad society, although certain members of the piracy gangs were showing an independence of spirit which made their control difficult.

Kuala Kurau was also one of the main sanctuaries for members of the Brotherhood fleeing from the arm of the law or lying low to await a favourable opportunity for further depredations. It comprises two villages, one of which lies on the main road from the Krian coast to Taiping, while the other is on the opposite side of the Kurau estuary, and is known in customary Malay fashion as 'Saberang', or 'across the water'. Saberang is situated on the edge of the swamps and creeks which form a confused and intricate network along the coast from here southwards. Any approach from across the estuary or from the sea can at once be seen, and refuge taken in the creeks.

The second headquarters was on a small island near Matang, where one of the executives, picturesquely known as the 'Crocodile', besides running a sundry goods business in Penang, smuggled rice into Matang in large quantities, and as a pay-off to the secret society underworld handed on information as to the movement of shipping and the nature of cargoes as a preliminary to arranging piracy on the Perak coast. He planned piratical attacks with the co-operation of the acknowledged Triad 'boss' of the area, Yeoh Ah Bah, head of the Ghee Peng Ho Society of Port Weld, and the latter's piracy chief, Tan Leng Lay of Gula, who recruited gangs from among the Yen Hai. Once a piracy had been committed, the prize was brought to Matang, bribes were paid to customs and police, and the goods were sent by road to Taiping, where other traders arranged sales, part of the proceeds of which were remitted to the 'Crocodile'. Rice, copra, rubber, Burmese tobacco, rope, and opium were among cargoes pirated, and to avoid piracy, merchants found it advisable to contact the 'Crocodile' and pay the fee demanded for a safe-conduct document. This was obtained for them from Tan Leng Lay himself, or from his personal representative at Matang, who became a sort of unofficial Harbour Master, checking all cargoes passing in or out of the port and making sure that tribute was paid to the gangster world.

The organization became known as the Matang kongsi, and included not only the traders interested in smuggling, but the gangs of pirates, extortioners, and kidnappers who were under the personal control of Tan Leng Lay. The kongsi ran its own secret society, the Ho Hup, the treasurer of which, of White Fan rank, took part in the smuggling and was also responsible for arranging kidnapping for ransom, selecting the victims, and arbitrating between them and the gangs on the terms for release.

Taiping, the main focus of population, and the hub of commerce, was the main market for the disposal of contraband goods. The town still retained something of the aura of the 1870s when, as Klian Pauh, it had been the stronghold of the Hai San Society. But the composition of its population had long since changed and had become predominantly Hokkien, while the Hakka and Cantonese mining communities of Larut had moved to the more prosperous Kinta valley.

Triad had revived at Taiping at the time of the Japanese surrender primarily because collaborators needed protection against MPAJA vengeance. This suited Yeoh Ah Bah of Port Weld who, in co-operation with Kuala Kurau, was organizing Triad resistance to the threat of MPAJA control of Taiping, where both traders and gangsters were anxious to prevent this valuable disposal centre of smuggled and pirated goods falling into Communist hands. On this basis of mutual co-operation the prewar Sin Ghee Society was revived, Yeoh Ah Bah acting as liaison between the society at Taiping and the coastal societies of Port Weld and Matang; with four other prominent members of the secret society underworld he recruited members and retained control of such matters as arbitration in disputes within the Brotherhood. A leading trader, the proprietor of a motor-lorry business, was given high Triad rank, and his lorries soon provided a channel of communication between the smuggler–pirates of the coast and the disposal centre at Taiping, besides conveying new recruits to initiation ceremonies whenever called upon to do so by Yeoh Ah Bah. Thefts of rice during transportation which had been the bane of those holding government contracts soon stopped when members of the Sin Ghee Society were diplomatically employed by the companies concerned. The Sin Ghee came to be known by the name of the musical association, the Kim Ho Hean, whose premises it used as a cover club. For some time it controlled all Triad activities in Taiping, other groups acknowledging its overall authority.

The coastal societies soon stretched from North Perak as far south as Pangkor Island, the Dindings estuary, and Lower Perak, and included, among others,

Ghee Peng Ho	at Port Weld,
Hup Ho	at Matang,
Aik Seng	at Sungei Kerang,
Aik Bun	at Kg Temerloh,
Aik Hing*	at Pasir Hitam and Trong,
Aik Kiu	at Pantai Remis,
Aik Chin	at Sungei Kg Penang Kechil, Pangkor,
Ghee Kee	at Lumut, Dindings,
Aik Soon	at Sungei Ayer Tawar, Dindings,
Chung Ghee	at Kg Koh, Dindings,
Aik Ghee	at Sitiawan, Dindings,
Aik Soon	at Telok Anson, Lower Perak,
Aik Ghee	at Bagan Datoh, Lower Perak,
Aik Sin	at Bagan Pasir, Lower Perak.

* Also called 'See Hai', i.e. 'Four Seas', the name of a fishermen's club, or 'Ma T'au', i.e. 'Jetty'.

Many of these were pirate groups operating from haunts extremely difficult of access.

By the end of 1946 the most important inland societies were the Sin Ghee, the Aik Ho, and the Aik Peng at Taiping, the Ghee Hup at Simpang (Taiping), with branches at Aulong and Changkat Jering, the Ghee Beng at Bagan Serai, the Aik Khoon at Selama, the Aik Beng at Kuala Kangsar, and the Chung Yi T'ong at Ipoh; all were linked with the coast. The Krian societies worked in close touch with Kuala Kurau, but the Aik Peng at Taiping and the Chung Yi T'ong at Ipoh acknowledged the authority of Pasir Hitam.

Inevitably, from May 1946, when the Penang influx began, there was a general acceleration of Triad criminal activities in North Perak as Penang thugs joined the piracy gangs at sea or the extortion and kidnapping gangs on land. Trouble spots were quickly reported at Kuala Kurau, Kuala Gula, Kuala Sanga, Kuala Trong, and Kuala Jarum Mas. Further south, in July, one junk-load of Penang 'Brethren' landed at Lumut, and under cover of apparently innocuous benefit societies soon organized several Triad groups in the Dindings and Lower Perak areas, thus extending Triad activities down the entire length of the Perak coast.

Inland from Kuala Kurau, Bagan Serai became a Triad headquarters for Krian. Already in March 1946 many recruits from the Krian coast had been initiated into the Brotherhood at one of Ooi Ah Soh's last ceremonies in Penang. Early in July several hundred more were initiated near Nibong Tebal, and when the new headquarters was opened on 15 August, the Sin Ghee sent gifts and held a celebratory feast attended by several Penang and Kedah members. A week later a red eagle[2] painted on a three-foot board, together with large portraits of Sun Yat-sen and Chiang Kai-shek were also ordered for the new branch by the Brethren in Taiping.

The red eagle and the portraits symbolized an alliance between Triad and KMT interests, for as in Penang, Province Wellesley, and Kedah the KMT sought to use the North Perak societies as a 'strong arm' against the Communists. By mutual agreement, Triad groups began to operate under cover of the SMCYYC, and the Corps made use of the influence of the Triads to propagate its own political principles and to secure support for future KMT schemes. In Taiping itself, an additional branch of the Sin Ghee, the Aik Ho, recruited several hundred new members during the last few months of the year, and together with the Sin Ghee adopted the practice of issuing badges in the form of a KMT flag in place of the more usual initiation document.

Ong Keng Hooi, the General Secretary of the Penang Ang Bin Hoey committee, was reported to be very active in this political sphere in Perak, particularly during October and November 1946. From two headquarters at Kuala Kurau and Trong he operated inland from Bagan Serai, through Taiping, to Sungei Siput, and along the coast from Kuala Kurau to Pangkor. Like Ooi Ah Soh in Kedah, he made contact in November with the Chinese emissary, Tai Kwee Sheng, on the latter's visit to KMT and SMCYYC branches in Malaya, and contingents of Sin Ghee and Aik Ho members from Taiping joined with others from Penang in operations against the Communists in the Dindings area later that month.[3]

But important though Penang influence was in North Perak, the primary cause of the acceleration of Triad activity was the beginning of a serious struggle within the ranks of the local Triad Brethren, where the authority of the long-established leaders on the coast, such as Yeoh Ah Bah of Port Weld, was challenged by the outlaw and pirate chief, Tan Leng Lay. This young man was born at Kuala Gula, a few miles south of Kuala Kurau, and, like it, surrounded by a confused network of creeks. He was initiated into the Triad Brotherhood during the Japanese Occupation, became a Straw Sandals[4] as leader of a gang, and during the postwar interregnum was active in the Triad resistance against the MPAJA. The gang was concerned in extortion and robbery which alienated his fellow-clansmen in Gula. As a result, three of the clansmen, a father and two

---

[2] A red eagle represents a 'Hung Hero'. The pronunciation of the characters for both expressions is the same (Hung Ying), though the characters are different.

[3] See below, p. 382.   [4] See App. 1, pp. 530–1.

sons, were taken up the creeks by the gang and stabbed to death by Tan Leng Lay, who believed that one of the sons was an MPAJA reservist and that the other was a police informer. A few months later, in February 1946, the gang rounded up during the night two more families of clansmen in Gula, including the village headman, two women, three boys under 16 and two girls aged 12 and 8, ten or eleven persons in all. All were tied with ropes and taken by sampans up the creeks where they were stabbed or shot to death by Tan Leng Lay, who seemed to have developed a mania for killing. Again, the reason was said to be that the families had turned against him and were therefore potential police informers. Two of the boys, though stabbed through the neck, survived and reached a police station. Tan Leng Lay and his men took to the creeks and began to form an independent coastal Triad gang. Triad ruffians from the bagans and some from Penang joined him, and soon he had an armed band of 20 or more, which, by 1948, was over 50 strong and had secured the subservience of many coastal villages.

In the concealment of the coastal mangrove swamps Tan Leng Lay set up his Triad headquarters, which he called the Ang Soon Tong (Hokkien), (Cantonese: Hung Shun T'ong), the Hung Obedience Hall, the title of the original Second (Cantonese) Lodge of the Hung Brotherhood. By his followers he was called Tai Koh (Elder Brother), and by the police he was generally known as 'The Leper' through a confusion of the Chinese pronunciations of 'Elder Brother' (Tai Koh) and 'Leper' (T'ai Koh). He was also known as Tai Koh Wah, through a mistranscription of 'Tai Koh-ah', the familiar form of 'Elder Brother'.

Established Triad leaders regarded him as an upstart, but he became a law unto himself, a homicidal maniac, difficult to eliminate because of the band of killers with whom he was surrounded. Efforts made by the police to capture him were unsuccessful. The ill effects of the Occupation were still felt in the force which was badly served in respect of trained personnel, launches, motor transport, and information. Tan Leng Lay had three fast motor launches (formerly air force rescue craft), and his contacts kept him well informed of police moves. He was first located in May 1947 in the Larut estuary, and when the police got on to his trail he moved from one place to another, finally to Bagan Che Hakim on the north bank of the Trong estuary. His gang lived by robbery and piracy, and among its members Tan Leng Lay was extremely popular, for he did not, like most leaders, demand the whole proceeds and dole out a little to the band, but let them retain most of the loot so long as they kept him in funds. He was thus able, according to one source, to use his men as 'hunting hawks and dogs', and they served him faithfully, while he himself was able to indulge his craving for opium to the full.

He riveted his control upon the coast from Gula to Pantai Remis, and became the dominating power in North Perak, arrogating to himself the right to discipline any wayward members of the Brotherhood, and to order the death of Triad officials merely on the complaint of his own unscrupulous followers that an offence against Triad law had been committed. In an ever-widening area he assumed the role of arbiter of Triad affairs, and demanded tribute from the various Triad headmen, most of whom were too terrified to refuse. The 'Crocodile' of Matang paid him $500 monthly, Yeoh Ah Bah contributed $300 monthly, and was asked for more, and every opium den down the coast paid him a percentage of its profits. Even in Kuala Kurau he had his spies, and a communication centre.

But through fear of arrest he was forced to confine his activities to piracy on the open sea, brief visits to the coastal bagans, and the holding of trials in the inaccessible swamps. Though rabidly anti-Communist, he was unable to participate in the Triad–KMT alliance because he dared not appear in the open. But he adopted his own methods of campaign, and emulating the traditional example of the first Grand Master of the Hung Family, Ch'an Kan Nam, the Taoist priest who had directed the five refugee monks to disperse into the provinces of China to raise troops and money for their campaign against the Manchus, he sent five of his followers, each having the rank of 'Tiger' General ('51') to Taiping to extract money and to purchase arms to be used against the enemies of Triad in Malaya—the Communists. The 'Tigers' appear to have operated within the Sin Ghee, but eventually formed a society which came to be known as the Aik Peng. The original five 'Tigers' were supported by twenty or thirty non-ranking members. They were heavily armed, and engaged in extortion and kidnapping to an unprecedented degree. In particular, they sought as their victims any of known Communist sympathies.

The Aik Peng soon became the most notorious of all the societies in the Taiping area and attracted the most vicious of the hooligan elements. It was under the aegis of the oldest, most respected and feared sinseh of the district, Tua P'ui Ka, usually known by the prestige title of Kwun Lam, and to whom the rarely-used code number '489' was applied to denote his high standing in the Triad hierarchy. His specialized knowledge of Triad ceremonial induced an equivalent fear in the hearts of those Brethren whose knowledge of such matters was rudimentary. At the time of the formation of the society he was over 60 years old. The Five 'Tiger' Generals of the Leper were 'crowned' by him, and this enhanced their prestige and power.

The 'Tigers' operated from the Matang area, in co-operation with the Ho Hup gangs, but their depredations soon brought them into conflict not only with Yeoh Ah Bah at Port Weld, whose position Tan Leng Lay was determined to usurp, but with the Sin Ghee leaders in Taiping, and with Lim Ah Hah, the powerful sinseh of the Ghee Hup Society at Simpang. The Triad code permitted extortion from non-members as a proper means of livelihood, but there was frequent rivalry between societies as to the right to kidnap any particular victim. On one occasion the towkay of a rubber factory in Ayer Kuning, Taiping, was kidnapped by four members of the Aik Peng but was rescued by a Ghee Hup gang led by one of his own employees. He was later recaptured by the Aik Peng just as he was about to be initiated into the Brotherhood by Lim Ah Hah. The matter went to arbitration, when the Triad code was upheld. The rescuer was sentenced to twelve lashes for intervening on behalf of his towkay, a non-member, and the latter was ordered to pay $3,000 to his original kidnappers for ransom. Lim Ah Hah lost face. Furthermore, the head of the Ghee Hup at Simpang received a demand from Tan Leng Lay for $10,000 to be paid within a week as compensation for the insult offered to the 'Tigers'.

This in itself was a contravention of the Triad code, for although *non*-members were legitimate targets for extortion, members of the Brotherhood were protected. The 'Tigers' ignored this rule, sending letters demanding money from shopkeepers who already belonged to the Brotherhood, and the Taiping society leaders began to draw together to counter this menace. On Yeoh Ah Bah's instructions, the Aik Ho was formed in Taiping by a White Fan with the express purpose of breaking the power of the 'Tigers' and protecting Triad members against their extortionate demands, but the new society found that mere verbal protests were met by a challenge to 'fight it out'. The Leper himself, claiming that he was short of funds, made no attempt to restrain his gang, and even a peace offering of $1,000 collected by the Aik Ho from societies in Taiping, Selama, and Bagan Serai was of no avail, and the extortion continued.

For the Chinese population as a whole, the Triad network was so intricate that no business transaction could be completed without meeting Triad levies. Most men of any standing found it necessary to join a society or suffer the ruination of their business, or be kidnapped and held for ransom. Entrance fees ranged from $36 and a monthly subscription of $5 for a working man to £360 or even $3,600, plus a monthly subscription of $50 for shopkeepers or estate owners. Even so, such was the climate of fear that the necessity to secure protection resulted in initiation ceremonies of as many as 500 recruits taking place within a few miles of Taiping.

The ruthless nature of Triad power was shown when two pork-butchers who attempted to join the Aik Peng Society disappeared completely. Years later it became known that at the ceremony they were denounced by another pork-seller (who had a grudge against them) as being members of the Wa Kei, a rival fraternity at enmity with the Triad groups. They were then eliminated.

Early in 1947, after failing to prevent the depredations of the 'Tigers' by diplomatic methods, the officials of the Sin Ghee and the Aik Ho called upon Yeoh Ah Bah, as the senior Elder Brother of the district, to hold a disciplinary tribunal before which Tan Leng Lay should be arraigned for permitting his gang's breach of the Triad code, but Yeoh Ah Bah was afraid to move. Already a White Fan from Kuala Trong and a Straw Sandals from Ipoh had been condemned to death by Tan Leng Lay for breaches of Triad rules. The White Fan had consorted with the widow of a deceased member of the Brotherhood, and had misappropriated $4,000 extorted from a charcoal-kiln owner instead of paying the money into the society's funds. The Straw Sandals had committed adultery with the wife of a Brother in Ipoh. Both delinquents were killed by being tied in sacks and thrown into the sea, and those who carried out the sentences were suitably rewarded. Tan Leng Lay himself assisted in the second ritual murder, but when, by an exceptionally able piece of detective work, three of his helpers were arrested in January 1947, he had gone back to his swamps.

In an attempt to fight it out with the 'Tigers' the Aik Ho Society formed its own strong-arm squad, but this action, together with a number of kidnappings by the Leper's men, led to the intervention of the police, and the arrest of some of the Aik Ho leaders.

During 1947 Taiping became notorious among Chinese merchants as a place to be avoided at all costs. No man was safe from the kidnapping gangs of the Aik Peng, and once captured, failure to pay ransom meant certain death. Another vicious group of Triad kidnappers operated further inland at Kuala Kangsar, under the auspices of the Aik Beng Society, and by December, when ten of its members were arrested and charged with membership of a Triad society, no fewer than twenty-five kidnappings were laid at its door, but in no case would witnesses give evidence in court.

The most notable kidnapping of the year was that of a prominent Chinese community leader of Sungei Bakap, Province Wellesley, who in April 1947 was taken from his home, bound, and after being transferred three times from boat to boat was placed under guard at the bottom of a small sampan in the swamps, where he remained for over fifty days, despite a full-scale military and air operation mounted to search for him. He was eventually traced to the mouth of the Selinsing river and was rescued by the police, who shot his guard dead. There is reason to believe that this particular kidnapping had not been authorized by Tan Leng Lay, and that when the intense police activity which followed caused him to leave Perak, he left instructions that the kidnappers themselves should be killed when found.

Police action kept Triad leaders on the run. In February 1947 Yeoh Ah Bah found it advisable to leave Perak, not only because of a police probe but also because he and a fellow Triad official, the treasurer of the Sin Ghee, had been reported to Tan Leng Lay on a charge of embezzling Triad funds. Refusing to attend an enquiry to which they were summoned, both men were sentenced to death *in absentia*, and joined by the sinseh, Lim Ah Hah, who also had earned Tan Leng Lay's displeasure, and by the Red Rod[5] of the Aik Ho who feared police arrest, they fled southwards to the Selangor coast. There they were soon gainfully employed for several months in holding initiation ceremonies among refugees from Bagan Si Api Api in Sumatra, who in September 1946 had fled from an Indonesian attack and had found shelter in Port Swettenham, Pulau Ketam, Port Dickson, and Kuala Selangor. By August 1947 a considerable number of these refugees had returned to Bagan Si Api Api, well provided with arms through Yeoh Ah Bah, and on arrival they formed their own (Overseas Chinese) Self-Protection Corps to police the area.

No sooner had they done so than they were joined by Tan Leng Lay and his gang, who, tired of being trailed from place to place by the Perak police, moved over to Sumatra and settled themselves in the bamboo swamps, a short distance from the village. From his retreat Tang Leng Lay planned the removal of all rivals along the Malayan coast and of certain Triad leaders who, in his opinion, were guilty of breaches of Triad law. Among those who had earned his displeasure were the old Ticchiu headman of Tanjong Piandang, Chia Ling Ngai, the leader of Cell 12, Penang, the treasurer of the Aik Kiu at Pantai Remis; the head of the Ang Bin Hoey in Malacca, and certain influential traders in Kuala Kurau. His instructions were carried out by a section of his gang operating from Port Weld.

The community at Tanjong Piandang, a Tiechiu fishing village with the usual smuggling facilities five miles to the north-west of Kuala Kurau, had always been of independent spirit, disinclined to tolerate outside interference. It was not only a Tiechiu bagan, whereas those further south were, mostly, Hokkien, but it was further differentiated by being, according to police report, a Third Lodge Triad Society, the other coastal societies being, by this time, of Second Lodge allegiance.

Tan Leng Lay's gang, operating with some bad elements in Saberang, Kuala Kurau, found an opportunity for extortion in Tanjong Piandang. In October 1947 the proprietor of a shop there received a demand for $5,000 from the gang under threat of death. The proprietor, a Triad member, went to Chia Ling Ngai,

[5] A Triad headman. See App. 1, pp. 530–1.

to seek his good offices in arranging a settlement. Chia decided that this demand
was an intrusion by outsiders into his territory and advised the shopkeeper to
report if anyone came to collect the money. The gang asked a Hokkien member
living in Tanjong Piandang to approach the shopkeeper about payment. It was
then agreed that $480 would be paid the next day, and the shopkeeper reported
this arrangement to Chia, so that when the go-between went to collect the
money he was arrested by Chia's men and taken to the jungle where Chia
delivered judgement. He said that for one 'Brother' to extort money from another
was an offence punishable with death, and sentenced the prisoner to 'a ride
in the sea'. At this moment the prisoner's wife appeared and pleaded for her
husband's life. Chia relented and released him with a warning not to repeat
such an action. There the matter ended, or so it seemed.

Later on the Leper's men in Kuala Kurau plotted to kidnap the elderly proprietor of a small shop in Tanjong Piandang, who was not a Triad member.
The news reached his son, a Triad member, who asked Chia for protection, as
a result of which members of the Leper's gang who arrived at the village to do
the kidnapping were arrested by Chia and his men. They were taken to the Fish
Traders' Association, the organizational centre of the village, above which Chia
lived, and of which he was the president. There, Chia said that intruders coming
to commit extortion or kidnapping without his consent would be 'taken for a
ride in the sea'. The accused refused to admit that they planned to kidnap the
old man and as there was no evidence, they were released. But before leaving,
they were warned that if they did not heed Chia's advice, or raised a gang to
make war on him, he would inform the police and ask for their assistance.

The gang returned to Kuala Kurau to discuss the matter with their confederates. They decided that Chia was violating Triad law by preventing 'Brethren'
from earning an honest living and was protecting a non-member; no true Triad
'Brother' would threaten to call in the police. They denounced him as a traitor,
and added that he had diverted Triad funds to his own use. Chia was ordered
to attend at Kuala Kurau for enquiry into his action, but he refused to go.

On the night of 6 November a motor-boat arrived at Tanjong Piandang from
Kuala Kurau, and a party of men rowed ashore in two sampans. They were
joined by others who had come by road. The gang went to the Fish Traders'
Association and called to Chia upstairs. Unaware of the identity of his visitors,
Chia came down and was eventually shot, after which the gangsters called the
villagers together and announced that they had killed a traitor. The Triad verse
relating to the killing of the traitor 'Ah Ts'at' was left on the table as a reminder.

After this two of the gang crossed to Penang, where the leader of Cell 12 of
the Ang Bin Hoey was accused of embezzling $25,000, the proceeds of an opium
piracy. The two stabbed him to death, extorted $1,200 from the members of
his cell as their reward, and returned to Kuala Kurau. Meanwhile, forty-eight
hours after the Tanjong Piandang murder, other members of the gang had gone
south to Pantai Remis where, on the night of 8–9 November, they had killed
the treasurer of the local Triad group, also on the charge of misappropriating
funds and refusing to obey a summons to an enquiry. Further south Malacca
was the next place to receive the attention of the Leper's thugs, and on
11 November the independent and unco-operative leader of the local Triad
group was shot as he cycled along the street and later died.

The Leper's hand then reached out to Kuala Kurau itself, where a wealthy

Chinese merchant and community leader had urged the local Triad officials to avoid criminal acts which would bring the village into disrepute, and to resist the demands of the Leper's gangsters to kidnap and extort in the area. On the night of 26 November, after the merchant's movements had been closely watched for several days, ten members of the Leper's gang arrived by motor-boat from Port Weld with the intention of kidnapping him for ransom. One of the gang went inside his shop and at the point of a gun forced the intended victim to hand over his keys. Fortunately word reached the police, who arrived in time to arrest this man, though the others fled. Four went by motor-boat towards Port Weld where they were intercepted but jumped overboard and escaped into the mangrove swamp; the others escaped in sampans. A second attempt made on 28 November was abandoned on the approach of a police boat. The two most important officials of the Kuala Kurau society resigned from office and went to Penang.

Finally, on 8 December, several members of this same gang again visited Malacca, intending to take control. But they were recognized by the local gang, and two of the intruders were shot, though not fatally, and were later arrested by the police. Four others got back to Port Weld, and the remainder went over to Bagan Si Api Api to report to the Leper.

Over the months the Chinese population of Bagan Si Api Api had become disillusioned. Originally, in August, they had welcomed the accession of strength represented by the Leper and the forty members of his well-armed gang. But they soon found that the newcomers were a law unto themselves and had no intention of obeying the behests of the village elders. Within a few days of their arrival they had pirated five ships in the vicinity, much to the consternation of the local community, who feared that piracy would give the village a bad name and attract the notice of the authorities, and that another massacre by the military such as had occurred in 1946 might be expected. They also feared that they might be accused of complicity in the murders of Triad officials which were taking place along the Malayan coast on the Leper's instructions.

One such murder had even occurred at Bagan Si Api Api itself. The Leper sent to Singapore for a sinseh called the 'Cockroach' who was accused of having officiated at a ceremony though not fully qualified, and though the charge was denied, the man was strangled in the house where the Leper was living. The Committee of the Self-Protection Corps then decided that the Leper was too much of a liability, and that he must be warned that the lawless conduct of his followers must stop. This was a direct challenge to the position of overlordship which Tan Leng Lay had assumed, and his relations with the local Chinese deteriorated.

He took swift action, including an order to his gang to recruit additional members to reinforce his guard at Bagan Si Api Api and to raise contributions from all Triad societies in north Malaya, but before these schemes could get under way he was asked to be present at a further meeting of the Committee of the Self-Protection Corps held because the piracies had continued and the gang had become increasingly arrogant. The discussion lasted so long that one of the Leper's 'Tigers', who had previously been instructed to go and get him if he were detained by the local people, insisted on forcing his way into the building and shot the guard when he resisted. In the fracas that followed the village headman was shot dead in front of the building.

The enraged villagers then decided that the only solution was to exterminate the gang. There is little doubt that the close ties existing between them and Yeoh Ah Bah strengthened their determination. They surrounded the gangsters in their camp in the bamboo swamp and shot all who were present, sparing only the Leper's wife, who tried unsuccessfully to parley for a cease fire. While sparing her life, they removed her jewellery. It is believed that about thirty of the gang were killed, but several members had put out to sea on a piratical venture just before the attack. They escaped to the Malayan coast, although a second boat was intercepted and all on board, with the exception of two Hainanese engineers, were killed. Tan Leng Lay's widow regarded the massacre as the vengeance of the 'Cockroach', whose ghost, she said, had appeared in the hut on the two previous nights with such clarity that on the second occasion the Leper had fired at it with his pistol.

The elimination of these pirates, robbers, extortioners, and murderers early in January 1948 temporarily relieved the population of the Perak coast of an intolerable burden of fear, and allowed such of the established and more 'conservative' local Triad leaders as had survived to resume something of the authority which had been threatened by the emergence of the Leper. The police, too, were thankful to hear the news, the more so because the slaughter had happened outside Malayan jurisdiction, and they were not faced with the distasteful duty of bringing to book those who had performed a public service by eliminating these criminals.

Certainly, by the end of 1947, the CID Headquarters of the Malayan Union were fully aware of the extent of the threat offered by the Triad societies, and the suggestion was made that a specialized headquarters staff was needed to deal with this problem. Already the timely strengthening of the CID staff at Malacca in August 1947 had prevented the development of serious secret society trouble in that State. In September a new registry devoted to collecting information concerning Triad members throughout Perak had been set up in Ipoh, under a Chinese police officer, and on 17 November a CID branch in Taiping began to function. Early in 1948 similar branches were established in Lower Perak and in South Perak, but further development, particularly in the form of a central clearing-house at Malayan Union Headquarters, was considered essential.

Meantime, the emergence of Tan Leng Lay and the outrageous exploits of his gang had so antagonized the locally-recognized Triad leaders of North Perak, all of whom feared for their lives, that a stream of information began to flow to the police from Triad sources anxious to see the gang destroyed. This development, aided by close co-operation from Penang, helped the police to take more effective action. A raid on Saberang (Kuala Kurau) on the night of 10–11 December 1947 was followed by another on No. 10 Matang on 28 December, when a number of documents were discovered. These revealed that the premises were a Matang link of the Kim Ho Hean in Taiping, and led to the immediate arrest of the Taiping leader whose lorries had carried smuggled goods from the coast to the disposal centre. The Kim Ho Hean closed its doors and other arrests followed, including the notorious 'Crocodile' of Matang and the White Fan who had acted as go-between in kidnapping cases in that area. All three men were banished and the smuggling organization at Matang was disrupted. Tan

Ah Hai, the 'Harbour Master' of Matang, was arrested in June 1949 and was also banished.

An examination of the books of the 'Crocodile' revealed the extent of the bribery and corruption at Matang, Port Weld, and Penang, and letters from the public indicated the relief felt by traders at the downfall of this 'second government' which had so oppressed them. Much was revealed concerning links between Matang and Taiping and about secret society methods of extortion and intimidation.

In June 1948 banishment action was initiated to include Yeoh Ah Bah, and three known leaders of the piracy gangs of Port Weld and Matang, together with several members who were already in police hands. Yeoh Ah Bah evaded arrest. In November 1947 he was reported to have returned to Port Weld, but was then said to have left for the Malacca coast. He was never discovered by the police, and died in Sepatang (Port Weld) in February 1949 without their being aware of his presence.

As for the piracy gangs, on the death of Tan Leng Lay, Teh Siew Huat, the leader of the killers responsible for the November 1947 murders, after his fortunate escape from Bagan Si Api Api, had gathered together all remaining members of the gang and had taken refuge in the Matang swamps. Before long he was in control of the coast, and his men became known as the 'Sepatang gang'. It was not until 16 November 1948 that he was eventually run to earth and arrested with four others in an isolated house at Sungei Derhaka (Matang). One sten-gun, a Luger pistol, and a quantity of ammunition were found in their possession. All five were charged with illegal joint possession of firearms, and on 20 January 1949 Teh Siew Huat was sentenced to death.

He was succeeded not by Tan Ah Leng, his second-in-command, also 'wanted' by the police, but by Loh Cheang Yeow, who had previously been personally responsible for producing before Tan Leng Lay for judgement those culprits accused of breaches of the Triad code. More recently, Loh Cheang Yeow had won the admiration of the gang by daring to fire at the police who were attempting to arrest him in a coffee-shop. Thereafter he became the outlaw of the coast, and the natural successor to the Leper as the organizer of piracy and protection.

Documents recovered in the raid at Sungei Derhaka revealed that the house was used as a Triad headquarters and had been the scene of an initiation ceremony as late as 19 September 1948 (17/8 moon). Twenty-four recruiters had brought sixty-five initiates, and fees of $36 and $21 had been paid. Not many initiation ceremonies were discovered. Tua P'ui Ka, the sinseh of the Aik Peng, had fled to Telok Anson when police action in Taiping became too penetrating. Lim Ah Hah remained for some time in Selangor but eventually returned to Taiping, and was arrested at Simpang in July 1949. He was banished from Malaya, and was later reported to be in Sumatra. Ng Ah Nam (Ooi Ah Nam), a sundry shopkeeper and crab collector living at Sungei Karang, who for years had been a member of the Yen Hai and who acted as sinseh at many initiation ceremonies on the coast, first took refuge at Pasir Hitam, but was eventually arrested and banished in 1954.

By the end of 1949 only one member of the Big Five who had recruited members for the revived Sin Ghee still remained in Taiping. Of the other four, Yeoh Ah Bah was dead, Lim Ah Hah had been banished and was in Sumatra, the treasurer of the Sin Ghee who had fled from Tan Leng Lay's wrath in February 1947 had returned to Perak, been arrested, and banished to China where, according to later reports, he was killed by the Communists, and the fifth member of the group had gone to Sumatra.

Thus in Matang, Port Weld, and Taiping the crowded stage cleared. One by one most of the prominent players disappeared, but there were others anxious and willing to take their places in the cast.

The Dindings and Lower Perak

Down the remainder of the Perak coast, from Pantai Remis to the Bernam river estuary, in the Dindings and Lower Perak, a similar drama was being enacted.

During the Japanese Occupation a section of the MPAJA had a headquarters on the mainland in the swamps behind Lumut and Sitiawan, and there were a few OCAJA guerrillas on Pangkor Island. The Lumut coast was the scene of several secret landings from submarines of individual British and Chinese members of Force 136 who were met by MPAJA agents and were conducted to a jungle headquarters of the resistance movement in the hills behind Kampar, in the Kinta valley.

The local Chinese population around Sitiawan, overwhelmingly Hokchiu (from Foochow in Fukien Province), and speaking their own difficult language, contributed generously to the support of the MPAJA, to whom their linguistic isolation served as a shield, and although the Japanese undoubtedly recruited spies and informers to watch for these landings, no member of Force 136 was ever betrayed in this area.

Despite Communist domination, and although little authentic information is available concerning the activities of Triad groups as such in the Dindings area during the Occupation, it is reasonable to assume that in this time of stress and danger self-protection Triad groups were in existence, particularly in isolated bagans on the coastal fringes. Certainly once the Occupation ended there was clear evidence of a swift upsurge of Triad activity. In the first place, Sino-Malay tension in the adjacent Perak river valley resulted on several occasions in 1945 and 1946 in serious communal incidents, and caused many Chinese in the Dindings to seek personal protection within secret society groups lest the trouble spread to the coast. Again, as in the Krian and Matang districts, there was intense inter-Chinese rivalry, and Triad societies which formed at Pangkor, Lumut, Sitiawan, Kampong Koh, and Sungei Ayer Tawar to organize the coastal smuggling or to act as protection groups were rapidly caught up in the political antagonism which developed in those areas between Chinese Nationalist groups and the remnants of the Communist MPAJA.

For despite the help given to the MPAJA during the Occupation by the Hokchiu inhabitants of the Sitiawan district, the period of the interregnum was one of widespread terror. Exactions imposed by the MPAJA during their brief period in the saddle were on a vast scale, and the leader of the organization in this area was said to have benefited by $100,000, part of which came from trading in looted rubber. On Pangkor Island the Communist People's Committee sentenced to death some fifty persons, including shopkeepers and labour contractors, whose main crime appears to have been their failure to satisfy the demands of the committee. The victims were taken to Tanjong Hantu (the Haunted

Promontory) and there executed and buried in a common traitors' grave, where their remains were later discovered.

In the early months of the British Military Administration, however, the grip of the Communists was loosened as an investigation into the executions led to the arrest of some of the leading MPAJA personnel. The KMT and the SMCYYC were now able to establish themselves, and eventually to enlist the aid of Triad groups with the common aim of eradicating the Communists. According to one SMCYYC leader, the Triad societies functioned as a Peace Preservation Corps, charged with the righteous duty of eliminating the Communists who were disrupting the life of the community. The Communists, on their part, concentrated upon the subversion of labour, in the Rubber Workers' Union and among the fishermen of the coast, a policy which embittered relations between labourers and employers.

A crisis was reached on China's National Day, 10 October 1946, when the Communists, including the NDYL, the Labour Union, the Women's Union, and the ex-MPAJA, decorated their premises and staged demonstrations. A motor-lorry, owned by a notorious ex-MPAJA leader, flying a hammer-and-sickle flag and containing members of the NDYL, was attacked in Kampong Koh. The tyres were slashed and the driver and occupants assaulted. During the next few days a number of the leaders of the Communist Front organizations in several of the villages were abducted, and a general anti-Communist movement began during which the signboards and flags disappeared from the premises of the various Communist organizations throughout the district, and 200 or 300 known Communist supporters took refuge in the swamps. Those of their assailants who were arrested by the police for participation in this campaign were bailed out by a leading official of the SMCYYC, while the Communist-controlled Chinese press of Ipoh called upon the Government to suppress the 'bandits of Sitiawan'.

The Chinese Consul at Kuala Lumpur, an earnest ex-university lecturer on his first consular assignment, anxious for the good name of the Chinese community, visited Sitiawan in an attempt to restore harmony, and was reported to have remarked during a speech that every party should preserve its own principles and not interfere with others. He hoped that under British rule, when all societies were recognized, the members of the Hung Brotherhood would operate openly, like the democratic T'ongs of America, and abandon their previous secrecy. He was certain that if the Hung Brotherhood could obtain registration, no accidents would happen in future.[6] Like most of his compatriots, the Consul was confused as to the state of the law. The prewar provisions under which societies were required to register were no longer operative. But his intent was clear, namely, that the Hung Brotherhood should receive official recognition by the Malayan Government.

Pangkor was the scene of the next clash. With a population of about 8,000 inhabitants the island was entirely dependent upon the fishing industry for its existence, apart from the quantum of smuggling usual to such places. Two-thirds of the proprietors of the fishing firms owning the boats and gear and marketing the fish were Hokkiens, the rest were Cantonese, Tiechiu, or Hainanese. Politically, also, the majority were inclined towards the KMT.

On the other hand, most of the fishermen were Cantonese, with a considerable

[6] *Kwong Wah Yit Poh*, 28 Oct. 1948.

admixture of Hainanese. Before the war there were two Fishermen's Associations, one Hainanese and Communist in sympathy, the other Cantonese, managed mainly by labour headmen and contractors who had no strong political interests but who, like the proprietors of the fishing firms, had KMT sympathies. During the Japanese Occupation, however, when popular opinion supported the Communist anti-Japanese movement, the control of the Cantonese Association passed into the hands of younger members who were active supporters of the Communists, and so after the war the entire labour force, though not composed of indoctrinated Communists, was controlled by Communist-dominated Associations.

These Associations had also acquired financial resources. In addition to the extensive extortion which went on during the Interregnum, a cess of 50 cents a pikul was levied on all fish caught, 20 cents being allocated to the MCP and 30 to the labour Associations, bringing in an income of some $4,000 monthly to the party, and $6,000 monthly to the Associations. A further collection 'for the relief of the poor' brought in 1,000 bags of rice and 1,000 tins of oil, all of which were used or sold for the benefit of the Communist leaders. Nor were the Fishermen's Associations the only channels through which Communist influence could be exercised, since there were also the usual political organizations of the Communist Front, even including a New Democratic Children's Corps for those between the ages of 8 and 15.

Faced on the one hand by this strong Communist influence among the labour force, and subjected on the other to pressure from Triad fugitives from the Penang Ang Bin Hoey in concert with KMT enthusiasts, the employers decided to come to terms with the Triad group, and agreed to form a Merchants' Association to be called the Aik Cheng Mutual Aid Society, and to hold an inauguration ceremony on 17 November 1946. In this decision they were strongly encouraged by the leaders of the SMCYYC, the only Nationalist organization on the island, who had been closely linked with the Triad groups of the Sitiawan area during the recent attempts to uproot Communist organizations in that district.

On 17 November, in the darkness of the early morning hours, 100 or more men landed secretly on the east coast of Pangkor Island and made their way along the shore to the village of Sungei Pinang Kechil. They were Triad reinforcements from Penang, Kuala Kurau, Kuala Kangsar, Taiping, Trong, Pantai Remis, and Sitiawan, who were determined that the Aik Cheng inauguration ceremony should take place without Communist interference and that the Communists should be made fully aware of the new Association's strength. The expenses of their journey had been met by the SMCYYC.

The opening ceremony took place without disturbance, although the NDYL which was housed close by showed its contempt for the new Association by flying its flag at half-mast. This insult undoubtedly annoyed the Triad visitors who were spoiling for a fight, and who in retaliation abducted a Hainanese coffee-shop keeper and took him to the mainland despite pursuit by the police. Although the ensuing riot was quelled, uneasiness continued. Fishing was at a standstill, for the fishermen declared that they were afraid to take out the boats at night lest they should be attacked by Triad fighters, and the proprietors reported that Communist elements had threatened to burn down the entire village.

The authorities decided to establish a police station in the most suitable building, the premises of the Aik Cheng Association, which had remained closed since the riot. While taking over, Triad documents were discovered, together with a list of over 400 members of the Association who had been admitted to membership of the Hung Brotherhood. The Association was a cover for a Triad society.

Well aware that Triad societies were unlawful, the Committee members at once offered to dissolve the Association and to donate their funds to charity, but they were still liable to prosecution. With the collapse of the organization and the withdrawal or removal of those 'foreign' Triad elements who had arrived to 'protect' the new Association, tension lessened, and with additional police precautions a compromise was eventually reached and the economic life of the island revived. The Communists appeared to have won the first round, but the political struggle was not yet over, and there was soon a particularly gruesome epilogue.

In a plank and atap house near Kampong Koh in the Sitiawan district, the owner of a small rubber holding, surnamed Chu, lived with his family, including not only his wife and small child but his parents, brothers and sisters, and a servant girl, fourteen in all. Late in 1946, when Triad elements began to prevail in the area, Chu applied for membership of the Brotherhood in order to protect himself from the depredations of its members, but his application was refused. Possibly he was Communist-tainted, or the sum he offered may have been inadequate.

On 3 January 1947 Chu informed the police that there were bad characters at the back of his holding, and as a result of a raid on a hut in the swamp the coffee-shop keeper who had been kidnapped from Pangkor Island on 18 November was found and rescued, after having been a prisoner for weeks.

Retaliation came swiftly. At midnight on 9 January, when Chu's household was asleep, a gang of five men approached and threw a hand-grenade through a downstairs window. After a second explosion flames rose to the upper storey. Those who in desperation jumped out of the windows were set upon by the gang and beaten to death. Others perished in the flames. Chu himself escaped, but eight of his household died. Three of the gang were eventually arrested, but evidence was insufficient to support a prosecution. They were subsequently banished to China.

After the outbreak of the Emergency in June 1948 Chu joined up with the Communists in the jungle. Whether his heart had always been with them or whether he hoped to revenge himself on his enemies will never be known, for he was killed in an encounter between the police and his band in February 1949. But the 'Sitiawan Outrage' will live in the minds of the people of the district as an example of the ruthless vengeance which overtakes those who defy the Triad Brotherhood.

Throughout 1947 members of Triad societies in the Dindings continued their anti-Communist activities with the covert support of the KMT which could thus stimulate action against the common enemy without being directly involved in overt criminal acts. But when in August Triad members abducted and murdered five Chinese estate workers near Pantai Remis, including a high-ranking Communist Commissioner who was not only recruiting for the Communist-controlled Rubber Workers' Union but was believed to be in possession of information as to the whereabouts of an MCP arms dump in the Dindings, increased police attention proved an embarrassment, and certain KMT officials urged their allies to moderate their activities. There are indications that the murder was connected with an attempt by the Leper's coastal gangs to obtain additional arms before leaving Perak for Sumatra. As to this, the gangs were forestalled, for only nine days before the abduction the Perak police had uncovered a large buried arms dump in the swamps four miles from Ayer Tawar.

The Triad picture in Lower Perak is in certain respects similar to that of Matang and Taiping, for Telok Anson, the main Triad centre, and the port serving both the Perak river and the Lower Perak districts, was the southern importing and distributing centre of the smuggling network organized with Japanese connivance from Kuala Kurau, with an all-Perak coverage. Merchants in this port who acted as distributors of smuggled goods prospered exceedingly during the Occupation, but as all who prospered were inevitably regarded as Japanese collaborators by their less fortunate compatriots, they feared retribution when the Occupation ended, particularly at the hands of the MPAJA, and turned to the traditional Triad groups for protection. Among the first of the Triad societies in Lower Perak were Hokkien groups of the Yen Hai, including the Aik Soon at Telok Anson, which operated under cover of a Benevolent Society, the Aik Ghee at Bagan Datoh, and the Aik Sin at Bagan Pasir, all three of which sprang into being to protect smugglers and distributors and to maintain a grip of the coast. These societies worked in co-operation with similar groups further north in the Dindings, Matang, and Krian, and the Aik Soon became particularly powerful. All ships reaching Telok Anson paid tribute to the society, and cargoes belonging to non-members were frequently confiscated. In the town Tiechiu shops were targets for extortion. Small businesses were dunned for $400, $500, and $800, and larger firms who dared to resist blackmail found themselves faced with demands which reached $50,000 in some cases. Kidnapping for ransom on land and piracy at sea were rampant.

The Yen Hai groups were not alone in the field, for with a revival of Triad in the Kinta valley other societies extended their activities into Lower Perak, and by the end of 1947 six Triad societies were on record in Telok Anson. The demands of these rivals added to the turbulence of the scene and accounted for much of the crime among the Chinese. When the depredations of lawless bands of Malays and Indonesians were also taken into account the crime figures for Lower Perak were the highest in the State.

One society was unmasked in January 1948 through an investigation into the murder of a Malay who had been found drowned in a sack in September 1947 near the Telok Anson railway wharf. He had given information to the Customs Department concerning an opium-smoking saloon, upon which the proprietor of the saloon and other interested parties collected $1,600 to pay the killers of a Triad society to eliminate him. It transpired that a minor Customs official, a Chinese, was the secretary of the society concerned. The uncovering of the lodge premises, the seizure of many Triad documents, and the arrest of three of the society leaders disrupted the organization. It was discovered that at the end of 1947 the society had 558 members among the Chinese business community of Telok Anson, several of whom testified that they had joined through fear and threats from the society's officials. Entrance fees totalling more than $15,000 had been paid, ranging from $21 to $360, and sinsehs from Taiping had officiated at initiation ceremonies held in the near-by jungle.

Kinta

Further inland the extensive mining area of the Kinta valley, stretching from north of Ipoh southwards to Kampar, was the scene of an important postwar development. Not only was there a widespread revival of secret societies among members of the large Chinese population, but the MCP, fully cognizant of the appeal of such societies to the labouring masses, attempted to control the revival by penetrating the Hung Brotherhood and winning over Triad members to its own support.

It met with some success, for it was helped by contacts made during the Occupation. Many Triad members had joined the MPAJA to save their own skins, and participated in the resistance movement in Perak with the guerrillas. Once the Occupation ended they returned to their villages. The majority were neither necessarily indoctrinated Communists nor supporters of their MPAJA comrades, but some were subject to Communist pressure because of this wartime association, and it is known that certain Triad members were sent back to their homes specifically 'to direct the Hung Brotherhood'.

Nowhere did the MPAJA emerge in greater strength after the Occupation than in the Kinta valley. Led by prewar Communists, heavily armed, with an external organization designed to deal with propaganda, supplies, communications, and subscriptions, and equipped with spies and assassins who could eliminate 'traitors', the guerrillas were the vanguard of Communist control. When eventually the British took over, and later, when the MPAJA disbanded, Communist activity continued among the thousands of Chinese who formed the bulk of the labour forces on the tinfields, and an era of strikes and general labour unrest, engineered through the Perak Federation of Trade Unions and the Perak Rubber Workers' Union in particular, undermined government attempts to restore peace and order and to rehabilitate the tin and rubber industries.

The situation was made worse by the depredations of innumerable armed robber gangs who descended upon the villages, and by rising communal feeling between Malays and Chinese, which resulted in disturbances at Manong in November 1945, at Bota the following month, and at Bekor in March 1946. The personal efforts of H.H. the Sultan of Perak and of Mr Lau Pak Kuan, the Chinese community leader, succeeded in calming communal fears, but tension remained, and crime continued. This is illustrated in the following all-Perak table which indicates the contrast between 1946 and the four prewar years:

Year	Murder	Gang robbery with murder	Robbery with murder	Gang robbery	Robbery	Total
1946	63	3	1	124	338	529
1939	19	—	2	9	22	52
1938	20	—	2	6	35	63
1937	17	—	—	4	4	25
1936	13	—	4	—	15	32

Source: Perak Police *AR*, 1946

In Penang and along the North Perak coast the Communist threat had been contained by the Triad societies reinforced by KMT support, but when, early in

1946, a similar movement attempted to develop in Kinta, it faced certain diffi-culties. Politically, Communist power in Kinta was still widespread, and greatly feared. Ethnically, the Kinta Chinese population differed widely from the pre-dominantly Hokkien groups of Penang and the Perak coast, for the majority were either Cantonese or Hakka, with a small minority of Hokkiens and Tie-chius.[7] Further, the Kinta Triad groups were divided among themselves, and lacked the cohesion and unity of purpose which characterized both Penang and North Perak through the Ang Bin Hoey. Although there were undoubtedly some who appreciated the advantages of an overall Triad organization, no such grouping took place.

Among the Cantonese and Hakkas, the Triad societies which revived belonged, in the main, either to the Ghee Hin (Cantonese: Yi Hing) or to the Hai San (Cantonese: Hoi San), still distinguishable as the two main contestants of the early mining days in Larut, whence the original mining community had migrated in the 1880s. At the same time large numbers of Cantonese and some Hakkas joined Triad's greatest rival in the 'protection' of the Cantonese community, the Wa Kei Society. The Hokkien and Tiechiu minorities, particularly in the Ipoh area, formed groups which co-operated with the societies on the Perak coast.

Ipoh, the commercial and communication centre of the Kinta valley, was of particular importance to the coastal smugglers and pirates for the inland dis-tribution of illicit goods, and after the liberation one Triad centre was soon in operation on the Chemor Road, while at Chamberlain Road in Ipoh town the Chung Yi T'ong (Hall of Loyalty and Righteousness) was established. This society, with a strong Hokkien membership, was linked not only with Port Weld and Pasir Hitam but with smuggling gangs in the Dindings, through the Chung Ghee Benevolent Association of Kampong Koh.

Two initiation ceremonies were held at Chemor Road, and two at Pusing, a few miles south-west of Ipoh, and conveniently situated on north–south and east–west roads, which was the headquarters of both Cantonese Ghee Hin and Hai San, and became the hub of the Triad revival under the auspices of these two societies. The Ghee Hin operated under cover of the Yin Ngee Seah and was led by an officer of the SMCYYC who was strongly opposed to Communism. The Hai San operated under cover of an unobjectionable, non-political, charit-able organization, whose committee members were all reputable local shop-keepers, mine and estate owners.

The Hai San leader, who had joined the MPAJA during the Occupation to avoid elimination, had become a member of the MCP, and on the liberation had been engaged in Communist propaganda in Ipoh. When the propaganda corps was disbanded, he returned to Pusing, and together with a Triad sinseh, Sit Toh Sang, he revived the Hai San. Through his leadership the MCP hoped to control this Triad faction, and in the early stages he rallied strong support for the party from among Triad members, many of whom participated in the local Communist May Day procession.

By July 1946 Triad groups had spread in all directions. To the west societies came into existence at Siputeh, Parit (on the Perak river), and Bruas, whence Pusing influence spread southwards to Lumut and Sitiawan. South of Pusing

[7] According to the 1947 census, of the 107,000 Chinese male population of Kinta, Cantonese formed 46 per cent, Hakkas 32 per cent, Hokkiens 9 per cent, and Tiechius 5 per cent (Census Report, 1947, Table 36, adapted).

there were Hai San groups at Tronoh and Tanjong Tualang, where the MCP was still in control. Another Hai San society was formed to the east at Batu Gajah. North of Pusing a string of societies came into existence at Papan, Lahat, Menglembu, Ipoh, and Chemor. At Menglembu there was a branch of the Ghee Hin under an old sinseh whose four sons had been MPAJA members, and from Lahat southwards the influence of the '108' Society filtered through Langkat into Lower Perak.

Side by side with this renaissance of the Ghee Hin and the Hai San came a resurgence of the Wa Kei, branches of which were established at Ipoh, Menglembu, Tronoh, Tanjong Tualang, and Sungei Siput north, Gopeng, and Kampar. In all cases they operated under cover of Benevolent Associations, whose titles frequently included the characters 'Wa K'iu' (Overseas Chinese). The ritual leader of the Triad revival was the Hakka sinseh, Sit Toh Sang, a member of the Hai San Society of Pusing with great prestige among all the Triad groups as far south as the Dindings.

Throughout Kinta the various Triad groups raised funds through the usual channels—extortion letters, kidnapping for ransom, and 'protection', and the arrival from Penang in mid-1946 of Ang Bin Hoey fugitives anxious to make a living increased these activities. But it was not until September 1946 that the policy decision to implement the Triad clauses of the Societies Enactment enabled the Perak police to take action against Triad organizers as such. A raid on the sinseh's house at Menglembu produced Triad initiation diplomas and also evidence of close co-operation with the Communist Party, including entry forms for joining the Reserve Party of the MPAJA. In January 1947 Sit Toh Sang was arrested in Pusing and convicted of possession of Triad documents. He was sentenced to two years' imprisonment and later banished.

After his removal there were new developments in Pusing. For some time, as the power of the Hai San had grown, its leader had gradually drifted away from the MCP. He now began to co-operate with the Ghee Hin, and the two societies combined to form a branch of the Perak Mining Employees' Association. This was a KMT-inspired trade union backed by prominent Chinese mining employers and labour contractors who were determined to retain control of the tin-mining industry. It had been formed to counteract the activities of the Communist-inspired Perak Mining Labourers' Union. The Hai San leader became the Vice-President of the new Association, secret society elements assisted in recruitment, and the new union's influence spread widely in the Gopeng–Ipoh area, and also reached Tanjong Tualang, the Communist stronghold.

In Ipoh police action was taken against the Hokkien groups. On the night of 9–10 April the headquarters of the Chung Yi T'ong was raided and six members arrested. The hall of the house was decorated with Triad scrolls and a drawing of a red eagle was also found. In the garden six buried grenades were unearthed, and when enquiries led to a further raid on a house in Theatre Street, two books containing Triad documents were recovered.

In May a small atap hut on the Chemor Road was also raided and proved to be another Triad centre. Triad documents and articles connected with an initiation ceremony were found inside, as well as 171 initiation diplomas with the names of those initiated and of the sinsehs who had performed the ceremonies. These diplomas facilitated further enquiries, and interrogations revealed that most members had been initiated as a result of threats. The Chung Yi T'ong

cc

was gazetted as an illegal society. Many Triad leaders went into hiding and others left Ipoh.

By May 1948 police pressure had resulted in some diminution of Triad activity in Chemor, Ipoh, and Pusing, but Menglembu and Lahat remained heavily infected. At Sungei Siput north, Gopeng, and Kampar the Wa Kei was very strong. In South Perak Communist influence was being challenged by Triad societies at Bidor and Tapah, where gambling on a large scale was known to be organized. Banir village, near Tapah, was a keen centre for Triad recruiting and initiation. Ceremonies were held in rubber estates, the only approaches to which were through villages which could easily give warning.

The MCP had not succeeded to any extent in winning over Triad members to their support, particularly after the debacle in Pusing in 1947 and the subsequent formation of the Perak Mining Employees' Association. Nevertheless they retained strong influence in areas where they had operated during the Occupation. These included Tanjong Tualang to Degong, Degong to Ayer Kuning (on the Bidor–Telok Anson Road), and Bidor to Tanjong Malim, especially Ulu Slim. Cameron Highlands was also under Communist control. In these areas dwelt 'the Communist army in waiting', units of the MPAJA which had never been disclosed.

Upper Perak: The Malayan Overseas Chinese Self-Defence Army

The efforts made by the KMT throughout Perak to align the Triad societies on their side in opposition to the Communists have already received notice, but the determination to oppose Communism went much further than that, for, in the upper reaches of the Perak river, the KMT maintained a secret armed guerrilla group to be called upon should the MCP attempt to take control of Malaya by force of arms. This had been developed from a remnant of the wartime non-Communist pro-KMT guerrillas, and although not Triad in origin, had within its ranks Triad personnel, and had contact with Triad groups outside.

In December 1945, when the Communist MPAJA disbanded, it was intended that the KMT-sponsored guerrillas, the OCAJA, would at the same time hand in their arms and disband. They did in fact parade for this purpose, but at the last moment, on account of some alleged insult which has never been satisfactorily explained, they refused to disband and marched off again, still fully armed.

In June 1946 disbandment of part of the main group in Perak was achieved by negotiation, but a considerable body, in two sections, withdrew to their wartime bases in the jungles of Upper Perak, one around Grik and the other around Lenggong. A third group remained in being over the border in Kelantan. During the latter part of 1946 and the first half of 1947 further efforts were made by the Government, with the help of the Chinese Consul and a number of prominent ex-KMT guerrillas, to get into touch with these three groups and induce them to disband on payment of the usual terms, together with a free passage to China for any who wanted to go there. Despite a number of promising starts and the expenditure of a considerable sum of money, nothing came of these negotiations, and by the middle of 1947 it was clear that they had broken down. In the light of what was later discovered, it is doubtful whether there was ever any genuine intention to disband. A large proportion of the arms handed in by those who surrendered in 1946 were unserviceable, and much of the negotiation with those still in the jungle turned on their insistence on being recognized as official troops and being employed by the Government.

In November 1947 it was reported that a recruiting campaign was taking place in the region north of Ipoh with the object of forming at Lenggong an army to be trained as KMT-disciplined effectives in case the Communists became belligerent in Malaya. Investigations followed, and early in 1948 it was confirmed that this force was actually in existence, and that it controlled an area of some 600 square miles, roughly pear-shaped, extending from beyond Grik in the north, spreading down both sides of the Perak river and the main road, and narrowing to a finish near Kati, some ten miles north of Kuala Kangsar.

From 1 January 1948 the force adopted the new title of Malayan Overseas Chinese Self-Defence Army (MOCSDA). Its total strength is difficult to assess; one estimate of 800–1,000 is probably an exaggeration, and it is likely that there were not more than 400 active military members, including the Kelantan group which had come across to Lenggong in November 1947, when the reorganization had taken place.

A factor which added to the potential danger of this 'army' was that the area under its control included a large Chinese agricultural population of Kwangsais, and MOCSDA itself was largely Kwangsai in composition. During the war years the district had been developed by Kwangsai squatters, who produced considerable crops of tobacco and ginger. It was natural that the section of the OCAJA formed in the area during the war should also be Kwangsai and should have developed a technique of living off their fellow cultivators. The knowledge that there was this reserve of able-bodied agriculturalists who could at any time be transformed into fighters and who were under the orders of MOCSDA increased the sense of power in the minds of the leaders and supporters of the force, making them the less inclined to accept the terms offered by the Government.

By April 1948 enough information had been collected to enable a combined police–military expedition to be undertaken against a number of MOCSDA camps. The first target, Ayer Karah, proved to be a camp and a training depot, complete with parade ground, flagpole, targets, offices, and all the paraphernalia for military training. Portraits of Sun Yat-sen and Chiang Kai-shek and Chinese Nationalist flags adorned the main hall. The camp and the training school were sited on the tops of hills, with the undergrowth well cleared to provide an unimpeded field of fire from the rifle pits dug round the crests. Jungle trees had been left unfelled so that complete cover from air observation was retained. Other camps were found at Grik and Kati, and from all these places documentary evidence of the activities of the organization was obtained.

Besides the guerrilla army there was a Civil Administration Corps, headed by a former OCAJA leader who had settled in Kuala Kangsar and had acquired as allies a local Triad group which had been part of the MPAJA in the Perak river valley south of that town. Freed from the domination of the Communists at Pusing, they had entered into a junior partnership with MOCSDA, and their leader became a close associate of the civil director. Further south, in the Tanjong Tualang area, a directive centre had been set up in December 1947, in control of 200 men, and it was also proposed to expand in the Manong–Bruas–Siputeh triangle, where MOCSDA had close links with a local Triad organization.

Funds for the maintenance of the guerrilla 'army' were provided by taxation.

The Upper Perak region was divided into four districts, each under a 'Civil Administrator'. Within each district there were further divisions and subdivisions. Families were grouped into clusters of thirty called 'Kaps', and each of these clusters had a headman responsible for the collection of taxes from the families under his control. A number of Kaps, perhaps thirty or more depending upon the distribution of the population, were formed into a 'Koi', which again had its headman responsible for the collection of taxes from the constituent Kaps. These headmen of Kois and Kaps were exempt from taxation. There was a poll-tax of $1 monthly on each adult, male or female, aged 16 or over. Agricultural produce was taxed through the dealers to whom it was sold for marketing: rubber at 50 cents a pikul, tobacco at $5 a pikul, though $8 in Grik, where the extra $3 was exacted for the maintenance of the SMCYYC. Beans paid $1 a pikul, ginger $1.50, and padi one-tenth in kind. Dealers' books were checked weekly by officers appointed by the Civil Administrator. Goods vehicles were taxed at $50 monthly, while the bus company paid $400. There was a sliding scale of taxation of businesses. Large shops paid $100 monthly, normal shops $60, and small ones $10. The administration also promoted its own trading company, had interests in tin-mining, and was negotiating the purchase of a rubber estate. Permits to promote gambling were issued to produce additional revenue. Finally, the MOCSDA Administration had its own courts with a military officer as Judge, before which those infringing the regulations of the Administration were brought.

From statements made by cultivators it is clear that the system of taxation had been in operation for two years, but that from August 1947, when committee meetings were held and a reorganization was planned on a commercial basis with a new scale of taxation, the organization was improved and extended, bringing the whole area under the control of MOCSDA. It was in August 1947 that the proposal to expand the 'army' was taken, and the recruiting campaign began. The training camp was built in November 1947.

In the police–military operations which began in April 1948 the main MOCSDA force avoided contact and moved off, probably over the Kelantan and Siamese frontiers, but a few prisoners were taken. Rewards were offered for the capture of the Commander. Leaders who were arrested were quite frank that the purpose of the 'army' was to be in position, ready for the third world war which was believed to be imminent, and prepared to repulse the attempt which would be made by the Communists to take control in Malaya.

Documents captured during the operations linked the organization with the KMT and the Chinese Consulate. The go-between was a major of the Chinese National Army who was captured on his way to deliver a document to the MOCSDA army informing them of the projected attack by government forces. He stated that as the Malayan Government was unable and unwilling to take any counter-measures against the Communists, it was incumbent upon the overseas Chinese to provide their own shield of defence. From the time of the opening of the operations, strenuous efforts were made by Chinese Consular officials and KMT leaders to persuade the Government to take over MOCSDA as an official defence corps. Despite the fact that the Commander was a 'wanted' man, it was common knowledge that he could be reached if addressed 'care of the Chinese Consulate-General, Singapore'.

The immediate effect of the military operation in Upper Perak was the release of the population from the heavy pressure of MOCSDA. As usual, once official action was taken to remove the pressure, information was forthcoming from those who previously had been too frightened to say anything about it, and had for two years, unknown to the Government, endured this form of tyranny. That this should have been possible is a modern object-lesson in the power of fear over a large Chinese community, and is an example of the way in which an organization of this nature can establish itself and arrange for its own support through a pattern of pressure well understood by and acquiesced in by the community.

Long before the operation against MOCSDA could be pushed to a satisfactory conclusion, the Emergency had begun, and all the troops and police available were required to combat the new threat. This added weight to the supporters of MOCSDA to induce the Government to take over the organization as an anti-Communist unit, but their proposals were not accepted because of the political issues involved. Some of the members thereafter resumed their original employment as agriculturalists, others remained with the rump of the 'army' and returned to the old hunting grounds, demanding from the cultivators arrears of taxes from April 1948, when the organization was disrupted. But the response was not so ready. The power of MOCSDA had been challenged, and though not overthrown, had lost the sanction of inevitability. Gradually the fortunes of these outlaws waned in keeping with those of the KMT whose leaders were the targets of the assassination squads of the new Communist army. In April 1949 the remnants of MOCSDA still remaining in Upper Perak surrendered. There were 90 men in all, of whom 56 were embodied as special constables and worked with the jungle squads of the military–police formations in the Kuala Kangsar area; 33 were resettled in Upper Perak, and 1 went to China at his own request. The arms surrendered included 2 Bren guns, 11 Sten guns, 41 rifles, 21 pistols, 4 shot-guns, 35 grenades, and over 10,000 rounds of ammunition.

Thus ended an organization which the KMT leaders and the Chinese Consular officials had hoped would provide the core for an armed movement to oppose the Communists and establish KMT rule over the Chinese community of Malaya.

17

TRIAD ACTIVITY ON THE MALAYAN MAINLAND, 1945-8, II

1. SELANGOR

ALTHOUGH the reports for the more southerly States of the peninsula are not as comprehensive as are those for Penang and Perak, there is enough information to enable the main features to be distinguished.

In Selangor the immediate postwar scene was characterized by many acts of vengeance on the part of the MPAJA and by an attempt to rivet Communist control upon the countryside. Once again, as in Kinta, the objective was the control of labour, not only on the wharves of Port Swettenham but in the coal mines at Batu Arang and the tin mines and rubber estates throughout the State. Kajang, a strongly Communist district south of Kuala Lumpur, received particular attention, for it was intended that in the eventual Communist revolt planned to drive the British from Malaya, Kajang should be the first 'Liberated Area'.

But the Communist leaders were not unchallenged, for armed gangs of extortioners operating under high-sounding titles on the pattern of the hill bands well known in the Chinese legends were among the first to prey upon the population. One of these groups, the Green Dragon Mountain gang, a criminal gang reputed to use a Triad ritual and responsible for many murders during the Occupation, continued to terrorize the area around Kuala Lumpur until mid-1947. With a membership of over 100, and led by Liew Ngit Sing, it first operated south of the capital. In September 1945 it captured the police station at Salak South, and was only driven out after a battle with the military in which several members of the gang were killed, and others wounded and captured. Later, as a result of negotiations, these prisoners were released in return for the surrender of arms, but sufficient weapons were secretly retained to enable the gang to continue to blackmail shopkeepers in the area. Any failure to 'co-operate' resulted in abduction for ransom, and even death after ransom had been paid.

It is recorded that for a time the gang received sanctuary and financial support from a Triad group which formed in Serdang, but after several months' activity Liew Ngit Sing was arrested in May 1946. He was rescued in September by his followers who ambushed the police escort taking him from court to gaol. In January 1947 he was again captured, with five others, and was eventually sentenced to seven years' imprisonment on charges of abduction with intent to murder. Meantime, several members of the gang had moved north to Batu Caves. Others went east to Ampang, where they were discovered in May 1947 after joining with another smaller group, the Tiger Tamers. They had continued their career of extortion and abduction, but when some members were arrested no victims would give evidence in court, and action was taken under the Banishment Ordinance.

In October 1947 those of the gang who had remained in their original haunts at Serdang were attacked by a rival group which called itself the Malayan Chinese People's Self-Defence Corps. This was led by Lee Loy, reputed to have been an MPAJA executioner during the Japanese Occupation. Immediately after the war, with fourteen kindred spirits from Selangor and Perak, he had gone to Padang Besar on the Perlis–Siam border. There he organized large-scale gambling and preyed upon the smugglers thronging the town. In 1946, when Triad gangsters from Penang, Province Wellesley, and Kedah began to intervene, Lee Loy came to a working agreement with a group of ex-KMT guerrillas from Kaki Bukit, and the combined gang operated under his leadership in Padang Besar until early 1947, when the return to more normal conditions on the border and an unwelcome increase of police attention caused the entire group to retire to Kaki Bukit. But relationships, both criminal and political, were uneasy, internal dissensions soon broke out, and after a gun-battle behind Kaki Bukit town in which three of his men were killed, Lee Loy was dethroned and returned with his followers to his old haunts in Selangor, leaving his previous allies in sole control at Kaki Bukit.

Within a short time he reappeared in the Serdang area of Selangor at the head of a band of thirty well-trained, heavily armed ex-guerrillas, intent upon the elimination of local rivals, the Green Dragon Mountain gang. His second in command was a boy of sixteen, who had escaped from the Selangor Boys' Home by flourishing a pistol which had been smuggled in to him in a loaf of bread. Dressed in black and white uniforms with hammer and sickle badges, and carrying a red flag also with that emblem, the gang embarked upon a campaign of murder and extortion, giving receipts for 'contributions' received to encourage the illusion that they were a properly-constituted group working for the good of the people.

Their campaign against the Green Dragon Mountain gang began on 12 September, when they attacked the village of Serdang. They dragged the president of the local Chinese Association into the street and murdered him, exchanged shots with the local police, plastered the village with violent anti-British and anti-Government posters, and before leaving, demanded tribute from all and sundry under pain of death. During October they discovered the hideout of their rivals, whose leader committed suicide by jumping into a mining pool; large quantities of ammunition and several cases of hand-grenades then fell into their hands.

Information furnished by Wa Kei Society members led to the location of Lee Loy's gang at Sungei Buloh, five miles north-west of Kuala Lumpur. The group was surprised by a police party, and in the ensuing gun-battle Lee Loy and two others were killed. Pursuit of the gang continued, and in December the young deputy chief was arrested in Pudu, Kuala Lumpur, negotiating for the purchase of a revolver, with a loaded Luger pistol at his waist.

As in Perak, the Communist challenge in Selangor was met by an immediate Triad revival in the coastal areas, particularly in Pulau Ketam, Port Swettenham, Klang, and the bagans of Kuala Selangor and Kuala Langat. A slightly later revival centred upon Kuala Lumpur and spread into Ulu Selangor and Ulu Langat.

On the coast, within the Triad ranks there were two contestants for power, the Yen Hai or coastal group, and the Luk Tai or land group, which came to be known in police circles as the 'Sea Gang' and the 'Land Gang'. The coastal group was very strongly influenced by Yeoh Ah Bah of Port Weld, and was closely linked with Cell 12 of both Perak and Penang. The Land Gang, on the other hand, looked to Cells 4 and 21 in Penang for support.

The Sea Gang was similar in every respect to the Triad groups of the coastal bagans in Perak. Like their brethren further north, members were mostly Hokkiens, and as fishermen and smugglers they were in constant contact, one group with another. Pulau Ketam, a small island nine miles west of Port Swettenham, was their headquarters. This island, four miles long by two miles wide, was a natural stronghold for smugglers and for secret society activity, for contact could easily be made with steamers entering and leaving Port Swetten-ham and with smaller vessels trading along the coast; also it was only seventy-five miles from Sumatra and the Triad stronghold of Bagan Si Api Api with which its inhabitants had close personal contact. At the same time it was far enough away from the Selangor mainland to be assured of privacy and freedom from too much attention from police or customs officials. No one could approach Pulau Ketam without being seen, and all strangers arriving at the village jetty were regarded with grave suspicion. The swamps adjoining the village provide convenient hiding-places when occasion demands for smuggled arms, chandu, or fugitive members of the Triad Brotherhood, and the island provides an excellent site for initiation ceremonies.

While Pulau Ketam was the headquarters, the ritualistic centre, and the refuge of the Sea Gang, Port Swettenham was the hub of its power, the source of much of its income, the scene of its depredations, and the centre of its recruit-ment. A Chinese company, which was formed immediately after the liberation to work the port, was swiftly dominated and 'protected' by the Sea Gang, whose leaders were the power behind its authority. In the 'stream', the loading and off-loading labourers were Chinese, at the wharves they were more usually Indian, but whatever their race, Triad ruled. All Chinese were forced to become members of the Brotherhood. An attempt by Communist agents to infiltrate the wharf labour and to stage a strike late in December 1945 was quickly frus-trated by the Company's labour supervisor, a Triad member of White Fan rank and head of the Sea Gang, who promptly enlisted a squad of 'strong-arm' men from Kuala Lumpur and forced the strikers back to work. No Triad employee was ever dismissed by the Company, which cared for wives and families of those who were detained or imprisoned for their misdeeds or who found it advisable to abscond.

Financially, the Sea Gang reaped a rich harvest. Consigners or consignees paid a toll on every lighter loading or off-loading in the 'stream' and on every lorry-load of goods loading or off-loading on the wharves. The Port Swettenham –Klang road was watched by the gang to see that none escaped this payment. In the town gambling haunts, opium dens, brothels, shopkeepers, hawkers, and the like, paid 'protection' money. At sea the pirating of cargoes and the smug-gling of arms and opium was controlled by the gang, not only in the Port Swettenham approaches but along the entire Selangor coast.

Late in September 1946 the Sea Gang was unexpectedly reinforced when nearly 2,500 Chinese refugees arrived from Bagan Si Api Api after an attack by Indonesian troops, when they had all, men, women, and children, taken to their boats and sailed eastwards, seeking refuge on the Malayan coast. They arrived destitute, were cared for in the first instance by their compatriots and by the Social Welfare Department, and were then temporarily distributed until such time as conditions improved and they could return to Sumatra; 1,600 stayed at Pulau Ketam, 550 at Kuala Selangor, 150 at Tanjong Karang, 100 at Port Swettenham, and 40 at Port Dickson on the coast of Negri Sembilan. They were received with surprising friendliness and were rapidly absorbed into the local population. Official attempts were made to find new homes for them in Dutch territory, and a camp on one of the Rhio islands was offered but was rejected by a deputation of refugees who visited the proposed site. They all remained in Selangor for several months, and then, on receiving reports that Bagan Si Api Api was again peaceful, one party went back in June 1947 to start rebuilding their village. Gradually most of the refugees returned, although a number remained in the Selangor coastal villages.

The significance of this influx lay in the fact that the male refugees were all initiated Triad society members, linked through their own society with the Yen Hai of the Malayan coast. Their arrival in Selangor was a direct stimulus to local Triad activity. From information obtained several years later, it seems that they actively recruited new members by the traditional forceful methods, particularly in the bagans around Kuala Selangor, and towards the end of 1946 they urged Yeoh Ah Bah, Lim Ah Hah (the sinseh), and two other Triad leaders from Taiping to come south, hold initiation ceremonies, and generally strengthen the coastal Triad organization. As has already been indicated, the invitation was most opportune as the Leper was threatening the authority and lives of these officials in North Perak, and in February 1947 these Taiping leaders arrived in Selangor and spent several remunerative months on the coast. By May 1947 at least seven initiation ceremonies had been held at Pulau Ketam, two more at Tanjong Karang, and another at Sekinchang. The combined membership of Pulau Ketam, Port Swettenham, and Klang was estimated at this time to be 11,000, of whom 3,000 were said to be on Pulau Ketam. In August a special police coastal patrol operating between Port Swettenham and Pangkor reported that the Sea Gang had an almost complete grip on all Chinese who worked along the Selangor coast. Smuggling and black-marketing were taking place on an enormous scale.

Yeoh Ah Bah returned to North Perak in November 1947, but before he left Selangor he presided at yet another initiation ceremony at Pulau Ketam late in September, when some 80 new members were admitted. He was supported by an official from Sumatra, and initiates included 20 from Taiping, 40 from Telok Anson and Kuala Selangor, and the remainder from Sepang (Kuala Langat) and Malacca.

The authority of the Sea Gang was firmly established but it was not un-challenged. Although its operations in Selangor centred mainly on Port Swetten-ham, Pulau Ketam, and the bagans of the coast, these activities overflowed to Klang, six miles inland, on the main road and railway to Kuala Lumpur and the interior. There the Land Gang had been set up by members of the Penang Cell 21, who drifted southwards after the break-up of the Ang Bin Hoey in Penang in May 1946. This gang was said to have its headquarters at Bukit Changgang (Kuala Langat), and it may have had a refuge on an island near

Kuala Sepang, but its main operative centre was Klang, where it endeavoured to control all rackets, offering protection to merchants and their goods in return for a toll, and providing similar facilities for coffee-shops, amusement parks, petty traders, and hawkers. At one time members of Cell 4, Penang, also attempted to establish themselves in Klang but they eventually joined forces with Cell 21.

Inevitably there was dissension between the Sea and Land Gangs, for their zones of 'protection' were constantly overlapping. The main conflict concerned the right to smuggle opium, claimed by the Sea Gang as their monopoly, but when importers of illicit chandu in Klang decided to accept the protection of the Land Gang, matters reached a climax, and to strengthen their own hand the Sea Gang invited Yeoh Ah Bah, as the Elder Brother of the coast, to Selangor. Open hostilities broke out. Early in March 1947 one leader and a member of the Land Gang were killed by orders of the Sea Gang. Three weeks later the Land Gang retaliated by killing a leader of the Sea Gang. In May nine members of the Land Gang attempted to circumvent the payment of protection money to their rivals on the importation of smuggled chandu by going out in a small boat to a ship in Port Swettenham harbour to buy direct a consignment of chandu, said to be worth over $20,000. The Sea Gang intervened, killed 3 of the 9 interlopers, and confined the remaining 6 until the Hokkien Association of Klang negotiated for their release.

A fight for supremacy was then planned to take place near Sepang, and both gangs sought reinforcements as far afield as Penang, Ipoh, and Malacca, but a temporary compromise was reached on the advice of the Taiping leaders.

It was at this stage that the police were able to take decisive action. Strengthened in May 1947 by the gazetting of both gangs as unlawful societies, they arrested a prominent leader of the Sea Gang at Port Swettenham and the leader and six members of the Land Gang operating in Sungei Pelek and Sepang. For a time gangster activities quietened down, although both sides tried to get permission from the Taiping leaders to call in Triad members from Sumatra to kill detectives in Klang believed to be responsible for the information which had led to the arrests. The Sea Gang also intensified its collection of special subscriptions, ranging from $108 to $360, and succeeded in winning the support of a Chi Kung Tong group at Sultan Street, Kuala Lumpur, under cover of which it began to operate.

The inland Triad revival based on Kuala Lumpur had originated a few miles north of the capital at Setapak, a small village which during the Japanese Occupation had formed part of the civilian supply organization for the Selangor MPAJA headquarters in the near-by hills. The organizers were a group of pre-war Hokkien Triad members, some of whom, as in Penang, had links with the '108' Society in Singapore. They followed the example of Penang in adopting the title Ang Bin Hoey and in setting up a central controlling committee, dividing the Kuala Lumpur area into 'cells', supervisors of which attended central committee meetings. But they had no centralized headquarters premises, and their authority was far less comprehensive than that of the Penang society. For unlike Penang, or even the Selangor coast, the Chinese community in the Kuala Lumpur district was not primarily Hokkien but was predominantly Cantonese and Hakka, whose Triad groups, when formed, maintained a degree of independence incompatible with complete Hokkien domination. And the rival Wa Kei Society was already in the field. It had revived immediately after the war, partly in opposition to the Communists' bid for power but also to ensure that under the new British policy of freedom of association Wa Kei, and not Triad, should control the secret society world. A further element in the Wa Kei revival was the desire to retain control of the organization of public lotteries in which some members of this society had been engaged during the Japanese Occupation.[1]

Under these circumstances, although the Ang Bin Hoey was able to count upon the support of its own cells, had liaison links with both Port Swettenham and Klang, and was ultimately able to depend to a limited extent upon the support of certain Cantonese and Hakka Triad gangs and societies who were prepared to resist the pretensions of the Wa Kei, it was nevertheless unable to establish itself in the supreme position achieved by Triad both in Penang and along the Perak and Selangor coasts, and the Kuala Lumpur scene remained one of incessant struggle between Triad and Wa Kei.

Besides its central organization, the Ang Bin Hoey developed seven sub-branches in the Kuala Lumpur area. Of these the cell at Chow Kit Road was the most powerful, but others rapidly came into existence at Setapak, Gombak, Sentul Pasar, Kepong, Pahang Road ($2\frac{1}{2}$ miles), and Klang Road ($4\frac{1}{2}$ miles). Villages further afield also soon formed part of the network, and initiation ceremonies under Kuala Lumpur auspices were held as far away as Bentong in Pahang.

The central committee was controlled by a Triad leader of outstanding personality, Tan Hong Piew, who, though handicapped because he had been blinded by vitriol in 1929, was regarded with unusual reverence because of his gift of oratory and his extensive knowledge of Triad ritual and practice.

With the exception of an English-speaking Chinese who acted as liaison officer between the society and outsiders, and who made arrangements for the legal defence of arrested members, the majority of the central committee were cell leaders who were actively engaged in the usual secret society pursuits. Recruitment by intimidation was widespread and membership grew, particularly in places of large employment such as the Ng Teong Keat Biscuit Factory at Setapak, the Lee Rubber Company at Gombak, the railway workshops at Sentul Pasar, and the Lucky World Amusement Park in Kuala Lumpur town. Stall-holders, shopkeepers, brothel-keepers, opium dens, travelling theatrical

1

Chinese by Tribe

	Hokkien	Tiechiu	Hakka	Cantonese	Hainanese
K. Lumpur (Mun.)	21,385	5,668	20,330	54,066	6,616
(Rest)	17,448	2,694	35,967	18,338	2,940
Ulu Selangor	7,963	1,085	15,723	12,639	1,141
Ulu Langat	8,805	814	17,468	5,179	738
Klang	24,194	5,239	3,159	6,579	3,624
K. Selangor	10,907	807	1,369	1,206	997
K. Langat	16,288	1,624	2,690	1,277	1,823

Source: Census Report Malaya 1947, Table 96 (adapted).

troupes, and the like paid protection money. Members of the Hokkien Black Cat Opera Troupe, performing at the Lucky World, admitted, when later arrested, that they had joined the Ang Bin Hoey in Penang in order to ensure freedom from molestation during their tour of the mainland.

After the official gazetting of the Ang Bin Hoey as an unlawful society in May 1947, the Selangor cells either went underground or operated under cover-associations. At Serdang the Seng Kong Athletic Association, which also provided funeral benefits, was used by the Ang Bin Hoey as a meeting-place and gambling club. Applicants for membership who had not already been admitted to the Hung Brotherhood were required to undergo a 'mosquito net' ceremony of initiation before being permitted to join. Members included Hokkiens, Cantonese, and others, and there was a Hokkien sinseh for the initiation of Hokkien candidates, and a Cantonese sinseh for the Cantonese. At funeral processions the Association's banner, a white flag with a red border, was carried. This was similar to the flag used in Larut in the 1870s as the symbol of Second Lodge (Ghee Hin) foundation. Branches were opened at Kepong in 1948 and at Ampang Street, Kuala Lumpur, in 1952.

The Kuala Lumpur cells of the Ang Bin Hoey, like the Sea Gang, also arranged to operate under cover of the Chi Kung Tong, the prewar Association of Fui Chiu Hakkas which, together with the Cantonese Chung Woh Tong, had revived in Kuala Lumpur in 1946.[2] Also based at Kuala Lumpur were three Cantonese Triad gangs, the Kwan Luen (Military United), the San Kwan (New Military), and the Sap Sam Yau (Thirteen Comrades), all of which had affiliations with Singapore societies.

The Kwan Luen and the San Kwan were prewar societies, each connected with the Kwan Kee of Singapore. The Kwan Luen was resuscitated in Kuala Lumpur in 1946 by a Singapore agent, assisted by a local leader who was employed as a mechanic on a dredge at Sungei Way, and it eventually made its headquarters at Setapak. Members included mining and engineering labourers and trishaw riders who paid an entrance fee of $2.10. The gang used the titles of Triad ranks but employed a simplified initiation ceremony. It engaged in the usual pursuits of criminal gangs and was resolutely opposed to the Wa Kei.

The San Kwan had existed in prewar Kuala Lumpur as the Kwan Kee, a society of strong Hakka and Cantonese membership using a Triad ritual. During the Japanese Occupation it changed its name to San Kwan, and after the liberation began to operate in the Pudu and Ampang districts, with headquarters in a local temple. It adopted a simplified ritual and was particularly engaged in promoting gambling, smuggling opium, and 'protecting' members of Chinese opera troupes. Its membership was smaller than that of the Kwan Luen and was estimated at about 200. Details of the Thirteen Comrades gang are not available.

In March 1948, reinforced by the support of the fighter strength of these allies, the Ang Bin Hoey challenged the Wa Kei to an organized fight to decide the question of control of underworld rackets in the Kuala Lumpur area. Since 1945, when the Kepong branch emerged, the Wa Kei had become very powerful, with branches in Kuala Lumpur town, Pudu, Setapak, Ampang, Kajang, Sungei Besi, Serdang, Rawang, Serendah, and Ulu Yam, most of them operating

[2] See below, pp. 429–33.

under cover associations, all of which paid liberal funeral benefits. The principal organizer was a vermicelli seller from Kuala Lumpur, Cheah Siew, alias Kor Hor Chut, who became known as the 'self-appointed King of Wa Kei'.

It would be wrong to infer that the purpose of these Associations was to engage in criminal pursuits. Basically they were formed as social clubs where members, many of whom were shopkeepers, traders, and contractors, could meet, drink, and gamble in the evening. They also filled a need by providing protection both from the Communists and from the demands of Triad gangsters. But within the Brotherhood were groups of members whose main activities and sources of livelihood were the organization of public gaming (often in the premises of the Associations) and the promotion of illicit opium dens. One such group which, with Japanese compliance, had managed the public Chee Fah lottery[3] throughout the Occupation continued to thrive on this business until November 1946 when the lottery was officially prohibited. Thereafter bribery of police detectives (many of whom were members of the Wa Kei) became increasingly prevalent. By 1948 membership in Selangor, Perak, Negri Sembilan, and Pahang ran into thousands, and in Kuala Lumpur town in particular constant war was waged with Triad gangs by groups of Wa Kei thugs because of disputes concerning zones of 'protection'.

On 23 March 1948 a fight developed outside the Lucky World Amusement Park and continued far into the night, though broken up several times by the police. The Wa Kei finally withdrew, with two of their men seriously injured.

The Wa Kei were also faced with the enmity of the MCP, and on 4 May a meeting of sixty Wa Kei leaders was held in Kuala Lumpur, at which it was decided to offer help to the Government against the Communists, particularly by passing information to the police. On 19 May three Wa Kei and three Ang Bin Hoey representatives met and agreed that in future, in order to avoid police interference, they would settle their disputes by negotiation, and not by fighting.

Meantime, severe police action had followed the big society fight. On 9 May the leader of the Chow Kit Road Triad cell was arrested and later banished. A large number of membership forms and receipt books were found in his possession relating to the formation of yet another cover-association, in which the San Kwan gang was particularly interested. This was the Tong Yik Mutual Aid Association, open to all members of the Triad Brotherhood.

The outbreak of the Communist revolt increased the urgency for police action against those liable to disturb the public peace. In June three leaders of the Sap Sam Yau gang were arrested, together with a Japanese doctor whom they had harboured since the liberation. They were all discovered packing large quantities of medical stores which were to be taken by the doctor to the MCP forces in the near-by jungle. In July five important leaders of the Sea Gang at Port Swettenham and Sepang were arrested, as were two members of the Chow Kit Road cell, Kuala Lumpur, who had been bodyguards of the leader. Early in August Tan Hong Piew, the blind leader of the Selangor Ang Bin Hoey central committee, was also taken into custody, and in September four leaders of the Kwan Luen and one leader of the San Kwan gangs were arrested. This action disrupted the cells and dispersed their allies, the Cantonese and Hakka gangs, and for some time Triad activities in Selangor subsided.

[3] See below, p. 444.

2. PAHANG

The adjacent States of Pahang and Negri Sembilan were both influenced by the revival of Wa Kei and Triad activities in Selangor.

In Pahang, where the Wa Kei with its centre at Bentong and branches at Raub, Mentekab, and Kuala Lipis had been in existence for many years before the Pacific War, activities completely ceased during the Japanese Occupation. The Wa Kei leader was arrested by the Japanese and died in 1942, and the society's activities ceased. But on the liberation, taking advantage of the lawlessness of the transition, the society resuscitated, though for a time the strength of the MPAJA groups in the area prevented much development. As early as January 1946, once the MPAJA had been disbanded, an important organizer of the Wa Kei in Kuala Lumpur arrived in Bentong accompanied by six active members. They opened a restaurant which served as a Wa Kei meeting-place and as premises where large-scale gambling could be organized. By the end of the year some prewar officials of the society had been installed and 120 members enrolled; branches had also been opened at Raub and Manchis. Progress was checked when gambling was prohibited by the police, but in 1947 new premises were bought and a cover-club established which soon had a membership of several hundred in addition to contributors to a Benevolent Scheme. As usual, a criminal nucleus organized the collection of protection money from local traders, promoted gambling, and committed extortion and assaults.

The Bentong Wa Kei kept in touch with other branches of the society in the Federation, particularly with Kuala Lumpur, and was a strong rival of the Triad and later of the Chung Woh Tong groups which made their appearance in Pahang. It remained the inveterate enemy of Communism, and the strength of its grip on the Chinese of Bentong was demonstrated after the outbreak of the Emergency in 1948, for the Communists were never able to penetrate the town and when, in due course, a Home Guard was formed, the great majority of officers and men were Wa Kei members. The small branch at Manchis, however, did not survive but closed down when the district was overrun by the terrorists.

Kuantan, on the east coast and close to the Pahang Consolidated Company's tin lode mine, was also a Wa Kei centre. In 1941 it was reported that about 80 per cent of the Chinese in the town were members. Later, when the Japanese occupied the country, several were killed, but after the liberation the society was resuscitated under cover of a social club. Only Cantonese were recruited or allowed to enter the club, and membership comprised mostly building labourers and mechanics.

Little detail is available concerning Triad societies during the immediate post-war period in this State. A Ghee Hin group developed in Bentong with links to Kuala Lumpur and Setapak, and a Triad society was formed in Kuantan, though not as strong as the Wa Kei. Attempts made to form a branch of the Chung Woh Tong in Kuantan were unsuccessful. The main society influence throughout the State was Wa Kei.

3. NEGRI SEMBILAN

In Negri Sembilan records of the secret society position in the early postwar years are again very scanty, though such as are available indicate that from a focus in Seremban and spreading to other areas of Chinese population there was a revival of Triad and Wa Kei societies.

In 1946 a group of prewar Ghee Hin Hokkien Triad members, influenced by their compatriots in Kuala Lumpur and Klang, set up a Triad branch in Seremban. From a headquarters established in a local rubber factory they formed a central committee, organized six town cells on the Kuala Lumpur model, and started the usual 'protection'. Other Triad groups linked with Seremban also came into existence at Mantin (on the main Seremban–Kuala Lumpur road), at Port Dickson on the coast, and at Kuala Pilah and Bahau to the east. Groups probably existed at Tampin and Gemas, although specific information is not available.

As usual, recruitment took place among workers in factories, Chinese tappers on estates, and miners in the tinfields, and shopkeepers were pressed into joining. Progress among the fishermen of Port Dickson was stimulated by the influx in June 1946 of Triad members from Sumatra, but in the Bahau area, which had been a centre of MPAJA activity during the Occupation and where there was a substantial Hakka population of left-wing sympathy, Triad organizers faced a Communist challenge, and in July 1948 were frustrated in an attempt to operate under cover of a Chi Kung Tong branch, established by agents from Sultan Street, Kuala Lumpur. In a fight which took place, the branch leader was killed by Chinese communists, who were reported to be members of the rival left-wing Chi Kung Tong group.

In Seremban itself Triad was challenged by Wa Kei. Organized, as in Pahang, by the same Kuala Lumpur leader, Kor Hor Chut, this society operated under cover of a local musical association and concentrated upon the organization and protection of gambling. Other Wa Kei branches were formed at Mantin and Kuala Pilah, and later on the mines at Lukut and on the rubber estates in the Bahau area. But once the Emergency began activities of both societies subsided throughout the State.

4. MALACCA

Brief reference has already been made to the shooting of the chief Malacca Triad leader by order of the Leper, in November 1947, and to the subsequent failure of an attempt by the latter's gang to seize control of Triad activity in the State.[4]

Malacca, with its old connexions with the Ghee Hin and Hai San, was naturally the scene of a Triad revival after the Japanese Occupation. Here, too, the MCP was making a serious and successful attempt through the trade unions to control the labouring population in the port and the countryside, and also rival gangsters from Singapore were seeking opportunities for black-marketing, smuggling, and extortion.

The local Triad initiative was seized by a retired Malacca detective who some time in 1946 was initiated into the Hung Brotherhood in Penang as a member of Cell 16. This cell, whose large membership of 3,500 was drawn from among farmers, fishermen, and local traders, included certain MCP sympathizers.

In Malacca the ex-detective established a trishaw business, and took the lead

[4] See above, p. 376.

in building up a Triad organization initially financed by protection money extorted from businessmen by a strong-arm group of thugs for whom he procured
guns. As his 'protection' terms were high ($3,600, $7,200, and $10,800, accord-
ing to the status of the merchant concerned) he was soon very wealthy, and
became the chief figure in the Malacca underworld, where he was greatly feared
because of his previous police contacts. His Triad headquarters was established
in Malacca town at his house in Bunga Raya, and branches were formed at
Bachang and at Sungei Rambai, a coastal village convenient for smuggling
activities. Initiation ceremonies at which Ooi Ah Hoo (a sinseh from Penang
and a member of Cell 16) is reported to have officiated were held on Pulau Besar,
an island off the coast, and another is known to have been held at Sungei
Rambai.

MCP influence in Malacca was strong, but the Triad headman drew many of
its supporters into the Triad net, and before long there was an unusually large
admixture of Communist elements in his organization. Of a group of opium
smugglers who became important-ranking members of the society several were
active Communists and ex-members of the MPAJA, and some were officials
in the Communist-controlled union among building labourers, in the sawmills,
the Harbour Board, and the rubber factories. Two other leaders, however, had
worked for the Japanese Naval Intelligence during the Occupation. One of
these men became head of the society's strong-arm gang, and the second organized a combined Triad–MCP extortion racket whereby all lorries entering
Malacca town from outstations paid a toll of $5, plus 10 per cent of the hire
charge. Similar co-operation developed in several outlying villages such as
Belimbing, Machap, Bemban, and Sungei Rambai, and scattered KMT elements
found it advisable to disguise their political sympathies lest they be molested.
The bulk of the Chinese population either paid protection money or joined the
Triad groups, and even after May 1947 when the 'Bunga Raya Boys' were
gazetted as an unlawful organization, intimidation continued.

The local supremacy of the Triad headman was threatened by the intervention
of external Triad interests. With the Hung Brotherhood temporarily beaten in
Penang and subjected to growing police pressure in North Perak and Selangor,
Malacca seemed to offer a possible alternative as a coastal headquarters. But
when, in June 1947, the supervisor and seven members of Cell 15 of the Penang
Ang Bin Hoey arrived in Malacca intending to hold initiation ceremonies, they
were informed by the Triad headman that his territory extended to a five-mile
boundary round the town and that they could not operate within that zone.
Once they had been shown the extent of his armoury, the newcomers abandoned
their proposal to fight it out and, very disgruntled, returned to Penang.

Aware of these developments, the police took steps to strengthen the section
of the Malacca CID concerned with secret society activity, and on 20 August
raided the Kong Yik Club, the Chi Kung Tong Malacca headquarters. These
premises were discovered already prepared for a Triad initiation ceremony, and
all present (eleven Hakkas and two Tiechius) were arrested. As in Kuala Lumpur,
Triad groups had begun to operate under cover of the Chi Kung Tong. A visit
from Yeoh Ah Bah and the subsequent initiation of a group of Malacca recruits
at Pulau Ketam late in September were added indications of Malacca's growing
importance in the Triad world.

A threat to the local Triad headman's authority now developed from within his own group. Some of his men, discontented with his distribution of profits, formed an independent gang and began to commit robberies. As this was contrary to his policy of avoiding open crime, he called upon them to return their arms, and when they refused, expelled them from his territory. In revenge, they joined the Leper's coastal gang, reported that the Malacca headman had turned government informer and had exceeded his powers by refusing to allow the Penang party to start initiation ceremonies in Malacca, thus depriving them of a livelihood. On the strength of these accusations his elimination was ordered, and he was shot on 11 November.

Surviving leaders of his Malacca organization took swift steps to safeguard their own position, and when the Leper's gang made their second visit to Malacca on 8 December, intent upon further eliminations, the local gang, informed of their arrival, attacked first and seriously wounded two of their opponents, while the others fled. Less than a month later, the destruction of the Leper and his gang at Bagan Si Api Api ended the feud.

Early in 1948 there were some successful prosecutions on charges of possession of Triad documents or for participating in the management of a Triad society. The increase in police powers under the Emergency Regulations led to the arrest of known gangsters and to the finding of detailed lists containing the names of 430 members of the MCP, some of whom were also officials of the Malacca Triad groups. These included the opium smugglers and several members of the strong-arm gang, nearly all of whom were arrested and many subsequently banished. This action simultaneously disrupted both the Communist and the Triad groups in Malacca.

5. JOHORE

The upsurge of Triad in Johore was in part influenced by communal disturbances which broke out as early as 21 August 1945 when Malays attacked the MPAJA who were attempting to take over control in the Batu Pahat area. Subsequent unrest caused Chinese to seek protection within their traditional societies. Thereafter several factors, including rivalries within Triad, between Triad and Wa Kei, and between Triad and the MCP, particularly in central Johore, all contributed to a turbulent postwar scene throughout the State.

The west coast ports of Muar and Batu Pahat, overwhelmingly Hokkien and old centres of strong KMT influence, successfully resisted Communist infiltration. Their wharf labourers, mainly recruited from Singapore, were strongly Triad, and in Muar appear to have belonged mostly to the '24' and '08' Singapore Triad groups, although there was some penetration by Cell 21 from Klang via Malacca. Local Chinese merchants and their labour contractors in both ports ensured that through labour associations (the Industrious Chinese Workers' Association and the Wharf Labourers' Association) firm control should be exercised over the workers, and strikes and similar troubles avoided. Both ports were centres of opium smuggling, and the operators were protected by gangs of fighters drawn from the secret societies. In this business there was a link between Triad groups in Muar and Malacca. The arrest of a piracy gang at Muar in March 1948 caused a temporary lull in these activities.

In the smaller south-west ports of Pontian and Kukup, in Johore Bahru district, and in the Kota Tinggi area in the south-east and the Pengerang

DD

Peninsula secret societies revived, linked with Singapore. Loading coolies in Pontian, workers in the pineapple factories along the Johore Bahru–Skudai road, Fui Chiu Hakkas engaged in timber-felling, rattan-collecting, and in saw-mills in the area around the 17th mile on the Kota Tinggi road, Hokkien fisher-men in the Sidili and Mawai areas, and Tiechiu market-gardeners in the lonely hamlets of Pengerang were all involved. Throughout the southern area extor-tioners terrorized the poorer sections of the Chinese community, and shop-keepers found it expedient to meet demands for subscriptions.

From the scanty information available it would appear that Singapore repre-sentatives from the Triad '24' group and from the non-Triad Tiechiu Sa Ji Society were both active in south Johore, the Sa Ji becoming increasingly powerful after 1949.

During the Japanese Occupation, Johore had been a strong centre of anti-Japanese resistance, and after the war many of the toughest and most irrespon-sible ex-members of the MPAJA gathered together in an area of central Johore bordering the railway. For a distance of ten miles on each side of the track, and stretching from Bekok in the north to Kulai in the south, they operated in gangs, and this area, with Kluang as the focal point, became the main battle-ground over which the MCP and the swiftly-forming Triad and Wa Kei secret society groups struggled for control of the Chinese community.

Kluang, situated where the west–east road from Batu Pahat to Mersing crossed the main north–south railway line, with a Chinese population of over 40,000 divided into three large groups of Hokkiens, Hakkas, and Cantonese, with a considerable addition of Hainanese and a sprinkling of Tiechius, was an obvious centre for complicated secret society developments with a political trend, for it was subject to Triad and Wa Kei influences from both Kuala Lumpur and Singapore, and was the centre of a strongly Communist area.[5] As early as 1946 Triad was evident in Segamat and Bekok and spread from these centres to the neighbouring villages of Bukit Siput and Pekan Jabi, and to extensive Chinese squatter areas such as Kangkar Cha'ah.

In September 1946 a Triad society calling itself the Chung Yi T'ong (Hall of Loyalty and Righteousness) was formed at Kluang by two Hakka organizers from Kuala Lumpur. It operated under cover of a local club and by pressure recruited members from all walks of life: merchants, contractors, shopkeepers, market-stall holders, squatters from the near-by village of Yap Tau Sah (notorious as a Triad hotbed), and even former members of the MPAJA. Initiation ceremonies were conducted by an elderly Hakka sinseh from Kuala Lumpur, and the society's influence spread rapidly northwards along the railway line to Niyor, Chamek, and Paloh, and southwards to Rengam and Layang-Layang.

The success of the Chung Yi T'ong in luring members from leftist labour unions aroused the enmity of the Communist groups in the area, but in addition

5

Area	Hokkien	Tiechiu	Hakka	Cantonese	Hain-anese	Total
Kluang	10,873	1,307	11,691	10,944	3,515	41,317

Source: Census Report Malaya 1947, Table 36.

there were rivalries among the Triad fraternity. In April 1947 a Triad sinseh from Yap Tau Sah village was shot dead in Kluang. He had arrived from Pusing (Perak) a few months earlier, but whether his death was due to Communist enemies or Triad intriguers was never established. It may well have been that his arrival provided a second Triad nucleus which leaders of the Chung Yi T'ong would not tolerate.

For a time Chung Yi T'ong activities slackened, but Perak influence in the area was exercised through a small coffee-shop in Bekok with the sign 'Hing Tai' (Brothers) whose proprietor had arrived in Johore in 1946 after organizing Triad societies in Perak, and who was known to travel between Kluang, Sungei Cha'ah, Bekok, and Segamat.

It was reported that in Kluang town a group of prominent KMT leaders had met secretly and formed a Triad branch to try to prevent the spread of Communist influence down the Kluang–Mersing road, and to extend their own influence to the Ayer Hitam, Batu Pahat, and Yong Peng areas. Although they became powerful in the town and received help from organizers in Kuala Lumpur, they were unable to penetrate Batu Pahat or Muar in the west, Jemaluang or Mersing in the east, or any part of the south with the exception of Kulai, for in each of the other districts some society was already in being and did not welcome interlopers.

More important than the incursions from Selangor and Perak was the Triad influence from Singapore which flowed along the railway from Johore Bahru to Gemas. In April 1947 cards inscribed 'Iron Dragon Society' (Thit Leong) of the '36' Group were found in a kongsi-house near Skudai. In July the Tarzan hooligan gang from Tiong Bahru in Singapore was operating in Johore Bahru. In August arrests in Paloh included members of sub-branches of the '108' group.

By September central Johore had become Malaya's major crime field. In October a combined police–military operation ('Vermin') cleared out some of the gangs and succeeded in reducing the monthly total of armed robberies from 17 to 3, but nevertheless in November it was reported that groups claiming to be Triad were in operation at Skudai, Senai, and Kulai, with major organizations at Kluang and Labis. Further north at Siding, near Segamat, a Triad initiation ceremony was raided by the police in December when the sinseh, 2 other officials, and 13 initiates were arrested. Together with the usual documents and altar furnishings, a carefully-primed hand-grenade was found at the site. The promoters were members of the Singapore '328' Society, and more of its members were arrested in February and March 1948 at Kulai.

Even more active than the Triad societies was the Wa Kei, which was revived early in 1946 at Bekok by Kor Hor Chut, the Wa Kei 'king'. It operated under cover of the Chue Lok Association with a prominent labour contractor as its principal organizer. As in other States, membership was drawn mainly from among the Cantonese, with some Kwangsais and Hakkas of the lumbering and sundry goods trades. Contractors, anxious to avoid Communist domination, urged their labourers to join, and in so doing they became the particular targets of MCP hostility.

Towards the end of 1946 the Wa Kei moved its headquarters to Kluang, and during the next eighteen months, under the cloak of branches of the Johore Chinese Mutual Aid Association, spread its activities eastwards to Jemaluang, Mersing, and Endau, northwards to Gemas, and southwards to Kulai and

Senai. As these were all areas of Communist influence, one of the first results of the Communist revolt in mid-1948 was the elimination of many Wa Kei leaders.

Two societies of Triad origin and political aims, the Chung Woh Tong and the Chi Kung Tong, added their own small quota to the general ferment. Representatives of the former from Kuala Lumpur arrived in Kluang in February 1947 and established branches in Kluang and Jemaluang, recruiting Cantonese, Kwangsais, and Hakkas. The Chi Kung Tong followed suit with branches at both places, but neither society aroused much enthusiasm and both were overshadowed by the main Triad and Wa Kei groups.

6. SUMMARY

In the area which became the Federation of Malaya it is clear that during the early postwar years the removal of Japanese control and the declaration of the new British policy of freedom of association resulted in a renascence and proliferation of Triad societies everywhere. This was augmented in some areas, particularly in Penang and along the Perak coast, by the need for mutual protection within certain groups, usually those which had collaborated with the Japanese, and had thus become anathema to the Communist-controlled guerrilla forces.

The idea of an open, lawful confederation of Triad societies, a Malayan headquarters of the Brotherhood capable of playing its part in the social and political arenas, presented itself to some of the organizers of the revived societies, particularly at Penang, probably in emulation of current trends in China. But others, notably the group at Kuala Kurau, and later the Leper on the Perak coast and at Bagan Si Api Api in Sumatra, aimed at an overall control-centre of the Brotherhood, whether lawful or unlawful.

Coupled with these organizational experiments went the exploitation of the newly-formed or revived societies by the inevitable hooligan elements within them, using the power and prestige of the Brotherhood for criminal ends— robbery, extortion, abduction, and murder. Added to this was the enforcement of penalties, including that of death, upon offending members who transgressed the code of the Brotherhood.

The widespread influence of Triad was recognized by both the MCP and the KMT, each of which deliberated how best to attract and utilize this movement for its own purposes.

On the one hand, in such zones as Kedah, Kinta (Perak), Ulu Selangor, Bahau (Negri Sembilan), Malacca, and Central Johore, the wartime absorption of Triad members into the ranks of anti-Japanese organizations brought such recruits into close contact with Communist groups, and created relationships which tended to persist after the peace, when the MCP made its all-out attempt to control labour. The Communist doctrine and that of the Triad Brotherhood had one principle in common, in theory at least, namely, the supremacy of the common man. Both organizations were thus attractive to the masses, but this very similarity meant that they were rivals, for although the Communists wished to supplant the Triad influence in the hearts of the common people, and were prepared to infiltrate into the Triad societies in an attempt to advance their own cause, they were reluctant to compromise with a body whose activities were so remote from the avowed ideals of the party. Furthermore, labourers in general were often uncertain of their own individual loyalties—whether towards Communist-inspired labour unions or towards the local Triad society, and their allegiance often wavered according to which body seemed at any particular time to be the more powerful.

The KMT, on the other hand, was less concerned with ideologies, and found in the Triad societies a valuable weapon to fight the Communists. This was particularly true in the Perak coastal areas, and at one time there was a tendency in police circles to regard Triad as the 'strong arm' of the KMT. Events in the Sitiawan Pangkor districts lent credibility to this view, but although there were links and relationships between individuals or groups by means of which KMT and Triad organizations could work together in a common cause, or more correctly against a common enemy, this did not mean that Triad was necessarily and ideologically aligned with the KMT wherever these groups existed. Many individuals, it is true, were members both of Triad and KMT and, as with Chinese religions, simultaneous membership presented no problem, but of the two organizations, the tradition, ritual, and power of Triad were the older and more irresistible, and the tradition of Triad was independence.

The Wa Kei, the Cantonese–Hakka Brotherhood of Triad derivation, though invariably opposed to the Hokkien–Tiechiu groups of direct Triad lineage on account of rivalry of control over 'protection' zones, was indomitably opposed to Communism; consequently, in areas of Cantonese predominance, Wa Kei and the KMT were frequently found in association.

Finally, apart from the usual run of Triad societies there were the two specialized Triad groups working under the cover of social clubs, the Chi Kung Tong and the Chung Woh Tong, both of which floundered along uncertainly copying the shifts taking place in China, with the Chi Kung Tong inclining to the left and the Chung Woh Tong to the right.

The overwhelming upsurge of Triad in Penang and North Perak in 1945–6 and the subsequent spread throughout the peninsula resulted in a reversion to a position akin to that which had existed before 1890 in which secret societies were the paramount irresistible force in the Chinese community. This increased the immense problems faced by a depleted and still ill-equipped police force confronted with an unprecedented crime wave throughout the country.

The first steps to control by the Government were the declaration made in September 1946 that the provisions of the prewar law outlawing Triad societies would be enforced, and the decision to make use of the powers of banishment in suitable criminal cases. These were followed by the inclusion of the anti-Triad provisions in the new Societies Ordinance which came into force on 1 April 1947, and by the gazetting of nine societies as unlawful in May of that year. Most important of all was the introduction of the Emergency Regulations in June 1948 which, though framed to deal with the Communist revolt, gave to the Executive wide powers of arrest and detention of persons likely to cause a breach of the peace.

Once again, the difficulty of dealing with this particular oriental problem by the application of legal principles and techniques derived from Western ethical standards and designed to deal with Western social conditions was becoming apparent.

18

SINGAPORE, 1945–8

No information of any secret society activity in Singapore during the Japanese Occupation has been traced. After the British surrender in February 1942, the Japanese at once screened the entire Chinese male population of the island, and among the thousands who failed to satisfy the investigators and were taken off to the beaches or were towed out to sea in barges and shot were a proportion of secret society members who, although confined by the British at the beginning of the war, had been released in the general gaol delivery ordered immediately before the fall of Singapore. Some of those who survived the Japanese interrogations bought their lives by agreeing to work as informers to the Kempeitai, and on liberation by the British in September 1945, many of these men associated themselves with the so-called 'patriotic societies', which were merely hooligan gangs participating in the wave of armed robbery, looting, blackmail, and extortion which swept over the island. Over the next few months immense profits were made from the theft during transit from the docks of military and RAF stores—particularly clothing for which there was a tremendous demand—carried on mainly by drivers and clerical staff of the Services in conjunction with the gangs, and traffic in arms with the Netherlands Indies became a profitable field for members of the underworld.

Side by side with these hooligan activities a powerful Communist movement exerted heavy pressure through the General Labour Union, and labour organizations connected with the Union attracted the unemployed and the riff-raff who in earlier years had formed the main body of secret society ruffians. For several months innumerable strikes organized in pursuance of a policy of systematic piecemeal attacking of employers were supported by funds collected from shopkeepers by strong-arm members of the Union and its satellites using the familiar technique of demand with implied menace. But in February 1946 the Communists failed in their attempt to challenge the authority of the Government by holding processions throughout the town ostensibly to mourn the loss of Singapore to the Japanese in 1942 but in reality to celebrate a Day of Remembrance for the defeat of the British on that occasion, and the firm handling of the issue by the Government made it plain that the latitude which had been allowed to subversive elements, and in particular to the Communist organizers in the period of intoxication after the liberation was at an end. The arrest of many of the leaders dampened the enthusiasm of the agitators, and from then onwards the underworld in Singapore began to regroup on the familiar secret society pattern of prewar years.

A tremendous resurgence of secret societies resulted. Many Hokkien and Tiechiu prewar societies quickly resuscitated under the traditional grouping of '8', '18', '24', '36', and '108'. New societies also formed, some of those belonging to the '24' and '36' and many components of the '108' adopting numerical designations in lieu of Triad titles. Hence the '969' of the '24' group, the '329' and the '666666' of the '36' group, and, among others, the '303', '404', '505', '707', '808', '909', and the '760', of the '108' group. The '969' of the '24' group eventually developed nine branches, and the '329' of the '36' group and the '303' of the '108' group three each. Many of the new societies were composed of men of different Chinese dialects, and in some cases Malays and Indians were included. Most of these groups were criminal gangs rather than ritualistic secret societies.

An important revival was that of the prewar independent Sa Ji, the Tiechiu society which re-established its headquarters in River Valley Road. Seven branches were formed elsewhere throughout the island, and although there was no overall organization individual headmen invariably acknowledged the authority of the main branch, the Lau Yong Heng, whose headman was consulted in all important matters.

Among the Cantonese societies the prewar Heng and the Khwan Yi groups were swiftly in the field. The Heng formed three new societies, the Loh Wah, the Heng Fuk, and the Heng Khiu, and the Khwan Yi formed five new groups, the Tai Chap Wui, the San Kwan, the Khwan Luen, the Khwan Kei, and the Khwan Fatt. In times of trouble the 'Heng' looked for assistance to the Hokkien '18', and the Khwan Yi sought the help of the '24'. In addition to the Heng and the Khwan Yi groups, other important Cantonese revivals of the Man Yi group included the Wui Kwan, the Thit Kwan, the Woh Kei, and the Wa Khiu.

A new society called the Chap Sah Tai Poh (Thirteen Princes)—a name taken from the thirteen main cards of the mahjong table—became important in the postwar scene. Its membership was at first confined to Hokch'ias, and the society became part of the '18' group. After a year of existence its name was changed to Chap Sah Io (Thirteen Comrades), and from a headquarters at Johore Road it developed nine branches in the town. This society became very powerful, its members protecting the Chap Ji Ki lotteries. Over the years a number of its leaders were banished, and its membership was later extended to include Malays, Indians, and other Chinese, such as Hakkas and Cantonese.

The admixture of Malays and Indians within certain Chinese societies was a development of the postwar secret society scene which added considerably to the intensity of inter-gang rivalry, and was particularly marked between the '329' of the '36' group and the Choan Gi Ho of the '18' group. The '329' consisted of Malays, Indians, and Chinese, with Malays predominating. Members of the Choan Gi Ho were mostly Chinese, but absorbed a gang of Malays in order to gain assistance in their fights with the '329'. This feud continued over the years, becoming particularly virulent in May 1948, and only the arrest of Northern Indian (Sikh) and Malay leaders of the '329' eventually restrained these gangs from further violence.

The resuscitation of secret societies and the formation of criminal gangs operating under the cloak of such societies and fighting one another for control of 'protection areas' was one factor contributing to the turmoil which developed in Singapore in the postwar years, but the ease with which arms could be procured, the presence of thousands of criminals who in normal circumstances would not have been at large, the general dislocation of employment, the lack of rice, and the overall shortage of supplies also created a climate favourable to crime. The total number of seizable offences reported in 1946 was 14,187 as compared with 6,893 in 1938, and 4,702 in 1937, and there was no doubt that in 1946 a large number of cases went unreported. Most prevalent of all were armed robberies, 960 as compared with 117 in 1938 and 28 in 1937. House-breaking and theft were 1,520 as compared with 567 in 1938.

Faced with this unprecedented crime wave, and in particular with the existence of the innumerable armed gangs, the police urged the reintroduction of the pre-war Societies Ordinance. In July 1946 a raid on Pulau Minyak, in the swamps of the Kallang Basin where the Sa Ji was 'protecting' rice-smuggling, resulted in the seizure of eighteen revolvers and pistols, a hand-grenade, and a large quantity of ammunition, and further raids in the Jalan Besar area resulted in the seizure of loaded rifles and pistols belonging to the Heng Khiu Society. By August it was estimated that of the 100 Hokkien and Tiechiu societies existing at the time, 50 were active, and in forwarding to the Government details of 9 of the most prominent Hokkien, Tiechiu, and Cantonese societies the police suggested that the case for suppression was not only as strong as that of 1889, but was further aggravated by the reaction which had followed the Japanese Occupation and the long years of war.

The Singapore Government, like that of the Malayan Union, had been required under the postwar policy of freedom of association to abandon the pre-war controls and to introduce fresh legislation under which societies would be at liberty to exist without applying for registration, but might, if their conduct endangered the peace or welfare of the State, be declared unlawful. From the inception of Civil Government on 1 April 1946, strong opposition had been raised by the Singapore Government and its advisers to this policy, and in October 1946, following the lead of the Malayan Union, it was decided that use could be made of those sections of the prewar Societies Ordinance which outlawed Triad societies provided that the Attorney-General was satisfied that there was a *prima facie* case to answer.

This decision meant that Triad groups were banned, but this had little or no effect upon the activities of the secret society gangs, the majority of whose members could not be shown to be initiated Triad Brethren, and who continued with their routine of extortion, robbery, and inter-gang fights, frequently flaunting their gang membership by wearing insignia of identity, normally in the form of small metal badges with enamelled fronts, bearing the number of the gang or characters showing its name. On occasion, additional items included in the design were crossed flags, a star, a swastika, a dragon, or a tiger, emblems used by particular societies. Belt buckles similarly adorned were also popular. Membership certificates, usually a small printed card, though sometimes a small piece of cloth, printed from a wooden block, were useful during extortion activities, and at Chinese New Year, greeting cards, of a type which could be bought locally ready-printed with New Year greetings, were frequently embellished by rubber stamp, wooden 'chop', or pen, with the name of a particular society or gang. These cards were left at the premises of shopkeepers with the information that the distributor would call later for an appropriate seasonal gift, and no one was ever in doubt as to what was intended, or as to the inadvisability of failing to comply.

Throughout 1947 Singapore was disturbed by inter-secret society warfare. In January severe rivalry between the Hokkien '108' and the '36' was eventually resolved, but not until various clashes had resulted in one murder, one attempted murder, eight kidnappings, and several cases of assault. The '108' had been supported by the Sa Ji, and by the Goh Chhin (Five Stars) and the Thirteen Comrades of the '18' group.

During April the interplay of secret societies and trade unions was brought to light at the Aik Hoe Rubber Factory where the workers were members either of the Rubber Workers' Union or of the Engineering Workers' Union. The former union was associated with and protected by the Thirteen Comrades, and the latter by the '329' of the '36' group. Workers who were members of the Thirteen Comrades tried to coerce others of the rival union to pay subscriptions to this society, and a typical feud ensued resulting in several armed clashes in which one bystander was killed, a leader of the '329' was shot dead, and another member wounded. Clashes continued during May with shooting and throwing of hand-grenades, and in June one member of the '329' was murdered at the Aik Hoe Factory. In revenge, one of the Thirteen Comrades was abducted by the '329', and was fortunate in contriving to escape. Eventually, a settlement was reached through the intervention of the management of one of the amusement parks which was under the influence and protection of the '329', and was afraid of possible repercussions within the park should the dispute continue.

Another feud flared up in June between the Sa Ji and the '108', the origin being an attempt by members of the '108' to extort money from a man who proved to belong to the Sa Ji. A number of fights took place, members of the '108' demonstrated at North Boat Quay, an area under the protection of their rivals, and later abducted a member of the Sa Ji and threatened him with burial alive. Thereafter, the Sa Ji publicly posted a challenge in New Market Road calling upon the '108' to fix a time and place for a decisive battle. Police vigilance and the arrest of some of the leaders prevented the fight, but in July a member of the '108' was shot dead by members of the Sa Ji, and later the '108' retaliated by abducting and seriously assaulting two of their enemies.

These feuds were between Hokkien gangs, or Hokkien and Tiechiu gangs, but there were also disputes which involved both Hokkien and Cantonese gangs. One started in July (1947) between the Loh Wah of the Heng group, a gang of mixed membership, and the Lo Kwan of the Khwan Yi group, composed of Cantonese only. The question at issue concerned the sale of 'black-market' tickets at the Jubilee and Majestic Cinemas. A meeting between the two gangs was arranged but failed to reach a settlement, and a fight ensued in which a Hokkien member of the Loh Wah was stabbed and died. Thereupon the Hokkien '18' group offered their support to the Loh Wah gang, while the Cantonese Khwan Yi and the Hokkien '24' group (which was at enmity with the '18') joined forces with the Lo Kwan.

While the body of the murdered man was lying in a funeral parlour the premises were visited by detectives who discovered a large number of costly wreaths bearing the inscriptions of well-known secret societies, including the Heng Woh and the Heng Fatt, both of which were Cantonese societies opposed to the Lo Kwan. To each wreath was attached a card offering the condolences of the society concerned. The funeral which took place the following day passed off without incident owing to the presence of strong police patrols, but this was just the type of funeral at which a violent secret society outbreak might be expected. Eventually, the corpse made a solitary journey to the grave, the mourners, of whom there were several hundreds, having abandoned the procession on the appearance of a large force of detectives.

The same pattern of feuds and fights between rival gangs, mainly belonging to Hokkien secret societies, continued during the rest of 1947 and until the middle of 1948. Between January and June of that year there were 20 gang fights in which either firearms or knives were used, 7 society men being killed and 9 passers-by injured. In addition, there were several fights in which aerated waterbottles were used. These were favourite weapons of the thugs, and were to be found in every street. Two attempts were also made to murder Hokkien detectives. In the second of these the assailant fired five rounds at the detective without hitting him, but the detective shot his man dead.

Meanwhile, in March 1947 the Secretary of State had authorized the enforcement of the prewar Societies Ordinance in Singapore, provided that amendments were introduced to permit the unhampered existence of political parties in order to encourage the development of an electoral system in the Colony. Registration of societies under the old Ordinance was resumed on 15 April 1947 and met with general approval although opposed by political groups, possibly because in announcing the proposed resumption of registration the Government did not at the same time make clear how the special position of political parties would be protected.

The representative of the MCP declared that his party would not apply for registration unless the Government abolished the existing legislation dealing with sedition and banishment, but added that the party wished to make it clear that it not only did not object to registration in principle, but would request the Government to extend recognition to the MCP as a legal political organization, just as the Communist Party had been recognized in other parts of the British Empire since the war.[1] He may have seen in the system of registration a possibility of obtaining official acknowledgement of the legal existence of the Communist Party. At the end of April, however, doubtless upon instructions from other party officials, he declared that the MCP could not accept the Ordinance under any circumstances, and on 11 May twelve other political or quasi-political organizations resolved to demand the repeal of the Ordinance.

Already the Government had decided to introduce an amendment exempting from its provisions any association which the Governor in Council might by order declare to be a political association. At a meeting of the Advisory Council held on 29 May to consider this proposed amendment the Acting Colonial Secretary briefly reviewed the reasons for reimposing the Ordinance. He said that Singapore was experiencing a situation similar to that which existed in 1890 when the Colony was ruled by secret societies which terrorized peaceful citizens. It was to deal with such a situation that the Societies Ordinance was first enacted. He then referred to the existing widespread prevalence of extortion, usually committed in the name of some society. Before the re-enforcement of the Ordinance such societies were not unlawful, and it had been necessary for the police to prove definite criminal acts against individuals before any action could be taken. In normal circumstances it might reasonably be argued that such powers were adequate, but the existing circumstances were far from normal. The police were seriously hampered by lack of witnesses due to intimidation by the gangs of extortioners and robbers. It was not expected that secret societies

[1] *Straits Times*, 11 Apr. 1947.

would cease to exist as a result of the enforcement of the Societies Ordinance, but its enforcement would give the police an extra weapon.

The amendment concerning political parties came into force on 12 June 1947, and fifteen associations were excluded from the operation of the Societies Ordinance under this new provision, and were thus allowed to function freely. Although the purpose of this amendment was to stimulate the growth of local political parties with a view to introducing a form of representative government based on popular franchise, it not only legalized the existence of local political parties such as the Malayan Democratic Union, the MCP and its satellites, the MPAJA Ex-Comrades Association, the NDYL, and the Singapore Women's Federation, but also opened the door to China-based political parties such as the KMT, the SMCYYC, and the CDL, which were all declared by the Governor in Council to be political associations. All these societies had, in fact, been openly in existence in the 'free for all' period since the liberation, and had striven with zest to increase their influence among the Chinese in Malaya. As in China, these groups saw in the promotion of popular Triad organizations the possibility of extending their own power, and from mid-1946 it was apparent that in addition to the re-formation of secret society gangs based on the prewar pattern which was already taking place, there were other influences at work in Singapore (as in Penang and Kuala Lumpur) attempting to draw secret society members into a comprehensive political Triad association.

Among those involved in Singapore were the refugee leaders of the Penang Ang Bin Hoey, the president, Teoh Teik Chye, and the secretary-general, Ong Keng Hooi. In July 1946 the *Nanyang Siang Pao* (26 July) published an article concerning the clashes and quarrels between the secret societies in Singapore, which were particularly severe at the time between the '108' and the '36' groups, and stated that 'several brave and wise members' of the Penang Ang Bin Hoey were trying to effect a settlement and to unify the societies into a Triad Association which would be law-abiding and have an acknowledged place in society.

Late in September cyclostyled handbills purporting to be a Manifesto issued by the Singapore Society of Brethren of the Hung Family on the occasion of its inception were distributed at the Great World Amusement Park. The Manifesto attributed the corruption and degeneration of the postwar Hung societies to the absence of a central leading organ. Members had been engaged in armed conflict with fatal results on many occasions. Some had gone to the extent of selling the interests of the Brotherhood, while some, using the name of the society, had committed acts of extortion, intimidation, robbery, and looting. By such disgraceful behaviour the lives of the Hung society's elders had been endangered, peace and order had been disturbed, and the members were despised by the local Government and by the public as 'hooligans and social pests'. Members were urged to amend their ways, and to remember that the tradition of the Brotherhood required them to render service in the interests of their country and fellow countrymen. It was the aim of the newly-organized Singapore society to win the co-operation of all Triad members in establishing a new China under a government of the people by the people for the people, and the society 'approved and supported the policy drafted by the China Hung Family Democratic Party, and the policy of the Malayan Branch of the China Hung Mun Chi Kung Tong, all of which aimed at the establishment of a united China with a democratic government'. At the same time posters were pasted on walls in the streets, and the headquarters of the '108' and '36' secret society groups were approached through the post. All documents were stamped with the seal of the Singapore Society of Brethren of the Hung Family, and were similar in tone to the hand-bills which had been distributed in Penang a few weeks earlier.

Although the origin of these handbills and posters was not definitely established at the time, they clearly represented an attempt to arouse interest in the political situation in China and in the reorganization of the Brotherhood as a political force along the lines which had recently been debated by the Chi Kung Tong in America and on the China coast, and which had borne fruit in the creation of the Hung Family Democratic Party announced by Szeto Mei-tang in Shanghai on 1 September 1946. During November it was reported that Penang officials of the Ang Bin Hoey were attempting to establish a headquarters in Singapore, and were in touch with the '108', the '36', and the Thirteen Comrades, but it was not until the arrest of Teoh Teik Chye in mid-December 1946 for his previous activities in Penang that the extent of proposed developments in Singapore was discovered.

Although he was involved in the Singapore scheme the main stimulus came from prominent officials of the KMT and the Chinese Consulate working in conjunction with certain veteran Triad leaders of Singapore. The underlying object was to organize political and financial support for the KMT against the Communists, in Malaya and in China. Already ten initiation ceremonies had been held in Singapore under the auspices of the new society of 'Brethren of the Hung Family', and an important Triad personage came from China to help to organize the proposed Triad combination. Teoh Teik Chye, still recognized as the head of the Ang Bin Hoey in Penang, and addressed by Singapore Triad leaders as 'Elder Brother', was to be restored to power, and Ooi Ah Soh, the notorious sinseh of Penang, was to visit Singapore to discuss developments in North Malaya with the Singapore Triad leaders.

The arrest and banishment of the Penang leaders did not deter others, for the publicity given in the Chinese vernacular press in Malaya to the attempts being made in China and America to organize the Brotherhood as a political force had increased the community's awareness of the potentialities of a centralized Triad foundation. Local opportunists in Singapore, in Triad, economic, and political circles, were quick to see the possible advantages of being connected with a movement in support of a strong government in China which they all confidently expected to emerge from the postwar settlement, and from which they hoped to benefit.

During 1947 and the early months of 1948 attempts to harness the large Triad potential of Singapore to the use of China-based political parties continued. In February 1947 one individual appeared, describing himself as the 'Officer-in-Charge of the Singapore Preparatory Office of the Malayan China Hung Mun Chi Kung Tong, and President of the Siam Branch'. He was accompanied by some Penang Triad members, and made contact with the Put Ko Society of the '108' group. He appears to have been discredited and disappeared from Singapore, only to reappear in Penang in December as a representative of the Sultan Street group of the China Chi Kung Tong of Kuala Lumpur, attempting unsuccessfully to form a branch of that organization. He was believed to be a member of Cell 12 of the Penang Ang Bin Hoey.

In July 1947 Chiu Yuk, the veteran organizer of the Chi Kung T'ong in

America and China, applied for a permit to visit Malaya, but was refused because of the Triad nature of his organization. He had intended to work not only for the unification of the Hung Brethren within one all-embracing lodge but to establish branches of the Min Chi Tang, which in the political and financial spheres would advance the well-being of postwar China, and in this he had been assured of the support of the KMT. Although his visit was disallowed, and although on 6 September Szeto Mei-tang announced in Shanghai that he had abandoned the attempt to organize the Min Chi Tang in China, Chiu Yuk continued his efforts to influence the Chinese in Malaya, and not only corresponded with certain Triad members of Singapore, but deputed his nephew, Chiu Cheong Heng, to make preliminary enquiries in Malaya generally as to the possibility of forming a combined Triad organization.

As a result, early in October an informal approach was made to the authorities by a Hokkien group, one of whom appeared to be in contact with Chiu Yuk. They proposed that the secret societies of Singapore should be unified within an organization to be called the Malayan Hung Mun Chi Kung Tong, which would apply for registration under the Societies Ordinance, but would hope to be granted the same status as other political and public organizations. Draft rules and regulations were submitted which proved on examination to be almost identical with those issued in the Manifesto of the Min Chi Tang in China, though with additions reminiscent of the Ang Bin Hoey of Penang. The promoters, none of whom was a prominent member of the Chinese community, and who, from their addresses, came from areas notorious for secret society activities, claimed that they had already been promised the co-operation of some of the leading secret societies, and hoped to be able to put an end to the faction fights that were so distracting Singapore, and to encourage the growth of mutual goodwill between members of the Brotherhood.

Six weeks later (18 November) they made formal application for registration as a society. They included the prefix 'Hung Mun' in their title, and were instructed, pending consideration of their application, not to carry on activities. Before the end of the month there were comments in the *Chung Shing Yit Pao* (26 November 1947) concerning 'political opportunists' who used the term 'Hung Family' for greater pull and influence, and quoting as an example Szeto Mei-tang. The following day, the *Sin Chew Jit Poh* announced the impending formation of the 'Headquarters for Singapore Branches of the China Hung Mun Chi Kung Tong'.[2]

On 2 December the original application for registration of the Hung Mun Chi Kung Tong in Singapore was superseded by another, supported by different persons known to be connected with the CDL. The new leaders, thought to be men of greater influence, had been induced by the original promoters to push the application with the authorities. The rules submitted had been redrafted, but the title of the society remained the same, the 'Objects' were exemplary, and membership was open to 'anyone of the Hung Brethren' subject to approval by the executive committee, to other Chinese subject to a three-month probationary period, and to non-Chinese as Honorary Members.

One of the new promoters said that through this organization members could be educated and made 'law-abiding and peace-loving' and that it would be a bulwark against Communist agitation (particularly among the labourers, many

[2] *Sin Chew Jit Poh*, 27 Nov. 1947.

of whom were members of the Brotherhood) but would never become the tool of any political party. He quoted as an example the unsuccessful efforts made by the KMT (in China and in Singapore) to absorb the Brotherhood.

Meanwhile, although no official recognition was yet forthcoming, recruitment began, and a number of clandestine initiation ceremonies were held. Internally, there were soon difficulties in the way of harmonious relationships between would-be organizers of a combined Hung organization and the individual leaders of the component societies, and all attempts by the new promoters to control the finances of the Triad groups were fiercely resisted by their leaders.

Chiu Yuk's nephew, Chiu Cheong Heng, described as the representative of the Shanghai headquarters of the Hung Mun Chi Kung Tong Lodge, also attempted in vain in Singapore and on the Malayan mainland to rally the jealous Triad groups into a combined organization, and late in March 1948 returned to China, admitting failure. Nor were independent KMT efforts in Kedah any more successful, since every Triad group was watching the outcome of the Hung Mun Chi Kung Tong's application for registration in Singapore.

Matters came to a head in March 1948. At the beginning of the month an Indian living in the Bukit Timah area addressed a letter to the District Judge, Singapore, informing him that lorry-loads of Chinese had been seen by him disappearing down side roads off Clementi Road. A watch was kept by the police, and at dawn on 5 March eighty-eight Chinese were arrested as they emerged from the bushes on to the road after attending a Triad initiation ceremony, and the majority had a fresh needle-prick at the tip of the middle finger. Most of those arrested were Hokkien labourers employed on the docks or in boat-building yards, others were sampan men or small shopkeepers. Sixty-seven pleaded guilty to a charge of having taken part in an initiation ceremony, most of the others claiming that they had gone under duress.

A search of the site of the ceremony produced a beheaded cockerel buried just below the soil, and half-burnt remnants of Triad emblems. The initiation fee had been $10.80, and the ceremony was the seventh arranged by the Hung Mun Chi Kung Tong organization. It was estimated that in all some 500 people had been initiated, but no information had reached the police.

Through these arrests the police discovered the identity of several of those responsible for the organization of the initiations and the chief officials were later arrested and banished. On 12 May the application for registration of the Hung Mun Chi Kung Tong as a political party was officially refused, and a few days later the cases of those arrested at the Clementi Road initiation ceremony were heard in the district court. After commenting upon the lack of public co-operation with which the police were usually faced, the District Judge imposed sentences upon the prisoners ranging from three to thirty months' rigorous imprisonment. Proceedings for banishment against forty-five of those sentenced were taken at a later date.

Later in the month there was another important arrest when Ong Keng Hooi, secretary-general of the Penang Ang Bin Hoey, who was in hiding in Singapore, was discovered. He was concerned with the promotion of the initiation ceremonies, and hoped to play an important part in the future of the combined Triad organization. In order to avoid banishment he had applied for a false birth certificate. His case was transferred to Penang, and he was subsequently banished. No further overt attempt to resuscitate the proposal of a Triad combination was made for some considerable time.

As in the Federation of Malaya it was the outbreak of the Communist revolt in mid-1948 and the introduction of the Emergency Regulations which primarily enabled the police to contain the rising power of the Triad gangs. Already during the latter part of 1947 a monthly average of 100 of their leading members had been arrested, interrogated, and photographed under the few provisions of the Societies Ordinance which at the time were permitted to be used, but most of those arrested were released within twenty-four hours as required by law, and in very few cases was there enough evidence to warrant prosecution. With the enforcement of the Emergency Regulations on 24 June 1948, introduced to inhibit the spread to Singapore of the threat to peace caused by the Communist uprising in the Federation, and in part designed to provide for the arrest and detention of persons who seemed likely to be a danger to public order, first on the police list came those who were working for the Communist cause, but large numbers of known secret society members were also swept in on the grounds that they were potentially dangerous at a time when the Communist Party might be expected to use any means to foster public disorder. Of a total of 1,400 arrests of all categories made under the Emergency Regulations in 1948, only 227 were still under detention at the end of the year. Of the remainder, some had been banished, some repatriated to China at their own request, but the majority had been released either unconditionally or under Direction Orders requiring them to be indoors at night and to report to the police from time to time. Many of the secret society members arrested under the regulations were restricted in this way.

Extensive use was made of powers under the Banishment Ordinance. In the eighteen months ending in September 1948, nearly 1,000 alien Chinese had been recommended for banishment by the police, and in over 900 of these cases banishment was approved. Some recommendations were in respect of criminals with several convictions, others concerned opium smugglers, traffickers in women, or gambling promoters. In so far as these activities were normally coupled with secret society members it is safe to say that the majority of the banishees were active members of secret societies.

Before the end of July 1948 the MCP and the NDYL were removed from the list of associations recognized as political parties excluded from the operation of the Societies Ordinance in Singapore, while other Communist satellites ceased to exist as organizations. The Malayan Democratic Union, having failed to obtain the public support for which it had hoped, and conscious of the drawback of having been closely associated with the 'leftist' groups, dissolved itself voluntarily on 20 June, but it was not until May 1949 that the KMT and the CDL were deleted from the list and were required to conform to the provisions of the Societies Ordinance.

The introduction under the powers conferred by the Emergency Regulations of a system of registration of the entire population, with the requirement that each individual must apply for an identity card bearing his particulars, his photograph, and his thumbprint or signature, greatly strengthened the hands of the police. The identification of the individual had always been the greatest single administrative difficulty in dealing with the large Chinese population in Malaya, and on many occasions the proposal to introduce registration had been considered only to be rejected as an unwarranted interference with the liberty of the subject. But with the threat to security presented by the revolt of the MCP, registration was accepted in the Federation and in Singapore, to the anger of the insurgents, whose policy thereafter included robbery of identity cards from individuals. Introduced as a temporary measure, in so far as the Emergency Regulations were themselves temporary, registration of the population with the issue of identity cards proved to be so useful, not only to the authorities but to the individual, that it was regarded as generally desirable, and permanent legislation passed in both territories made provision for its continuation.

Because the Emergency Regulations were introduced so soon after the re-implementation of the Societies Ordinance, it is not possible to say with certainty whether the provisions of the Ordinance would, in themselves, have proved adequate to control the serious secret society threat which had developed by the middle of 1948. In the light of subsequent events it is highly improbable that they would have sufficed, and it is beyond doubt that the use by the Executive and by the police of the powers bestowed by the Emergency Regulations led to a rapid diminution in crime in general and in secret society crime in particular, in Singapore and in the Federation. At last the stage had been reached where, as suggested by the Governor of Penang in 1825 when first faced with the problem of secret societies, it had become necessary to dispense with 'the stricter judicial forms applicable to ordinary occasions in the apprehension of suspected persons', although in 1948 the unusual procedure had at least legislative sanction.

19

SECRET SOCIETIES AND THE MALAYAN COMMUNIST PARTY

1. THE REVOLT OF THE MALAYAN COMMUNIST PARTY

DURING the period 1948–60 Malaya was convulsed by the outbreak of armed revolt by the MCP which, while affecting the Chinese community in particular, brought the whole population into serious danger and overshadowed for several years the threat of secret societies. The story of the revolt has been told in detail elsewhere, and only an outline is necessary here as a background to a detailed discussion of the relation between the MCP and the secret societies.

Despite the open co-operation with the British against the Japanese, the MCP had never swerved from its secret intention of driving the British from Malaya and ultimately setting up a Communist republic backed by a Communist army. Late in 1945 it was agreed that the party's policy should be peaceful penetration rather than immediate armed revolt, and considerable success was achieved in the penetration of labour unions and some of the newly-formed political groups, while a vituperative anti-British campaign was conducted in the vernacular press. Nevertheless, by the end of 1947, except in the labour field, the fortunes of the MCP were at a low ebb. The extension of government control, improved economic conditions, the expansion of the Chinese Nationalist associations, and the drastic action in some areas of the anti-Communist Triad and Wa Kei groups, had combined to loosen the Communist grip. Although still able to promote a number of strikes, the MCP influence appeared to be on the wane, and the armed outbreak in April 1948 took the Governments of Malaya by surprise.

There were three main reasons for the MCP's change of plan:

1. The lack of success of peaceful penetration.

2. The discovery that the secretary-general of the party, Loi Tek, had, during the Japanese period been responsible for the death of many Communist leaders by secretly betraying them to the Japanese. Loi Tek disappeared in March 1947 after being accused by a colleague of deviation and by the end of the year enquiries had confirmed his treachery. This revelation led the central committee to have doubts about the policy of peaceful penetration which he had advocated, fearing that this might be another aspect of his duplicity.

3. The instructions issued by the Cominform to the Communist parties of Southeast Asia to stage revolts under the banner of national liberation movements in order to embarrass the colonial powers. These instructions were passed to delegates from the various areas (including Malaya) at a Communist-sponsored Southeast Asia Youth Conference at Calcutta in February 1948. At

a meeting in March the central committee of the MCP adopted this plan, and condemned Loi Tek's previous policy as one of 'opportunist deviation'.

The revolt began with a general strike at the Singapore Harbour Board in April, and spread in May to the ports of Penang and Port Swettenham, as well as to rubber estates and tin mines, where Chinese contractors were murdered, pay-rolls robbed, buildings burned, and labour forces intimidated. In June there were 119 incidents with the usual targets plus attacks on estate managers, police stations, and a number of KMT leaders. The MCP had called for total mobilization of the MPAJA, whose name was changed to the Malayan People's Anti-British Army. Faced with what was clearly a widespread and well-organized campaign of murder, the Federation Government between 16 June and 5 July issued a series of Emergency Regulations authorizing arrests without warrant, and detention by order of the Chief Secretary for a period of two years with provision for the renewal of such orders. The death penalty for the possession of arms was also prescribed. Action was taken under the Societies Ordinance to outlaw the MCP, the NDYL, the MPAJA Ex-Comrades' Association, and the Ikatan Pembela Tanah Ayer Melayu, a Malay leftist body.[1] Singapore introduced Emergency Regulations on 24 June, and withdrew the exclusion from the operation of the Societies Ordinance previously granted to the three Communist groups mentioned above.[2]

In an attempt to gain some political support, the MCP in January 1949 announced their plan for a Malayan People's Democratic Republic, and changed the name of the Malayan People's Anti-British Army to the Malayan Races Liberation Army. Public support was not, however, forthcoming. On the contrary, the numbness and inertia initially induced in the Chinese community by the sudden and violent Communist attack began to dissipate as government forces were strengthened and as supplies were denied to the rebels by removing squatters from the jungle fringe into guarded village communities. In February 1949 a group of Chinese leaders, realizing that the passivity of their community was jeopardizing their political prospects, formed a Malayan Chinese Association (MCA) whose avowed objects included the preservation of inter-communal relations, and support for the Government in quelling the revolt. There was an immediate response, especially among the non-English-speaking Chinese, some of whom were KMT members, and by the end of the year over 100,000 members were enrolled and branches had been organized in all the States and most of the districts of the Federation.

By 1954 it was clear that the armed revolt would not succeed, and greater emphasis was placed by the MCP on subversion, the more so because political developments were taking place designed to lead to independence. On the eve of the first Federal elections in July 1955, an offer was made by the MCP to negotiate with the British for an end to the fighting. This was rejected, but when the newly-elected Government came to power it proclaimed a limited amnesty and offered surrender terms. As a result, a meeting was arranged with the MCP leader, Chin Peng, whose stipulation that the MCP should be granted legal status and freedom of action was refused. An MCP document written in 1955 and discovered in 1956 made plain the intent of this stipulation. It said:

[1] *FMGG*, 13, 23 July 1948, 2nd suppl., GN 2037, 23 July.
[2] Sing. GNs 216 & 217, 23 July 1948.

Undoubtedly our tactics today are to join the Tunku in a common effort to get rid of the colonial rule of the British imperialists. After there is a state of peace we can immediately win over more support of the broad masses of the people and go a step further by overthrowing the Tunku's bourgeoisie dictatorship and changing it to a joint dictatorship of all races and strata.[3]

Discussions with the Colonial Office for the creation of an independent state came to fruition on 31 August 1957 when independence was proclaimed. The political structure of the Government (developed in 1953) was an alliance between three communal parties—UMNO, the MCA, and the Malayan Indian Congress.

Military operations in the jungle dragged on for another three years, but by May 1959 the whole of the country with the exception of one area round Sungei Siput in Perak had been cleared of rebels, and the armed revolt was virtually dead. In July 1960 the Emergency was declared to be at an end. The remnants of the Communist forces under Chin Peng took refuge in the Malaya–Siam border country where they have remained ever since as a Communist 'army in waiting'. But Communist subversive penetration of political parties, labour unions, youth organizations, and other groups of popular appeal, continued with increasing vigour, backed by the powerful and triumphant CCP which, through the press, literature, radio, films, schools, and business contacts, directed a never-ending stream of propaganda at the overseas Chinese in Southeast Asia.

2. TRIAD–MCP RELATIONS

One question of vital importance to the Government of the Federation once the Emergency was seen to be a widespread movement was whether the mass of members of the Triad Brotherhood, with their far-reaching interconnexions and their propensities to violence, would join the Communists. It was known that intermingling between Triad and Communist already existed upon an individual basis. It was also known that there was resentment in Triad circles because of the intensive police action to which they had been subjected during 1947 and early 1948.

But the MCP and Triad were basically rivals. Each was anxious to control the masses, well aware of the advantages that would accrue, and prepared to deal ruthlessly with all opposition. Their difference was ideological; whereas the MCP preached Marxism and aimed at introducing a soviet system of government, the Triad groups offered the protective shield of a traditional social organization which they hoped to resuscitate, and were not concerned with political theories. Primarily, therefore, this rivalry for power was a cause of cleavage between Communists and Triads. On the whole, antipathy rather than co-operation was the keynote of their relationships in the immediate postwar period, and at the beginning of the terrorist campaign secret society members were among the first Communist victims, sharing the fate of KMT members and labour contractors, many of whom were members of the Wa Kei. Of the Triad casualties, the Hai San leader in Pusing was killed in his house by a terrorist mobile unit because of his role in forming the Perak Mining Employees' Association which had frustrated the Communist attempt to control the local labour forces.[4] Thereafter, as police action swept into detention many Triad

[3] F/M Leg. Co. Paper 23 of 1959, p. 17.   [4] See p. 387 above.

leaders in several States, Triad society activities were dislocated, and Triad members, fearing further arrests or the attention of terrorists, became chary of attracting notice.

At first during the Emergency (June–July 1948) Triad–Communist rivalry seemed to be continuing, though a number of Triad members joined in the revolt, some (particularly in Malacca) from sympathy with the Communists, others because they sought excitement, or resented police action, or were intimidated through previous MPAJA membership and fear of arrest under the Emergency Regulations. Such apparent links as were discovered were on an individual basis, and were not attributable to any organizational approach. But later there were indications, particularly in Kinta (Perak) and North Malaya, that the Communist rebels were co-operating with small secret society groups. In August 1948 a document found in a terrorist hut near Tronoh (Kinta) spoke of a decision to employ 'well-tried bad elements' (which undoubtedly included Triad gunmen) to carry out assassinations. In Penang certain members of Cells 4 and 12 of the Ang Bin Hoey, encouraged by their leaders, were found to be helping the Communists. In Selangor a leader of the former Green Dragon Mountain Gang and several of his followers enlisted in the Communist armed forces, and after a period of training reappeared in Serdang to carry out their old extortion activities, this time in the name of the Malayan People's Anti-British Army.[5] In Menglembu (Kinta) some Wa Kei and Communist elements co-operated in running Chee Fah gambling as a means of mutually raising funds. And although certain Communist leaders were reported strongly opposed to any form of collaboration, and Triad groups in the Taiping area remained allegedly impervious to Communist infiltration, these incidents were straws in the wind.

As early as September 1948 some Communist leaders in Singapore, alarmed by the way in which terrorism was alienating the sympathies of the Chinese masses, saw the need to win the sympathy, if not the co-operation, of the lower middle classes—the artisans, clerks, and small shopkeepers. It was suggested that attempts should be made to win over the rank and file of the KMT and the secret societies, and for this it was considered necessary to develop 'Front' organizations, to be called the Anti-British League. This idea spread to the mainland. In February 1949 a document recovered at Siputeh (Kinta) stated: 'Under the work of the organization of the Anti-British Backing-Up Society is the task of winning over the co-operation of Malay soldiers, and members of the Triad society . . .'

There were also rumours (confirmed in March 1949 by documentary evidence recovered from a wounded terrorist) that propaganda along the North Perak coast, Province Wellesley, South Kedah, and Penang was urging Triad–Communist co-operation within a Communist-controlled Anti-British Alliance. There was even a suggestion that all Triad societies should unite and form a Pan-Malayan unit with this object in view. This approach exploited anti-imperialism and national patriotism (in support of Communist China). It emphasized the sufferings of Triad members at the hands of a repressive Malayan Government, and suggested that the Brotherhood should take revenge by assuring the success of the revolt, for, if it failed, the societies would again be oppressed. Further, since national patriotism was a Triad characteristic, and as the CCP would shortly either govern the whole of China or would control a

---

[5] See pp. 392–3 above.

local coalition Government (and thus, by inference, be worthy of support), it was seemly that in Malaya Triad and Communist should unite against an anti-Triad and anti-Communist Government. It was stressed that the Communist campaign was directed solely against the British, who should be driven out of Malaya.

But in proposing such an alliance organizers of the Communist Front in North Malaya had overplayed their hand. Given the very mixed nature of the Triad societies in the area, all with numerous Communist sympathizers and ex-MPAJA members, such a proposal was not surprising, but when the matter was considered by officials of the MCP as distinct from leaders of the satellite groups (the NDYL, the Federation of Trade Unions, and the Ex-Service Men's Association of the MPAJA), the proposal was denounced as a grave error in policy which might conceivably lead to an increase in the strength of the Triad groups at the expense of the party. It was foreseen that differences in political and economic outlook would make continued collaboration difficult, and sooner or later trouble would arise, and 'friends would then become enemies'.

It was therefore recommended that instead of an alliance with Triad on a group basis, the MCP, working independently, should concentrate upon recruiting individual Triad members into an Anti-British Alliance. Such recruits were to be urged to encourage fellow members of the secret societies to join the Alliance, and were to be allowed in certain circumstances to raise funds from merchants for the maintenance of armed units. In this way Triad influence on the masses might be used to win popular support for the armed revolt, without jeopardizing Communist leadership and control.

Although this policy was adopted, the MCP's basic distrust of the Brotherhood remained, and was expressed forcibly in a document discovered in Johore in February 1949:

> Secret Societies are organizations of robbers. They have no definite aims and no political beliefs. They are concerned solely with their own self-interest. They are capable on the one hand of being utilized by the British Imperialists or the Kuomintang, or, on the other hand, of joining the revolution.
>
> For this reason, we should penetrate them by political methods, and persuade their members to join the revolution. We should try to win them over by proposing to reorganize their society. If they refuse to be reorganized, they may be permitted to exist only if they do not oppress the masses, or oppose us.
>
> They are vagabonds, and it is very difficult to correct them. So when we receive them, or reorganize them, we should be on our guard, and should give them political education to improve them in the course of the National Liberation struggle.

A letter written by the secretary of the Selangor State Committee of the MCP, Chan Lo, and recovered from the body of a terrorist leader killed at Gombak (Selangor) in May 1950, expressed similar sentiments:

> Triad personnel are elements of a decadent society, ostensibly patriotic, but in reality self-seeking. When once tempted by offers of money they will commit all sorts of crime. Care should be taken to avoid arousing their suspicion. They should be given political teaching, and their societies should be reorganized under different names, such as the 'Righteous Killer Squad', the 'Blood and Iron Volunteer Corps', and the 'Anti-British Protection Corps'.

Certainly experience over the years fully justified Communist fears of the unreliability of Triad members as allies. Early in 1949 branches of the Anti-British Alliance were formed in Penang, Province Wellesley, and South Kedah.

In Perak, Taiping remained aloof, and in Krian, secret society leaders, well known to the police, were cautious. Further down the Perak coast, particular attempts were made to influence the Yen Hai groups, and Chinese community leaders were asked for financial and material aid, and for help in recruiting new members of the Anti-British Alliance. In some specious propaganda, 'Brothers of the Hung Brotherhood' were especially mentioned as desirable recruits: 'They are noted for their bravery and unity, and we enthusiastically hope that they will rise, bring their arms, and join hands with us to overthrow British imperialism. Then only will there be a glorious future in which we can enjoy liberty and happiness.'

In Penang, where Cells 4, 12, and 15 of the Ang Bin Hoey were known to have Communist sympathies, progress towards co-operation was initially checked when the police arrested four prominent cell leaders, but even so some Triad gunmen joined the Communist assassination squads. During 1949 and 1950 Penang Triad members on the whole seemed uninterested in politics and more intent upon trying to revive prewar Triad societies, for their own protection and to defend their gambling activities. When these attempts failed (again frustrated by police action) some Triad individuals turned to the Communists, impressed by their growing power and hoping for support in their unlawful pursuits. In 1951 a Triad group in Jelutong was permitted to co-operate in collecting subscriptions, but the Communists soon found that funds were being misappropriated, and they feared that Triad members of the Anti-British Alliance were acting as spies. Several suspects were assassinated, and the Communist Branch Committee member who had agreed to the original arrangements was dismissed. In Province Wellesley in January 1952, one prominent Triad leader who had joined the terrorists committed suicide after surrender to the police in an attempt to evade an investigation into his peculation and the vengeance of his Communist accusers; another leader who had shared in the profits was killed by the Communists. Clearly, the prognostication 'friends will then become enemies' was being fulfilled.

Triad–Communist relations continued to deteriorate. By June 1952 Triad members were leaving Penang and joining the armed mobile units of the Kinta Valley Home Guard.[6] About July 1952 further recruitment of Triad members into the ranks of the Penang Anti-British Alliance was forbidden by the MCP on security grounds, and a rigorous investigation into the affairs of Party members and 'sympathizers' was begun in a determined effort to remove the Triad elements and to create a small, reliable, and politically-pure Communist group.

A Communist document recovered near a terrorist camp in the Relau Hills, Penang, in January 1953 proved to be an investigation form for recruits from secret societies. There were forty-nine questions asking the name of the society, the reason for joining, the rank held, and the identity of leaders and members. Questions were also asked concerning any criminal record of robbery or assault, the names of accomplices and the owners of guns, whether arrested, escaped, or betrayed, whether tried in court, whether a lawyer had been engaged, the term of imprisonment or of police supervision. Questions on police detectives ('running dogs') asked who were the best and who the worst? How many were known, and was contact still made with any of them? Who had recommended

6 See pp. 441–2 below.

that the member should make common cause with the Revolution? Why had he joined, and when? Finally, it was suggested that if the secret society member had any confession to make to the organization, he would be well advised to take the opportunity to do so. Later investigations revealed that by August 1953 no fewer than fifty Triad members had been eliminated in Penang by the Communists since the outbreak of the Emergency.

If in Penang Triad–Communist relations were strained, by the autumn of 1952 it was clear that throughout the Federation very little progress had been made by the MCP in winning or organizing mass support, and the problem of how best to attract the revolutionary potential of Triad to the Communist cause remained unsolved.

As far as is known, no reference to secret societies occurred in policy documents issued by the MCP Politburo (as distinguished from comments by local party leaders) until October 1951, when on Moscow's instructions the Chinese revolutionary model was adopted, and the MCP began to restrict military operations and emphasize the formation of Communist Front organizations. Part of the October Directives then issued stated that 'members of Triad Societies would not normally be eliminated unless they collected subscriptions from the masses by intimidation, acted as running dogs or spies, or were gangsters operating against the Party'. In a further Directive concerned with mobilizing public opinion and winning over the masses, instructions were given to form a United Front against Imperialism, by utilizing existing organizations 'including unlawful forms of mass organization', which would appear to include Triad societies, though nothing more specific was stated, nor was there any guidance on how best to wean Triad elements from their old allegiance.

The significance of these instructions becomes more apparent in the light of current affairs in China, where in January 1951 secret societies were outlawed, and in a subsequent campaign waged for months against 'counter-revolutionaries' many of those accused of utilizing 'feudalistic secret societies to engage in anti-revolutionary activities'[7] were condemned to death or to lifelong imprisonment. In Malaya, these measures struck terror into the hearts of secret society banishees awaiting shipment to China, but although the Communist Government in China had ruthlessly eliminated secret society elements who had posed an active, seditious threat, the basic Communist policy remained that of winning over and absorbing the secret society rank and file into Communist people's organizations. Outside China the CCP was fully prepared to make use of secret societies for its own ends, appreciating that in Malaya, for instance, the local party, seeking power, still needed to consider how best to bring to its own support the influence exercised by the societies upon the masses. Thus, following the CCP line, the October Directives represented a policy of discrimination, and the MCP, while liquidating proved enemies and purging its own ranks of undesirable elements, sought (though with some misgivings) the co-operation of those members of the secret societies whose loyalties were not actively committed against it.

Although there was still considerable divergence of opinion within the higher ranks of the MCP on the relative merits of armed revolt and subversive penetration, in Selangor Yang Kuo, vice-secretary-general of the party and a close friend and mentor of the secretary-general, Chin Peng, had no doubt on the matter.

[7] Keesing, 1950–2, p. 11419A, *Ta Kung Pao* (Hong Kong), 23 Feb. 1951.

Writing to Chin Peng in the middle of 1952 he attributed the failure of the party to date to their underrating the strength of the British and overrating their own. He urged the formation of a Racial Independence United Front, in which all races, various levels of society, political parties, associations, guilds, and individuals might be brought together in a common stand against Imperialism, and the subordination of all terrorist military activity to that end. Although his advice did not prove wholly acceptable, in October (1952) unexpected developments in Selangor (possibly activated by the CCP) played into his hands, and brought at least the question of secret society–Communist relations into renewed prominence.

It has been revealed from captured documents relating to the period October–December 1952 that the party secretary for Selangor, Chan Lo, was at that time giving serious, though cautious, consideration to an offer of co-operation from the Chi Kung Tong, Kuala Lumpur (a branch of the China Chi Kung Tong which had become part of the CCP's United Front), on the basis of their mutual interests. An account of the negotiations made it clear that if the Chi Kung Tong could prove its good faith to the satisfaction of the State Committee secretary, the latter would recommend it as a cover organization to further MCP plans to infiltrate into towns and urban areas, to indoctrinate the youth and intelligentsia, and possibly to promote contact with the Chinese People's Government through the medium of the Tong's leading personalities.[8]

Probably stimulated by the Chi Kung Tong's approach, the Selangor State Secretariat of the MCP issued two pamphlets in November (1952).The first, intended for party consumption only, was entitled 'Opinions connected with the Present Activities', and devoted several pages to the 'Question of Secret Societies', viewed from a political angle. Both Triad and Wa Kei societies were said to be the product of capitalism—either associations of vagrants and unemployed for criminal purposes, or organizations of labourers excluding all but 'brothers'. It was felt that the latter, being manual workers, would 'easily accept the influence and leadership of the Revolution'.

In a brief but perspicacious account of the secret society scene in Selangor there were references to the Sea Gang and the Land Gang on the coast, who, recruited from fishermen, wharf, godown, and transport workers, frequently fought one another over smuggling and other interests. In what direction their political sympathies lay was not known. As for the Triad and Wa Kei groups in the interior, the Triad leaders were secret society members of long standing, and included small shopkeepers, owners of small estates, and heads of labour gangs. They were described as being politically 'left' ('inclined towards democracy') although it was admitted that there were KMT members within their ranks. Their attitude towards the revolution was said to be one of 'either neutrality or sympathy', and the Chi Kung Tong was described as their open political organization.

In contradistinction, the Wa Kei, though a derivative of Triad, and including in its membership manual workers, farmers, shop assistants, and small and medium capitalists, enrolled as its most important members the big contractors, their foremen, and headmen, who were responsible for recruiting and controlling labour on the estates and mines. With gangster elements from the towns, and some members of the Detective Force of the police, these contractors were said

---

[8] See pp. 435–6 below.

to form the core of the Wa Kei, and as politically the society was in the grip of the KMT, its policy was 'pro-British, anti-Communist, anti-Revolution, and anti-Democracy'. 'Triad and Wa Kei stand opposed to each other', the MCP commented.

Both Triad and Wa Kei were said to use intimidation to recruit members, and both operated under cover of legitimate Benevolent Societies and clubs from which they drew funds. In trade union activities the party had clashed with both Triad and Wa Kei, only to a slight extent with the former, but to a very serious extent with the latter, and since the armed revolt began the Wa Kei had been among the party's worst enemies, its members acting as spies for the British imperialists.

In a long analysis it was then admitted that the party's past approach to the secret societies, especially as reflected in dealings with 'reactionary contractors', had been too uncompromisingly ultra-left. Insufficient consideration had been given to distinguishing between the obstinate reactionaries and those who had been forced to join the societies in order to continue their livelihood. The latter formed the mass of the people, and might be regarded as politically neutral. They must be won over, and not antagonized by the extermination of their leaders without any explanation. In future, the great mass of manual workers and peasants who formed the lower strata of the secret societies must be regarded as a basic party objective, to be won over, united, and organized, although care must be taken to guard against the infiltration of undesirable elements into any organization so formed. Even reactionary members of secret societies were not to be eliminated unless proved to be 'in league with the enemy to destroy the Revolution'. In such cases, the offender

should be treated as an enemy spy and proclaimed as such. That he is a contractor, or secret society leader, or a responsible officer of any other organization should not be announced. If he is neither in league with the enemy nor an enemy spy, but only exploits and oppresses the people, or is only reactionary in his speech, then he is not to be exterminated (special cases excepted). Instead, he should be warned, and punished, and won over politically.

Finally, there should be no direct negotiation with the Triad societies as such, and no interference with Benevolent Societies, or with any other organization run by the secret societies as long as no compulsion was used to force the masses to join them. Such associations should be infiltrated by the party with the object of eventually gaining control. This process would take time, and should on no account be hurried, for it had to be admitted that secret society influence over the masses was far stronger and more deeply-rooted than that of the party. Any attempt to seize control would only result in conflict, and the societies, being stronger, might easily prevail, and expel members of the party, whose future work would then be made more difficult. (There can surely be no greater confirmation of the fundamental importance of the secret society complex in the Chinese community of modern Malaya than this frank assessment by the Selangor State Committee of the MCP.)

The second pamphlet, 'An Announcement to the Brethren of the Various Secret Societies', was prepared jointly by the Headquarters of the 1st Regiment of the Malayan Races Liberation Army and the MCP Selangor State Commitee, and carried the authority of 'Central'. It was addressed to Triad society members only, and was later sent by post to certain Triad leaders and Benevolent Societies in Selangor. It urged the secret societies to join in a United Front against British Imperialism.

In order to demonstrate the supposed close affinity between Communism and the basic principles of the secret societies (whose criminal complexion was frankly recognized) the MCP adopted a fulsome method of approach. It claimed that the secret societies throughout Selangor all stemmed from the Hung Brotherhood, originally an organization of the peasants in China to combat the oppression of feudal aristocrats, landlords, and villains. The Brotherhood, chivalrous, righteous, and courageous, had fought against injustice, had plundered the rich to help the poor, and above all had been inspired by strong national sentiment, opposing for centuries foreign aggression. But these lofty aims and ideals had been overlaid in 'colonial Malaya' through contact with 'a capitalist hegemony where the concept of selfish individualism prevailed'. Loafers and vagabonds had infiltrated the societies, had oppressed the masses, and for financial gain had helped foreign capitalists oppose the trade unions. They had also attempted to undermine the revolutionary war effort, and the party had therefore been compelled to adopt punitive measures causing unfortunate misunderstandings between itself and the societies. But basically there were no insoluble contradictions between the secret societies, the MCP, or the trade unions; all were working for the welfare of the masses, and although the criminal elements which had crept into the societies deserved punishment, their existence did not necessarily mean that the societies as a whole were evil. 'As withered twigs are apt to be found on a big tree, so will black sheep be found in a large family'. It was to those society members who had remained 'honest' and 'honourable' in their dealings with the public that the party extended an invitation to forget the past, and to join the United Front against British Imperialism. The 'Announcement' ended with a warning to members to learn from the tragic fate of those in China who had opposed the Communists.

The whole pamphlet was an example of the kid-glove approach recommended in the document of guidance. Even the final sentence was in the nature of a warning rather than a threat—a reminder of the inevitability of the victory of the revolution, in Malaya as well as in China, and an exploitation of the traditional desire to be found on the winning side. As far as is known, no such appeal was issued by any of the other State or Regional Committees of the party. Its appearance in Selangor may well be attributable to the existence in that state of the Malaya headquarters of the China Chi Kung Tong, which the CCP hoped to use as a channel of communication with Chinese in Malaya, and to the presence of Yang Kuo, who appreciated that the revolt in Malaya must be replaced by a policy of peaceful subversion, and that the success of any United Front entailed the support of members of the Triad societies, who must be won over and not antagonized.

3. THE CHINA CHI KUNG TONG AND THE MCP

The attempts being made in China by all political groups to bring the Hung Brotherhood into the political arena, and the consequent formation of rival Triad political parties, the Min Chi Tang and the China Chi Kung Tong, were reproduced in Malaya. In particular, cleverly disguised efforts of Communist agents from China operating within the local China Chi Kung Tong to encourage the MCP to bring members of Triad societies into its revolt increased the potential seriousness of an already grave threat to public security.

Postwar Chi Kung Tong activities in Malaya were throughout very closely linked with the China scene, and Selangor, in particular, was concerned with the China Chi Kung Tong which, under the leadership of the nephew of the founder of the party, the late General Ch'en Chiung-ming, had been revived in Hong Kong in May 1946, ostensibly as a result of Chiang Kai-shek's announcement that all political parties would be invited to send their representatives as delegates to the proposed forthcoming National Assembly. That this postwar China Chi Kung Tong was in reality a *new* party, penetrated and financed by the CCP in opposition to the Min Chi Tang (the political manifestation in China of the Hung Mun Chi Kung Tong), but using the façade of the old China Chi Kung Tong to disguise the new, was not common knowledge either in China or Malaya. Nor was it generally known that through the overseas branches of the China Chi Kung Tong the CCP was seeking a means of communication with Triad members of overseas Chinese communities for its own political purposes.

In response to a letter sent in June 1946 by the China Chi Kung Tong's headquarters in Hong Kong, the old Chi Kung Tong in Selangor began to revive its activities. In September 1946 a preliminary meeting of members who were still interested in its affairs was held at the party's previous headquarters, the Kung Seong club, Sultan Street, Kuala Lumpur. It was agreed that the party should be re-formed, and so the China Chi Kung Tong of the Malayan Union came officially into existence in December 1946 at the club's premises.

Its political programme was to oppose the dictatorship of the KMT, and to assist the party in China to gain power within the Chinese Government, but the Kuala Lumpur leaders had little understanding of the issues involved. They were dazzled by the prospect and prestige of becoming known entities in the political life of China, and locally the initiation of new members meant an income for the officials in addition to a share of the gaming proceeds of the Kung Seong club.

But dissensions soon arose, centred, typically, on money matters, and at the end of the year a new president was elected. He proved to have a keen eye for the financial benefits of his position, and claimed that as president he was *ex-officio* president of the Chi Kung Tong and entitled to the control of the revenues from initiations. The claim was resisted, and a split occurred in the party widened three months later by a further dispute on dividing the gaming revenue. The party president and some forty followers then broke away and established themselves under the title 'Selangor Branch of the China Chi Kung Tong'. They temporarily made their headquarters in a room in the Fui Chiu Association building at 7 Foch Avenue, offered to them by the 'open' representative of the MCP in Selangor. This building, which housed the Fui Chiu (Hakka) Association, was mainly occupied by the MCP and its satellite associations, and the invitation so hospitably extended to the splinter Chi Kung Tong was a shrewd move to draw this organization over to the left. An earlier suggestion that the Chi Kung Tong should co-operate with the MCP had not been accepted, but it was now inevitable that constant contact would have its effect and pave the way for the closer co-operation for which the Communists were angling.

The Sultan Street section remained in being, retaining the title Malayan

Union Headquarters of the China Chi Kung Tong, and in May 1947 both sections were invited to send representatives to what was called the Third Conference of the China Chi Kung Tong, held in Hong Kong. ('Third' Conference cleverly maintained the historic sequence of the original China Chi Kung Tong's conferences, the first in 1923, the second in 1931.) In addition to their secretary, the Foch Avenue group sent a former East River (Canton) guerrilla officer. Sultan Street sent a member of many years' standing.

At the conference, held under the presidency of General Li Chi-shen, the personal jealousies of the Kuala Lumpur factions received scant sympathy. Only the Foch Avenue delegates were permitted to attend the actual sessions, although the Sultan Street delegate was allowed to state his case. All three delegates were abruptly told to compose their differences, and were reprimanded for allowing personal matters to interfere with the interests of the party. An official order (dated 15 May 1947) was issued instructing the two factions to reunite, and a committee for adjustment and re-registration was appointed under the supervision of Kon Voon Sem, a veteran and respected leader of the Fui Chiu community in Selangor and a long-standing member of both the Kung Seong club and of the Chi Kung Tong. He had not, however, concerned himself with the affairs of the revived party, as he was occupied with matters concerning the CDL, branches of which were forming in Malaya. He was surprised to hear of his arbitrary appointment but nevertheless accepted.

On 30 August, shortly after the delegates had returned from Hong Kong and before the adjustment committee met, the Foch Avenue group entertained representatives of the press and of all the Communist satellite associations, informing them that it had been recognized as the official Malaya headquarters of the China Chi Kung Tong. In a spate of congratulatory speeches the MCP and labour leaders urged close co-operation, and the celebration ended in an atmosphere of mutual friendliness. On 6 September the first meeting of the adjustment committee was held. It decided upon the details of the registration of members, and appointed a preparatory committee to form a Malaya Branch of the China Chi Kung Tong. The Sultan Street leader refused to co-operate, and it was clear that there was little prospect of reconciliation. Nevertheless, arbitrators were appointed from among prominent members of the Hakka community, and negotiations for the reunion of the two groups continued during October. But despite certain concessions made by Foch Avenue, Sultan Street refused to come to terms, and at a so-called All-Selangor Meeting held on 9 November accused the Foch Avenue group of being under Communist control, and advocated that an independent Chi Kung Tong should be run on neutral political lines from the Kung Seong club. A party signboard was to be erected at Sultan Street, recruitment pressed forward, new branches formed, and a further meeting held on 30 November to elect office-bearers. Informed of these developments, Foch Avenue referred the matter back to Hong Kong and received official instructions that the Sultan Street group should recognize Kon Voon Sem's authority, and should register as a branch with the Hong Kong headquarters.

Details of the disagreement together with the gist of the Hong Kong ruling were published by Foch Avenue in the leftist press.[9] This publicity caused much annoyance at Sultan Street, where, as previously arranged, an 'All-Malaya

[9] *Min Sheng Pao*, 28 Nov. 1947 and *Nan Chiao Jit Poh*, 2 Dec. 1947.

Meeting' was held on 30 November, attended by over seventy 'delegates', the great majority of whom came from various parts of Selangor, although there was a sprinkling of representatives from Perak, Penang, Negri Sembilan, Pahang, and Johore. The election of standing and executive committees was postponed, but a committee of nine members was formed to 'protect the party', and in a published account of the meeting the Sultan Street group announced that they were carrying out the instructions of the central headquarters in establishing their branch headquarters at the Kung Seong club to convince all concerned that theirs was not 'an illegal organization', as alleged by Foch Avenue.[10]

And so the deadlock remained, the two rival groups maintaining their separate identities and each claiming to be the authentic representative of the China Chi Kung Tong. There is no doubt, however, that the Foch Avenue group was recognized by the Hong Kong central committee as the authentic headquarters for Selangor and also for Malaya, and that the Sultan Street group was cold-shouldered.

These petty squabbles received publicity in the local Chinese vernacular press, although due prominence was given to certain more important developments in the wider Chi Kung Tong field, including Chiu Yuk's grandiose conception of a Federation of Triad Societies in South China, Indo-China, Siam, Indonesia, and Malaya, and Szeto Mei-tang's announcement in Shanghai in September 1947 that he was withdrawing from politics, and intended to concentrate upon leading the Hung Brotherhood in reconstruction projects for the rehabilitation of China.

As all China-based political parties with overseas branches were already engaged in seeking financial aid ostensibly for the rehabilitation of the homeland, this emphasis upon the possible role of the Hung Brotherhood caused an increase of activity in Malaya, and from Kedah to Singapore, the KMT, the CDL, and CCP sympathizers began to seek Triad support for their various political projects. Since the local Government had proscribed Triad societies as such, they one and all attempted to organize this support under the title Chi Kung Tong, the Kuala Lumpur political party.

The secret arrival from Hong Kong of a nephew of Chiu Yuk, charged with the task of encouraging the formation of a combined Hung Mun Chi Kung T'ong (Lodge) in Malaya, and the announcement in the Chinese press in December 1947 that an application, sponsored by a prominent merchant in Singapore, had been forwarded to the Registrar of Societies for the registration of the headquarters in Singapore of a Triad political party, to be called the Hung Mun Chi Kung T'ong, added to the bewilderment of the Malayan Chinese public.

A KMT official in Perak, commenting upon the plethora of reports concerning the formation of 'Chi Kung Tong' branches, admitted that there were both 'left' and 'right' Hung factions in existence, and that it was difficult to classify them. Early in December Foch Avenue found it necessary to explain publicly that although it had close historical relations with the Hung Brotherhood it was unrelated to the Hung Mun Chi Kung Tong at that time so active in Singapore.[11] A few weeks later, the Min Chi Tang headquarters in Hong Kong stated that it had no connexion with any overseas Chi Kung Tong organization,[12] and in Kedah Triad members who were being urged to join a KMT scheme for the formation of a Chi Kung Tong organization, insisted that the words 'Hung

[10] *Chung Shing*, 3 Dec. 1947.   [11] *Nan Chiao*, 2 Dec. 1947.   [12] Ibid. 26 Feb. 1948.

Mun' should appear in the title of any new Chi Kung Tong branch in recognition of the Brotherhood's past services to the cause of democracy.

Both sections of the China Chi Kung Tong at Kuala Lumpur participated in the political race for expansion. In October 1947 Foch Avenue attempted to establish a branch at Bukit Mertajam, Province Wellesley, and secretly distributed pamphlets in Penang. In November two Foch Avenue representatives approached local Triad societies in Segamat, Siding, and Labis, in Johore, suggesting amalgamation with the China Chi Kung Tong as the only political party representing the Hung Brotherhood. Some Hakka members supported them, but Hokkien members said they were uninterested in politics. Early in 1948 Foch Avenue held the usual annual meeting to elect office-bearers. Kon Voon Sem remained in overall control of the Preparatory Malaya Chi Kung Tong Committee and a significant election as an ordinary member of the Selangor Executive Committee was that of Tan Hong Piew, the blind but able leader of the Kuala Lumpur Triad groups and an influential figure in the underworld, with known Communist leanings. Still more significant was his appointment as vice-president of the Malaya Chi Kung Tong committee under Kon Voon Sem.[13]

As their earlier attempts to expand had made little headway Foch Avenue officials decided to renew the campaign, and representatives were appointed to organize new branches in north Malaya, south Malaya, and Singapore. Their efforts were fruitless; in the north people were said to be frightened to join lest the Government should take action against them, in the south it was said to be impossible to convince people that the Chi Kung Tong was a political party and not a Triad society.

Initially Sultan Street was more successful than its rival. The two prewar branches at the Kung Yiu club, Raub (Pahang), and the Kung Yik club, Malacca, revived, and in August a new branch was formed in Klang, followed by considerable activity in the Kuala Selangor, area, where recruits were encouraged to attend a Triad initiation ceremony on Pulau Ketam early in November. As tension with Foch Avenue increased, recruitment was intensified, frequently by intimidation, and at the time of the meeting of 30 November Sultan Street claimed to control thirteen 'branches' in Selangor, as well as groups in Perak, Penang, Pahang, Negri Sembilan, and Johore.[14] This claim was exaggerated. To try to increase his own personal power and financial resources, the leader of the Sultan Street group had cast his net wide in Triad waters. But most of the 'delegates' who attended the meeting of 30 November were not genuine Chi Kung Tong members interested in the party's political aims, but Triad leaders seeking a refuge from police attention and a Chi Kung Tong cover for their activities, and in return 'protecting' the gaming which was being carried on with the president's connivance. In the political field, contact was made with Chiu Yuk's nephew, who visited Selangor in an attempt to form a united Hung Lodge, and there was some dallying with KMT elements who, Sultan Street hoped, would provide the initial finances necessary for the opening of a Chi Kung Tong branch in Penang.

A preliminary office was opened there on 27 December 1947. A signboard was erected, an announcement that the branch was prepared to register members

[13] *Min Sheng Pao*, 13 Feb. 1948.   [14] *Chung Shing*, 3 Dec. 1947.

appeared in the Chinese press,[15] and the Chinese Consul in Penang was officially informed. Several thousand enrolment forms were printed and distributed, and were sent in particular to each of the twenty-two Ang Bin Hoey cells in Penang, with the suggestion that as Government had 'approved' the formation of the China Chi Kung Tong in Kuala Lumpur there could be no objection to it elsewhere. The Ang Bin Hoey could therefore use the new branch as a cloak, and thus recover its former position in the Triad world. But the Ang Bin Hoey cell leaders remained unimpressed. They were awaiting the result of the Hung Mun Chi Kung Tong application for registration in Singapore before making any move, believing that it would be refused. They also suspected that despite recent assertions of loyalty to the KMT, Sultan Street's political sympathies lay with the CDL. Furthermore, they themselves were being approached by KMT leaders who again under the title Chi Kung Tong were attempting to rally Triad elements in support of Chiang Kai-shek, hard-pressed by the Communists in China. This movement, part of a wider scheme organized from Singapore, aimed in North Malaya at uniting the Triad members in Kedah, Penang, and North Perak with similar groups in Siam.

As with Foch Avenue, none of Sultan Street's efforts prospered. The president, unpopular because he was dictatorial and had mishandled the club finances, was dropped from the committee, and went to Hong Kong on business in February 1948. Those officials who had been in contact with Chiu Yuk's nephew concerning the possible foundation of an All-Malaya Hung Mun Chi Kung T'ong were disappointed, for he returned to Hong Kong late in March (1948), reporting to Chiu Yuk that conditions for its formation were 'most unfavourable' in Singapore and in the Federation. As for Penang, after trying for several months to establish the new branch, the Sultan Street leaders abandoned the attempt in May 1948, after the Singapore Government had officially refused to register the Hung Mun Chi Kung Tong in the Colony.

The outbreak of the MCP revolt and the introduction of the Emergency Regulations gravely hampered any continuation of Chi Kung Tong activity in Malaya. In July (1948) Foch Avenue 'suspended external activities' on instructions from Hong Kong, and in August two of its committee members, including the Triad leader Tan Hong Piew, were arrested with Communist sympathizers. A number of the party's rank and file then took to the jungle, and those who remained in the towns effaced themselves.

Sultan Street maintained a precarious existence for some time, attempting to raise funds through lotteries and a mutual aid society. In December 1948 its previous president returned from Hong Kong, where he had made his peace with the China Chi Kung Tong headquarters (who as part of the Democratic Front were now clearly on the winning side in China), and announced that he had been entrusted with the task of uniting the two factions; but no official amalgamation took place. Kon Voon Sem declared that Chi Kung Tong activities had ceased, and when the new Societies Ordinance came into force in September 1949 neither side applied for registration. Despite protests by some of its members, Sultan Street took down its signboard, but gambling and Triad initiations continued secretly at the Kung Seong club until the middle of 1950 when official action was taken to close the premises.

While in Malaya the China Chi Kung Tong was on the wane, in China

[15] *Sin Pin Jit Poh*, 27 Dec. 1947, and *Kwong Wah Yit Poh*, 30 Dec. 1947.

it was becoming more important as the CCP not only began to defeat the KMT in the field but skilfully rallied to its banner those democratic groups, including the China Chi Kung Tong, who sought a broad-based Government in place of the KMT dictatorship. In April 1949 Kon Voon Sem went to Peking as a Malaya Chi Kung Tong delegate to the forthcoming People's Political Consultative Council, summoned by Mao Tse-tung ostensibly to consider the views of all members of the Democratic Front and to formulate an acceptable policy. He remained in China, becoming a member of the Central People's Council, chairman of the Chi Kung Tong and the CDL in Kwangtung Province, and adviser to the Overseas Affairs Commission in Canton, forming a very useful link between the CCP, the MCP, and the China Chi Kung Tong in Malaya. Other prominent Foch Avenue office-bearers made their way to China but the nucleus of a Foch Avenue China Chi Kung Tong group remained in Kuala Lumpur. Joined by certain self-seekers from Sultan Street, and assisted by a few active newcomers, this nucleus was to attempt, when occasion arose, to carry out the behests of their Chi Kung Tong 'brothers' in China. For although the Chi Kung Tong branches in Malaya had officially closed, and external activities had apparently ceased, before the end of July 1949 instructions came from Kon Voon Sem in China to 'select executive talents in Malaya for future use'. During the next few months Chi Kung Tong members in Kuala Lumpur read in the local press of the discussions taking place in Peking, whither the China Chi Kung Tong, as part of the Democratic Front, had sent six representatives, including Kon Voon Sem. In September they listened to the broadcasts in which Chan Ki Yau and Szeto Mei-tang expressed their support of the Common Programme, promising to mobilize Chi Kung Tong members overseas to assist in the construction of the new democratic fatherland. In January 1950, at a restaurant in Kuala Lumpur, they celebrated the British recognition of Communist China with a dinner party and bought Chinese Victory Bonds. In April they heard of the establishment of the headquarters of the China Chi Kung Tong in Canton, with Kon Voon Sem as vice-chairman, and read of the proceedings of their party's Fourth Representatives' Conference, where once again their leaders pledged loyalty to the Chinese People's Government and promised to mobilize overseas support.

But throughout 1950, although interested in these developments in China, local members of the China Chi Kung Tong in Kuala Lumpur, seriously hampered by the Emergency Regulations and the new Societies Ordinance, feared to engage in any overt activities. One Sultan Street leader with left sympathies hoped to utilize for Chi Kung Tong purposes the Triad members of the Hung Kwan Society, which was rapidly expanding thanks to renewed Triad–Wa Kei hostility in Selangor, but he was unable to find an appropriate organizer among the more senior of the former Chi Kung Tong members.

But this situation did not remain static, for when in 1951 the People's Government took action in China against counter-revolutionaries, extended its land-reform programme, and sought support for its campaign in Korea, an intensification of effort was required from all members of the United Front both at home and abroad. Early in the year word was received in Kuala Lumpur that a general meeting of the China Chi Kung Tong would be held in Canton, and it was suggested that representatives from Malaya should attend. This meeting was preceded in March by a conference of the United Front and the CCP's

South China Bureau, and the China Chi Kung Tong conference in Canton held early in April 1951 confirmed a decision already taken that the party's duty was to lay a strong foundation for its expansion outside China, facts which were broadcast by Peking radio.

A representative from Kuala Lumpur attended the Chi Kung Tong conference as Malayan delegate, and was flattered by the warmth of his reception and by being elected a member of the central executive committee of the conference. He returned to Malaya in July, charged with the duty of reorganizing the local Chi Kung Tong to carry out a definite policy, which included assisting Malayan Chinese students to go to China for further studies, encouraging the despatch of money to China as contributions or investments, spreading anti-KMT propaganda, and eulogizing the administration and the rapidity of reconstruction in the New China. For a few months there were some slight stirrings of revival among the Kuala Lumpur leaders. A small group met secretly from time to time to discuss how best to further this programme. Eventually, a few students were assisted to China, a few contacts were made with Chinese schools, a little money was collected, and there was some communication with Chi Kung Tong members in other parts of Malaya, but there was no specific organization—only the small group of so-called 'responsible persons'; nor was the policy prescribed pursued with any great energy or urgency.

But gradually, from behind the façade of old Chi Kung Tong leadership, new activators emerged. In January 1952 one of General Li Chi-sen's previous emissaries, who had spent some years incognito in Kuala Lumpur and had recently been in Canton when the decision was taken to purge the Chi Kung Tong of 'counter-revolutionary and unpure elements', returned to Selangor as a liaison officer between the local Chi Kung Tong groups and the Canton headquarters, charged with keeping Kon Voon Sem informed of developments in Malaya. In Penang a self-claimed refugee from China became quietly active in building up Chi Kung Tong influence, and in Kuala Lumpur a young Chi Kung Tong member played his part as one of the 'responsible persons' in furthering the expansion of activities as ordered by Canton. It was he who in October 1952 caused a fluttering in the dovecots by the direct approach to the MCP in the Selangor jungle to which reference has already been made. There are some grounds for believing that he had been specifically sent to Malaya from China to bring about such a Triad–Communist rapprochement, in furtherance of the policy of forming a United Front, but it has also been suggested that, disappointed by lack of advancement, he was merely attempting to impress the CCP with his ability and enthusiasm in order to secure an official appointment in China.

Details of this approach became known to the authorities late in January 1953 when several letters were recovered during military operations near Kuala Lumpur. In the first of these letters, dated 23 October 1952, a District Committee member of the MCP at Ulu Klang reported to the District Committee chairman, Ampang, that the Chi Kung Tong intended to form a 'People's Righteous Corps' and had asked for Communist support. The Corps, to be formed initially in Kuala Lumpur ('our own town'), would later be extended to other areas. Its object was to take action against any secret society whose activities were harmful to the masses and to the MCP. The letter made it clear

FF

that this meant action against the Wa Kei Society, the rival and enemy of the Triad groups in Kuala Lumpur and the interior of Selangor and also the sworn enemy of the Communists. There can be no doubt that this implied that the Chi Kung Tong planned to form a striking force which would attack the Wa Kei in compliance with the request of the Triad groups, and it is probable that they hoped to get armed support from the MCP. There was no further mention of this corps in the correspondence, but the prospect of contact with the Chi Kung Tong was welcomed by the District Committee chairman of the MCP as being of assistance in its work in Kuala Lumpur and in furnishing a means of approach to the Communist Party leaders in China. The contact was reported to more senior Selangor Communist officials, together with details of the Chi Kung Tong's current assignment from Canton, but information concerning the extent of the Chi Kung Tong's alleged youth work made singularly little impression upon the Selangor State Committee. Writing late in December 1952, the Selangor State secretary of the MCP, Chan Lo, though willing to continue the liaison, insisted upon increased security precautions and a clarification of the Chi Kung Tong's political views. He particularly wished to know whether Chi Kung Tong leaders regarded China or Malaya as their home country, and what their attitude was to British imperialism. As for youth work, he recommended that the Chi Kung Tong should concentrate on forming an open and legal organization within which students could be organized under cover of cultural activities.

This evidence seems to show that although the MCP had not expected to be contacted by the China Chi Kung Tong, they were quick to see the advantages of co-operation, and their swift production in November of the two documents concerned with Triad–Communist relations[16] indicated that some of their leaders appreciated the advisability of a renewed approach to the Triad societies along more diplomatic lines than in the past, while not ignoring the proposal to form a corps to oppose a mutual enemy, the Wa Kei Society.

During the first half of 1953 the small nucleus of the Chi Kung Tong's 'responsible persons' continued to carry out their Canton assignment, and some of them also assisted the MCP by distributing propaganda received from China and by sending copies of the MCP's 'Announcement' to known Triad leaders. But this was the limit of their achievement. They themselves adopted the title 'People's Righteous Corps', but an alleged attempt to persuade Triad members to join a so-called 'Revolutionary Corps of the Hung People' (Hung Mun Kak Sun Tuen) attracted a mere thirty or forty recruits, although membership was said to carry with it an assurance of protection by the China Chi Kung Tong headquarters in Canton in the event of banishment to China.

Independently, the MCP made their own contacts in Setapak with Tan Hong Piew, the blind leader of the Selangor Ang Bin Hoey, and through him a second channel was formed early in 1953 for the encouragement of Triad co-operation and for the distribution of copies of the 'Announcement'. But although in return the MCP seems to have given some assurance of local protection, it gave no practical help in the form of arms to combat the Wa Kei in Selangor.

Both links were summarily broken in May 1953 when the police began an all-out campaign against known Triad leaders in Selangor, including some of those who had been concerned in this liaison. Action against the Chi Kung

---

[16] See above, pp. 426–8.

Tong was postponed until December (1953), by which time the identity of the main contacts had been established and the scope of their operations revealed. The detention of the main activator early in January 1954, and his subsequent banishment to China several months later, dislocated Chi Kung Tong activity. Although about the time of his arrest the Selangor State Committee of the MCP approached the Chi Kung Tong headquarters in Canton asking whether the Triad societies in Malaya were assisted by the Chi Kung Tong, and, if so, whether the writer could be assisted to make contact with them for purposes of mutual co-operation, as far as is known, no such contact was renewed.

Certain features of these attempts to form a bridge between Triad and the MCP through the Chi Kung Tong are worth noting.

The first is the difference of opinion between locally-orientated and China-orientated groups within the MCP. Part of the strength of the MCP was its claim to be fighting for the cause of national liberation by the Malayan peoples. Throughout the whole of postwar activities in Malaya it claimed to be a 'Malayan' party, repudiating any suggestion that it was directed by the CCP. It is therefore understandable that the MCP leaders as a group had received no instructions from the CCP concerning the utilization of the Chi Kung Tong.

But there were some members of the MCP, particularly Yang Kuo of Selangor, who realized the futility of the armed revolt and urged the formation of a United Front on the China model. In a volte face, such a policy was also skilfully recommended by Russia in 1951 after the Sino-Soviet pact of 1950 had given her a base in the Far East from which to spread Russian influence.

If the Malayan revolt had never taken place, it is likely that the MCP would have retained its legal status, there would have been no anti-Communist military campaign, and no organization of the Chinese residents in Malaya to resist Communism. Instead, Communist pressure would have been exerted in a gradual process of winning over the Chinese population through labour associations and culture groups, so that they would become attuned to the idea of a Communist China, and would proudly acclaim the new Government in China as the champion of the Chinese nation. Regarded in this light, the Malayan revolt was a liability to the Chinese Communist Government unless it had succeeded, for it tended to align the large Chinese population against Communism, whereas the United Front technique would have opened the way to win over a large section of this community. This was the true potential danger of an organization such as the Chi Kung Tong, not so much that it might have been of some direct practical help to the MCP in their revolt, but that by providing a channel for the infiltration of schools and associations throughout the country it might have influenced the Chinese community in Malaya in favour of the Communist régime in China, and thus weakened their resistance towards Communism in general and the MCP in particular.

As for Triad–MCP links, any Triad offers to help the MCP were based on self-interest. In 1952 the fact that the Communists were doing well in Malaya was an inducement to be on good terms with the winning side, and in 1952–3 the Triad groups, particularly in Selangor, wanted weapons to help them in their fight against the Wa Kei, and hoped to get them from the Communists.

Triad support of the Chi Kung Tong was on a different basis, for this was in origin a Triad organization. Whereas the Hung Brotherhood was outlawed in

Communist China, and Triad members banished from Malaya feared possible execution, the Chi Kung Tong, as a member of the United Front, had some standing there, so that any support of its activities in Malaya might well favour a banishee.

20

TRIAD ACTIVITIES IN THE FEDERATION OF MALAYA, 1948–55

1. GENERAL

I N the early stages of the Emergency reconsideration was given by the Federation Government to the Societies legislation. Since April 1947 a registration system based on the prewar Societies Ordinance had been in force in Singapore, and it was proposed that a similar system should be introduced in the Federation, a policy supported by the new High Commissioner[1] and the new Commissioner of Police.

A new Ordinance on the lines of the prewar Enactment came into force on 1 September 1949, as Ordinance No. 28 of 1949. It applied only to societies established in the Federation, or having their headquarters or places of business there. These were styled 'Local Societies', all of which were required to apply for registration. Thereupon, they might be either registered or exempted, and every local society which was neither registered nor exempted was deemed to be an unlawful society.

Societies using a Triad ritual were declared to be unlawful, and possession of Triad documents was an offence.

The Registrar was bound to refuse registration if he was satisfied that a society was connected with any group of a political nature outside Malaya and that it was likely to be used for any purpose prejudicial to peace, welfare, or good order, and the High Commissioner was empowered to order the dissolution of any society (registered or exempted) which was being used for any such purpose.

Persons convicted of being office-bearers, or of managing or assisting in the management of an unlawful society, were liable to a fine of $5,000 or to imprisonment for a maximum of three years. The penalty for membership or for attending a meeting of such a society was a fine of $1,000 or imprisonment of up to one year, and there was a similar penalty for persons permitting a meeting of such a society in premises occupied or controlled by them. Persons attending a meeting of a Triad society or found in possession of Triad documents were liable to a fine of $2,000 or up to two years' imprisonment.

With the passing of this Ordinance the wheel came full circle. The experiment of complete freedom of association was abandoned. In the Malayan Union under the voluntary scheme of registration introduced in 1947 only 208 societies had registered, whereas in 1938 under the system of compulsory registration, 2,660 societies were either registered, exempted, or recorded. Although the voluntary system gave to a society a legal status, registration was unpopular, partly because

---

[1] Sir Edward Gent was killed in an air crash in July 1948. He was succeeded by Sir Henry Gurney.

the only societies the Registrar could call upon to register were those suspected of being used for unlawful purposes. Registration was thus regarded by many as the mark of doubtful respectability, for there was nothing to distinguish the society which had registered voluntarily from its neighbour which had been required to register. The 1949 Ordinance restored the prewar position in which registration was the normal status, exemption being granted to such societies as were, by their nature, unlikely ever to need financial or police supervision.

In 1951 amendments were introduced by which the Registrar might refuse registration of a society connected with a political group outside Malaya, whether or not it seemed likely to be used for purposes prejudicial to peace, etc., but must refuse registration of any society likely to be so used, or which, in his opinion, was undesirable.[2] Further amendments were passed in 1953 and 1954 to tighten control over societies which had as one of their objects the provision of death benefits for members or their dependants. An inordinate number of such societies had sprung up many of which were swindling the public, and the additional provisions inserted in the Ordinance brought the finances of such societies under supervision.[3]

The new Ordinance was an additional potential deterrent to Triad activities, but the problems presented by the Communist revolt continued to demand the unremitting efforts of the police, and those Triad leaders who had escaped the first spate of arrests in 1948 began to take advantage of this diversion of police attention. Gradually the strength of the secret societies began to increase, accelerating from 1950 onwards as some of the leaders originally detained under the Emergency Regulations were released and began to return to their old haunts.

Meantime, although individuals, either willingly or through pressure, joined in the Communist revolt, Triad members in many areas and Wa Kei members generally were opposed to the rebels and were to some extent fighting the Government's battle. It was fully appreciated by the authorities, for instance, that at Kepong in Selangor and at Bentong in Pahang the Home Guards were Wa Kei to a man and dominated the inhabitants of their areas in the fight against the terrorists. Chinese leaders were, of course, equally aware of this alignment, and in January 1950 an indirect approach was made to the Government through the agency of a leading Chinese merchant in Singapore suggesting that the formation of a central Malayan organization of Hung Brethren would be the best method of combating the Communist threat. It was argued that such a body working through representatives in each state would encourage the Chinese people, and in particular the squatters near the jungle, to withdraw support from the Communists and to inform against them. This organization would also, it was said, be able to induce such of the 'bandits' as had Triad backgrounds and connexions to surrender with their weapons, provided that this was done secretly, to the organization which would be empowered to pay rewards, arrange for the issue of identity cards, and to settle the bandits into civilian life or arrange for their return to China if they so wished. Throughout, emphasis was laid upon avoidance of any participation by the Government in these arrangements, and, indeed, it seemed that the intention was to evolve a system of control through the headmen of various clans and associations similar to an extended form of the Capitan system. It was noteworthy that KMT leaders were involved in the proposed plan.

[2] Ord. 23 of 1951, FM.   [3] Ords 11 of 1953 & 12 of 1954, FM.

A year later, in January 1951, an anonymous letter received by the special Post Box 5,000 urged the Government to mobilize and arm the Triad groups of Penang and Perak against the Communists, expressing the opinion that if this were done the Emergency would end within six months. The writer claimed that Triad had already given proof of its anti-Communist sentiments in its fight against the Communists in the Dindings. Lists of Chinese in Penang, Kuala Kurau, Taiping, and Ipoh who would assist the Government in this project were enclosed, and consultation with these leaders was strongly advised. Once again the list included known KMT leaders. Neither of these two suggestions was acceptable to the Government, for the political implications clearly were that Triad and KMT would receive official recognition, would evade the prohibitions imposed by the new Societies Ordinance, and would expect and demand representation in the counsels of government. The door would be open for the government of the Chinese in Malaya by a Triad KMT body strongly attached to the Nationalist Government of Formosa.

Later, however, an armed, anti-Communist organization, consisting largely of secret society personnel with strong KMT backing, actually came into existence with the consent and assistance of the Government, though at the time of its proposed formation no hint was given of either Triad or KMT participation. This occurred because of the intensity of the Communist attacks on the Kinta valley mines in late 1951 and early 1952, which caused the leading Perak Chinese to propose that a mobile armed force should be raised to protect the mines, replacing the static guards who were being overrun. Government approval was eventually given to the raising of such a force within the framework of the Home Guard organization, though not without misgiving, for there was a flavour of a private army about the proposal. The cost was shared between the Government and the mine-owners, the latter contributing $8 a pikul of tin-ore produced in the area covered by the scheme. The force, named the Kinta Valley Home Guard, was based on Ipoh, Batu Gajah, and Kampar, and the first parade was held in June 1952 with 163 men, later to increase to an operational strength of 1,600. But from the start there were internal rivalries and tensions. Among the forty officers, twenty-four had been trained in military or police academies in Nationalist China. They were strong KMT supporters and were secretly subsidized by a group of Chinese mine-owners who also had KMT attachments. The rest of the officers included several Wa Kei members, and as each group competed for overall control, there was constant friction.

In the ranks, the rapidity of recruitment had precluded any thorough check of individual antecedents, and a fairly high percentage of undesirable elements was admitted, including not only convicted criminals—who, on discovery through checking of fingerprints, were discharged—but also a large number of secret society members. Locally-recruited Wa Kei members, most of whom were Cantonese or Hakkas, formed 60–70 per cent of the early intake, but there were also Triad members, recruited along the Perak coast and in Penang, mainly Hokkiens, Hokchius, or Tiechius, who in the main were members either of the Perak coast Yen Hai groups, or of the Ngai Loke Athletic Association, a 'self-defence' (Kwun T'au) club which had been formed at Penang soon after the war but had been refused registration in 1950. By the end of 1952 it was estimated that about half the force belonged to Wa Kei or Triad in almost equal proportions, and that the rest were uncommitted.

Tension between the rival groups caused considerable trouble and indiscipline. Each group tried to keep promotions in its own hands and tended to refuse to obey orders given by officers and n.c.o.'s of its rivals. In mid-1953 it was announced that the force would be reduced by the discharge of secret society members. This caused not only a spate of hurried resignations but the spectacle of officers submitting for dismissal lists of members of rival societies alleged by them to be undisciplined trouble-makers. In the end, a reasonably-disciplined force 900 strong and of good morale, was developed under the command of a former European police officer, assisted by seven other European officers distributed between headquarters and the three groups into which the force was divided. But even after the removal of the most active secret society elements, undoubtedly a fair proportion of Triad and Wa Kei remained, with the latter predominating. Although inadequate training and bad shooting precluded any early spectacular successes against the Communists, the presence of these armed and mobile groups deterred attacks on the mines. From January 1954 some successful encounters led to a marked improvement in morale, Communist attacks further diminished, mines were enabled to reopen, and production increased. The crisis in the tin industry was over.

Thus in Perak, within the framework of the Kinta Valley Home Guard, Wa Kei and Triad members, despite their mutual antagonism, were of assistance to the Government in opposing Communist attacks, but in Selangor the situation was different, for there antagonism developed into a serious threat to the public peace as the two societies fought each other for the control of public gaming.

2. SELANGOR

Triad throughout Selangor had been seriously disrupted by the arrests of 1948. All overt activities in Port Swettenham and Klang had ceased, and in Kuala Lumpur town, where their allies the Kwan Luen, the San Kwan, and the Sap Sam Yau gangs had also been weakened, the Ang Bin Hoey cells went underground. In the country districts, particularly those near the jungle, Triad members, in conjunction with the rest of the Chinese population, were frequently intimidated by the terrorists, though some, including the Triad groups at Setapak, found little difficulty in reverting to the role of food suppliers which they had previously filled during the Japanese Occupation.

If Triad became weaker, Wa Kei remained powerful. Operating secretly from a headquarters in Kuala Lumpur, with strong under-cover branches in Setapak, Kepong, Serdang, and Kajang, its membership rose to an estimated 2,300 in 1950 in Selangor, with an overall membership of 10,000 in the Federation as a whole. In Kuala Lumpur its gambling activities were 'protected' by a strong-arm gang, the Thirteen Princes, for the pact of May 1948 whereby Triad and Wa Kei had agreed to settle disputes by negotiation was soon abrogated.

In 1949 some Triad members joined the Kwan Luen (thereafter sometimes known as the Hung Kwan) but still proved to be no match for the Wa Kei. A number of fights early in 1950 merely resulted in a fresh series of arrests which further weakened Triad and Kwan Luen, although the Wa Kei did not emerge unscathed. Five Kwan Luen leaders were arrested under the Banishment Ordinance, together with one each from the Ang Bin Hoey, the Chi Kung Tong, and the Wa Kei.

Nevertheless, during 1951 the Kwan Luen again revived, and hooligan elements from the defunct Sultan Street Chi Kung Tong formed themselves into the Yee Sap Yat Hing (Twenty-one Brothers) specifically to oppose the Thirteen Princes of the Wa Kei. In March the Red Rod of the Setapak Cell of the Ang Bin Hoey was arrested and detained for Min Yuen[4] activities, but by that time other Triad leaders who had been arrested at the beginning of the Emergency were being released, and in June (1951) Tan Hong Piew returned to Setapak after three years' detention, on bond of $500 and under restricted residence. The release of these leaders coincided with the beginning of a gradual easing of the Emergency situation as successful military operations on the part of the security forces and the change of policy from armed revolt to political subversion on the part of the MCP led to a lull in the shooting war, a circumstance which provided an additional stimulus to secret societies to expand their influence.

Before 1951 was out, there were warnings that Triad was gaining strength in Penang and Perak, and Selangor did not lag behind. By March 1952 a revival of Cell 12 had begun on the Selangor coast at Pulau Ketam and Port Swettenham, reputedly with support from Bagan Si Api Api in Sumatra. In Klang Cell 21, operating under cover of Benevolent Societies, resumed activities, and by April 1952 there were reports of initiation ceremonies being held in the suburbs of Kuala Lumpur, with a sinseh from Klang officiating. In June the organization of the Chee Fah lottery in Kuala Lumpur, 'protected' by the Wa Kei, and their ever-growing power in the field of gaming exacerbated the Triad gangs, who, despite all their efforts, could not penetrate the Chee Fah organization or share in the profits. Towards the end of the year (by which time the Red Rod of the Hokkien Triad groups had returned to Setapak from detention) the situation gravely deteriorated, particularly after Triad attempts to recruit reinforcements from among employees of the local bus companies were frustrated when they threw in their lot with the Wa Kei instead.

Serious disorders began on 12 December with a trivial incident in which a Triad member driving a car in Kuala Lumpur knocked over two tins of oil at a bus station and attempted to leave without apologizing to the owner, a Wa Kei member. The driver was attacked by employees of the bus station, and although a few days later a Triad emissary attempted to effect a reconciliation, asking for the usual compensation for the assault, the request was refused, with resultant loss of 'face' for Triad.

Fighting soon spread to Setapak, Chow Kit Road, and Pudu, involving Wa Kei and Triad and their supporting gangs, besides the employees of three Chinese bus companies. A Triad–Wa Kei fight at Setapak on the night of the 18th was followed by attacks with stones and bottles on buses travelling through Triad areas, drivers and conductors being assaulted. Several arrests were made, but very few of the prisoners were identified by the victims.

On the 20th, at Chow Kit Road, a Wa Kei workman employed by a wealthy local contractor was attacked by six Triad hooligans and seriously hurt. It was rumoured that an all-out fight between Wa Kei and Triad would take place in which reinforcements from Penang, Perak, Pahang, and Negri Sembilan would participate, but stern police warnings to certain Triad leaders in Setapak on the consequences of any further disturbances had a calming effect, although the Triad groups were far from accepting defeat. Almost immediately trouble broke

[4] Civilian organization for providing supplies and information to the MCP guerrillas.

out elsewhere. On 25 December there were serious disturbances in Klang between rival Triad gangs, and on the 27th a Detective Sub-Inspector was shot dead in Seremban as a result of Wa Kei–Triad rivalry concerning the local Chee Fah lottery. In renewed disturbances in Klang in mid-January (1953) Malay and Indian hooligan elements were brought from Port Swettenham, and further reinforcements from Chow Kit Road, Kuala Lumpur, were reported to be standing by.

Meantime, the Chee Fah lottery in Kuala Lumpur continued in full operation. Chee Fah is a game of thirty-six characters or numbers from which the promoter selects one, and writes it on a piece of paper which traditionally should be sealed in a box hung up in public at the headquarters of the lottery, in full view, so that no tampering can take place. Printed riddles or rhymes purporting to contain clues to the winning number are issued. Punters study the riddles and place their bets with collectors. Sometimes 'late wires' or verbal tips are given to favoured patrons of the game to encourage last-minute stakes. The odds paid to those who hit the winner are 30 to 1, and if the lottery is properly conducted it is a reasonable gamble. But in Kuala Lumpur in 1952 and 1953 it was not to be expected that the promoter would defy the law by hanging up the winning number in public and thus inviting the attention of the police. The promoters took full advantage of this circumstance by waiting until the betting slips had all been collected, then declaring the least-backed number as the winner. That this procedure was possible or even probable was no deterrent, for members of the public, habituated to similar gaming syndicates during the Japanese Occupation, were only too willing to participate, and the popularity of the lottery was spectacular.

Originally, three syndicates operated Chee Fah lotteries in Kuala Lumpur and suburbs, but after the two smaller ones at Salak South and Batu Road closed, the big syndicate functioned unrivalled at Pudu. Its huge success was largely due to the organization for the collection of bets. An army of collectors and their runners covered every section of the town and the near-by villages, and agents included the smallest roadside coffee-stall, petty tradesmen, and big gamblers who were frequently themselves bookmakers. In the Chee Fah organization itself the syndicate was the Big Bank, other smaller syndicates or operators running sub-banks, and usually 'laying off' part of their collections with the Big Bank in order to avoid a possible loss which they could not sustain.

Bets varied from a few cents to hundreds of dollars, although the majority were under $2, but the betting was so widespread that the Big Bank had a daily intake of some $60,000, sub-banks collected anything from $2,000 to $6,000 daily, while small operators in the villages gathered in $200 to $300. Collectors received ten per cent of all bets, and it was customary for winners to give them $2 on every $30 win. Only a fraction of the money collected was ever required to cover the payment of winners, and the business prospered exceedingly.

Women everywhere were strong supporters, and went to fantastic lengths, dreaming, praying, divining, in their efforts to find the winning character. Much of their housekeeping money was squandered, and small shopkeepers complained that business suffered. Even the rubber tappers whose wages had been reduced in the economic recession of 1952 bought tickets in the hope of winning the Chee Fah jackpot.

In September 1952 some action was taken by the police against runners and collectors found in possession of Chee Fah tickets and lists, but to little effect, for the offenders paid their fines of $2,000 or $3,000 without difficulty. The talk of the town was that the big 'bookies' and operators were safe because they had placed their bribes in the right places, but the problem was not quite so simple. The law against public gambling was very difficult to enforce against promoters unless they openly conducted a Common Gaming House to which the public was admitted, and the promoters of the Chee Fah lottery (which could claim to be as much a game of skill as the Football Pools in England) found little difficulty in avoiding incriminating evidence.

There was a further stumbling-block. The MCA, formed in February 1949 to help in the anti-Communist campaign, had been permitted to promote lotteries, the proceeds of which were used to some extent for helping to settle Chinese squatters who were uprooted by the Government and resettled in 'New Villages'. Though ostensibly confined to members of the Association, these lotteries were in fact accessible to all, and were just as much public lotteries as was the Chee Fah. (It was not until June 1953, with the prospect of popular elections ahead, that a ban was placed on the promotion of lotteries by political parties, and the MCA lotteries ceased.)

Late in 1952 the press gave publicity to the widespread nature of the Chee Fah lottery, and announced that because of this publicity the headquarters had moved to a more secluded place. The *Sunday Times* of 28 December and 4 January 1953 carried banner headlines referring to 'Chee Fah, the Great Rhyme Swindle', and told of the 'Crooked Empire of Mr X, the Kingpin of this Colossal Swindle', who, it was said, was more closely guarded than the High Commissioner. According to the press, 'slippery Mr X' had only one worry, the fear of being deported.

The Chee Fah 'King' was indeed well known to the police, but the case against him was difficult to substantiate, and the $10,000 which his liason officer was reputed to distribute monthly in bribes made concrete evidence the harder to find, and so in the markets, the coffee-shops, the buses, and the villages, the chief topic of conversation remained Chee Fah. For a few weeks after the press publicity, the Chee Fah 'King' appears to have handed over the running of the lottery to certain of his underlings, and some sort of compromise between the Triad and Wa Kei gangs was arranged whereby Triad 'protected' the operators in the outskirts of the capital, and Wa Kei 'protected' within Kuala Lumpur town itself. In the meantime, Triad sought allies.

The Government feared that radical repressive action against the societies would weaken the only elements based on the Chinese masses which were resisting the Communist threat. This applied particularly to the Wa Kei, whose uncompromising opposition repelled Communist infiltration in various areas throughout the Federation. Triad groups had also helped to prevent Communist infiltration, particularly on the Perak coast. The situation was complicated by the knowledge that many police detectives were linked with Wa Kei or Triad societies, and that owing to essential concentration upon Emergency problems little information was available in official archives concerning secret society personnel, organization, or activity. Nevertheless, no Government could view with equanimity a possible recrudescence of secret society power such as had swept through Malaya during the period between the Japanese Occupation and the outbreak of the Communist revolt, nor could a continuation of the current gang fights in urban areas, widespread corruption, or the illegal promotion of public lotteries be tolerated. It was clearly necessary that secret societies should be brought under some measure of control, and their criminal activities ended.

Early in January 1953 the Government established a central Secret Societies Suppression Branch of the Federal CID Headquarters, at Kuala Lumpur, to concentrate upon collecting information as to the size of the problem, the extent to which secret society influence had spread, and the political sympathies of the various groups. All police contingents were asked to report to Federal Headquarters on the secret society position in their areas, instructions were issued for the collection and codification of information concerning their personnel, and a Central Registry was opened. Wherever staff was available, individual state Secret Societies Suppression Branches were also formed, but agents from Federal Headquarters worked in the various states bringing in information independently in addition to that supplied by local contingents. Thus at last, four and a half years after the previous attempt to set up a centralized Secret Societies Branch, it was possible to continue the work that had been interrupted by the Emergency in June 1948.

The collection of information was essential, but with the discovery late in January 1953 that certain members of the Chi Kung Tong and the Selangor Triad group at Setapak were in communication with the MCP, and that the terrorists were planning to make a special attempt to win over the local Triads, came the realization that, in Selangor at least, Triad societies were not only a criminal problem but also a potential security risk, and active measures became imperative.

On the instructions of the High Commissioner[5] the matter was discussed early in March by a small committee which in addition to police representatives included the Director of Operations and the Secretary for Chinese Affairs. It was decided that action should be initiated in Kuala Lumpur, and that in the first instance, in order not to disrupt sources of information, arrests should be selective, and should be confined to those secret society members known to be engaged in criminal activities, until a more detailed knowledge of the structure and personalities of the societies was obtained. It was also decided that where possible liaison committees should be set up in the various states under the chairmanship of the local Secretary for Chinese Affairs and including representatives of the CID and of the Special Branch of the police. These committees were to meet monthly, and were to pool their information.

Within a matter of days the police made their first strike. Receiving information that about 60 Triad recruits were to be initiated at Setapak on the night of 19–20 March they raided the ceremony, which, after two changes of location, was being held in a banana grove. With the co-operation of an Army Searchlight Unit, they succeeded in arresting 30 men who were either fleeing from the scene or were discovered hiding in houses in the vicinity, although many others escaped; 25 of those arrested were Hokkiens.

Investigations revealed that although a few initiates lived in Selangor, the majority had been brought from as far afield as Batu Pahat (Johore) and Kuala Kurau (Perak), a particularly large group coming from Bahau and Kuala Pilah (Negri Sembilan), where Triad was known to be expanding. From articles found

---

[5] Sir Gerald Templer, appointed in January 1952. Sir Henry Gurney was assassinated by Communist guerrillas in October 1951.

on the site the ceremony had clearly been a full-scale Triad initiation, obviously intended to admit into the Hung Brotherhood new members of Triad societies widely distributed throughout the Federation.

All those arrested were remanded in custody, and the case was heard in court on 23 April. During the investigation the Secret Societies Suppression Branch acquired a very considerable amount of information concerning organization and leadership, and although large funds were swiftly collected by Triad leaders to pay the fees of counsel who were briefed for the defence of 11 of the defendants, 15 of those arrested were convicted of attending a Triad meeting and each sentenced to 2 years' imprisonment. On appeal two of these sentences were reduced to 18 and 15 months respectively. Three others arrested were acquitted, and twelve cases were withdrawn.

These court proceedings aroused widespread interest. Several letters were sent to Post Box 5,000, one of them alleging that while the police were raiding the initiation ceremony, other Triad members were holding a meeting near-by with MCP representatives. Another letter written after sentences had been pronounced regretted that only 'small fry' had been arrested, and that the leaders (some of whom were named) had escaped. This letter, too, alleged that the Triad group at Setapak was in league with the MCP and was operating as part of the Min Yuen in that area. During April several members of the public brought to the police copies of the MCP 'Announcement', which they had received through the post.

Early in May the police had sufficient information to take further action, and application was made to the Government for the issue of twenty-three warrants of arrest and detention under the Banishment Ordinance in respect of Triad leaders in Kuala Lumpur. These were issued on 28 May, and 22 arrests made including once more the blind leader of Setapak, Tan Hong Piew, and all those of his group who had been in contact with the MCP. They also included all members of the Triad central committee, leaders of all cells, three leaders of the Twenty-one Brothers gang, and three prominent members of the Pahang Road cell whose 'protection' activities had been particularly oppressive. After enquiry, eleven of those arrested were banished to China, nine were sentenced to restricted residence (two for life, four for ten years, and three for five years), and two were released. Tan Hong Piew, treated as a special case, was among those whose residence was restricted for ten years. It was considered that although he was influential in Triad circles in Setapak, banishment was too harsh a sentence in view of his blindness and family circumstances. Instead it was decided to exclude him from the districts of Kuala Selangor, Kuala Langat, Klang, and Kuala Lumpur; this was expected to curb any future activities on his part.

The arrests of the twenty-two Triad leaders in Kuala Lumpur gave the Secret Societies Suppression Branch additional information on Triad organization in Klang and Port Swettenham. In July a drive was instituted in Klang after the 'protection' activities of members of Cell 21 had led directly to the murder of the manager of a Tiechiu Wayang which was appearing at the Great World Amusement Park. Aware that it would be necessary for him to purchase 'protection' the unfortunate man had arranged to provide an older leading member of Cell 21 with ten complimentary tickets for each show, but younger members of the gang who had not, apparently, profited from this transaction entered the Wayang and refused to pay. This caused a disturbance in which a Chinese police constable was assaulted, and the gang later decided to avenge themselves upon the manager for loss of 'face'. Two Tamils and a Malay were hired to assault the victim, who was so badly beaten that he died in hospital without recovering consciousness.

In an attempt to break Triad power in Klang the police arrested several members of Cells 4, 12, and 21, and the drive continued to Port Swettenham where further members of these cells were arrested. Of all these, twelve were banished, and most of the others were put on restricted residence for periods of from one to fifteen years. Two of those arrested were required to enter into bonds with sureties of $1,000 for one year.

Meantime, once the way was cleared by the cessation of the MCA lottery, the police in Kuala Lumpur turned their attention to the promoters of the Chee Fah lottery. In June (1953) they arrested the five principal members including the Chee Fah 'King', his two brothers, a cousin, and a fifth who was unrelated but who held high Wa Kei rank at Hot Springs, Setapak, and was heavily involved in several gambling promotions in Kuala Lumpur town. The cousin, who already had three previous convictions for opium offences, was banished to China, and the others were restricted for life to residence in Kuala Kubu, forty miles from Kuala Lumpur, although these sentences were modified in 1955 to exclusion from Selangor. Many of the smaller Chee Fah operators fled. Others volunteered information which enabled the police to form a clear picture of the multitudinous ramifications of the lottery, the use of cover organizations, club gambling, and corruption. During the investigations one police officer was offered $3,000 monthly if he would turn a blind eye, and it was suggested to another senior police officer that if the lottery were permitted to continue for a further four months, during which time the promoters hoped to make a final $100,000 profit, he would benefit to the extent of $30,000 or $40,000. The offer was accompanied by a promise that at the end of the four months the promoters would finally 'retire', but the offers were refused.

The arrests of the Chee Fah syndicate caused grave anxiety in Wa Kei ranks, particularly among those who were also promoting Fan Tan and Pai Kow gambling.[6] An early raid in Pudu in June caused a notorious Fan Tan centre to close, and its promoter, a high-ranking Wa Kei official who had been distributing heavy bribes to the local police, went into hiding. He was arrested early in 1954 and put under restricted residence. Another Wa Kei associate of similar rank, who had been operating Pai Kow gambling in Pudu under cover of a club in the area, and who was a leader of the Thirteen Princes who had terrorized the district during the operation of the Chee Fah lottery, also fled. He eventually returned to Kuala Lumpur and opened an opium saloon, but was arrested and in December was excluded from the district for ten years. These two arrests, with several others of lesser importance, checked for a time the Fan Tan and Pai Kow gambling activities in the Pudu area.

In a different category was the arrest in early November (1953) of the self-styled Wa Kei 'King', Cheah Siew, alias Kor Hor Chut, already noticed as being connected with the postwar revival of the Wa Kei in Selangor, Pahang, and Johore, and whose energy and personality had enabled him to play an important role in Selangor Wa Kei organization from time to time. He maintained that the

---

[6] Fan Tan: stakes laid on the number of counters left (1, 2, 3, or 0) after counting out from a random pile four at a time. Pai Kau: gambling game with dominoes and dice.

Wa Kei Society sided with the Government against Communism, pointing to the success of those Home Guards which were largely Wa Kei as compared with other Home Guards. He emphasized that if the Wa Kei organization were disrupted in such areas, the resulting vacuum would be filled by the Communists. This factor had already determined the official policy of selective action against individuals of the Wa Kei society responsible for criminal activities rather than against those responsible for the organization of the society, a policy which remained as a general guide, but, as the police were to discover, it was difficult to apply this selective treatment without disrupting the fabric when it was known that the organization as a whole was invariably supported by the 'protection' of gaming, brothels, opium saloons, and other similar activities. Cheah Siew was excluded from Selangor for fifteen years, and went to Malacca, and in February 1954 the head of the society in Kuala Lumpur, who had held office since 1949, was taken into custody and was excluded from Selangor.

From May 1953 onwards action was taken against clubs which were known to be cover associations for either Wa Kei or Triad activities. By the end of the year six clubs had been closed down in Kuala Lumpur. All were used as gambling resorts, and included the Seng Kong Athletic Association, where both Triad and left-wing Chi Kung Tong activities were taking place, and four clubs which were found to be covers for Wa Kei. The power to dissolve undesirable societies was widely used. At the end of 1953 it was reported that throughout the Federation since the Societies Ordinance had come into force in 1949, 188 societies had been closed. Of these, twenty-three were closed because they were used by secret society members, while many of the remainder were used as professional gambling dens. Strong police action continued throughout 1954 and early 1955, and during that period seven Kuala Lumpur clubs were closed for illegal gambling activities.

These various measures had the effect of establishing for a time a reasonable degree of public peace, and certain Chi Kung Tong arrests removed the danger of Triad–MCP co-operation from the political arena. But in the criminal field the respite was brief. In March 1955 Chee Fah revived in Kuala Lumpur, operated by remnants of the 1953 organization who had escaped arrest and backed by the Chee Fah 'King', who had been allowed to leave Kuala Kubu on condition that he did not return to Selangor, but who had gone to near-by Seremban in Negri Sembilan, whence he hoped to operate the lottery by telephone. Although he abandoned this scheme and departed to Singapore, and although an important Wa Kei Chee Fah promoter who had eluded the police in 1953 was arrested in Kuala Lumpur in June 1955, Chee Fah continued in the capital, and by July had spread to Klang and Port Swettenham.

Its revival brought new life to the Triad and Wa Kei gangs, for although the main Triad leadership had been dispersed and the Wa Kei organization dislocated, the gangs quickly re-formed. The Kwan Luen had received an access of strength in 1953 when Ang Bin Hoey members, left leaderless because of the police arrests, had joined forces with them. The Twenty-one Brothers also revived, and a new gang, the Yee Woh See (Righteous Accord Society), organized in January 1955, with a membership of fifty or sixty youths, became affiliated, operating in Pudu and Loke Yew Road areas of Kuala Lumpur. Three Wa Kei gangs appeared, including not only the Thirteen Princes and the Ten Tigers of Kwangtung (Kong Tung Sap Fu), the latter established in 1952 in the Madras

Theatre area, but the Eighteen Disciples (Sap Pat Loh Han), a group of youths who became active in Pudu.

Once more the police were faced with the task of breaking up these gangs. Arrests and banishments of the leaders of the Twenty-one Brothers and the Thirteen Princes reduced the incidence of gang fights and in time the Chee Fah, the Fan Tan, and the Pai Kow gambling was again checked. Thus, although the 1955 scene in Selangor showed the resilience of the secret societies, which after two years of concentrated police action were still prepared to re-enter the arena, nevertheless, the Secret Societies Suppression Branch of the CID, with its sources of information and the capacity to use such information effectively, was a deterrent which had not previously existed, and afforded some hope that the societies would eventually be brought under effective control.

3. PENANG

Throughout the Federation there was an upsurge of secret society criminal activity in 1953–5, while a political threat was also in evidence in certain States.

In Penang, on the outbreak of the Emergency in 1948, the police arrested fifteen Ang Bin Hoey leaders, including some who were known to be attempting to swing their fellow members into the Communist camp, but this action did not eradicate Triad activity. The twenty-two Ang Bin Hoey cells remained, and although most of them were inactive, gangster elements, despite the removal of many of their leaders, were still on the look-out for means of continuing to earn the easy money to which they had become accustomed. As already noted, during the second half of 1948 they formed a succession of gangs, all of which, with the exception of the New Ang Bin Hoey, were broken up by the police.[7]

In the absence of any central organization of the societies this process of fragmentation continued, and in March 1949 there were signs that attempts were being made to resuscitate certain prewar societies, including the Sin Ghee Hin, the Sin Tai Kwan, the Ke Iau San, and the Sin Khien Khoon, all of which in 1945 had merged with the Ang Bin Hoey. These societies began to re-form as individual groups, the Sin Ghee Hin from Cell 18, the Sin Tai Kwan from members of Cell 1, the Ke Iau San from Cell 12, and the Sin Khien Khoon from Cells 12 and 20. Timely information enabled the police to take action, and this development was checked in its early stages.

For a time Triad groups contented themselves with running illegal gambling under the cover of clubs. By the end of 1949 Cell 20 had organized a gambling centre at Tanjong Bungah, frequented by Ang Bin Hoey members, but this was quickly raided. In January 1950 five former leaders of the Ang Bin Hoey in Balik Pulau were warned by the police for their gaming activities, and in February 1950 Cells 4, 12, 20, and 21 were reported to be concentrating on gambling. Other Triad members who found Penang no longer sufficiently rewarding moved across to Kuala Kurau in North Perak, where they engaged in gambling, extortion, and piracy, although no longer on the scale of the hey-day of the Ang Bin Hoey. Between January and June 1950 four piracies were reported off the coast between Krian and Pulau Rimau, but the cargoes, all rubber, were small, their total value being only $16,000.

During March 1950, in an attempt to form an organization free from the

7 See above p. 354.

domination of the old cell leaders, who were well known to the police, and were therefore a liability, certain young members of Cells 2, 19, and 21 tried to form a new society in the Jelutong area, which adopted the name New Ang Bin Hoey, later changed to Tok Lip Tong (Specially-formed Society). This group disintegrated on the arrest of their principal leader, previously a member of Cell 19 of the Ang Bin Hoey, and the members dispersed.

By 1951 continued police action had seriously weakened the entire framework of the Ang Bin Hoey, and with this weakening, Triad's old enemy, the Communist Party, came into prominence. Underworld gangsters who had hitherto used fear of the Ang Bin Hoey as their principal weapon switched to using the name of the MCP for extortion purposes. This brought the vengeance of that party upon their heads. In the first three months of 1951 four Ang Bin Hoey members were shot dead by the MCP and two more were wounded. Even when certain members of Cell 20 came to an understanding with Communist elements in Jelutong, relationships were characterized by fights, kidnappings, and Communist courts of enquiry. Later in 1951 assassinations began again, with an ever-increasing Triad death roll which continued to rise throughout 1952, and in 1953 all semblance of Triad–MCP co-operation, of which there had been some evidence in the rural areas, disappeared. In the town gangs of Triad derivation resumed their normal operations, reinforced by supporters from Singapore and by refugees from the police action in Kuala Lumpur.

The resulting picture was very different from that of 1945–6. The majority of the Ang Bin Hoey cells remained inactive, and cell leaders known to the police kept discreetly in the background. No central committee existed and no initiation ceremonies were held, perhaps because pressure by the police had already removed so many sinsehs in Penang. Instead, elements of certain cells began to operate as criminal gangs apparently independent of all Triad control, adopting tattooed insignia in lieu of initiation, but choosing titles which were distinctly reminiscent of Triad.

Perhaps the most important was the '108' (or '08') reputedly formed by Triad members in March 1953 as an offshoot of the '108' in Singapore and closely linked with '108' members in Kuala Lumpur. The membership rapidly grew and it was supported by the Skeleton Gang (Kut Thow Tong), another derivative of the Ang Bin Hoey organized at this time, whose leaders belonged to Cells 4, 18, and 20, and which drew its membership from among trishaw riders, pickpockets, and hooligans. It 'protected' prostitutes, opium-den keepers, and hawkers. The insignia of the '108' was a tattooed tiger's head, and the Skeleton Gang's mark of identity was a tattooed skull and cross-bones. Simultaneously the Red Flower Society (Ang Hua T'ong), recalling the Red Flower Pavilion of the Triad initiation ceremony, made its appearance, said to be a branch of the '48 Dots' Society in Kuala Lumpur, in turn recalling the 48 drops of water on the tomb of the 'Myriad Cloud Dragon', three for each of sixteen Chinese characters.[8] Its founder, the treasurer of the Penang branch of the '48 Dots' Society, was a white Fan of Cell 4 of the Ang Bin Hoey, and the majority of the Red Flower Society were Triad members, this particular group including pickpockets, petty-thieves, and black-marketeers of cinema tickets.

In July 1953 the Eight Immortals was organized from among former members of the Ngai Loke Athletic Association (the Kwun T'au club closed down in 1950),

[8] See App. 1, pp. 527, 529.

some of whose members had joined the Kinta Valley Home Guard in 1952. It was active in George Town, particularly in gang fights, as was the Axe Gang (organized by a fireman in the local Fire Brigade), members of which were tattooed with an axe-head on the left arm. The organizer was a member of Cell 1 of the Ang Bin Hoey, two of his section leaders were 'Tiger' Generals of Cell 20, and most of the gang were Triad members. 'Protection' was given to keepers of opium dens, hawkers, and street stall-holders, and there was a gang of fighters who could be hired to commit assaults. Two other gangs which appeared before the end of 1953 were the Gang of Gods and the Praying Party, but neither appears to have survived. The Praying Party battened upon gamblers in the 100 Characters and 1,000 Characters lotteries, falling into trances, prophesying winning numbers, and extorting from the winners when the prophecy fortuitously proved correct.

There is no doubt that the police drive in Selangor during the early months of 1953 caused a number of suspects to run to Penang, and helped to foster the formation of these new gangs. Persons believed to be leaders were called up and warned by the police, and some of the groups dissolved quietly, but others, particularly the Skeleton Gang, continued to give trouble. The Wa Kei, which had first intruded on the Penang scene in 1950, also began to make its presence felt, recruiting its members from the Cantonese community, and in April 1954 rivalry between members of the Skeleton and the '108' gangs on the one hand, and Wa Kei members on the other, led to violence.

In January and February 1955 the Wa Kei–'108' feud broke out again, curbed for a time by the arrests of four '108' members who were given sentences of six months' imprisonment. Meantime, six new gangs appeared, formed by members of the Ang Bin Hoey, and all six with names of Triad significance. They were the Two Swords and Seven Stars, the Octagon Gang, the Golden Eagle, the '308', the Faithful Hearts, and the Righteous Dragon and Tiger.

The Two Swords and Seven Stars, an extortion gang seventy strong, operated in Batu Gantong, Kampong Bahru, and Thean Teik Estate, and was organized by a member of Cell 20 who was later arrested under the Restricted Residence Ordinance. Its emblem was two crossed swords set in a circle of seven stars. The Octagon Gang, formed by a notorious Straw Sandals of Cell 4, who also had connexions with the Communists in Penang, organized piracy at Batu Maung and also operated in George Town along Bridge Street. Its members were labourers and sampan rowers, about 200 strong, and the gang was powerful and much feared. The Golden Eagle, a 'protection' gang formed in Jelutong by a member of Cell 4, co-operated with the '308', which was interested in small-scale gaming at Perak Road market and other town areas. The Faithful Hearts, said to be an offspring of the '48 Dots', formed originally by an organizer from Singapore, had between 20 and 30 members, all between the ages of 17 and 25. They attempted to control the black market in cinema tickets, and also hired themselves out for assault. The Righteous Dragon and Tiger Gang was a vicious group of pickpockets, thieves, and robbers, the majority with several convictions, who earned the reputation of being the best fighters in Penang.

The newcomers were unwelcome interlopers in the gangster world, and in June the older-established gangs, the '108', the Skeleton, and the Eight Immortals formed themselves into the Three United (Sam Hup T'ong), with the dual purpose of strengthening their opposition to the Wa Kei and maintaining their own supremacy. Four of the new gangs banded themselves together in opposition. The Wa Kei, meantime, retained its isolation from all other gangs.

Despite preventive police patrols over a period of several weeks, a serious fight took place on the night of 30 July between the Three United and the Faithful Hearts, and thereafter these two alliances, having apparently been formed for the purpose of this challenge, dissolved. It was not until early December that the '108' renewed its attack on the Wa Kei, and on that occasion the police, forewarned, arrested seven of its members, two of whom were found to be in possession of electric light bulbs filled with hydrochloric acid.

By the end of 1955, the Ang Bin Hoey cells, with the possible exception of Cell 20, had receded into the background. In general, 'ritualistic Triad' was moribund and hooligan gangs occupied the Penang stage. But the year ended with information that in Province Wellesley one Triad initiation ceremony had been held in October and another in December, both for initiates to the '108'. This society, formed in the Province in mid-1955, was not related organizationally to the '108' of Penang. It was sponsored for the most part, by older men, all Hokkiens, and took the place formerly held by the Ang Bin Hoey, which was known to exist as late as the end of 1953 in Butterworth, Bukit Mertajam, and Nibong Tebal. The society spread rapidly, developed nine cells, and gained the support of some Chinese members of the Federation Regiment stationed at Butterworth, who were used by the society as 'fighters'. The initiation ceremony held on 9–10 December at a small hamlet, Kampong Sungei Puyu, PW was missed by the police, who arrived on the scene an hour too late, but it indicated that ritualistic Triad in a rural area like the Province was still able to survive, although in Butterworth itself the gangster scene was similar to that of George Town on Penang Island.

Police action against secret societies in Penang during the first five years of the Emergency had been concentrated upon preventing any Triad–Communist co-operation in the rural areas, particularly in the Balik Pulau district, and in controlling the emerging criminal gangs in Penang town, but the advent of Triad fugitives from Selangor in 1953 caused more stringent action to be taken. In August 1953 the first meeting of the Secret Societies Liaison Committee between the Secretary for Chinese Affairs and representatives of the Special Branch and the CID of the police was held, and in April 1954, as a result of the Triad–Wa Kei rivalry, a small Secret Societies Suppression Branch was also set up. From January 1955, when secret society suppression was decentralized from the Federal capital to police contingents, the local police had greater scope to initiate action, and besides the usual arrests for rioting or extortion, the practice of calling up suspects for interrogation, warning, and on occasion photographing and fingerprinting, was adopted on a large scale.

Three leaders of the Skeleton Gang were arrested in December 1954 and one was later banished, the other two being placed on Restricted Residence. Action was also taken against two leaders of the '48 Dots' and one of the Two Swords and Seven Stars. In September 1955 the first court conviction was obtained for membership of an unlawful society on the evidence provided by tattoo marks. A member of the '108', tattooed with a tiger's head on the shoulder, was sentenced to four months' rigorous imprisonment and a fine of $100. In December a member of the '360' group of Singapore, arrested in Penang and known to be a member of the '108' in Singapore and of the Twenty-one Brothers in Kuala

Lumpur, was sentenced to one year's imprisonment and a fine of $100. He was tattooed on the arm with a dragon and a sword.

4. KEDAH

As in 1945–6 society activities in Penang and Province Wellesley had strong repercussions in the adjacent States of Kedah and Perak. With the outbreak of the Emergency in 1948, most of the known Triad Leaders in Kedah were arrested and repatriated to China, and the Ang Bin Hoey cells became dormant until mid-1952. In mid-1953 two gangs appeared in Alor Star, one, the '303', formed by an Ang Bin Hoey member of 'Straw Sandals' rank, the other, the '48 Dots', connected with the Penang Triad gang of the same name. So-called 'charitable' fun-fairs provided an opportunity for secret society men from Penang and Taiping to operate gaming stalls and to make local Triad contacts, but when gambling developed to such an extent that many Malays lost the profits of their padi harvest, the authorities stepped in to ban the fairs. Subsequent action in Penang and Kedah against leaders of the '48 Dots', and in Alor Star against the local leader of the '303', brought these gangs under some control, but at the beginning of 1955 the '08', a splinter of the Penang Ang Bin Hoey, was formed in Sungei Patani, and at the end of the year there was still considerable activity by Triad members in the areas of Alor Star, Gurun, and Kulim.

Far more troublesome than the Chinese societies in Kedah at the time were the Malay secret societies, in particular the Bintang Lima (Five Stars) and the Kain Merah (Red Cloth). The Bintang Lima, originally formed in 1938, had begun as a political party and degenerated into a criminal organization. It operated along the Kedah–Perlis border, and its members were from time to time involved in murder, robbery, and extortion. After a revival in 1945–6, police action caused it to disintegrate, but in 1952 its influence was again felt along the coastal strip north and south of Alor Star. Its favourite technique was to steal water-buffaloes from Malay padi-growers and hold them to ransom. In 1955 part of the society moved south to Padang Serai, east of the Province Wellesley border, and there formed the Kain Merah Society. Members wore a red kerchief on their heads or painted the mudguards of their bicycles red.

In May 1955 four leaders of the Bintang Lima were arrested, and two of them were later put on restricted residence, but both Malay societies were still active at the end of the year.

5. PERAK

Despite the severe police action taken during 1948 and 1949, Triad survived in Perak, particularly in the coastal areas, always difficult to control and almost inaccessible to the police. In the swamps around Trong, Loh Cheang Yeow, the Leper's successor, continued his elusive life with a small bodyguard, and until 1955 evaded all attempts to flush him from his lairs. In Kuala Kurau the inevitable smuggling and gambling continued, although on a more restricted scale, and in Taiping some of the old Triad groups began to re-form. Elsewhere, however, the severity of the Communist attacks, the continuance of the revolt, and fear of the powers exercised by the authorities under the Emergency Regulations acted as deterrents to any overt Triad activity, and the societies kept very quiet.

Later in 1951 the old sinseh, Tua P'ui Ka, reappeared in Taiping from his refuge in Telok Anson, and as a result during 1952 a Triad revival gradually gathered momentum in the Taiping and coastal areas. The Sin Ghee, though still in existence, remained inactive, as did the Aik Ho, but the Ghee Hup revived, followed by the notorious Aik Peng, which in 1953 held three initiation ceremonies. On the coast, where the Ghee Peng Ho at Port Weld and the Hup Ho at Matang remained dormant, the Aik Hin at Pasir Hitam and Trong revived activity, with Loh Cheang Yeow in close contact. Further south, three initiation ceremonies were held at Pantai Remis and another at Lumut, while on 2 September at both Port Weld and Trong feasts were held in celebration of the Triad Ancestral Day (the 25th day of the 7th Moon) with over 100 members at each. Only the initiated understood that these feasts, held ostensibly in honour of the 'Ten Spirits', referred to the spirits of the Five Former and the Five Later Ancestors of the Triad Brotherhood. At a similar celebration in the following year at the See Hai club at Pasir Hitam, 200 members attended.

Although Hokkien Triad groups dominated the coast from North Perak to Telok Anson, as they had done in 1946–7, inland from Taiping, at Kuala Kangsar, Ipoh, Kampar, and Tapah, there were reports in mid-1953 that Cantonese and Hakka societies were recruiting new members. In emulation of the Triad gangs in Penang and Kuala Lumpur, the Eight Immortals (Pat Sin T'ong) appeared in Ipoh, and the New Military (San Kwan) in Kampar, the latter about 100 strong, including some former members of the Kinta Home Guard.

The Wa Kei societies also made their presence felt, particularly in Kampar and in that area of Kinta lying between Ipoh and Tronoh, the traditional home of the society. Despite a setback late in 1949 when most of their cover-clubs were refused registration under the new Societies Ordinance and were obliged to close down, the Wa Kei groups enlarged their membership and zones of operation. By 1953 there were over 6,000 members in Perak. As usual, the majority were Cantonese, and were numerous among the detectives, the special constables, and the Home Guards.

A new area of developing Wa Kei activity was Taiping, where in 1951 a group calling itself the Eighteen Disciples was formed under cover of a Musical and Dramatic Association which operated also as a Mutual Aid Society. This group was not a gang of young hooligans but a body of middle-aged men, some of whom had businesses in the town. Its members not only provided a gambling nucleus, but were the vital centre of Wa Kei influence in Taiping, strongly opposing the Triad societies. The possibilty of secret societies taking an interest in the future political life of Perak was illustrated during the campaign for the first election of Town Councillors at Taiping in August 1954, when the unsuccessful candidates included one member of the Eighteen Disciples and one known Triad member.

By mid-1953, police action to stem the rising ride of activity in Perak became imperative, but as the first essential was to obtain information concerning the individual leaders primarily involved, arrests, as in Selangor, were on a strictly limited and selective basis, confined in the first instance to the Triad groups who posed the main threat. In September the sinseh, Tua P'ui Ka, was arrested.

Because of his age and his long residence in Malaya he was not banished to China but was confined to Kampar under the Restricted Residence Ordinance. His enforced absence from Taiping, and the arrest of three representatives who had conferred with Cell 4 in Penang concerning the formation of a Special Service Squad which was to take action against the informers and detectives who were assisting the police in the offensive against the societies, checked the activities of the Aik Peng. In the Kinta district the expulsion of secret society members from the Kinta Valley Home Guard, the break-up of the New Military gang in Kampar, and the arrest and banishment of the leader of the Eight Immortals in Ipoh, at least decreased the confidence of the Triad groups, although the Ipoh gang soon revived under new leaders and a new name, the Twenty-one Brothers.

During 1954 police action continued in the Taiping area. Early in the year the Ghee Hup leader at Simpang was arrested and restricted to Ipoh, and in May another prominent leader of the Aik Peng was arrested and restricted to Kampar. On the coast the arrest of a sinseh and his banishment to China deprived the Yen Hai groups of their chief ritual expert, but it was not until March 1955 that the real menace of the coast, Loh Cheang Yeow, was run to earth. This operation entailed a house to house search in Bagan Kuala Larut, a village on stilts in mangrove-covered mud swamps, during which Loh Cheang Yeow, after killing a detective with a Sten gun, escaped to the swamp where he was eventually cornered and killed.

For the first time for many years the inhabitants of the Trong estuary and the adjacent coast ceased to pay tribute to an overlord. But while Loh Cheang Yeow was alive he ruled the coast, and in the settlement of disputes his word was law. After his death old feuds and quarrels emerged, in particular, a dispute about the ownership of cockle beds north of Port Weld which before 1939 were natural breeding grounds for cockles, worked mainly by Port Weld Tiechius. Thereafter, for some years, no cockles appeared, and a mainly Hokkien syndicate (of the surname Ong) then reintroduced cockle seed and applied for a Temporary Occupation Licence. Meanwhile the Port Weld cockle-pickers raided the beds and formed a society (in October and November 1955) which they called Ang Bin T'ong (Society of the Ang—or Hung—People), to oust the Hokkien syndicate and to assist their own members who had been arrested by the police after the raid. The society spread rapidly down the Perak coast to the Trong estuary uniting all smaller clans against the powerful Ong clan, which seemed to be making a bid to monopolize the coast. In retaliation, the Ong faction formed the Pek Beng (White Clear) Society.

The Ang Bin T'ong soon extended its activities beyond the mere raiding of cockle beds and interference with the traditional smuggling traffic of its rivals, and itself became a menace on the coast, protecting and extorting in the usual Triad manner. Although police action succeeded in preventing any large-scale clash between the two groups, the Ang Bin T'ong continued to flourish, and trouble was never far distant.

6. PAHANG

Although the Wa Kei remained the dominant society in Pahang, Triad and Chung Woh groups also emerged during 1948–55 and were invariably opposed to the Wa Kei. Owing to the demands made upon the police by the Emergency, no serious attempt to assess the position was made until early 1954, when, as part of the campaign against secret society activities throughout the Federation, a Secret Society Liaison Committee for Pahang was set up in Kuala Lipis, and first met in May 1954.

The Wa Kei was still very strong in Bentong town and in some near-by New Villages, and was particularly active in the Home Guard. Kuantan Wa Kei was believed to be organizing opium smuggling, Raub Wa Kei existed as a small offshoot from Bentong, and lorry-drivers on convoy route to Kuala Lumpur were reported to be attempting to organize a Wa Kei branch at Temerloh. A Triad society was known to exist at Bentong, and others were believed to exist at Mentakab, Temerloh, Triang, and Raub. The Chung Woh Tong had become active in Bentong and in Ketari New Village (fifteen miles away), and the Chi Kung Tong was believed to exist in isolated areas.

Enquiries made after the first meeting of the Liaison Committee revealed that the Wa Kei at Bentong had over 300 initiated members and 1,000 contributors to the Benevolent Scheme. A new branch at Kuala Padah had taken the place of Manchis, which had ceased activities at the beginning of the Emergency. The Wa Kei's interest in the New Villages in the Bentong district was also confirmed.

Triad activities and membership in Bentong had also greatly increased during 1953. Intimidation was used to obtain recruits, who were taken to Setapak in Selangor for initiation. During 1954 Triad activity spread to Karak village. Under vigorous leadership membership soon reached 200, and by the end of the year there had been three clashes with the Wa Kei Home Guard members. Triad societies were also found at Pertang and Ketari New Villages, and among timber-cutters from Negri Sembilan who travelled up the railway into the Kuala Krau, Jerantut, and Kuala Lipis areas.

By the end of 1955 Triad membership in the Bentong district was estimated at 300–400, and the Triad groups were in close association with the Chung Woh Tong, most of whose members also belonged to the KMT, and were operating under cover of the Chinese Young Men's Association. There were, however, some Triad members in Bentong and Karak who had joined the left-wing Pan-Malayan Rubber Workers' Union.

The Chung Woh Tong, already known in postwar Malaya in Selangor, Perak, Johore, and Singapore, did not begin to operate in Pahang until 1950, and its appearance at this time was due partly to the situation created in Malaya by the introduction of the Societies Ordinance of September 1949, and partly to the outbreak of the Korean War in mid-1950.

With the introduction of the Societies Ordinance all local KMT branches officially closed down, but sought to use the Chung Woh Tong (which was attempting to operate under cover of social clubs) not only as a 'strong-arm' body, but as a cover for its own continued existence underground. Meantime, the outbreak of the Korean War and the prospect of American aid for Chung Woh Tong guerrillas who might harass the Chinese Communists on the China mainland caused an increase in Chung Woh Tong attempts at recruitment in Hong Kong and Malaya and in their efforts to raise funds ostensibly to finance an 'Anti-Russian–Anti-Communist Army' in China. They hoped thus to demonstrate their worthiness to be counted among the reliable members of the Third

Force working for the introduction of a democratic government in their home-land.

Chung Woh Tong activities in Pahang began at Bentong among Cantonese, Kwongsai, and Hakka youths attending a class for instruction in the Chinese art of self-defence. The group was encouraged by KMT members in Bentong, particularly after the visit of the Malayan Chinese Mission to Formosa late in 1952, which renewed the enthusiasm of supporters of Nationalist China in Malaya. In Bentong a committee was secretly formed which included Chung Woh Tong, KMT, and SMCYYC leaders and several Triad members. Chung Woh Tong initiation ceremonies were held in Bentong and adjacent New Villages, and by March 1953 the society was reported to have between 150 and 200 members, recruitment taking place under cover of the Chinese Young Men's Association. It thus threatened to become a powerful rival of the Wa Kei. Though both were anti-Communist, the Wa Kei was mainly concerned with its own local fortunes whereas the Chung Woh Tong was linked with the KMT and with politics in China, where it hoped to gain prestige through an invasion of the mainland by forces from Formosa. When this was not forthcoming, some of the local enthusiasm evaporated and from the end of 1955 Chung Woh Tong influence in the Bentong area waned, leaving the Wa Kei as the principal influence, with the Triad societies as the main rivals.

In Kuantan attempts to form a Chung Woh Tong branch failed and police interest in the chief organizer caused him to leave Kuantan hastily by plane, and to take refuge ultimately in Kluang, Johore.

7. NEGRI SEMBILAN

Activity in Negri Sembilan during this period was closely connected with Selangor, and was based, particularly in Seremban, upon Triad–Wa Kei rivalry for the control of gambling, which reached a climax in December 1952. Thereafter, a decision taken early in 1953 by the Triad leaders in Selangor to embark upon a widespread recruitment campaign strongly affected Negri Sembilan, especially Kuala Pilah and Bahau, and subsequent police action weakened the Triad groups to the advantage of the Wa Kei.

After an initial period of society inactivity from the outbreak of the Emergency in mid-1948, the Wa Kei was the first to show signs of revival. Affiliated to its Kuala Lumpur headquarters, and still operating in Seremban under cover of the Yan Fung Musical Research Society, its aim as in Kuala Lumpur, was the control of Chee Fah and Chap Ji Ki lotteries. In March 1950 its cover club was re-registered as the Yan Fung Amateur Musical Association and it embarked upon an ambitious project in which 125 of its Wa Kei members formed a syndicate and contributed $100 each to finance large-scale gambling in a house in Seremban town. A protection scheme for the gambling was organized, certain local detectives were persuaded to join the society, and the goodwill of others was financially assured. Nevertheless this highly profitable resort was raided by the police in August 1950, the premises were closed down, and in July 1951 the cover society was dissolved.

After consultation with representatives from Kuala Lumpur, the Wa Kei began to operate underground. A strong drive for membership was made, particularly among fitters and mechanics in the motor trade, and by the end of 1951 its power was once again in the ascendant. Extortion and protection rackets increased, subsidiary headquarters were opened, and large-scale clashes inevitably occurred with the Triad groups which by this time had also emerged in strength.

The banning of the Ang Bin Hoey in May 1947 had prevented its branches from continuing to exist openly, and subsequent attempts by Triad members to operate under cover of Chi Kung Tong branches particularly those of right-wing persuasion, brought upon them the vengeance of Communist terrorists, who early in the Emergency killed several Chi Kung Tong leaders in the Bahau area of Negri Sembilan. Although three Chi Kung Tong initiation ceremonies were held in the Bahau district during 1949, the Communists retained control of this strongly Triad area, and the exhibition of their ruthlessness combined with the fear of police action engendered by the additional powers of arrest conferred under the Emergency Regulations discouraged Triad activity within Negri Sembilan for some time. But in September 1950 an application was made to register the Kiau Yew Benevolent Society (Overseas Friends Benevolent Society), whose headquarters were said to be in Klang (Selangor), and whose organizers in Negri Sembilan (five of whom proved to be members of the Ghee Hin) wished to operate the society from the premises of the Lee Rubber Company's factory in Seremban, whose employees were known to be Triad members almost to a man.

This application was refused in May 1951, but meantime the organizers had already held an initiation ceremony in October 1950 on the Seremban–Labu road, when thirty-five initiates (mostly small shopkeepers from Seremban, Lukut, and Port Dickson) had been admitted, and over the ensuing months had made considerable headway in organizing protection activities. Even after registration of the cover society had been refused the group continued to function, and a further initiation ceremony was held in June 1951, when Hinghwa trishaw riders were brought into the fold.

Meantime, control of gambling remained in the hands of the Wa Kei, and towards the end of 1951 and during 1952 several clashes occurred between the rival societies, but none was decisive. The Triad society penetrated the ranks of the Auxiliary Police volunteers, but although numerically and financially stronger than the Wa Kei, found it necessary to call in aid from other districts when fights occurred. The Wa Kei, on the other hand, set up another cover organization, the Negri Sembilan Chinese Engineering Employees' Union, and in November 1952, following the example of the Wa Kei in Kuala Lumpur which had organized a lottery in June, began to operate a Chee Fah lottery in Seremban.

For two months the lottery flourished, bringing wealth and prestige to the Wa Kei. For this a Detective Sub-Inspector of Police, believed to be a member, was largely responsible, but he had promised protection both to the Wa Kei and to the Ang Bin Hoey, not only to the Chee Fah lottery but also to the Triad-protected gambling stalls in the newly-opened Coronation Amusement Park, and was accepting 'protection money' from both societies. Angered by this duplicity, a 'Tiger' General of the Triad society shot the Sub-Inspector dead in the street on the night of 27 December, though before dying the victim shot and killed his assailant. This double killing, coinciding with the serious rioting in Kuala Lumpur and Klang, and with the scandal of the Chee Fah in Selangor, was an added factor in the Federation Government's decision to take action against the secret societies. In Seremban intensive police action against Triad and Wa Kei groups led to the closing down of the Coronation Amusement Park and to several successful raids on Chee Fah establishments which resulted in convictions in court. With the elimination of these sources of revenue and rivalry peace was temporarily restored, but the societies remained in being, and in March 1953, after the closing of several of its haunts, the Wa Kei took its revenge against an alleged informer by throwing acid in his face.

Meantime, as a result of the contacts made in Selangor between the Chi Kung Tong, the MCP, and certain Ang Bin Hoey leaders at Setapak, and the Triad decision to form an armed striking force (the Hung Kak) with which to oppose the Wa Kei, rural Triad elements in Negri Sembilan (particularly in Kuala Pilah and Bahau) were subjected to pressure from Triad recruiting agents from outside, and at the initiation ceremony held at Setapak on the night of 19–20 March 1953, and successfully raided by the Selangor police, no fewer than 19 would-be initiates from Negri Sembilan were arrested, of whom 11 (5 from Bahau and 6 from Kuala Pilah) were sentenced to 2 years' rigorous imprisonment, and 8 others acquitted. A further 2 were believed to have escaped arrest. This setback did not stop the recruitment, and in October there was a small initiation ceremony at Rasah at which 11 new members were admitted. But thereafter, two Seremban leaders, both sinsehs and both Hakkas, fled to China, and severe police action against Negri Sembilan Triad leaders began. Early in November the 'external affairs' officer in the Seremban Triad group was arrested and was restricted to reside in the north of the state. Other prominent leaders either surrendered or fled, and inevitably the weakening of the Triad groups resulted in an increase of Wa Kei power, while younger and less influential Triad members tended, as elsewhere in the Federation, to form new gangs, freed from the restraint of their elders.

Throughout 1954 the older Triad members remained inactive, but in March–April a certain reorganization took place when a society was formed for the protection of market stall-keepers and hawkers, of whom some 200 were enrolled. Another group, all Hinghwas, the majority of whom were Triad initiates, was organized upon the Triad model under the leadership of a vermicelli-maker and his assistant, an opium smuggler. The Triad groups also had members in the Federation Regiment which was stationed in the state. But except in Seremban, where it was admitted that hooligan members were active, secret societies were said to be dormant. Neither the Triad nor the Wa Kei were holding initiation ceremonies, the mere payment of a subscription being sufficient proof of membership. The main sources of society revenue were opium, prostitutes, and gambling, of which opium was the most important, and towards the end of the year no fewer than fifty opium dens were flourishing in Seremban.

A severe fight in Seremban town on the night of 9 August when fifteen Chinese soldiers of the Federation Regiment supported by about the same number of Chinese civilian members of the Ang Bin Hoey clashed with Wa Kei members removed any complacency concerning the secret society situation. In the fight, belts, steel scrapers, and motor-cycle chains were used, and four Federation Regiment men and five civilians were injured, one of the latter fatally.

A Chinese member of the Federation Regiment who was formerly a special constable until his dismissal in 1952, and who had later joined the Kinta Valley Home Guard for about six months and had eventually enlisted in the Federation Regiment, was arrested and charged with murder. The Hinghwa section of the Ang Bin Hoey collected $1,500 and the rest of the Ang Bin Hoey in Seremban collected a similar sum on behalf of those members who had taken part in the clash, and the leader of the Market and Hawkers' Society, who had been responsible for enlisting the aid of the Federation Regiment, fled to Singapore, where he was at once arrested for possession of Triad documents and sentenced to four months' rigorous imprisonment. After the clash, it was admitted by the police authorities that the Ang Bin Hoey was strong in Seremban, Kuala Pilah, and Bahau, and that the Wa Kei was strong in Seremban, Mantin, Titi, Kuala Pilah, and Durian Tipus. Each society had about 800 members in Seremban. Action was also taken against Wa Kei leaders in Seremban and Kuala Pilah.

The year 1955 was marked by the spread of Triad activities among the Chinese labour forces who worked on the large estates. Chinese New Year provided the Triad leaders in Seremban with the opportunity to organize gambling in several small towns and New Villages in the neighbourhood. On 28 February an initiation ceremony held at Nilai was raided by the police, and eight initiates, four of whom had pricks on the middle finger of their left hand, together with the sinseh, were arrested coming away from the ceremony. The court case failed on the grounds that the police had not actually seen the ceremony in progress, and on the sinseh's assertion that no Triad ceremony would ever be held on the seventh day of a Chinese month. In March a further initiation was held, this time at Bahau, where the initiates were drawn from Kuala Pilah and Bahau, but the sinseh was, once again, from Seremban. On 30 September he initiated four new members from Mantin, allegedly in his own house. In November Tampin New Village, in the south of the State and on the Malacca border, became an important recruiting centre, and recruiters from Malacca, assisted by local Ang Bin Hoey members had soon organized a Triad group of about 100 members.

During the year there were several minor Wa Kei–Triad clashes, and Wa Kei members took to carrying narrow-bladed daggers, sharpened triangular files, and scrapers, concealed in pump cases on their bicycles. During December the frequency of gang fights kept the police on the alert, and on the 31st Triad members attending a funeral procession armed themselves with iron rods and sticks. Wa Kei members near the cemetery did the same, and a very surly crowd dispersed only after the police had fired a shot.

8. MALACCA

In Malacca, the timely strengthening of the secret society section of the CID in August 1947, and its success in discovering the identity of 430 MCP members, including many with Triad affiliations, crippled both Communist and Triad organizations for some years. Very little is known of any secret society activities, except that in mid-1951 five Ang Bin Hoey members left for Bagan Si Api Api (Sumatra), and in Malacca town a group of some fifty hooligans (remnants of Triad and other gangs) began to operate as the Plumflower gang. In 1953 their leader left for Klang and did not return, and by 1955 their activities had subsided. In 1953 the official Secret Society Liaison Committee set up in Malacca found very little upon which to report. About 1,500 Hokkien Triad members among fishermen and petty traders were believed still to exist in such old centres as Sungei Rambai, Bachang, and Malacca town, but all three branches were inactive, and their members known. Four long-established Benevolent Associations, originally of Triad origin, also existed in Malacca town. From time to time Triad members from Kuala Lumpur anxious to 'protect' opium smuggling, and others from Kluang (Johore) interested in gambling promotion, visited Malacca, but were not successful in setting up any local organization. In June 1952 and February 1953 Cantonese wayangs from Kuala Lumpur on visits were accompanied by Wa Kei strong-arm men, but these Wa Kei members made no attempt to interfere in local affairs and left with the troupes. During 1953 there were some unsubstantiated reports of attempts to organize a Wa Kei branch, consisting of Cantonese and Hakka elements in Malacca territory, but as far as was known, such attempts were unsuccessful. In February 1954 a number of '108' members from Singapore seeking new areas for operations visited Malacca, and were followed in May–June by a few members of the '24' gang who tried to extort from prostitutes. But all these interlopers soon returned to their original bases.

It was not until late in 1955 that severe police pressure in Negri Sembilan caused a seepage of Triad activity over the Malacca border. In September there were reports that new initiates at Mambau (south-west of Seremban) had been promised assistance from Malacca Triad, and that in future initiation ceremonies would be held in Malacca territory. In December there was a report that a new secret society sub-branch was being formed in Taboh Naning New Village (a few miles east of Tampin, in Malacca territory), in which Hakkas and Hoi Luk Fung Cantonese were co-operating.

9. JOHORE

Johore, where the Communist revolt was particularly violent, and where secret societies were immediately affected, was in strong contrast to the comparative peace and inactivity of Malacca. Of the forty Communist incidents reported in the Federation of Malaya during May 1948 when the Emergency was getting under way more than half were in Johore, and at the end of July, when the monthly total had risen to 250, Johore still headed the list, with Selangor, Perak, and Pahang following closely.

Johore estate contractors and their headmen who had weaned labourers away from the Communist-controlled unions and had persuaded them to join secret societies, particularly the Wa Kei, were specific targets, and in Bekok village, where the first postwar Johore branch of the Wa Kei had been formed in 1946, the Communist terrorists attacked in June 1948. One Wa Kei member was killed and its chief active leader was severely wounded. He and his family fled to Selangor, and thereafter the branch ceased to exist. But elsewhere, operating from its headquarters in Kluang, and still under the cover of the Chinese Mutual Aid Association, the Johore Wa Kei increased in strength, partly, no doubt, because of the comparative immunity from arrest earned by members through their leaders' Federation-wide offer to give information to the Government against the Communists. By 1952–3 membership in Johore had reached 1,700 and it supplied most of the members of the Home Guards. Its operations against the Communists in the Jemaluang area were particularly valuable and kept the terrorists out of a remote district which otherwise might well have become a Communist 'liberated area'. At the same time the power of the society as a whole enabled a section of its members to proceed with the usual promotion of gambling, intimidation, and extortion from which it obtained its finances.[9]

Triad groups, often associated with Singapore societies, also came to the notice of the police. Members of a Singapore Triad society discovered at an initiation ceremony near Segamat in December 1947, were arrested and banished. In February and March 1948 other members of the same society operating at Kulai were also arrested. With the outbreak of the Emergency police action intensified. There were more arrests in the Segamat area, particularly at Bukit Siput, Pekan Jabi, and Sungei Cha'ah. In July the arrest and banishment of the leader of the Chi Kung Tong branches at Segamat and Kluang, formed only a few months earlier by representatives from Foch Avenue, Kuala Lumpur, curbed that society's activities. A revival of the Triad Chung Yi Tong in Kluang, under cover of the Min Sian Shee club, was frustrated, when registration of the cover society was refused in July 1950. In the south the powerful Singapore Tiechiu society, the Sa Ji, appeared under cover of a Musical Society established in 1949 and soon had 1,000 members in Johore Bahru, Skudai, and Pontian Kechil. The Sa Ji, as always, was particularly active among workers in the pineapple factories, in Johore and Singapore.

Despite the Emergency Singapore secret societies continued to influence Johore Bahru during 1950–2. The Sa Ji remained in control of the workers in the pineapple factories, and in 1950 a splinter gang of the '24' group (Singapore) was also organized, operating in Johore Bahru, Tampoi village, and Skudai.

Bus employees in Johore Bahru were members of the Chap Sa Io (Thirteen Comrades) of the '18' group (Singapore), but when during bus-company troubles the Singapore branch refused to take action in Johore Bahru, the local members turned for help to a new non-Triad Johore group, the Youth Co-operative Society, formed originally by the management of the Johore Bahru cinema to eject rowdies. This society soon degenerated into a 'protection' gang, drawing membership from among trishaw riders and youths who worked at the Singapore Naval Base but who lived in Johore Bahru. During 1952 this gang had many clashes with the police.

Batu Pahat, still a KMT stronghold, remained comparatively peaceful under the protection of its well-organized Triad wharf labour until 1949, when thug gangs and rival Triad groups from Kluang and Singapore penetrated the town. Extortion and assaults caused an exodus of wealthy Chinese merchants to Singapore, and a group of community leaders decided to buy off the thugs individually, a method which, with the co-operation of some police detectives, proved effective. A similar situation arose in 1951 when the Woh Kei Society from Singapore established a branch in Batu Pahat and recruited members from the Cantonese and Hakka communities. Once again the organizers were bought off by the community leaders and returned to Singapore. Later still,

---

[9] Wa Kei membership in Johore, 1952, was estimated as follows:

Segamat area (Bekok, Jementah, Buloh Kasap, Batu Anam, Gemas) . .	700
Kluang area (Paloh, Rengam, Layang-Layang)	6–700
Kulai area (Ayer Bemban, Senai, Sedenak)	200
Mersing area (Endau, Jemaluang)	300

the arrival of gangster elements from Kluang and the formation of extortion groups which easily terrorized such victims as waitresses and hawkers again disturbed the peace of the town.

Muar presented a similar picture. Local gangs of extortioners began operations in 1951. For a time they were held in check by the Triad society of wharf labourers which, financed by the proceeds of a local amusement park, and backed by several influential merchants, took preventive measures. Would-be Wa Kei interlopers from Seremban were also kept out of the town. But in 1952 trouble began again when some Surrendered Enemy Personnel together with some gangsters from Muar began assaults and extortions. Large-scale screening operation by the police in October brought relief.

The firm police action against Triad members in Selangor in 1953 caused some of them to take refuge in Johore where they proposed to set up a central Triad headquarters at Kluang, but arrests by the Johore police prevented this, and raids on suspected Triad premises at most of the towns and villages in the State kept the societies in check. The Chung Woh Tong at Jemaluang was raided in July and further activities prohibited. In April an important Wa Kei leader at Jemaluang (where Wa Kei was the dominant power) had been arrested, and early in 1954 Wa Kei leaders from Jemaluang and Kluang were summoned to Police Headquarters in Kuala Lumpur and warned that all extortion activities by their members must cease. As a result, at Kluang in April, and in Jemaluang in May 1954, the cover associations under which the Wa Kei had operated decided to close down, the register of members at Kluang was burnt by its president, and the head of the Jemaluang branch left for Singapore. Thereafter, apart from collecting subscriptions from its members, the society became inactive for some time, although its organization remained.

Many Wa Kei members carried on their duties in the Home Guards, and on the night of 19 October (1954) Communist terrorists who attacked Jemaluang were beaten off by a Home Guard patrol consisting almost entirely of Wa Kei members. The terrorists unsuccessfully tried to capture the power station and left posters on the perimeter fence, appealing to the inhabitants for support and alleging that the introduction of 'White Areas' was merely a ruse to hide the fact that the British army in Malaya was under strength.

Police action against Triad groups included the dissolution in January 1954 of the Triad cover, the Industrious Chinese Workers' Association, of Batu Pahat, but with the removal of the control previously exercised by this Association hooligan gangs appeared with repeated clashes over 'protection' areas. Similar gangster activities often stimulated from Singapore occurred in other parts of the State. In May two members of the Thirteen Comrades arrived in Segamat from Singapore, but were arrested after sending out extortion letters. A previous member of the '08' Triad society, an inhabitant of Labis, returned to his home town after spending several years in Singapore and attempted to form an extortion gang. In Johore Bahru the '24' group was active and its leader arrested, while the local branch of the Singapore Sa Ji, though apparently inactive, was known to have over 400 members in the pineapple factories in the Skudai–Johore Bahru area.

Later, in 1955, the State Liaison Committee concerned with secret societies recorded the non-committal view that the situation was not entirely quiet but that adequate information was still not available.

21

SINGAPORE, 1949–55

ALTHOUGH the widespread arrests made under the Emergency Regulations in 1948 resulted, as in the Federation, in a pronounced lull in secret society activities in Singapore throughout 1949, the police continued to make frequent visits to the known meeting-places or pangkengs of the gangs, to opium dens and coffee shops reputed to be secret society haunts, and make full use of their powers of arrest. Clashes between gangs occurred from time to time, but on the whole the situation remained quiet, with the police very much in control.

But early in May 1950 there were signs of renewed recruitment. It was reported that contributions were being solicited ostensibly for the building of a temple, and that the receipts were stamped with a seal of Triad significance. The police raided an address in Pickering Street, seized three seals and several receipt books bearing the name Tho Hng Sin Sia (Peach Garden Spirit Society), and discovered that one of the books was stamped in addition with the seals of the Incense Master (Lo Chu) and of the treasurer. The Incense Master was arrested on the premises, charged with the possession of Triad documents, and sentenced to one year's imprisonment. He was later banished to China. The treasurer was also arrested, together with an elderly Triad veteran believed to be the chief organizer who was also banished.

Investigations revealed that the Tho Hng Sin Sia had been inaugurated early in 1948 to encourage recruitment from among men of the surnames Low, Kuan, and Teo, for the initiation ceremonies being organized at that time by the promoters of the Hung Mun Chi Kung Tong in Singapore. This recruitment ceased after the eighty-eight arrests at Clementi Road on 5 March 1948, but in May 1950 was being renewed. The name Tho Hng (Peach Garden), when associated with the names of the Low, Kuan, and Teo clans,[1] was of particular significance, suggesting sworn brotherhood of the Peach Garden of the Three Kingdoms period in China, which formed a basic part of Triad tradition. A Peach Garden temple, if built, could serve not only as a place of worship, but as a focus for Triad organization in Singapore. The arrests of the society's officials prevented further immediate developments.

From the outbreak of the Communist revolt there had always been the possibility that the MCP might seek to make use of secret society gangsters, and in 1950, when the Communist threat in Singapore changed from propaganda to violence, it was found that secret society members had become involved. In December fourteen Chinese youths were arrested at No. 1 Muar Road. Communist documents were discovered, and investigations revealed that these men had been implicated in a number of identity-card robberies. All belonged to secret societies, some to the Choan Gi Ho ('18' group), some to the Tarzan

[1] In Mandarin Liu, Kuan, and Chang.

gang ('18' group), and some to the Gi Tong Hin ('24' group). Again in June 1951, it was discovered that a number of secret society gangsters in the Silat Road area were also connected with the MCP. Fifty-nine were arrested under the Emergency Regulations. All belonged to the Anti-British League (a subsidiary of the MCP) and were members of the Gi Kung Tong ('18' group). Some admitted having committed various offences instigated by the League, such as arson of public transport vehicles, identity-card robberies, and distribution of MCP propaganda.

Meanwhile, strong police action against the MCP, including the arrest of four members of the Singapore Town Committee in May 1950 and of the English-speaking branch of the Anti-British League in January and February 1951, the capture of the printing-press of the *Freedom News* in July 1951, and the unmasking of various Communist centres dislocated the Communist organization. In 1952 open defiance was abandoned in favour of a return to secret penetration of labour and student ranks. Open outrages decreased by 90 per cent, public distribution of propaganda was negligible, but some serious attacks were made against individuals, and once again use was made of secret society gangsters who, at Communist instigation, were responsible for the shooting of a bus-driver of the Singapore Traction Company in November 1952, of a male Chinese in January 1953, and of a detective in May 1953.

On the general question of whether it was appropriate that the powers granted by the Legislature for the purpose of countering the threatened subversive acts of the MCP should continue to be used for the control of secret society members unconnected with the party, there were, from 1951, some misgivings in official circles, and with the continuance of comparative calm in the underworld, relaxations of policy were progressively introduced. In mid-1951 a ruling was made that when it was well established that a person was a secret society member against whom there was no conviction or other specific information of activity during the Emergency, no Detention Order would be issued, but there might be a Direction Order controlling his night movements and requiring him to report to the police. A year later the policy was further relaxed so that the powers under the Emergency Regulations were not to be used to detain persons of criminal type against whom there was no evidence of subversive activities or sympathies, although this did not preclude the making of Direction Orders in suitable cases. Eight persons within this category still under detention were released on Direction Orders, while forty-seven others whose detention had been suspended were similarly treated. From the beginning of 1953 even the issue of Direction Orders for this category of persons was discontinued, and secret society members had thus no longer to fear the power of the Emergency Regulations provided that they avoided subversive activities.

As was to be expected, the use of powers under these Regulations had undoubtedly resulted in a reduction of secret society activity and in a decrease in crime generally, but towards the end of 1952 there were signs of deterioration, and from mid-1953 onwards the police were perturbed to find that despite their most vigorous efforts, crime attributable to society members and to organized society groups was increasing. During the first six months of the year there were 60 secret society clashes as against 25 during the whole of 1952, and by the end of the year figures of serious crime showed that reports of robbery had risen from 10 in 1949 to 33 in 1953. At the time it was estimated that there were 360 secret societies in Singapore, of which 136 were active, including 110 Hokkien and Tiechiu societies, 18 Cantonese, and 8 Malay or Indian. Apart from the powerful Tiechiu Sa Ji with its seven branches, the majority of the Hokkien and Tiechiu societies were still organized in the same five groups, '8', '18', '24', '36', and '108', but there were no permanent group heads, or leaders, or headquarters. Matters of importance to the whole group were occasionally discussed by headmen of component societies in a convenient coffee-shop, but despite some measure of mutual allegiance there were frequent clashes between societies within any group, and the '24' and the '108' were perpetually at war with one another. Among the Cantonese, Hakkas, and Hainanese were twenty-five societies, still grouped under the Man Yi, the Heng, and the Khwan Yi,[2] while in addition to these Chinese societies, Indian, Malay, and Eurasian youths had banded themselves together in search of 'easy money' under such names as Tarzan, Heroes, B.29, Flying Tiger, and Black Atom Bomb. Eight thousand members of the Hokkien and Tiechiu societies were on police record, of whom 75 per cent were listed as 'active'; of 1,400 members of Cantonese societies on record, 34 per cent were active, and of 500 recorded members of the Malay and Indian groups, 20 per cent were active. Although gangs of mixed membership existed, and gave considerable trouble (in 1953 five secret society murders and two attempted murders were traced to mixed societies), nevertheless the Chinese societies remained the principal problem. Once again attention was called by the police to the diminishing effectiveness of the Banishment Ordinance in view of the increasing proportion of society members who were local-born and were therefore not subject to this law. Local-born members were estimated to be about 80 or 85 per cent of the whole. Nevertheless, 350 Banishment Orders were carried out in 1953. Only thirty-three of these were Orders made in the current year, the balance had been made during the period 1947–52 in respect of persons who had evaded arrest.

The police also took the view that the Societies Ordinance was of little use for dealing with the criminal gangs of the type found in Singapore. Although some of the members were full initiates of the Triad Brotherhood, many were not, nor was there any form of ritual initiation into the gangs which could be brought within the Triad sections of the Societies Ordinance. Though some of the Hokkien and Tiechiu societies had pangkengs or headquarter premises, these usually consisted merely of a room in a shop-house, used by members for sleeping and almost devoid of furniture or any distinguishing feature. Without some sort of documentary evidence it was practically impossible to prove that any aggregation of individuals constituted a 'society' within the meaning of the law. It was further claimed by the police that the taking of photographs and fingerprints of suspected gangsters under the provisions of Section 22 of the Ordinance was no longer a deterrent of any importance. Persons summoned for examination in this way could not be detained for longer than twenty-four hours, whereupon they returned to their old pursuits. The gangsters had now become habituated to this routine, knowing that nothing more was to follow.

As a result of representations made to the Government by the police calling

[2] The Man Yi was also called Ch'at Fong Pat Min (Seven Cardinals, Eight Faces). The Heng was also called the Ng Fong Luk Min (Five Cardinals, Six Faces). The Khwan Yi was also called the Sam Fong Si Min (Three Cardinals, Four Faces). The 'faces' were the number of societies originally in the group.

HH

for more drastic legislation, a review of the existing laws was undertaken to discover whether all the provisions which could be brought into play against the gangs were being employed, but it was found that the only provision of law which had not been fully used was Section 75 of the Criminal Procedure Code which provided for the binding over by the court of persons who appeared likely to commit a breach of the peace. During the last few weeks of the year (1953) thirty-two gang leaders were bound over in this way, but it was soon clear that the indirectness of this form of attack produced no significant results, and deliberations on the possibility of devising fresh legislation to deal with the problem continued.

In order to strengthen police pressure against the gangs a reorganization of the CID was undertaken whereby, from 1 March 1954, a separate Secret Society Branch was formed. Within this branch were three sub-branches, one for Hokkien and Tiechiu, one for Cantonese (including Hakka and Hainanese), and a third for Indian and Malay societies. Shortly after its formation the branch received information of the recent holding of a Triad initiation ceremony near a quarry on the outskirts of the city, and of a proposal to hold another in the same area. Arrangements were made for transmission to the police of the date of the ceremony when known, but it was not until 12 October that warning came. After the ceremony was known to have started, police ambushes were placed on all paths leading to the site, and during the night 36 men were arrested as they left the scene. The usual paraphernalia of an initiation was discovered, and subsequently 31 of those arrested pleaded guilty to charges of membership and attending a meeting of an unlawful society, and received sentences of five months' rigorous imprisonment.

The Secret Society Branch continued to wage a brisk campaign against the gangs, and by the end of the year 2,920 men had been arrested for enquiry, of whom 384 were photographed and placed on record under the provisions of Section 22 of the Societies Ordinance, and 55 were convicted in court on charges of being members of unlawful societies. Twenty of these convictions concerned men who had tattoo marks relating to their societies on their bodies. In January 1954 the police had become aware of this practice of tattooing, which, at first sight, appeared to be a peculiar method of identification for gang members to adopt, but which fell into the same category as the wearing of badges relating to their societies which was a general practice just after the liberation. But whereas at that time all societies were lawful because of the non-operation of the Societies Ordinance, since the reintroduction of the Ordinance in April 1947 such societies were unlawful, and it was a measure of the scant regard paid to the powers of the police as compared with the powers wielded by the societies that members were prepared to go about in public displaying large tattoo designs on their bare arms or bare chests indicative of the gangs to which they belonged. Admittedly, most of the designs were cabalistic, with meanings hidden from the non-member, but many had the number of the society or group worked into the pattern. The possession of such a distinguishing mark warned all with whom the member came in contact that he was 'protected', and therefore not lightly to be accosted. It also tended to convey the impression, common throughout the world in circles in which tattooing is adopted, of being formidable, and invested the wearer with an aura of bravado very useful when making demands upon others.

It was perhaps fortunate for the police that in the early cases of this nature brought to court the accused pleaded guilty to membership of an unlawful society, for it might have been difficult to prove to the satisfaction of a court that a particular design was, in fact, used only by members of a certain society. But as the number of cases grew, and with them the number of admissions made by wearers of these designs, the police were able to proceed with some confidence. So much so, that individuals were discovered who, fearing prosecution, had had tattoo marks removed by the application of strong acid which burned through all the skin layers into the flesh, leaving ghastly open wounds. There were others who voluntarily went to the detective station to report that they had unknowingly been tattooed with designs which, it appeared, were the marks of secret societies. In such cases, if the man was not known to be a society member, no prosecution ensued, but persons convicted by the courts for wearing these tattoos were sentenced to 1–5 months' imprisonment. Even so, these prosecutions concerned only a minute proportion of the active secret society membership.

Consideration by the Government of the possibility of introducing more stringent laws to deal with the gangsters resulted in the preparation of a Bill providing for Corrective Training and Corrective Detention on the lines of the provisions of the UK Criminal Justice Act, 1948, Sections 21 and 22. The Preamble declared the Bill to be 'An Ordinance to provide new methods of dealing with members of, or persons connected with, unlawful societies . . .'.

As originally drafted, powers were given to the courts (High Court and District Court) whenever a person of 18 years of age or more was convicted of certain offences set out in the schedule, and was a member of or connected with an unlawful society, to pass a sentence of corrective training for a term of not less than 3 and not more than 7 years. In similar circumstances, a person of 30 years of age or more might receive a sentence of preventive detention for a term of not less than 5 and not more than 14 years. Other provisions empowered the courts to prohibit a person from being out of doors between 7 p.m. and 6 a.m., and to require him to notify his movements and any change of address to the police whenever ordered by the court to execute a bond for keeping the peace, or to be subject to police supervision. In such cases, the court had first to be satisfied that the person was a member of or connected with an unlawful society.

The Bill laid it down that a certificate signed by a Deputy Superintendent of Police or by the Registrar of Societies should be conclusive proof of membership or connexion with an unlawful society. This provision gave rise to some public uneasiness, and when the Bill was referred to a Select Committee of the Legislative Council on 13 April 1954, among several proposed amendments was one stating that the certificate from the police or the Registrar of Societies was not to be accepted as conclusive proof, but was merely to be *prima facie* evidence of the facts stated therein. It was left to the courts to decide whether or not the evidence produced was sufficient to be acceptable as proof. There was one other amendment of importance. The original Bill provided for the admission as evidence in court in such cases of statements made to police officers of a certain rank. This was a well-known provision of law in the United Kingdom and in some Colonies, but the Select Committee by a majority of three to two decided against its inclusion. In its amended form the Bill was passed in October

1954 as the Criminal Justice (Temporary Provisions) Ordinance 1954. It was a temporary measure to be in force for one year only, though the Governor in Council was empowered to extend its operation for further periods of not more than twelve months at a time.

The Ordinance was brought into force on 1 April 1955, but at the end of the year the police reported that it had been of very limited assistance as, in the main, it was effective only after convictions, and these were notoriously difficult to obtain. Of 65 certificates tendered in court by the police, only 18 were accepted though there were still some cases pending at the end of the year. The police did not regard the Ordinance as an effective substitute for the most potent weapon of the past—the Banishment Ordinance. Some of the prisoners were acquitted and others had their charges reduced to a lower category to which the new law did not apply. In any case, because of the difficulty of getting witnesses to testify, the number of cases that could be brought before the courts at all was so small that the effect on the societies was negligible.

The year 1955 was indeed one of great difficulty in Singapore. There was both political ferment and industrial unrest, and the secret societies took advantage of any disturbance to further their own ends. Early in the year a new Constitution was brought into force under which elections were to be held in April for a newly-constituted Legislative Assembly with a membership of 32, of whom 25 would be elected, 4 would be nominated by the Governor, and 3 (the Chief Secretary, whose change of title from that of Colonial Secretary denoted a change of function, the Attorney-General, and the Financial Secretary) would be *ex-officio* members. In place of the Executive Council there was to be a Council of Ministers to include the Governor and the 3 officials, together with the leader of the majority party (who was to have the title of Chief Minister) and 5 other members nominated by him as Ministers. Transitional in character, the Constitution was designed to pave the way for full self-government, by enabling a political party to hold a majority in the elected Assembly, and to gain experience at ministerial level, although for the time being finance, defence, internal security, and external affairs were in the hands of official members, responsible to the Governor.

The forthcoming election naturally stimulated local political activity. Nor were members of China-based political parties slow to take advantage of the situation, and once again, as in 1946 and 1947–8, attempts were made by both KMT and 'middle-of-the-road' groups to organize the secret societies into a combined association, partly, and avowedly, as a means of preventing inter-society faction fights and creating a bulwark against growing Communist penetration of student ranks and trade unions, but also as a means of increasing their own local power and advancing the policy of their particular party in China. (A similar development was noticeable in Hong Kong at this time, where KMT attempts were made to organize members of right-wing trade unions as the Hung Mun Yi Yuen Tong, a new manifestation of the Min Chi Tang.)

The KMT was quickly in the field in Singapore. Already in mid-1954 an enthusiastic member of the party, who was also a committee member of the MCA, had been urged from Formosa to counter Communist influence among Chinese students and to encourage their return to Nationalist China for advanced studies. His efforts materialized in February 1955 in the attempted formation of a so-called Youth Party, to be sponsored by the MCA, with a membership drawn from the secret societies. Under discipline and control and indoctrinated against Communism, the promoters asserted that these youths could be transformed into law-abiding citizens. What was certain, though undeclared, was that this organization would be used to support candidates in the coming elections.

A meeting of leaders of secret societies was called on 20 February and was attended by some 200 representatives. A central committee of 17 members was elected, and proposals to establish 25 branch committees, one for each electoral ward, were passed. But when, in due course, it was discovered that the Government would not countenance such an organization, the scheme was dropped. The attempt had one beneficial result in that it provided a medium through which the leaders of the '108' group and the '24' group, which had long been opponents in a vicious feud, were brought together at a meeting of reconciliation, though this proved to be only a temporary respite.

The elections held on 2 April were contested by five parties and ten independents, and when the Labour Front won the largest number of elective seats its leader, Mr David Marshall, was invited to form a Government. Supported by two nominated members and by the three official members, he formed a coalition with the UMNO–MCA–Singapore Malay Union group whose three seats gave him an overall majority in the Assembly.

For some weeks before the elections there had been vigorous campaigning during which scathing denunciations of the colonial system were made by some of the candidates, maintaining that the people were oppressed and that deliverance was at hand. The business of canvassing was one which secret society men found most congenial, and most of the candidates, knowingly or unknowingly, made use of such men in their campaign organizations. Usually they were not employed as a group but individually, and it may well be that many of the candidates were unaware of the connexions of these helpers. The helpers, on the other hand, were well aware of the value of participation, and made it clear to detectives that if their candidate were elected they would then have a member of the legislature to whom they could appeal if in trouble.

In some instances the influence of secret societies was of greater effect than this account implies. In the report of a Commission of Enquiry into Corrupt, Illegal, or Undesirable Practices at Elections, published in 1958, it was stated with reference to the general election of 1955 that apart from intimidation the practice of secret society members accompanying the voters to polling stations was used 'as a convenient procedure for the payment of bribes to voters'. The report stated:

A voter is told that he will get a bribe for voting for the candidate, provided the candidate is successful at the election. The secret society member accompanying the voter to the Polls will note his name and address and, after the election if the candidate is successful, payment will be made as promised. But even here intimidation plays its part, because if a candidate is not successful and there is a serious discrepancy in the number of votes expected to be cast for him, a voter who did not vote as directed would not only have missed the opportunity of earning his bribe, but would also fear investigation and punitive action by the secret society.

Reference was made to a statement by one of the defeated candidates (a European) to the effect that public meetings had proved to be of little value to him in his campaign, and that the intervention of secret societies had been an important factor in the election. This was only the opinion of one man, a defeated candidate of European nationality, but there was undoubtedly a general feeling among the Chinese public also that the secret societies had played a part, though not, perhaps, a dominant part in the elections.

There was, however, no alignment of secret society groups with particular political parties. In one area, members of a particular society group were to be found working for one party, while elsewhere members of the same group were working for a rival party. For this reason, and because of the special police precautions which were taken, there was no outbreak of inter-society trouble arising from the participation of members in the election campaign. But it was noticeable that once the elections were over and the new Government had settled in, there were several occasions when secret society members under arrest sought the protection of the Assemblyman elected for their area.

Here, again, it would be improper to suggest that the Assemblymen concerned were cognizant of the manner of life of these men, or were necessarily under the influence of the societies. The Assemblyman was approached by a constituent with a story of unwarranted arrest by the police, and felt it to be his duty to make enquiries, the more so if the person concerned had been an active supporter of his candidature during the elections. But it was clear that the society members believed or hoped that the new Constitution offered a prospect of weakening the power of the police in their attempt to overcome the menace of the gangs.

In addition to the ferment caused by the changing constitutional pattern and the exuberance of the participants in the elections, a number of industrial disputes became matters of public concern because of the contempt for law and order shown by many of the striking groups, and the intimidation, threats, sabotage, and riots which accompanied the strikes. Along with this went a campaign of hatred directed against the police by the strikers and their supporting demonstrators organized by the Chinese Middle Schools' Union, which had a strong Communist bias.

Since 1951, when police action had caused the Communist Party in Singapore to abandon open violence in favour of subversion, Communist agents had concentrated upon the placing of underground workers within the trade unions and the Chinese Middle Schools, a policy which was approved by the CCP as likely to win the support of labourers and students. To further this policy, an able labour organizer was introduced to members of the Singapore Anti-British League some time in 1952. By 1953 he had become the president of the Amalgamated Malayan Pineapple Workers' Union. In 1954 he was appointed vice-president of the newly-founded Singapore Factory and Shop-Workers' Union, and in 1955 became the head of another new union, the Farmers' Association. This man was also on record as a member of the Gi Ho secret society of the '18' group, and as an active protagonist of the united front of the MCP he expanded Communist influence through the organizations over which he exercised control, exploiting Communist celebrations days, wage grievances, and problems of the farming population, and pressing with Front propaganda in educational circles. This Communist penetration was not confined to labour and student organizations, but spread in 1955 to the political field, when the People's Action Party (PAP), formed from various shades of left-wing opinion, contested the elections in April, and although only winning three seats became the most active part of the opposition in the Assembly.

Soon after taking office, the newly-elected Government of Singapore found itself challenged by a campaign of militant trade unionism. The most important of these disputes was that of the Hock Lee Bus Company which dragged on for many weeks, leading finally to a riot on 12 May 1955 in which four people were killed, two of them members of the police force. Although not responsible for the outbreak of the riot, secret society members took advantage of the opportunity provided by the disturbances to join in assaults on the police, and from then onwards there was an increase in crimes of violence, in many of which secret society gangsters were implicated.

One of the first acts of the new Government at the first meeting of the Legislative Assembly held on 26 and 27 April had been to revoke some of the Emergency Regulations as an earnest of the fulfilment of election pledges. One of these Regulations empowered the Commissioner of Police to impose a curfew whenever he deemed it to be necessary. On 13 May, the day after the Hock Lee riot, the Government found it necessary to restore this power of curfew, and on the 16th an emergency meeting of the Legislature was called to confirm this action. Leaders of the PAP were then accused of relations with a group of unions concerned with the strikes which was alleged to have encouraged the recalcitrance of the strikers and to have incited the workers to revolt. For its part, the Government was subjected to counter-accusations of ineptitude. What is certain is that the increased activities of Communist-penetrated unions, both of workers and of students, coupled with the climate of political ferment to which the inflammatory language of some of the candidates at the elections had contributed, provided a favourable opportunity for the spreading of discord and incitement to revolt by the Communist front organizations, leading to civil disturbance in which the mob—including secret societies—participated.

There were many more industrial disputes later in the year, some of which affected public utilities. The worst attempts at sabotage were made at the gas-works, at the power station, and at the civil airport. In most of the strikes there was obstruction by the strikers and opposition to action by the police to remove them, while intimidation was widespread. On fifty-one occasions attempts were made to burn motor vehicles, usually belonging to European owners. Despite the offer of large rewards by the police, no information was forthcoming.

Under these conditions, with the police constantly occupied with duties arising from the industrial troubles, secret societies found a congenial climate for their operations. It may be, too, that they were encouraged in the belief that a new era was dawning by the cancellation in June of nine Banishment Orders in respect of secret society men who were thereupon released from prison. Seven of these men had been participants in the initiation ceremony held in October 1954. During the year there was a serious increase in crime, and of the 39 murders committed (as compared with 19 in 1954) 11 were attributable to secret society gangsters (as compared with 4 in the previous year).

The Emergency Regulations which had provided such useful material for candidates in the election campaign as evidence of an 'oppressive' colonial Government ceased to have effect from 21 October 1955, for on that date the declaration of a state of emergency lapsed and was not renewed. Like the proclamation of 1872 under the Preservation of the Peace Act, the proclamation of a state of emergency had lasted a long time. The 1872 proclamation was in force for thirteen years, though originally intended for use only at times of riot and disorder. The proclamation of 1948 persisted for seven years, but unlike the earlier one this proclamation had been brought before the Legislative Council of Singapore every three months for renewal, and on each such occasion a review of the state of emergency was given to the House and members had the opportunity (which was frequently used) of criticizing the operation of any of the Emergency Regulations.

But the new Government of 1955 decided that a state of affairs which had continued for seven years could not with propriety be regarded as an emergency. Nevertheless, during the first few months in the life of this Government, the spectacular increase in the power of Communist-controlled labour unions known as the Middle Road Group which were responsible for most of the industrial turmoil made it clear to the ministers that some of the extraordinary powers contained in the Emergency Regulations must be retained until peace was restored. Another factor to be considered was the anxiety of the Federation Government that powers to deal with Communists should not be relaxed lest Singapore should become a refuge and a base of organization for the jungle war in the Federation. It was a difficult decision for the new Government to take, particularly for the Chief Minister who, during his election campaign, in unmeasured terms had roundly condemned the use by the Government of the powers conferred by the Emergency Regulations. But a Bill was introduced in September embodying those powers which it was thought necessary to retain, to continue in force for a period of three years.

The new law was known as the Preservation of Public Security Ordinance, reminiscent of the Preservation of the Peace Act of 1867. The 1955 Ordinance (25 of 1955) came into force on 21 October of that year, the day on which the proclamation of a state of emergency expired, and its main provisions concerned the power to order detention. The section creating this power read:

> 3 (I). If the Governor in Council is satisfied with respect to any person that, with a view to preventing that person from acting in any manner prejudicial to the security of Malaya or to the maintenance of public order therein or the maintenance therein of essential services, it is necessary to do so, the Chief Secretary shall by order under his hand make an order directing that such person be detained for any period not exceeding two years.

The only essential difference between this provision and that of the Emergency Regulation which it replaced was that under the new Ordinance it was necessary for the Governor in Council to be satisfied, whereas under the old Regulations it was necessary only for the Chief Secretary to be satisfied as to the necessity for issuing an Order. But in the matter of appeal there was a more significant difference. Under the old Regulations an appeal against an Order was made to an advisory committee presided over by a Judge, and the committee made its recommendation to the Governor. Under the new law, the Appeal Tribunal, consisting of two Judges and one District Judge, had discretion to revoke, amend, or confirm an Order. The police were empowered to arrest without warrant and detain pending enquiries any person in respect of whom the police officer had reason to believe that there were grounds which would justify his detention under the provisions of the Ordinance, or that he had acted or was about to act in any manner prejudicial to the public safety or the maintenance of public order. Detention in such cases might extend to sixteen days if the necessary enquiries could not be completed earlier. The Commissioner of Police was again empowered to impose curfew, provided that no order of curfew could remain in force for longer than forty-eight hours unless confirmed by the Governor in Council. Power was also given to take photographs and fingerprints of persons detained under the provisions of this Ordinance.

The new Ordinance, like the former Regulations, made no mention of Communists, Communism, or subversion. Nevertheless, the context in which it was introduced was that of Communist subversion, and the powers under the new law were not used to effect the arrest and detention of criminals unconnected with subversive movements. This legislation, therefore, had no direct effect on the powers of the police to control the activities of the gangs. It did, however, renew the power to deal with subversive elements who were exploiting the labour unions and were thus creating a climate of insecurity in which the activities of the gangs thrived. This was a matter of some importance, for by the end of the year there had been 275 strikes with a consequent wave of general unrest. There had been only 8 strikes in 1954, and 4 in 1953.

At the same time as the new Ordinance was introduced another law, the Criminal Law (Temporary Provisions) Ordinance (26 of 1955), was passed. Its provisions included the prohibition of strikes and lockouts in essential services, and power to restrict the display of national emblems. The police were empowered to disperse assemblies of ten or more persons in any place, public or private, whenever the Chief Secretary had declared that an immediate threat to public peace existed. Persons in possession of explosives with intent to endanger life or property were liable to a sentence of imprisonment for life and to whipping, as were also those who consorted with them. Provision was made for the trial of offences under the Ordinance to be held *in camera* should the court consider this to be expedient, and any statement freely made by an accused person to a police officer of or above the rank of Inspector was admissible as evidence in trials under the Ordinance.

In addition to these legislative attempts to improve the situation, the police themselves not only took direct action against secret society members whenever possible but waged an unremitting war against gambling houses, lottery promoters, and opium-smoking saloons, all of which were closely connected with secret societies in that their personnel was invariably composed of secret society men and their existence depended upon the protection of the societies. For the function *par excellence* of secret societies was the protection of unlawful enterprises. Not that lawful undertakings escaped the net of protection—the shopkeeper, the market-stall holder, the licensed hawker, all paid their toll—but unlawful enterprises such as gambling houses, opium saloons, unlicensed hawkers, or brothels had a special attraction because the managements, by virtue of the illegality of their trade, feared to make any complaint to the authorities, and greater tribute was therefore extorted by the protector.

Some idea of the extent of the work of the Narcotics and Gambling Sections of the CID may be gleaned from the figures on page 476.

Shortly after the coming to power of the new Government in April 1955 came further proposals to organize a combination of secret societies, sponsored this time by those enthusiasts who had made an earlier attempt in December 1947 but had been refused in May 1948. The promoters apparently hoped that

	1953	1954	1955	1956	1957
Narcotics					
Searches of saloons		3,796	3,720	3,149	2,541
Opium pipes collected		2,978	1,787	1,749	2,053
Opium lamps collected		2,879	1,571	1,543	1,678
Persons charged in court		1,851	989	1,070	656
Gambling					
Premises searched	688	588	540	878	620
Gambling found	480	420	348	643	518
Persons arrested	1,437	920	885	1,216	401
Value of bets on Chap Ji Ki documents seized ($000)	323	525	241	207	6
Fines imposed ($000)	146	234	198	97	12
Persons sentenced to gaol	22	32	53	48	1
Clubs dissolved	8	6	6	2	—

Source: CID *ARs*, 1955–7.

the newly-elected Government, faced with the insoluble problem of ever-increasing gang warfare and with an epidemic of Communist-inspired industrial troubles, would welcome a plan which might be doubly effective by absorbing the secret societies under one controlling body whose influence would be used to counter the Communists.

The first indications of this movement became apparent in July 1955, when a representative of the promoters urged a member of the US Information Service to use his influence to help the proposed association to obtain registration. The Registrar of Societies who was discreetly sounded gave no encouragement, but over the next few months there were repeated reports that leading Chinese businessmen, important members of political parties, and even ministers had been approached. By the end of November Objects and Rules had been drawn up, the intention being to apply for official recognition as a 'party' to be called the South East Asia Hung Mun Chi Kung Tong. As an incentive to acceptance by the Government the sponsors undertook to assist in maintaining peace and order, in settling labour unrest, and in resisting the Communist threat. Furthermore, the 'party' would encourage its members to 'co-operate on the basis of a reasonable wage' whenever workers were required by the Government for construction purposes. In return it was suggested that if at any time the Government should grant citizenship rights, special facilities should be given to members in making applications in order to raise the prestige of the 'party'.

Provision was made for branches to be set up in various districts and States, with sub-branches in towns. Membership was divided into four categories—founder-members (i.e. those of the original Hung Mun Brotherhood), life-members, ordinary members, and patron members. Patron members only were exempted from undergoing the traditional and secret religious rites of initiation which were obligatory for all others joining the 'party'.

It was clear that a Triad organization was envisaged whose members would be bound by the full ritual and oaths and would be subject to the Triad disciplinary code. But by the end of 1955 the application for registration had still not been submitted to the Registrar, and in the meantime, despite the new laws and the pressure kept up by the police on the gangs, clashes between rival secret societies and crime attributable to their members continued to increase. In November 1955 the feud between the '24' and the '108' groups flared up again. The question at issue was the protection of areas around Sago Street and Chulia Street, and a meeting of leaders of the two groups took place in a coffee-shop to try to settle the matter by negotiation. When the talks failed, the gangs set upon one another with bottles from the coffee-shop and knives from near-by hawkers' stalls. More than 60 men took part in the various affrays of which there were 7 throughout the night. Five members whose ages ranged between 17 and 20 years were seriously slashed or stabbed and 4 bystanders were injured. On this occasion the police had information of the possibility of a fight, and had called in leaders of the two groups to warn them not to disturb the peace.

The *Straits Times*, in commenting on the 'Empire of the Hoodlums', remarked:

The most disturbing fact about this little gang war is that the gang bosses thought nothing of waging battle quite openly and on quite an impressive scale. Despite repeated warnings on the part of the authorities that they are determined to 'beat the secret society gangs' of which three hundred and sixty-eight are known to the Police, the gangs operate as boldly as ever. The fight helped convince the shopkeepers and tradesmen who are 'protected' by these gangsters that the Police are not the shield they should be. The difficulties under which the Police have to work are notorious, but shopkeepers living in the shadow of the gangs are impressed only by the strength of the gangs and the inability of the Police to deal with them. The reasons are academic. . . . Secret society activity far from declining shows renewed and returning vigour.

This assessment was correct. The gangs were steadily getting the upper hand.

22

FEDERATION OF MALAYA, 1956–65

1. GENERAL

THE main political development of the period 1956–8 was the achievement of self-government by the Federation on 31 August 1957. Measures taken by the police to ensure that no untoward incidents marred that occasion reached their peak just before Independence Day, and continued to have effect for several months afterwards.

The secret society world naturally received much attention. The setting up of a special section in each police contingent to deal with secret society suppression had enabled a closer watch to be kept and facilitated the recording of known or suspected members on police files. Nevertheless, during 1956, the occurrence of Triad initiation ceremonies in Perak, Negri Sembilan, and Malacca, and the discovery of a number of new societies in several States were indicative of the persistence of Triad tradition despite the increased police surveillance. But although the year's record was one of frequent minor incidents, clashes between rival gangs, and constant police pressure, the situation was under control. In some cases where attendance at an initiation ceremony or possession of Triad documents or involvement in fighting could be proved, action was taken in court, but more frequently recourse was had to procedure under the Banishment of the Restricted Residence Enactments.

The year 1957 opened inauspiciously with a series of disturbances in Penang (see below), where one clash in particular served as a warning of what could happen in the very sensitive state of public opinion in the months immediately preceding the grant of independence. Throughout the country there was a notable increase of 'Kwun T'au' parties, groups for instruction in the Chinese art of self-defence, including stratagem and the cult of invulnerability, and one secret society leader in Perak who was conducting a recruiting campaign frankly declared that after the grant of independence, when the British left, the Chinese would have to look after themselves and therefore needed the protection of the Triad Brotherhood.

On the Malay side there was an increase in the number of groups formed for instruction in *bersilat*, the Malay art of self-defence which again is frequently extended to include invulnerability techniques. In addition to restraining both Chinese and Malays from these pursuits, a drive against known secret society members was begun in February under the code-name of Operation Pukat (Fishing Net). The intention was to remove as many hooligans as possible from the scene before the independence celebrations on 31 August and so minimize the risk of disturbances which, in the highly emotional atmosphere and the thronging of the crowds, might well have had most serious consequences.

Suspects already listed were called in, and some important leaders detained. Others were photographed and warned. In this way throughout the country many hundreds of secret society men and gangsters passed through police hands.

During the independence celebrations all went well, and there was no sign of trouble anywhere in the Federation. But it is noteworthy that despite the wide sweep of the Pukat, a number of Triad initiation ceremonies were reported, one in Selangor (where the police drive was most intensive) only six miles from Kuala Lumpur in June, several in Malacca territory, and one in Negri Sembilan.

The technique of calling in all known suspects for interrogation and warning was continued through 1958. This in itself may have had a deterrent effect, but, in addition, the knowledge obtained through these interrogations by the specialized sections of the police enabled them to take further action through applications for the issue of Banishment or Restricted Residence Orders. Enquiries held under the relevant laws resulted in the banishment of 17 men and the placing of 130 on restricted residence. The cumulative effect of such action throughout 1957 and 1958 was to be seen in the progressively decreasing number of serious incidents in most States, though clashes still occurred. There were only eight secret society murders during the year. An investigation took place into the penetration by secret societies of the armed forces of the Federation, particularly the Federation Regiment which had a high proportion of Chinese rank and file. In September it was announced that over sixty men had been discharged on this account.

Legislative Action

At the time of the Penang riot in January 1957 (p. 484) it was realized that the permanent legislation dealing with the maintenance of public order was inadequate to deal with the situation, and recourse was had to the Emergency Regulations which were not designed for this purpose but for the suppression of the seditious movement of the MCP. In order to transfer some of these powers to the permanent legislation a Bill was published in September 1958 with the title of Public Order Preservation Bill, providing for the issue of proclamations in any areas for a period not exceeding one month at a time. Once such a proclamation was issued, the Government were empowered to introduce a number of controls which would not otherwise be lawful. These included the imposition of curfew, the closing of roads, the removal of onlookers or looters, the forbidding of assemblies or processions, the calling in of arms, the exclusion of agitators from specific areas, and the prohibition of publication, verbal or otherwise, of words likely to be prejudicial to the restoration of public order or to incite to disobedience of the law or the causing of violence. The Bill was passed by an overwhelming majority on 25 October. Though not specifically directed against secret societies, for these powers could clearly not be used in the day-to-day struggle between the police and the societies, it was generally believed that by thus showing its determination to maintain order the Government had increased public confidence.

Despite the reduction in serious crime during 1957 and 1958 the Government were far from satisfied that all was well. As was discovered in Singapore, the system of calling in suspects and then releasing them after questioning, while producing an initial spell of quietude, lost its efficacy when members of the underworld realized that as a rule no punishment was involved, and business could proceed as usual.

Consideration was therefore given to tighter control through legislation similar to that introduced in Singapore in 1958 which provided for preventive detention by order of the Executive without trial by the courts.[1] At a press conference in February 1959 Tunku Abdul Rahman talked of the 'growing menace' of secret societies and stated that the terms of the Constitution in the Federation precluded the adoption of a law of this nature. A different approach was therefore necessary, and a Prevention of Crime Bill was introduced with the following 'Objects and Reasons'.

In recent times the activities of secret society members, gangsters, extortioners and other criminals have markedly increased. If vigorous action is not taken to repress them, they are likely to become a dangerous menace. Experience shows that the ordinary procedure of the criminal law is inadequate, largely because the victims of these organized gangs and societies are too terrorised to be willing to give evidence in open court. Formerly the activities of criminals of this type were to some extent controlled by the application of the Banishment law, but this is not available against Federal citizens. . . . It is accordingly necessary, if society is to be defended effectively, to provide new methods for preventing the growth of criminal societies and criminal activities.

The machinery through which it was hoped to achieve this control was the maintenance of a register of persons who, after enquiry, were found to be members of secret societies or criminal gangs, smugglers of drugs, traffickers in women, promoters of unlawful gaming, or habitual criminals or other undesirable persons. Before entry in the register it would be necessary for the police to satisfy the enquiry officer that there was sufficient evidence to justify the presumption that the person in question fell within one of these categories. Those registered were liable to police supervision for five years, and to have their movements restricted. To enable them to be readily recognized, their Identity Cards were to be marked with a large black cross. Should they be convicted of any offence during their period of registration, they were liable to double the normal penalty and to whipping. Provision was made for appeal to the Minister against registration, and for the removal of names from the register after a period of good behaviour. The Bill was passed by the unanimous decision of the Legislature on 19 February, and came into force on 1 April 1959.

The political event of the year was the election of a new House of Representatives on 20 August. There had been considerable weakening of various opposition parties through the arrest, from October 1958 onwards, of over 300 individuals classed as 'subversives'. The last batch of these was rounded up only six days before the election, a circumstance which evoked critical comment from opposition leaders. At the election, the main political combination, the Alliance, was returned to power with 70 seats out of 104.

The Constitution provided that before it could be amended there must be a favourable vote of two-thirds of the total number of members of both the Senate and the House of Representatives. The Alliance Government now had a sufficient majority to ensure the adoption of any constitutional amendments thought to be necessary.

At the opening of the new Parliament on 19 April it was announced that the

[1] See below, pp. 511–14.

Government intended to introduce a number of amendments to the Constitution. Among these was one which would permit the adoption of preventive detention. It was also stated that it was proposed to declare the official end of the Emergency on 31 July, and that before that date legislation would be introduced to incorporate many of the powers conferred by the Emergency Regulations into the permanent law.

The Bill to amend the Constitution was passed by the House of Representatives after an acrimonious debate on 25 April by 75 votes to 13, many of the Opposition members having left the House when a division was called. On 20 June the promised legislation to replace the Emergency Regulations was introduced in the lower House and passed through all stages. It was passed by the Senate on 6 July, and under the title 'Internal Security Ordinance' provided that should the Yang di Pertuan be satisfied that it was necessary to prevent any person from acting in a manner prejudicial to the security of Malaya or of any part thereof, he could order his detention for a period which might extend to two years. Alternatively, restrictions could be imposed upon his activities relating to his employment, residence, participation in politics, and movements at night. Provision was made for an appeal, against either detention or restriction, to an Advisory Committee consisting of a Judge and two other persons, whose advice would be tendered to the Yang di Pertuan. Each case was required to be reviewed every six months by an Advisory Board.

As in Singapore, the law was intended primarily to deal with persons found promoting subversion, replacing a similar Emergency Regulation under which over 300 people had been arrested since October 1958 when a drive against Communist penetration had begun.[2]

To deal with the gangsters, an amendment to the Prevention of Crime Ordinance was passed empowering the police to arrest without warrant persons registered under the Ordinance who were found loitering or consorting with other registered persons. This extension of powers was strongly criticized by a member of the Opposition, Mr D. R. Seenivasagam, a lawyer, who considered that the police were not to be trusted with such powers. Commenting on this, the *Straits Times* in a leader (29 June) remarked: 'All legislation of this kind is ugly and can be abused. The gangster activity against which this Ordinance is aimed is even uglier, and the ordinary processes of law are quite incapable of dealing with it.' There was general acceptance of the need for extended powers, a feeling that had been reinforced by a police report in May which revealed that 120 new gangs had been formed in the previous 15 months, offshoots of Triad and Wa Kei, and, for the most part, concerned in extortion in the new villages created during the Emergency. Fifteen thousand secret society men were known to the police, and of these 350 had been registered under the Prevention of Crime Ordinance.

As promised, the state of emergency, first proclaimed in June 1948, was duly declared to be ended on 31 July 1960. This, however, brought no abatement of the pressure exerted by the criminal gangs upon the public. Indeed, from this time onwards it would appear that their activities increased, with mounting figures of gang robbery, robbery, and extortion, including kidnapping of wealthy Chinese.

The establishment by the Singapore Government in June of a penal reform

[2] White Paper on Penetration of Communism, 24 Feb. 1959.

centre at Pulau Senang revived interest in the proposal which had received the assent of the Federal Government two years earlier to create such a settlement in Federation territory. On 3 October it was announced that an island off Pulau Tioman on the east coast had been chosen for this purpose. An added reason for setting up such a centre was said to be that China was now unwilling to accept criminals banished from Malaya. The *Straits Times* in a leader on 4 October commended the proposal, remarking that gangsterism was as serious a menace as ever. No such reformatory settlement was, however, established.

Details of secret society activities in the various States during 1960 are not available but crime statistics for the first nine months published in December showed that there had been a sharp rise in gang robberies and cases of extortion. In Selangor there were 275 of each of these, while in Perak there were 43 gang robberies and no fewer than 412 cases of extortion. At Malacca there would appear to have been a recrudescence of the Chee Fah lottery, for the police made 66 raids on Chee Fah agencies during the year.

In the House of Representatives on 21 April 1961, the leader of the People's Progressive Party (Mr D. R. Seenivasagam) accused the Youth Section of the MCA of recruiting thugs and gangsters of the Wa Kei Society and using them for intimidation at elections, and these allegations were supported by a member of the Socialist Front. It was said that a special fund had been subscribed from which to pay the costs of defence of any of its members brought to trial, and that free legal advice was available from Senator Yeoh, a lawyer. The Senator later vigorously denied any association between the MCA Youth and any secret society, and accused Seenivasagam of having originally used gangsters in his election campaigns and of having provided free legal advice for them. Action taken by the MCA Youth (said to number 50,000) he said, was simply in self-defence against this form of intimidation. Whatever the origin of the practice may have been, it seems certain that the MCA Youth organization did send truckloads of its members to places where elections were being held, ostensibly to keep the peace.

The incidence of kidnapping for ransom by gangs throughout the country also increased during the year, and in May a decision was taken to introduce legislation on the same lines as a Bill published by the Singapore Government authorizing the death penalty for this offence, and providing penalties of up to seven years' imprisonment for any person negotiating a ransom. The Minister for Justice, Mr Leong Yew Koh, in commending the Bill to Parliament emphasized the serious menace of the societies by saying: 'The steel grip which the secret societies have on the vast bulk of the Malayan Chinese community is really frightening.'

There were indications in 1962 that crime was still increasing and that the pressure of the societies was certainly no less. Statistics for gang robberies and robberies for the first quarter of the year showed an increase of between 40 and 50 per cent over those of the previous year which, in their turn, had been considerably higher than those for 1960. The King's Speech at the opening of Parliament in April referred to the threat to public order posed by secret societies and gangs of thugs, and to the inadequacy of existing laws to deal with the problem. New laws were under consideration, and the public were asked to render every possible assistance and co-operation.

During 1963, as indeed during much of 1962, matters criminal were largely overshadowed by matters political in the local press. Since April 1961, when Tunku Abdul Rahman first put forward for consideration the suggestion of forming a Federation of Malaysia comprising the Federation of Malaya, the State of Singapore, and the Borneo territories of Sabah (formerly North Borneo), Sarawak, and Brunei, there had been consultation between various representative bodies from all these countries. There were also vigorous objections raised by opposition parties in the Federation and Singapore, leading to drastic action by each of these two Governments against left-wing leaders. The date originally set for the inauguration of the new Malaysia was 31 August 1963, but at the last moment plans were disrupted by the violent reactions of President Sukarno of Indonesia (who had previously expressed approval of the proposals), and proceedings were stayed while a referendum in the Borneo territories was held. Eventually the Federation of Malaysia (though without Brunei, which declined to join) was brought into being on 16 September 1963, in the face of vociferous protests by Sukarno, who promptly instituted the campaign of 'confrontation' with military support which continued until June 1966.

It would seem that the news of these political shifts and developments so fully occupied the attention of the press that there was room for little else, though it is evident that despite the vast powers now possessed by the Government for detention without trial of suspected criminals, the public were still dismayed by the tyranny exercised by the gangs with near-impunity.

In 1964 attention was still largely centred on the troubles besetting the new Malaysia from without: the persistent pressing of the claim by the Government of the Philippines to part of the territory of Sabah, and the continuing confrontation by Indonesia, in the execution of which there were not only raids and infiltration in the Borneo territories by Indonesian armed forces but also attacks on the Malay peninsula itself by raiding parties landed on the Johore coast (August) and dropped into central Johore by parachute (September).

In January there was, once again, a reference to the proposal that a penal settlement should be established on an off-shore island. The Minister of the Interior stated that a committee had considered the proposal, but the contents of its report were not revealed and it was announced that the idea had been shelved. There was, apparently, some difficulty in persuading the Government of the State concerned to agree to the use of an island for this purpose. No doubt, too, the failure of the Pulau Senang experiment in Singapore in the previous July had a dampening effect.[3]

The use of secret society personnel for subversive purposes was revealed at the end of the year when it was announced that twelve self-confessed secret society men, since arrested, had been trained for sabotage in Indonesia and then sent back to Malaya to engage in such activities. Between June and October they had been responsible for four hand-grenade attacks, the derailment of a train, the placing of a bomb in the Malacca Club, and the partial destruction of an electric pylon in Malacca territory. The Minister for Home Affairs assured the House of Representatives that every effort was being made to keep the secret societies under control, and that their activities were well contained by the police. Since the introduction of the register of criminals (April 1959), 1,237 undesirable characters had been registered and many others were kept under restricted residence.

[3] See below, pp. 520–3.

In 1965 there was an important constitutional development. Incompatibility between political leaders in Singapore and the Federation of Malaya led, on 9 August, to a change in the composition of the Federation of Malaysia by the exclusion of the State of Singapore.

Turning to the record of incidents in the several States of the Federation during 1956–65, it should be noted that examination of detailed police records and reports for the purposes of this study ceased at the end of 1958. Thereafter such information as was obtainable from the press and from official publications has been used, but as these are comparatively meagre sources, from 1959 onwards, the information given here can only serve as a postscript to the main study.

2. PENANG

In Penang in 1956 Triad showed signs of revival. Early in the year a 'New Cell 12' of the Ang Bin Hoey was discovered, formed by five members of the old Cell 12 with some members of other cells. It had close links with Kuala Kurau and aimed at recruiting 1,000 members. Another old cell, No. 20, was also reorganized as 'New Cell 20', closely associated with the '308' Society, and, like it, at enmity with the '08' Society with which it had street clashes.

A series of disturbances by Chinese and Malay hooligan gangs began in January 1957 on the occasion of the celebration of the centenary of the establishment of the Municipal Commission. Some heat had been engendered at the elections for the newly-constituted City Council in the previous December when the Malay voters confidently expected to win a majority of the seats and consequently to elect the first Mayor whose name was freely quoted. In the event, Chinese won most of the seats, and a Chinese Mayor was elected. Openly and officially there was no friction on this account, but there is no doubt that the communal partisanship of Chinese and Malay hooligans contributed to the outbreak which occurred on 2 January during a procession forming part of the celebrations. A clash between a Chinese Lion Dance troupe in the procession and a group of Malays flared into a mob affray in which Chinese youths attacked Malays and assaulted a Chinese Police Inspector who tried to control the crowd. During the ensuing week four Chinese and a Malay were killed by being waylaid, and there were, in all, eighty-eight cases of assault. Appeals by community leaders and by Tunku Abdul Rahman who visited Penang helped to calm the atmosphere and vigorous seeking-out of known gang members by the police reduced the chances of trouble spreading.

Thereafter the secret society section of the police was reinforced under a fresh head of the CID, and an intensification of pressure began through the arrest of suspects, the collection and carding of information, and applications for warrants of arrest and detention wherever possible. This drive merged into Operation Pukat, but nevertheless in March there were two society murders near the Wembley Amusement Park involving members of the Eight Immortals (Pat Sin). Otherwise the record shows only minor extortion cases in one of which an offshoot of the Wa Kei calling itself the New Flower (San Fa) was concerned, until November when a fight between the Two Dragons and Tiger (Yi Leung Hoh) and the Wa Kei occurred in Cintra Street, during which parangs, daggers, and acid were used. Eight men were arrested, three of whom were 'wanted' in connexion with a murder in Serembam.

In 1958 nearly 1,000 persons were interrogated by the police. The only disturbances of the peace were a few minor clashes and assaults from which one death resulted. Among the gangs involved were the Eight Immortals, the Double Tiger Mountain, the Canton Ten Tigers, the Red Flower (Hung Fa), the Garden gang (Hua Huen), the '24' gang, and New Cell 20. In May the police intervened to prevent a planned trial of strength between the Eight Immortals and the Double Tiger Mountain gangs. Nine youths of the latter were arrested and turned out to be students of two Chinese High Schools: the Chung Ling and the Han Chiang. Information had been received in January that four of the gangs had penetrated these schools, and after the May incident the school authorities were prevailed upon to take disciplinary action which reduced the threat. During the last four months of the year no incidents at all were recorded, a quite remarkable state of affairs, particularly in the light of the announcement by the Chief Minister in April 1959 that there were 2,500 secret society members organized in 24 groups known to the police in Penang.

3. KEDAH AND PERLIS

In 1957 police action in these states was mainly directed against the Malay Bintang Lima (Five Star) gangs, first in north Kedah and Perlis and later in central Kedah where, towards the end of the year, four of these gangs were found to exist round Gurun. Six leaders were arrested, of whom four were committee members of a Malay political party. A Chinese extortion gang reinforced by '08' members from Sungei Patani and Penang was rounded up in April. At the end of the year there was a report of the formation of a new Triad society at Baling. Action against the Malay gangs continued in 1958 at Alor Star, Gurun, Yen, and Baling. Convictions were obtained against some of the leaders for theft, attempted extortion, and possession of offensive weapons. One man who had just returned from Mecca was restricted to residence on Pangkor Island; others were restricted for five years with one year's police supervision. In Perlis the Black Coat gang (Jubah Hitam) was reported to be responsible for most of the crime. It was about thirty strong, mostly Malays with a few Chinese.

4. PERAK

In Perak in 1956 there was considerable society activity, particularly on the coast and in Kinta. At Kuala Kurau, where the Ong clan reigned supreme, and where the Triad gangs maintained their traditional role of protecting smuggling, there was some internal friction. As in Penang, both New Cell 12 and New Cell 20 made their appearance, causing realignment of allegiances. But the chief trouble spot was Port Weld, where the Hokkien–Tiechiu struggle for power between the Ong clan on the one hand and the Behs and Lims on the other, which had continued since the death of the 'Pirate King', Loh Cheang Yeow, in March 1955, became very bitter in May 1956. Early that month the Behs organized an initiation ceremony in the swamps near Port Weld when several new members were admitted into their society, the Ang Bin T'ong. The Ongs decided on a trial of strength and on the 14th of the month sixty members of the rival factions assembled at Port Weld village, and only intervention by the police prevented a serious incident. Despite police reinforcements the pot still simmered. Two further initiation ceremonies were held by the Ang Bin T'ong in June and July, both at Bagan Hamida, near Matang.

Inland, in Ipoh and the Kinta valley, several new societies appeared. The '108' (or '08'), formed in Ipoh in 1955, became very powerful in 1956. Its leaders penetrated the North Malaya Commercial and Industrial Employees' Union which they used as a cloak for their activities, and the society's membership increased to over 400. Its influence covered areas in Ipoh town, Pasir Pinji, and Falim, and spread as far south as Telok Anson, where employers were intimidated into joining the society and contributing to its funds. Another gang came to light in April, formed by a Cantonese from Penang who had arrived in Ipoh late in 1955 and had organized evening classes in the Chinese art of self-defence at Menglembu. He was a member of the notorious Ngai Loke Society in Penang, and collected 20 or 30 youths to re-form the Eight Immortals, thus arousing the enmity of the remnants of the original society of that name which, after reorganizing as the Twenty-one Brothers, had later become the New Pasir Puteh gang, operating in Pasir Puteh and Pasir Pinji. A serious fight between the rivals took place in Ipoh in mid–July when two members of the New Pasir Puteh gang were stabbed to death by the Eight Immortals, and a third was badly wounded.

Elsewhere in the mining areas of Batu Gajah and Pusing there was activity among Cantonese societies in the guise of social clubs. Triad gangs with such names as the Little Heroes and the Dragon and Tiger Society appeared in some of the New Villages, and later there were reports that the manager of a mine at Pusing had accepted the demand of local Triad leaders that he should pay a protection fee of one dollar for every pikul of tin-ore produced. In Kampar, Tanjong Tualang, and Tanjong Rambutan the Wa Kei had become very active.

During the second half of the year a number of warrants of arrest and detention were issued by the Government under the Banishment and Restricted Residence Enactments, though not as many as the police recommended. Early in July a prominent leader of the '108' in Ipoh, who was concurrently the vice-president of the North Malaya Commercial and Employees' Union, was arrested on a banishment warrant, together with another '108' leader in Telok Anson.

In August 34 warrants of arrest and detention were issued, 8 for Taiping, 2 for Telok Anson, and 24 for Ipoh. Arrests included 4 leaders of the Ang Bin T'ong and 2 of the Pek Beng at Port Weld, another '108' leader at Telok Anson, and 11 members of the Eight Immortals who had been involved in the July fight with the New Pasir Puteh. Late in September a raid was made on Tanjong Rambutan, where for months the Wa Kei had been pursuing a vigorous recruiting campaign, and 11 arrests checked developments. By the end of the year, 13 banishments and 12 restricted residence orders had been confirmed and several others were pending.

The reaction of the gangs to this steady pressure was to call a meeting at Menglembu in July of representatives of the '108', the '303', and the Eight Immortals, together with other Triad members, some of whom came from as far afield as Singapore, Penang, and Kuala Lumpur. It was proposed that all should affiliate in an alliance to be known as the Woh Kei Society (not to be confused with the Wa Kei) and that 50 per cent of the receipts of each group should be paid to a central fund to be used for the assistance of members 'on the run' or in need of legal expenses. It would be the duty of all affiliates throughout the country to harbour such refugees, thus, it was suggested, circumventing the increased dangers flowing from the police reorganization. There were also proposals for importing members from other areas to eliminate police officers or informers who were over-zealous.

It is unlikely that any of the constituent parties would, in practice, have parted with such a substantial portion of their income on this basis, but negotiations continued throughout the year. Meantime the '108' in Ipoh changed its name to the Hung Hop T'ong (Triad United), moved its headquarters, stepped up its recruiting, and held an initiation ceremony. On the coast all members of the Ang Bin T'ong at Port Weld were required to contribute a minimum of $30 to a fund to be used to obtain the release of the society's leaders recently arrested, while the See Hai, the notorious fishermen's club at Pasir Hitam on the Trong estuary (mainly of the Lim clan), collected funds to build a new clubhouse.

In 1957 four new gangs were reported in new villages round Ipoh: the Heavenly Gang (T'in Fong Pong), the Young Swallows (Siew Fei Ying), the Double Tiger Mountain (Siong Foo San), and the New '08' (San Leng Pat), while at Kuala Gula a New Ang Bin Hoey came into being. Nevertheless Operation Pukat kept trouble to a minimum and only six minor clashes were reported. The number of secret societies existing throughout Perak at the end of the year was given as 52, of which 38 were Triad and 14 Wa Kei. There are no comparable figures for the rest of the Federation.

With Independence Day safely past, and less stringent police control, incidents became more frequent, and there were reports of minor cases of assault or attempted extortion from most centres: Ipoh, Falim, Menglembu, Taiping, Sitiawan, Kuala Kangsar, and Pangkor Island. Several of these were stabbing affrays or assaults with parangs, and the gangs involved included the '08', Twenty-one Brothers, Double Tiger Mountain, Woh Kei, Wa Kei, Eight Immortals, Flying Tigers, and Little Heroes. Early in May at Pangkor Island an outbreak occurred between Chinese secret society men and Malay gangs. Eight houses were burnt down, 1 man killed and 10 injured; 2,000 of the 10,000 inhabitants of the island fled to the mainland. The Public Peace Preservation Ordinance of 1958 was invoked and the police were reinforced. A curfew was imposed and all weapons called in. After a few days of tension, with police present in force, goodwill committees were formed and fears were dissipated. The incident, like that at Penang early in 1957, was a sharp reminder of the rapidity with which serious civil disturbances could arise, particularly in areas dominated by secret societies and especially when communal antipathies were involved. It also demonstrated the need for legislation such as the Public Peace Preservation Ordinance to enable action to be taken at a moment's notice.

At Menglembu in June one death resulted from the stabbing of a Woh Kei man by Wa Kei members, and in December the decomposed body of a man, believed to be a Double Tiger Mountain member, was found on a sandbank in the Kinta river. He had been wounded in the skull. Two men were found in possession of Triad ritual writings, one at Menglembu in February and the other at Gopeng in July. The police made repeated raids and night checks on gangster haunts, and obtained five warrants against members of the Ang Bin T'ong at

Port Weld who had fostered the tension arising from the dispute over the ownership of the cockle beds. Similar action was taken against five members of the Ang Bin Hoey at Kuala Gula. In December it was discovered that three Triad gangs in the Ipoh area had amalgamated. They were the Siew Ying Hung, the Pat Sin, and the Hung Hop. Taking one word from each of these titles, the new society called itself the Siew Pat Hung. In the following month this group was responsible for a particularly vicious example of inter-gang warfare at Menglembu when several members attacked nine Wa Kei men who were playing cards, hacking two men to death with parangs and wounding one.

In February 1961 the well-known pattern of a secret society fight during a funeral procession was repeated at Ipoh involving the Wa Kei and the '08'. On the morning of 11 April, in Menglembu, three gangsters stabbed a youth four times in the stomach and beat him as he ran into a coffee-shop. Though the street was crowded, no one intervened, and no information was forthcoming. Other instances of extortion and assault in the area were believed to have gone unreported. Shops had taken to closing before dusk to avoid trouble, and food-stalls, usually well patronized, were deserted. There had been 10 major gang clashes in 12 months resulting in 2 deaths. On 23 July there was another affray during a funeral procession at Menglembu with two men seriously wounded. For some time the Siew Pat Hung had been increasing in strength and was believed to have 400 members in Ipoh and 700 throughout Perak. The police arrested 11 leading members during July. In the same month there was a spate of robberies at tin mines near Ipoh, perpetrated by gangs who removed valuable items of machinery such as Diesel fuel pumps which were in short supply, using this technique to demand protection money from the owners. On 6 August a leading Chinese mine-owner was murdered at his home in Ipoh by a gang attempting to kidnap him. In November, 13 Restricted Residence Orders were issued against leaders of the Siew Pat Hung, and other arrests that month included 7 members of the '08' and 30 gangsters at Kampar, detained for enquiry. In December five 'Tiger' Generals, including the head of the Green Dragon Society, were arrested in Ipoh and one in Taiping, and later in the month there was yet another instance of a gang clash at a funeral, involving the Siew Pat Hung and the Koh Kee societies.

Ipoh was again in the news in May 1962 when there was a clash between the Wa Kei and the '08'. Ten members of the Eighteen Disciples, a Wa Kei splinter group, were served with orders of restricted residence, bringing the total of secret society men placed on such orders in Perak since April 1959, when the Prevention of Crime law came into force, to 201. In September the Minister of Justice declared that Ipoh had more serious crime than any other place in the Federation and that the gangsters there seemed to be thriving. It was his view that the imposition of whipping in addition to prison sentences was having a salutary effect. Even the quiet hill-station of Cameron Highlands had been invaded: a gang in June held up sightseers from a bus at a footbridge and demanded toll under threat of 'acid'.

In January 1963 the police began a review of the list of 450 gangsters who were on restricted residence with the intention of removing restrictions from those who had been of good behaviour. It was, however, still necessary to apply for additional orders, and in May leaders of the Wa Kei, the Eight Immortals, and the Canary gang were served with such orders.

5. SELANGOR

Police action, begun in 1965 against Chee Fah promoters and Triad and Wa Kei gangs in Selangor, continued in 1956, and by May Kuala Lumpur was cleared of Chee Fah. The organization disintegrated with the arrest of six remaining small operators in Klang and a Hainanese promoter who tried to bribe a police inspector to allow the lottery to continue. In October the arrest, for banishment, of a notorious leader of the newly formed '51' gang at Klang, helped to discourage the coastal groups. In the Kuala Lumpur, Sepang, and Salak areas, where the old Triad–Wa Kei antagonism flared up occasionally, intensified police action included the arrest of five members of the Eighteen Disciples in August and of the leader of a criminal gang in November.

As Kuala Lumpur was to be the scene of an important international gathering for the independence celebrations at the end of August 1957, every precaution was taken to prevent any civil disturbance. The special secret societies section of the police was strengthened, and information about every known or suspected secret society member or gangster was collected and carded. In July application was made for 44 warrants of arrest and detention, and in August for a further 59. The majority of the men concerned were from the Kuala Lumpur area (but 14 were from Klang) and when the celebrations took place, despite the quite exceptional crowds, no untoward incident occurred.

This police drive was the most comprehensive ever staged, and yet, on 19 June, a Triad initiation ceremony was performed at Kent Estate, only six miles from the centre of Kuala Lumpur town. The police, however, were warned in advance and managed to arrest eight participants, though many must have escaped for the paraphernalia at the site indicated that a full-scale ceremony was in progress, believed to have been sponsored by the '08' Society. Arrests under the warrants previously issued continued throughout the year, but the gangs were not eradicated, and in November a dispute over protection areas led to the murder of a headman of the '360' gang who was stabbed and hacked to death near the Chinese Assembly Hall in Kuala Lumpur by two members of the Twenty-one Brothers Society.

Next year (1958) only eleven assaults attributable to societies were reported, involving the Thirteen Princes, Two Dragons and Tiger, Kwan Luen, '108', '360', Canton Ten Tigers, and Twenty-one Brothers. There were two deaths from stabbing. The visit of the Canadian Prime Minister to Kuala Lumpur in November was the occasion of an intensified security check in which 200 doubtful characters were interrogated.

In February 1959, the year in which Tunku Abdul Rahman spoke of the 'growing menace' of secret societies, the police at Kuala Lumpur seized a cache of weapons assembled in readiness for a fight between the '360' and the Wa Kei, in which it was expected that 200 would have participated. The weapons included 19 acid bulbs, 10 parangs, and 7 bicycle-chain whips. Towards the end of 1960 the police began another round-up operation. Sixty-six men were arrested in December and 142 in January 1961, the object being to reduce the incidence of crime at the Chinese New Year (15 February). But even so there were eight gang robberies and sixteen other robberies in the State during January. In May in Kuala Lumpur in broad daylight two youths were murdered. One was stabbed and clubbed to death outside a cinema by a gang of ten, and the other was called out of a coffee-shop by four gangsters and slashed to death with parangs. Scores of people were present but no one intervened or gave information. Another youth was stabbed seriously during the afternoon of 10 July. At Klang in June a wealthy Chinese rubber merchant was kidnapped by an armed gang in full view of a bus-load of people but no report was made by them. The law providing the death penalty for kidnapping was passed in July but did not come into force until August. On the day the law was passed, a 13-year-old boy, son of a wealthy Chinese miner, was kidnapped.

On 4 May 1962 there was an attempted kidnapping in Kuala Lumpur in which the victim, having resisted, was shot dead. Three days later, several Senators spoke in Parliament of a 'crime wave'. The death penalty for kidnapping was said to be ineffective, and there were many murders and robberies. It was suggested that secret societies were encouraged by lack of employment and that they had extended their activities from Singapore. The crime figures were referred to as 'staggering', and there was 'appalling fear' among the people.

The Minister for Internal Security (Dato' Ismail) in reply declared that if members of the public would not come forward and report to the police, there was little that could be done even if the police force were doubled and new laws were introduced. As for kidnapping, 'as long as millionaires insisted on paying large ransoms rather than face their civic responsibilities, then I don't know how we are ever going to overcome the problem'. This reply was not well received, for the 'millionaire' was required to face not only civic responsibilities but certain torture and death, and, as was pointed out, people lived in such fear that they dared not report. Among other incidents in May, acid was thrown by a gang of eight at a man near Kuala Lumpur, and in June seven holds-ups or robberies were reported in the press, including the robbing of a goldsmith's shop in Kuala Lumpur by a gang who got away with $35,000 worth of jewellery. Early in the month, a judgement of the Federal Appeal Court revealed the surprising fact that under a section of the Penal Code which had remained unaltered since its original introduction, whipping with a rattan was mandatory in cases of conviction for gang robbery. In July a Chinese businessman was kidnapped in Kuala Lumpur and released four days later. He denied that any ransom had been paid. The assailants were later arrested. Chee Fah lotteries again appeared in the news when forty persons alleged to be concerned in their operation in Kuala Lumpur and Seremban were arrested. At the end of the month a police conference was held to consider the increase of crime, and once again emphasized that no effective improvement could be expected until eye-witnesses were prepared to give evidence. This conclusion was no more helpful than the minister's remark about millionaires, for the whole essence of the problem lay, as it had always lain, in the very fact that witnesses were not prepared to give evidence.

In a leader of 16 May 1963 the *Straits Times*, commenting on an audacious pay-roll grab in a crowded main street of Kuala Lumpur, declared that the year's crime sheet for the town was getting as bad as it was in the early postwar years when the police force had little morale and the crooks too many guns. It referred to half a dozen shopkeepers and as many householders who had been the victims of armed gangs. 'The protection racket,' it said, 'as the police know but will never admit, is flourishing as never before. There is a wave of the same kind in Ipoh and Penang. . . . There are few towns of any size where violent crime has not increased.' Thereafter no further comments on the crime situation in Kuala Lumpur appeared, but in 1965 there were said to be fifteen secret societies in Selangor, among them the Kwan Luen, the '08', the Small Plum Blossom (Siu Mui Fa), the Eighteen disciples, the '360', the '303', the Twenty-one Brothers, and the Tiger and Dragon.

6. PAHANG

In Pahang in 1956 the Wa Kei maintained the supremacy which it had already established during 1955. In February 1956, when the first local elections were held at Benta Sebrang, Wa Kei intimidation was said to be responsible for the very small polls, only 29 per cent voting in Benta Sebrang and 37 per cent in Benta town, the majority of whom were Malays. It was believed that the Wa Kei, in order to secure the election of their own men, effectively warned voters not to support other candidates, and as a result many voters, particularly MCA members, did not vote, and leading MCA candidates were defeated.

In June there was evidence of increasing Wa Kei–Triad enmity in Bentong, several clashes took place in August, and in November prior information enabled the police to prevent a very serious fight arranged to take place at Telemong between the Wa Kei and a combined force of Triad and Chung Woh Tong. During that month, too, a secret society sub-branch of the CID was at last set up based on Bentong. In December, after the Wa Kei had stabbed a Chung Woh Tong member who had refused to join their society and had killed a man who had intervened in the attack, about thirty Chinese, led by a local bus-driver, met together in Kuala Lipis to plan a recruiting drive for Triad and Chung Woh Tong, to secure their own safety in the event of further Wa Kei intimidation.

The sharp rivalry between Triad and Wa Kei continued in 1957, and the Chung Woh Tong, aligned with Triad, was also active. A San Yi Hing (Triad) was formed in Kuala Lipis in April, and in June the Triad group in Bentong split into two factions, 'New' and 'Old', for reasons which were not discovered. There was evidence of considerable liaison between the Pahang Chung Woh Tong and branches of the same society in Singapore and Selangor. The society held an initiation ceremony in September at Pertang village.

The same pattern continued through 1958 when about fifty incidents, assaults, and threats of assault, were reported, mostly in the Bentong area and invariably involving one or other of the three main societies. The most serious case occurred in July when a gang of the '360' from Kuala Lumpur threw five acid bombs into a coffee-shop, injuring five Wa Kei men. Six assailants were arrested. A typical case of 'protection' took place at Sungei Lui, a New Village, in February. A Lion Dance team from Selangor arrived to give performances there, and shortly afterwards three jeep-loads of Chung Woh Tong men from Sungei Ruan appeared, sent for the leader of the team, and demanded 70 per cent of his takings. No conclusion was reached, and the jeeps circled through the village several times as a display of strength, but were stopped by the police on the way out. One vehicle escaped, but in the others parangs, daggers, and a bicycle chain were found, and the sixteen occupants were arrested.

A Triad–Wa Kei incident occurred on a Bentong estate where the kepala (headman or overseer), a Wa Kei man, dissatisfied with some of his labourers who were Triad men, dismissed them and replaced them with Wa Kei men and was attacked by the Triad labourers reinforced by other members.

There was one case of discovery of documents, a man in a Bentong hotel being found in possession of a written booklet of Wa Kei ritual verses and code words. In April 1961, at Kuantan, 24 people were arrested attending a Triad initiation ceremony at a Chinese cemetery at 8 o'clock at night. Among them were two Malays and a young Sikh. Surprisingly, too, one of those in attendance was an 18-year-old Chinese girl.

7. NEGRI SEMBILAN

As in Pahang, the main feature of the secret society scene in 1956 in Negri Sembilan was the rivalry between Triad and Wa Kei. Both sides were busy recruiting, and the police found it necessary to take special precautions at Chinese New Year by calling in and warning known leaders. Six weeks later, on the night of 24 March, a Triad initiation ceremony was held in the Chinese cemetery at Tampin, and the police, forewarned, intervened but only managed to arrest six men, including the sinseh. Five of these were convicted and sentenced to imprisonment. In April there was a Triad–Wa Kei fight with knives when two men were badly wounded. In addition to prosecutions when possible, the police made full use of the procedures under the Banishment and Restricted Residence laws. Triad was reported to be active in ten areas, including Kuala Pilah, Bahau, Jelebu, Rembau, and Tampin, and the Wa Kei in six areas, including Mantin, Nilai, Lukut, and Port Dickson.

During the first half of 1957 there was apprehension of racial conflict on the declaration of independence, particularly in the country districts, and mass recruiting for both Triad and Wa Kei was reported from ten separate areas in April. In order to ensure greater concealment from the police, initiation ceremonies were sometimes replaced by a simple form of introduction of new members to old. In June there were reports of the formation of Chinese boxing clubs from eight places, membership varying from ten to fifty. These were invariably linked with either Triad or Wa Kei groups. In conformity with Operation Pukat, all known society leaders were warned to keep the peace and were closely watched.

A joint meeting of Wa Kei representatives from Seremban, Kuala Pilah, Dangi, Ladang Geddes, and Bahau was held at Jelebu in July at which the death benefit for members was fixed at $200, with an additional $150 to be paid to parents or dependants. Legal fees incurred in court actions by the police against members were to be met by subscriptions from all members, and all members were enjoined to attend funerals of members so that rival societies would appreciate the strength of the Wa Kei. One Triad initiation was reported, held, unknown to the police, at Sungei Nipah near Port Dickson, but only fourteen recruits were enrolled. During the last three months of the year three new Triad societies appeared, the Gi Tiong Hin in Seremban, the Thirteen Comrades linked with Singapore, at the Lee Rubber Factory, Seremban, and the '108' at Tampin with membership of over 100. There was one case of possession of Triad documents at Jelebu in December.

Although few incidents were recorded in 1958, there were two deaths as a result of gang clashes. The leader of the Flying Dragon Society (Fei Lung

T'ong), formed in March at Rahang Kechil, died after being assaulted by members of the Kwan Luen of Kuala Lumpur, and in December members of the Flying Dragon, armed with daggers, sickles, parangs, and chains, assaulted a Chung Yee Woh member, causing his death. This was said to be avenging a previous assault.

At a Triad funeral at Bahau in March it was noted that Triad members from Seremban, Tampin, and Kuala Pilah were present, and at a similar funeral at Tampin in May about 300 members from various parts of the state and from Malacca attended. One case of possession of written Triad verses was recorded at Rahang, and reports of the formation of 'Yankee Gangs' by Malays came from Ulu Berenang (30 members) and Kampong Talang, Kuala Pilah (12 members).

In a drive to induce a greater measure of confidence between police and public, 10,000 leaflets in English and Chinese were distributed in September 1962 urging the public to co-operate by giving information about secret societies, and promising that complete secrecy would be maintained as to sources of information. Such exhortations, however praiseworthy, rarely produce results, for it is the common belief that the secret societies, through their connexions with detectives and informers, will, sooner or later, uncover the sources.

8. MALACCA

The only notable features during 1956 were an influx of Wa Kei labourers for work on the Federation Regiment Camp at Sungei Udang (the contractor was a well-known Wa Kei supporter from Kuala Lumpur), and a Triad initiation ceremony held in May in a private house at which, it was said, 46 men and 1 woman were present. The organizer fled when investigations began, and no authentic details were obtained. Two urban gangs, the Lau Kwan Teo (a Triad gang of Peach Garden surnames) and the Fourteen Names (Chap Si Beng)—non-Triad—engaged in minor assaults and extortion.

In 1957 there were signs that both Triad and Wa Kei were strengthening their ranks by recruitment and influencing the labour unions. There were also serious gang fights in March involving among others the Lau Kwan Teo and the Fourteen Names, and further fights in May and June. A number of Triad initiations were held. In February two were held on an estate at Sungei Rambai, to which initiates came from Johore, Malacca, and Negri Sembilan, and another ceremony was being arranged. There were also reports of a number of 'mosquito-net' ceremonies[4] having been held in a squatter area of Malacca. In April a ceremony with simplified ritual was held at a temple at Kampong Pantai when 26 members of the Transport Workers' Union were admitted, and on 5 October there was a ceremony on Pulau Besar, off the Malacca coast, by members of the Lau Kwan Teo. Later in the month the police interrupted a ceremony in rather clumsy fashion, resulting in the shooting of two of the participants, one of whom died. Thirteen others were arrested. In November the police were warned that three political parties contesting the Municipal elections had employed gangsters to campaign for them. A close watch was kept on their activities and no trouble occurred. In March 1958 a cyclist was arrested and found to have two acid bulbs in his toolbag—the first appearance of acid bombs in Malacca. He

[4] See App. 1, p. 530.

and three others (who escaped) were said to be Triad members who intended to use the bombs against a police officer in the secret societies section. In September there was a fight between the '108' gang and the Yee Hup Woh in which bicycle chains and daggers were used, and one man died. Apart from these, the incidents recorded were of a very minor nature in which the Sa Kang, '108', '21', and '36' gangs were mentioned. An initiation ceremony at which 20 new members were enrolled was held in May in the Chinese cemetery, 7th mile, Muar Road, but the police were not forewarned.

9. JOHORE

Johore in 1956 was affected from June onwards by an influx of secret society gangsters fleeing from 'Operation Dagger' in Singapore.[5] Johore was an obvious refuge, and by the end of the year forty-eight men with tattoo patterns relating to Singapore societies had been charged with membership of unlawful societies. They had been found in all corners of the State, and, indeed, similar arrests took place throughout the Federation, even as far away as Kelantan and Trengganu. An attempt to link up refugees from the Singapore '108' and '303' with a local society in a 'Triangle' gang was frustrated by the police through the arrest of the Singapore men at Batu Pahat, but another Triangle gang, probably on the same lines, was reported to exist at Kluang. Tampoi was another area frequented by Singapore gangsters, and the arrest in November 1956 of the leader of the local '24' gang on a banishment warrant caused the Singapore gangster refugees to move on. Throughout the State Lion Dance teams and Chinese boxing classes sprang up as a prelude to independence, and, as elsewhere, were associated with local secret societies.

Police pressure kept incidents at a low level in 1957. Eighteen more tattooed men were arrested and charged; a '56' gang appeared in Kluang, and a '108' at Gemas Bahru, but no details of development were given. A number of assaults at the United Malayan Pineapple Factory at Skudai in 1958 arose from society allegiances. The trade union, as might be expected, had a large element of Sa Ji men, and to counteract this influence two kepalas recruited a gang of Sio Gi Ho men from Singapore for work at the factory and to show the union officials that they were not all-powerful. This led to cases of intimidation and assaults which quietened down after a police investigation and the prosecution of the management for not keeping a proper labour register as required by law. Apart from an attempt to kidnap a Chinese estate manager in November 1960, which was frustrated by a police ambush, reports of society activities in Johore in these later years were remarkably few.

10. KELANTAN

As in Kedah and Perlis, most of the criminal activity was conducted by Malay gangs which, in Kelantan, were armed with small axes and were known as Kapak Kechil (small axe) gangs. In 1954 there were on average twenty-five cases of assault monthly. A police drive beginning in 1957 with the imposition of restricted residence in many cases reduced the numbers by 1960, and at the end of the year these gangs were said to have been suppressed. But in August

[5] See below, p. 497.

1962 it was reported that there had been 107 assaults with weapons during the previous seven months, mainly by Kapak Kechil gangs. Clearly there had been a recrudescence of this specialized form of Malay gang activity.

Though the information covering the years 1959–65 is fragmentary, there is no reason to believe that any significant change in the basic impact of secret societies on the Chinese community took place during this period in the Federation of Malaya.

23

SINGAPORE, 1956–65

1. 1956–9

DURING the first six months of 1956 secret society activity continued to increase. During May and June there were 70 occasions on which gang fights were prevented by police intervention. The incidence of armed robbery rose to double that of the similar period in 1955. Gangsters armed themselves with home-made daggers and knuckle-dusters, and cycle chains fitted with handles were also used, while in preparation for gang fights, cases of aerated waters, wooden poles, and wooden stools such as were used at hawkers' stalls were placed in readiness in dark corners of streets and alley-ways to be used as weapons of assault.

This general deterioration in the secret society scene led to renewed attempts by certain China-looking groups to bring the societies under centralized control. In particular, the promoters of the Southeast Asia Hung Mun Chi Kung Tong redoubled their efforts, but their subsequent attempts to enlist the support of members of the Labour Front, and their redrafting of the proposed society's rules were in vain. Under no circumstances were they prepared to forgo the secret initiation of members, or the taking of the Triad oath, without which, they contended, they would be unable to maintain control over their members. The Government, on the other hand, were well aware of the danger of delegating to a Triad organization their primary duty of maintaining order. In any case, as the law stood, all Triad organizations were unlawful, and unless the Legislature was prepared to rescind this prohibition, which was unlikely, it was not possible to recognize a society which was avowedly Triad. But not until September 1956 did the promoters finally abandon their attempts to persuade the Government that the formation of a comprehensive Triad organization would be an effective instrument for controlling the unruly elements of the underworld.

In the meantime the KMT group had also re-entered the field, to support the existing Singapore Government, to oppose Communism, and to prevent lawlessness. They also aimed at gaining the support of 'big business', and winning over the secret societies to form the rank and file of a Chinese Nationalist society to promote local KMT interests and to form a channel through which KMT influence might penetrate. This resulted in the proposed formation of a Federation of Industry and Commerce which should further develop the trading prospects and industrial expansion of Singapore, and an attempt to create a 'chivalrous' society, which was to be in the nature of a welfare organization into which secret societies of all groups were to be recruited. The principal promoter was the organizer who had attempted to form the Youth Corps in February 1955.

Early moves began in May, but according to a report which appeared in the *Singapore Standard* on 5 May, certain members of the underworld swiftly took advantage of the current political climate to post 'invitation cards', stamped with a Triad seal, urging businessmen to become Triad members (at an entrance fee of $100 and a monthly subscription of $50), and to employ as their body-guards 'tough young men' guaranteed to have no previous gangster records. Other sources reported that owners of cargo lighters were being approached for contributions of $100 each.

On 10 June a meeting was held at a Chinese club in Singapore, attended by nearly 500 men representing about 175 secret societies of all groups, together with a number of leading KMT supporters. Also present was an emissary from Formosa who, according to the Chinese press, was a Triad 'Elder Brother' who had been banished from Indonesia in the previous year, and who, after spending some time in Formosa, had recently visited the Philippines, Hong Kong, and Siam, and in Malaya had made contact with several prominent leaders of the overseas Chinese community in Kuala Lumpur, Ipoh, Penang, Malacca, and Singapore.[1] His avowed purpose was the improvement of trade relations between Malaya and Nationalist China, but an account of his visit which appeared in the *Free China Magazine*, published in Taipeh in July 1956, con-firmed his interest in the unification of secret societies as a means of strengthen-ing KMT influence among overseas Chinese in Southeast Asia.

The meeting of 10 June resulted in a decision to form an association to be called the Chung Yi Tsung Sheh (General Association of Loyalty and Righteous-ness) which should support the local Government, oppose the spread of Com-munism, and, by settling disputes between its own component societies, should prevent the frequent recourse to violence which had disturbed the peace of Singapore. In later discussing this decision with the CID the promoters admitted that any reference to Triad had been deliberately omitted from the title of the Association, and stated that members would not be initiated, nor would there be any binding oath. Furthermore, they hoped that as branches of the Associa-tion spread throughout Singapore, individual secret societies would disappear. Although the Association was avowedly anti-Communist, its sponsors insisted that it was not a KMT organization, and asserted that one of its aims was to obtain local citizenship for its members.

The authorities were not deceived, and before action could be taken by the promoters to prepare rules and submit an application for registration they were informed that the Government could not countenance such a development. Although fully aware of the need for a new approach to the whole problem of counteracting the criminal activities of the secret societies, it was realized that the public of Singapore would immediately recognize the proposed organization as a Federation of Secret Societies, whose organizers and sponsors were primarily concerned in uniting secret societies under this banner for political purposes, and that prevention of lawlessness was only a very secondary consideration.

In June 1956 there was a change of government leadership, when Mr Marshall, the Chief Minister, was succeeded by Mr Lim Yew Hock.

In an attempt to stem the tide of gangster fights, an all-out police drive, known as 'Operation Dagger', began on 16 July with the declared objects of reducing the incidence of violent crime, preventing secret society clashes and

---

[1] *Kung Shang Pao*, issues 3 & 4 of 19 & 22 June 1956 (Singapore mosquito paper).

gang fights, and through police action making movement of armed gangsters in Singapore more difficult. The whole of the resources of the police force were brought into use during this operation, and the main targets were members of the underworld between the ages of 16 and 26. Between the hours of 7 p.m. and midnight, spot checks were made at coffee-shops, amusement parks, and other places of public resort, to search suspects for arms and to keep gangsters on the move. Road blocks were set up after dark to check for arms and on the number-plates of cars. Areas frequented by the gangs were cordoned off and systematically searched, as were back-lanes and other dark spots, while persons loitering in suspicious circumstances or suspected of being secret society members were arrested, particularly those bearing tattooed symbols.

The immediate result was a disorganization of the gangs. Many members went into hiding or fled to the Federation, where some were arrested by the Federation police while prospecting for fresh fields to exploit. In Singapore itself a number hid themselves in the lighters which thronged the Singapore river, others in the brothels of the city, until both types of refuges were 'flushed'.

During the first six weeks of 'Operation Dagger', 922 suspects were screened, of whom 736 were found to be already on record as members of secret societies. Gradually the incidence of serious crimes diminished, decreasing from 731 in June to 660 in July and to 610 in August. There were no gang fights, and only two incidents took place in which secret societies were involved, as compared with 97 in the previous six months.

At the same time further consideration was given to the possibility of introducing yet additional legislation to control the gangs, and attention was directed to the basic problem of why gangs and secret societies existed, and how best to prevent their coming into being. In his address to the Legislative Assembly on 29 August 1956 the Governor admitted that the Government had been gravely concerned by the danger to the public welfare from gangsters, secret societies, armed violence, and corruption, and said he was determined to continue to take strong action to remove these threats. In that task the Government appealed confidently for the co-operation and support of the public, which were essential. It was intended to do everything possible to foster moral welfare by the encouragement of healthy youth activities and by ensuring, as far as might be, that young people received proper moral teaching and guidance. The Government was anxious that parents should give more care to watching over the characters and occupations of their children.

These were brave words, but when it came to considering how such a policy should be implemented, the problem proved to be as elusive as ever. The leader of the PAP, Mr Lee Kuan Yew, in endorsing the desire of the Government to stamp out 'armed thuggery, intimidation, extortion, and all unlawful pursuits organized by unlawful gangs' rightly pointed out that although Boys' Clubs might help, the problem could never be tackled successfully unless the questions of education and employment opportunities were also tackled.

'Operation Dagger' continued, but despite the best efforts of the police it gradually ceased to be effective. With the realization that the powers of the police and the courts, though unsettling and irritating, were not a serious danger to their continuance in the business of protection, extortion, and blackmail, so long as the victims could be induced not to complain, the gangs started to re-form. In September there were five gang fights, and during October nineteen impending gang fights were thwarted by the intervention of the police. Then, on the night of 25 October, began the Chinese Middle School riots which gave members of the underworld an opportunity to take their revenge for the police pressure to which they had been subjected.

The Communist attempt to form a United Front of the masses by penetration of legal organizations, particularly those concerned with students and labourers, had gathered momentum during 1956. A year earlier registration of a Chinese Middle Schools Students' Union had been approved by the Registrar of Societies, Singapore, with the proviso that the Union should not participate in politics or industrial disputes. The Union was gazetted on 5 December (1955), but the proviso was, from the beginning, ignored. During 1956 the Union, jointly with other bodies, took an increasing part in political meetings and in political action and agitation. Within the Middle School members of the Union Committee organized a 'Study for action' campaign ('Hsieh-Hsih') on the Communist model, and dominated not only the discipline, organization, and policy of Chinese education but the Committees of Management, principals, and teachers.

The arrogance and recalcitrance of the Union leaders made action imperative. On 18 September (1956) three members of the staff of the Chung Cheng High School and two primary schoolteachers were arrested under the Banishment Ordinance. Also detained (under the Preservation of Public Security Ordinance) was a student of the Chung Cheng who was connected with the 'Hsieh-Hsih' movement. At the same time two Communist Front organizations, the Brass Gong Musical Association and the Women's Federation, were dissolved. On 24 September the Singapore Chinese Middle Schools Students' Union was itself dissolved, and a week later its president was arrested. On 10 October four more students were arrested, and the Minister of Education ordered the dismissal of two teachers and 142 students who had taken part in subversive activities.

The response of the remaining leaders of the union was to call a sit-down strike of the students of the Middle Schools, and the riots that broke out on 25 October were the result of the eviction of Chinese students who had camped in the grounds of the Chung Cheng High School and the Chinese High School for fifteen days, and had refused to leave. The students were supported by members of the Communist-controlled trade unions, who came to their aid in the same way as the students had aided them during the Hock Lee riots in May 1955. Support also came from the mob in general, including secret society gangsters.

Disorders began on the roads leading to the Chung Cheng and the Chinese High Schools, and by the morning of 26 October had become widespread. It was estimated that thousands took part in the rioting in Bukit Timah Road, when police and civilian vehicles were either burnt out or severely damaged. A crowd of 300 rioters attacked uniformed police close to the Chung Cheng school, and a similar crowd attacked the Geylang Police Station but was dispersed by a police charge. The mobs then directed their attacks against Europeans, and against the police wherever found.

With the aid of the military and a detachment of police from the Federation, the worst of the disorders were over by 27 October, and by 2 November quiet was restored, but the cost was 12 killed by police and military action, 4 being students; 127 people (including 26 police and servicemen) were injured, there were 2 cases of acid-throwing, and a Boyanese (Malay) driver of a City

KK

Council van was battered to death by rioters, an event which almost led to an outbreak by other Malays against the Chinese. As it was, two Chinese shops were damaged by Malays, but the efforts of Muslim leaders to persuade their co-religionists to be calm succeeded in preventing further trouble.

In addition to 375 arrests of persons connected with specific offences during the riots, the CID arrested 256 known secret society men in the disturbed areas. The secret societies neither caused nor directed the riots, but as in 1864, because of the organization of the mob within the various societies, the gathering of a crowd to take part in a civil disturbance was easily and expeditiously accomplished. On such occasions it is not necessary for this section of the public to be ideologically aligned with those who begin a riot. It is enough that there is a challenge to constituted authority, an opportunity for revolt and looting which those who are brought up in the secret society tradition cannot resist.

On 27 October action was also taken against 234 members of the Singapore Factory and Shop Workers' Union and the Bus Workers' Union, all of whom were detained under the Preservation of Public Security Ordinance. The able organizer of the Singapore Factory and Shop Workers' Union had already been arrested under a banishment warrant on 18 September, and several prominent leaders were included in the October arrests, among them Mr Lim Chin Siong, a member of the Legislative Assembly, and other members of the left wing of the PAP. But arrests even on this scale deterred neither the Communist Front supporters nor the secret societies. By the end of the year, the Singapore Factory and Shop-Workers' Union had re-formed as the Singapore General Employees' Union, again infiltrated by Communist organizers, and by March 1957 secret societies of the '108' and '24' groups, after a few minor incidents, had renewed their implacable feud.

A hint of the possible alignment of secret society groups with political parties was given in an article which appeared early in 1957 in *The Torch*, the organ of the Liberal–Socialist Party. It was suggested that the police had been successful during 'Operation Dagger' in suppressing gangs which were opposed to the Chief Minister, whereas Gang 24 was permitted to operate freely. From this it may be deduced that the writer of the article was of the opinion that Gang 24 supported the Chief Minister. Official examination of the background of 1,707 persons arrested did not support this allegation, but clearly the writer of the article was of the opinion that the societies had by then political affiliations.

The advent in June 1957 of bye-elections for the Legislative Assembly in the constituencies of Cairnhill and Tanjong Pagar brought again into public discussion the possibility of the influence of secret societies in elections, and the acting Chief Minister declared that the Government was determined to do its utmost to ensure that the contest would be conducted in an orderly manner and that neither candidates nor their workers would be subjected to intimidation or pressure from secret societies. An intensification of 'Operation Dagger' was ordered in the constituencies, directed against hooligans who were engaged in tearing down posters of candidates not supported by them.

No complaints were made to the police of any use of secret societies during the elections, but at the next meeting of the Assembly, on 18 July, Mr Lee Kuan Yew (PAP) introduced a motion calling for a Commission of Enquiry into allegations of corrupt practices by candidates. During the debate a number of speakers alleged that there had been corrupt practices involving secret societies, and it was clear that Chinese public opinion was in no doubt as to the truth of these allegations. The motion was passed unanimously, and on 2 September 1957 a Commission was appointed. Its report, which will be examined later, was submitted on 22 March 1958.

Throughout the rest of 1957 there was increasing public concern over the realization that the police were no longer able to exert reasonable control over the unlawful pursuits of the societies. In July a conspiracy was discovered to murder a member of a society of the '108' group. Thirteen conspirators were arrested, but as usual the evidence was insufficient to warrant court proceedings. All were members of the same society who had decided to kill a fellow member who had turned prosecution witness in a case of murder involving other 'Brethren'. Public affrays continued without abatement. On 1 September a party of detectives on rounds in Chin Nam Street discovered on the five-foot way a number of parangs, daggers, motor-cycle chains, and pieces of iron piping, obviously placed in readiness for a fight. On the night of the 17th a Chinese temple at Siok Wee Road was searched after information had been received that weapons would be found there, and the police recovered 4 parangs, 3 bottles and 4 bulbs containing sulphuric acid, a ceremonial sword, 4 wooden poles, 2 iron chains, an iron rod, 4 lengths of iron-piping, and 29 steel blades.

Also, from July onwards, the situation was further complicated by a series of well-organized kidnappings of wealthy members of the Chinese community. In the first of these the victim was the son of a merchant, the sum demanded for his release was forthcoming, and he was set free the same day. No report was made to the police. In August there were two cases (in one of which the sum of $1,500,000 was demanded as ransom, but the kidnappers were foiled by the bravery and determination of the victim's wife), one followed in September, two in October, and two in November. Though not organized by secret societies, it later transpired that the principal gang concerned was headed by an experienced secret society member who used others from Triad groups to carry out detailed observation of the movements of the projected victims, and to arrange for the provision of cars and the detailed planning of the operation. In addition to the kidnappings many more extortion letters were received by Chinese shopkeepers, and in October acid was used on two occasions in gang fights.

The police stepped up their campaign against the gangs by introducing 'Operation Pereksa' (Examination). During October, in addition to the intensive measures carried out by the Secret Societies Branch of the CID, the uniformed police examined no fewer than 19,641 persons, of whom only three were found to be in possession of offensive weapons. On 17 November a large-scale search of the Bukit Timah area was undertaken with the assistance of troops in an attempt to discover the hideout of the kidnappers, but was unsuccesful. Two similar wide sweeps were carried out by the police alone in other areas during the following week, again without success.

At the end of November, deeply concerned about the wave of kidnapping against which they felt themselves to be powerless, members of the Chinese Chamber of Commerce met to consider the position, and the meeting was widely publicized by both the Chinese and the English press. The president was reported to have said that victims of extortions and kidnappings were not confined to millionaires, 'but that hawkers, petty businessmen, and others with little money were also threatened'. Another member declared that nearly every shop in South Bridge Road had received extortion letters, another remarked that never had Singapore seen such outrageous defiance of law and order. Yet another was reported as saying that Singapore was being ruled by terror, and that the public was worse off than in Japanese days.

The merchants were understandably perturbed, and there was a noticeable tendency for wealthy members of their community to set off on journeys abroad to escape the unwelcome attentions of the kidnap gangs. Others bought themselves bullet-proofed motor-cars or travelled always with armed escorts, and had their homes well-fenced and protected by guard dogs. But not everyone could take such precautions.

A letter sent by the Chamber to the Chief Secretary invited his attention to the grave concern of the people of Singapore over the apparent deterioration of . . . internal security as reflected in the recent frequent reports in the Press of flagrant defiance of law and order such as extortion, kidnapping, gang fights, hooliganism, rape, juvenile delinquency, and politicians' manoeuvres with secret societies for electoral purposes or interference with the Police in suppressing gangsterism or secret societies' activities.

The letter went on to suggest that the situation called for a new and drastic approach with positive public co-operation, which might not have been possible hitherto either because of existing limitations of the law, or public funds, or the lack of practical arrangement for public co-operation. A Commission of Enquiry was proposed, consisting of trusted members of the public free from political party affiliations, to enquire into the various aspects of the problem, which were enumerated. The letter finally enquired whether the Emergency Regulations could be implemented to combat the existing crime wave.

It might have been a more helpful gesture had the Chamber itself instituted a campaign for public co-operation, for it was the reluctance of victims to complain and of witnesses to give evidence in cases involving secret societies that led to demands that the police should be fortified by abnormal powers. And just as former Governments consisting of a majority of European officials had been reluctant to introduce powers which went beyond the code of justice accepted in the United Kingdom, so, in 1957, a Government consisting for the most part of elected members of local people, whose policy was decided by a Council of Ministers of whom all but three were elected, found itself in the same quandary. But whereas the reluctance of earlier Governments had to some degree been conditioned by the outlook of the Secretary of State and Parliament in Britain, that of the new Government was more concerned with its reputation among the people of Singapore. This Government was the first step away from the colonial tradition, and it was necessary to make a gesture of removal of restrictions on the liberty of the subject, certainly not to assume powers and practices outside the normal framework of the law, for although the law was a colonial importation it was also the basis of the democratic idea which permeated the rising political parties. Already the popularity to be gained from the masses by the removal of the Emergency Regulations had largely been offset by the introduction of the Preservation of Public Security Ordinance, and the proposal to go still further and to apply unusual powers not only to the particular problem of the Communist menace but also to the regular problem of secret societies was disconcerting.

The fact remained that despite constant review of the laws in force and consideration of possible amendments or new laws, the only positive result in recent years had been the introduction of a penalty of imprisonment with or without flogging for throwing acid, and a small amendment of the Minor Offences Ordinance to deal more effectively with the carrying of dangerous weapons in public places. While these new provisions were in themselves welcomed by the police, the effect on the problem faced was negligible, and by the end of 1957 the stage had been reached when almost the only means of police control of secret societies was that of action under Section 12 of the Societies Ordinance for arrest and investigation of suspected members. Such action was both un-satisfactory and temporary, for should no grounds for prosecution be found, release was imperative within twenty-four hours, a provision well known both to members of the societies and to the general public.

The extent to which the police used such powers as were at their disposal may be judged from the following table covering the period 1954–7.

	1954	1955	1956	1957
Secret society fights	30	24	25	150
Secret society murders	4	11	4	10
Arrests under s.12(I) of the Societies Ordinance	2,920	3,205	3,821	5,024
Convictions under this section, mainly tattoos	55	4	119	3
Placed on record by the Registrar of Societies	384	73	170	230
Secret society members recommended for banishment	38	32	20	1
Orders of Banishment issued	17	9	9	nil
Ordered on conviction to undergo corrective training			5	1
Ordered on conviction to submit to curfew and police supervision			24	nil

When to these figures are added those of the activities of the Narcotics and Gaming Branches of the CID, and regard is had to the thousands of people stopped and searched by the uniformed police during 'Operation Dagger' and 'Operation Pereksa', it will be seen that police activity was on a considerable scale. But despite the heavy pressure exerted through these channels, the results were not commensurate with the effort, and it was clear, from the number of secret society fights and murders which took place, that the police drive against the gangs was unsuccessful and that something more effective was needed if public confidence was to be restored.

The use of the term 'secret societies' to describe the existing problem was, in some degree, misleading. Very few societies with full Triad ritual were function-ing in Singapore. The so-called secret societies which had plagued the island since 1945 had little ritual or formal organization and but small funds. They were, in effect, criminals' protection societies. The members, who for the most part were under 30, changed their allegiance frequently, and although most of the violent crimes against the public in Singapore were committed by secret society men, very few crimes were organized by societies themselves. The majority were committed by individual thugs or gangs of thugs who expected to retain all or nearly all the proceeds of their crimes, and who looked to their secret society only for protection against prosecution and against rival gangs. Gangs of criminals within the societies ran gambling, smuggling, vice, and extortion rackets, provoked gang fights, and intimidated the public, and the problem had become, therefore, one of crime in general and of the fear inspired by gangsterism in particular rather than an organized war by the secret societies against the Government. During 1957 the figures of crime of the types in which these societies indulged had greatly increased. There were 150 gang fights as compared with 30 in 1954, 24 in 1955, and 25 in 1956. The figures for kidnapping, extortion, and assault had similarly increased, and hospital figures showed a startling increase in the number of knife and parang wounds treated.

It was recognized that the existing problem of secret societies, gangsterism, and crime was essentially social and economic. Most members of societies and most of the criminals of Singapore were young men from poor homes, with no education, and little prospect of obtaining interesting or remunerative honest employment. But even if an improvement of economic conditions, active and expensive educational and club work among the children (and parents) in the poorer parts of the city, organization for self-protection among such groups as hawkers, and effective action by the police against gambling and against the middlemen, procurers, traffickers, souteneurs, brothel keepers, and persons who lived on the earnings of prostitutes, reduced the attractions and profits of gangsterism, juvenile delinquency could only be eradicated over a period of years, and the immediate need was to preserve the peace of Singapore. For that purpose it was necessary to rely on a strong police force backed by strong legislation and having the confidence of the public.

In attempting to deal with the crime wave the police had encountered several difficulties. Proceedings under the Banishment Ordinance were infrequent, because very few secret society members had both been convicted of crimes of violence and had been born outside Malaya. Furthermore, tattoo marks, insignia, and society documents were rarely found, and these convenient means of identifying members were therefore no longer available to secure convictions under the Societies Ordinance or preventive detention under the Criminal Justice (Temporary Provisions) Ordinance. Magistrates had proved unwilling to bind over persons brought before them under the Criminal Justice (Temporary Provisions) Ordinance on the uncorroborated evidence of police officers, while Section 3 of the Ordinance, providing for corrective training and preventive detention, could only be used if a conviction had first been obtained, and as it was almost impossible to persuade any victim or witness of gang violence to testify in court, this section was little used. Even where convictions had been obtained against gangsters, the court had frequently imposed very lenient sentences which were far from being deterrent.

Several proposals were put forward for strengthening the current law to enable the police to take more effective action, including increased penalties, corporal punishment for all crimes of violence, prosecution of persons found at the scene of a disturbance or escaping therefrom, and finally that the Government should have powers, similar to those under the Preservation of Public Security Ordinance, for detaining without trial known secret society leaders and members for corrective training or preventive detention. It was felt that the enactment of such legislation for a limited period of perhaps six months might be sufficient to enable the police to bring under control the gangster activities which were rapidly getting out of hand, and it was along such lines that discussions took place during the early weeks of 1958.

During the second half of 1957 the Government was faced not only with the ever-increasing activity of the secret society gangs, and with an unprecedented wave of kidnapping, but with renewed Communist subversion, and in August took action to counter Communist penetration of the PAP, several left-wing trade unions, and certain sections of the Chinese press. Under the Preservation of Public Security Ordinance, 38 arrests were made. They included 19 leaders of the Central Cultural and Education Committee of the PAP or its propaganda sections in the various branches, 15 leaders of 10 of the 32 left-wing trade unions, and 4 members of the staff of the *Sin Pao*, a Chinese newspaper which had played an important role in the co-ordination of Communist Front activities.

The attempted penetration of the PAP was of particular importance. At the annual conference of the party held on 4 August, only five of the 'moderate' leaders were re-elected to the central executive committee. This was part of the policy decided by the left-wing Middle Road unions that they would reduce the majority of the moderates in the PAP although they themselves were not yet ready to take over. Their plan failed when both Mr Lee Kuan Yew and Dr Toh Chin Chye, though elected, refused their appointments, and the extremists were obliged to take office. But on 22 August 5 of the 12 newly-elected members of the central executive committee were arrested, and the remaining 7 members constituted themselves as an emergency committee. Later, on 20 October, Mr Lee Kuan Yew offered them twelve 'safe' names to be voted for or against as a team. The offer was accepted, and at a meeting at which some 700 members of the PAP were present, the 'moderates' resumed control of the party.

In September the authorities had also taken action against renewed subversion within the Chinese Middle Schools. On the 25th, forty-eight students were arrested, and on the following day similar action was taken against the principal of the Chung Cheng High School. Twenty-nine of the students were later released, but Detention Orders were issued against the remaining nineteen, and the school principal was banished to China.

In December there was renewed political activity in Singapore in connexion with elections held on the 21st for the 32 seats of the reconstituted City Council, and four parties, the Liberal-Socialists, the Labour Front, the PAP and the Workers' Party (newly formed by Mr David Marshall), together with two Independents, contested the wards. The results showed, on the one hand, a spectacular fall in the number of seats held by the Liberal-Socialists, who, though previously holding a majority of seats in the Council, and though contesting all the 32 seats in the elections, won only 7. On the other hand, the PAP won 13 seats out of the 14 contested, and the Workers' Party won 4 out of 5 contested.

The success of the PAP and of the Workers' Party was attributed to the enthusiastic assistance of Chinese youths of school age, and both parties received strong support from the Chinese-speaking and pro-Communist sections of the community. The PAP's success was also due, in part, to the full support which it received from all its branches. The differences between the moderates and the extreme leftists within the party were temporarily shelved.

Reports that all the political parties and some of the Independents contesting the elections had the active support of secret society personnel is a factor relevant to this study, and at the time gave added substance to fears already expressed during the year.

Throughout 1958 the political scene in Singapore was dominated by final preparations for the achievement of independence already promised for 1959. Of these preparations, those connected with the elections which were an essential preliminary to the introduction of the new Constitution were of particular importance. There was danger not only that leaders of the Communist Front might capture the Government of the new State, but that through intimidation and corruption carried out by secret societies during the elections real freedom of voting might be jeopardized.

The decision taken by the Secretary of State for the Colonies that those detained for subversion in Singapore should not be allowed to sit as members of the first Legislative Assembly under the new Constitution was an attempt to counter the first threat, and the legislation enacted as a result of the publication of the report of the Commission of Inquiry into Corrupt, Illegal, or Undesirable Practices at Elections, laid upon the table of the Assembly on 14 April 1958, reduced the opportunities for coercion previously seized by the secret societies.[2]

The report confirmed that in the elections of June 1957, undue influence had been exerted on voters by secret society members. Indeed, the Commissioners expressed the opinion that, in their view, by far the greatest threat to free and honest elections lay in the existence of secret societies and the intervention of their members on such occasions. They added:

> In the case of offences committed by members of secret societies or persons enjoying their protection, it is virtually impossible to get witnesses to testify in Court against the offenders. The basic factor responsible for that state of affairs is the public sense of insecurity which we can well appreciate. Unless and until the Police are in a position to deal adequately with the secret societies in Singapore and eliminate them as a factor in the life of the community, members of the public cannot reasonably be expected to come forward and give evidence in Court which would expose them to certain and ruthless reprisal by the secret societies.[3]

Referring to the evidence of one witness described as having 'extensive knowledge of the subject', and who was of the opinion that the ordinary person in the lower middle class considered that he got better protection from the secret societies than he did from the Government, the Commission commented on the difficulties facing the police because of the acceptance of secret societies by certain sections of the population, and remarked:

> The result of the inability operating under the present laws to rid the country of secret societies and to secure the punishment of offences committed by their members has instilled in the minds of the public a fear of the power of secret societies and a lack of confidence in the Police to deal with them and to afford protection against their activities.[4]

The fear was certainly there, but it was an ingrained, traditional fear deriving from the age-long social pattern in China. Once more the Commission was

[2] Sing. Leg. Ass., Cmd. 7 of 1958.   [3] Ibid. p. 33, para. 81, & p. 12, para. 15.
[4] Ibid. pp. 12–13, paras 17 & 19.

reiterating the opinion so frequently expressed in the past that the laws in force in Singapore under the British judicial system were inadequate to eliminate or control these societies or to protect the public from their depredations, mainly because the victims could not be persuaded to bear witness against the aggressors.

The report gave details of the methods of operation of the societies at elections:

> Canvassing for votes by members of secret societies is based on intimidation, which depends for its effectiveness on the premise that the canvasser is known to the elector as a member of a secret society. The threat may be expressed or implied, but in either case the gist of it is that the elector may expect harm from the society after the election, if he should fail to vote as directed. Very often merely the fear of incurring the displeasure of the secret society is sufficient compulsion in the mind of a voter in daily proximity to secret society gangsters to induce him to vote as directed by the secret society canvasser.[5]

The report then dealt with the practice of candidates on election day sending out their supporters to collect voters and transport them in cars to the polling stations. The practice provided great scope for exploitation, because a secret society member, either as passenger or driver, accompanied the elector to the polling station giving him last-minute instructions on how to vote. Moreover, the society member waited while he cast his vote and then took him home, thus maintaining the sense of intimidation because, according to the evidence heard, the voter had little faith in the secrecy of the ballot and 'considerable faith in the ability of the secret societies to get to know things supposed to be secret'. This sense of intimidation operated among people inexperienced in elections and with an exaggerated idea of the omniscience of secret societies; it was accentuated when society members demanded to see their identity cards and noted the particulars against a copy of the electoral roll.

This was a very true description of the role of the secret society canvasser and of the ingrained fear on which he worked. Equally true was the statement in the report concerning another style of intimidation:

> The prevention or discouragement of electors from going to the polling stations is a comparatively simple task for members of a secret society. . . . They know the political leanings of the electors in their locality, and on election day by a show of force in the streets they prevent, or at least discourage, electors considered to be supporters of an opposing candidate from leaving their homes or shops. There is, however, little or no overt intimidation. They loiter in groups disporting the symbol of the candidate they favour, and electors who would vote for another candidate are afraid to go by. The more venturous electors would be simply told to go home. This form of control is particularly effective to prevent electors from entering cars provided by an opposing candidate to take them to the polling stations. There is, of course, nothing to prevent a voter from accepting a lift to the polling station in the car of the candidate supported by the gangsters, and then voting for another candidate; but this is not readily appreciated among the less educated people of Singapore. Moreover, where there is secret society intimidation in the streets in support of a candidate, there is an understandable fear that there will be secret society members in the cars provided by that candidate, who will intimidate the voter into voting for him.[6]

The result of the Commission's investigation of specific incidents which were alleged to have occurred during the bye-elections in June 1957 were also given in the report. The Commissioners stated that from the nature of that evidence

[5] Ibid. p. 13, para. 21.   [6] Ibid. p. 14, para. 23.

they formed the opinion that only part of the picture had been revealed to them, and that the full extent of the intervention by members of secret societies was still a matter of conjecture.[7] Even so, the report revealed that societies belonging to the '108', the '36', the '24', the '18', and the independent Sa Ji groups, had all played their part, and that certain society leaders had been particularly active.[8]

Although some of the candidates later complained that they were not given the opportunity to cross-examine witnesses and challenged the findings of the Commission on points concerning their own dealings with secret society members, no one attempted to deny that the picture drawn was a true representation of the place occupied by the societies in the life of the people and a correct outline of the tactics used by their members at elections. Nor were such manifestations of secret society interest in elections confined to Singapore. They existed in the Federation wherever there were Chinese eligible to vote.

The employment of secret society members in election campaigns was only one section of the enquiry of the Commission, which was required to investigate corrupt, illegal, or undesirable practices at elections whatever their origin. The Commission's recommendations included proposals for the registration of canvassers, the prohibition of canvassing on the day of the election, of the provision of private transport to take voters to the polling stations, of the display of anything on vehicles to indicate connexion with any candidate or party, and of persons loitering within a radius of 200 yards of a polling station, all of which were designed to prevent the intimidatory activities already described. It is noteworthy that most of these recommendations related to restrictions which are not considered to be necessary in England, and that, once again, something beyond the provisions of English law was deemed necessary to protect the public in Singapore.

Perhaps the most surprising of the conclusions reached was that compulsory voting was the most important single measure that could lead to the elimination of the types of corrupt practices that had occurred. The Commission believed that, by increasing the field of the franchise, compulsory voting would reduce the significance of any corrupt influence which might be exercised over sections of the electorate, and would obviate the need for candidates and their supporters to induce electors to exercise their franchise.[9] This may be too sanguine an estimate. Certainly compulsory voting would not seem to affect any of the modes of intimidation set out in the report. On the contrary, it would widen the field for intimidation, for whereas under a voluntary system a voter might stay at home and avoid pressure, under a compulsory system anyone attempting to avoid his duty, like anyone else committing an unlawful act, would give the secret society a lever to use against him. He must vote or the society members would report him, and the rest of the intimidation to compel him to vote for a particular candidate would continue as before. However, the idea of compulsory voting had been a subject of public discussion for some time because of the smallness of the poll under the voluntary system, and doubtless this influenced the Commission. In due course, most of its recommendations, including the system of compulsory voting, were embodied in the Legislative Assembly Elections Ordinance, passed on 3 March 1959.

Meanwhile, on 23 April 1958, nine days after the Commission's report had

[7] Sing. Leg. Ass., Cmd. 7 of 1958, p. 15, para. 29.
[8] Ibid. pp. 15–20, paras 29–42.   [9] Ibid. p. 34, paras 85–6.

been laid on the table of the House, the Government had made a legislative attack on the gangs by introducing, on a Certificate of Urgency, its proposals for strengthening the powers of the police through amendments to the Criminal Justice (Temporary Provisions) Ordinance and the Penal Code.

The secret society crime wave of 1957 had continued into 1958. There were fights in January and February, and fights and an initiation ceremony in March. Throughout these months during which the '108' and the '24' were at one another's throats, there was a deplorable increase in the use of acid during fights and in premeditated attacks, and on one occasion a member of the '24' hurled electric light bulbs filled with acid into two lorries taking labourers to work, injuring seven men. Another disturbing factor was the discovery that schoolboys were joining the gangs in ever-increasing numbers, not only boys from the Chinese schools which had always provided a reservoir for new entrants but also boys from English schools which had hitherto been reasonably free from such contacts. The virus had also infected the Singapore Infantry Regiment, and 56 men (representing 10 per cent of the force) were discharged for secret society activities.

After debate, the following amendments to the Criminal Justice (Temporary Provisions) Ordinance were passed with only one dissentient voice:

1. The court was given power to impose preventive detention or a course of corrective training on those found guilty of offences included in the Schedule to the Ordinance without requiring proof of membership of a secret society. This gave the courts a wider discretion than formerly, but did not overcome the difficulty of obtaining adequate evidence to obtain a conviction.

2. In order to counter the practice adopted by gangsters who had been engaged in a fight or were about to be so engaged of dropping their weapons on the arrival of the police and assuming the role of innocent onlookers, powers were given to police officers not below the rank of Inspector to arrest persons found in suspicious circumstances in the vicinity of a gang fight. Thereafter, provided such persons could be shown to be either members of an unlawful society or to have been placed on record by the Registrar of Societies, they could be required by a court to enter into a bond to keep the peace. The court was given power to make curfew orders on such persons, and breach of the bond entailed liability to imprisonment not exceeding twelve months, or to a fine of $1,000, or to both.

3. Finally, the carrying of knives or offensive weapons in public, loitering with intent to commit a seizable offence, and offences under the Corrosive Substances Ordinance (1956) were added to the list of scheduled offences. These were types of offences frequently committed by persons associated with gang warfare.

Despite the anxiety expressed by all members who spoke on the Bill that some way should be found to put an end to the menace of the gangs, there was considerable disquiet about giving the police powers to arrest onlookers. More than one speaker alleged that the police detectives were all ex-secret society men and would use this new power to avenge themselves on former enemies by falsely informing their Inspectors that innocent individuals were connected with societies while permitting the real gangsters to operate under their protection. The problem was how to give the necessary power to the police to enable them to bring the gangsters to justice without, at the same time, exposing innocent persons to the abuse of authority.

The Leader of the Opposition (Mr Lee Kuan Yew) considered that should attempts be made to bring standards and patterns of law and order from a foreign land which did not suit local condictions, chaos would result. Neither the democratic system, nor its rules, laws, and enactments could be transplanted wholesale. He admitted that the basic causes of secret society violence were social and economic, but until those causes were remedied there was need for certain restrictive action lest the secret societies should turn their attention not only to extortion but to the overthrow of the existing political order. While opposing the extremes of the Japanese, who beheaded secret society members, and of the Russians, who sent such offenders to work camps where they were reorientated into the 'right way of thinking', it was necessary to find a solution which would act as an effective counter and even as a deterrent. He hoped the Bill would answer the need.

The amendments to the Penal Code were designed to permit the courts to impose heavier penalties for certain offences. For committing an affray the maximum imprisonment was raised from one month to one year, and the maximum fine from $100 to $1,000. For kidnapping or abduction the maximum sentence was raised from seven to ten years, and, in addition, the court was empowered to order whipping for these two offences. In explanation of the reintroduction of whipping, the Chief Secretary admitted that although modern penal reform was antipathetic to the use of corporal punishment, those principles of reform, if they were to achieve their purpose, required the existence of conditions which it had regrettably to be admitted did not exist in Singapore. The thugs who took part in crimes of violence were not, for the most part, susceptible to the sympathetic treatment which those principles symbolized. No objections were raised in the Assembly to the amendments, and, indeed, one member was very strongly of the opinion that the enhanced penalties for kidnapping and abduction were still inadequate. Certainly, the proposals as brought before the House were far less stringent than might have been expected from the original drafts. During preliminary discussions the essential recommendation that the Government should have powers similar to those under the Preservation of Public Security Ordinance for detaining without trial known secret society leaders for corrective training or preventive detention had been dropped. Modifications had also been made concerning corporal punishment, which was to be provided only as an alternative punishment for crimes of kidnapping and abduction, and not as a mandatory punishment, while the provision for prosecution of persons found at the scene of a disturbance or escaping therefrom included safeguards for persons with reasonable excuse.

The amendments passed on 23 April 1958 came into force on 2 May, but the situation continued to deteriorate, and on 12 June still further powers were given to the police by the Legislative Assembly under the Societies Ordinance, the Gaming House Ordinance, and the Betting Ordinance, to enable police officers not below the rank of Assistant Superintendents to enter and search premises in which they had reason to believe that offences against these laws were being committed, without the necessity of having to obtain a warrant from a Magistrate.

In addition to the augmentation of police powers, an attempt was made to establish closer contact between the police and the public. At the end of June a Police Week was held during which some of the main police stations were thrown open to the public, and talks were given on various topics of police activity. The Police Week was amazingly popular, and crowds thronged to the police stations as though to a theatrical show. As a result, the experiment was extended to other police stations both in the city and in rural areas with equal success.

But qefore the new powers conferred in May and June could be given a reasonable period of trial, or the policy of encouraging the public could get beyond the initial stage, Singapore was swept by a wave of gangster crime which caused shock and alarm. Already in April, May, and June there had been a further 89 gang fights. In June alone 44 persons were injured in such fights, and in July Hokkien secret societies were responsible for 4 murders and the wounding of over 40 people, half of them seriously. Most of these casualties occurred during affrays between the '24' group and the '108' group, and in addition another feud between the '36' and the '108' was in full swing. The feuding groups instituted curfews upon each other, and organized battles in which 20, 30, or 50 men a side participated, whilst members seen on the city streets by a rival group were assaulted at sight.

A notable feature of the assaults was the number of young schoolboys involved. One 12-year-old boy was stabbed eight times and tortured by a juvenile gang, and a youth was admitted to hospital after having been savagely beaten by a gang of ten boys aged between 10 and 15. The police made many raids on known gang headquarters and on premises where fights were about to take place. Frequently the information on which they acted came by telephone from members of the public in areas where gangsters were seen to be congregating, and this was a welcome change from the usual apathy. Invariably the usual paraphernalia of offensive weapons was found—parangs, spears, daggers, poles, and aerated water bottles, together with bottles or bulbs of acid.

August began even more viciously than July. On the second of the month a petrol-kiosk attendant was admitted to hospital in a serious condition after having been assaulted by ten thugs. Another man had a serious knife wound inflicted during an early morning attack. A fireman was battered to death and another man stabbed to death. Two days later a youth of 15 belonging to the '108' was kidnapped from near his home by young gangsters of the '24' group. By 10 August eight people had been killed and twenty-four seriously injured during the previous six weeks.

This wave of crime caused widespread alarm, and on 11 August the Chief Minister announced that the Government had approved an emergency plan (Operation Sapu) to deal with the gang leaders. From 5 p.m. each evening and throughout the night the police combed the haunts of the gangsters looking for known members and especially for leaders, and on 13 August, in view of what the Chief Secretary described as the 'extreme gravity' of the worsening position, the Government introduced on a Certificate of Urgency a Bill amending not the Criminal Justice (Temporary Provisions) Ordinance, but the Criminal Law (Temporary Provisions) Ordinance.

The purpose of the amending Bill was to empower the Chief Secretary to issue Orders of Detention in respect of persons who had been associated with activities of a criminal nature, and whose detention had been shown, to his satisfaction, to be necessary 'in the interests of public safety, peace and good order'. The consent of the Public Prosecutor was necessary before an Order of Detention could be issued by the Chief Secretary, and although the original detention was not to exceed six months, extensions of such Orders were permitted up to a total of two years. An Advisory Committee was constituted to which all Orders were to be submitted, together with the grounds for making the Order. The Committee would then report to the Governor in Council, who would cancel or confirm the Order. Any police officer might, without warrant, arrest and detain any person in respect of whom he had reason to believe there were grounds which would justify his detention by an Order of the Chief Secretary. Such police detention could extend to sixteen days should this be necessary for purposes of enquiry.

In introducing the Bill, the Chief Secretary remarked that the House needed no reminder of the current situation regarding enforcement of law and order because of the activities of secret societies. He referred to the steady increase in gangsterism over a long period and to the recent serious increase in crime. There had been 157 gang fights in the first six months of the current year as compared with 150 in the whole of the previous year (1957) which in itself was six times as high as the figure for 1956. In the six weeks since 1 July 1958 there had been 51 fights and 6 murders attributable to secret society activities, and the incidence of housebreaking and theft was already double that of previous years. He declared that the basic reason why the police were unable to deal with the menace was the intimidation of the public by members of the gangs so that no one was prepared to give evidence in court. He added:

It is only the exceptional gravity of the present state of gang lawlessness which impels the Government to seek these exceptional powers for immediate use. No democratic government would like to curtail the liberty of any individual by executive action. This Government is no exception. But when there is no other means of restoring peace and good order and removing the dark shadow of terrorism which is spreading over the lives of innocent citizens, the Government has not only no alternative, but a positive duty to the public to take that action.

He went on to say that the powers in the Bill would be used against the leaders of the gangs, not against the rank and file.

Only one Independent member opposed the Bill; other speakers regarded it as an unfortunate necessity. The debate was noteworthy for the support given by Mr Lee Kuan Yew (PAP), himself a lawyer, to the contention that the normal judicial processes were inadequate. There were, in his view, three alternatives—either the gangsters were brought to trial, or allowed to continue as they were going, or locked up without trial. The PAP preferred to bring them to trial if possible. But, he continued, as every practising lawyer in town knew, the police admitted they could no longer deal with the situation. The gangsters knew the procedure by heart. The police would arrest them and lock them up for twenty-four hours. When they were produced in court they got two others to stand bail and the case was postponed. When the case came up for hearing, the witnesses decided that it was not healthy to say anything and the gangsters were acquitted. The situation was either to surrender, admitting that the judicial process was inadequate and that the law was beaten by the gangsters, or to decide to do something about it. Mr Lee then went on to make the accusation that important members of the Government party, the Labour Front, consorted with known thugs and members of secret societies. He was referring to a bye-election for the City Council held recently in July during which there were mutual recriminations by the Labour Front and the PAP alleging the use of secret society gangsters for purposes of intimidation during the election campaign.

The Bill was passed, and the Ordinance came into force on 15 August as Ordinance 25 of 1958. At the same meeting of the Assembly another Bill was introduced to implement many of the recommendations of the Commission of Inquiry into Corrupt, Illegal or Undesirable Practices at Elections. Some of its provisions were designed to minimize the participation of secret society gangsters in election campaigns, and it was referred to a Select Committee.

The passing of the amended Criminal Law (Temporary Provisions) Ordinance meant that the Government at last openly admitted that the position postulated by Bonham in 1830 had been reached when he said: 'So long as the present judicial system exists in these Straits, it appears to me totally out of the question to put down the Hwuys.' True, the structure of the societies had changed, but the basic characteristic, intimidation of the populace, remained the same, and for that reason the main problem to be faced had not changed. Once the secret societies had been prohibited by law in 1890, the key to their control lay in the Banishment Ordinance and in the pressure which the Chinese Protectorate with its counter-ramifications throughout the Chinese community was able to exert. The operation of the Banishment Ordinance and the activities of the Chinese Protectorate were both acts of the Executive outside the framework of the normal judicial system. But by 1958, with the youth of the population almost entirely local-born, the Banishment Ordinance had lost its power, and with the abolition of the Chinese Protectorate this channel of influence had been removed, although it is probable that with modern developments in the underworld and among Chinese labour its influence would, in any case, have waned.

In place of the previous controls, the new law now introduced another extra-judicial power to be used by the Executive, but one of far less potency than that of the Banishment Ordinance. Detention for six months or even for two years was not to be compared with banishment to China. In the first case the culprit, fit and fattened after a safe sojourn in the hygienic confines of a detention camp, returned to his avocation refreshed and renewed. In the other he found himself removed for ever from the lush pastures of Singapore or the Federation of Malaya, and thrown back into the dangerous battleground of the underworld in China where others were already jealously guarding their perquisites and killing was no murder.

Nevertheless, despite the lesser value of the new power thus sanctioned, the date, 13 August 1958, is one to be remembered in the annals of Singapore, for it was then publicly proclaimed and accepted that the complex machinery of the law fashioned in accordance with British concepts of justice was inadequate to enable the Government to fulfil its primary function, that of maintaining order. Furthermore, this decision was reached and endorsed not by a Government of colonial bureaucrats, nor by a council of British business tycoons, but by a Legislative Assembly of which more than three-quarters of the members were elected by popular franchise, and the majority of whom were Chinese. (It should, however, be remarked that most of this majority were Western-educated.) A crisis in the impact of the culture patterns of East and West had been reached, not this time merely in the minds of the non-indigenous ruling class, who might be suspected of overestimating the danger through lack of contact with the masses, but in the minds of the local-born inhabitants, who might be expected

to interpret with some accuracy the feelings of the people around them. Moreover, this action was taken by a Government which knew full well that it not
only laid itself open to the charge of undemocratic tyranny but might well
estrange a significant proportion of the voters among the sansculottes of the
city. To such a degree were the Assemblymen convinced of the immediate danger
to the peace of the State presented by the secret societies. It is significant, too,
that the Opposition did not attempt to make political capital out of the un-
enviable position in which the Government found itself. On the contrary, the
need was recognized, and all political parties supported the unusual legislation,
only two Independent members voting against it. In the local English-language
press the Ordinance was referred to as 'probably the most widely-welcomed
legislation of recent years'.[10]

The police at once began a campaign of arrests of known gang leaders, and
by the end of the year 145 had been placed in detention. But the fights continued
—27 in September, 27 in October, 30 in November, and 35 in December. The
disturbing total for the year was 332. They had involved 14 deaths (in addition
to two other secret society murders) and injury to 285 persons, 25 of whom were
victims of acid attacks.

Politically, the last two months of 1958 were a period of some ferment as
various parties began to prepare for the vital elections to be held in May 1959.
On 10 November (1958) the Chief Minister, Mr Lim Yew Hock, announced the
formation under his leadership of a new political party, the Singapore People's
Alliance (SPA), designed to unite members of the Labour Front, the Liberal-
Socialists, and the Workers' Party in common opposition to the PAP. This move
was only partially successful, as the original parties were not dissolved but continued in existence despite loss of leaders and members. Meanwhile, the PAP
carried out extensive internal reorganization. It purged itself of extremists,
created a special cadre membership, re-registered all members, and reaffirmed its
aim of creating an 'independent, democratic, non-Communist, socialist Malaya'.

The terms of the new Constitution resulting from the final talks held in London
in May 1958 were published in Singapore on 27 November. There was to be a
State of Singapore, with full powers of internal self-government under a Yang
di-Pertuan Negara. Responsibility for defence and external affairs was reserved
to the United Kingdom Government through a High Commissioner resident in
Singapore. There was to be a Legislative Assembly of 51 elected members with
power to choose its own Speaker, and a Cabinet over which a Prime Minister
who commanded the confidence of a majority in the Assembly would preside.
The final power in matters of internal security was to lie with an Internal
Security Council which would include three representatives each of the Singapore and United Kingdom Governments and one ministerial representative from
the Federation Government who would, in effect, have the decisive vote.

At a forum of political parties held in Singapore on 29 November 1958 the
leader of the rump of the Labour Front publicly stated that he had already
received fifteen reports that one political party (by inference the SPA) was using
strong-arm men to canvass in certain areas in the customary secret society
tradition. The revelation by the PAP in February 1959 that a fund of $500,000
(Malayan) had been deposited in an American bank in Singapore by an organization in America at the disposal of a Minister of the Government did

[10] *Sunday Times*, 21 Sept. 1958.

nothing to improve the prospects of the SPA, and when the elections for the newly-constituted Legislative Assembly took place on 30 May 1959, contested by 14 parties and 34 Independents, the PAP won 43 seats, polling 283,799 of the 524,420 votes. Of the remainder, 4 seats were won by the SPA, 3 by UMNO, and 1 by an Independent. Only 5 members of the previous Legislature were returned to the new Assembly.

As the *Straits Times* pointed out in a leader on 1 June, while the opposition could have been much stronger but for the split vote, it was equally plain that in terms of an effective majority in the House, a united election front embracing every non-PAP party and every Independent would not have made any practical difference. The PAP won all the seven straight fights, and in twenty-three other constituencies every one of their candidates polled more than the combined votes of their opponents. Split vote or no, the polling had justified the PAP's claim to the support of a majority of the voters.

2. 1959–65

The new Government, headed by Mr Lee Kuan Yew, the English-educated socialist leader of the moderates in the PAP, took office early in June 1959, but only after the Governor had agreed to the release from detention of eight prominent left-wing PAP members arrested for subversion in October 1956 and August 1957. Otherwise Mr Lee refused to take office, an action, of course, designed to retain the support of the left wing of the PAP. Those released were all left-wing labour union officials whose influence on the unions was very great, particularly among the non-English-speaking Chinese trade union members, many of whom were attracted to Communism. While fully prepared to accept the challenge of these left-wing leaders rather than antagonize their supporters, it was Mr Lee's policy to persuade the Chinese masses in Singapore that their future prosperity and happiness lay not in Communism or in loyalty to China but in democratic socialism, in the development of a Malayan consciousness and loyalty, and in an eventual political merger between Singapore and the Federation.

But this was a long-term policy; the immediate necessity was to win the support of moderate opinion in order to prevent a flight of capital which he well knew would endanger the success of the social and economic projects which were the basis of the PAP programme. He therefore proceeded to arm his Government with powers to counter subversion and to subdue the secret society gangs which were disrupting the peace.

The gangs were the first target. As early as June 1959 it had already become clear that the special powers of detention adopted in August 1958 had not led to the hoped-for improvement. Detention without punishment or any form of compulsory work had proved to be ineffective, and ring-leaders were replaced almost as quickly as they were detained. In June 1959 the new Government made determined attempts through the tightening of certain licensing laws to rid Singapore of drug-peddling, gambling, and prostitution, in all of which pursuits secret societies were involved, but it was soon found advisable to introduce further legislation to increase the penalties for crimes of violence which, despite the 1958 legislation, showed no signs of abating.

In August, therefore, another Bill to amend the Criminal Law (Temporary

LL

Provisions) Ordinance was presented to the Legislative Assembly proposing amendments to the detention provisions of increased stringency. It provided that, with the consent of the Public Prosecutor, the Minister for Home Affairs, in the interests of 'public safety, peace, and good order', might order the detention of any person associated with criminal activities for a period of one year instead of six months, or alternatively that such a person should be under police supervision for a period not exceeding three years. All orders under the Ordinance were to be reported to an Advisory Committee within twenty-eight days. The Committee would then report to the Yang di-Pertuan Negara, who would confirm, reject, or vary the order.

Any person under police supervision contravening any order or conditions imposed upon him was, on conviction, liable to imprisonment for not more than three years or not less than one year, and the same punishment applied to persons under police supervision who knowingly consorted or habitually associated with others who were under supervision. Furthermore, those under police supervision who committed any of the crimes set out in the Third Schedule (which included offences under the Societies Ordinance, the Penal Code, the Minor Offences Ordinance, the Arms Offences Ordinance, the Firearms and Ammunition (Unlawful Possession) Ordinance, and the Corrosive Substances Ordinance) were, on conviction, liable to double the normal penalty and to whipping. All persons detained or subject to police supervision were to be issued with a special identity card, and any person making false statements regarding his identity was liable to a fine of $5,000 or to imprisonment not exceeding three years or to both. The Yang di-Pertuan was empowered to extend the validity of any order of detention for a year, and to extend the period of police supervision indefinitely.

These amendments were approved at the September meeting (1959) of the Legislative Assembly. At the same meeting amendments to the Criminal Procedure Code passed their Second Reading and were referred to a Select Committee. This amending Bill sought to increase the powers and jurisdiction of the criminal district and police courts, enabling them to impose heavier sentences and to hear some cases previously reserved for the High Court. It also sought to allow cautioned statements made to police officers not below the rank of Inspector to be admitted in court as evidence, and to dispense with trial by jury except in capital cases.

Meanwhile, crimes of violence continued. During September a gang of thirty youths set upon a police patrol with parangs and broken bottles. Another gang of seventeen killed a petty tradesman who had resisted their extortion. A young man was stabbed to death in a coffee-shop, a family of six were the victims of an acid attack, and in Changi Gaol 200 gangsters detained there fought a battle with knives, iron piping, and bottles. The *Straits Times* of 5 October had the following comment:

Each act of violent crime and secret society activity in Singapore offers fresh justification of the abnormal powers with which the Government has armed itself and the police, and reinforces the case for adding to them if by so doing the battle against gangland can be assisted. Public support for tough action is no problem. . . . The question turns rather on the effectiveness of severe physical punishment, short of Kempeitai methods, as a deterrent.

A move against political subversion was made on 14 October when, on a certificate of urgency, the Government sought the approval of the Legislative

Assembly to the extension of the Preservation of Public Security Ordinance for five years, and asked for sanction to abolish the Appeal Tribunals set up under the original Ordinance in 1955, replacing them by Advisory Committees which would make recommendations to the Yang di-Pertuan Negara on cases which came up for review. This amendment restored the original position obtaining previously under the Emergency Regulations. Other amendments were designed to give the Minister for Home Affairs greater flexibility in the exercise of his powers. A person could be placed under restrictions without having first been detained, the categories of persons upon whom restrictions could be imposed were extended, and the restrictions could apply not only to residence but also to employment and activities.

In introducing the Bill, the Prime Minister stressed that the final answer to the Communist challenge was not this type of legislation which entailed giving the Executive emergency or extraordinary powers. The economic, social, and political conditions and the battles in those fields would, he said, decide whether Singapore, and indeed Malaya, would go from strength to strength as a democratic State in which the more tolerant features of human civilization were preserved while the economic needs and necessities were rapidly met, or whether the totalitarian system would succeed the democratic State to cater for these economic needs. The powers for which approval was being asked could only provide a temporary damper against those who set out to wreck the democratic State.

The extension of the life of the Ordinance for a further five years was un-opposed in the Assembly, but there was considerable debate on the abolition of the executive appellate tribunal. This had previously been discussed at a PAP meeting held in October attended by representatives of all fifty-one PAP branches, when the Prime Minister in his capacity as secretary-general of the party explained that although an election pledge had been given to retain the Appeal Tribunal, representations from the Judges had caused the Government to reconsider. In the Assembly debate he emphasized that, in principle, the responsibility for the detention or release of a person under such extraordinary powers could not rest with the judiciary, and with the passing of the Bill the Singapore Government assumed complete and undivided responsibility for safe-guarding security, subject only to the overriding authority of the Internal Security Council, with whose directives the Government was obliged to conform.

Before any intensive drives under the amended laws were instituted, a people's war against gangsters and lawless elements was proclaimed, to be preceded by an amnesty of sixteen days during which gangsters were urged to break with their societies and report to the Advocate General. In all, 818 availed themselves of this opportunity, and although this was but a small proportion of the 10,000 secret society members believed to exist in Singapore, the project had a good psychological effect and reduced public sympathy for those subsequently detained or placed under police supervision.

Increased police activity followed the amnesty, and there was some decrease in the number of secret society incidents. By the end of the year, 276 suspects were under detention and 187 were under police supervision. In court, the Secret Societies Branch of the CID charged 721 persons with a variety of offences, and a record quantity of offensive weapons was seized, including 257 bottles and bulbs of acid. Nevertheless, the annual total of 402 secret society incidents showed an increase of 20 per cent over the 1958 total. There was also an increase in the total of street robberies, house-breakings, and thefts of vehicles, and of 50 murders 7 were due to secret society clashes. Gang fights did not entirely cease, and in December there was a severe clash between 30 members of the '108' and the '24' gangs in the Aljunied–Geylang area in which 5 men were splashed with acid and 2 were hacked with parangs. During a running fight, one member of the '24' carried the new State flag of Singapore on which has been embroidered in Chinese the characters: 'Faithful Red Army, Cantonese Section'.

Clashes of a particularly vicious nature continued during January and February 1960. The peak was reached in May with 38 incidents, but thereafter activities decreased and the annual total was almost 40 per cent less than in 1959. Arrests under the Criminal Law (Temporary Provisions) Ordinance were the main deterrent, and increased police patrols helped to keep down affrays. This improvement was, however, offset by a severe outbreak of kidnapping for ransom organized by two powerful syndicates and causing grave apprehension among wealthy Chinese businessmen. Ten incidents were reported, and another three went unreported. Although not organized by secret societies as a society activity, the kidnappings were the work of gangs whose members were secret society men, though not all of one society. The leader of the main gang was run to earth and shot dead by the police during a gun battle on 24 August. The leader and several members of the second group were later detained, and in all 87 arrests were made.

Further legislative action was taken to strengthen the hands of the Government by amendments to the Criminal Procedure Code, the Societies Ordinance, the Citizenship Law, and the Banishment Ordinance. Amendments to the Criminal Procedure Code while in Select Committee had evoked protests from the Bar Committee in January 1960 against the proposal to render admissible in evidence statements made to police officers by accused persons. As a result the Select Committee formulated rules governing the taking of such statements, and the revised Bill was accepted by the Assembly on 14 April. At the same time the jury system was discontinued except in cases which might involve the death penalty or which had been notified in the Gazette as being subject to jury decision.

Amendments to the Societies Ordinance, described by the Minister as 'an ancient and venerable piece of legislation', were first proposed in January 1960, and caused much discussion. Enhanced penalties designed to discourage the formation of secret societies or other 'undesirable and shady societies' often used as haunts for secret societies or as gaming clubs under their protection evoked little adverse comment, but the provision that all societies (including political ones) must apply for registration aroused considerable resistance from Opposition ranks, particularly from Mr David Marshall, leader of the newly-formed Workers' Party.

During the debate the Prime Minister reminded members of the Assembly that even cultural and sporting associations were not always what they professed to be, as the previous Government well knew. It was one thing to say that an association had been formed for the blowing of flutes or the banging of brass gongs, but it was another to get members to practise such arts (a reference to the innocent titles of previous subversive Communist Front organizations).

After reference to a Select Committee the Bill was passed in May and came into operation on 22 July 1960.

Under the new Ordinance (37 of 1960) every society was required to register. There was no longer a category of exempted societies, nor were Freemasons or political associations excluded. The Registrar was empowered to refuse permission to register if satisfied that a society was liable to be used for unlawful purposes or for purposes prejudicial to public peace or to good order, or if it would be contrary to the national interest for a particular society to be registered. These provisions contained a significant extension of the powers of the Executive. As some concession to those who had so strongly opposed the inclusion of political associations in the ambit of the Ordinance, the Registar was restrained from ordering such an association to furnish him with minutes of any meeting, or any list of members, and in the drafting of the Ordinance emphasis was placed upon his duty to register a political society and not upon his right to refuse.

These provisions were unlikely to be of much assistance to the police in their campaign against the gangsters, but might be expected to help the Government to control the development of subversive associations. Of more importance to the police was a new provision to the effect that in prosecutions under the Ordinance evidence of repute might be adduced to show that a person was a member of a society, and that a particular society was in existence. In addition, the maximum penalty for membership of an unlawful society or for permitting meetings to be held on premises, or for possession of Triad documents was raised from six months' imprisonment to three years, while that for assisting in the management of an unlawful society was increased from three years to five. Furthermore, no officer of a society ordered to be dissolved might hold office in any other society without the written permission of the Minister for a period of three years after the dissolution.[11]

While the Societies Ordinance was under consideration, changes were introduced in the citizenship law. Under a Citizenship (Amendment) Bill published on 9 April 1960, the existing qualification of two years' residence for citizenship was increased to not less than eight years' residence out of the preceding twelve years, and the qualification for naturalization was raised from eight to ten years' residence in the preceding twelve years. An important provision empowered the minister to deprive a person of his citizenship should his activities prove to be prejudicial to the security of Malaya or to the interests of public safety, peace, and good order; a provision which was to have important repercussions on the powers of banishment. For a Banishment (Amendment) Bill which passed into law in September 1960 enabled the Government to banish or expel a person, whether a British subject or an alien, whose subversive or criminal activities made him an undesirable resident. Previously British subjects whether born in Singapore or elsewhere were not banishable, but under the new law the only persons not banishable were Singapore citizens. When it is remembered that the Government also had the power to deprive a person of his Singapore citizenship (even though born in Singapore) in the interests of security, safety, peace, and good order, it will be seen that in this combination of powers the Government possessed a very potent weapon.

[11] Sing. Leg. Ass. Deb., vol. 12, no. 2, 14 Jan. 1960; *Straits Times*, 5 Jan., 14 Jan., 4 May 1960; *Sing. GG*, Suppl. 41 of 22 July 1960, pp. 839–45; GN S183.

All the matters mentioned above—increased powers of arrest, detention and supervision without trial, and enhanced punishments for offenders—were penal measures, but another and more constructive aspect of the Government's attempt to solve the gangster problem was the introduction during 1960 of two experiments in social therapy. The first, of a preventive nature, was the formation of a Work Brigade in Singapore, the second, a reformative measure, was the opening of a Penal Settlement on the 200-acre island of Pulau Senang ('Isle of Ease') twelve miles south of Singapore near Raffles Lighthouse, where modern methods of rehabilitation were to be tried in an open camp 'with only the sea for walls'. It had long been thought that lack of work or occupation was one of the primary causes of the drift of youths into secret societies and a life of crime, and it was hoped that a Work Brigade would curtail this drift and have the dual merit of giving young members a sense of purpose and effort, and creating a source of labour for both skilled and unskilled trades.

The Brigade was recruited in the main from youths and girls who had just left school but had not yet found suitable employment. The scheme envisaged a possible 5,000 recruits who were to be housed in rural camps in groups of 50 to 100 or 150. Essentials of housing, food, clothing, and material needs were provided, and sufficient work and leisure to enable recruits to lead a corporate life, to co-operate in working, studying, and recreation, and to take pride in contributing to the cause of national construction, for their duties were to include the construction of roads and irrigation canals, the reclamation of land, and other public works projects.

The decision to set up a rehabilitation centre for secret society gangsters was a development of particular importance. A similar scheme had been suggested in 1958 in the Federation of Malaya but, though not officially abandoned, was moribund. In Singapore the unsatisfactory prison conditions brought about by the detention of hundreds of men for prolonged periods coupled with the lack of new prison building led to the appointment of a Prisons Inquiry Commission under the chairmanship of Mr Devan Nair who had previously been a political detainee. From among its members an *ad hoc* Committee was appointed to make proposals for an urgent solution to the serious problems arising in the prisons from the presence there of persons detained under the Criminal Law (Temporary Provisions) Ordinance 1955. The Committee's report of 15 January 1960 contained detailed proposals for setting up a rehabilitation centre on Pulau Senang. The scheme was accepted by the Government, and work on the island by detainees started in May.

In the early stages the men were kept within their secret society groups, but soon began to mingle, and this mingling was later adopted as the official policy. As between the detainees and the staff, the aim was to establish mutual trust as the basis of their relationship, and the Superintendent of the Camp (Mr D. S. Dutton) was a dynamic, enthusiastic, and dedicated officer. It was hoped that the skills and disciplines of work and the benefits of education received in the camp would enable the detainees to take their places in the community as decent working citizens, and that a year on the island followed by six months in a Work Brigade might be a reasonable period in which to effect the change.

The scheme (which was restricted to detainees of Singapore citizenship) was a positive attempt, through hard work, education, and example, to come to grips with the economic, social, and moral aspects of the secret society problem under conditions which were very different from the normal prison atmosphere and yet safeguarded the public. It also had the practical advantage of providing an additional place of detention, a matter of some importance, for the large number of local-born youths among the gangsters, coupled with the increasing reluctance of the People's Government of China to accept as banishees even those who were born in China, had greatly decreased the effectiveness of the Banishment Ordinance, while the amended legislation permitting detention without trial had led to a large increase in the number of persons to be accommodated.

The number of occupants of the camp rapidly increased, and by October 1961 there were more than 400 men in camp; 76 had been released to a Work Brigade in Singapore, and of these 6 had found government jobs and 2 had returned to their previous work with the City Council. Some were employed in the camp as settlement attendants. In the Legislative Assembly in April 1962, the Minister for Home Affairs referred to the drop in the figures for attempted murder, extortion, acid-throwing, stabbing, and assault. The Criminal Law (Temporary Provisions) Ordinance remained the major weapon against the gangsters, and he told the House that 804 known gangsters were being held under it. Of these, 85 had been in prison for more than three years and 235 for more than two years. The majority were on Pulau Senang. He also stated that since the camp opened in June 1960, 135 men had been released. The scheme seemed to be working well.

However, the first sign that all was not well came in April 1963 when an Assistant Settlement Officer was attacked with a changkol[12] by a man ordered to report to a senior officer for a disciplinary offence. Others joined in the attack, and 14 were later removed from the island. Three weeks later 8 detainees out of a party of 25 being taken by boat to the island escaped after attacking the crew and the solitary warder and forcing the crew to return to harbour waters. On 6 July 13 carpenters who had worked late into the previous night refused to work further overtime on Saturday and were forthwith sent back by the Superintendent to Changi Gaol. This was the punishment most disliked, for it cancelled the period already spent on the island and made release once more remote. The carpenters expressed their resentment to their friends who, after their departure, turned their minds to plans of revenge. News of this was passed to the Superintendent through detainees who heard that a plot was being hatched, but he was not disposed to regard it seriously. On 12 July he was secretly warned that a revolt was imminent. He radioed Singapore but stated that he considered that the malcontents were in a minority and that there were plenty of detainees who would stand by him to resist them. He did not think it necessary to send a police party to the island, but took the precaution of having all the boats but one quietly removed to a neighbouring island to prevent escapes.

At the time of the planning of the rehabilitation centre it had been decided as a matter of policy that no firearms should be kept there. Staves and wicker shields were the only articles of defence available. Despite the sanguine outlook of the Superintendent, orders were given in Singapore for an armed party of police to go to the island, but by the time they arrived the rioting had begun and ended.

There were 318 detainees in camp at the time (about 60 more being on a visit to Singapore) and the riot broke out just after 1 p.m. when they were being

[12] A hoe-shaped digging tool.

mustered for gardening after the lunch break. They took up their changkols, parangs, and other gardening tools and suddenly a number of the men, variously estimated at between 70 and 90, attacked the warders and cut them down with changkols and parangs. The mob then armed themselves with iron piping and bottles and moved towards the administration block where the Superintendent (Dutton) and his assistant (Tailford) were in the radio room summoning help from Singapore. A barrage of bottles (1,600 of them) was kept up on members of the staff near the building and a series of attacks were launched and repulsed, but eventually the mob overcame the defenders. Tailford was stabbed in the right temple and overpowered, and the rioters set fire to the building. Dutton was attacked and hacked to death and his body thrown into the flames. Most of the supervisory staff were attacked and injured. Three more were hacked to death, and the body of one, a warder, was also thrown into the flames. The remainder of the camp buildings were splashed with petrol and kerosine and set alight, and the generator smashed. Within forty minutes the camp was reduced to a shambles while the 200 or more non-participants made no attempt to intervene. The rioters hoisted a detainee's shirt on the flagstaff and sat down in the shade of a tree to sing extempore songs of triumph to the accompaniment of guitars. A few of the ringleaders set off in the boat towards Indonesian waters but were later cut off by customs and police launches.

The first to land on the island after the alarm had been given both by siren and by the firing of Very lights were a group of about thirty Malays from a near-by island armed with spears, followed immediately by a party of Marine police, but the riot was over. They were faced with a scene of desolation but no resistance. The experiment of a prison without walls to which so much thought, endeavour, and enthusiasm had been given ended as a charred ruin.

Most of the detainees were removed to Singapore, and eventually 58 were brought to trial, a trial which, as the Lord President of the Court of Appeal later remarked, by reason of its length, the number of persons involved, and the horror of the events to which it related was probably unparalleled in the legal history of Malaya. It lasted for sixty-four days spread over four months before Mr Justice Buttrose and a special jury. The case ended on 13 March 1964 when 18 of the accused were condemned to death on charges of murder, 11 were sentenced to three years' imprisonment for rioting with deadly weapons, 11 sentenced to two years' imprisonment for rioting, and 11 acquitted. The 18 condemned to death appealed to the Federal Court of Malaysia which sustained the original judgement, and the Privy Council held that further appeal was unjustified. All 18 were hanged at Changi Gaol on 29 October 1965.

In the light of many previous encouraging reports which had been written about Pulau Senang, the savage riots of 12 July 1963 came as a great shock to Singapore and as a bitter disappointment to those who had sponsored and supported the reform scheme. Conjecture was rife as to the cause of failure. It was suggested that too much had been attempted too soon, that the initial success of the settlement had lowered the guard not only of the men in charge but also of those responsible for putting so large a number of men in this one settlement, that the supervisory guard was too small to cope with 400 detainees, all able-bodied youths of criminal proclivities and secret society connexions, that the selection of detainees sent to the island was not sufficiently strict and the extent to which secret society influence persisted not sufficiently recognized, that the employment of former detainees as subordinate staff led to corruption and discrimination, and that the decision to have no firearms on the island was unsound. A study of the evidence given at the trial (21 volumes) provides no specific clue beyond the fact that the trouble was undoubtedly precipitated by the action of the Superintendent in sending away the thirteen carpenters. Most, or all, of the above factors may well have had a place in the creation of the climate in which the riot plan was hatched. The Court of Appeal in its judgement referring to the scheme to 'transmogrify persons thought to be dedicated to a life of crime into useful and virtuous citizens' remarked, smugly: 'We are not concerned with the merits of that scheme or to speculate whether some aspects of it may merit a modest place in the history of human folly. Nor is it any concern of ours to examine the legality of some of the things that were done in pursuance of it.' And again: 'had there been firearms available the present proceedings might not have been necessary'.

An enquiry into the causes and circumstances of the riot was ordered by the Singapore Government but was suspended during judicial proceedings. When Singapore became part of Malaysia on 16 September 1963, matters concerning public security, police, and prisons were among those which were transferred to the Central Government. The enquiry was quietly abandoned, and no further move was made to repeat this experiment in rehabilitation.

The period during which the Pulau Senang centre was in existence was one in which the Singapore Government were largely preoccupied with political matters: in containing the threat of the Communists within the PAP and through labour and student movements, and in considering the suggestion made by Tunku Abdul Rahman in May 1961 that a constitutional merger should take place between the Federation of Malaya, Singapore, and the British Borneo territories to form a Federation of Malaysia.

Towards the end of 1960 there were signs of conflict within the PAP when Mr Ong Eng Guan, former Minister for National Development, of the left-wing group, resigned from the party. In May 1961 he stood for election as an independent and defeated his PAP opponent. The split in the party widened when some of the Political Secretaries appointed by Mr Lee Kuan Yew (when he obtained their release from detention at the time of assuming office) were publicly critical of the Government's policies. This was particularly evident in the labour field and led to a split in the PAP-sponsored Trade Union Congress, the left wing being led by Mr Lim Chin Siong. In July three Political Secretaries were dismissed from office and thirteen left-wing PAP members of the Legislative Assembly were dismissed from their positions on all committees. The rebels formed themselves into a new party, the Barisan Socialis (Socialist Front), headed by Dr Lee Siew Choh, leaving the PAP with a majority of only one in the Assembly.

Thereafter the battle was joined between the Barisan and the PAP on almost all topics, but particularly on labour matters and on the proposals to join the new Malaysia. The TUC swung to the left and was dissolved by the Government, whereupon Lim Chin Siong formed a Singapore Association of Trade Unions (SATU) embracing the many Communist-influenced and left-inclined unions. A bitter struggle ensued for the control of the unions which dominated the China-looking sections of labour, and a series of strikes by these unions began and continued through 1962. In November of that year five of these trade unionists were arrested for distributing Communist literature. In February 1963 113 people were arrested by order of the Internal Security Council which, at the same time, issued a pamphlet on *The Communist Conspiracy* explaining the way in which the unions and other 'Front' organizations were being penetrated with the object of overthrowing the Government, establishing a Communist base, and undermining the proposed formation of Malaysia, preparations for which were by this time well advanced.

In May the police conducted an extensive sweep through the underworld in search of armed leaders of gangs concerned in a spate of robberies, pay-roll snatches, and murder. The *Straits Times* on 16 May, in a leader concerning the prevalence throughout the country of armed robbery and violent crime, re-marked: 'There is more armed robbery in broad daylight in Singapore than for years past. . . . Yet the special powers . . . given the police to help them fight the secret societies obviously are still not sufficient to prevent fresh waves of vicious crime.' It called upon the public to assist the police by providing informa-tion and co-operation.

The date fixed for the inauguration of Malaysia was 31 August, but because of the implacable opposition of Indonesia, the date was postponed to enable a team appointed by the Secretary-General of the United Nations to carry out an on-the-spot investigation to ascertain whether the majority of the people of Sarawak and Sabah were genuinely in favour of the proposed federation. This being established, the inauguration took place on 16 September.

Mr Lee Kuan Yew decided upon an immediate election with a view to obtain-ing confirmation of his policy. At the shortest notice the election was held on 22 September and resulted in an overwhelming victory for the PAP, which secured 37 out of the 51 seats contested. The Barisan obtained 13 seats. The Singapore Alliance Party (formed on similar lines to the ruling Alliance Party in the Federation of Malaya) fielded 42 candidates but won no seats.

Under the Constitution of Malaysia, matters concerning police and security fell to be dealt with by the Central Government, and the policy of eradicating Communist influence from educational, labour and 'Front' organizations was energetically continued once the new Government had been elected. On 26 September twenty members of Nanyang University were arrested for pro-Communist activities. Tan Lark Sye, a wealthy industrialist and founder of this Chinese-language university, was alleged to have actively and persistently col-laborated with an anti-national group of Communists in the university, and proceedings were begun to remove his Singapore citizenship.

On 3 October the dissolution of five associations was ordered. They were associations of Rural Residents, Country People, Hawkers, and Stall-holders, and were alleged to be political associations for agitation and for recruiting Communists. On 8 October fourteen leaders of SATU, including three Barisan members of the Legislative Assembly, were arrested as they were making arrangements for a roster of strikes for political purposes. Two other Barisan Members of Assembly thought it advisable to disappear, and in due course applied to the Speaker for leave of absence from the Assembly. On 13 November the Government refused to permit the registration of SATU (which at this time had 29 affiliate unions) under the Trade Union Ordinance, and about the middle of December 108 teachers in Chinese schools (including 12 principals) were dismissed for alleged involvement in Communist activities.

Events thereafter may be rapidly summarized. During 1964 kidnapping of wealthy Chinese continued and the police made repeated surprise screenings of sections of the populace, stopping as many as 3,000 people a day in an endeavour to lay hands on members of the extortion gangs. In June 52 students of Nanyang University were arrested for subversive activities, and in July about 100 students were expelled and 50 of the non-academic staff dismissed. All were concerned with Communist infection.

On the Prophet's Birthday (21 July) a Muslim procession led to severe communal riots between Chinese and Malays. This was a public manifestation of the growing incompatibility of the PAP policy vigorously advocated by Mr Lee Kuan Yew, stressing the need to recognize the political equality of all citizens of Malaysia irrespective of race, and the UMNO policy strenuously propounded by some of its leaders, insisting that the Malays were the indigenous people and that they had a special position in the country and in its governance.

The outbreak was exploited by hooligans and Indonesian sympathizers eager to cause disruption in furtherance of Sukarno's policy of non-recognition and 'confrontation' of the new Malaysia. In the first few days 32 people were killed and some 200 injured. A drive by the police against secret society members roped in 550 men for detention under the Criminal Law Ordinance which was extended for a further five years. Incidents continued sporadically until September (8 killed and 60 injured in clashes in 48 hours early in the month). Goodwill committees set up in Singapore, Johore, and throughout Malaya eventually led to a lowering of the temperature and avoided the spread of trouble throughout the country which might well have happened. In December details were issued of the training of secret society men by Indonesia in sabotage, and of the specific plots, including the communal disorders, in which they had been employed before being arrested.

Despite the dangerous atmosphere, the public argument between the two political groups continued with little abatement, and this led Tunku Abdul Rahman and his advisers to decide that if trouble was to be avoided, Singapore must leave the Federation of Malaysia forthwith. This decision having been taken, Mr Lee Kuan Yew was informed on 9 August 1965 that Singapore was no longer accepted as a member of the Malaysian Federation. The leaders of the Singapore Government, once they had recovered from their shock, elected to become a Republic within the Commonwealth and assumed full responsibility for the government of the island State.

In this atmosphere, secret society matters became of secondary importance. The powers conferred by the Criminal Law (Temporary Provisions) Ordinance were freely used to keep the gangsters off the streets while political and constitutional issues kept the Government fully occupied.

The conclusion to be reached after a close study of developments in Malaya from the end of the eighteenth century to the present day is that the potential danger to the people and the Governments of Malaysia and Singapore deriving from the deeply-entrenched tradition of Chinese secret societies still persists and will require not only the sternest measures of control but also the wisest measures of social reconstruction and education if it is to be kept at bay. The price of peace is eternal vigilance.

APPENDIX 1

Traditional History

The traditional history places the origin of the Brotherhood in the Manchu dynasty of Ch'ing. The year of foundation varies in different versions, but the most usual is 1674. The story relates how the emperor, hard-pressed by invading tribes, issued a proclamation calling for volunteers, in response to which the monks of Shao Lin Monastery in Fukien province went to the frontier and, by a series of stratagems and the use of supernatural powers, defeated the enemy and saved the country. In return the monastery was granted special privileges, and the abbot was given a seal bestowing imperial authority. A later monarch was advised that the abbot used these powers to defy the local government, and that the monastery should be destroyed. This was done through the treachery of a renegade monk known as 'Number Seven' (Ah Ts'at) who revealed the secret approaches to the monastery, enabling a troop of soldiers to set fire to the building.

Five of the monks who escaped and were pursued by the soldiers passed through a series of vicissitudes, being rescued from each peril by supernatural intervention. When halted by a river, a boatman arrived to ferry them across; when hungry, a fruit-seller appeared; when faced by a junction of three streams where a two-plank bridge was destroyed, three stepping stones miraculously emerged. During the journey a white metal censer was found bearing the characters 'Overthrow the Ch'ing, Restore the Ming', and eventually they reached the temple of Kao Ch'i (Cantonese: Ko Hai) or High Brook, near to the Black Dragon river.

These five monks are known as the Former Five Ancestors, or, concisely, as the Five Ancestors, and during a fight with the imperial troops they were again saved, this time by five horse-dealers known as the Later Five Ancestors or the Five 'Tiger' Generals.

In a cave near the temple of High Brook lived a solitary scholar who had been removed from an official post for supporting the people, and retired to the White Stork Grotto to devote himself to the study of Taoism and the supernatural arts. His name was Ch'en Chin Nan (C: Ch'an Kan Nam), and he agreed to join the group to form a Brotherhood with the aim of freeing the people from oppression by overthrowing the Manchu dynasty and restoring the Chinese dynasty of Ming. At the Red Flower Pavilion, part of a near-by monastery, they bound themselves by a blood-oath in imitation of the Peach Garden Heroes, by pricking their fingers, squeezing the blood into a bowl of wine, and drinking in turn while swearing the oath. Ch'en Chin Nan was chosen as the leader with the title of Grand Master or Master of the Incense, and the Brotherhood adopted the title of 'Hung' as their family name, from the reign title of the first Ming emperor, with the watchword 'Yi' (Justice). The first Grand

---

[1] Limitations of space restrict this account to summary form.

Assembly of inauguration of the Hung Brotherhood was held on the 25th day of the 7th moon.

At this stage a youth claiming to be Prince Chu, a grandson of the last Ming emperor appeared. This was an auspicious omen, and they said: 'Let us follow the will of Heaven in carrying out our rightcous cause', a phrase that was adopted as a precept of the Brotherhood.[2] An army was recruited with a Van-guard leader named Su Hung Kuang (C: So Hung Kwong) who was also given the title of T'in Yu Hung (C: T'in Yau Hung) or 'Heaven Protect Hung'. They were joined by a giant of a priest called 'Wan Yun Lung (C: Man Wan Lung) or 'Myriad Cloud Dragon' who, as a youth, had killed an oppressive official and became a monk to evade the law. He was appointed to be the Elder Brother or Generalissimo of the movement.

In a battle with the imperial troops the Hung army was defeated and the Generalissimo slain. An octagonal tomb was built, a nine-storied pagoda erected, and a three-cornered monument set up in his honour, bearing sixteen characters, each prefixed by the three dots of the character for 'water'. When the funeral was ended it was found that the Prince Chu had disappeared, and the Grand Master announced that the time was not propitious for the extermina-tion of the Ch'ing dynasty. He proposed that the Brethren should disperse to propagate the virtues and aims of the Brotherhood among the masses, in the fields and highways, and along the rivers and lakes. They then divided into five Lodges, each headed by one Former and one Later Ancestor, and dispersed throughout the country, each to an allotted region. Each Lodge had a coloured flag, a basic number, two watchwords, and a distinctive seal. (See table p. 532.)

It is probable that this history is entirely fanciful, based on some local happen-ing in Fukien province round which a legend has been woven. The monastery story is obviously borrowed from the famous monastery of Shao Lin in Honan, where the monks practised the arts of fighting and strategy, and where the Indian patriarch Bodhidharma (introduced into the Triad legend as Ta Mo = dharma) lived.[3] Items from historical romance, from legend, from Confucianism, and from the whole religious complex of astral-worship, ancestor-worship, Buddhism and Taoism are added, and a composite legend created.

Triad Ritual

The important ritualistic feature of Triad is the initiation ceremony, having symbolic affinity with the journey of the Five Ancestors, combined with borrow-ings from the ritual of the Heroes of Liang Shan, and from rituals of other religions. There are accounts of the ceremony available from several sources (see note on sources, p. 534). Each version differs in particular items, but all follow the same basic pattern. The summary here given is founded on informa-tion obtained in postwar Malaya. Variations are found, attributable sometimes to faulty transmission of verbal or written verses, sometimes to deliberate intent —to distinguish one Lodge or one society from another—and sometimes to ignorance on the part of those preparing and performing the ceremony.

In Malaya the ceremony may take place in a temple or in club premises, but is usually held in a clearing in the jungle, or in a rubber estate, or in a Chinese graveyard, or some such isolated place, after nightfall, the only light being that

[2] Usually translated as 'Obey Heaven and act righteously'.
[3] See Pelliot, *T'oung Pao*, xxv (1928), pp. 444–8.

of flickering candles which accentuates the eeriness of the surroundings. A rectangular space is marked out with sticks and string to form the 'City', entrance to which is by the East Gate. (Oval and circular 'Cities' have also been known.) Candidates (New Horses) are brought by 'Horse Leaders' and sponsored by a 'Guarantor Maternal Uncle'. They pay an entrance fee, usually $1.08 or a multiple thereof. Before the rites begin, the various 'furnishings' of the city are put in place. Strips of paper (usually red) are hung up along the 'walls' naming various shrines: to Kuan Ti and Kuan Yin among others. Towards the west end of the enclosure an altar is erected made of rough posts with planks. Hanging above it is a strip of paper, usually red but sometimes yellow or green, bearing characters in black for 'Hung Obedience Hall' usually shortened to a cipher form peculiar to Triad. There are also the characters for 'Red Flower Pavilion', and, written vertically, the names of the Five Ancestors and the Five 'Tiger' Generals, together with names of other legendary persons of Triad ritual or connected with Buddhist or Taoist mythology. This represents the ancestral tablets arranged on the altar for worship.

In the centre of the altar table is a bowl or tin representing a peck measure, and styled the City of Willows.[4] It should contain rice, though sand is sometimes found, and thrust into or standing on the rice are a ruler, scissors, mirror, sword or knife, abacus, balance, fan, pen brush, red rod, miniature standard with the characters for 'Commander of the Three Armies', many small triangular coloured paper flags with Triad characters, a 'Warrant Flag' bearing the character 'Command', and five joss sticks for the ancestors. Outside the peck-measure are the 'Hung Lamp' (a wick-light), three small cups of tea and five of wine, a saucer of oil with seven lighted wicks (the Dipper again), red candles, pipe and tobacco, straw sandal, an umbrella, ink and inkstone, threads of five colours, fruits, perhaps green twigs and leaves of paper cash (as used at funerals), a china bowl, and three 'Hung' cash. Hanging in front of the altar may be a paper slip with the characters 'Heaven and Earth Circle', indicating that a hoop should stand below the altar.

Between the altar and the East Gate down the middle of the enclosure are three arches of branches, or of sticks and string, representing three portals. The first (from the east) bears the characters 'Hung Gate' and also 'Grand Assembly of the Hung People'. The second is labelled 'Hall of Loyalty and Righteousness' (Chung Yi T'ong), and the third may have 'City of Willows' or 'Red Flower Pavilion'. Behind the altar are a piece of paper representing a 9-storied pagoda, and one with 16 characters prefixed by the 3-dot water radical. Elsewhere in the enclosure are paper slips representing the 2-plank bridge, 3 shops (Man Hop, Yi Hop, Woh Hop), 3 stepping stones, a hill or heap of fire (joss papers), and possibly an orchard.

For the setting up of each item there is a ritual verse which is chanted by the sinseh in charge of the ceremony who performs priestly functions throughout. He invokes the spirits of the ancestors and invites them to enter the peck measure and also installs the officials who will take part in the ceremony—each with a ritual verse. While this is taking place, old members stand round the inside of the enclosure, while 'New Horses' wait outside the southern 'wall' observing

---

[4] The peck measure represents the Dipper or Plough in Ursa Major for which the same character is used. It, and some of the articles placed in it, are also used in some Taoist ceremonies.

these preliminary incantations. Old members and candidates alike have made preparation by removing shoes and jackets, discarding all metal articles such as rings, belt-buckles, and cash, taking the right arm out of the shirt sleeve so that the right shoulder is bared (a variation bares the left shoulder), tucking inwards the left point of the shirt collar, and turning the left trouser-leg upwards (inwards) three folds (some versions say the right leg). The old members wear a narrow fillet of red cloth round the head while candidates wear a white fillet.

When all is ready, the candidates, whose names have been written on a sheet of paper by a clerk outside the enclosure, are marshalled by the Vanguard who, after going through the motions of mounting a horse, leads the New Horses round the outside in an anti-clockwise direction before appearing at the East Gate where he is challenged by one of the two guardians who asks for his credentials. Then follows an interchange of ritual phrases, after which the guardian reports to the sinseh who stands by the altar. The Vanguard is then subjected to a very lengthy formal catechism by the sinseh, through set question and answer, covering in great detail a variety of objects with Triad associations. Thereafter the candidates are admitted. In some versions there is a washing of the face and a wiping with a towel either at the beginning or the end of the ceremony. Each candidate holds a lighted joss-stick, head downwards, between his palms, and they proceed, often in twos, on one knee and one foot through the three portals. At each one are two guardians armed with real or imitation swords or parangs, who demand, again by set question and answer (as to which the candidates are instructed on the spot) assurances of loyalty and secrecy. The pressure of a sword on the back of the neck brings home the nearness of the death penalty for betrayal, and the ritual stubbing out of the joss sticks on the ground typifies the ease with which their lives can be extinguished. They are also required to swear that they will not interfere with the wives and daughters of fellow members.

On arrival at the altar which purports to be in the Red Flower Pavilion, the left middle finger of each candidate is pricked with a needle (a variant is the right finger) and blood expressed into a bowl of red wine, the mixture being known as the Hung wine or Red Flower wine. (In some versions the finger is dipped in the mixture and sucked in a particular way.) They then crawl through a hoop below the altar (though there may be only a paper tag to represent this) symbolizing their birth into the family of Hung, all of whose members are of one mother—Earth. Thereafter they worship at the pagoda of 'Myriad Cloud Dragon', sip purifying water, buy fruit, and go through the motions of passing under the bridge, crossing stepping stones, jumping over the heap of fire, and, perhaps, going through an orchard.

After a pause, the oath-taking ceremony begins. A white cock is killed as a symbol of the traitor 'Ah Ts'at' (sometimes the cock is not white) and all new members touch the corpse with a knife held with hands crossed in a special fashion, while they swear secrecy. The sinseh reads out the 36 oaths, together with the rules, prohibitions, and punishments, and the bowl of Hung wine, balanced on a sword or parang, is offered to each to sip as the blood bond of loyalty and secrecy, witnessed by all the old members and by the spirits of the Five Ancestors and of all the other gods invoked. The punishments already recited make it clear that traitorous members can expect not only the vengeance of fellow members by knife and strangulation but also that of the ancestors and the gods through death by thunder, lightning, or the tearing of the flesh by wild dogs.

There may be additional features: the burning of the papers containing the oaths, etc., and perhaps the list of the new members' names, and the mixing of the ash in the Hung wine before sipping; the breaking of the bowl containing the residue of the Hung wine; the passing of a Hung coverlet over the heads of the kneeling candidates, or the touching of the head of each with the Red Rod; and the 'eating of the iron ball' (hard-boiled duck's egg). At some stage towards the end of the ceremony, the new member should receive three Hung cash (sometimes by gesture only). Throughout, everything is contrived to terrify the candidates into the belief that the slightest transgression will result in the direst punishment, and by the end of the ceremony, they are completely committed. The proceedings take several hours, and should last until dawn, symbolizing the emergence from darkness into light.

Triad writings often refer to the ceremony as a theatrical play of five and a half acts. There are variations, but the following is typical:

Act 1. Grand Assembly of the Hung People.

Act 2. Teaching the sons in the Hall of Loyalty.

Act 3. Stabilize the country and behead the traitors.

Act 4. Eating (or buying) fruit at the head of the bridge (or: in front of the steps).

Act 5. Drinking water at the side of the bridge.

Half Act. Eating the Iron Ball, or Brethren meet in unity, or Meeting of old and new incense.

The ceremony can be much shortened, the briefest form being known as a 'Mosquito-net' ceremony. This takes place indoors with none of the usual paraphernalia and only a few of the ritual items.

After completion of the initiation rites, a further ceremony may be held at which the sinseh confers ranks. This is done, again with ritual verses, by placing gold paper badges (as used in temple ceremonies) in the fillets of the recipients, an investiture carried out in the presence of all members to ensure that all are aware of the authority conferred. It is not unusual for initiation ceremonies and the conferment of ranks to cover several separate societies. The decision as to what ranks are to be conferred rests, naturally, with the governing body of each society. Instruction of new members in secret signs and language does not normally take place at a ceremony, but is undertaken individually (for a fee) by those holding White Fan rank in any society.

The designations of office-bearers and their code numbers are as follows: Ordinary member: 49; Five Tiger General (Fighter): 51; Straw Sandals (Messenger, negotiator, agent): 432; Red Rod (Disciplinary officer, often headman of the society): 426; White Fan (Ritual teacher): 415.

The certificate or diploma given to each member after initiation usually has written upon it the names of a number of officials participating in the ceremony. Among these may be found the following:

Master of the Incense pot (or censor) (Lo Chue). This is the title of the sponsoring authority, either a society or, at times, an individual.

2 Hukwang, China, 1841. The Censor for Hukwang sent this Diploma to the Emperor with a Memorial complaining against the Sam Hop Wui throughout five or six provinces.
(A. Wylie, *Chinese Researches*, p. 124.)

3 Shanghai, 1853. Diploma used by the Triad rebels at Shanghai.
(A. Wylie, *Chinese Researches*, p. 135.)

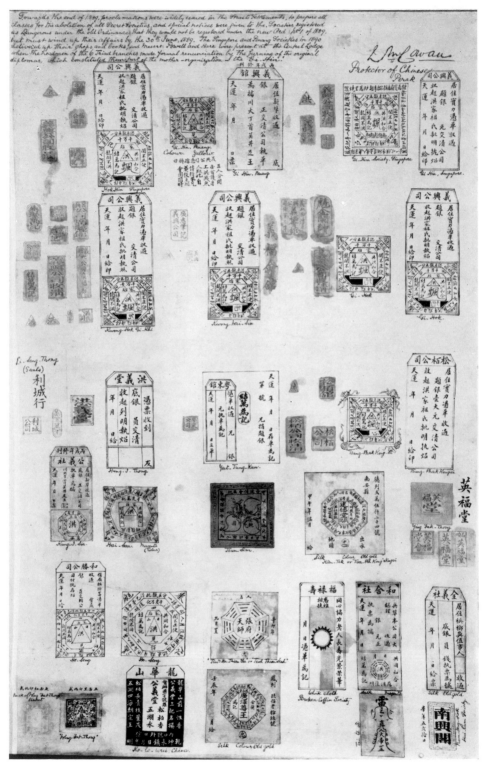

4 Cowan's Wall-Sheet of Diplomas, 1897.

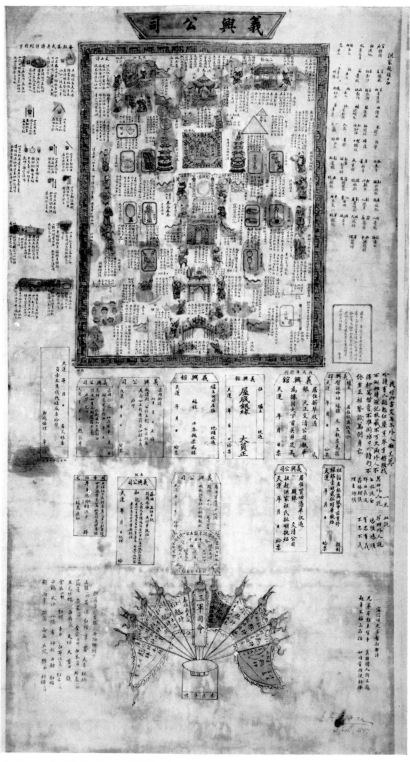

5 Cowan's Wall-Sheet, 1897, showing verses, documents, and altar-flags of the Ghee Hin Society.

6 Diploma of a First Lodge society, but bearing the cipher of the Second Lodge. Sitiawan, 1922.

7 Diploma of a Third Lodge society, but bearing the cipher of the Second Lodge.

8 A simple form of membership receipt on cloth. Ipoh, 1923.

7

6

8

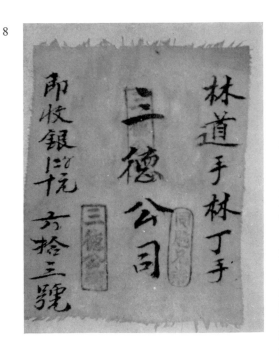

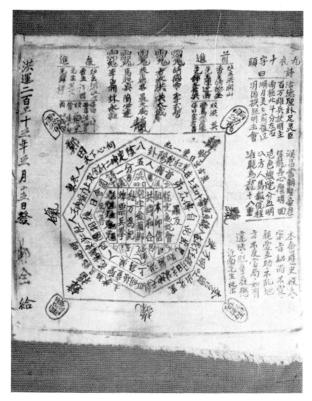

9 Ang Bin Hoey Diploma Penang, 1946.

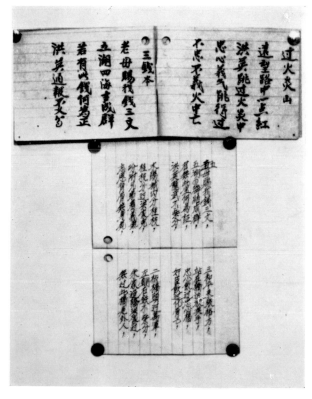

10 Pages of Triad ritual note-books. Penang, 1946.

11, 12 Triad altar in jungle, Kuala Lumpur, 1957.

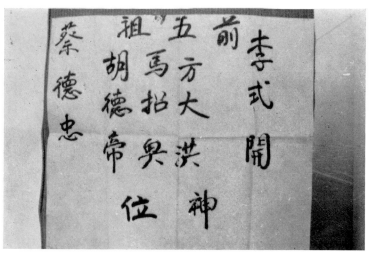

13 Simple form of Ancestral Tablet sheet.

14 The City of Willows; The Heaven and Earth Circle; The Flaming Mountain; The Orchard; The Well of Three Rivers; The Two-planked Bridge; and (centre) The Hung Hero ('Hero' written upside down).

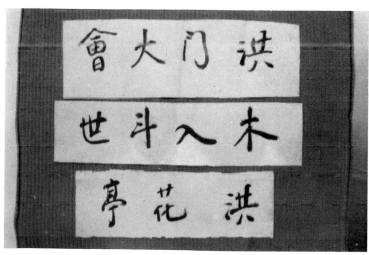

15 Grand Assembly of the Hung People. The four characters on the Peck Measure. The Hung Flower Pavilion.

Documents from Triad ceremony, Malacca, 1957.

16 Ghee Hin Token Tomb, Johore Bahru. Built 1921.

17 Wa Kei Token Tomb, Menglembu, Perak. Built 1948.

18 Wa Kei Token Tomb, Kuala Lumpur. Built 1951.

Master of Incense (Heung Chue). The person responsible for all the arrange-ments connected with the ceremony (but not for the ritual). Often the Elder Brother of the sponsoring society, and may also perform the function of Red Rod at the ceremony. Confusion has arisen over this title which is sometimes applied to the sinseh because the first Master of Incense was Ch'an Kan Nam.

Sinseh (Cantonese: sinshang). Sometimes called the 'Dishevelled Hair'. He is normally an experienced White Fan and may conduct all the initiation cere-monies for any of the societies in a given area. Sometimes called a Ch'an Kan Nam; shortened to 'Kan Nam', or, in colloquial Hokkien, 'Kwun Lam'. There is some evidence that a very experienced sinseh may be given the code number of 489.

Vanguard (Sin Fung). The person appointed to function as Vanguard at a ceremony. Obviously one well-versed in the responses.

Guarantor Maternal Uncle (Po K'au). The guarantor of the candidate.

Horse Leader (Tai Ma). The introducer of the candidate.

The form of diploma varies greatly; sometimes it is merely a piece of red paper on which is written the flag-colour and the watchwords of the Lodge to which the society belongs, together with the name and number of the member and details of the officials present at the ceremony. At other times the traditional octagonal pattern is used with ritual couplets whose characters are arranged in ordered displacement. Usually, too, there are a number of composite characters which, when disentangled, form a ritual phrase, or ciphers composed of parts of several ritual characters, or characters made esoteric by prefixing another character such as Tiger or Dragon or Lightning. The numbers 3, 8, 21, derived from the stroke structure of the character 'Hung', may also be found, and it is a common feature of Triad ritual and practice to use, instead of the normal character 'Hung', the character for its homophone meaning 'Red'.

Within a society the principal officers are the Elder Brother, the Second Brother, and the Third Brother. Together they form the centre of control. The Elder Brother may also be the Red Rod, the disciplinary officer. The Second Brother is a 'civil' official, a White Fan who keeps the books, seals, and docu-ments of the society, and copies of the oaths, rules, punishments, etc. The Third Brother is a 'military' official with the rank of Straw Sandals and in control of the fighters.

The 36 oaths prescribe the acts which a Brother must avoid, and the punish-ment inflicted by Heaven or the Five Ancestors on those who disobey, as well as the more immediate punishments to be inflicted by the society. The rules, prohibitions, and punishments are usually merely variations on the same theme. The main items prohibited are: Disobedience to parents, Adultery with the wife or sister of a Brother, Betrayal of a Brother to obtain his wife, Marrying the widow of a deceased Brother, Betrayal of a Brother for reward, Robbing, cheating, or slandering a Brother and refusing to help him in trouble or in a fight, Usurping the functions of a sinseh, Betrayal of the secrets of the Brother-hood, and introducing a government officer (secretly) as a candidate for member-ship. In modern versions, one of the heavenly retributions is death by motor car which seems to be accepted as just as fortuitous as death by lightning, drowning, tigers, or wild dogs. Among the penalties inflicted by the society are

MM

death by knives, 'eating the vermicelli' (being tied up with ropes), and 'death by bath' (being tied up, usually in a sack, and drowned.

THE FIVE LODGES

The supposed distribution of the five Lodges throughout China, together with their distinguishing marks, are given below. The tidy arrangement of distribution by provinces bears no relation to actual practice, at least if the coverage of these Lodges in Malaya is any guide, for societies of the first three lodges are found, and they are not restricted to members from the provinces shown in the table.

Lodge	Provinces	Title	Flag	Base number	Watchwords (Cantonese)
No. 1	Fukien and Kansu	Green Lotus Hall Phoenix Divn	Black	One-nine	Kong and Piu (Ornate)
No. 2	Kwangtung Kwangsi	Hung Obedience Hall Golden Orchid Divn	Red (Crimson)	Twelve	Hung and Shau (Longevity)
No. 3	Yunnan Szechuan	Family Royal Hall Lotus Chapter Divn	Vermilion (or Yellow)	Nine or Four-nine	Lui and Hop (Accord)
No. 4	Hunan Hupeh	Consult Heaven Hall Elegant Cloister Divn	White	Two-nine	K'ei and Woh (Harmony)
No. 5	Chekiang Kiangsi	Vast Change Hall Obtain Fortune Divn	Green (or Blue)	Four-seven	T'ai and T'ung (United)

Of the early Hoeys in Malaya, the Ho Seng was First Lodge, the Ghee Hin Second Lodge, and the Hai San Third Lodge, and each used the appropriate flag, base number, and watchwords. These distinguishing characters have also been found on membership certificates of various Triad societies in Perak in more recent years. The strong influence of the Ghee Hin seems to have resulted in the use of its titles, at times, as applicable to Triad in general, no matter of which Lodge. This is particularly true of the cipher form used for 'Hung Obedience Hall' which has been found at the head of membership certificates of societies belonging to Lodges other than the second. Similarly the seal of the Second Lodge—the character Hung in a triangle—is used by all Lodges.

It may be noted, too, that of the nine components of the central Ghee Hin body in Singapore, one, the Ts'ung Paak, did not, like the others, use the title Ghee Hin on its certificates, seals, and other documents. It is said, also, to have used white characters on a black ground for the central banner in the peck-measure at initiation ceremonies. It is conceivable that it may have been a First or Fourth Lodge society willing to associate with the other Ghee Hin, Second Lodge societies in the central body, but maintaining its separateness by refusing to employ the title of the Second Lodge. This is merely conjecture.

THE CENTRAL GHEE HIN BODY IN SINGAPORE

Very little is known of the organization of the central Ghee Hin body in Singapore which would seem to have been a conference of leaders of the various sections, but was not itself a registered society, presumably because its membership was less than the statutory ten persons.

Major Low, writing in 1840–1,[5] mentioned meetings of the T'in Tei Wui (as the Ghee Hin was then known) being held at a temple 'in the outskirts of the suburbs at Kampong Glam'. This was probably the central temple usually described as being situated in Rochore, but there is no indication of the date of its foundation.[6]

Vaughan, writing in 1878, described this temple as being a large 'open-roomed' building about 60 feet wide and 120 feet long, with extensive kitchens on each side, 30 to 40 feet wide, extending the whole length of the building, capable of cooking dinner for several hundred men. Downstairs there were two halls separated by an open paved courtyard. These halls were used only for feasting. Upstairs there were also two halls, the front one used on important occasions for enquiries by the elders into complaints against other societies or for large initiation ceremonies. The other hall upstairs was the main hall or lodge and contained the shrine of the tablets of the Five Ancestors, together with carved cabinets containing the tablets of deceased officers of the Ghee Hin which were worshipped at the appropriate times.

Members of all nine branches feasted together on two festival days at a cost of 20 or 30 cents each. Within the branches, no event of importance such as the election of an Elder Brother, or a sinseh or other officer was carried into effect without communication with the parent body.

Pickering, writing in the same year as Vaughan, gave the dates of feasting and theatricals as the 25th of the First and the 25th of the Seventh Moon, the latter being the foundation day of the Triad Brotherhood.

Stanton (p. 40) called the Grand Lodge the Kwong Wai Shiu. This was the title of the Cantonese section, which, though it may well have been the senior branch, was not the central body.

The ancestral tablets of notable deceased Ghee Hin members are still to be found in a small temple in Lavender Street called the Hung Ka Temple.

[5] Buckley, i. 365–6.
[6] The area was known to the Chinese as Goh Choh (Five Ancestors), which may be the origin of 'Rochore'.

APPENDIX 2

THE earliest English-language source was 'The Triad (Secret) Society' by Dr Milne, a Protestant missionary of Malacca, written in 1821 but not published until after his death when it appeared in the *RAS Trans.*, i. 240–50. 'The Chinese Secret Triad Society of the Tien-ti-huih', by Lieut. Newbold and Major-General Wilson of the Madras Army, read to the same society in January 1840 but not published till 1841, contains much interesting information about this society gathered mainly in the Straits Settlements. It would seem that the authors believed that the swearing of the oath in the Peach Garden was synonymous with the founding of the Triad Society. A short account of the initiation ceremony is given, together with a translation of the 36 oaths.

Dr Hoffman's more detailed 'Triad Ritual' appeared in 1848 and 1853, while Vaughan's 'Notes on the Chinese of Pinang' (1854), in addition to describing the various types of Chinese organizations in Penang, including five societies of Triad type, gave a short account of an initiation ceremony which, from later evidence, was of the Ho Seng Society.

Another most interesting article on the Triad Society, with prints of the diplomas used by the Triad rebels at Amoy and Shanghai in 1853, appeared in the *Shanghae Almanac* for 1854. This, too, is anonymous, but was written by Alexander Wylie and is reproduced in the collection of his writings, *Chinese Researches*, published in 1897.

In 1854 John Kesson of the British Museum published *The Cross and the Dragon*, which contained a section on Chinese secret societies and gave a very short account of Triad ritual, a copy of the 36 oaths (in translation), and a reproduction of a membership diploma. Part of this information seems to have been taken from Newbold, and part from a book called *Thien, Thi, Hoi'h*, by a German missionary, E. H. Roettger, who had lived in the Dutch East Indies.

But it was not until 1866 that a comprehensive documented description of the Triad ritual appeared in Schlegel's *Thian Ti Hwui; the Hung League or Heaven and Earth League*. This still remains the basic guide (though he occasionally falls into error) with the supreme advantage that it includes the Chinese characters for the ritual verses. (This work was reprinted in 1956 by the Government Printer, Singapore.)

In 1868 the Report of the Penang Riot Commission contained at App. 17 an account of the initiation ceremony and translations of ritual verses of the Penang Ghee Hin Society. An unfinished account given in 1878–9 by W A. Pickering, the first Protector of Chinese, Singapore, of the traditional history and of an initiation ceremony attended by him at the Ghee Hin headquarters in Singapore, was published in the *JSSBRAS*, vols i & iii. Vaughan's *Manners and Customs of the Chinese of the Straits Settlements* (based on his earlier article) was published in Singapore in 1879. William Stanton's 'The Triad Society or Heaven and Earth Association' was reprinted in book form in Hong Kong in 1900, from vols xxi & xxii of the *China Review*, and in 1925 *The Hung Society or the Society of Heaven and Earth*, by J. S. M. Ward and W. G. Stirling, was published in London. Mention should also be made of an article by James Hutson published in the *CJSA* in October, November, and December 1928 (vol. ix, nos 4, 5, & 6). This was a translation from a book in Chinese by Amane Hirayama, of which there are several editions, the earliest seen being that published by the Research Institute of the South Manchurian Railway in January 1925. Hutson translated the traditional history and the actual history from this work, much of which appears to have been taken from Stanton's book. He did not translate the portion dealing with the ritual. Important, too, is the small book by Favre published in 1933 under the title *Les sociétés secrètes en Chine*.

There are also several Chinese-language printed sources none of which was published earlier than 1911, and most of which have appeared during the last thirty years. They are mentioned in the Bibliography. In using them care is needed to establish whether they refer to the Ko Lao Hui, the Ch'ing Pang, or the Triad Society, all of which are referred to as the Hung Brotherhood but have different rituals. In recent years a number of popular romances in printed form have appeared concerning the Hung Brotherhood. For the most part they elaborate the traditional history at great length, but some, such as the *One Hundred and Twenty Comrades*, contain short descriptions of the ritual of the Triad Society.

Information has also been obtained from a number of unpublished sources, among them the Clementi Book (in the author's possession) containing impressions from the wood blocks and seals handed in at the dissolution of the societies in Singapore and Penang in 1890, and two large wall-sheets prepared by a Triad member in 1897 for William Cowan, an officer of the Chinese Protectorate in Malaya. One of these has replicas of the membership diplomas and seals of various societies, including those dissolved in 1890, and the other has a pictorial representation of the Ghee Hin rites, together with reproductions of documents and paraphernalia used by the society, and some of the secret message-signs formed by the arrangement of tea-cups and chopsticks.

But the most interesting sources have come to hand through the author's long association (beginning in 1921) with the Department of Chinese Affairs (Chinese Protectorate) in Malaya. In particular the years from 1946 onwards, when an upsurge of Triad activity took place, were most fruitful. Documents seized by the police included Chinese manuscript booklets containing portions of the versified ritual and sometimes brief notes on some of the appurtenances. Scores of participants in initiation ceremonies were interrogated, by police officers and by the author. Some were in police custody, others were brought to light through underground channels. In general, the evidence of initiates was rather disappointing. During the ceremony the 'New Horses' are so bewildered and terrified that they are frequently unable to remember clearly the sequence of events or the meaning of what they do. And as the ceremony is usually performed at night in the dim light of a few candles with the initiate, for most of the time, in a bowed position with head bent low, he has little opportunity for close scrutiny.

In a different category are the old members who have attended several ceremonies, and especially the sinsehs who conduct them. Many of these were questioned, and some were extremely co-operative for a variety of reasons. A

MM 2

few had been arrested and become police agents; others were prepared to tell all they knew if it was certain that they were to be sent to China so that their local contacts would not be able to accuse them of betraying the Brotherhood in return for a promise of release. There were others, too, who, though reluctant at first, became quite enthusiastic in talking of these matters with someone who had some knowledge of their craft, and one man was so angry when it was suggested that he was bogus that he proceeded to prove that he was genuine. Others, on the contrary, were not to be moved from their secrecy and silence.

A most striking feature was the very low standard of knowledge of most of the sinsehs questioned. What they knew had been learned by rote and was limited by the deficiencies of their instructors. Whenever obvious errors in ritual verses were pointed out, the sinseh's reply was invariably that he only knew what he had learnt. Enquiry as to any esoteric meaning behind the ritual met with a completely blank response. To any particular question the answer invariably was: 'there is a verse about that' which they recited at once. That was their authority and they probed no further. It was readily admitted that many so-called sinsehs had only a very shaky knowledge of the ritual. They are, one and all, very alive to the financial potentialities attached to the exercise of their craft, and it is possible to meet a sinseh who will quietly declare that the whole business is a lot of mumbo-jumbo through which they extract a livelihood from a credulous public.

One old sinseh who had long retired to the respectability of keeping a shop was prevailed upon to write out a short history of Triad in China and Malaya as he understood it, together with a description of the organization of a society and an account of the ritual, secret signs, and expressions, amounting, in all, to 120 pages. In parts it varies from other information, but it has been a most useful guide when working through fragmentary documents, and when piecing together the story of postwar Malaya. One other, most useful, source has been the articles and documents seized by the police at initiation ceremonies. These were frequently photographed at the site and then removed for further examination.

In general, allowing for variations, the basis of the ritual used today is approximately the same as that analysed by Schlegel in 1866, and many of the verses found in modern manuscript sources are exactly the same as those quoted by him. One difference is worthy of comment. Some of the published sources cited above tell of the pricking of the fingers of all those present at the ceremony, old members as well as initiates, and most of them say that the Hung wine is drunk by all. On the other hand, in the evidence given before the Penang Riot Commission (1868) a member of the Ghee Hin (Oh Wee Kee) stated that each *new* member drank. It seems likely that the original intention was to establish a blood communion between all members, but the modern practice is that only the new members are pricked, and only they drink the Hung wine, which would seem to be in accordance with the Penang Ghee Hin practice.

Ward and Stirling (vol. i, App. pp. 176–9) describe a ritual of the 'Three Dots' Society which they regard as a separate Brotherhood from Triad. Wynne develops this theme in *Triad and Tabut* (pp. 128–51). Both descriptions rely on the same source, an article by C. B. Cooper, a Malayan-born lawyer of Johore, written in 1924, and published in the *Malayan Police Magazine* of March 1933. It is the opinion of every sinseh with whom the present writer has discussed this ritual that it is undoubtedly Triad, but that some of the items had been misinterpreted to, or by, Cooper. Without going into details, it may be said that there is no reason to doubt that the title 'Three Dots' Society is a commonly-used expression to denote a Triad society. The earliest use of this title that has been traced occurs in an extract from the Canton Register of 15 Oct. 1831, quoted in the *Chinese Repository*, iv (1836), pp. 415–25.

APPENDIX 3

Name	Supposed strength	Tribe	Meeting houses
1. Ghee Hin	15,000	Hokkien	Rochore
2. Chen Chen Kow	1,000	Tew Chew & Kay	N.B. Road
3. Ghee Hok	800	Tew Chew	Carpenter St
4. Hysam	6,000	Kokien & Tew Chew	Cross St
5. Hen Bing	500	Hokien	S. Bridge Rd
6. Choo Leong	500	Hokien	Upper Hokien St
7. Hock Bing	600	Hokien & Hylam	Upper Nankin St
8. Ang Bang	400	Hokien	Teluk Ayer St
9. Gee Sin	1,500	Tay Chew	Java Rd
10. Gee Kee	1,500	Kay & Tay Chew	Bench Rd
11. Gee Soon	1,500	Hokien & Hylam	Campong Bencoolen
12. Ghee Hin	2,500	Hylam	Honkong St
13. Cho Koon	3,500	Tew Chew	New B. Rd
14. Ghee Hin	4,000	Macao	Rochore

Note: The names and addresses of the headman which appear in the original have here been omitted.

The spelling given above is that of the original list and shows discrepancies, e.g. 'Tay Chew' and 'Tew Chew' for the same thing (Tiechiu). 'Kay' represents 'Kheh' (Hakka). No. 4, 'Hysam' should be 'Hysan', and there is a peculiarity, too, about its membership which seems to be Hokkien and Tiechiu. Though not impossible this would be an unusual combination, and it differs from the usual composition of the Hai San elsewhere which was predominantly 'Macao', mainly Hakka. It may be that what was intended was 'Kay and Tew Chew'. 'Bench Rd' should be 'Beach Rd', 'New B. Rd' is 'New Bridge Rd', 'N.B. Rd' may be the same or 'North Bridge Rd'. There is no mention of the Ts'ung Paak Kwun, the Hakka affiliate of the Ghee Hin, but it is possible that this is to be found in No. 2, Chen Chen Kow. No. 13, Cho Koon, is the Tiechiu Ghee Hin (Tio Kun). No. 7, Hock Bing, may be the Hok Hin. It is noteworthy that the Ghee Hok is shown as a Tiechiu society. Several of the societies would seem to have disappeared by the time of the registration of 1877, or else not to have been regarded as 'Dangerous Societies'.

The list, dated 1 May 1860 and signed by C. B. Plunket, Acting Commissioner of Police, Singapore, is to be found in printed form as an enclosure to Cavenagh's Despatch No. 108 of 5 June 1860, together with a letter from Plunket dated 24 April 1860 (IOL, Proceedings Home Judicial, Range 206, vol. 64).

APPENDIX 4

STATE OF REGISTERED SOCIETIES AT THE END OF 1889

Singapore

Name	Premises	Office-bearers	Members
Ghee Hin (Hokkien)	China St	478	18,973
Ghee Hok	River Valley Rd	396	14,487
Ghee Khee Kwang Hok	Beach Rd	97	6,466
Hok Hin	North Canal Rd	162	14,317
Kwong Wai Shiu	Victoria St	61	4,877
Ts'ung Paak	Upper Nankin St	60	7,413
Hong Ghee Thong	Upper Chinchew St	15	402
Lee Seng Hong	South Bridge Rd	5	407
Yuet Tong Kun	Banda St	5	415
Heng Sun	Havelock Rd	42	559
TOTAL		1,321	68,316

Source: Sing., Ch. Protect. *AR*, 1889, Table E (*SSGG*, 14 Apr. 1890, p. 858).

Penang

Name	Premises	Office-bearers	Members
Ghee Hin	Church St	245	75,000
Kien Tek	Armenian Lane	50	21,000
Ho Seng	King St	92	14,000
Chun Sim	King St	9	2,450
Hai San	Beach St	13	850
TOTAL		409	113,300

Note: In Singapore and Penang the figures for membership include all names in the registers. Owing to deaths and removals, it is possible that only 50 per cent remained.

Source: Pg Ch. Protect. *AR*, 1889, Table J (*SSGG*, 11 Apr. 1890, p. 862).

Malacca, 1888

	Members
Ghee Hin	6,487
Ghee Hin (Macao)	527
Hai San	515
TOTAL	7,529

Source: Mal. *AR*, 1888 (*SSGG*, 5 July 1889, pp. 1270–96).

APPENDIX 5

THE KIEN TEK SOCIETY OF PENANG AND THE TOA PEK KONG DEITY[1]

THE reasons for the formation of this society are readily understandable. The early Chinese immigrants in Penang were mainly 'Macaos' from Kwangtung and Kwangsi, and formed the labouring and artisan communities. The Hokkiens, smaller in numbers, were predominantly shopkeepers and traders, many of whom had come from Malacca and other near-by territories where they had long been established. The differences of province, language, customs, and occupation led the Hokkiens to combine for mutual support and the protection of their own interests. China-born Hokkiens formed their own society, the Chun Sim, in 1826 to protect themselves against the overbearing pretensions of the Macao Hoeys, and for similar reasons the Kien Tek was founded in 1844. There were, however, still some Hokkiens who remained in the Ghee Hin.

The tutelary deity of the society, Toa Pek Kong (Old Great-uncle), still exists in part of the old Kien Tek premises in Armenian Lane, Penang, in the Hok Tek (Fuk Tak) shrine belonging to the Poh Hock Seah, an association composed of the leaders of the local-born Hokkien community which, on the official dissolution of the Kien Tek in 1890, undertook to continue the ceremonial worship of the deity at this shrine. It consists of three figures representing three early Hakka immigrants, Chang Li, a teacher, Ch'iu Siu Chin, a charcoal maker, and Ma Fu Chun, a blacksmith, who became sworn brothers and whose graves may still be seen at Tanjong Tokong where a temple, Sea Pearl Temple, has been built in their honour. The gravestone of Ma bears a date corresponding to 1809, though it is said that the temple was built some ten years earlier. Like the sister temple to the same deity in Penang town, this was a Hakka foundation, and during the period of the Kien Tek Society there was great antagonism between the Hokkien and the Macao communities, for the former wished to monopolize the temple for their ritualistic ceremony on the fifteenth day of the first moon each year. The matter was eventually settled by arbitration, the Hokkiens using the temple on the fifteenth and the Macaos on the sixteenth.

There is still a survival of the Hokkien ceremony. Each year on the fifteenth, a censer in a carved carrier is taken from the Armenian Lane shrine to the Tanjong Tokong temple where, in the evening, members of the Poh Hock Seah assemble and take possession to the exclusion of non-members. (This, at times, still meets with dissent and verbal opposition.) The grill gates are locked, and a simple ceremony of worship with lighted joss-sticks is conducted by a Taoist priest, at the end of which the joss-sticks held by the members are stubbed into the censer. The electric lights are turned out, and the crowd outside waits tensely for the revivification of the god. This is performed by the president of the society who blows upon the ashes, and by a secret means causes a tongue of flame to shoot up in the darkness, to the great relief of the watching crowd, for the spirit is with them for another year.

[1] See above, p. 75.

The members of the Poh Hock Seah then settle down to a dinner (paid for from the society's funds) at tables a little way off from the temple. The censer of ash is taken back in procession to the shrine in Armenian Lane. In this way the last shadow of the ritual of the Kien Tek is still maintained. This, at least, is the legend and ceremony as known in Penang. It may be that other places have their own legends, for Toa Pek Kong is worshipped by Chinese throughout Malaya and the adjacent lands as the god of good fortune, particularly concerned with the fortunes of the pioneer overseas community. His name has passed into the Malay language as Topekong, applied to any deity in a Chinese temple, sometimes found in the variant form Dato' Peking. From it, too, derives the Malay word Tokong, meaning a Chinese temple or shrine.

The Penang Riot report of 1868, though giving a reasonably full account of the Ghee Hin ritual, does not deal with that of the Kien Tek in the same detail. We know, however, that candidates had their fingers pricked, that the blood was mixed with wine, and that all members drank of the mixture while pledging themselves to be all of one heart. The oath and the names of new members were written on a piece of yellow paper which was burnt after being read out by the secretary. The titles of some of the office-bearers were the same as those used in Triad: First, Second, and Third Elder Brother, the sinseh, and the Red Rod, but despite these similarities it is doubtful whether the Kien Tek was a Triad society and a member of the Hung Brotherhood. An original print of its membership 'seal' appears in the Clementi Book, and there are facsimiles on Cowan's Wall-sheet and at p. 102 of Wynne (with a translation open to challenge). There is no similarity between the phrases in these diplomas, however they may be arranged, and those used in Triad diplomas, and there is a significant absence of the character 'Hung'. The rule prohibiting members from joining any one of the three Triad societies in Penang tends to support the assumption that the Kien Tek was not a Triad foundation, and that instead of the Five Ancestors it adopted the local Toa Pek Kong as its tutelary deity. On the other hand, a very old Triad sinseh whose uncles had been connected with the Kien Tek was emphatic, when questioned by the present writer, that it was part of the Hung Brotherhood. It is, however, conceivable that by this he merely meant that it was a secret brotherhood with a blood-oath.

It is tempting, because of the similarity of titles, to connect this society with the 'Kwan Tec' which fought the Ghee Hin in Singapore in 1846. Unfortunately the characters for the title 'Kwan Tec' are not known, but it is not impossible that there may be some connexion. In the early 1840s the Dutch authorities at Rhio were uprooting the Kwan Tec Society from their territory, and it may be that some of these refugees arrived in Penang (as they did in Singapore) and stimulated the formation of the Kien Tek. But this is conjecture.

One other conjecture which can be ruled out is made by Wynne (pp. 101, 130). It is that this society was identical with, or the counterpart of the Ghee Hok Society of Singapore. Both the Kien Tek and the Ghee Hok existed side by side at Penang from 1875 onwards, and the latter society was composed mainly of Tiechius[2] and used a Triad diploma.[3]

In contemporary documents the Kien Tek is sometimes called the Kien Hok; this title derived from the transposition of the characters for Hokkien.

[2] Pg *AR*, 1885.   [3] Clementi Book and Cowan's Wall-sheet.

APPENDIX 6

'FOUR DISTRICTS' AND 'FIVE DISTRICTS'

THE use of the terms 'Four Districts' and 'Five Districts' in relation to the three Larut wars from 1861 onwards needs some elucidation.

These terms are well known within the Cantonese community. The Four are: Sin Neng (now called T'oi Shan), San Wui, Hoi P'eng, and Yan P'ing, and they form a cluster in the south-west of Kwangtung province. The Five are: Nam Hoi, P'un Yue, Shun Tak, Tung Kwun, and Heung Shan (now called Chung Shan). These latter are the 'home districts' of Canton, surrounding the capital and extending down the estuary of the Pearl river. Their inhabitants regarded themselves as true Cantonese, and looked upon people from the Four Districts as marginal Cantonese speaking an outlandish dialect.

The Four Districts are known in Cantonese as the Sz Yip, and in Hokkien as See Kwan (properly See Koain). The Five Districts are known as Ng Yuen, or Ng Tai Yuen (Five large districts): in Hokkien these become Go Kwan (properly Goh Koain) and Goh Toa Kwan. Note that Chen Shang is not one of the Five Districts, though it is contiguous with two of them.

In contemporary documents of the Larut wars of 1861 and 1865, the terms Four Districts and Five Districts are not to be found, for the simple reason that men from these districts were not involved. These wars were between men from the Fui Chiu (Waichow) prefecture and men from the Chen Shang district. By 1872 the position had changed and the war was between men of Sin Neng and adjacent districts (the Four Districts) and men of Chen Shang. It was not until about August 1872 that men of the Five Districts were brought into the fight by the Chen Shang men, and this was done through Low Sam, the Mentri's agent.

There was, and still is, in Penang an association called the Ng Fuk T'ong (Hall of Five Blessings) founded in 1857, most of whose members were from the Five Districts. Membership was open to men of other districts except the Four Districts who were not eligible. The districts eligible were set out in the Rules: the first five being the Five Districts and the sixth, Cheng Shan. With this background it is possible to understand how the Five District men came to be linked with the fortunes of the Cheng Shan men. The first documentary mention of the entry of the Five Districts into the fray is in a statement made to Speedy by Ong Ah Yu on 18 October 1872, who told of an attack by '1,000 armed Chinese of the Goh Tay Kwan tribe'.[1] Campbell (Acting Lieut. Governor) in a memorandum of 19 October talked of a faction called 'In Tye Yoon' (i.e. Ng Tai Yuen) incited by the Chen Shang men against their common enemy.[2] In a covering letter Campbell talked of the recovery of the Chen Shangs 'with the aid of another faction'.[3] Other documents also fit this explanation, e.g. the Sz Yip petition of 3 May 1873[4] which, after recounting the expulsion of the

[1] C.1111, p. 13.   [2] Ibid. p. 16.
[3] Ibid. p. 10.   [4] Ibid. pp. 146–7.

Chen Shangs in February–March 1872, said: 'After that, the Mentri entered into an agreement with a kongsee named "Ang Tye Yon".'[5]

It may be noted, too, that neither Campbell's memorandum nor that of C. J. Irving, who visited Larut in April and May 1872,[6] makes any mention of the Five Districts in the early stages of the fight in February 1872. The translation of dates in the Sz Yip petition is faulty, but from another document it would seem that this accession of strength to the Chen Shang side occurred in August 1872.[7]

The first writer to give the names Four Districts and Five Districts to the two sides retrospectively from the beginning of the Larut troubles in the 1860s was A. M. Skinner in his Précis of Perak Affairs written on 10 January 1874,[8] and this mistake was immediately repeated by Braddell in his report dated 28 January.[9] Thereafter successive writers have relied on these two documents and the mistake has been perpetuated.

[5] The printed version in C.1111 gives 'Ong Tye You', which is a miscopying from the MS in the Singapore archives of 'Ang Tye Yon'.
[6] C.1111, p. 127. [7] Report of Koh Boon An, CDPL, No. 26.
[8] C.1111, pp. 114–25. [9] Ibid. pp. 160, 176.

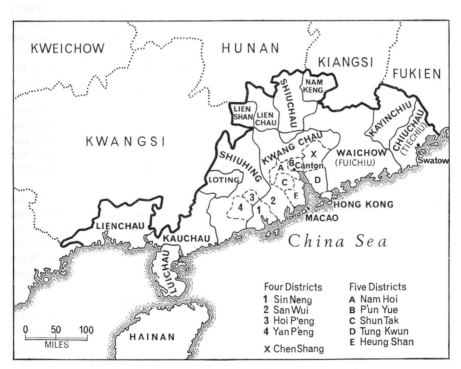

4. Kwangtung: 'Four Districts' and 'Five Districts'

APPENDIX 7

THE Wa Kei Brotherhood is quite separate from Triad and is frequently found in opposition, but it has adapted certain items from Triad ritual verses and nomenclature to its own much simpler ritual practice.

The following condensed account is based on interrogation of leaders of the Wa Kei Society, and on examination of MS notebooks found in possession of members.

The initiation ceremony is usually held in the premises of the club under cover of which the local Wa Kei Society works. A space on the floor is set out as an altar with the picture of Kuan Ti, or the characters for his name, as the central item of worship. There are no Five Ancestors, though the term City of Willows is found in its verses. Standing on the altar space are also two red candles and an incense pot containing four joss-sticks. Four is the basic number of the society. There is also a small bowl of water with a knife laid across it, point towards the front, and sweets of four colours. The official conducting the ceremony is known, as in Triad, as 'Sin Shang' (teacher) but the ritual is so simple that it can readily be learnt.

Candidates are brought forward by a Maternal Uncle (K'au Pa) and their names are listed. As in Triad, they remove all articles of metal from their persons and take off their shoes. The whole of the torso is bared. The Sin Shang and the Maternal Uncle take up their positions squatting on the floor with their backs to the altar space, the Uncle being on the Sin Shang's left. The candidates kneel on both knees facing them, if possible, four at a time, and each is given a lighted joss-stick by the Maternal Uncle which is held, Triad fashion, between the palms head downwards. The Sin Shang chants four oaths, one sentence at a time, each sentence being repeated by the candidates. After each oath the joss-sticks are extinguished by stubbing on the ground or dipping in the bowl of water, and a fresh lighted stick is provided. When all four are extinguished they are picked up by the initiates and held right way up to be relighted by the Maternal Uncle. This is known as 'Gathering the Incense' (Wui Heung).

The Sin Shang recites a prayer which the initiates repeat, thereafter placing their joss-sticks right way up in the incense pot. The slip of paper bearing the names of the candidates is then burnt, and the ashes stirred into the bowl of water with the point of the knife. With the tip of the knife still in the water, the bowl is proffered to each new member to sip, and thereafter each is given a coloured sweet to eat. This concludes the ceremony.

The oaths cover the following items: non-interference with the womenfolk of a Brother; assistance to a Brother in a quarrel with an outsider, if the former seems to be in the right, otherwise exhortation; refraining from harbouring a grudge against a Brother, helping a Brother in distress with food, money, and by other means, and not refusing his plea. One version was discovered containing a fifth clause, warning the candidate not to join the Triad or other secret society, and not to join the Communists. This was in an area where the Wa Kei was in conflict with both these groups. There are the usual visitations from Heaven should the oaths be broken.

Throughout the ritual there is much emphasis on Kuan Ti, and the phrase which usually accompanies representations of this god is frequently used: Loyal of heart and righteous of spirit (Chung Sam Yi Hei). The number four is constantly employed, the four characters Shui, Luk, P'eng, On (peace on water and land) repeatedly appear, and one title of the society is the 'Four Character Society' (Sz Koh Tsz). Another is 'Four Hole Society' (Sz Koh Lung) from the four square 'holes' in the character 'Wa' of Wa Kei. Most of the secret hand signs are made with four fingers. The numbers 21 and 31 are also frequently found in verses of the society, both deriving from the formation of the character 'Wa'.

Of particular interest are two Wa Kei tombs, in the Chinese cemeteries at Menglembu and Kuala Lumpur. There is no corpse in either, the tombs are there as a focus of worship for the Wa Kei Brethren. The one at Menglembu, the traditional centre of Wa Kei in Perak, bears the date 7th day of 3rd moon, equivalent to 15 April 1948, together with a diagram of a cent piece and the inscription: 'Overseas Chinese Descendants, Tutelary Deity, Meeting Place. Erected by the Choh Heng T'ong'. This last is the name by which the Malayan Lodge of the Wa Kei is known. The Kuala Lumpur tomb, dedicated in 1951, bears the title 'Kwong Wa'. On each side of the main inscription is a smaller one, and the first and last characters of these two lines when placed together form the motto: 'Shui Luk P'eng On.' That the Brotherhood should, as recently as 1948 and 1951, have set up these 'ancestral tombs' is an indication of the strength of the postwar revival of the Wa Kei Society in the Federation of Malaya.

ABBREVIATIONS USED IN CITING OFFICIAL SOURCES

Act. Sec.:	Acting Secretary
AR:	*Annual Report*
App.:	Appendix
Beng.:	Bengal
CDPL:	Corresp. relating to the Disturbances in Perak and Larut
Commr, Dy Cmmr:	Commissioner, Deputy Commissioner
COD:	Colonial Office Despatch
Col. Sec.:	Colonial Secretary
Conf.:	Confidential
Cons:	Consultations
Corresp.:	Correspondence
CP:	Chinese Protectorate
CSO:	Colonial Secretary's Office
doc.:	document
EPO:	Enquiry into the Complicity of Chiefs in the Perak Outrages, 1876
FMS:	Federated Malay States
Ft Cornwallis/ William:	Fort Cornwallis/William
GD:	Governor's Despatch
GG:	Government Gazette
GN:	Gazette Notification
GOI:	Government of India
Gov.	Governor
Leg. Co.	Legislative Council
Lett.	Letter(s)
Mal.:	Malacca
Mgte:	Magistrate
Mtg:	Meeting
Ord.:	Ordinance
P. of C.	Protector of Chinese
PEP:	Perak Enquiry Papers
Pg:	Penang
PLC:	Proceedings of Legislative Council
PRCR:	Penang Riots Commission Report
Pres.:	President
RCs:	Resident Councillor(s)
Reg.:	Regulation
Sel.:	Selangor
Sel. Ctee:	Select Committee
Sing.:	Singapore
SS:	Straits Settlements
Supt:	Superintendent

SELECT BIBLIOGRAPHY

1. OFFICIAL SOURCES

THE archives at the Singapore National Library (formerly Raffles Library) contain internal correspondence up to 1867 as well as letters and despatches to and from India for that period. They also contain despatches to the Colonial Office from 1867 onwards. Enclosures to despatches are not, however, usually included in the Singapore archives, but may be found in the library of the India Office for the Indian period and at the Public Record Office, London for the Colonial Office period. It is not always easy to trace despatches in the India Office Library as they may be in different departmental series, e.g. General, Judicial, Foreign (Political). Those in the Public Record Office are in Series CO 273, and usually contain enclosures and Colonial Office minutes. This series also contains copies of some documents earlier than 1867.

The Singapore archives also contain a volume of Correspondence relating to the Disturbances in Perak and Larut, 1862–73 (CDPL), another comprising material collected by the Commission appointed in 1876 to enquire into the complicity of the Chiefs in the Perak Outrage (EPO), with a Précis of Evidence and an Abridgement of Evidence, and three volumes of 'Perak Enquiry Papers' (1876–7) (PEP), containing the full statements of witnesses examined at the enquiry.

Parliamentary Papers

The principal Parliamentary Papers covering the subject are:

C.465*	1872	Recent Proceedings &c. (Selangor)
C.1111	1874	Correspondence relating to certain Native States, &c.
C.1320	1875	Further correspondence &c.
C.1505	1876	Further correspondence &c. (Malacca, Perak, Selangor, S. Ujong)
C.1505–1	—	Maps and sketches for C.1505.
C.1512	1876	Further correspondence &c. (Perak & S. Ujong)
C.1709	1877	Further correspondence &c. (Perak & S. Ujong)
C.2410	1879	Instructions to British Residents and other papers

Straits Settlements, *Proceedings of Legislative Council* (annual)
Particularly useful for their Appendices containing reports submitted by Commissions.

—— *Minutes of Executive Council*

Government Gazettes

Annual Reports: Straits Settlements and Federated Malay States
   Postwar: Singapore and the Federation of Malaya

Special Papers

Legislative Assembly, Singapore, Sessional Papers:

  Cmd. 53 of 1956: Singapore Chinese Middle Schools Students' Union
  Cmd. 33 of 1957. The Communist Threat to Singapore

 * Owing to overprinting, it is difficult to discern whether this figure is 465 or 466, but the next Paper (C.1111) refers to it as 465.

Cmd. 7 of 1958: Report of the Commission of Inquiry into Corrupt, Illegal, or Undesirable Practices at Elections

Cmd. 14 of 1959: Communist Literature in Singapore

Federation of Malaya Legislative Council
Paper No. 23 of 1959: The Communist Threat to the Federation of Malaya

2. CHINA BACKGROUND

(a) *Works in Chinese*

Ch'en Ching Chu. *Hung-men ch'i-hsieh* (Wonderful Heroism of the Hung Family). Hong Kong, Hsiang Chi Bookshop, 1952. 4 vols.

Romantic history.

Chu Lin. *Hung-men chih* (Record of the Hung Family). Shanghai, Chung Hua Book Co., 1947–8.

Detailed history of Hung Brotherhood. Ritual verses and phraseology of Ko Lao Hui and Ch'ing Pang, and illustrations of Hung documents.

Hirayama Amane. *Chung-kuo pi-mi she-hui shih* (History of Chinese Secret Societies). S. Manchurian Railway Research Dept, 1925.

History, organization, ritual, oaths, etc., of the Triad society. Partly trans. by Hutson (q.v.). Close resemblance to Stanton's book (1900).

Hui-tang ti lai-chi tsu-chih (History and Organization of Societies). Singapore, *Sin Chew Weekly*, 20 & 27 Dec. 1956.

Hung-men pi-mi li-shih (History of Hung Family Secrets). Hong Kong, Hsiang Chi Bookshop, n.d. 2 vols.

Triad traditional history and ritual. Popular account of the Red Flower Pavilion, the Five Ancestors, and the City of Willows.

Hung men sou-pi (Investigation of Hung Family Secrets). Macao, Hung Fuk Publishing Co., 1957.

Mostly Ko Lao Hui with some Triad usage.

Liu Lien-k'o. *Pang-hui san-pai-nien ke-ming shih* (A History of 300 Years' Revolutionary Activities of the Secret Societies). Macao, Liu Yuan Publishing Co., 1942.

Lo Erh-kang. *T'ien-ti Hui wen-hsien lu* (Records of the Heaven and Earth Society). Shanghai Book Publishing Co., 1948.

Origins and subdivisions of the Hung Brotherhood.

Pai-erh yu (One Hundred and Twenty Comrades). Hong Kong, Hsiang Chi Bookshop. 3 vols.

Triad novel set in Canton City. Some ritual detail.

Wang Ch'ao-ch'in. *Kuo-min ke-ming yün-tung* (National Revolutionary Movements). Formosa.

Wang Fu-luan. *Hua-Ch'iao yü chung-kuo ke-ming* (The Overseas Chinese and the Chinese revolution). Hong Kong, Asia Press Ltd.

Wei, The Ven. *Chung-kuo pang-hui Ch'ing, Hung, Han Liu* (Chinese gangs and societies; Green, Red, and Han Liu). Shanghai Literature Co., 1948.

Note: A number of additional Chinese sources are cited by Chan Wing-tsit in *Religious Trends in Modern China* (q.v.), pp. 156–61.

(*b*) *Works in European languages*

Ball, J. Dyer. *Things Chinese*. Shanghai, 1925.

Boyle, F. Chinese Secret Societies. *Harper's Magazine*, Sept. 1891.

Brewitt-Taylor, C. H. *Romance of the Three Kingdoms or States* (trans.). Shanghai, 1929. 2 vols.

Brine, Cdr. *The Taeping Rebellion in China*. London, 1862.

Buck, Pearl S. *All Men Are Brothers* (trans.). London, 1933.

Burkhardt, V. R. *Chinese Creeds and Customs*. Hong Kong, 1953.

Cameron, M. E. *The Reform Movement in China, 1898-1912*. Stanford, Calif., 1931.

Chan Wing-tsit. *Religious Trends in Modern China*. New York, Columbia UP, 1953.

Ch'en, J. and R. Payne. *Sun Yat-sen; a Portrait*. New York, 1946.

Chiang, Siang-tseh. *The New Rebellion*. Washington, 1954.

A Chinese Secret Society (Ch'ing Pang). *China Review* (London), Dec. 1934.

The Chinese Repository (Hong Kong, 1833-44), vols. i, iv, v, xiv, xv, xviii.

Cordier, H. Sociétés secrètes chinoises. *Revue d'Ethnographie*, vii (1888).

Coulet, G. *Les sociétés secrètes en terre d'Annam*. Saigon, 1926.

Couling, S. *Encyclopaedia Sinica*. Shanghai, 1917.

Courant, N. Les associations en Chine. *Annales des Sciences Politiques* (Paris), xiv (1899).

De Groot, J. J. M. Militant Spirit of the Buddhist Clergy. *T'oung Pao*, 1891.

—— *Sectarianism and Religious Persecution in China*. Amsterdam, 1903-4. 2 vols.

De Korne, J. C. *The Fellowship of Goodness*. Michigan, 1934.

—— Sun Yat-sen and the Secret Societies. *Pacific Affairs*, Dec. 1934.

De Riencourt, A. *The Soul of China*. London, 1959.

Dubarbier, G. Les sociétés secrètes en Chine. *La Nouvelle Revue*, ser. 4, yr 49 (1948).

Eitel, E. J. History of the Hakka People. *China Review*, ii (1873-5).

Favre, B. *Les sociétés secrètes en Chine*. Paris, 1933.

Giles, H. A. *Freemasonry in China*. Shanghai, 1890.

Glick, C. and Hong Sheng-hwa. *Swords of Silence*. New York, 1947.

Guenon, R. *La grande Triade*. Paris, 1899.

Hail, W. J. *Tseng Kuo-fan and the T'ai P'ing Rebellion*. New Haven, Conn., 1927.

Hoffman, Dr Triad Ritual. *Chinese Repository*, xviii, June 1849.

Hsiao Kung-ch'üan. *Rural China: Imperial Control in the Nineteenth Century*. Seattle, 1960.

Hugh, A. Y. Significance of Secret Societies in Chinese Life. *China Weekly Review*, 10 Sept. 1927.

Hughes, G. The Small Knife Rebels. *China Review*, i (1872-3).

Hutson, J. Chinese Life in the Tibetan Foothills. *New China Review*, Feb. 1920.

—— Chinese Secret Societies. *China Journal of Science and Arts*, ix/4, 5, & 6 (1928); x/1 (1929).

Isaacs, H. R. *Five Years of KMT Reaction*. Shanghai, 1932.

—— *The Tragedy of the Chinese Revolution*. Stanford, Calif., 1951 (1st ed., 1938).

Jackson, J. H. *Water Margin* (trans.). Shanghai, 1937. 2 vols.

Kesson, J. *The Cross and the Dragon.* London, 1854.

Kuo Ping-chia. *China: New Age and New Outlook.* London, 1956.

Levy, H. S. Yellow Turban Religion and Rebellion at the end of Han. *Journal of American Oriental Society,* lxxvi (1956).

Lin Yueh-hwa. *The Golden Wing.* London, 1947.

Lindley, A. F. *Ti-Ping Tien-Kwoh; the History of the Ti-Ping Revolution.* London, 1913.

Martin, B. *Strange Vigour; a Biography of Sun Yat-sen.* London, 1944.

Mason, C. W. *The Chinese Confessions of C. W. Mason (Ko Lao Hui).* London, 1924.

Maybon, P. B. *Essai sur les associations en Chine.* Paris, 1925.

Meadows, T. T. *The Chinese and their Rebellions.* 1856. Stanford, Calif., Academic Reprints, 1953.

Milne, W. The Triad (Secret) Society in China. *Royal Asiatic Society Transactions,* i/2 (1827), pp. 240–50.

——, trans. *The Sacred Edict.* Malacca, 1817.

Morse, H. B. *In the Days of the Taipings.* Salem, Mass., 1927.

Pelliot, P. La secte du Lotus Blanc et la secte du Nuage Blanc. *Bulletin de l'École d'Extrême Orient,* iii (1903).

—— Review of J. S. M. Ward and W. G. Stirling, *The Hung Society. T'oung Pao,* xxv (1928).

Playfair, G. M. H. Chinese Secret Societies. *China Review,* xv (1886–7).

Pulleyblank, E. G. *The Background of the Rebellion of An Lu-shan.* London, 1955.

Purcell, Victor. *The Boxer Uprising.* London, 1963.

Schlegel, G. *Thian Ti Hwi, The Hung League or Heaven and Earth League.* Batavia, 1866, reprinted Singapore, 1956.

Schram, Stuart R. Mao Tse-tung and Secret Societies. *China Quarterly,* July–Sept. 1966.

Shih, U. Y. C. Some Rebel Chinese Ideologies. *T'oung Pao,* xliv (1956).

Stanton, W. The Triad Society or Heaven and Earth Association. *China Review,* xxi & xxii (1899), reprinted Hong Kong 1900.

Staunton, Sir G. T. trans. *Ta Tseng Leu Lee; the fundamental laws . . . of the Penal Code of China.* London, 1810.

Steiger, G. N. *China and the Occident; Origin and Development of the Boxer Movement.* New Haven, Conn., 1927.

Sun Yat-sen. *Memoirs of a Chinese Revolutionary.* London, 1918.

Tan, C. C. *The Boxer Catastrophe.* New York, 1955.

T'ang Leang-li. *The Inner History of the Chinese Revolution.* London, 1930.

Tien Tsung. Chinese Secret Societies. *Orient Magazine* (Hong Kong), Sept. 1952–Jan. 1953.

Wang, Y. C. Tu Yueh-sheng, 1888–1951. *Journal of Asian Studies,* May 1967.

Ward, J. S. M. and W. G. Stirling. *The Hung Society, or The Society of Heaven and Earth.* London, 1925. 3 vols.

Werner, E. T. C. *Myths and Legends of China.* London, 1922.

—— *A Dictionary of Chinese Mythology.* 1932.

Williams, S. W. *The Middle Kingdom.* New York, 1900–1. 2 vols.

Wylie, A. Chinese Researches. Shanghai, 1897. (Article on secret societies written for *Shanghai Almanac,* 1854.)

3. MALAYA

Anderson, J. Considerations relating to the Malay Peninsula. *JIA*, viii (1854). Reprinted *JMBRAS*, xxxv, pt 1 (1962).

Anson, Sir A. E. *About Others and Myself*. London, 1920.

Begbie, Capt P. F. *The Malay Peninsula*. Madras, Vepery Mission Press, 1834.

Bird, Isabella. *The Golden Chersonese*. London, 1879.

Blythe, W. L. Historical Sketch of Chinese Labour in Malaya. *JMBRAS*, xx, pt 1 (1947); Corrigenda, xxi, pt 1, 1947.

—— The Interplay of Chinese Secret and Political Societies in Malaya. *Eastern World*, Mar.–Apr. 1950.

Braddell, T. *Singapore and the Straits Settlements*. Pinang Gazette Press, 1858.

—— *Statistics of the British Possessions in the Straits of Malacca*. Penang, 1861.

Brimmell, J. H. *A Short History of the Malayan Communist Party*. Singapore, 1954.

—— *Communism in South East Asia*. London, 1959.

Buckley, C. B. *An Anecdotal History of Old Times in Singapore*. Singapore, 1902. 2 vols.

Burney, H. *The Burney Papers: printed by order of the Committee of the Vajira-nana National Library*. Bangkok, 1910–14. (Printed for private circulation.) 15 vols.

Cameron, J. *Our Tropical Possessions in Malayan India*. London, 1865.

Cavenagh, Sir O. *Reminiscences of an Indian Official*. London, 1884.

Chen Ta. *Chinese Migrations, with special reference to Labour Conditions*. Washington, 1923.

Clodd, H. P. *Malaya's First British Pioneer; the Life of Francis Light*. London, 1948.

Comber, L. F. *Chinese Secret Societies in Malaya*, 1800–1900. New York, 1959.

Coope, A. E. The Kangchu System in Johore. *JMBRAS*, xiv, pt 3 (1936).

Cooper, C. B. Notes on the Sa Tiam or Three Dot Brotherhood, 1924. *Malayan Police Mag.*, Mar. 1953.

Cowan, C. D. Early Penang and the Rise of Singapore. *JMBRAS*, xxiii, pt 2 (1950).

—— Sir Frank Swettenham's Perak Journals, 1874–6. *JMBRAS*, xxiv/4 (1951).

—— *Nineteenth Century Malaya*. London, 1961.

Cowgill, J. V. Chinese Place Names in Johore. *JMBRAS*, ii (1924).

Croockewit, J. H. The Tin Mines of Malaya. *JIA*, viii (1854).

Cullin, E. G. and W. F. Zehnder. *The Early History of Penang, 1592–1827*. Penang, 1905.

Dennys, N. B. *A Descriptive Dictionary of British Malaya*. London, 1894.

Doyle, P. *Tin Mining in Larut*. London, 1879.

Freedman, Maurice. Immigrants and Associations: Chinese in Nineteenth-Century Singapore. *Comparative Studies in Sociology & History*, ii/1 (1960).

Gullick, J. M. Captain Speedy of Larut. *JMBRAS*, xxvi/3, Nov. 1953.

—— *Malaya*. 2nd ed. London, 1964.

Hall, W. T. *Report on Tin Mining in Perak and Burma*. Rangoon, 1899.

Hill, A. H. The Hikayat Abdullah. *JMBRAS*, xxviii/3 (1955).

Jackson, R. N. *Pickering: Protector of Chinese*. Kuala Lumpur, 1965.

Kennedy, J. *A History of Malaya*. London, Macmillan, 1962.

552 *The Impact of Chinese Secret Societies in Malaya*

McNair, J. F. A. and W. D. Bayliss. *Prisoners Their Own Warders*. London, 1899.

Makepeace, Walter and others, eds. *One Hundred Years of Singapore*. London, 1921. 2 vols.

Maxwell, T. P. Benson. *Our Malay Conquests*. London, 1878.

Middlebrook, S. M. and J. M. Gullick. Yap Ah Loy. *JMBRAS*, xxiv/2 (July 1951).

Miller, Harry. *Menace in Malaya*. London, Harrap, 1955.

Mills, L. A. British Malaya, 1824–67. *JMBRAS*, iii/2 (1925).

—— and associates. *The New World of Southeast Asia*. Minneapolis, 1949.

Morrah, P. The Kinta Gangs. *Malayan Police Mag.*, xxii/1 (1951).

Newbold, T. J. *Political and Statistical Account of the British Settlements in the Straits of Malacca* . . . London, 1839. 2 vols.

—— and F. W. Wilson. The Chinese Secret Society of the Tien-Ti-Huih. *JRAS*, vi (1840–1).

Onraet, R. H. *Singapore; a Police Background*. London, 1946.

Parkinson, C. Northcote. *British Intervention in Malaya*, 1867–77. Singapore, 1960.

Pickering, W. A. The Chinese in the Straits of Malacca. *Fraser's Mag.*, Oct. 1876.

—— Chinese Secret Societies and Their Origin. *JSBRAS*, i (1878) & iii (1879).

Purcell, Victor. The Big Five of Penang (Chinese Kongsis Past and Present). *Straits Times Annual*, 1939.

—— *The Chinese in Malaya*. London, 1948.

—— *The Chinese in Southeast Asia*. 2nd ed. London, 1965.

[Read, W. H.]. *Play and Politics; Recollections of Malaya by an Old Resident*. London, 1901.

Sadka, E., ed. The Journal of Sir Hugh Low; Perak, 1877. *JMBRAS*, xxvii/4 (1954).

Song Ong Siang. *One Hundred Years' History of the Chinese in Singapore*. London, 1923.

Stirling, W. G. The Coffin-Breakers' Society. *JMBRAS*, iv, pt 1 (1926).

Swettenham, Sir F. *British Malaya*. London, 1906.

—— *Malay Sketches*. London, 1895.

—— *Footprints in Malaya*. London, 1941.

Thio, E. *The Singapore Chinese Protectorate*. Kuala Lumpur, Univ. of Malaya, 1952.

[Vaughan, J. D.]. Notes on the Chinese of Pinang. *JIA*, viii (1854).

—— *The Manners and Customs of the Chinese of the Straits Settlements*. Singapore, 1879.

Vetch, R. N. *Life of Lieut.-General Sir Andrew Clarke*. London, 1905.

Westerhout, J. B. Notes on Malacca. *JIA*, ii (1848).

Wilkinson, R. J. *A History of the Peninsular Malays* . . . 3rd ed. Singapore, 1923.

—— Sungei Ujong and Notes on Negri Sembilan. *JSBRAS*, 1921.

Windstedt, Sir R. O. A History of Negri Sembilan. *JMBRAS*, xi, pt 3, 1934.

—— A History of Malaya. *JMBRAS*, xii, pt 1 (1935).

—— A History of Perak. *JMBRAS*, xii, pt 1 (1934).

—— A History of Selangor. *JMBRAS*, xii, pt 3 (1934).

Wray, L. *The Tin Mines and Mining Industries of Perak*. Taiping, 1894.

Wynne, M. L. *Triad and Tabut*. Singapore, 1941. (Distributed 1957.)

GLOSSARY

atap: thatch made from leaves of the nipah palm.
Babas: Straits-born Chinese.
bagan: a jetty; also applied to estuarine fishing villages.
betel nut: fruit of the areca palm.
bhang: intoxicating liquor prepared from Indian hemp.
chandu: opium prepared (by cooking) for smoking.
Chinchews: Hokkiens from the Chuan Chiu prefecture in Fukien province.
chinting: outdoor officer.
Dato': honorific title.
ganja: same as bhang.
Hoey (Hokkien), Wui (Cantonese): an association. Commonly used in early
    Colonial days to mean a secret society.
Jamadar: Indian police officer.
kangchu: Chinese headman of a river.
kangka: Chinese river settlement.
Kling: a native of southern India.
kongsi: any partnership or group with a common interest.
Kwun Lam: a senior Triad ritual official.
nakhoda: ship's captain.
nibong: a palm which furnished a hard black wood used for spears, fences,
    roof battens, etc.
pangkeng: a sleeping bed platform, a dormitory. Also applied to a gang head-
    quarters.
parang: a Malay chopping knife.
Penghulu: Malay village headman.
samseng: a hooligan, gangster.
sinkeh: new arrival.
sinseh: a corrupt form of the Hokkien pronunciation Sien Sih (Cantonese Sin
    Shang) meaning teacher. In Triad usage it denotes the ritual expert who
    performs priestly functions at initiation ceremonies. Though corrupt, this
    form is used throughout the book because it is commonly found in police
    records and is widely accepted by the public.
sireh: the leaf of a vine in which betel nut and prepared lime are wrapped for
    mastication.
tabut: a Hindu processional emblem.
tongkang: large cargo lighter.
towkay: an employer.
twakow: cargo ship.
wayang: theatrical performance.

GENERAL INDEX[1]

Abdul Rahman, Tunku, 421, 480, 483–4, 523, 525
Abdul Samad, Sultan of Selangor, 118–20, 172–3
Abdullah, Raja of Klang, 118, 172–3
Abdullah, Sultan of Perak, 177–8, 180–7, 191–2, 194, 249
Abdullah b. Abdul Kadir, 47–49
Abu Bakar, Sultan of Johore, 241
Adamson, W., 154, 157, 229, 231, 236
Ah Kwee, Capitan, see Chang Keng Kwee
Ahmad, Panglima Besar, 189
Ahyas, 44
Ali, Sultan of Perak, 125, 177
Amoy, refugees from, 75–76, 79–80
Anson, Col., 132–4, 139–40, 146–7, 155–7, 168, 180–3, 185

'Baba' Chinese, 58
Bagan Si Api Api, 354, 363, 375, 377, 379, 394–5, 406, 443, 461
Bain, N. K., 270
Banishment: post-war policy, 9, 358–9; Peace Preservation Ord. and, 129, 143–8, 198, 206, 210, 215–17; naturalized British subjects, 135, 143–4, 147–9; Straits-born Chinese, 206, 211, 305, 467, 513; effectiveness of, 206, 341, 348, 467, 504, 513; Societies Ord. (1889) and, 229–31; British subjects, 229–31, 246–7; Enactment (FMS, 1899), 260, 294
Banishees: (SS), 146–8, 210, 220, 223, 243–7, 285, 287–8, 297–8, 301–2, 315; Perak, 270, 272; FMS, 291–4; Singapore, 417, 467, 473, 500, 503; MU, 358–62, 393; F. of M., 447–9; Chinese People's Republic unwilling to receive, 482, 521
Ord. (SS, 1888), 302, 341; enacted, 7, 224; amended, 215–17, 247–8, 289–90, 519
See also Restricted residence
Barnes, W. D., 260
Bencoolen, 41, 84

Benevolent societies, see Friendly societies
Bengal, 39–40, 64, 66–69, 74; see also India, Government of
Birch, A. N., 177, 178 n.
Birch, E. W., 260
Birch, J. W. W., 154, 159, 165, 174, 188, 190–192, 194
Black, J. A., report by, 296 n., 307–9
Blundell, E. A., 72–75, 116; governorship of, 82–103
Boey Yu Kong, 132, 134–5, 142, 146–7
Bonham, S. G., 58–60, 64
Bonsor, Mr, 227, 230 f.
Boon Swee, see Chong Bun Sui
Braddell, T., 98, 129, 133, 144, 147, 149, 151, 175, 190, 213
Brooke, Raja, 92
Brotherhood, Chinese cult of, 16
Brown, F. S., 98, 127, 133, 146–7, 149–51, 154
Buckingham and Chandos, Duke of, 136–138
Buckley, C. B., 76, 79
Buddhism, 15, 17, 20–21
Burney, Capt. H., 50
Butterworth, Govr, 68–70, 77–78, 80–82, 167
Buttrose, Mr Justice, 522

Cairns, Lt-Govr, 219
Campbell, G. W. R., 178–81, 184, 542–3
Cantonese, 233–4; and Hakkas, 23, 175; settlement in Malaya, 43–45, language, 44; and Hokkiens, 50, 76; and Larut war, 175–6; in Perak, 320, 381–2, 386, 441; in Selangor, 320, 368–9, 396–9; in Johore, 404–6; Singapore gangs, 297, 301, 306–7, 309, 311–13
Societies, 50–51, 142, 207, 286–7, 291–3, 295, 306, 309–11, 318, 320–1, 381–2, 386, 397–9, 405–6, 409–10, 441, 455, 458, 462–3, 467, 486

[1] The names of secret societies and of political and other organizations appear in a separate index on pp. 563–6 below. Societies known not by names but by numbers are grouped together at the end of this. To avoid overloading an unusually long index, a few minor societies and gangs have been omitted.

The abbreviations used for 'Federated Malay States', 'Singapore', and so on need no explanation, except that 'F. of M.' stands for either the Federation of Malaya or that of Malaysia.

Ho Cheo Tek, 67
Ho Ghi Siu, 175–80, 182–3, 186–7
Ho Yam Ko, 67
'Hoey', meaning of word, 50 n.
Hoey Kwans, 295, 298
Hoffman, Dr, cited, 534
Hoi Luk Fung: Hakkas, 198 n.; Cantonese, 462
Hokch'ias, 44, 285–6, 299–300, 307
Hokchius, 44, 285–6, 318, 380, 441
Hokkiens, 176, 233–4, 369, 381, 386–7, 396–8, 403–4; settlement of, in Malaya, 41, 43–45, 49–51, 55–56; language, 44; Hokkien-Tiechiu hostility, 76–80, 155–6, 163–4, 202, 286, 298–9, 301, 312, 375–6, 384, 456, 485–6; societies, 129, 142, 207–8, 243–6, 285, 287–8, 291, 293–5, 299, 313, 318–19, 396–8, 401, 407, 441, 455, 462, 467, 538–40;—Singapore gangs, 303, 306–8, 311–13, 408–12
Hong Kong, 6, 8, 27, 32–33, 141 n., 197, 199, 222, 226–7; police, 212, 235–6
Hung Wu, Emperor, 20
Hussein, Syed, 113, 115
Hussey, Mr, 268–9
Hutson, J., cited, 535

Ibbetson, R., 50, 53
Ibrahim, Ngah (the Mentri), 121–5, 175, 177–185, 187–8, 190, 192, 194
Identity cards, 417–18, 480, 515
Immigrants, Chinese, 22–23, 39–45; why they joined societies, 1–2, 14; indentured workers, 43; ill-treatment and protection of, 43, 164–71, 197; provinces of origin, 43–44; kidnapping of, 168–9, 203–4; no. of, 222, 284–5, 287, 296 n., 302, 322; women, 323
Immigration: effect of cessation of, 12; attitude of European community, 5, 65, 167–71, 212, 322;—of Chinese community, 168–9, 322; control of, 165–71, 200, 284–5, 296, 301–2, 321–2; Ordinances, 169–70, 197, 204–5, 212–14, 296
India, Government of: effect of liberalistic policy, 4; and administration of SS, 39–40; and Singapore riots, 77–78; and policy towards societies, 77–78, 80–82, 89–91, 101, 105–7, 111–13, 116; and police, 69, 93, 101; transfer of SS from, 89, 126–8; and Penang riots (1857), 94–98; State Prisoners Act, 102; and intervention in Malay States, 118, 124–125, 127
Indians, 84, 92, 94, 138, 284–5, 338; processions and festivals, 83–85, 130–1, 205; and secret societies and gangs, 105, 113, 115, 142, 270, 409; see also under Police
Indonesia, 483, 524
Internal Security Ord. (F. of M., 1959), 481

Interpreters, 5, 157–8, 197, 212; see also Chinese language
Irving, C. J., 175 n., 177, 543
Irving, E. A., 162–3
Ismail, Dato', 490
Ismail, Raja (the Bendahara), 177–8, 183, 192, 194
Ismail, Raja, of Klang, 173

Ja'far, Sultan of Perak, 121–2, 125
Jackson, Supt, 69
Jamadars, 66
Japan, Japanese: occupation of Malaya, 8, 327–30, 380;—aftermath of, 330–3, 365; and societies in China, 24, 30–32; secret societies in, 31; anti-Japanese activities in Malaya, 281–3, 289, 316–17, 351
Jawi-Pekans, 105, 130, 138, 150
Jervois, Mr, 263–4
Jervois, Sir W., 192–3, 199, 201, 210, 249
Johore, 7, 41, 330; gambling and lotteries, 244–5, 289; British Adviser accepted, 288; Emergency, 462; Indonesian raids, 483
Societies: (1890–1919), 240–1, 287–9, 291, 320–1; (1920–41), 307, 311, 313, 317; (1945–8), 330, 403–6; (1948–65), 446, 462–4, 494
Juma'at, Raja, 118, 172

Ka Yin Chius, 118–19, 173–4, 189, 192–3, 255
K'ang Yu-wei, 279
Karl, E., 197, 205, 215
Kedah: early history, 39–40, 46, 49; societies in nineteenth century, 113, 115; gambling, 245; Malay societies, 265, 485; Triad, Communists and KMT (1945–8), 330, 352–3, 363–8, 406; Emergency, 422–3; societies (1948–65), 454, 485
Kelantan, 330, 388–9, 494–5
Kemp, Mr, 268
Kesson, J., cited, 535
Khehs, see Hakkas
Khoo Chye, 138, 145, 148
Khoo Hong Chooi, 176, 178
Khoo Mah Pean, 138, 145, 148
Khoo Poh, 134–5, 147–8
Khoo T'ean Tek, 102–3, 111, 131–2, 134–5, 138–43, 145, 148
Khoo Teng Pang, 75, 139
Khor Khum, 339–44, 359–60, 363–4, 366
Kidnapping, 154, 304, 373–6, 481–2, 490, 501–502, 518, 525; see also under Immigrants
Kim Ho Hean, 370, 378
Kimberley, Lord, 160, 174, 181, 184
King, S. E., 296 n., 209–10
Kinta, 258; tinfield, 250–1; Japanese occupation, 328, 330, 380, 406; Chinese tribes, 368, 386; Emergency, 422, 424, 441–2, 452, 456

(1945–8), 329–30, 338–63, 382; (1948–1965), 422–5, 450–4, 484–5
See also Province Wellesley
Perak: (before 1874), 4, 42, 49, 122, 125; British intervention, 180–1; under Residential system, 190–2, 249–54, 257–8; Japanese occupation, 328–30, 332; People's Committees, 330; Emergency, 421–2, 424, 440–1
Societies: (1875–1900), 250–61; (1900–41), 290–4, 317–19; (1945–8), 363, 368–91, 399, 405–7; (1948–55), 441–2, 454–6; (1955-65), 478, 482, 485–8; Malay societies, 261–75
See also Dindings; Kinta; Krian; Kuala Kurau; Larut; Piracy
Peranakans, 130
Perlis, 363–5, 368, 485
Pickering, W. A., 533–4; Interpreter, 5, 157–158; Protector of Chinese, 5–6, 199, 205; and policy towards societies, 6, 197–221, 224–34, 256; and intervention in Malay States, 185–7, 189–90, 193, 249; and Chinese immigration, 197; and kidnapping of sinkhehs, 203–4; Registrar of Chinese Societies, 205; and gambling, 219–20; attack on, 220, 222, 243; retires, 234–5
Pilfert, Mr, 209–10
Piracy, 173, 188, 329, 450; (1945–8), 333, 339, 343, 346, 348–50, 353–4, 368–72, 376–9, 386
Plunket, C. B., 80, 114, 132, 156–8, 161–3, 165, 198–9, 538
Poh Teng Sang, 360–1
Police, 2–5, 8–11, 64–66, 85–86, 89–93, 101, 136–8, 153–60, 197, 212, 229–30, 301, 378; recruitment of Chinese, 2, 5, 63–64, 66, 101, 159–60, 165–6, 212, 321, 378;—from Hong Kong, 235–6; society headmen as special constables, 3–4, 108, 112, 129, 143–4, 161; Indians in, 66, 101, 115, 229;—Sikhs, 253, 258, 321; detectives first appointed, 101; Clementi Smith Commission, 211–12; reorganized (1927–1930), 295, 306, 313; takes over functions of Chinese Protectorate, 295–6; Armed Police Reserve, 300–1, 321; Ordinance (1925), 301; state of after war, 331, 354; Secret Societies Suppression Branches, 446–7, 450, 453, 468; statistics of action by (1954–7), 503; need for stronger legal backing, 503–4
Police supervision, 480, 485, 516
Political parties, 337; origins of, 7–8, 279–280
Politics, 337; participation of societies, 7, 10, 242, 362, 365, 406, 482, 493, 500, 513–14; political associations and Societies Ordinances, 357, 412–13, 417, 439–40, 519;

attempt to unite secret societies, 470–1, 475–6, 496–7
Popejoy, Inspector, 312–13
Powell, F., 237 n., 239, 241–2, 254–6
Preservation of Public Security Ord. (Sing., 1955), 474–5, 502, 504–5, 517
Prevention of Crime Ord. (F. of M., 1959), 480–1
Prevention of Crimes Ord. (SS, 1902), 288; Enactment (FMS), 292
Processions, 83–85, 87, 94–97, 99–100, 113, 141, 198, 220, 525
Prostitution, 204, 214, 224, 245, 307, 311, 313
Protector of Chinese, *see* Chinese Protectorate; Pickering, W. A.
Province Wellesley, 41, 44, 75, 130, 132–4, 150, 181, 289; societies (to 1900), 47, 113, 115, 198, 205, 209–10; (1900–19), 285; (1945–8), 353, 363–5, 375; (1948–65), 422–4, 453
Public Order Preservation Bill (F. of M., 1958), 479
Public Peace Preservation Ord. (F. of M., 1958,), 487
Pulau Senang, 13, 520–3

Raffles, Sir S., 39, 41, 43, 127, 166
Read, W. H., 120, 127, 145–7, 149, 151 n., 154, 160, 166, 204, 208, 216–18, 220; Larut war and British intervention, 184–6
Restricted Residence, 271–2, 452–4, 456, 478–480, 485–6, 488, 492, 517
Restrictions on employment, etc., 481, 517
Revenue farms, 55–56, 128, 178, 188 n., 287; in Malay States, 190–3, 250–2, 254
Riccard, H., 215
Ridges, H. G., 259
Rioting, place of, in Chinese politics, 202–3
Robinson, Sir W., 210
Rodger, Mr, 254–5
Roettger, E. H., cited, 534

Sarawak: Hakka rising, 92–94; societies declared illegal, 147
Sarib, 'Che, 262
Schlegel, G., cited, 534, 536
Schultz, Capt., 254–7
Scott, T., 127–9, 146, 149, 151, 166, 168–70, 223
Scott, W. R., 151, 154, 169–70
Seah Eu Chin, 156
Secret Societies Liaison Committees, 446, 453, 457
See Kwan, *see* Four Districts
Seenivasagam, D. R., 481–2
Selangor: (to 1874), 40, 49, 118–20, 172–4; tinfields, 42, 61, 118–20, 254; British intervention and Residential system, 188, 192–3, 254; MPAJA resistance, 328;

INDEX OF SOCIETIES AND ORGANIZATIONS

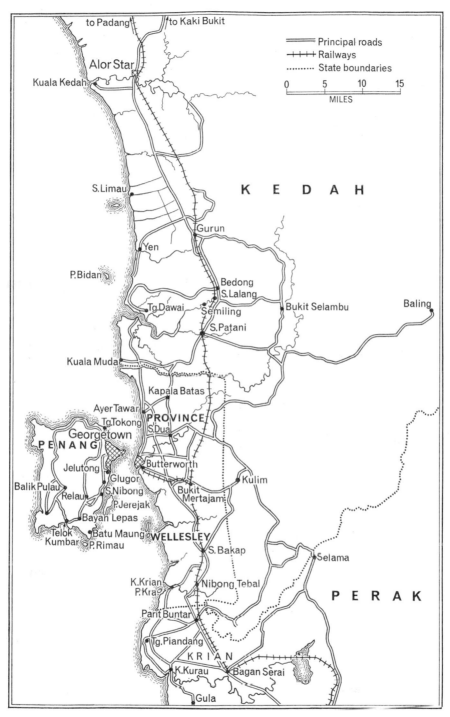

5. Kedah, Province Wellesley, Penang, and North Perak (Krian)

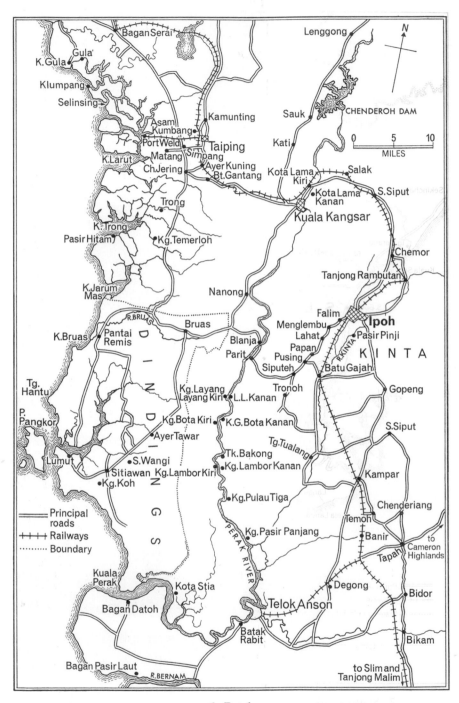

6. Perak

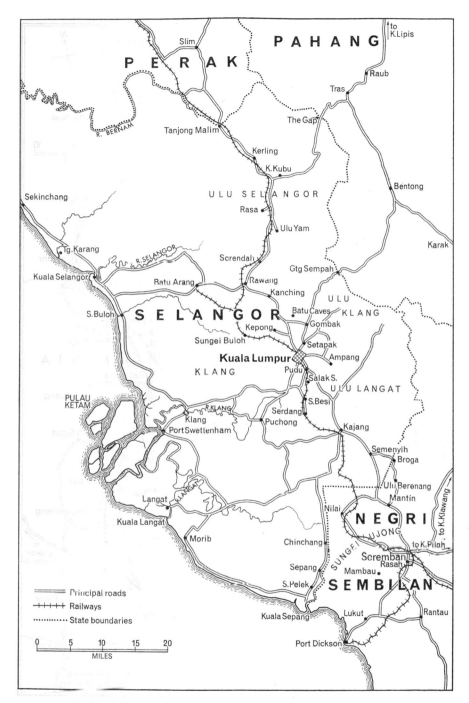

7. South Perak, West Pahang, Selangor, and Negri Sembilan

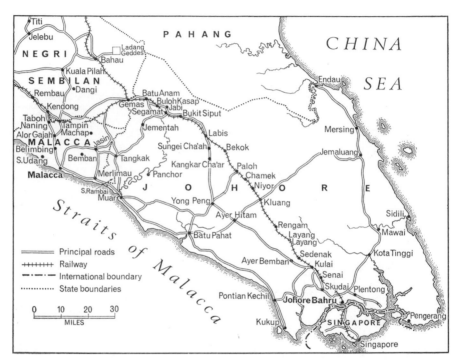

8. Johore, Malacca, and East Negri Sembilan